# Basics of Research Methods for Criminal Justice and Criminology

### THIRD EDITION

**MICHAEL G. MAXFIELD**
John Jay College, City University of New York

**EARL R. BABBIE**
Chapman University

WADSWORTH
CENGAGE Learning™

Australia • Brazil • Japan • Korea • Mexico • Singapore • Spain • United Kingdom • United States

**WADSWORTH**
CENGAGE Learning™

*Basics of Research Methods for Criminal Justice and Criminology*, **Third Edition**
Michael G. Maxfield and Earl R. Babbie

Senior Acquisitions Editor: Carolyn Henderson Meier

Senior Assistant Editor: Erin Abney

Editorial Assistant: Virginette Acacio

Media Editor: Ting Jian Yap

Senior Marketing Manager: Michelle Williams

Marketing Assistant: Jack Ward

Senior Marketing Communications Manager: Heather Baxley

Senior Content Project Manager: Christy A. Frame

Creative Director: Rob Hugel

Senior Art Director: Maria Epes

Senior Print Buyer: Karen Hunt

Rights Acquisitions Account Manager, Text and Images: Roberta Broyer

Production Service: Anne Talvacchio, Cenveo Publisher Services

Copy Editor: Susan Zorn

Cover Designer: Riezebos Holzbaur Design Group

Cover Image: Getty Images/Superstudio

Compositor: Cenveo Publisher Services

For product information and technology assistance, contact us at **Cengage Learning Customer & Sales Support, 1-800-354-9706.**

For permission to use material from this text or product, submit all requests online at **www.cengage.com/permissions.** Further permissions questions can be e-mailed to **permissionrequest@cengage.com**.

Library of Congress Control Number: 2011925887

Student Edition:

ISBN-13: 978-1-111-34691-1

ISBN-10: 1-111-34691-7

**Wadsworth**
20 Davis Drive
Belmont, CA 94002-3098
USA

Cengage Learning is a leading provider of customized learning solutions with office locations around the globe, including Singapore, the United Kingdom, Australia, Mexico, Brazil, and Japan. Locate your local office at www.cengage.com/global.

Cengage Learning products are represented in Canada by Nelson Education, Ltd.

To learn more about Wadsworth, visit www.cengage.com/wadsworth.

Purchase any of our products at your local college store or at our preferred online store www.cengagebrain.com.

Printed in the United States of America
1 2 3 4 5 6 7 15 14 13 12 11

*To Max Jacob Fauth and Laine Ellen Fauth*
*To Evelyn and Henry Babbie*

# Brief Contents

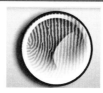

# Contents

# Preface

Since the first edition of *Research Methods for Criminal Justice and Criminology* (*RMCJC*) was published in 1995, we have been delighted to hear comments from instructors who have used the text—and from a few who do not use it! Although it is always gratifying to learn of positive reactions, we have also listened to suggestions for revising the book through its six editions. Some colleagues suggested trimming the text substantially to focus on the most important principles of research methods in criminal justice. Students and instructors are also increasingly sensitive to the cost of college texts.

As a result, we introduced *Basics of Research Methods for Criminal Justice and Criminology* about six years ago. Our objective in producing that text was fivefold: (1) retain the key elements of the parent text; (2) concentrate on fundamental principles of research design; (3) appeal to a broad variety of teaching and learning styles; (4) retain salient examples that illustrate various methods; and (5) reduce less-central points of elaboration and the examples used to illustrate them. That proved to be more challenging than we initially thought. At one point we were tempted to do something simple like drop two chapters, wrap the result in a soft cover, and declare what was left to be the basics. Fortunately that sentiment was reined in and we pursued a more deliberate approach that involved planning from the ground up.

*Basics* is shorter, more concise, and focused on what we believe is the most central material for introductory courses in research methods. Rather than simply offering a truncated version of the full text, *Basics* has been crafted to appeal to those seeking a more economical alternative while retaining the big book's highly successful formula. Many instructors teaching shorter courses, or courses where students are better served by concentrating on basic principles of criminal justice research, have used the *Basics* edition. Others, especially instructors teaching introductory graduate courses, prefer the more extensive coverage offered in *RMCJC*.

# Goals and Objectives

Criminal justice has always been a fascinating topic for students, partly because it is the stuff of news stories, fiction, and much popular entertainment. Criminal justice research goes behind and beyond the headlines to address important questions of *who*, *what*, *why*, and *how*. *Who* is involved as offender, victim, and justice professional? *What* is the nature and frequency of different kinds of crime and disorder problems, and what new problems are emerging? *Why* are incidents happening in particular places, and why are offenders involved in particular patterns of behavior? *How* are different kinds of offenses committed? *How* should justice agencies prevent and respond to problems of crime and safety?

Our primary goal in writing this edition is unchanged: to help students learn how to conduct research to answer these and related questions. Toward that end, certain principles have guided our revision of each edition of the text. Our intent is to:

- provide a careful description of the varied options for doing research in criminal justice.

- clarify and demystify what is traditionally a difficult subject for students at all levels.

- illustrate research methods with examples that are informative and interesting.

- incorporate new approaches that reflect methodological developments in the field.

- emphasize the application of criminal justice research to real-world problems and justice policy examples.

- bridge the gap between authors, instructors, and students by drawing on examples of our own research, especially research conducted with student colleagues.

# Organization of the Text

The third edition of *Basics of Research Methods for Criminal Justice and Criminology* has 11 chapters:

- Chapter 1, "Criminal Justice and Scientific Inquiry," introduces research methods. Material in this chapter describes how social scientific inquiry differs from other ways of learning things. This chapter also advises students on how to select research topics, conduct a literature review, and write a research proposal.

- Chapter 2, "Ethics and Criminal Justice Research," examines how research has the potential to harm subjects, and the obligations of researchers to minimize the risk of such harm. Examples illustrate the range of ethical issues in justice research and the steps researchers take to address them.

- Chapter 3, "General Issues in Research Design," describes basic features of all research studies that have to be considered when planning a research project. These include causation, the time dimension, and different fundamental avenues for criminal justice inquiry.

- Chapter 4, "Concepts, Operationalization, and Measurement," considers these central topics. All research requires some sort of measurement, and this chapter examines its key elements. As an in-depth example of measurement, we describe different approaches to measuring crime—a fundamental dependent and independent variable in criminal justice research.

- Chapter 5, "Experimental and Quasi-Experimental Designs," examines how to plan research that has explanatory purposes. Research design involves a collection of building blocks that can be combined in different ways. We emphasize the flexibility of research designs, drawing on interesting and creative examples.

- Chapter 6, "Sampling," describes approaches to selecting subjects for research. We cover the two general categories of probability and nonprobability sampling, describing different subtypes in each category. The basics of probability theory are introduced as key principles underlying sampling and statistical significance.

- Chapter 7, "Survey Research and Other Ways of Asking Questions," explores traditional survey research and other types of interviewing. Changes in technology continue to affect how surveys are conducted. Focus groups are described as tools for developing surveys or drawing detail from survey responses.

- Chapter 8, "Field Research," includes discussion of qualitative approaches as well as more structured environmental surveys. Examples illustrate the use of different approaches.

- Chapter 9, "Agency Records, Content Analysis, and Secondary Data," covers data extracted from administrative records as well as data series regularly collected by researchers and government agencies. Examples illustrate the wide range of research opportunities supported by data from different secondary sources.

- Chapter 10, "Evaluation Research and Problem Analysis," focuses on applied research that aims to improve criminal justice policy. The chapter describes how problem analysis is increasingly used in justice agencies to reduce crime and related problems.

- Chapter 11, "Interpreting Data," introduces data analysis techniques widely used in criminal justice research. Descriptive and explanatory approaches are explained and illustrated with examples.

# What's New in This Edition

In preparing this third edition, we stayed with what has proved to be a popular formula. But we have also responded to suggestions from reviewers, colleagues, and instructors who used earlier editions.

### Theory Pull-Outs

To underscore the importance of theory in all phases of research, we have added special types of examples to several chapters. Some of these are drawn from articles recently published in the *Journal of Research in Crime and Delinquency (JRCD)*, which I have edited for the past three years. Scholars sometimes write to ask whether their work might be suitable for publication, and I always respond: "*JRCD* publishes theory-based empirical research…." The theory-based examples in this edition of *Basics* illustrate this in different ways.

### Expanded Examples of Student Research

Reviewers and colleagues have often commented positively on the use of examples from student research in earlier editions and in the larger text. As a result, we have included more of these throughout the book, many in featured boxes.

Highlighting student research serves different purposes. First, it amplifies what some colleagues call the "over-the-shoulder" tone of the text, in which readers feel they are experiencing more than just words on a printed page. Second, student research examples embody the kind of collaborative supervision that exists between students and faculty. Third, we have great familiarity with the details of work by our students. Such details are rarely described in published articles, and being able to report them adds behind-the-scenes information not readily available elsewhere. Finally, Earl and I believe the examples presented here are topical and inherently interesting to readers. Among the new examples in this edition are projects that address terrorism, human trafficking, sex offenders, and crime at bus stops. The first three are well-known topics, while the last is an example of a seemingly humble problem that will be meaningful to most people living in large urban areas.

We have also made the following specific changes in each chapter:

- **Chapter 1** has been extensively revised to provide an overview of criminal justice research the way it is commonly taught. On the advice of reviewers, basic principles of social science research have been revised and moved to Chapter 3. Chapter 1 now presents material on how to plan research, and how to write a research proposal. This includes guidance on how to conduct a literature review. The revised opening chapter better reflects what most instructors do in the first class or two.

- **Chapter 2** includes new material on the institutional review boards that oversee the protection of human subjects in social science research. The chapter also describes important new research on the question of crime displacement, something that is usually overstated as an ethical problem in applied research.

- **Chapter 3** now presents an expanded discussion of social science research foundations, with content formerly in Chapter 1. We have streamlined discussion of validity threats by moving some of this important material to Chapter 5 where it can be more clearly linked to topics in research design.

- **Chapter 4** reorganizes some discussion on conceptualization in response to comments from reviewers and colleagues who have used earlier editions of the book.

- **Chapter 5** clarifies some discussion of experiments. Material on threats to validity formerly in Chapter 3 has been selectively added here, reducing the potential for repetition that some users perceived in earlier editions.

- **Chapter 6** clarifies basic sampling concepts. We describe new examples of creative approaches to nonprobability sampling. Sections on probability sampling have been consolidated. To beef up our discussion of qualitative field research, we added a simple table to illustrate the systematic field sampling of available subjects in a public place.

- **Chapter 7** adds information on the continually evolving climate for survey research, partly drawing on a book I co-edited in 2007, *Surveying Crime in the 21st Century*. New examples link survey and sampling technology. Material on aging telephone survey technology has been cut to make room for our discussion of newer directions in survey research.

- **Chapter 8** expands discussion of qualitative approaches to field research, including a new example based on student research. Galma Jahic combined archival data and field interviews with public officials in Bosnia and Herzegovina to study human trafficking for her dissertation research at Rutgers University. Another new example describes how former colleague Ron Clarke and I learned about seaport operations in the post-9/11 era. Our field observations of container handling at a huge port helped us understand the problem of vehicle theft for export. This chapter also presents brief descriptions of qualitative field research on corrections and policing. Finally, we draw on recent books by Dina Perrone and Ko-lin Chin to illustrate field research on drug use in dance clubs, and drug production in the Golden Triangle of Southeast Asia.

- **Chapter 9** features a more concise discussion of content analysis. A new box illustrates the use of agency records and content analysis to examine recruitment by terrorist organizations in Turkey. This is another example of student research, in this case a dissertation by a Rutgers student who is now a police chief in the Turkish National Police. A hypothetical example of new data collection has been replaced by a discussion of how researchers worked with Pennsylvania State Police to collect new data on traffic stops.

- **Chapter 10** includes incremental updates to the section on problem analysis that was introduced in the previous edition. A new example describes an evaluation of a time-series study of auto theft in Australia. This evaluation illustrates how the timing of different policy initiatives makes it possible to use time-series designs for evaluation.

- **Chapter 11** updates crime data in certain examples. A new example draws on a hot-button topic—identity theft. We describe data from the National Crime Victimization Survey to estimate identity theft victimization. Univariate and bivariate examples are presented.

# Learning Tools

### The Research Writer for Criminal Justice CD-ROM

Included as a CD-ROM, this new version of the *Research Writer for Criminal Justice* helps students tackle the task of writing research reports by taking some of the mystery out of the endeavor. It provides a template that guides students through the process of writing a research report, from the beginning idea to the documentation of the last source. Moreover, students can access helpful hints and tips as they write with just a click of a button. They can also e-mail their work at any stage of the process to their instructor, and they can even export their work to Microsoft Word where the document will be formatted in a style consistent with standard research projects. We hope students find this CD-ROM exciting and helpful.

### Ancillary Materials

To access additional course materials, please visit www.cengagebrain.com. At the CengageBrain.com home page, search for the ISBN of your title (from the back cover of your book) using the search box at the top of the page. This will take you to the product page where these resources can be found.

A number of supplements are provided by Cengage Learning to help instructors use *Basics of Research Methods for Criminal Justice and Criminology* in their courses and to aid students in preparing for exams. Supplements are available to qualified adopters. Please consult your local sales representative for details.

## For the Instructor

***Instructor's Resource Manual with Test Bank***    An improved and completely updated *Instructor's Resource Manual with Test Bank* has been developed for this text. The manual includes key terms, detailed chapter outlines, chapter summaries, activities and assignments, and internet resources. Each chapter's test bank contains questions in multiple-choice, true–false, fill-in-the-blank, and essay formats, with a full answer key. The test bank includes the page numbers in the main text where the answers can be found. Finally, each question in the test bank has been carefully reviewed by experienced criminal justice instructors for quality, accuracy, and content coverage. Our "Instructor Approved" seal, which appears on the front cover, is our assurance that you are working with an assessment and grading resource of the highest caliber.

***ExamView® Computerized Testing***    The comprehensive *Instructor's Resource Manual* described above is backed up by ExamView, a computerized test bank available for PC and Macintosh computers. With ExamView you can create, deliver, and customize tests and study guides (both print and online) in minutes. You can easily edit and import your own questions and graphics, change test layouts, and reorganize questions. Using ExamView's complete word-processing capabilities, you can enter an unlimited number of new questions or edit existing questions.

***PowerPoint Slides***    Handy Microsoft PowerPoint slides outline the chapters of the main text in a classroom-ready presentation to help you make your lectures engaging and to reach your visually oriented students. The presentations are available for download on the password-protected website and can also be obtained by e-mailing your local Cengage Learning representative.

***The Wadsworth Criminal Justice Video Library***    So many exciting new videos— so many great ways to enrich your lectures and spark discussion of the material in this text! Your Cengage Learning representative will be happy to provide details on our video policy by adoption size. The library includes these selections and many others.

- **ABC® Videos.** ABC videos feature short, high-interest clips from current news events as well as historic raw footage going back 40 years. Perfect for discussion starters or to enrich your lectures and spark interest in the material in the text, these brief videos provide students with a new lens through which to view the past and present, one that will greatly enhance their knowledge and understanding of significant events and open up to them new dimensions in learning. Clips are drawn from such programs as *World News Tonight, Good Morning America, This Week, PrimeTime Live, 20/20,* and *Nightline,* as well as numerous ABC News specials and material from the Associated Press Television News and British Movietone News collections.

- **Cengage Learning's "Introduction to Criminal Justice Video Series"** features videos supplied by the BBC Motion Gallery. These short, high-interest clips from CBS and BBC news programs—everything from nightly news broadcasts and specials to CBS News Special Reports, *CBS Sunday Morning, 60 Minutes,* and more—offer additional classroom enrichment.

- **Films for the Humanities.** Choose from nearly 200 videos on a variety of topics such as elder abuse, supermax prisons, suicide and the police officer, the making of an FBI agent, and domestic violence.

*Criminal Justice Media Library*   Cengage Learning's Criminal Justice Media Library includes nearly 300 media assets on the topics you cover in your courses. Available to stream from any web-enabled computer, the Criminal Justice Media Library's assets include such valuable resources as Career Profile Videos featuring interviews with criminal justice professionals from a range of roles and locations, simulations that allow students to step into various roles and practice their decision-making skills, video clips on current topics from ABC® and other sources, animations that illustrate key concepts, interactive learning modules that help students check their knowledge of important topics, and Reality Check exercises that compare expectations and preconceived notions against the real-life thoughts and experiences of criminal justice professionals. The Criminal Justice Media Library can be uploaded and used within many popular learning management systems. You can also customize it with your own course material. You can also purchase an institutional site license. Please contact your Cengage Learning representative for ordering and pricing information.

## For the Student

*Careers in Criminal Justice Website*   *(available bundled with this text at no additional charge)* Featuring plenty of self-exploration and profiling activities, the interactive Careers in Criminal Justice Website helps students investigate and focus on the criminal justice career choices that are right for them. Includes interest assessment, video testimonials from career professionals, resumé and interview tips, and links for reference.

***CLeBook***    CLeBook allows students to access Cengage Learning textbooks in an easy-to-use online format. Highlight, take notes, bookmark, search your text, and, in some titles, link directly into multimedia. CLeBook combines the best aspects of paper books and ebooks in one package.

***Current Perspectives: Readings from InfoTrac® College Edition***    These readers, designed to give students a closer look at special topics in criminal justice, include free access to InfoTrac College Edition. The timely articles are selected by experts in each topic from within InfoTrac College Edition. They are available free when bundled with the text and include the following titles:

- Cyber Crime
- Victimology
- Juvenile Justice
- Racial Profiling
- White-Collar Crime
- Terrorism and Homeland Security
- Public Policy and Criminal Justice
- Technology and Criminal Justice
- Ethics in Criminal Justice
- Forensics and Criminal Investigation
- Corrections
- Law and Courts
- Policy in Criminal Justice

# Acknowledgments

Several reviewers made perceptive and useful comments on various drafts of the book. We are especially grateful to them for their insights and suggestions:

Michael Birzer, Wichita State University

Jason Clark-Miller, Texas Christian University

Angela West Crews, Marshall University

Deborah Eckberg, Metropolitan State University

Melissa Fenwick, Western Connecticut State University

Aric Frazier, Vincennes University

Kathy Johnson, University of West Florida

Kent R. Kerley, University of Alabama at Birmingham

Satenik Margaryan, Montclair State University

Jerome McKean, Ball State University

Heidee McMillin, Lewis-Clark State College

Michael Montgomery, Tennessee State University

Kathy Oborn, Pierce College

Denny Powers, South University–Columbia

Bradford W. Reyns, Southern Utah University

Marc Riedel, Southeastern Louisiana University

Melinda Schlager, Texas A&M University–Commerce

Benjamin Steiner, University of South Carolina

Quanda Stevenson, University of Alabama

PJ Verrecchia, York College of Pennsylvania

Brenda Vose, University of North Florida

Hsiao-Ming Wang, University of Houston–Downtown

As usual, a number of students at the Rutgers University School of Criminal Justice offered advice, feedback, and contributions for this and earlier editions. I thank: Dr. Carsten Andresen (Travis County Department of Community Corrections and Supervision); Dr. Gisela Bichler (California State University–San Bernardino); Stephen Block; Dr. Sharon Chamard (University of Alaska); Dr. Niyazi Ekici (Turkish National Police); Shuryo Fujita; Dr. Galma Jahic (Istanbul Bilgi University, Turkey); Dr. Jarret Lovell (California State University–Fullerton); Nerea Marteache; Dr. Marie Mele; Dr. Nancy Merritt (National Institute of Justice); Dr. Melanie-Angela Neuilly (Washington State University); Dr. Dina Perrone (California State University–Long Beach); Gohar Petrossian; Stephen Pires (Florida International University); Dr. James Roberts (University of Scranton); Dr. William Sousa (University of Nevada–Las Vegas); Dr. Christopher Sullivan (University of Cincinnati); and Dr. Sung-suk Violet Yu (John Jay College of Criminal Justice).

I'm also pleased to thank my new students at John Jay College for their contributions: Kevin Barnes-Ceeney, Katharine Boyd, Cory Feldman, Brittany Hayes, Amber Horning, Karen Pepper, and Cyann Zoller.

Finally, Earl and I are very grateful for the patient, professional assistance from project manager Anne Talvacchio at Cenveo Publisher Services and the people at Cengage: Carolyn Henderson Meier, Michelle Williams, Christy Frame, Erin Abney, Virginette Acacio, and the entire book team.

Mike Maxfield

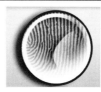

# About the Authors

**Michael G. Maxfield** is Professor of Criminal Justice at John Jay College, City University of New York. He is the author of numerous articles and books on a variety of topics, including victimization, policing, homicide, community corrections, and long-term consequences of child abuse and neglect. He has served as editor of the *Journal of Research in Crime and Delinquency* since 2008. Maxfield received his PhD in political science from Northwestern University.

**Earl R. Babbie** graduated from Harvard University before enlisting in the U.S. Marine Corps. He received his PhD from the University of California–Berkeley, and began teaching shortly thereafter. Credited with defining research methods for the social sciences, Dr. Babbie has written several texts, including the best-selling *The Practice of Social Research*.

# PART 1

# An Introduction to Criminal Justice Inquiry

What comes to mind when you encounter the word *science*? What do you think of when we describe criminal justice as a social science? For some people, science is mathematics; for others, it is white coats and laboratories. Some confuse it with technology or equate it with difficult courses in high school or college.

Science is, of course, none of these things per se, but it is difficult to specify exactly what science is. Scientists, in fact, disagree on the proper definition. Some object to the whole idea of social science; others question more specifically whether criminal justice can be a social science.

For the purposes of this book, we view science as a method of inquiry—a way of learning and knowing things about the world around us. Like other ways of learning and knowing about the world, science has some special characteristics. We'll examine these traits in this opening set of chapters. We'll also see how the scientific method of inquiry can be applied to the study of crime and criminal justice.

Part One lays the groundwork for the rest of the book by examining the fundamental characteristics and issues that make science different from other ways of knowing things. Chapter 1 begins with a look at native human inquiry, the sort of thing all of us have been doing all our lives. We'll also consider research purposes and the basics of how to design a research project.

Chapter 2 deals with the ethics of social science research. The study of crime and criminal justice often presents special challenges with regard to ethics. We'll see that most ethical questions are rooted in two fundamental principles: (1) research subjects should not be harmed, and (2) their participation must be voluntary.

The overall purpose of Part One, therefore, is to construct a backdrop against which to view more specific aspects of research design and execution. By the time you complete the chapters in Part One, you will be ready to look at some of the more concrete aspects of criminal justice research.

## CHAPTER 1

# Criminal Justice and Scientific Inquiry

*People learn about their world through a variety of methods, and they often make mistakes along the way. Science is different from other ways of learning and knowing. We'll consider errors people commonly make and how science tries to avoid them, different purposes of research, and principles for designing a research project.*

## INTRODUCTION

*Criminal justice professionals are both consumers and producers of research.*

Spending a semester studying criminal justice research methodology may not be high on your list of "Fun Things to Do." Perhaps you are, or plan to be, a criminal justice professional, and you are thinking, "Why do I have to study research methods? When I graduate, I'll be working in probation (or law enforcement, or corrections, or court services), not conducting research! I would benefit more from learning about probation counseling (or police management, or corrections policy, or court administration)." Fair enough. But as a criminal justice professional, you will need to be a consumer of research. One objective of this book is to help you become an informed consumer of research.

For example, findings from a pioneering experimental study of policing, the Kansas City Preventive Patrol Experiment, appeared to contradict a fundamental belief that a visible police patrol force prevents crime. Acting as a consumer of research findings, a police officer, supervisor, or executive should be able to understand how that research was conducted and how the study's findings might apply in his or her department.

Most criminal justice professionals, especially those in supervisory roles, routinely review various performance reports and statistical tabulations. A continually growing number of research reports may now be found on the Internet. For example, the National Criminal Justice Reference Service (NCJRS) was established to archive and distribute research reports to criminal justice professionals and researchers around the world. Many such reports

are prepared specifically to keep the criminal justice community informed about new research developments and may be downloaded from the NCJRS website (www.ncjrs.gov). An understanding of research methods can help decision makers critically evaluate such reports and recognize when methods are properly and improperly applied. The box titled "Home Detention" describes an example of how knowledge of research methods can help policy makers avoid mistakes.

Another objective of this book is to help you produce research. In other courses you take or in your job, you may become a producer of research. Probation officers sometimes test new approaches to supervising or counseling clients, and police officers try new methods of dealing with recurring problems. Many cities and states have a compelling need to evaluate services provided to offenders released from prison or jail. Determining whether changes or existing programs are effective is an example of applied research. A problem-solving approach, rooted in systematic research, is being used in more and more police departments and in many other criminal justice agencies as well. Therefore, criminal justice professionals need to know not only how to interpret research accurately, but also how to produce accurate research.

## WHAT IS THIS BOOK ABOUT?

*This book focuses on how we know what we know.*

This book focuses on how we learn. Although you will come away from the book knowing many things you don't know right now, our primary

**HOME DETENTION**

Home detention with electronic monitoring (ELMO) was widely adopted as an alternative punishment in the United States in the 1980s. The technology for this new sanction was made possible by advances in telecommunications and computer systems. Prompted by growing prison and jail populations, not to mention sales pitches by equipment manufacturers, criminal justice officials embraced ELMO. Questions about the effectiveness of these programs quickly emerged, however, and led to research to determine whether the technology worked. Comprehensive evaluations were conducted in Marion County (Indianapolis), Indiana. Selected findings from these studies illustrate the importance of understanding research methods in general and the meaning of various ways to measure program success in particular.

ELMO programs directed at three groups of people were studied: (1) convicted adult offenders, (2) adults charged with a crime and awaiting trial, and (3) juveniles convicted of burglary or theft. People in each of the three groups were assigned to home detention for a specified time. They could complete the program in one of three ways: (1) successful release after serving their term, (2) removal due to rule violations, such as being arrested again or violating program rules, or (3) running away or absconding. The agencies that administered each program were required to submit regular reports to county officials on how many individuals in each category completed their home-detention terms. The accompanying table summarizes the program-completion types during the evaluation study.

| | Convicted Adults (%) | Pretrial Adults (%) | Juveniles (%) |
|---|---|---|---|
| Success | 81 | 73 | 99 |
| Rule violation | 14 | 13 | 1 |
| Abscond | 5 | 14 | 0 |

These percentages, reported by agencies to county officials, indicate that the juvenile program was a big success; virtually all juveniles were successfully released.

Now consider some additional information on each program collected by the evaluation team. Data were gathered on new arrests of program participants and on the number of successful computerized telephone calls to participants' homes.

| | Convicted Adults (%) | Pretrial Adults (%) | Juveniles (%) |
|---|---|---|---|
| New arrest | 5 | 1 | 11 |
| Successful calls | 53 | 52 | 17 |

As the table shows, many more juveniles were arrested, and juveniles successfully answered a much lower percentage of telephone calls to their homes. What happened?

The simple answer is that the staff responsible for administering the juvenile program were not keeping track of offenders. The ELMO equipment was not maintained properly, and police were not visiting the homes of juveniles as planned. Because staff were not keeping track of program participants, they were not aware that many juveniles were violating the conditions of home detention. And because they did not detect violations, they naturally reported that the vast majority of young burglars and thieves completed their home detention successfully.

A county official who relied on only agency reports of program success would have made a big mistake in judging the juvenile program to be 99 percent successful. In contrast, an informed consumer of such reports would have been skeptical of a 99 percent success rate and searched for more information.

*Source:* Adapted from Maxfield and Baumer (1991) and Baumer, Maxfield, and Mendelsohn (1993).

purpose is to help you look at how you know things, not what you know.

## Two Realities

Ultimately, we live in a world of two realities. Part of what we know could be called our *experiential reality*—the things we know from direct experience. If you dive into a glacial stream flowing down through the Canadian Rockies, you don't need anyone to tell you the water is cold; you notice that all by yourself. And if you step on a piece of broken glass, you know it hurts without anyone telling you. These are things you experience.

The other part of what we know could be called our *agreement reality*—the things we consider real because we've been told they're real, and everyone else seems to agree they are real. A big part of growing up in any society, in fact, is learning to accept what everybody around us "knows" to be true. If we don't know those same things, we can't really be a part of society. Ideas about gender, race, religion, and different nations that you learned as you were growing up would fit in this category. We may test a few of these truths on our own, but we simply accept the great majority of them. These are the things that "everybody knows."

To illustrate the difference between agreement and experiential realities, consider preventive police patrol. The term *preventive* implies that when police patrol their assigned beats they prevent crime. Police do not prevent all crime, of course, but it is a commonsense belief that a visible, mobile police force will prevent some crimes. In fact, the value of patrol in preventing crime was a fundamental principle of police operations for many years. A 1967 report on policing for President Lyndon Johnson by the President's Commission on Law Enforcement and Administration of Justice (p. 1) stated that "the heart of the police effort against crime is patrol.... The object of patrol is to disperse policemen in a way that will eliminate or reduce the opportunity for misconduct and to increase the probability that a criminal will be apprehended while he is committing a crime or immediately thereafter."

Seven years later, the Police Foundation, a private research organization, published results from an experimental study that presented a dramatic challenge to the conventional wisdom on police patrol. Known as the Kansas City Preventive Patrol Experiment, this study compared police beats with three levels of preventive patrol: (1) control beats, with one car per beat; (2) proactive beats, with two or three cars per beat; and (3) reactive beats, with no routine preventive patrol. After almost one year, researchers examined data from the three types of beats and found no differences in crime rates, citizen satisfaction with police, fear of crime, or other measures of police performance (Kelling et al. 1974).

Additional studies conducted in the 1970s cast doubt on other fundamental assumptions about police practices. A quick response to crime reports made no difference in arrests, according to a research study in Kansas City (Van Kirk 1977). And criminal investigation by police detectives rarely resulted in an arrest (Greenwood 1975).

We mention these examples not to attack routine law enforcement practices but to show that systematic research on policing has illustrated how traditional beliefs—as examples of agreement reality—can be misleading. Simply increasing the number of police officers on patrol does not reduce crime because police patrol often lacks direction. Faster response time to calls for police assistance does not increase arrests because there is often a long delay between the time when a crime occurs and when it is reported to police. Clever detective work seldom solves crimes because investigators get most of their information from reports prepared by patrol officers, who in turn get their information from victims and witnesses.

Traditional beliefs about patrol effectiveness, response time, and detective work are examples of agreement reality, a "reality" that a surprising number of people still embrace. In contrast, the research projects that produced alternative views about each law enforcement practice represent experiential reality. These studies are examples of **empirical**[1] research, the production of knowledge based on experience or observation. In each case, researchers conducted studies of police practices and based their conclusions on observations and experience. Empirical research is a way of learning about crime and criminal justice, and explaining how to conduct empirical research is the purpose of this book.

## The Role of Science

Science offers an approach to both agreement reality and experiential reality. Scientists have certain criteria that must be met before they will agree on the reality of something they haven't personally experienced. In general, an assertion must have both *logical* and *empirical* support: it must make sense, and it must agree with actual observations.

---

1. Words set in boldface are defined in the glossary at the end of the book.

For example, why do earthbound scientists accept the assertion that it's cold on the dark side of the moon? First, it makes sense because the surface heat of the moon comes from the sun's rays. Second, scientific measurements made on the moon's dark side confirm this logical explanation. So scientists accept the reality of things they don't personally experience—they accept an agreement reality—but they have special standards for doing so.

More to the point of this book, however, is that science offers a special approach to the discovery of reality through personal experience. Epistemology is the science of knowing; methodology (a subfield of epistemology) might be called the *science of finding out*. This book focuses on criminal justice **methodology**—how social scientific methods can be used to better understand crime and criminal justice policy. To understand scientific inquiry, let's first look at the kinds of inquiry we all do each day.

## PERSONAL HUMAN INQUIRY

*Everyday human inquiry draws on personal experience and secondhand authority.*

Most of us would like to be able to predict how things are going to be for us in the future. We seem quite willing, moreover, to undertake this task using causal and probabilistic reasoning. First, we generally recognize that future circumstances are somehow caused or conditioned by present ones. For example, we learn that getting an education will affect what kind of job we have later in life, and that running stoplights may result in an unhappy encounter with an alert traffic officer. As students, we learn that studying hard will result in better examination grades.

Second, we recognize that such patterns of cause and effect are probabilistic in nature: the effects occur more often when the causes occur than when the causes are absent—but not always. Thus, as students, we learn that studying hard produces good grades in most instances, but not every time. We recognize the danger of ignoring stoplights without believing that every such violation will produce a traffic ticket.

The concepts of causality and probability play a prominent role in this book. Science makes causality and probability more explicit and provides techniques for dealing with them more rigorously than does casual human inquiry.

However, our attempts to learn about the world are only partly linked to personal inquiry and direct experience. Another, much larger, part comes from the agreed-on knowledge that others give us. This agreement reality both assists and hinders our attempts to find out things for ourselves. Two important sources of agreement reality—tradition and authority—deserve brief consideration here.

### Tradition

Each of us is born into and inherits a culture made up, in part, of firmly accepted knowledge about the workings of the world and the values that guide our participation in it. We may learn from others that planting corn in the spring will result in the greatest assistance from the gods, that the circumference of a circle is approximately 3.14 times its diameter, or that driving on the left side of the road (in the United States) is dangerous.

Tradition, in this sense, has some clear advantages for human inquiry. By accepting what everybody knows, we are spared the overwhelming task of starting from scratch in our search for regularities and understanding. Knowledge is cumulative, and an inherited body of information and understanding is the jumping-off point for the development of more knowledge.

### Authority

Despite the power of tradition, new knowledge appears every day. Throughout life we learn about new discoveries and understandings from others. However, our acceptance of this new knowledge often depends on the status of the discoverer. For example, you are more likely to believe a judge who declares that your next traffic violation will result in a suspension of your driver's license than your parents when they say the same thing.

Like tradition, authority can both help and hinder human inquiry. We do well to trust the judgment of individuals who have special training, expertise, and credentials in a matter, especially in the face of contradictory arguments on a given question. At the same time, inquiry can be greatly hindered by the legitimate authorities who err within their own special province. Biologists, after all, do make mistakes in the field of biology, and biological knowledge changes over time. Criminal justice research sometimes yields mistaken results, and we are wise to accept research findings with caution even if they come from experts. The box

titled "Arrest and Domestic Violence" illustrates the problems that can result when criminal justice policy makers accept too quickly the results from criminal justice research.

Inquiry is also hindered when we depend on the authority of experts speaking outside their realm of expertise. Consider a political or religious leader, lacking any biochemical expertise, who declares marijuana to be a dangerous drug. The advertising industry plays heavily on this misleading use of authority by having popular athletes discuss the value of various sports drinks and having movie stars evaluate the performance of automobiles.

 **ARREST AND DOMESTIC VIOLENCE**

In 1983, preliminary results were released from a study on the deterrent effects of arrest in cases of domestic violence. The study reported that male abusers who were arrested were less likely to commit future assaults than offenders who were not arrested. Conducted by researchers from the Police Foundation, the study used rigorous experimental methods adapted from the natural sciences. Criminal justice scholars generally agreed that the research was well designed and executed. Public officials were quick to embrace the study's findings that arresting domestic violence offenders deterred them from future violence.

Here, at last, was empirical evidence to support an effective policy in combating domestic assaults. Results of the Minneapolis Domestic Violence Experiment were widely disseminated, in part because of aggressive efforts by the researchers to publicize their findings (Sherman and Cohn 1989). The attorney general of the United States recommended that police departments make arrests in all cases of misdemeanor domestic violence. Within five years, more than 80 percent of law enforcement agencies in U.S. cities adopted arrest as the preferred way of responding to domestic assaults (Sherman 1992, 2).

Several things contributed to the rapid adoption of arrest policies to deter domestic violence. First, the experimental study was conducted carefully by highly respected researchers. Second, results were widely publicized in newspapers, in professional journals, and on television programs. Third, officials could understand the study, and most believed that its findings made sense. Finally, mandating arrest in less serious cases of domestic violence was a straightforward and politically attractive approach to a growing problem.

Sherman and Berk (1984), however, urged caution in uncritically embracing the results of their study. Others urged that similar research be conducted in other cities to check on the Minneapolis findings (Lempert 1984). Recognizing the need for more research, the U.S. National Institute of Justice sponsored more experiments—known as replications—in six other cities. Not everyone was happy about the new studies. For example, a feminist group in Milwaukee opposed the replication in that city because it believed that the effectiveness of arrest had already been proved (Sherman and Cohn 1989, 138).

Results from the replication studies brought into question the effectiveness of arrest policies. In three cities, no deterrent effect was found in police records of domestic violence. In other cities, there was no evidence of deterrence for longer periods (6 to 12 months), and in three cities, researchers found that violence actually escalated when offenders were arrested (Sherman 1992, 30). For example, Sherman and associates (1992, 167) report that in Milwaukee "the initial deterrent effects observed for up to thirty days quickly disappear. By one year later [arrests] produce an escalation effect." Arrest works in some cases but not in others. In responding to domestic assaults, as in many other cases, it's important to carefully consider the characteristics of offenders and the nature of the relationship between offender and victim.

After police departments throughout the country embraced arrest policies following the Minneapolis study, researchers were faced with the difficult task of explaining why initial results must be qualified. Arrest seemed to make sense; officials and the general public believed what they read in the papers and saw on television. Changing their minds by reporting complex findings was more difficult.

Both tradition and authority, then, are double-edged swords in the search for knowledge about the world. Simply put, they provide us with a starting point for our own inquiry, but they may lead us to start at the wrong point or push us in the wrong direction.

# ERRORS IN PERSONAL HUMAN INQUIRY

*Everyday personal human inquiry reveals a number of potential biases.*

Aside from the potential dangers of relying on tradition and authority, we often stumble when we set out to learn for ourselves. Let's consider some of the common errors we make in our own casual inquiries and then look at the ways science provides safeguards against those errors.

## Inaccurate Observation

The keystone of inquiry is observation. But quite frequently we fail to observe things right in front of us or mistakenly observe things that aren't so. Do you recall what your instructor was wearing on the first day of this class? If you had to guess now, what are the chances you would be right?

In contrast to casual human inquiry, scientific observation is a conscious activity. Simply making observations in a more deliberate way helps to reduce error. If you had gone to the first class meeting with a conscious plan to observe and record what your instructor was wearing, you would have increased your chances of accuracy.

In many cases, using both simple and complex measurement devices helps to guard against inaccurate observations. Suppose that you had taken photographs of your instructor on the first day. The photos would have added a degree of precision well beyond that provided by unassisted human memory.

## Overgeneralization

When we look for patterns among the specific things we observe around us, we often assume that a few similar events are evidence of a general pattern. The tendency to overgeneralize is probably greatest when there is pressure to reach a general understanding, yet overgeneralization also occurs in the absence of pressure. Whenever overgeneralization does occur, it can misdirect or impede inquiry.

Imagine you are a rookie police officer newly assigned to foot patrol in an urban neighborhood. Your sergeant wants to meet with you at the end of your shift to discuss what you think are the major law enforcement problems on the beat. Eager to earn favor with your supervisor, you interview the manager of a convenience store in a small shopping area. If the manager mentions vandalism as the biggest concern, you might report that vandalism is the main problem on your beat, even though other business owners and area residents believe that drug dealing contributes to the neighborhood problems of burglary, street robbery, and vandalism. Overgeneralization leads to misrepresentation and simplification of the problems on your beat.

Criminal justice researchers guard against overgeneralization by committing themselves in advance to a sufficiently large sample of observations and by being attentive to how representative those observations are. The **replication** of inquiry provides another safeguard. Replication means repeating a study, checking to see whether similar results are obtained each time. The study may also be repeated under slightly different conditions or in different locations. The box titled "Arrest and Domestic Violence" describes an example of why replication can be especially important in applied research.

## Selective Observation

Another danger of overgeneralization is that it may lead to selective observation. Once we have concluded that a particular pattern exists and have developed a general understanding of why, we will be tempted to pay attention to future events and situations that correspond with the pattern and to ignore those that do not. Racial, ethnic, and other prejudices are reinforced by selective observation.

Research plans often specify in advance the number and kind of observations to be made as a basis for reaching a conclusion. For example, if we wanted to learn whether women are more likely than men to support long prison sentences for sex offenders, we would plan to make a specified number of observations on that question. We might select a thousand people to be interviewed. Even if the first 10 women supported long sentences and the first 10 men opposed them, we would continue to interview everyone selected for the study and record each observation. We would base our conclusion on an analysis of all the observations, not just those first 20 respondents.

## Illogical Reasoning

People have various ways of handling observations that contradict their judgments about the way things are. Surely one of the most remarkable creations of the human mind is the maxim about the exception that proves the rule, an idea that makes no sense at all. An exception can draw attention to a rule or to a supposed rule, but in no system of logic can it prove the rule it contradicts. Yet we often use this pithy saying to brush away contradictions with a simple stroke of illogic.

What statisticians call the *gambler's fallacy* is another illustration of illogic in day-to-day reasoning. According to this fallacy, a consistent run of good or bad luck is presumed to foreshadow its opposite. An evening of bad luck at poker may kindle the belief that a winning hand is just around the corner; many a poker player has stayed in a game too long because of that mistaken belief. Conversely, an extended period of good weather may lead us to worry that it is certain to rain on our weekend picnic.

## Ideology and Politics

Crime is, of course, an important social problem, and a great deal of controversy surrounds policies for dealing with crime. Many people feel strongly one way or another about the death penalty, gun control, and long prison terms for drug users as approaches to reducing crime. There is ongoing concern about racial bias in police practices and sentencing policies. Being tougher on sex offenders

seems to be a favorite topic of state legislatures. Ideological or political views on such issues can undermine objectivity in the research process. Criminal justice professionals may have particular difficulty separating ideology and politics from a more detached, scientific study of crime.

Criminologist Samuel Walker (1994, 16) compares ideological bias in criminal justice research to theology: "The basic problem … is that faith triumphs over facts. For both liberals and conservatives, certain ideas are unchallenged articles of faith, almost like religious beliefs that remain unshaken by empirical facts."

Most of us have our own beliefs about public policy, including policies for dealing with crime. The danger lies in allowing such beliefs to distort how research problems are defined and how research results are interpreted. The scientific approach to the study of crime and criminal justice policy guards against, but does not prevent, ideology and theology from coloring the research process. In empirical research, so-called articles of faith are compared with experience.

## To Err Is Human

We have seen some of the ways that we can go astray in our attempts to know and understand the world and some of the ways that science protects its inquiries from these pitfalls. Social science differs from our casual, day-to-day inquiry in two important respects. First, social scientific inquiry is a conscious activity. Although we engage in continual observation in daily life, much of it is unconscious or semiconscious. In social scientific inquiry, we make a conscious decision to observe, and we stay alert while we do it. Second, social scientific inquiry is a more careful process than our casual efforts. We are more wary of making mistakes and take special precautions to avoid doing so.

Do social scientific research methods offer total protection against the errors that people commit in personal inquiry? No. Not only do individuals make every kind of error we've looked at, but social scientists as a group also succumb to the pitfalls and stay trapped for long periods.

## PURPOSES OF RESEARCH

*We conduct criminal justice research to serve various purposes.*

Criminal justice research, of course, serves many purposes. Explaining associations between things like police patrol and crime levels is one of those purposes; others include exploration, description, and application. Although a given study can have several purposes, it is useful to examine them separately because each has different implications for how we structure research.

### Exploration

Much research in criminal justice is conducted to explore a specific problem, known as **exploratory research**. A researcher or official may be interested in a crime or criminal justice policy issue about which little is known. Or perhaps an innovative approach to policing, court management, or corrections has been tried in some jurisdiction, and the researcher wishes to determine how common such practices are in other cities or states. An exploratory project might collect data on a measure to establish a baseline with which future changes will be compared.

For example, heightened concern over drug use might prompt efforts to estimate the level of drug abuse in the United States. How many people are arrested for drug sales or possession each year? How many high school seniors report using marijuana in the past week or in the past month? How many hours per day do drug dealers work, and how much money do they make? These are examples of research questions intended to explore different aspects of the problem of drug abuse. Exploratory questions may also be formulated in connection with criminal justice responses to drug problems. How many cities have created special police or prosecutor task forces to crack down on drug sales? What sentences are imposed on major dealers or on casual users? How much money is spent on treatment for drug users? What options exist for treating different types of addiction?

Exploratory research in criminal justice can be simple or complex, using a variety of methods.

A mayor who is anxious to learn about drug arrests in his or her city might simply phone the police chief and request a report. Estimating how many high school seniors have used marijuana requires more sophisticated survey methods. Since the early 1970s, the National Institute on Drug Abuse has supported nationwide surveys of students regarding drug use.

### Description

A key purpose of many criminal justice studies is to describe the scope of the crime problem or policy responses to the problem. In **descriptive research**, a researcher or public official observes and then describes what was observed. Criminal justice observation and description, methods grounded in the social sciences, tend to be more accurate than the casual observations people may make about how much crime there is or how violent teenagers are today. Descriptive studies are often concerned with counting or documenting observations; exploratory studies focus more on developing a preliminary understanding about a new or unusual problem.

Descriptive studies are frequently conducted in criminal justice. The FBI has compiled Uniform Crime Reports (UCR) since 1930. UCR data are routinely reported in newspapers and widely interpreted as accurately describing crime in the United States. For example, 2008 UCR figures (Federal Bureau of Investigation 2009) showed that Nevada had the highest rate of auto theft (611.6 thefts per 100,000 residents) in the nation and Maine had the lowest (89.3 per 100,000 residents).

Descriptive studies in criminal justice have other uses. A researcher may attend meetings of neighborhood anticrime groups and observe their efforts to organize block watch committees. These observations form the basis for a case study that describes the activities of neighborhood anticrime groups. Such a descriptive study might present information that officials and residents of other cities can use to promote such organizations themselves. Or consider research by Bruce Jacobs and associates (Jacobs, Topalli, and Wright 2003) in which they describe the motivations for carjacking, how offenders select targets, and how carjacking differs from other types of robbery.

## Explanation

A third general purpose of criminal justice research is to explain things. Reporting that urban residents have generally favorable attitudes toward police is a descriptive activity, but reporting *why* some people believe that police are doing a good job while other people do not is an example of **explanatory research**. Similarly, reporting why Nevada has the highest auto-theft rate in the nation is explanation; simply reporting auto-theft rates for different states is description. A researcher has an explanatory purpose if he or she wishes to know why the number of 14-year-olds involved in gangs has increased, as opposed to simply describing changes in gang membership.

## Application

Researchers also conduct criminal justice studies of an applied nature. **Applied research** stems from a need for facts and findings with specific policy implications. Another purpose of criminal justice research, therefore, is its application to public policy. We can distinguish two types of applied research: evaluation and policy/problem analysis.

Applied research is often used to evaluate the effects of specific criminal justice programs. Determining whether a program designed to reduce burglary actually had the intended effect is an example of evaluation. In its most basic form, evaluation involves comparing the goals of a program with the results. If one goal of increased police foot patrol is to reduce fear of crime, then an evaluation of foot patrol might compare levels of fear before and after increasing the number of police officers on the beat on foot. In most cases, evaluation research uses social scientific methods to test the results of a program or policy change.

The second type of applied research is the analysis of general justice policies and more specific problems. What would happen to court backlogs if we designated a judge and prosecutor who would

handle only drug-dealing cases? How many new police officers would have to be hired if a department shifted to community policing? These are examples of *what-if* questions addressed by policy analysis. Policy analysis is different from other forms of criminal justice research primarily in its focus on future events. Rather than observing and analyzing current or past behavior, policy analysis tries to anticipate the future consequences of alternative actions.

Similarly, justice organizations are increasingly using techniques of problem analysis to study patterns of cases and devise appropriate responses. Problem-oriented policing is perhaps the best-known example, in which crime analysts work with police and other organizations to examine recurring problems. Ron Clarke and John Eck (2005) have prepared a comprehensive guide for this type of applied research.

Our brief discussion of distinct research purposes is not intended to imply that research purposes are mutually exclusive. Many criminal justice studies have elements of more than one purpose. Suppose you want to examine the problem of bicycle theft at your university. First, you need some information that describes the problem of bicycle theft on campus. Let's assume your research finds that thefts from some campus locations have declined but that there was an increase in bikes stolen from racks outside dormitories. You might explain these findings by noting that bicycles parked outside dorms tend to be unused for longer periods of time and that there is more coming and going among bikes parked near classrooms. One option to further reduce thefts would be to purchase more secure bicycle racks. A policy analysis might compare the costs of installing the racks with the predicted savings resulting from a reduction in bike theft.

Incidentally, the Center for Problem-Oriented Policing has published an extremely useful guide on the problem of bicycle theft (Johnson, Sidebottom, and Thorpe 2008). In addition to its substantive value, this guide is an example of applied research that can be conducted and used by justice professionals. Visit the website www.popcenter.org for more information and examples.

# HOW TO DESIGN A RESEARCH PROJECT

*Designing research requires planning several stages, but the stages do not always occur in the same sequence.*

We've now seen how casual human inquiry can set us up for making mistakes, and we have summarized basic research purposes. But what if you were to undertake a research project yourself? Where would you start? Then where would you go? How would you begin planning your research? College courses on research methods in criminal justice often require students to design a research project. The rest of this chapter covers the basics of planning research and writing a proposal.

Every project has a starting point, but it is important to think through later stages, even at the beginning. Figure 1.1 presents a schematic view of the social scientific research process. Think of this as a sort of map that provides an overview of the whole process before we launch into the details of particular components of research.

## The Research Process

At the top of the diagram in Figure 1.1 are interests, ideas, theories, and new programs—the possible beginning points for a line of research. The letters (*A, B, X, Y*, and so forth) represent concepts such as deterrence or burglary. Thus, you might have a general interest in finding out why the threat of punishment deters some but not all people from committing crimes, or you might want to investigate how burglars select their targets. Question marks in the diagram indicate that you aren't sure things are the way you suspect they are. We have represented a theory as a complex set of relationships among several concepts (*A, B, E,* and *F*).

The research process might also begin with an idea for a new program. Imagine that you are the director of a probation services department and you want to introduce weekly drug tests for people on probation. Because you have taken a course on criminal justice research methods, you decide to design an evaluation of the new program before trying it out. The research process begins with your idea for the new drug-testing program.

Notice the movement back and forth among these several possible beginnings, represented by the arrows between the top boxes. An initial interest may lead to the formulation of an idea, which may fit into a larger theory, and the theory may produce new ideas and create new interests. Or your understanding of some theory may encourage you to consider new policies.

To make this discussion more concrete, let's take a specific research example. Suppose you are concerned about the problem of crime on your campus and you have a special interest in learning more about how other students view the issue and what they think should be done about it. Going a step further, let's say you have the impression that students are especially concerned about violent crimes such as assault and robbery, and that many students feel the university should be doing more to prevent violent crime. The source of this idea might be your own interest after being a student for a couple of years. You might develop the idea while reading about theories of crime in a course you are taking. Perhaps you recently read stories about a crime wave on campus. Or maybe some combination of things makes you want to learn more about campus crime.

Considering the research purposes discussed earlier in this chapter, your research will be mainly exploratory. You probably have descriptive and explanatory interests as well: How much of a problem is violent crime on campus? Are students especially concerned about crime in certain areas? Why are some students more worried about crime than others? What do students think would be effective changes to reduce campus crime problems?

## Getting Started

To begin pursuing your interest in student concerns about violent crime, you undoubtedly will want to read something about the issue. You might

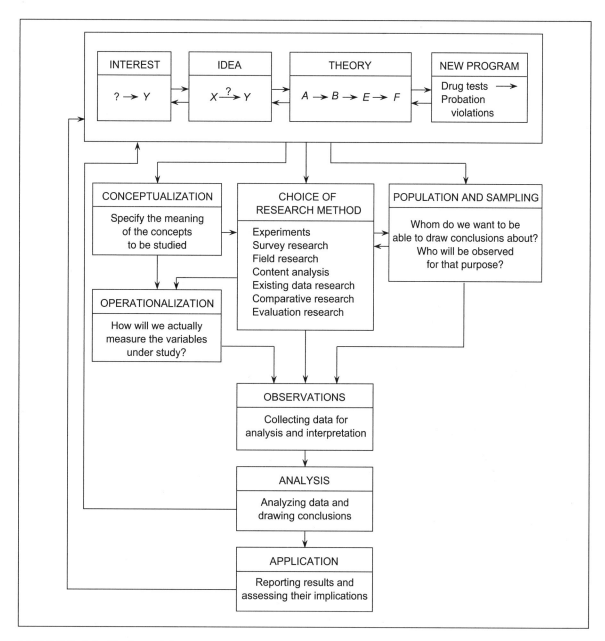

**FIGURE 1.1** The Research Process

begin by finding out what research has been done on fear of crime and on the sorts of crime that concern people most. Items posted on a campus website might provide information about violent crimes that occurred recently. In addition, you will probably want to talk to people, such as other students or campus police officers. These activities will prepare you to handle various decisions about research design. As you review the research literature, you should make note of how other researchers approached the problem and consider whether the same designs will meet your research objective.

What is your objective, by the way? It's important that you are clear about that before you design your study. Do you plan to write a paper based on your research to satisfy a course requirement or as an honors thesis? Is your purpose to gain information that will support an argument for more police protection or better lighting on campus? Do you want to write an article for the campus newspaper or blog?

Usually, your objective for undertaking research can be expressed in a report. The website for this book includes information that will help you with the organization of research reports. We recommend that you make an outline of such a report as the first step in the design of any project. You should be clear about the kinds of statements you will want to make when the research is complete. Here are two examples of such statements: "X percentage of State U students believe that sexual assault is a big problem on campus," and "Female students living off campus are more likely than females living in dorms to feel that emergency phones should be installed near buildings where evening classes are held." Although your final report may not look much like your initial image of it, outlining the planned report will help you make better decisions about research design.

## Conceptualization

We often talk casually about criminal justice concepts such as deterrence, recidivism, crime prevention, community policing, and child abuse; but it is necessary to specify what we mean by these concepts to do research on them. Chapter 4 will examine this process of **conceptualization** in depth. For now, let's see what it might involve in our hypothetical example.

If you are going to study student concerns about violent crime, you must first specify what you mean by *concern about violent crime*. This ambiguous phrase can mean different things to different people. Campus police officers are concerned about violent crime because that is part of their job. Students may have

two kinds of concerns. On the one hand, they might be concerned about crime in much the same way they are concerned about other social problems, such as immigration, health care, and the global economy. They recognize these issues as problems society must deal with, but they don't feel that the issues affect them directly; we could specify this concept as *general concern about violent crime*. On the other hand, students may feel that the threat of violent crime does affect them directly, and they express some fear about the possibility of being a victim; let's call this *fear for personal safety*.

Of course, you need to specify all the concepts you wish to study. If you want to study the possible effect of concern about crime on student behavior, you'll have to decide whether you want to limit your focus to specific precautionary behavior such as keeping doors locked or general behavior such as going to classes, parties, and football games.

## Choice of Research Method

A variety of methods are available to the criminal justice researcher. Each method has strengths and weaknesses, and certain concepts are more appropriately studied by some methods than by others.

A survey is the most appropriate method for studying both general concern and fear for personal safety. You might interview students directly or ask them to fill out an e-mailed questionnaire. As we'll see in Chapter 7, surveys are especially well suited to the study of individuals' attitudes and opinions. Thus, if you wish to examine whether students who are afraid of crime are more likely to believe that campus lighting should be improved than students who are not afraid, then a survey is a good method.

Other methods described in Part Three may be appropriate. Through content analysis (discussed in Chapter 9), you might examine postings on a campus blog and analyze what the writers believe should be done to improve campus safety. Field research (see Chapter 8), in which you observe whether students tend to avoid dark areas of the campus, will help you understand student behavior in avoiding certain areas of the campus at night. Or you might study official complaints made to police and college administrators about crime problems on campus. As you read Part Three, you'll see how other research methods might be used to study this topic. Usually the best study design is one that uses more than one research method, taking advantage of their different strengths.

## Operationalization

Having specified the concepts to be studied and chosen the research method, you now must develop specific measurement procedures. **Operationalization**, discussed in Chapter 4, refers to the concrete steps, or operations, used to measure specific concepts.

If you decide to use a survey to study concern about violent crime, your operationalization will take the form of questionnaire items. You might operationalize fear for personal safety with the question: "How safe do you feel alone on the campus after dark?" This could be followed by boxes indicating the possible answers "Safe" and "Unsafe." Student attitudes about ways of improving campus safety could be operationalized with the item "Listed below are different actions that might be taken to reduce violent crime on campus. Beside each description, indicate whether you favor or oppose the actions described." This could be followed by several different actions, with "Favor" and "Oppose" boxes beside each.

## Population and Sampling

In addition to refining concepts and measurements, decisions must be made about whom or what to study. The population for a study is that group about whom we want to be able to draw conclusions. Groups are usually made up of people, but we may wish to study a group of drug rehabilitation clinics. We are almost never able to study all the members of the population that interests us, so we often sample subjects for study. Chapter 6 describes methods for selecting samples that adequately reflect the whole population that interests us. Notice in Figure 1.1 that decisions about population and sampling are related to decisions about the research method to be used.

In the study of concern about violent crime, the relevant population is the student population of your college. As you'll discover in Chapter 6, however, selecting a sample requires you to be more specific than that. Will you include part-time as well as full-time students? Students who live on campus, off campus, or both? Many such questions must be answered in terms of your research purpose. If your purpose is to study concern about sexual assault, you might consider limiting your population to female students. If hate crimes are of special interest, you will want to be sure that your study population includes minorities and others who are thought to be particularly targeted by hate crimes.

## Observations

Having decided what to study, among whom, and by what method, you are ready to make observations—to collect empirical data. The chapters of Part Three, which describe various research methods, discuss the different observation methods appropriate to each.

For a survey of concern about violent crime, you might prepare an electronic questionnaire and e-mail it to a sample selected from the student body, or you could have a team of interviewers conduct the survey over the telephone. The relative advantages and disadvantages of these and other possibilities are discussed in Chapter 7.

## Analysis

We manipulate the collected data for the purpose of drawing conclusions that reflect on the interests, ideas, and theories that initiated the inquiry. Chapter 11 describes a few of the many options available to you in analyzing data. Notice in Figure 1.1 that the results of your analyses feed back into your initial interests, ideas, and theories. In practice, this feedback may initiate another cycle of inquiry. In the study of student concern about violent crime, the analysis phase will have both descriptive and explanatory purposes. You might begin by calculating the percentage of students who feel afraid to use specific parking facilities after dark and the percentage who favor or oppose each of the different things that might be done to improve campus safety. Together, these percentages will provide a good picture of student opinion on the issue.

Moving beyond simple description, you might examine the opinions of different subsets of the student body: men versus women; freshmen, sophomores, juniors, seniors, and graduate students; and students who live in dorms versus off-campus apartments. You might then conduct some explanatory analysis to make the point that students who are enrolled in classes that meet in the evening hours are most in favor of improved campus lighting.

## Application

The final stage of the research process involves using the research you've conducted and the conclusions you've reached. To start, you will probably want to communicate your findings so that others will know what you've learned. You will usually prepare some kind of written report. Perhaps you will make oral presentations in class or at a professional meeting. Or you might create a web page that presents your results. Other students will be interested in hearing what you have learned about their concerns about violent crime on campus.

Your study might also be used to actually do something about campus safety. If you find that a large proportion of students you interviewed believe that a parking lot near the library is poorly lighted, university administrators could add more lights or campus police might patrol the area more frequently. Crime prevention programs might be launched in dormitories if residents are more afraid of violent crime than students who live in other types of housing. Students in a Rutgers University class on crime prevention focused on car thefts and break-ins surrounding the campus in Newark, New Jersey. Their semester project presented specific recommendations on how university and city officials could reduce the problem.

## Thinking about Research Problems

One of the most important, yet surprisingly difficult, parts of the research process is specifying and framing your interest in a particular problem or question.

What are you interested in understanding? Surely you have several questions about crime and possible policy responses. Why do some juvenile gangs sell drugs whereas others steal cars? Why do particular neighborhoods near campus seem to have higher rates of burglary? How often are guns found in stop-and-frisk operations? Do sentencing policies discriminate against minorities? Do cities with gun control laws have lower murder rates? Is burglary more common in single-family homes or apartment buildings? Are sentences for rape more severe in some states than in others? Are mandatory jail sentences more effective than license suspension in reducing repeat drunk-driving offenses? Think for a while about the kinds of questions that interest and concern you.

To give you ideas about the many possible subjects for research, here are topics of papers written by students in the first class Michael Maxfield taught at John Jay College in fall 2010:

- Risk assessment in juvenile parole hearings
- The effect of religion and culture on attitudes about suicide
- Determining the extent to which arrest frequency is associated with substance addiction and mental illness
- Links between domestic violence and indirect spouse abuse after separation
- An exploratory study of pimps in Atlantic City, New Jersey
- An experimental study of attitudes toward sex offenders in Spain
- Whether sexual abuse by Catholic priests is a product of sexual preference or situational factors
- Community disorganization and crime on Native American lands

In most cases, researchers find themselves reworking or clarifying research problems as they learn more about a topic. That was the case for students in Maxfield's class. The student studying pimps was surprised to learn that only a minority of prostitutes in Atlantic City had anything like the classic worker/manager relationship with a pimp. That led to reframing the research to begin by classifying the different ways prostitutes worked with pimps and others playing pimplike roles.

In most cases, you're advised to begin with your own interests and experiences and then learn more about what research has been done. For example, the third topic listed above was examined by a student with considerable experience in correctional settings. She began with her observation that people arrested frequently for minor offenses often seem driven more by substance abuse and mental health problems than by any overt criminal intent. The student then conducted research to learn more about existing research on jail populations, and she revised her topic as she read more of the research literature.

Students sometimes have difficulty narrowing interests to researchable questions. We are all concerned about crime and justice problems to some degree, but our casual interests can be misleading. Reading research about crime and justice problems is a good way to get ideas about research topics and to see how social science addresses problems that are treated more casually in popular literature. The box "Getting Ideas about Research Questions" offers more advice in this regard.

## REVIEWING THE LITERATURE

*Researchers begin a research project with a review of the literature.*

Research should be seen as an extension of what has previously been learned about a particular topic. A review of the literature will tell you what's already known and not known. In most cases, you should organize your search of the literature around the key concepts you wish to study. Alternatively, you may want to study a certain population: corrections officers, sex offenders, drug counselors, computer hackers, and so forth. In any case, you'll identify a set of terms that represent your core interests.

Conducting a literature review has become both much easier and much more challenging with the expansion of information and search tools on the Internet. It's easier in the sense that much information can be accessed through the Internet without having to visit bricks-and-mortar libraries. Most colleges and universities now have online access to academic journals. Reports by government agencies and private organizations are readily available to anyone with access to the web.

Reviewing what others have found about a problem has become more difficult largely for the same reason: it's easy to access a seemingly endless supply of documents. This has produced a related problem of how to sort through all the information, separating research findings from the demented ramblings of ideologues and everything in between. After providing guidelines on how to find relevant literature, we'll suggest some cautionary strategies.

### General Strategies

Doing a literature review is basically a process of accumulating, sorting through, and synthesizing information. We all do this every day in different, usually informal ways. Doing a literature review for research is more systematic and deliberate, just like the research process in general. It's best to keep notes of articles, books, websites, or other things as you review them. Also keep in mind that research literature accumulates; research studies usually build on previous studies, as we noted in the box "Getting Ideas about Research Topics."

**Getting Started** Start with a book or an article that deals with your topic and expand from there. We'll call this your source document. Expanding can mean going both backward, consulting readings cited in your source document, or forward, in which you find later research that is based on your source document. For example, if you're interested in terrorism, you might read the book *Outsmarting the Terrorists* by Ronald Clarke and Graeme Newman (2006). In conducting your literature review, you would read the selected references shown in the book's bibliography.

But you would also be interested in later research that expands on what Clarke and Newman wrote in 2006. One of the best ways to do this is to use the website Google Scholar (http://scholar.google.com). Type "clarke newman outsmarting" in the search box, and one of the first references that pops up should be their book. In December

## GETTING IDEAS ABOUT RESEARCH TOPICS

Many people will have some idea of what sort of research question they are interested in, no matter how general the idea may be. Even so, it can be difficult for beginning researchers to get started. Here are some tips for finding and fleshing out preliminary ideas about research topics.

### Do an Internet Search, but Use Specialized Tools

For example, type this phrase into a Google search panel: "sex offender residency restrictions." In December 2010 this entry produced an estimated 98,700 results that included mass media stories, links to legislation, and many other types of sites. Then type the same phrase into a Google Scholar search panel (go to http://scholar.google.com). In December 2010 this yielded about 160 results of scholarly books and articles on the topic. Reading examples of these, or mass media stories for that matter, will give you ideas about how to begin research on sex offender residency restrictions.

### Replicate an Existing Study

Berenson and Appelbaum (2010) examined where sex offenders lived in two New York counties. They were interested in laws that required sex offenders to live a minimum distance from places like schools and other public facilities, as well as the effects that such laws have on housing choices for sex offenders. Two findings were noteworthy. First, 73 to 97 percent of existing housing units in the two counties were off-limits to sex offenders because they were too close to specified facilities. Second, and a consequence of the first finding, most sex offenders living in the two counties were in violation of the restrictions. What about in your city or county? Since data on where sex offenders live are widely available, you could conduct a similar kind of study in a different place.

### Follow Up on Recommendations for Further Research

Many research articles and books conclude by describing how subsequent research can add to knowledge. So if you find an article interesting, you might get an idea from the authors' suggestions for further research. For example, White and Loeber (2008) examined links between bullying in school, placement in special education programs, and later involvement in serious delinquency. They found that later delinquency often followed bullying, regardless of placement in special education programs. Their research was based on interviews over a period of years with students in Pittsburgh, Pennsylvania, schools. Near the end of their article, they recommend that future research use systematic observations of behavior in different types of school activity (p. 393). If you were interested in the problem of bullying or violence in middle schools, reading articles that report research on the topic could give you ideas about designing your own study.

### Ask Your Professor

If one of the requirements for your research methods course is to write a research proposal or actually do some research, you should find out what topics are of special interest to your instructor. This does not mean you should engage in idle flattery. Instead, think of your instructor as both an expert and a professional scholar, someone who is probably doing research for a book, scholarly article, or dissertation. Your professor is an expert in what research might need to be done in a particular area. Don't hesitate to ask for ideas, and be sure to use focused questions, like "What sorts of topics are you interested in?" That's better than asking something like "Can you give me some ideas? I don't know where to begin."

---

2010 this search showed that 64 subsequent publications had cited the book. Clicking on "cited by 64" produces a list of these publications, together with links to further information about the books or journals that cite Clarke and Newman. In this way, you can find out about more current research that's been published since your source document.

**Being Selective**   Sources like Google Scholar offer a built-in quality control by limiting your search to academic journals and related publications.

However, you may want to find other types of materials, such as government reports, or studies published by other types of organizations. Ronald Clarke and Phyllis Schultze offer a useful warning and guidelines: "Unlike scholarly books and journal articles, websites are seldom reviewed or refereed. You need to be critical of the information you use when it comes to the Web, because anyone can make a website that looks expert. In general, rely more heavily on those sites sponsored by colleges and universities, government agencies, and professional organizations" (Clarke and Schultze 2005, 24).

Some college or university libraries provide more detailed suggestions on how to evaluate information you discover in your research. For example, the Meriam Library at California State University Chico (2010) describes evaluation criteria referred to as the "CRAAP Test":

- Currency: Information timeliness
- Relevance: Does the information apply to your specific topic?
- Authority: The source of the information
- Accuracy: Is the information based on fact or opinion?
- Purpose: Why does the information exist? Why is it presented?

**Using a Library**  Although it is no longer necessary to visit a physical library to access many published research materials, libraries and librarians remain critical resources for research. Librarians can help you develop strategies for searching the literature and evaluating the different sources you find. Clarke and Schultze offer excellent advice on how to use different types of libraries. For research on crime and justice, the Don M. Gottfredson Library of Criminal Justice at Rutgers University, under the direction of Phyllis Schultze, is the best single resource available anywhere in the world, with unmatched physical and online resources. Visit the library through the World Criminal Justice Library Electronic Network at http://andromeda.rutgers.edu/~wcjlen/WCJ/.

## How to Read Scholarly Research

You don't read a social research report the same way you'd read a novel. You can, of course, but it's not the most effective approach. Journal articles and books are laid out somewhat differently, so here are some initial guidelines for reading each.

**Reading a Journal Article**  In most journals, each article begins with an abstract. Read it first. It should tell you the purpose of the research, the methods used, and the major findings. The abstract serves two major functions. First, it gives you a good idea as to whether you'll want to read the rest of the article. If you're reviewing the literature for a paper you're writing, the abstract tells you whether that particular article is relevant. Second, the abstract establishes a framework within which to read the rest of the article. It may raise questions in your mind regarding method or conclusions, thereby creating an agenda to pursue in your reading.

After you've read the abstract, you might go directly to the summary and/or conclusions at the end of the article. That will give you a more detailed picture of what the article is all about. Jot down any new questions or observations that occur to you.

Next, skim the article, noting the section headings and any tables or graphs. You don't need to study any of these things in your skimming, though it's fine to review anything that catches your attention. By the end of this step, you should start feeling familiar with the article. You should be pretty clear on the researcher's conclusions and have a general idea of the methods used in reaching them.

If you decide to carefully read the whole article, you'll have a good idea of where it's heading and how each section fits into the logic of the whole article. Keep taking notes. Mark any passages you think you might like to quote later on. After carefully reading the article, it's a good idea to skim it quickly one more time. This way you get back in touch with the forest after having focused on the trees.

If you want to fully grasp what you've just read, find someone else to explain it to. If you're doing the reading in connection with a course, you should have no trouble finding someone willing to listen. However, if you can explain it coherently to someone who has no prior contact with the subject matter, you'll know you have an absolute lock on the material.

**Reading a Book-Length Report**  The approach for articles can be adapted to reading a book-length report, sometimes also called a research monograph. These longer research reports cover the same basic terrain and roughly the same structure. Instead of an abstract, the preface and opening chapter of the book lay out the purpose, method, and main findings of the study. The preface is usually written more informally and so may be easier to understand than an abstract.

As with an article, it's useful to skim through the book, getting a sense of its organization, its use of tables and graphs, and its main findings. You should come away from this step feeling somewhat familiar with the book. Take notes as you go along, writing down things you observe and questions that are raised.

As you settle in to read the book more carefully, you should repeat this same process with each chapter. Read the opening paragraphs to get a sense of what's to come and then skip to the concluding paragraphs for the summary. Skim the chapter to increase your familiarity with it, and then read more deliberately, taking notes as you go.

It's sometimes okay to skip portions of a scholarly book, but this depends on your purpose in reading it in the first place. Perhaps only a few portions of the book are relevant to your research. However, if you are interested in the researcher's findings, you must pay some attention to the methods used (e.g., who was studied, how, and when?) to be able to judge the quality of the conclusions offered by the author.

## THE RESEARCH PROPOSAL

*Research proposals describe planned activities and include a budget and time line.*

If you undertake a research project—an assignment for this course, perhaps, or even a major study funded by the government or a research foundation—you will probably have to provide a research proposal describing what you intend to accomplish and how. We'll conclude this chapter with advice on how you might prepare such a proposal. As we do this, think of the research proposal as another way to get an overview of the research process.

### Elements of a Research Proposal

Some funding agencies have specific requirements for a proposal's elements, structure, or both. For example, in its research solicitation announcement for graduate research fellowships, the National Institute of Justice (NIJ) describes what should be included in research proposals, regardless of topic (National Institute of Justice 2010b). Your instructor may also have certain requirements for a research proposal you are to prepare in this course. Here are some basic elements that should be included in almost any research proposal.

**Problem or Objective**   What exactly do you want to study? Why is it worth studying? Does the proposed study contribute to our general understanding of crime or policy responses to crime? Does it have practical significance? If your proposal describes an evaluation study, then the problem, objective, or research questions may already be specified for you. For example, in its request for research on cybercrime and digital evidence recovery, the NIJ asked that proposals address forensic tools for specific electronic environments (National Institute of Justice 2010a, 3):

- Mobile cellular devices
- Internet-based (cloud computing) environments
- Voice-over-Internet Protocol (VoIP)
- Vehicle-based computer systems

In most cases, however, you will specify the research problem or objective.

**Literature Review**   As we described in the previous section, research begins by reviewing what others have said about your topic.

**Research Questions**   What specific questions will your research try to answer? Given what others have found, as stated in your literature review, what new information do you expect to find? It's useful to view research questions as a more specific version of the problem or objective described earlier. Then, of course, your specific questions should be framed in the context of what other research has found.

**Subjects for Study**   Whom or what will you study in order to collect data? Identify the subjects in general terms, and then specifically identify who (or what) are available for study and how you will reach them. Is it appropriate to select a sample? If so, how will you do that? If there is any possibility that your research will have an impact on those you study, how will you ensure that they are not harmed by the research? Finally, if you will be interacting directly with human subjects, you will probably have to include a consent form, as we describe in Chapter 2.

**Measurement**   What are the key variables in your study? How will you define and measure them? Do your definitions and measurement methods duplicate (which is okay, incidentally) or differ from those of previous research on this topic?

**Data Collection Methods**   How will you actually collect the data for your study? Will you observe behavior directly or conduct a survey? Will you undertake field research, or will you focus on the reanalysis of data already collected by others? Criminal justice research often includes more than one such method.

**Analysis**   Briefly describe the kind of analysis you plan to conduct. Spell out the purpose and logic of your analysis. Are you interested in precise description? Do you intend to explain why things are the way they are? Will you analyze the impact of a new program? What possible explanatory variables will your analysis consider, and how will you know whether you've explained the program impact adequately?

**References**   Be sure to include a list of all materials you consulted and cited in your proposal. Formats for citations vary. Your instructor may specify certain formats or may refer you to specific style manuals for guidelines on how to cite books, articles, and web-based resources.

**Schedule**   It is often appropriate to provide a schedule for the various stages of research. Even if you don't do this for the proposal, do it for yourself. If you don't have a time line for accomplishing the stages of research and keeping track of how you're doing, you may end up in trouble.

**Budget**   If you are asking someone to give you money to pay the costs of your research, you will need to provide a budget that specifies where the money will go. Large, expensive projects include budgetary categories such as personnel, equipment, supplies, and expenses (such as travel, copying, and printing). Even for a more modest project you will pay for yourself, it's a good idea to spend some time anticipating any expenses involved: office supplies, photocopying, computer disks, telephone calls, transportation, and so on.

As you can see, if you are interested in conducting a criminal justice research project, it is a good idea to prepare a research proposal for your own purposes, even if you aren't required to do so by your instructor or a funding agency. If you are going to invest your time and energy in such a project, you should do what you can to ensure a return on that investment.

## KNOWING THROUGH EXPERIENCE: SUMMING UP AND LOOKING AHEAD

*Empirical research involves measurement and interpretation.*

This chapter introduced the foundation of criminal justice research: empirical research, or learning through experience. Doing scientific research in criminal justice is different from the ordinary ways we learn about things because ordinary modes of inquiry have some built-in limits. The coming chapters describe how science tries to overcome such limits and biases.

We also considered the different purposes we may have in mind for conducting criminal justice research, ranging from exploration to examining links between policy action and justice problems.

Our advice on how to design a research project will be useful in two respects. First, it can serve as an annotated outline of what a typical research report would include, a guide for preparing a research report or proposal for this course. Second, Figure 1.1 and our discussion of how to design a research project offer an introduction and overview to later chapters.

Finally, it is helpful to think of criminal justice research as organized around two basic activities: measurement and interpretation. Researchers measure aspects of reality and then draw conclusions about what their measurements mean. All of us are observing all the time, but *scientific measurement* refers to something more deliberate and rigorous. Parts Two and Three of this book describe ways of structuring observations to produce more deliberate, rigorous measures.

The other key to criminal justice research is interpretation. Much of interpretation is based on data analysis, which is introduced in Part Four. More generally, however, interpretation very much depends on how observations are structured, a point we will encounter repeatedly.

As we put the pieces together—measurement and interpretation—we are in a position to describe, explain, or predict something. And that is what social science is all about.

## SUMMARY

- Knowledge of research methods is valuable to criminal justice professionals as consumers and producers of research.

- The study of research methods is the study of how we know what we know.

- Inquiry is a natural human activity for gaining an understanding of the world around us.

- Much of our knowledge is based on agreement rather than direct experience.

- Tradition and authority are important sources of knowledge.

- Empirical research is based on experience and produces knowledge through systematic observation.

- In day-to-day inquiry, we often make mistakes. Science offers protection against such mistakes.

- Whereas people often observe inaccurately, science avoids such errors by making observation a careful and deliberate activity.

- Sometimes we jump to general conclusions on the basis of only a few observations. Scientists avoid overgeneralization through replication.

- Scientists avoid illogical reasoning by being as careful and deliberate in their thinking as in their observations.

- The scientific study of crime guards against, but does not prevent, ideological and political beliefs influencing research findings.

- Different research purposes are exploratory, descriptive, explanatory, and applied.

- The research process is flexible, involving different steps that are best considered together. The process usually begins with some general interest or idea.

- A careful review of previous literature is an essential part of the research process.

- A research proposal provides an overview of why a study will be undertaken and how it will be conducted. It is a useful device for planning and is required in some circumstances.

## KEY TERMS

These terms are defined in the chapter where they are set in boldface and can also be found in the glossary at the end of the book.

| | | |
|---|---|---|
| applied research, p. 11 | empirical, p. 5 | methodology, p. 6 |
| conceptualization, p. 14 | exploratory research, p. 10 | operationalization, p. 15 |
| descriptive research, p. 10 | explanatory research, p. 11 | replication, p. 8 |

## REVIEW QUESTIONS AND EXERCISES

1. Review the common errors of personal inquiry discussed in this chapter. Find a newspaper or magazine article about crime that illustrates one or more of those errors. Discuss how a scientist would avoid making that error.

2. Briefly discuss examples of descriptive research and explanatory research about changes in crime rates in some major city.

3. Often things we think are true and supported by considerable experience and evidence turn out not to be true, or at least not true with the certainty we expected. Criminal justice seems especially vulnerable to this phenomenon, perhaps because crime and criminal justice policy are so often the subjects of mass and popular media attention. If news stories, movies, and TV shows all point to growing gang- or drug-related violence, it is easy to assume that these are real problems identified by systematic study. Choose a criminal justice topic or claim that is currently prominent in news stories or entertainment. Consult a recent edition of the *Sourcebook of Criminal Justice Statistics* (citation below) for evidence to refute the claim.

## ADDITIONAL READINGS

Clarke, Ronald V., and Phyllis Schultze, *Researching a Problem* (Washington, DC: U.S. Department of Justice, Office of Community Oriented Policing Services, 2005; http://popcenter.org/Tools/pdfs/researchingproblem.htm). Designed for justice professionals rather than researchers, this guide still offers very helpful advice on finding and interpreting research literature.

Hoover, Kenneth R., and Todd Donovan, *The Elements of Social Scientific Thinking*, 9th ed. (Belmont, CA: Wadsworth, 2007). This book provides an excellent overview of the key elements in social scientific analysis.

Levine, Robert, *A Geography of Time: The Temporal Misadventures of a Social Psychologist* (New York: Basic Books, 1997). Most of us think of time as absolute. Levine's book is fun and fascinating as he explores how agreement reality plays a major role in how people from different cultures think about time.

Maguire, Kathleen (ed.), *Sourcebook of Criminal Justice Statistics* (Washington, DC: U.S. Department of Justice, Office of Justice Programs, Bureau of Justice Statistics, annual; www.albany.edu/sourcebook). For 30 years this annual publication has been a source of basic data on criminal justice. If you're not yet familiar with this compendium, chapter 1 is a good place to start.

Tilley, Nick, and Gloria Laycock, *Working Out What to Do: Evidence-Based Crime Reduction* (London: Home Office Policing and Reducing Crime Unit, Crime Reduction Series, no. 11, 2002; www.homeoffice.gov.uk/rds/crimreducpubs1.html). One of many excellent publications from the British Home Office, this guide helps justice professionals develop policies based on empirical experience. The guide is clearly written and useful as an illustration of how practitioners use social science.

# CHAPTER 2

# Ethics and Criminal Justice Research

*We'll examine some of the ethical considerations that must be taken into account, along with the scientific ones, in the design and execution of research. We'll consider different types of ethical issues and ways of handling them.*

## INTRODUCTION

*Despite our best intentions, we don't always recognize ethical issues in research.*

Most of this book focuses on scientific procedures and constraints. We'll see that the logic of science suggests certain research procedures, but we'll also see that some scientifically "perfect" study designs are not feasible, because they would be too expensive or take too long to execute. Throughout the book, we'll deal with workable compromises.

Before we get to scientific and practical constraints on research, it's important to explore another essential consideration in doing criminal justice research in the real world—ethics. Just as certain designs or measurement procedures are impractical, others are constrained by ethical problems.

All of us consider ourselves ethical—not perfect perhaps, but more ethical than most of humanity. The problem in criminal justice research—and probably in life—is that ethical considerations are not always apparent to us. As a result, we often plunge into things without seeing ethical issues that may be obvious to others and even to ourselves when they are pointed out. Our excitement at the prospect of a new research project may blind us to obstacles that ethical considerations present.

Any of us can immediately see that a study that requires juvenile gang members to demonstrate how they steal cars is unethical. You'd speak out immediately if we suggested interviewing people about drug use and then publishing what they said in the local newspaper. But, as ethical as we think we are, we are likely to miss the ethical issues in other situations—not because we're bad, but because we're human.

## ETHICAL ISSUES IN CRIMINAL JUSTICE RESEARCH

*A few basic principles encompass the variety of ethical issues in criminal justice research.*

In most dictionaries and in common usage, ethics is typically associated with morality, and both deal with matters of right and wrong. But what is right and what is wrong? What is the source of the distinction? Depending on the individual, sources vary from religion to political ideology to pragmatic observations of what seems to work and what doesn't.

*Webster's New World Dictionary* (4th ed.) is typical among dictionaries in defining **ethical** as "conforming to the standards of conduct of a given profession or group." Although the relativity embedded in this definition may frustrate those in search of moral absolutes, what we regard as moral and ethical in day-to-day life is no more than a

matter of agreement among members of a group. And, not surprisingly, different groups have agreed on different ethical codes of conduct. If someone is going to live in a particular society, it is extremely useful to know what that society considers ethical and unethical. The same holds true for the criminal justice research "community."

Anyone preparing to do criminal justice research should be aware of the general agreements shared by researchers about what's proper and improper in the conduct of scientific inquiry. Ethical issues in criminal justice can be especially challenging because our research questions frequently address illegal behavior that people are anxious to conceal. This is true of offenders and, sometimes, people who work in criminal justice agencies.

The sections that follow explore some of the more important ethical issues and agreements in criminal justice research. Our discussion is restricted to ethical issues in research, not in policy or practice. Thus, we will not consider such issues as the morality of the death penalty, acceptable police practices, the ethics of punishment, or codes of conduct for attorneys and judges. If you are interested in substantive ethical issues in criminal justice policy, consult Jocelyn Pollock (2006) or Richard Spurgeon Hall and associates (1999) for an introduction.

### No Harm to Participants

Weighing the potential benefits from doing research against the possibility of harm to the people being studied—or harm to other people—is a fundamental ethical dilemma in all research. For example, biomedical research can involve potential physical harm to people or animals. Social research may cause psychological harm or embarrassment in people who are asked to reveal information about themselves. Criminal justice research has the potential to produce both physical and psychological harm, as well as embarrassment. Although the likelihood of physical harm may seem remote, it is worthwhile to consider possible ways it might occur.

Harm to subjects, researchers, or third parties is possible in field studies that collect information from or about persons engaged in criminal activity; this is especially true for field research. For example, studies of drug crimes may involve locating and interviewing active users and dealers. Scott Jacques and Richard Wright (2008) studied active drug sellers in Atlanta and St. Louis, recruiting subjects by spreading the word through various means. Collecting such information from active criminals presents at least the possibility of violence against research subjects by other drug dealers.

Potential danger to field researchers should also be considered. For instance, Peter Reuter and associates (1990) selected their drug-dealer subjects by consulting probation department records. The researchers recognized that sampling persons from different Washington, D.C., neighborhoods would have produced a more generalizable group of subjects, but they rejected that approach because mass media reports of widespread drug-related violence generated concern about the safety of research staff (Reuter, MacCoun, and Murphy 1990, 119). Whether such fears were warranted is unclear, but this example does illustrate how safety issues can affect criminal justice research.

Other researchers acknowledge the potential for harm in the context of respect for ethical principles. The box titled "Ethics and Extreme Field Research" gives examples of subtle and not-so-subtle ethical dilemmas encountered by a Rutgers University graduate in her study of drug use in rave clubs. For more information on this research, see Dina Perrone's book, *The High Life* (Perrone 2009).

More generally, John Monahan and associates (1993) distinguish three different groups at potential risk of physical harm in their research on violence. First are research subjects themselves. Women at risk of domestic violence may be exposed to greater danger if assailants learn they have disclosed past victimizations to researchers. Second, researchers might trigger attacks on themselves when they interview subjects who have a history of violent offending. Third, and most problematic, is the possibility that collecting information from unstable individuals might increase the risk of harm to third parties. The last category presents a new dilemma if

researchers learn that subjects intend to attack some third party. Should researchers honor a promise of confidentiality to subjects or intervene to prevent the harm?

The potential for psychological harm to subjects exists when interviews are used to collect information. Crime surveys that ask respondents about their experiences as victims of crime may remind them of a traumatic, or at least an unpleasant, experience. Surveys may also ask respondents about illegal behaviors such as drug use or crimes they have committed. Talking about such actions with interviewers can be embarrassing.

Some researchers have taken special steps to reduce the potential for emotional trauma in interviews of domestic violence victims (Tjaden and Thoennes 2000). One of the most interesting examples involves the use of self-completed computer questionnaires in the British Crime Survey (Mirrlees-Black 1999). Rather than verbally respond to questions from interviewers, respondents read and answer questions on a laptop computer. This procedure affords a greater degree of privacy for research subjects.

Recent developments in the use of crime-mapping software have raised concerns about the privacy of crime victims. Many police departments now use some type of computer-driven crime map, and some have made maps of small areas available to the public on the Web. Wartell and McEwen (2001) discuss how mapping raises new questions of privacy because individuals might be able to identify crimes directed against their neighbors. Researchers and police alike must recognize the potential for such problems before publishing or otherwise displaying detailed crime maps. For examples, see crime maps for cities in the San Diego metropolitan area (http://mapping .arjis.org).

By now, it should be apparent that virtually all research runs some risk of harming other people somehow. A researcher can never completely guard against all possible injuries, yet some study designs make harm more likely than others. If a particular research procedure seems likely to produce unpleasant effects for subjects—such as asking survey

## ETHICS AND EXTREME FIELD RESEARCH

Dina Perrone
California State University, Long Beach

As a female ethnographer studying active drug use in a New York dance club, I have encountered awkward and difficult situations. The main purpose of my research was to study the use of ecstasy and other drugs in rave club settings. I became a participant observer in an all-night dance club (The Plant) where the use of club drugs was common. I covertly observed activities in the club, partly masking my role as a researcher by assuming the role of club-goer.

Though I was required to comply with university institutional review board guidelines, published codes and regulations offered limited guidance for many of the situations I experienced. As a result, I had to use my best judgment, learning from past experiences to make immediate decisions regarding ethical issues. I was forced to make decisions about how to handle drug episodes, so as not to place my research or my informants in any danger. Because my research was conducted in a dance club that is also a place for men to pick up women, I faced problems in getting information from subjects while watching out for my physical safety.

### Drug Episodes and Subject Safety

I witnessed many drug episodes—adverse reactions to various club drugs—in my visits to The Plant. I watched groups trying to get their friends out of K-holes resulting from ketamine, or Special K. I even aided a subject throwing up. Being a covert observer made it difficult to handle these episodes. There were times in the club when I felt as though I was the only person not under the influence of a mind-altering substance. This led me to believe that I had better judgment than the other patrons. Getting involved in these episodes, however, risked jeopardizing my research.

During my first observation, I tried to intervene in what appeared to be a serious drug episode but was warned off by an informant. I was new to the club and unsure what would happen if I got involved. If I sought help from club staff or outsiders in dealing with acute drug reactions, patrons as well as the bouncers would begin to question why I kept coming there. I needed to gain the trust of the patrons to enlist participants in my research. Furthermore, the bouncers could throw me out of the club, fearing I was a troublemaker who would summon authorities.

As a researcher, I have an ethical responsibility to my participants, and as a human being, I have an ethical responsibility to my conscience. I decided to be extra cautious during my research and to pay close attention to how drug episodes are handled. I would first consult my informants and follow their suggestions. But if I ever thought a person suffering a drug

episode was at risk while other patrons were neither able nor inclined to help, I would intervene to the best of my ability.

### Sexual Advances in the Dance Club

The Plant is also partly a "meat market." Unlike most bars and dance clubs, the patrons' attire and the dance club entertainment are highly erotic. Most of the males inside the club are shirtless, and the majority of females wear extremely revealing clothes. In staged performances, males and females perform dances with sexual overtones, and clothing is partly shed. This atmosphere promotes sexual encounters; men frequently approach single women in search of a mate. Men had a tendency to approach me—I appeared to be unattached, and because of my research role, I made it a point to talk to as many people as possible. It's not difficult to imagine how this behavior could be misinterpreted.

There were times when men became sexually aggressive and persistent. In most instances, I walked away, and the men usually got the hint. However, some men are more persistent than others, especially when they are on ecstasy. In situations in which men make sexual advances, Terry Williams and colleagues (1992) suggest developing a trusting relationship with key individuals who can play a protective role. Throughout my research, I established a good rapport with my informants, who assumed that protective role. Unfortunately, acting in this role has had the potential to place my informants in physically dangerous circumstances.

During one observation, "Tom" grabbed me after I declined his invitation to dance. Tom persisted, grabbed me again, then began to argue with "Jerry," one of my regular informants, who came to my aid. This escalated to a fist-fight broken up only after two bouncers ejected Tom from the club.

I had placed my informant and myself in a dangerous situation. Although I tried to convince myself that I really had no control over Jerry's actions, I felt responsible for the fight. A basic principle of field research is to not invite harm to participants. In most criminal justice research, harm is associated mainly with the possibility of arrest or psychological harm from discussing private issues. Afterward, I tried to think about how the incident escalated and how I could prevent similar problems in the future.

### Ethical Decision Rules Evolving from Experience

Academic associations have formulated codes of ethics and professional conduct, but limited guidance is available for handling issues that arise in some types of ethnographic research. Instead, like criminal justice practitioners, those researchers have to make immediate decisions based on experience and training, without knowing how a situation will

(continued)

unfold. Throughout my research, I found myself in situations that I would normally avoid and would probably never confront. Should I help the woman over there get through a drug episode? If I don't, will she be okay? If I walk away from this aggressive guy, will he follow me? Does he understand that I wanted to talk to him just for research?

The approach I developed to tackle these issues was mostly gained by consulting with colleagues and reading other studies. An overarching theme regarding all codes of ethics is that ethnographers must put the safety and interests of their participants first, and they must recognize that their informants are more knowledgeable about many situations than they are. Throughout the research, I used my judgment to make the best decisions possible when handling these situations. To decide when to intervene during drug episodes, I followed the lead of my informants. Telling men that my informant was my boyfriend and walking away were successful tactics in turning away sexual advances.

respondents to report deviant behavior—the researcher should have firm scientific grounds for using that procedure. If researchers pursue a design that is essential and also likely to be unpleasant for subjects, they will find themselves in an ethical netherworld, forced to do some personal agonizing.

As a general principle, possible harm to subjects may be justified if the potential benefits of the study outweigh the harm. Of course, this raises a further question of how to determine whether possible benefits offset possible harms. There is no simple answer, but as we will see, the research community has adopted certain safeguards that help subjects to make such determinations themselves.

Not harming people is an easy norm to accept in theory, but it is often difficult to ensure in practice. Sensitivity to the issue and experience in research methodology, however, should improve researchers' efforts in delicate areas of inquiry. Review Dina Perrone's observations in the box "Ethics and Extreme Field Research" for examples.

## Voluntary Participation

Criminal justice research often intrudes into people's lives. The interviewer's telephone call or the arrival of a questionnaire via e-mail signals the beginning of an activity that respondents have not requested and that may require a significant portion of their time and energy. Being selected to participate in any sort of research study disrupts subjects' regular activities.

A major tenet of medical research ethics is that experimental participation must be voluntary. The same norm applies to research in criminal justice. No one should be forced to participate. But this norm is far easier to accept in theory than to apply in practice.

For example, prisoners are sometimes used as subjects in experimental studies. In the most rigorously ethical cases, prisoners are told the nature— and the possible dangers—of the experiment; they are told that participation is completely voluntary; and they are further instructed that they can expect no special rewards (such as early parole) for participation. Even under these conditions, volunteers often are motivated by the belief that they will personally benefit from their cooperation. In other cases, prisoners—or other subjects— may be offered small cash payments in exchange for participation. To people with very low incomes, small payments may be an incentive to participate in a study they would not otherwise endure.

When an instructor in an introductory criminal justice class asks students to fill out a questionnaire that she or he plans to analyze and publish, students should always be told that their participation in the survey is completely voluntary. Even so, students might fear that nonparticipation will somehow affect their grade. The instructor should therefore be especially sensitive to the implied sanctions and make provisions to obviate them, such as allowing students to drop the questionnaires in a box near the door prior to the next class.

Notice how this norm of voluntary participation works against a number of scientific concerns or goals. In the most general terms, the goal of generalizability is threatened if experimental subjects or survey respondents are only the people who willingly participate. The same is true when subjects' participation can be bought with small payments. Research results may not be generalizable to all kinds of people. Most clearly, in the case of a descriptive study, a researcher cannot generalize the study findings to an entire population unless a substantial majority of a scientifically selected sample actually participates—both the willing respondents and the somewhat unwilling.

Field research (the subject of Chapter 8) has its own ethical dilemmas in this regard. Often, a researcher who conducts observations in the field cannot even reveal that a study is being done, for fear that this revelation might significantly affect what is being studied. Imagine that you are interested in whether the way stereo headphones are displayed in a discount store affects rates of shoplifting. Therefore, you plan a field study in which you will make observations of store displays and shoplifting. You cannot very well ask all shoppers whether they agree to participate in your study.

The norm of voluntary participation is an important one, but it is sometimes impossible to follow. In cases in which researchers ultimately feel justified in violating it, it is all the more important to observe the other ethical norms of scientific research.

## Anonymity and Confidentiality

The clearest concern in the protection of the subjects' interests and well-being is the protection of their identity. If revealing their behavior or responses would injure them in any way, adherence to this norm becomes crucial. Two techniques—anonymity and confidentiality—assist researchers in this regard, although the two are often confused.

**Anonymity** A research subject is considered anonymous when the researcher cannot associate a given piece of information with the person. **Anonymity** addresses many potential ethical diffi-

culties. Studies that use field observation techniques are often able to ensure that research subjects cannot be identified. Researchers may also gain access to nonpublic records from courts, corrections departments, or other criminal justice agencies in which the names of persons have been removed.

One example of anonymity is a web-based survey where no login or other identifying information is required. Respondents anonymously complete online questionnaires that are then tabulated. Likewise, a telephone survey is anonymous if residential phone numbers are selected at random and respondents are not asked for identifying information. Interviews with subjects in the field are anonymous if the researchers neither ask for nor record the names of subjects.

Assuring anonymity makes it difficult to keep track of which sampled respondents have been interviewed, because researchers did not record their names. Nevertheless, in some situations, the price of anonymity is worth paying. In a survey of drug use, for example, we may decide that the likelihood and accuracy of responses will be enhanced by guaranteeing anonymity.

Respondents in many surveys cannot be considered anonymous because an interviewer collects the information from individuals whose names and addresses are known. Other means of data collection may similarly make it impossible to guarantee anonymity for subjects. If we wished to examine juvenile arrest records for a sample of ninth-grade students, we would need to know their names even though we might not be interviewing them or having them fill out a questionnaire.

**Confidentiality** A researcher who is able to link information with a given person's identity but promises not to is providing **confidentiality**. In a survey of self-reported drug use, the researcher is in a position to make public the use of illegal drugs by a given respondent, but the respondent is assured that this will not be done. Similarly, if field interviews are conducted with juvenile gang members, researchers can certify that information will not be disclosed to police or other officials. Studies using court or police records that include individuals' names may protect confidentiality by not including any identifying information.

Some techniques ensure better performance on this guarantee. To begin, field or survey interviewers who have access to respondent identifications should be trained in their ethical responsibilities. As soon as possible, all names and addresses should be removed from data collection forms and replaced by identification numbers. A master identification file should be created linking numbers to names to permit the later correction of missing or contradictory information.

Whenever a survey is confidential rather than anonymous, it is the researcher's responsibility to make that fact clear to respondents. He or she must never use the term *anonymous* to mean *confidential*. Note, however, that research subjects and others may not understand the difference. For example, a former assistant attorney general in New Jersey once demanded that Michael Maxfield disclose the identities of police officers who participated in an anonymous study. It required repeated explanations of the difference between *anonymous* and *confidential* before the lawyer finally understood that it was not possible to identify participants who were anonymous. In any event, subjects should be assured that the information they provide will be used for research purposes only and not be disclosed to third parties.

## Deceiving Subjects

We've seen that the handling of subjects' identities is an important ethical consideration. Handling our own identity as researchers can be tricky, too. Sometimes it's useful and even necessary to identify ourselves as researchers to those we want to study. It would take a master con artist to get people to participate in a laboratory experiment or complete a lengthy questionnaire without letting on that research was being conducted. We should also keep in mind that deceiving people is unethical; in criminal justice research, deception needs to be justified by compelling scientific or administrative concerns.

Sometimes, researchers admit that they are doing research but fudge about why they are doing it

or for whom. Cathy Spatz Widom and associates interviewed victims of child abuse some 15 years after their cases had been heard in criminal or juvenile courts (Widom, Weiler, and Cotler 1999). Widom was interested in whether child abuse victims were more likely than a comparison group of nonvictims to have used illegal drugs. Interviewers could not explain the purpose of the study without potentially biasing responses. Still, it was necessary to provide a plausible explanation for asking detailed questions about personal and family experiences. Widom's solution was to inform subjects that they had been selected to participate in a study of human development. She also prepared a brochure describing her research on human development that was distributed to respondents.

Although we might initially think that concealing our research purpose by deception would be particularly useful in studying active offenders, James Inciardi (1993), in describing methods for studying "crack houses," makes a convincing case that this is inadvisable. First, concealing our research role when investigating drug dealers and users implies that we are associating with them for the purpose of obtaining illegal drugs. Faced with this situation, a researcher would have the choice of engaging in illegal behavior or offering a convincing explanation for declining to do so. Second, masquerading as a crack-house patron would expose the researcher to the considerable danger of violence that was found to be common in such places. Because the choice of committing illegal acts or becoming a victim of violence is really no choice at all, Inciardi (1993, 152) advises researchers who study active offenders in field settings: "Don't go undercover."

## Analysis and Reporting

As criminal justice researchers, we have ethical obligations to our subjects of study. At the same time, we have ethical obligations to our colleagues in the scientific community; a few comments on those obligations are in order. In any rigorous study, the researcher should be more familiar than anyone else with the technical shortcomings and failures of the study. Researchers have an obligation to make those shortcomings known to readers. Even though it's natural to feel foolish admitting mistakes, researchers are ethically obligated to do so.

Any negative findings should be reported. There is an unfortunate myth in social scientific reporting that only positive discoveries are worth reporting (and journal editors are sometimes guilty of believing that as well). And this is not restricted to social science. Helle Krogh Johansen and Peter Gotzsche (1999) describe how published research on new drugs tends to focus on successful experiments. Unsuccessful research on new formulations is less often published, which leads pharmaceutical researchers to repeat studies of drugs already shown to be ineffective. Largely because of this bias, researchers at the Harvard University School of Dental Medicine have established the *Journal of Negative Observations in Biomedicine*, dedicated to publishing negative findings from biomedical research (www.jnrbm.com). In social science, as in medical research, it is often as important to know that two things are not related as to know that they are.

In general, science progresses through honesty and openness, and is retarded by ego defenses and deception. We can serve our fellow researchers— and the scientific community as a whole—by telling the truth about all the pitfalls and problems experienced in a particular line of inquiry. With luck, this will save others from the same problems.

## Legal Liability

Two types of ethical problems expose researchers to potential legal liability. To illustrate the first, assume you are making field observations of criminal activity, such as street prostitution, that is not reported to police. Under criminal law in many states, you might be arrested for obstructing justice or being an accessory to a crime. Potentially more troublesome is the situation in which participant observation of crime or deviance draws researchers into criminal or deviant roles themselves—such as smuggling cigarettes into a lockup in order to obtain the cooperation of detainees.

The second and more common potential source of legal problems involves knowledge that research subjects have committed illegal acts. Self-report surveys or field interviews may ask subjects about crimes they have committed. If respondents report committing offenses they have never been arrested for or charged with, the researcher's knowledge of them might be construed as obstruction of justice. Or research data may be subject to subpoena by a criminal court. Because disclosure of research data that could be traced to individual subjects violates the ethical principle of confidentiality, a new dilemma emerges.

Fortunately, federal law protects researchers from legal action in most circumstances, provided that appropriate safeguards are used to protect research data. Research plans for 2002 published by organizations in the Office of Justice Programs summarized this protection: "[Research] information and copies thereof shall be immune from legal process, and shall not, without the consent of the person furnishing such information, be admitted as evidence or used for any purpose in any action, suit, or other judicial, legislative, or administrative proceedings" (42 U.S. Code §22.28a). This not only protects researchers from legal action but also can be valuable in assuring subjects that they cannot be prosecuted for crimes they describe to an interviewer or field worker. Bruce Johnson and associates (1985, 219) prominently displayed a Federal Certificate of Confidentiality at their research office to assure heroin dealers that they could not be prosecuted for crimes disclosed to interviewers. More savvy than many people about such matters, the heroin users were duly impressed.

Note that such immunity requires confidential information to be protected. We have already discussed the principle of confidentiality, so this bargain should be an easy one to keep.

Somewhere between legal liability and physical danger lies the potential risk to field researchers from law enforcement. Despite being up-front with crack users about his role as a researcher, Inciardi (1993) points out that police could not be expected to distinguish him from his subjects. Visibly associating with offenders in natural settings brings some risk of being arrested or inadvertently being an accessory to crime. On one occasion, Inciardi fled the scene of a robbery and on another was caught up in a crack-house raid. Another example is the account Bruce Jacobs (1996) gives of his contacts with police while he was studying street drug dealers.

## Special Problems

Certain types of criminal justice studies present special ethical problems in addition to those we have mentioned. Applied research, for example, may evaluate some existing or new program. Evaluations frequently have the potential to disrupt the routine operations of agencies being studied. Obviously, it is best to minimize such interferences whenever possible.

**Staff Misbehavior**    While conducting applied research, researchers may become aware of irregular or illegal practices by staff in public agencies. They are then faced with the ethical question of whether to report such information. For example, investigators conducting an evaluation of an innovative probation program learned that police visits to the residences of probationers were not taking place as planned. Instead, police assigned to the program had been submitting falsified log sheets and had not actually checked on probationers.

What is the ethical dilemma in this case? On the one hand, researchers were evaluating the probation program and so were obliged to report reasons it did or did not operate as planned. Failure to deliver program treatments (home visits) is an example of a program not operating as planned. Investigators had guaranteed confidentiality to program clients—the offenders assigned to probation—but no such agreement had been struck with program staff. On the other hand, researchers had assured agency personnel that their purpose was to evaluate the probation program, not individuals' job performance. If researchers disclosed their knowledge that police were falsifying reports, they would violate this implied trust.

What would you have done in this situation? We will tell you what the researchers decided at the end of this chapter. You should recognize, however, how applied research in criminal justice agencies can involve a variety of ethical issues.

**Research Causes Crime**    Because criminal acts and their circumstances are complex and imperfectly understood, some research projects have the potential to produce crime or influence its location or target. Certainly, this is a potentially serious ethical issue for researchers.

Most people agree that it is unethical to encourage someone to commit an offense solely for the purpose of a research project. What's more problematic is recognizing situations in which research might indirectly promote offending. Scott Decker and Barrik Van Winkle (1996) discuss such a possibility in their research on gang members. Some gang members offered to illustrate their willingness to use violence by inviting researchers to witness a drive-by shooting. Researchers declined all such invitations (1996, 46). Another ethical issue was the question of how subjects used the $20 cash payments they received in exchange for being interviewed (1996, 51):

> We set the fee low enough that we were confident that it would not have a criminogenic effect. While twenty dollars is not a small amount of money, it is not sufficient to purchase a gun or bankroll a large drug buy. We are sure that some of our subjects used the money for illegal purposes. But, after all, these were individuals who were regularly engaged in delinquent and criminal acts.

You may or may not agree with the authors' reasoning in the last sentence. But their consideration of how cash payments would be used by active offenders represents an unusually careful recognition of the ethical dilemmas that emerge in studying active offenders.

A different type of ethical problem is the possibility of crime displacement in studies of crime prevention programs. Consider an experimental program to reduce street prostitution in one area of a city. Researchers studying such a program might designate experimental target areas for enhanced enforcement, as well as nearby comparison areas that will not receive an intervention. If prostitution is displaced from target areas to adjacent neighborhoods, the evaluation study contributes to an increase in prostitution in the comparison areas.

In a review of more than 200 evaluations of crime prevention projects, Rob Guerette and Kate Bowers (2009) report that the scope of displacement is limited. An earlier study by Rene Hesseling (1994) shows that the type of crime prevention action makes a difference, with displacement more common for target-hardening programs. For example, installing security screens on ground-floor windows in some buildings seemed to displace burglary to less protected structures. Similarly, adding steering column locks to new cars tended to increase thefts of older cars (Felson and Clarke 1998).

In any event, when it does occur, displacement tends to follow major policy changes that are not connected with criminal justice research. Researchers cannot be expected to control actions by criminal justice officials that may benefit some people at the expense of others. However, it is reasonable to expect researchers involved in planning an evaluation study to anticipate the possibility of such things as displacement and bring them to the attention of program staff.

**Withholding of Desirable Treatments** Certain kinds of research designs in criminal justice can lead to different kinds of ethical questions. Suppose researchers believe that diverting domestic violence offenders from prosecution to counseling reduces the possibility of repeat violence. Is it ethical to conduct an experiment in which some offenders are prosecuted but others are not?

You may recognize the similarity between this question and those faced by medical researchers who test the effectiveness of experimental drugs. Physicians typically respond to such questions by pointing out that the effectiveness of a drug cannot be demonstrated without such experiments. Failure to conduct research, even at the potential expense of subjects not receiving the trial drugs, would

therefore make it impossible to develop new drugs or distinguish beneficial treatments from those that are ineffective and even harmful.

One solution to this dilemma is to interrupt an experiment if preliminary results indicate that a new policy, or drug, does in fact produce improvements in a treatment group. Michael Dennis (1990) describes how such plans were incorporated into a long-term evaluation of enhanced drug treatment counseling. If preliminary results had indicated that the new counseling program reduced drug use, researchers and program staff were prepared to provide enhanced counseling to subjects in the control group. Dennis recognized this potential ethical issue and planned his elaborate research design to accommodate such midstream changes. Similarly, Martin Killias and associates (2000) planned to interrupt their experimental study of heroin prescription in Switzerland if compelling evidence pointed to benefits from that approach to treating drug dependency.

**Mandatory Reporting** The situation is somewhat murkier for researchers studying certain kinds of family violence. Following the Federal Child Abuse Prevention and Treatment Act of 1974, all states developed child protection agencies and adopted mandatory reporting laws. Specific provisions vary, but in general, people who learn about possible cases of child abuse must report them to designated state agencies. This certainly seems to be a worthwhile goal, but what about researchers who learn about possible child maltreatment in the course of a survey? In most states, such requirements apply only to health professionals and teachers. But in eight states, anyone who suspects a case of child maltreatment must report it to designated authorities.

Notice how this is consistent with one ethical principle—protection of human subjects by reporting possible victims—but at odds with another principle—confidentiality. A Bureau of Justice Statistics report on the protection of human subjects suggests that researchers warn subjects at the beginning of an interview that any information disclosed about child abuse must be reported to authorities

(Sieber 2001). But that threatens researchers' ability to learn about child abuse. Another approach, adopted by Lianne Woodward and David Fergusson (2000), is to interview subjects age 18 and older, asking about experiences of abuse victimization when they were children. This is an imperfect solution, but it illustrates the trade-offs between our interest in protecting research subjects and our interest in studying the phenomenon of child abuse. For more examples and guidance in this vexing research/ethical area, see Seth Kalichman's (2000) book, published by the American Psychological Association.

Research in criminal justice, especially applied research, can pose a variety of ethical dilemmas, only some of which we have mentioned here. See the additional readings at the end of this chapter for more information.

# PROMOTING COMPLIANCE WITH ETHICAL PRINCIPLES

*Codes of ethics and institutional review boards are two main ways of promoting compliance with ethical principles.*

No matter how sensitive they might be to the rights of individuals and possible ways subjects might be harmed, researchers are not always the best judges of whether or not adequate safeguards are used. In 1974, the National Research Act was signed into law after a few highly publicized examples of unethical practices in medical and social science research.[1] A few years later, what has become known as the **Belmont Report** prescribed a brief but comprehensive set of ethical principles for protecting human subjects (National Commission for the Protection of Human Subjects of Biomedical and Behavioral Research 1979). In only six pages, three principles were presented:

1.  *Respect for persons*: Individuals must be allowed to make their own decisions about participation in research, and those with limited capac-

ity to make such decisions should have special protection.

2.  *Beneficence*: Research should do no harm to participants, and seek to produce benefits.

3.  *Justice*: The benefits and burdens of participating in research should be distributed fairly.

Copious federal regulations have stemmed from these three principles. But in most cases, the research community has adopted two general mechanisms for promoting ethical research practices: codes of professional ethics and institutional review boards.

## Codes of Professional Ethics

If the professionals who design and conduct research projects can fail to recognize ethical problems, how can such problems be avoided? One approach is for researchers to consult one of the codes of ethics produced by professional associations. Formal codes of conduct describe what is considered acceptable and unacceptable professional behavior. The American Psychological Association's (2010) amended code of ethics is quite detailed, reflecting the different professional roles of psychologists in research, clinical treatment, and educational contexts.

Many of the ethical questions criminal justice researchers are likely to encounter are addressed in the ethics code of the American Sociological Association (1999). Paul Reynolds (1979, 442–449) has created a composite code for the use of human subjects in research, drawing on 24 codes of ethics published by national associations of social scientists. The National Academy of Sciences publishes a very useful booklet on a variety of ethical issues, including the problem of fraud and other forms of scientific misconduct (Committee on Science, Engineering, and Public Policy 2009).

The two national associations representing criminology and criminal justice researchers have one code of ethics between them. The Academy of Criminal Justice Sciences (ACJS) based its code

---

1. We'll consider one of these examples near the end of this chapter.

of ethics on that developed by the American Sociological Association. ACJS members are bound by a very general code that reflects the diversity of its membership: "Most of the ethical standards are written broadly, to provide applications in varied roles and varied contexts. The Ethical Standards are not exhaustive—conduct that is not included in the Ethical Standards is not necessarily ethical or unethical" (Academy of Criminal Justice Sciences 2000, 1).

After years of inaction, a committee of the American Society of Criminology (ASC) proposed a draft code of ethics in 1998, which drew extensively on the code for sociology. But no ethics code had been adopted as of January 2011, and the ASC withdrew its draft code from circulation in 1999. The ASC website includes the following statement on a page titled "Code of Ethics":

> The American Society of Criminology has not formally adopted a code of ethics. We would suggest that persons interested in this general topic examine the various codes of ethics adopted by other professional associations. (http://asc41.com/ethicspg.html)

Links to a number of ethics codes for social science associations are listed, including those listed above and the British Society of Criminology.

What can we make of the inability of the largest professional association of criminologists to agree on a code of ethics? The wide variety of approaches to doing research in this area probably has something to do with it. Criminologists also encounter a range of ethical issues and have diverging views on how those issues should be addressed. Finally, we have seen examples of the special problems criminologists face in balancing ethics and research. Not all of these problems have easy solutions that can be embodied in a code.

Even when they exist, professional codes of ethics for social scientists cannot be expected to prevent unethical practices in criminal justice research any more than the American Bar Association's Code of Professional Responsibility eliminates breaches of ethics by lawyers. For this reason, and in reaction to some controversial medical and social science research, the U.S. Department of Health and Human Services (HHS) has established regulations protecting human research subjects. These regulations do not apply to all social science or criminal justice research. It is, however, worthwhile to understand some of their general provisions. Material in the following section is based on the Code of Federal Regulations, Title 45, Chapter 4.6. Those regulations are themselves rooted in the *Belmont Report*.

## Institutional Review Boards

Government agencies and nongovernment organizations (including universities) that conduct research involving human subjects must establish review committees, known as institutional review boards (IRBs). These IRBs have two general purposes. First, board members make judgments about the overall risks to human subjects and whether these risks are acceptable, given the expected benefits from actually doing the research. Second, they determine whether the procedures to be used include adequate safeguards regarding the safety, confidentiality, and general welfare of human subjects.

Under HHS regulations, virtually all research that uses human subjects in any way, including simply asking people questions, is subject to IRB review. The few exceptions potentially include research conducted for educational purposes and studies that collect anonymous information only. However, even those studies may be subject to review if they use certain special populations (discussed later) or procedures that might conceivably harm participants. In other words, it's safe to assume that most research is subject to IRB review if original data will be collected from individuals whose identities will be known. If you think about the various ways subjects might be harmed and the difficulty of conducting anonymous studies, you can understand why this is the case.

Federal regulations and IRB guidelines address other potential ethical issues in social research. Foremost among these is the typical IRB requirement for dealing with the ethical principle of voluntary participation.

**Informed Consent** The norm of voluntary participation is usually satisfied through **informed consent**—informing subjects about research procedures and then obtaining their consent to participate. Although this may seem like a simple requirement, obtaining informed consent can present several practical difficulties. It requires that subjects understand the purpose of the research, possible risks and side effects, possible benefits to subjects, and the procedures that will be used.

If you accept that deception may sometimes be necessary, you will realize how the requirement to inform subjects about research procedures can present something of a dilemma. Researchers usually address this problem by telling subjects at least part of the truth or offering a slightly revised version of why the research is being conducted. In Widom's study of child abuse, subjects were partially informed about the purpose of the research—human development—one component of which is being a victim of child abuse, which the subjects were not told.

Another potential problem with obtaining informed consent is ensuring that subjects have the capacity to understand the descriptions of risks, benefits, procedures, and so forth. Researchers may have to provide oral descriptions to participants who are unable to read. For subjects who do not speak English, researchers should be prepared to describe procedures in the subjects' native language. And if researchers use specialized terms or language common in criminal justice research, participants may not understand the meaning and thus be unable to grant informed consent. Consider this statement: "The purpose of this study is to determine whether less restrictive sanctions such as restitution produce heightened sensitivity to social responsibility among persistent juvenile offenders and a decline in long-term recidivism." Can you think of a better way to describe this study to delinquent 14-year-olds? Figure 2.1 presents a good example of an informed consent statement that was used in a study of juvenile burglars. Notice how the statement clearly describes research procedures and also unambiguously tells subjects that participation is voluntary.

Other guidelines for obtaining informed consent include explicitly telling people that their participation is voluntary and assuring them of confidentiality. However, it is more important to understand how informed consent addresses key ethical issues in conducting criminal justice research. First, it ensures that participation is voluntary. Second, by informing subjects of procedures, risks, and benefits, researchers are empowering them to resolve the fundamental ethical dilemma of whether the possible benefits of the research offset the possible risks of participation.

**Special Populations** Federal regulations on human subjects include special provisions for certain types of subjects, called **special populations**, and two of these are particularly important in criminal justice research—juveniles and prisoners. Juveniles, of course, are treated differently from adults in most aspects of the law. Their status as a special population of human subjects reflects the legal status of juveniles, as well as their capacity to grant informed consent. In most studies that involve juveniles, consent must be obtained both from parents or guardians and from the juvenile subjects themselves.

In some studies, however, such as those that focus on abused children, it is obviously not desirable to obtain parental consent. Decker and Van Winkle faced this problem in their study of St. Louis gang members. See the box "Ethics and Juvenile Gang Members" for a discussion of how they reconciled the conflict between two ethical principles and satisfied the concerns of their university's IRB.

Prisoners are treated as a special population for somewhat different reasons. Because of their ready accessibility for experiments and interviews, prisoners have frequently been used in biomedical experiments that produced serious harm (Mitford 1973). Recognizing this, HHS regulations specify that prisoner subjects may not be exposed to risks that would be considered excessive for nonprisoner subjects. Furthermore, undue influence or coercion cannot be used in recruiting prisoner subjects. Informed consent statements presented to prospective subjects must indicate that a decision not to participate in a study will have no influence on work

You and your parents or guardian are invited to participate in a research study of the monitoring program that you were assigned to by the Juvenile Court. The purpose of this research is to study the program and your reactions to it. In order to do this a member of the research team will need to interview you and your parents/guardians when you complete the monitoring program. These interviews will take about 15 minutes and will focus on your experiences with the court and monitoring program, the things you do, things that have happened to you, and what you think. In addition, we will record from the court records information about the case for which you were placed in the monitoring program, prior cases, and other information that is put in the records after you are released from the monitoring program.

Anything you or your parents or guardian tell us will be strictly confidential. This means that only the researchers will have your answers. They *will not* under any conditions (except at your request) be given to the court, the police, probation officers, your parents, or your child!

Your participation in this research is voluntary. If you don't want to take part, you don't have to! If you decide to participate, you can change your mind at any time. Whether you participate or not will have no effect on the program, probation, or your relationship with the court.

The research is being directed by Dr. Terry Baumer and Dr. Robert Mendelsohn from the Indiana University School of Public and Environmental Affairs here in Indianapolis. If you ever have any questions about the research or comments about the monitoring program that you think we should know about, please call one of us at 274-0531.

---

*Consent Statement*

We agree to participate in this study of the Marion County Juvenile Monitoring Program. We have read the above statement and understand what will be required and that all information will be confidential. We also understand that we can withdraw from the study at any time without penalty.

Juvenile _____ Date: _____

Parent/Guardian _____

Parent/Guardian _____

Researcher _____

**F I G U R E  2.1**   Informed Consent Statement for Evaluation of Marion County Juvenile Monitoring Program

assignments, privileges, or parole decisions. To help ensure that these ethical issues are recognized, if an IRB reviews a project in which prisoners will be subjects, at least one member of that IRB must be either a prisoner or someone specifically designated to represent the interests of prisoners. Figure 2.2 presents a checklist required by the Rutgers University IRB for proposed research involving prisoners.

Regarding the last item in Figure 2.2, random selection is generally recognized as an ethical procedure for selecting subjects or deciding which subjects will receive an experimental treatment. HHS regulations emphasize this in describing special provisions for using prison subjects: "Unless the principal investigator provides to the [IRB] justification

in writing for following some other procedures, control subjects must be selected randomly from the group of available prisoners who meet the characteristics needed for that particular research project" (45 CFR 46.305[4]).

## Institutional Review Board Requirements and Researcher Rights

Federal regulations contain many more provisions for IRBs and other protections for human subjects. Some researchers believe that such regulations actually create problems by setting constraints on their freedom and professional judgments in conducting research. Recall that potential conflict between the

## ETHICS AND JUVENILE GANG MEMBERS

Scott Decker and Barrik Van Winkle faced a range of ethical issues in their study of gang members. Many of these should be obvious given what has been said so far in this chapter. Violence was common among subjects and presented a real risk to researchers. Decker and Van Winkle (1996, 252) reported that 11 of the 99 members of the original sample had been killed since the project began in 1990. There was also the obvious need to assure confidentiality to subjects.

Their project was supported by a federal agency and administered through a university, so Decker and Van Winkle had to comply with federal human subjects guidelines as administered by the university institutional review board (IRB). And because many of the subjects were juveniles, they had to address federal regulations concerning that special population. Foremost among these was the normal requirement that informed consent for juveniles include parental notification and approval.

You may immediately recognize the conflicting ethical principles at work here, together with the potential for conflict. The promise of confidentiality to gang members is one such principle that was essential for the researchers to obtain candid reports of violence and other law-breaking behavior. But the need for confidentiality conflicted with initial IRB requirements to obtain parental consent for their children to participate in the research:

> This would have violated our commitment to maintain the confidentiality of each subject, not to mention the ethical and practical difficulties of finding and informing each parent. We told the Human Subjects Committee that we would not, in effect, tell parents that their

child was being interviewed because they were an active gang member, knowledge that the parents may not have had. (Decker and Van Winkle 1996, 52)

You might think deception would be a possibility—informing parents that their child was selected for a youth development study, for example. This would not, however, solve the logistical difficulty of locating parents or guardians, some of whom had lost contact with their children. Furthermore, it was likely that even if parents or guardians could be located, suspicions about the research project and the reasons their children were selected would prevent many parents from granting consent. Loss of juvenile subjects in this way would compromise the norm of generality as we have described it in this chapter and elsewhere.

Finally, waiving the requirement for parental consent would have undermined the legal principle that the interests of juveniles must be protected by a supervising adult. Remember that researchers are not always the best judges of whether sufficient precautions have been taken to protect subjects. Here is how Decker and Van Winkle (1996, 52) resolved the issue with their IRB:

> We reached a compromise in which we found an advocate for each juvenile member of our sample; this person—a university employee—was responsible for making sure that the subject understood (1) their rights to refuse or quit the interview at any time without penalty and (2) the confidential nature of the project. All subjects signed the consent form.

*Source:* Adapted from Decker and Van Winkle (1996).

rights of researchers to discover new knowledge and the rights of subjects to be free from unnecessary harm is a fundamental ethical dilemma. It is at least inconvenient to have outsiders review a research proposal. Or a researcher may feel insulted by the implication that the potential benefits of research will not outweigh the potential harm or inconvenience to human subjects.

Many university IRBs have become extremely cautious in reviewing research proposals. See Richard Shweder's (2006) discussion for examples of problems resulting from this. Professional associations and research-oriented federal agencies have tried to offer guidance on what is and is not subject to various levels of IRB approval. Joan Sieber (2001) prepared an

analysis of human subjects issues associated with large surveys for the Bureau of Justice Statistics. Always alert for possible restrictions on academic freedom, the American Association of University Professors (2006) published a useful summary of how IRBs have come to regulate social science research.

There is some merit in such concerns; however, we should not lose sight of the reasons IRB requirements and other regulations were created. Researchers are not always the best judges of the potential for their work to harm individuals. In designing and conducting criminal justice research, they may become excited about learning how to better prevent crime or more effectively treat cocaine addiction. That excitement and commitment

- Does the research entail any possible advantages accrued to the prisoner through their participation in the research that impairs their ability to weigh the risk/benefits of the participation in the limited choice environment that exists in a prison? This comparison is to be made with respect to the general living conditions, medical care, amenities and earning opportunities which exist in a prison.
- Are the risks of the research commensurate with those that would be accepted by non-prisoner participants? Provide Rationale below.
- Is the information presented to the prisoners in the Consent Form or Oral consent script done so in a language understandable by the participants?
- Does the Consent Form explicitly state to the subject that "Do not tell us any information about past or future crimes that are unknown to the authorities as we cannot guarantee confidentiality of that information Additionally, I [the researcher] must report to the authorities information you tell me about harming yourself or other people, or any plans you have to escape."
- Does adequate assurance exist that parole boards will not take into account participation in the research when determining parole and that the prisoners were clearly informed of this prior to participation in the research?
- Describe what specific steps were taken to ensure that the Informed Consent Form includes information specific to the prisoner subject population. This is not necessary if the research is limited to data analysis.
- Is the selection of prisoner research participants fair and equitable and immune from arbitrary intervention by prisoner authorities? If not, has the PI provided sufficient justification for the implementation of alternative procedures?

*Source:* Adapted from Rutgers University Office of Research and Sponsored Programs document, available at: http://orsp.rutgers.edu/Humans/downloads/Prisoner%20PI%20Checklist.doc

**FIGURE 2.2** Excerpts from Checklist for Research Involving Prisoners

to scientific advancement may lead researchers to overlook possible harms to individual rights or well-being. You may recognize this as another way of asking whether the ends justify the means. Because researchers are not always disinterested parties in answering such questions, IRBs are established to provide outside judgments. Also recognize that IRBs can be sources of expert advice on how to resolve ethical dilemmas. Decker and Van Winkle shared their university's concern about balancing confidentiality against the need to obtain informed consent from juvenile subjects; together, they were able to fashion a workable compromise.

All colleges and universities have IRBs. Consult the City University of New York website (http://www.cuny.edu/research/ovcr/human-subjects-research.html) for an example, or visit the IRB website at your institution.

## ETHICAL CONTROVERSIES

*Examples illustrate how ethics is a problem in justice research.*

By way of illustrating the importance of ethics principles, together with problems that may be encountered in applying those principles, we now describe a research project that provoked widespread ethical controversy and discussion. This is followed by further examples of ethical questions for discussion.

## The Stanford Prison Experiment

Few people would disagree that prisons are dehumanizing. Inmates forfeit freedom, of course, but their incarceration also results in a loss of privacy and individual identity. Violence is among the realities of prison life that people point to as evidence of the failure of prisons to rehabilitate inmates.

Although the problems of prisons have many sources, psychologists Curtis Haney, Craig Banks, and Philip Zimbardo (1973) were interested in two general explanations. The first was the dispositional hypothesis—prisons are brutal and dehumanizing because of the types of people who run them and are incarcerated in them. Inmates have demonstrated their disrespect for legal order and their willingness to use deceit and violence; persons who work as prison guards may be disproportionately authoritarian and sadistic. The second was the situational hypothesis—the prison environment itself creates brutal, dehumanizing conditions independent of the kinds of people who live and work in the institutions.

Haney and associates set out to test the situational hypothesis by creating a functional prison simulation in which healthy, psychologically normal male college students were assigned to roles as prisoners and guards. The "prison" was constructed in the basement of a psychology department building: three 6 × 9 foot "cells" furnished with only a cot, a prison "yard" in a corridor, and a 2 × 7 foot "solitary confinement cell." Twenty-one subjects were selected from 75 volunteers after screening to eliminate those with physical or psychological problems. Offered $15 per day for their participation, the 21 subjects were randomly assigned to be either guards or prisoners.

All subjects signed contracts that included instructions about prisoner and guard roles for the planned two-week experiment. "Prisoners" were told that they would be confined and under surveillance throughout the experiment, and their civil rights would be suspended; they were, however, guaranteed that they would not be physically abused.

"Guards" were given minimal instructions, most notably that physical aggression or physical punishment of "prisoners" was prohibited. Together with a "warden," however, they were generally free to develop prison rules and procedures. The researchers planned to study how both guards and prisoners reacted to their roles, but guards were led to believe that the purpose of the experiment was to study prisoners.

If you had been a prisoner in this experiment, you would have experienced something like the following after signing your contract: First, you would have been arrested without notice at your home by a real police officer, perhaps with neighbors looking on. After being searched and taken to the police station in handcuffs, you would have been booked, fingerprinted, and placed in a police detention facility. Next, you would have been blindfolded and driven to "prison," where you would have been stripped, sprayed with a delousing solution, and left to stand naked for a period of time in the "prison yard." Eventually, you would have been issued a prison uniform (a loose overshirt stamped with your ID number), fitted with an ankle chain, led to your cell, and ordered to remain silent. Your prison term would then have been totally controlled by the guards.

Wearing mirrored sunglasses, khaki uniforms, and badges, and carrying nightsticks, guards supervised prisoner work assignments and held lineups three times per day. Although lineups initially lasted only a few minutes, guards later extended them to several hours. Prisoners were fed bland meals and accompanied by guards on three authorized toilet visits per day.

The behavior of all subjects in the prison yard and other open areas was videotaped; audiotapes were made continuously while prisoners were in their cells. Researchers administered brief questionnaires throughout the experiment to assess emotional changes in prisoners and guards. About 4 weeks after the experiment concluded, researchers conducted interviews with all subjects to assess their reactions.

Haney and associates (1973, 88) had planned to run the prison experiment for 2 weeks, but they halted the study after 6 days because subjects displayed "unexpectedly intense reactions." Five prisoners had to be released even before that time because they showed signs of acute depression or anxiety.

Subjects in each group accepted their roles all too readily. Prisoners and guards could interact with each other in friendly ways because guards had the power to make prison rules. But interactions turned out to be overwhelmingly hostile and negative. Guards became aggressive, and prisoners became passive. When the experiment ended prematurely, prisoners were happy about their early "parole," but guards were disappointed that the study would not continue.

Haney and colleagues justify the prison simulation study in part by claiming that the dispositional/situational hypotheses could not be evaluated using other research designs. Clearly, the researchers were sensitive to ethical issues. They obtained subjects' consent to the experiment through signed contracts. Prisoners who showed signs of acute distress were released early. The entire study was terminated after less than half of the planned 2 weeks had elapsed when its unexpectedly harsh impact on subjects became evident. Finally, researchers conducted group therapy debriefing sessions with prisoners and guards and maintained follow-up contacts for a year to ensure that subjects' negative experiences were temporary.

Two related features of this experiment raise ethical questions. First, subjects were not fully informed of the procedures. Although we have seen that deception, including something less than full disclosure, can often be justified, in this case deception was partially due to the researchers' uncertainty about how the prison simulation would unfold. This relates to the second and more important ethical problem: guards were granted the power to make up and modify rules as the study progressed, and their behavior became increasingly authoritarian. Comments by guards illustrate their reactions as the experiment unfolded (Haney, Banks, and Zimbardo 1973, 88):

> "They [the prisoners] didn't see it as an experiment. It was real and they were fighting to keep their identity. But we were always there to show them just who was boss."

> "During the inspection, I went to cell 2 to mess up a bed which the prisoner had made and he grabbed me, screaming that he had just made it.... He grabbed my throat, and although he was laughing, I was pretty scared. I lashed out with my stick and hit him in the chin (although not very hard), and when I freed myself I became angry."

> "Acting authoritatively can be fun. Power can be a great pleasure."

You can get a good impression of what guards and prisoners experienced by viewing videos of "arrest" and "prison" scenes available on the Internet. Search for "video Stanford prison experiment."

How do you feel about this experiment? On the one hand, it provided valuable insights into how otherwise normal people react in a simulated prison environment. Subjects appeared to suffer no long-term harm, in part because of precautions taken by researchers. Paul Reynolds (1979, 139) found a certain irony in the short-term discomforts endured by the college student subjects: "There is evidence that the major burdens were borne by individuals from advantaged social categories and that the major benefactors would be individuals from less advantaged social categories [actual prisoners], an uneven distribution of costs and benefits that many nevertheless consider equitable." On the other hand, researchers did not anticipate how much and how quickly subjects would accept their roles. In discussing their findings, Haney and associates (1973, 90) note: "Our results are ... congruent with those of Milgram[2] who most convincingly demonstrated the proposition that evil acts are not necessarily the deeds of evil men, but may be attributable to the operation of powerful social forces." This quote illustrates the fundamental dilemma—balancing the right to conduct research against the rights of subjects. Is it ethical for researchers to create powerful social forces that lead to evil acts?

## Discussion Examples

Research ethics is an important and ambiguous topic. The difficulty of resolving ethical issues cannot be an excuse for ignoring them. You need to keep ethics in mind as you read other chapters in this book and whenever you plan a research project.

To further sensitize you to the ethical component of criminal justice and other social research, we've prepared brief descriptions of real and hypothetical research situations. Can you see the ethical issue in each? How do you feel about it? Are the procedures described ultimately acceptable or

---

2. Here the authors refer to controversial research on obedience to authority by Lester Milgram (1965).

unacceptable? It would be very useful to discuss these examples with other students in your class.

1. In a study of "phishing," researchers obtain university e-mail addresses from a sample of undergraduate students. Bogus social networking messages are sent to participants to determine which features of messages are more likely to lure recipients to click on web links. The university computing services center has supplied the e-mail addresses, and the university IRB has approved the study.

2. In a federally funded study of a probation program, a researcher discovers that one participant was involved in a murder while on probation. Public disclosure of this incident might threaten the program, which the researcher believes, from all evidence, is beneficial. Judging the murder to be an anomaly, the researcher does not disclose it to federal sponsors or describe it in published reports.

3. While studying aggression in bars and nightclubs, a researcher records observations of a savage fight in which three people are seriously injured. Ignoring pleas for help from one of the victims, the researcher retreats to a restroom to write up notes from these observations.

4. In a study of state police, researchers learn that officers have been instructed by superiors to "not sign anything." Fearing that asking officers to sign informed consent statements will sharply reduce participation, researchers seek some other way to satisfy their university IRB. What should they do?

5. In the example mentioned in the section "Staff Misbehavior" (page 33), the researchers disclosed to public officials that police were not making visits to probationers as called for in the program intervention. Published reports describe the problem as "irregularities in program delivery."

## SUMMARY

- In addition to technical and scientific considerations, criminal justice research projects are shaped by ethical considerations.

- What's ethically "right" and "wrong" in research is ultimately a matter of what people agree is right and wrong.

- Researchers tend not to be the best judges of whether their own work adequately addresses ethical issues.

- Most ethical questions involve weighing the possible benefits of research against the potential for harm to research subjects.

- Criminal justice research may generate special ethical questions, including the potential for legal liability and physical harm.

- Scientists agree that participation in research should, in general, be voluntary. This norm, however, can conflict with the scientific need for generalizability.

- Most scientists agree that research should not harm subjects unless they willingly and knowingly accept the risks of harm.

- Anonymity and confidentiality are two ways to protect the privacy of research subjects.

- Compliance with ethical principles is promoted by professional associations and by regulations issued by the Department of Health and Human Services (HHS).

- HHS regulations include special provisions for two types of subjects of particular interest to many criminal justice researchers: prisoners and juveniles.

- Institutional review boards (IRBs) play an important role in ensuring that the rights and interests of human subjects are protected. But some social science researchers believe that IRBs are becoming too restrictive.

## KEY TERMS

anonymity, p. 29

*Belmont Report*, p. 34

confidentiality, p. 29

ethical, p. 25

informed consent, p. 36

special populations, p. 36

## REVIEW QUESTIONS AND EXERCISES

1. Obtain a copy of the Academy of Criminal Justice Sciences' (2000) code of ethics at this website: http://acjs.org/pubs/167_671_2922 .cfm. Read the document carefully. How would the code apply to the Stanford prison simulation?

2. Discuss the general trade-offs between the requirements of sound scientific research methods and the need to protect human subjects. Where do tensions exist? Cite illustrations of tensions from two or more examples of ethical issues presented in this chapter.

3. Review the box "Ethics and Juvenile Gang Members" on page 39), Although it is not shown in the box, Decker and Van Winkle developed an informed consent form for their subjects. Keeping in mind the various ethical principles discussed in this chapter, try your hand at preparing an informed consent statement that Decker and Van Winkle might have used.

## ADDITIONAL READINGS

Als-Nielsen, Bodil, Wendong Chen, Christian Gluud, and Lise L.Kjaergard, "Association of Funding and Conclusions in Randomized Drug Trials: A Reflection of Treatment Effect or Adverse Events?" *Journal of the American Medical Association* 290 (7, August 2003): 921-927. A brief, interesting and nontechnical analysis of research on the effects of new drugs. The authors find that research sponsored by drug companies is much more likely to find that drugs are effective, compared to research sponsored by nonprofit organizations. What do you make of that?

Committee on Science, Engineering, and Public Policy, *On Being a Scientist: Responsible Conduct in Research*, 3rd ed. (Washington, DC:National Academy Press,

2009). This monograph covers a range of issues, including research fraud and other misconduct by researchers. Although many of the issues are specific to the natural sciences, criminologists will find much valuable material.

Inciardi, James A., " Some Considerations on the Methods, Dangers, and Ethics of Crack-House Research," Appendix A in James A.Inciardi, Dorothy Lockwood, and Anne E. Pettieger(eds.),*Women and Crack Cocaine* (New York:Macmillan, 1993), pp. 147-157. In this thoughtful essay, Inciardi describes the dangers and depressing realities of field research in a crack house. Should a field researcher intervene when witnessing a gang rape in a crack house? Read this selection for Inciardi's answer.

# PART 2

# Structuring Criminal Justice Inquiry

At its base, scientific research is a process for achieving generalized understanding through observation. Part 3 will describe some of the specific methods of observation for criminal justice research. But first, Part 2 deals with the posing of proper questions, which is the structuring of inquiry. Posing questions properly is often more difficult than answering them. Indeed, a properly phrased question often seems to answer itself.

Chapter 3 addresses some of the fundamental issues that must be considered in planning a research project. We begin by considering some basic foundations of social science. Then we'll introduce different general approaches to doing research in criminal justice. Chapter 3 also examines questions of causation, the units of analysis in a research project, and the important role of time.

Chapter 4 deals with the specification of what it is we want to study—a process known as conceptu-

alization—and the measurement of the concepts we specify. We'll look at some of the terms that we use casually in everyday life, and we'll see how essential it is to be clear about what we really mean by such terms when we do research. Once we are clear on what we mean when we use certain terms, we are in a position to create measurements of what those terms refer to. The process of devising steps or operations for measuring what we want to study is known as operationalization. By way of illustrating this process, Chapter 4 includes an extended discussion of different approaches to measuring crime.

Chapter 5 concentrates on the general design of a criminal justice research project. A criminal justice research design specifies a strategy for finding out something, for structuring a research project. Chapter 5 describes commonly used strategies for experimental and quasi-experimental research. Each is adapted in some way from the classical scientific experiment.

## CHAPTER 3

# General Issues in Research Design

*Here we'll examine some fundamental principles about conducting empirical research, from the foundations of social science through causation, validity, the different units on which we conduct research, and the time dimension.*

# INTRODUCTION

*Certain principles guide all the different approaches to scientific research in criminal justice.*

Science is an enterprise dedicated to "finding out." No matter what we want to find out, though, there are likely to be a great many ways of going about it. Topics examined in this chapter address the foundations of social science, different general approaches to doing research in criminal justice, and elements of causation and time.

In practice, all aspects of research design are interrelated. They are separated here and in subsequent chapters so that we can explore particular topics in detail. We start by discussing basic principles of social science, those that apply to different broad approaches to conducting scientific inquiry.

Next, we examine causation in social science, the foundation of explanatory research, and the validity of statements about cause. We then consider units of analysis—the what or whom we want to study. Deciding on units of analysis is an important part of all research, partly because people sometimes inappropriately use data measuring one type of unit to say something about a different type of unit.

The chapter concludes with a discussion of alternative ways of handling time in criminal justice research. It is sometimes appropriate to examine a static cross section of social life, but other studies follow social processes over time. In this regard, researchers must consider the time order of events and processes in making statements about cause.

# FOUNDATIONS OF SOCIAL SCIENCE

*Social scientific inquiry generates knowledge through logic and observation.*

The two pillars of science are logic, or rationality, and observation. A scientific understanding of the world must make sense and must agree with what we observe. Both of these elements are essential to social science and relate to three key aspects of the overall scientific enterprise: theory, data collection, and data analysis.

As a broad generalization, scientific theory deals with the logical aspect of science, data collection deals with the observational aspect, and data analysis looks for patterns in what is observed. This book focuses mainly on issues related to data collection—demonstrating how to conduct empirical research—but social science involves all three elements. Figure 3.1 offers a schematic view of these three aspects of social science.

Let's now consider some of the fundamental things that distinguish social science from other ways of looking at social phenomena.

## Theory, Not Philosophy or Belief

Social scientific theory has to do with what *is*, not what *should be*. A **theory** is a systematic explanation for the observed facts and laws that relate to a particular aspect of life—juvenile delinquency, for example, or perhaps social stratification or political revolution. Joseph Maxwell (2005, 42) defines theory as "a set of concepts and the proposed relationships among these, a structure that is intended to represent or model something about the world."

Often, social scientists begin constructing a theory by observing aspects of social life, seeking to discover patterns that may point to more or less universal principles. Barney Glaser and Anselm Strauss (1967) coined the term *grounded theory* to describe this method of theory construction. Field research—the direct observation of events in progress—is frequently used to develop theories, or survey research may reveal patterns of attitudes that suggest particular theoretical explanations.

Once developed, theories provide general statements about social life that are used to guide research. For example, routine activity theory states that crimes are more likely to occur when a motivated offender encounters a suitable victim in the absence of a capable guardian (Cohen and Felson 1979). Mike Townsley and associates used routine activity theory to guide their research on "contagious" burglaries (Townsley, Homel, and Chaseling 2003). They argued that once burglars struck one

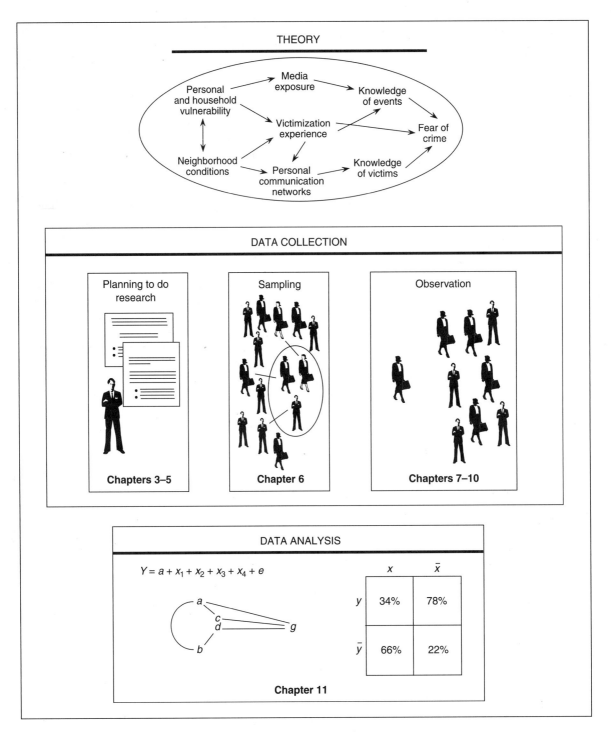

**FIGURE 3.1**  Social Science = Theory + Data Collection + Data Analysis

house in a neighborhood, they were more likely to break into nearby houses because they had become more familiar with an area and its potential targets. The research results were generally consistent with these expectations—burglary tended to cluster around houses of similar type in a neighborhood.

Townsley and associates used routine activity theory to generate a **hypothesis** about patterns of burglary. A hypothesis is an expectation about the nature of things derived from a theory. Taking a different example, a theory might contain the hypothesis "high school dropouts will have higher delinquency rates compared with youths enrolled in high school." Such a hypothesis could then be tested through research.

Drawing on theories to generate hypotheses that are tested through research is the traditional image of science, illustrated in Figure 3.2. Here we see the researcher beginning with an interest

in something or an idea about it. Next comes the development of a theoretical understanding of how a number of concepts, represented by the letters *A, B, C,* and so on, may be related to each other. The theoretical considerations result in a hypothesis, or an expectation about the way things would be in the world if the theoretical expectations were correct. The notation $Y = f(X)$ is a conventional way of saying that $Y$ (for example, auto theft rate) is a function of or is in some way caused by $X$ (for example, availability of off-street parking). At that level, however, $X$ and $Y$ have general rather than specific meanings.

In the operationalization process, general concepts are translated into specific indicators. Thus the lowercase $x$ is a concrete indicator of capital $X$. As an example, census data on the number of housing units that have garages ($x$) are a concrete indicator of off-street parking ($X$). This operationalization

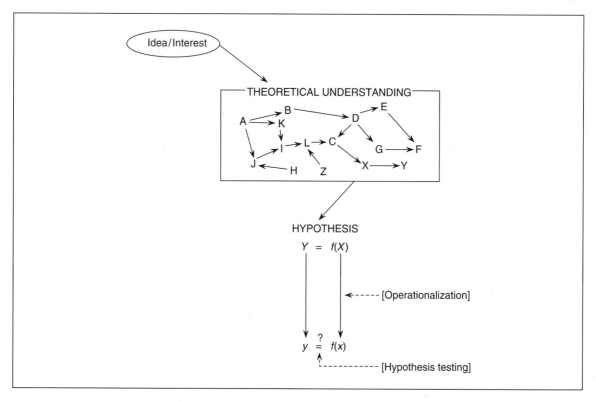

**FIGURE 3.2** The Traditional Image of Science

process results in the formation of a testable hypothesis: is the rate of auto theft higher in areas where fewer housing units have garages? Observations aimed at finding out are part of what is typically called **hypothesis testing**.

## Regularities

Ultimately, social scientific theory aims to find patterns of regularity in social life. This assumes, of course, that life is regular, not chaotic or random. That assumption applies to all science, but it is sometimes a barrier for people when they first approach social science.

A vast number of norms and rules in society create regularity. Only persons who have reached a certain age may obtain a driver's license. In the U.S. Supreme Court, only lawyers sit on the bench. Such informal and formal prescriptions regulate, or regularize, social behavior.

In addition to regularities produced by norms and rules, social science is able to identify other types of regularities. For example, teenagers commit more crimes than middle-aged people. When males commit murder, they usually kill another male, but female murderers more often kill a male. On average, white urban residents view police more favorably than nonwhites do. Judges receive higher salaries than police officers. Probation officers have more empathy for the people they supervise than prison guards do.

## What about Exceptions?

The objection that there are always exceptions to any social regularity misses the point. The existence of exceptions does not invalidate the existence of regularities. Thus it is not important that a particular police officer earns more money than a particular judge if, overall, judges earn more than police officers. The pattern still exists. Social regularities represent **probabilistic** patterns, and a general pattern does not have to be reflected in 100 percent of the observable cases to be a pattern.

This rule applies in the physical as well as the social sciences. In genetics, the mating of a blue-eyed person with a brown-eyed person will *probably* result in brown-eyed offspring. The birth of a blue-eyed child does not challenge the observed regularity, however. Rather, the geneticist states only that brown-eyed offspring are *more likely* and, furthermore, that a brown-eyed offspring will be born in only a certain percentage of cases. The social scientist makes a similar, probabilistic prediction, that women overall are less likely to murder anybody, but when they do, their victims are most often males.

## Aggregates, Not Individuals

Social scientists primarily study social patterns rather than individual ones. All regular patterns reflect the aggregate, or combined, actions and situations of many individuals. Although social scientists study motivations that affect individuals, **aggregates** are more often the subject of social scientific research.

A focus on aggregate patterns rather than on individuals distinguishes the activities of criminal justice researchers from the daily routines of many criminal justice practitioners. Consider the task of processing and classifying individuals newly admitted to a correctional facility. Prison staff administer psychological tests and review the prior record of each new inmate to determine security risks, program needs, and job options. A researcher who is studying whether white inmates tend to be assigned to more desirable jobs than nonwhite inmates would be more interested in patterns of job assignment. The focus would be on aggregates of white and nonwhite persons rather than the assignment for any particular individual.

Social scientific theories, then, typically deal with aggregate, not individual, behavior. Their purpose is to explain why aggregate patterns of behavior are so regular even when the individuals who perform them change over time. In fact, social science is not so much interested in people but rather variables.

## A Variable Language

Suppose someone says to you, "Women are too soft-hearted and weak to be police officers." You are likely to hear that comment in terms of what you know about the speaker. If it's your old Uncle Albert, who, you recall, is also strongly opposed to daylight saving time, zip codes, and computers, you are likely to think his latest pronouncement simply fits into his dated views about things in general. If the statement comes from a candidate for sheriff who is trailing a female challenger and who has begun making other statements about women being unfit for public office, you may hear his latest comment in the context of this political challenge.

In both of these examples, you are trying to understand the thoughts of a particular, concrete individual. In social science, however, we go beyond that level of understanding to seek insights into classes or types of individuals. In the two preceding examples, we might use terms like *old-fashioned* or *bigoted* to describe the person who made the comment. In other words, we try to identify the actual individual with some set of similar individuals, and that identification operates on the basis of abstract concepts.

One implication of this approach is that it enables us to make sense out of more than one person. In understanding what makes the bigoted candidate think the way he does, we can also learn about other people who are like him. This is possible because we have not been studying bigots as much as we have been studying bigotry.

Bigotry is considered a variable in this case because the level of bigotry varies; that is, some people in an observed group are more bigoted than others. Social scientists may be interested in understanding the system of variables that causes bigotry to be high in one instance and low in another. However, bigotry is not the only variable here. Gender, age, and economic status also vary among members of the observed group.

Here's another example. Consider the problem of whether police should make arrests in cases of domestic violence. The object of a police officer's attention in handling a domestic assault is the individual case. Of course, each case includes a victim and an offender, and police are concerned with preventing further harm to the victim. The officer must decide whether to arrest one or both parties,

or to take some other action. The criminal justice researcher's subject matter is different: does arrest as a general policy prevent future assaults? The researcher may study an individual case (victim and offender), but that case is relevant only as a situation in which an arrest policy might be invoked, which is what the researcher is really studying.

## Variables and Attributes

Social scientists study variables and the attributes that compose them. Social scientific theories are written in a variable language, and people get involved mostly as the carriers of those variables.

**Attributes** are characteristics or qualities that describe some object, such as a person. Examples are *bigoted, old-fashioned, married, unemployed,* and *intoxicated.* Any quality we might use to describe ourselves or someone else is an attribute.

**Variables** are logical groupings of attributes. *Male* and *female* are attributes, and *gender* is the variable composed of the logical grouping of those two attributes. The variable *occupation* is composed of attributes such as *dentist, professor,* and *truck driver. Prior record* is a variable composed of a set of attributes such as *prior convictions, prior arrests without convictions,* and *no prior arrests.* It's helpful to think of attributes as the categories that make up a variable. See Figure 3.3 for a schematic view of what social scientists mean by variables and attributes. Panel A lists both variables and attributes, mixing them together. Panel B separates these concepts to distinguish variables from attributes. Panel C presents variables together with the attributes they carry.

The relationship between attributes and variables lies at the heart of both description and explanation in science. We might describe a prosecutor's office in terms of the variable *gender* by reporting the observed frequencies of the attributes *male* and *female*: "The office staff is 60 percent men and 40 percent women." An incarceration rate can be thought of as a description of the variable *incarceration status* of a state's population in terms of the attributes *incarcerated* and *not incarcerated.* Even the report of family income for a city is a summary of

**A.**

| Some Common Criminal Justice Concepts |
|---|
| Female<br>Probation<br>Thief<br>Gender<br>Sentence<br>Property crime<br>Middle-aged<br>Age<br>Auto theft<br>Occupation |

**B.**

| Two Different Kinds of Concepts | |
|---|---|
| Variables | Attributes |
| Gender<br>Sentence<br>Property crime<br>Age<br>Occupation | Female<br>Probation<br>Auto theft<br>Middle-aged<br>Thief |

**C.**

| The Relationship between Variables and Attributes | |
|---|---|
| Variables | Attributes |
| Gender | Female, male |
| Age | Young, middle-aged, old |
| Sentence | Fine, prison, probation |
| Property crime | Auto theft, burglary, larceny |
| Occupation | Judge, lawyer, thief |

**FIGURE 3.3** Variables and Attributes

attributes composing the *income* variable: *$37,124, $64,980, $96,000,* and so forth.

The relationship between attributes and variables becomes more complicated as we try to explain how concepts are related to each other. Here's a simple example involving two variables: type of defense attorney and sentence. For the sake of simplicity, let's assume that the variable *defense attorney* has only two attributes: *private attorney* and *public defender*. Similarly, let's give the variable *sentence* two attributes: *probation* and *prison*.

Now let's suppose that 90 percent of people represented by public defenders are sentenced to prison and the other 10 percent are sentenced to probation.

And let's suppose that 30 percent of people with private attorneys go to prison and the other 70 percent receive probation. This is shown visually in Figure 3.4A.

Figure 3.4A illustrates a relationship between the variables *defense attorney* and *sentence*. This relationship can be seen by the pairings of attributes on the two variables. There are two predominant pairings: (1) persons represented by private attorneys who are sentenced to probation and (2) persons represented by public defenders who are sentenced to prison. But there are two other useful ways of viewing that relationship.

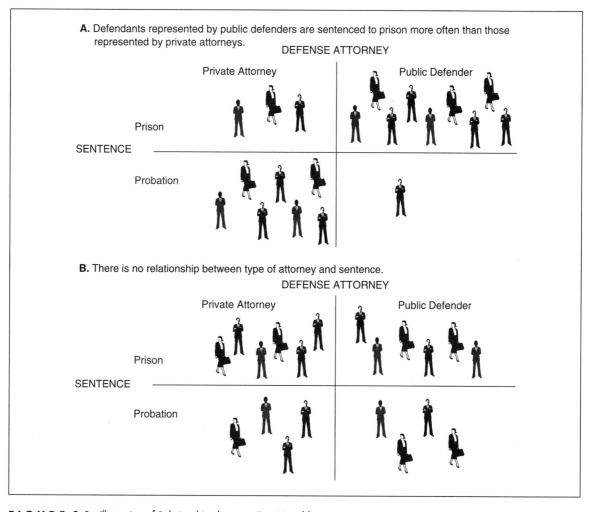

**F I G U R E  3.4**  Illustration of Relationships between Two Variables

First, imagine that we play a game in which we bet on your ability to guess whether a person is sentenced to prison or probation. We'll pick the people one at a time (not telling you which ones we've picked), and you have to guess which sentence each person receives. We'll do it for all 20 people in Figure 3.4A. Your best strategy in this case is to always guess prison because 12 out of the 20 people are categorized that way. You'll get 12 right and 8 wrong, for a net success score of 4.

Now suppose that we pick a person from Figure 3.4A and we have to tell you whether the person has a private attorney or a public defender. Your best strategy now is to guess prison for each person with a public defender and probation for each person represented by a private attorney. If you follow that strategy, you will get 16 right and 4 wrong. Your improvement in guessing the sentence on the basis of knowing the type of defense attorney illustrates what it means to say that the variables are related. You would have made a probabilistic statement on the basis of some empirical observations about the relationship between type of lawyer and type of sentence.

Second, let's consider how the 20 people would be distributed if type of defense attorney and sentence were unrelated. This is illustrated in Figure 3.4B. Notice that half the people have private attorneys and half have public defenders. Also notice that 12 of the 20 (60 percent) are sentenced to prison—6 who have private attorneys and 6 who have public defenders. The equal distribution of those sentenced to probation and those sentenced to prison, no matter what type of defense attorney each person had, allows us to conclude that the two variables are unrelated. Here, knowing what type of attorney a person had would not be of any value to you in guessing whether that person was sentenced to prison or probation.

## Variables and Relationships

Theories describe relationships that might logically be expected among variables. This expectation often involves the notion of *causation*: a person's attributes on one variable are expected to *cause* or encourage a particular attribute on another variable. In the example just given, having a private attorney or a public defender seemed to cause a person to be sentenced to probation or prison, respectively. Apparently there is something about having a public defender that leads people to be sentenced to prison more often than if they are represented by a private attorney.

Type of defense attorney and sentence are examples of independent and dependent variables, respectively. In this example, we assume that criminal sentences are determined or caused by something; the type of sentence depends on something and so is called the **dependent variable**. The dependent variable depends on an **independent variable**; in this case, sentence depends on type of defense attorney.

Notice, at the same time, that type of defense attorney might be found to depend on something else—our subjects' employment status, for example. People who have full-time jobs are more likely to be represented by private attorneys than those who are unemployed. In this latter relationship, the type of attorney is the dependent variable, and the sub-

ject's employment status is the independent variable. In cause-and-effect terms, the independent variable is the cause and the dependent variable is the effect.

How does this relate to theory? Our discussion of Figure 3.4 involved the interpretation of data. We looked at the distribution of the 20 people in terms of the two variables. In constructing a theory, we form an expectation about the relationship between the two variables based on what we know about each. For example, we know that private attorneys tend to be more experienced than public defenders. Many law school graduates gain a few years of experience as public defenders before they enter private practice. Logically, then, we would expect the more experienced private attorneys to be better able to get more lenient sentences for their clients. We might explore this question directly by examining the relationship between attorney experience and sentence, perhaps comparing inexperienced public defenders with public defenders who have been working for a few years. Pursuing this line of reasoning, we could also compare experienced private attorneys with private attorneys fresh out of law school.

Notice that the theory has to do with the variables *defense attorney, sentence,* and *years of experience,* not with individual people per se. People are the carriers of those variables. We study the relationship between the variables by observing people. Ultimately, however, the theory is constructed in terms of variables. It describes the associations that might logically be expected to exist between particular attributes of different variables.

## DIFFERING AVENUES FOR INQUIRY

*Social scientific research is conducted in a variety of ways.*

Three broad and interrelated distinctions underlie many of the variations of social scientific research: (1) idiographic and nomothetic explanations, (2) inductive and deductive reasoning, and (3) quantitative and qualitative data. Although it is possible to see them as competing choices, a good researcher masters each of these orientations.

## Idiographic and Nomothetic Explanations

All of us go through life explaining things; we do it every day. In our everyday explanations, we engage in two distinct forms of causal reasoning—idiographic and nomothetic explanation—although we do not ordinarily distinguish them.

Sometimes we attempt to explain a single situation exhaustively. You might have done poorly on an exam because (1) you had forgotten there was an exam that day, (2) it was in your worst subject, (3) a traffic jam caused you to be late to class, and (4) your roommate kept you up the night before with loud music. Given all these circumstances, it is no wonder that you did poorly on the exam.

This type of causal reasoning is **idiographic** explanation. *Idio* in this context means "unique, separate, peculiar, or distinct," as in the word *idiosyncrasy*. When we complete an idiographic explanation, we feel that we fully understand the many causes of what happened in a particular instance. At the same time, the scope of our explanation is limited to the case at hand. Although parts of the idiographic explanation might apply to other situations, our intention is to explain one case fully.

Now consider a different kind of explanation. For example, every time you study with a group, you do better on an exam than if you study alone. Your favorite team does better at home than on the road. You get more speeding tickets on weekends than during the week. This type of explanation—called **nomothetic**—seeks to explain a class of situations or events rather than a single one. Moreover, it seeks to explain efficiently, using only one or just a few explanatory factors. Finally, it settles for a partial rather than a full explanation of a type of situation.

In each of the preceding nomothetic examples, you might qualify your causal statements with phrases such as "on the whole" or "usually." You usually do better on exams when you've studied in a group, but there have been exceptions. Your team has won some games on the road and lost some at home. And last week you got a speeding ticket on the way to Tuesday's chemistry class, but you did not get one over the weekend. Such exceptions are an acceptable price to pay for a broader range of overall explanation.

Both idiographic and nomothetic approaches to understanding can be useful in daily life. They are also powerful tools for criminal justice research. The researcher who seeks an exhaustive understanding of the inner workings of a particular juvenile gang or the rulings of a specific judge is engaging in idiographic research. The aim is to understand that particular group or individual as fully as possible.

Rick Brown and Ron Clarke (2004) sought to understand thefts of a particular model of Nissan trucks in the south of England. Most stolen trucks were never recovered. Their research led Brown and Clarke to a shipping yard where trucks were taken apart and shipped to ports in France and Nigeria as scrap metal. They later learned that trucks were reassembled and sold to individuals and small companies. In the course of their research, they linked most thieves in England and most resellers abroad to legitimate shipping and scrap metal businesses. Even though Brown and Clarke sought answers to the idiosyncratic problem of stolen trucks in one region of England, they came to some tentative conclusions about loosely organized international theft rings.

In contrast to the idiographic study of Nissan truck theft, Pierre Tremblay and associates (2001) explored how a theory of offending helped explain different types of offender networks. After examining auto thefts over 25 years in Quebec, the authors concluded that different types of relationships were involved in different types of professional car theft. However, Tremblay and associates found that persons involved in legitimate car sales and repair businesses were key members in all networks. The researchers showed how complex relationships among people involved in legitimate and illegitimate activities helped explain patterns of car theft over a quarter century. This is an illustration of the nomothetic approach to understanding.

Thus social scientists have access to two distinct logics of explanation. We can alternate between searching for broad, albeit less detailed, universals (nomothetic) and probing more deeply into more specific cases (idiographic).

## Inductive and Deductive Reasoning

The distinction between inductive and deductive reasoning exists in daily life as well as in criminal justice research. You might take two different routes to reach the conclusion that you do better on exams if you study with others. Suppose you find yourself puzzling, halfway through your college career, over why you do so well on exams sometimes and poorly at other times. You list all the exams you've taken, noting how well you did on each. Then you try to recall any circumstances shared by all the good exams and by all the poor ones. Do you do better on multiple-choice exams or essay exams? Morning exams or afternoon exams? Exams in the natural sciences, the humanities, or the social sciences? After you studied alone or in a group? It suddenly occurs to you that you almost always do better on exams when you studied with others than when you studied alone.

This is known as the inductive mode of inquiry. **Inductive reasoning** (induction) moves from the specific to the general, from a set of particular observations to the discovery of a pattern that represents some degree of order among the varied events under examination.

There is the second, and very different, way you might reach the same conclusion about studying for exams. As you approach your first set of exams in college, you might wonder about the best ways to study. You might consider how much you should review the readings and how much you should focus on your class notes. Should you study at a measured pace over time or pull an all-nighter just before the exam? Among these musings, you might ask whether you should get together with other students in the class or study on your own. You decide to evaluate the pros and cons of both options. On the one hand, studying

with others might not be as efficient because a lot of time might be spent on material you already know, or the group might get distracted from studying. On the other hand, you can understand something even better when you've explained it to someone else. And other students might understand material that you've been having trouble with and reveal perspectives that might have escaped you.

So you add up the pros and the cons and conclude, logically, that you'd benefit from studying with others. This seems reasonable to you in theory. To see whether it is true in practice, you test your idea by studying alone for half your exams and studying with others for the other half.

This second approach is known as the deductive mode of inquiry. **Deductive reasoning** (deduction) moves from the general to the specific. It moves from a pattern that might be logically or theoretically expected to observations that test whether the expected pattern actually occurs in the real world. Notice that deduction begins with *why* and moves to *whether*, whereas induction moves in the opposite direction.

Both inductive and deductive reasoning are valid avenues for criminal justice and other social scientific research. Moreover, they work together to provide ever-more powerful and complete understandings.

## Quantitative and Qualitative Data

Simply put, the distinction between quantitative and qualitative data is the distinction between numerical and nonnumerical data. When we say that someone is witty, we are making a qualitative assertion. When we say that that person has appeared three times in a local comedy club, we are attempting to quantify our assessment.

Most observations are qualitative at the outset, whether it is our experience of someone's sense of humor, the location of a pointer on a measuring scale, or a check mark entered in a questionnaire. None of these things is inherently numerical. But it is often useful to convert observations to a numerical form. Quantification often makes our observations more explicit, makes it easier to aggregate and summarize data, and opens up the possibility of statistical analyses, ranging from simple descriptions to more complex testing of relationships between variables.

Quantification requires focusing our attention and specifying meaning. Suppose someone asks whether your friends tend to be older or younger than you. A quantitative answer seems easy. You think about how old each of your friends is, calculate an average, and see whether it is higher or lower than your own age. Case closed.

Or is it? Although we focused our attention on "older or younger" in terms of the number of years people have been alive, we might mean something different with that idea—for example, "maturity" or "worldliness." Your friends may tend to be a little younger than you in age but may act more mature. Or we might have been thinking of how young or old your friends look or of the variation in their life experiences, their worldliness. All these other meanings are lost in the numerical calculation of average age.

In addition to greater detail, nonnumerical observations seem to convey a greater richness of meaning than do quantified data. Think of the cliché "he is older than his years." The meaning of that expression is lost in attempts to specify how much older. In this sense, the richness of meaning is partly a function of ambiguity. If the expression meant something to you when you read it, that meaning came from your own experiences, from people you have known who might fit the description of being older than their years.

This concept can be quantified to a certain extent, however. For example, we could make a list of life experiences that contribute to what we mean by worldliness:

Getting married

Getting divorced

Having a parent die

Being fired from a job

Moving to another country

We could quantify people's worldliness by counting how many of these experiences they have had:

the more such experiences, the more worldly we say they are. If we think that some experiences are more powerful than others, we can give those experiences more points than others. Once we decide on the specific experiences to be considered and the number of points each warrants, scoring people and comparing their worldliness is fairly straightforward.

To quantify a concept like worldliness, we must be explicit about what we mean. By focusing specifically on what we will include in our measurement of the concept, as we did here, we also exclude the other possible meanings. Inevitably, then, quantitative measures will be more superficial than qualitative descriptions. This is the trade-off.

What a dilemma! Which approach should we choose? Which is better? Which is more appropriate to criminal justice research?

The good news is that we don't have to choose. In fact, by choosing to undertake a qualitative or quantitative study, researchers run the risk of artificially limiting the scope of their inquiry. Both qualitative and quantitative methods are useful and legitimate. And some research situations and topics require elements of both approaches.

## CAUSATION IN THE SOCIAL SCIENCES

*Causation is the focus of explanatory and evaluation research.*

One of the chief goals of social scientific researchers is to explain why things are the way they are. Typically we do that by specifying the *causes* for the way things are: some things are caused by other things.

At the outset, it's important to keep in mind that cause in social science is inherently probabilistic, as we noted earlier in this chapter. We say, for example, that certain factors make delinquency more or less *likely*. Thus, victims of childhood abuse or neglect are *more likely* to report alcohol abuse as adults (Schuck and Widom 2001). Recidivism is less *likely* among offenders who receive more careful assessment and classification at institutional intake (Cullen and Gendreau 2000).

## Criteria for Causality

We begin our consideration of cause by examining what criteria must be satisfied before we can infer that something causes something else. Joseph Maxwell (2005, 106–107) writes that criteria for assessing an idiographic explanation are (1) how credible and believable it is and (2) whether alternative explanations ("rival hypotheses") were seriously considered and found wanting. The first criterion relates to logic as one of the foundations of science. We demand that our explanations make sense, even if the logic is sometimes complex. The second criterion reminds us of Sherlock Holmes's dictum that when all other possibilities have been eliminated the remaining explanation, however improbable, must be the truth.

Regarding nomothetic explanation, we examine three specific criteria for causality, as described by William Shadish, Thomas Cook, and Donald Campbell (2002). The first requirement in a causal relationship between two variables is that the cause must precede the effect in time. It makes no sense to imagine something being caused by something else that happened later on. A bullet leaving the muzzle of a gun does not cause the gunpowder to explode; it works the other way around. As simple and obvious as this criterion may seem, criminal justice research suffers many problems in this regard. Often the time order connecting two variables is simply unclear. Which comes first: drug use or crime? And even when the time order seems clear, exceptions may be found. For example, we normally assume that obtaining a master's degree in management is a cause of more rapid advancement in a state department of corrections. Yet corrections executives might pursue graduate education after they have been promoted and recognize that advanced training in management skills will help them do their job better.

The second requirement in a causal relationship is that the two variables must be empirically correlated with each other—they must occur together. It makes no sense to say that exploding gunpowder causes a bullet to leave the muzzle of a gun if, in observed reality, a bullet does not come out after the gunpowder explodes.

Again, criminal justice research has difficulties with this requirement. In the probabilistic world of nomothetic models of explanation, at least, we encounter few perfect correlations. Most judges sentence repeat drug dealers to prison, but some don't. We are forced to ask, therefore, how strong the empirical relationship must be for that relationship to be considered causal.

The third requirement for a causal relationship is that the observed empirical correlation between two variables cannot be explained away as being due to the influence of some other variable that causes both of them. For example, we may observe that drug markets are often found near bus stops, but this does not mean that bus stops encourage drug markets. A third variable is at work here: groups of people naturally congregate near bus stops, and street drug markets are often found where people naturally congregate.

To sum up, most social researchers consider two variables to be causally related—one causes the other—if (1) the cause precedes the effect in time, (2) there is an empirical correlation between them, and (3) the relationship is not found to result from the effects of some third variable on each of the two initially observed. Any relationship that satisfies all these criteria is causal, and these are the only criteria that need to be satisfied.

## Validity and Causal Inference

Paying careful attention to cause-and-effect relationships is crucial in criminal justice research. Cause and effect are also key elements of applied studies, in which a researcher may be interested in whether, for example, a new mandatory sentencing law actually causes an increase in the prison population.

When we are concerned with whether we are correct in inferring that a cause produced an effect, we are concerned with the **validity** of causal inference. In the words of Shadish, Cook, and Campbell (2002, 34), validity is "the approximate truth of an inference.... When we say something is valid, we make a judgment about the extent to which relevant evidence supports that inference as being true or correct." They emphasize that *approximate* is an important word because one can never be absolutely certain about cause.

Researchers are mostly concerned with different **validity threats** in causal inference—reasons we might be incorrect in stating that some cause produced some effect. As Maxwell (2005, 106) puts it, "A key concept for validity is thus the validity *threat*: a way you might be wrong" (emphasis in original). Chapter 5 discusses different types of validity threats in detail, linking the issue of validity to different ways of designing research. Here we will describe how validity threats might emerge in examining possible relationships between drug use and crime.

## Does Drug Use Cause Crime?

Understanding causal statements about drug use and crime requires carefully specifying two key concepts—drug use and crime—and considering the different ways these concepts might be related. Jan Chaiken and Marcia Chaiken (1990) provide unusually careful and well-reasoned insights that will guide our consideration of links between drugs and crime. The three criteria for inferring cause—time order, empirical relationship, and eliminating alternative explanations—will guide our discussion.

First is the question of temporal order: which comes first, drug use or crime? Research summarized by Chaiken and Chaiken provides no conclusive answer. In an earlier study of prison inmates, Chaiken and Chaiken (1982) found that 12 percent of their adult subjects committed crimes after using drugs for at least two years, whereas 15 percent committed predatory crimes two or more years before using drugs. Studies of juveniles revealed similar findings: "About 50 percent of delinquent youngsters are delinquent before they start using drugs; about 50 percent start concurrently or after" (Chaiken and Chaiken 1990, 235).

Regarding an empirical relationship, many studies have found that some drug users commit crimes and that some criminals use drugs. Trevor Bennett and associates (2008) conducted summary analysis of 30 research studies on drug use and crime. They found that drug users were over three times more likely to be involved in crime than nonusers. So a statistical association between drug use and crime clearly exists.

What about the possible influence of other factors, things that might be related to both drug use and crime? Chaiken and Chaiken (1990, 234) conclude that "drug use and crime participation are weakly related as contemporaneous products of factors generally antithetical to traditional United States lifestyles." Stated somewhat differently, drug use and crime (as well as delinquency) are each deviant activities produced by other underlying causes. The presence of other factors suggests the relationship is not directly causal. Drug use and crime are linked, but each appears to be related to other variables.

To further consider the threats to the validity of links between drugs and crime, let's think for a moment about different patterns of each behavior, rather than assume that drug use and crime are uniform behaviors. Many adolescents in the United States experiment with drugs; just as many commit delinquent acts or petty crimes. A large number of adults may be occasional users of illegal drugs as well. Many different patterns of drug use, delinquency, and adult criminality have been found in research in other countries. Stephen Pudney (2002) and Trevor Bennett and Katy Holloway (2005) report on varying patterns of use in England and Wales, ranging from experimentation with marijuana to chronic heroin addiction. Because both drug use and crime take different forms, searching for a single cause-and-effect relationship misrepresents a complex process.

In further analysis Bennett and colleagues compared offending by type of drug use, finding that users of crack cocaine were more likely to be offenders than users of any other drug. They also found that the relationship between occasional marijuana use and delinquency among teenagers is different from that between occasional cocaine use and adult crime; each relationship, in turn, varies from that between crack cocaine addiction and persistent criminal behavior among adults.

Basic and applied research on the relationships among drug use and crime readily illustrates threats to the validity of causal inference. It is often difficult to find a relationship because there is so much variation in drug use and crime participation. A large number of studies have demonstrated that, when statistical relationships are found, both drug use and crime can be attributed to other, often multiple, causes. Different patterns among different population groups mean there are no readily identifiable cause-and-effect constructs. Because of these differences, policies developed to counter drug use among the population as a whole cannot be expected to have much of an impact on serious crime.

None of the above is to say that there is no cause-and-effect relationship between drug use and crime. However, research has clearly shown that there is no simple causal connection. For more on how questions of cause and effect emerge, see the box "Causation and Declining Crime in New York City."

## Introducing Scientific Realism

In our final consideration of cause and effect in this chapter, we revisit the distinction between idiographic and nomothetic ways of explanation. Doing research to find what causes what reflects nomothetic concerns more often than not. We wish to find causal explanations that apply generally to situations beyond those we actually study in our research. At the same time, researchers and public officials are often interested in understanding specific causal mechanisms in more narrowly defined situations—what we have described as the idiographic mode of explanation.

**Scientific realism** bridges idiographic and nomothetic approaches to explanation by seeking to understand how causal *mechanisms* operate in specific *contexts*. Traditional approaches to finding cause and effect usually try to isolate causal mechanisms from other possible influences, something you should now recognize as trying to control threats to validity. The scientific realist approach views these other possible influences as contexts in which causal mechanisms operate. Rather than try to exclude or otherwise control possible outside influences, scientific realism studies how such influences are involved in cause-and-effect relationships.

For example, we reviewed at some length the cause-and-effect conundrum surrounding drug use and crime. That review was framed by traditional nomothetic research to establish cause and effect. A scientific realism approach to the question would recognize that drug use and crime co-occur in some contexts but not in others.

We say that scientific realism bridges idiographic and nomothetic modes of explanation because it exhibits elements of both. Because it focuses our attention on very specific questions, scientific realism seems idiographic. Here's an example: "Will redesigning the Interstate 78 exit in Newark, New Jersey, cause a reduction in the number of suburban residents seeking to buy heroin in this neighborhood?" But this specific question is compatible with more general questions of causation: "Can the design of streets and intersections be modified to make it more difficult for street drug markets to operate?" Changing an expressway exit ramp to reduce drug sales in Newark is a specific example of cause and effect that is rooted in the more general causal relationship between traffic patterns and drug markets. Research by Nicholas Zanin and colleagues (2004) addresses both the idiographic explanation in Newark and the potential for broader applications elsewhere.

These illustrations of the scientific realist approach to cause and effect are examples of research for the purpose of application, a topic treated at length by British researchers Ray Pawson and Nick Tilley (1997). Application is a type of explanatory research, as we indicated in Chapter 1. In later chapters, we call on scientific realism as a strategy for designing explanatory research (Chapter 5) and conducting evaluations (Chapter 10).

Sorting out causes and effects is one of the most difficult challenges of explanatory research. Our attention now turns to two other important considerations that emerge in research for explanation and other purposes: units of analysis and the time dimension.

**CAUSATION AND DECLINING CRIME IN NEW YORK CITY**

Did changes in police strategy and tactics in New York City cause a decline in crime? That question is central to what became quite a spirited debate, a debate that centers our attention on causation. In fact, former police commissioner William Bratton (1999, 17) used language strikingly similar to what you will find in this chapter to argue that crime dropped in New York because of police action:

> As a basic tenet of epistemology ... we cannot conclude that a causal relationship exists between two variables unless ... three necessary conditions occur: one variable must precede the other in time, an empirically measured relationship must be demonstrated between the variables, and the relationship must not be better explained by any third intervening variable. Although contemporary criminology's explanations for the decline in New York City meet the first two conditions, they don't explain it better than a third intervening variable.

With these words, Bratton challenged researchers to propose some empirical measure of a variable that better accounted for the crime reduction. A number of researchers have advanced alternative explanations. Let's now consider what some of those variables might be.

**Changing Drug Markets**

After falling from 1980 through 1984, homicide rates in larger U.S. cities rose sharply through the early 1990s. This corresponded with the emergence of crack cocaine, a low-cost drug sold by loosely organized gangs that settled business disputes with guns instead of lawyers. The decline in crack use in the mid-1990s corresponded with the beginning of decreasing homicide rates. Alfred Blumstein and Richard Rosenfeld (1998) point to changes in crack markets as a plausible explanation—gun homicides and crack markets both increased and decreased together. Other researchers claim that changes in crack markets had some effect on violence (Johnson, Golub, and Dunlap 2000; Karmen 2000).

**Regression**

A common threat to validity in research on crime trends is regression to the mean. This refers to a phenomenon whereby social indicators move up and down over time, and abnormally high or low values are eventually followed by a return (regression) to more normal levels. Jeffrey Fagan and associates (Fagan, Zimring, and Kim 1998) present evidence to suggest that rates of gun homicide in New York were relatively stable from 1969 through the mid-1980s, when they began to increase sharply. Around 1991, rates began to decline, returning to approximate previous levels.

**Homicides Declined Everywhere**

Fagan and associates (1998) point out that although New York's decline was considerable, it was not unprecedented. Many large cities saw sharp reductions in homicide during the same period, and a few cities had even greater declines. Blumstein and Rosenfeld (1998) cite similar data, pointing out that sharp reductions in homicide rates occurred in cities where no major changes in policing were evident. This suggests that declining crime in New York was simply part of a national trend.

**Incapacitation**

The decline of homicide rates in the 1990s followed more than a decade of growth in incarceration rates in state and federal correctional facilities. According to the incapacitation argument, rates of homicide and other violent crimes declined because growing numbers of violent criminals were locked up. Some researchers have presented evidence to challenge that claim (Rosenfeld 2000; Spelman 2000).

**Economic Opportunity**

The early 1990s marked the beginning of a sustained period of economic growth in the United States. With greater job opportunities, crime naturally declined. A number of authors have cited this example of how change in one of the "root causes" of crime might have caused changes in rates of homicide and other serious crimes (for example, Karmen 2000; Silverman 1999), but none have offered any evidence to support it.

**Demographic Change**

Because violent and other offenses tend to be committed more by younger people, especially young males, a decline in the number of members in those demographic groups may be responsible for New York's reduced crime rate. Fagan and associates (1998) present data that show relatively stable numbers of 15- to 19-year-old males in New York, so it seems unlikely that demographic factors account for changes in crime rates. Additional analysis of demographic change has been conducted by Rosenfeld (2000) and James Alan Fox (2000).

**Continuation of a Trend**

George Kelling and William Bratton (1998) claim that crime declined in New York immediately following the implementation of major changes in policing. But other analysts argue that the beginning of the shift preceded these changes. Notice that this brings into question another of the three criteria for inferring cause by claiming that the effect—declining crime—occurred before the cause—changes in policing. Even more possible explanations have been offered, but those presented here are the most plausible and are most often cited by researchers. Andrew Karmen (2000, 263) offers a good summary of different explanations for New York's crime drop.

# UNITS OF ANALYSIS

*To avoid mistaken inferences, researchers must carefully specify the people or phenomena that will be studied.*

In criminal justice research, there is a great deal of variation in what or who is studied—what are technically called **units of analysis**. Individual people are often units of analysis. Researchers may make observations describing certain characteristics of offenders or crime victims, such as age, gender, or race. The descriptions of many individuals are then combined to provide a picture of the population that comprises those individuals.

For example, we may note the age and gender of persons convicted of drunk driving in Fort Lauderdale over a certain period. Aggregating these observations, we might characterize drunk-driving offenders as 72 percent men and 28 percent women, with an average age of 26.4 years. This is a descriptive analysis of convicted drunk drivers in Fort Lauderdale. Although the description applies to the group of drunk drivers as a whole, it is based on the characteristics of individual people convicted of drunk driving.

Units of analysis in a study are typically also the units of observation. Thus, to study what steps people take to protect their homes from burglary, we might observe individual household residents, perhaps through interviews. Sometimes, however, we observe units of analysis indirectly. We might ask individuals about crime prevention measures for the purpose of describing households. We might want to find out whether homes with double-cylinder deadbolt locks are burglarized less often than homes with less substantial protection. In this case, our units of analysis are households, but the units of observation are individual household members who are asked to describe burglaries and home protection to interviewers.

## Individuals

Any variety of individuals may be the units of analysis in criminal justice research. This point is more important than it may initially seem. The norm of generalized understanding in social science should suggest that scientific findings are most valuable when they apply to all kinds of people. In practice, however, researchers seldom study all kinds of people. At the very least, studies are typically limited to people who live in a single country, although some comparative studies stretch across national boundaries.

As the units of analysis, individuals may be considered in the context of their membership in different groups. Examples of groups whose members may be units of analysis at the individual level are police, victims, defendants in criminal court, correctional inmates, gang members, and active burglars. Note that each of these terms implies some population of individual persons. Descriptive studies having individuals as their units of analysis typically aim to describe the population that comprises those individuals.

## Groups

Social groups may also be the units of analysis for criminal justice research. This is not the same as studying the individuals within a group. If we study the members of a juvenile gang to learn about teenagers who join gangs, the individual (teen gang member) is the unit of analysis. But if we study all the juvenile gangs in a city to learn the differences between big gangs and small ones, between gangs selling drugs and gangs stealing cars, and so forth, the unit of analysis is the social group (gang).

Police beats or patrol districts might be the units of analysis in a study. A police beat can be described in terms of the total number of people who live within its boundaries, total street mileage, annual crime reports, and whether the beat includes a special facility such as a park or high school. We can then determine, for example, whether beats that include a park report more assaults than beats without such facilities or whether auto thefts are more common in beats with more street mileage. Here, the individual police beat is the unit of analysis.

## Organizations

Formal political or social organizations may also be the units of analysis in criminal justice research. An example is correctional facilities, which implies, of course, a population of all correctional facilities. Individual facilities might be characterized in terms of their number of employees, status as state or federal prisons, security classification, percentage of inmates who are from racial or ethnic minority groups, types of offenses for which inmates are sentenced to each facility, average length of sentence served, and so forth. We might determine whether federal prisons house a larger or smaller percentage of offenders sentenced for white-collar crimes than do state prisons. Other examples of formal organizations suitable as units of analysis are police departments, courtrooms, probation offices, drug treatment facilities, and victim services agencies.

When social groups or formal organizations are the units of analysis, their characteristics are often derived from the characteristics of their individual members. Thus a correctional facility might be described in terms of the inmates it houses—gender distribution, average sentence length, ethnicity, and so on. In a descriptive study, we might be interested in the percentage of institutions housing only females. Or, in an explanatory study, we might determine whether institutions housing both males and females report, on the average, fewer or more assaults by inmates on staff compared with male-only institutions. In each example, the correctional facility is the unit of analysis. In contrast, if we ask whether male or female inmates are more often involved in assaults on staff, then the individual inmate is the unit of analysis.

Some studies involve descriptions or explanations of more than one unit of analysis. Consider an evaluation of community policing programs in selected neighborhoods of a large city. In such an evaluation, we might be interested in how citizens feel about the program (individuals), whether arrests increased in neighborhoods with the new program compared with those without it (groups), and whether the police department's budget increased more than the budget in a similar city (organiza-

tions). In such cases, it is imperative that researchers anticipate what conclusions they wish to draw with regard to what units of analysis.

## Social Artifacts

Yet another potential unit of analysis may be referred to as *social artifacts*, or the products of social behavior. One class of social artifacts is stories about crime in newspapers or on television. A newspaper story might be characterized by its length, placement on front or interior pages, size of headlines, and presence of photographs. A researcher could analyze whether television news features or newspaper reports provide the most details about a new police program to increase drug arrests.

Social interactions are also examples of social artifacts suitable for criminal justice research. Police crime reports are an example. We might analyze assault reports to find how many involved three or more people, whether assaults involved strangers or people with some prior acquaintance, or whether they more often occurred in public or private locations.

At first, crime reports may not seem to be social artifacts, but consider for a moment what they represent. When a crime is reported to the police, officers usually record what happened from descriptions by victims or witnesses. For instance, an assault victim may describe how he suffered an unprovoked attack when he was innocently enjoying a cold beer after work. However, witnesses to the incident might claim that the "victim" started the fight by insulting the "offender." The responding police officer must interpret who is telling the truth in trying to sort out the circumstances of a violent social interaction. The officer's report becomes a social artifact that represents one among the population of all assaults.

Records of different types of social interactions are common units of analysis in criminal justice research. Criminal history records, meetings of community anticrime groups, presentence investigations, and interactions between police and citizens are examples. Notice that each example requires information about individuals but that social interactions between people are the units of analysis.

## The Ecological Fallacy

We now briefly consider one category of problems commonly encountered with respect to units of analysis. The **ecological fallacy** refers to the danger of making assertions about individuals as the unit of analysis based on the examination of groups or other aggregations.

As an example, suppose we are interested in learning about robbery in different police precincts of a large city. Let's assume that we have information on how many robberies were committed in 2010 in each police precinct of Chicago. Assume also that we have census data describing some of the characteristics of those precincts. Our analysis of such data might show that a large number of robberies in 2010 occurred in the downtown precinct and that the average family income of persons who live in downtown Chicago (the Loop) was substantially higher than in other precincts in the city. We might be tempted to conclude that high-income downtown residents are more likely to be robbed than are people who live in other parts of the city—that robbers select richer victims. In reaching such a conclusion, we run the risk of committing an ecological fallacy, because lower-income people who did not live in the downtown area were also being robbed there in 2010. Victims might be commuters to jobs in the Loop, people visiting downtown theaters or restaurants, passengers on subway or elevated train platforms, or homeless persons who are not counted by the census. Our problem is that we examined police precincts as our unit of analysis, but we wish to draw conclusions about individual people.

The same problem will arise if we discover that incarceration rates are higher in states that have a large proportion of elderly residents. We will not know whether older people are actually imprisoned more often. Or, if we find higher suicide rates in cities with large nonwhite populations, we cannot be sure whether more nonwhites than whites committed suicide.

Don't let these warnings against ecological fallacy lead you to commit what is called an *individualistic fallacy*. Some students approaching criminal justice research for the first time have trouble reconciling general patterns of attitudes and actions with individual exceptions they know of. If you read a newspaper story about a Utah resident visiting New York who is murdered on a subway platform, the fact remains that most visitors to New York and most subway riders are not at risk of murder. Similarly, mass media stories and popular films about drug problems in U.S. cities frequently focus on drug use and dealing among African Americans. But that does not mean that most African Americans are drug users or that drugs are not a problem among whites.

The individualistic fallacy can be especially troublesome for beginning students of criminal justice. Newspapers, local television news, and television police dramas often present unusual or highly dramatized versions of crime problems and criminal justice policy. These messages may distort the way many people initially approach research problems in criminal justice.

## Units of Analysis in Review

The purpose of this section has been to specify what is sometimes a confusing topic, in part because criminal justice researchers use a variety of different units of analysis. Although individual people are often the units of analysis, that is not always the case. Many research questions can more appropriately be answered through the examination of other units of analysis.

The concept of units of analysis may seem more complicated than it needs to be. Understanding the logic of units of analysis is more important than memorizing a list of the units. It is irrelevant what we call a given unit of analysis—a group, a formal organization, or a social artifact. It is essential, however, that we be able to identify our unit of analysis. We must decide whether we are studying assaults or assault victims, police departments or police officers, courtrooms or judges, and prisons or prison inmates. Without keeping this point in mind, we run the risk of making assertions about one unit of analysis based on the examination of another. The box titled "Units of Analysis in

**UNITS OF ANALYSIS IN THE NATIONAL YOUTH GANG SURVEY**

In 1997, the third annual National Youth Gang Survey was completed for the federal Office of Juvenile Justice and Delinquency Prevention (OJJDP). This survey reflects keen interest in developing better information about the scope of youth gangs and their activities in different types of communities around the country. As important and useful as this effort is, the National Youth Gang Survey—especially reports of its results—illustrates how some ambiguities can emerge with respect to units of analysis.

A variety of methods, often creative, are used to gather information from or about active offenders. Partly this is because it is difficult to systematically identify offenders for research. Studying youth gangs presents more than the usual share of problems with units of analysis. Are we interested in gangs (groups), gang members (individuals), or offenses (social artifacts) committed by gangs?

Following methods developed in earlier years, the 1997 National Youth Gang Survey was based on a sample of law enforcement agencies. The sample was designed to represent different types of communities: rural areas, suburban counties, small cities, and large cities. Questionnaires were mailed to the police chief for municipalities and to the sheriff for counties (National Youth Gang Center 1999, 3). Questions asked respondents to report on gangs and gang activity in their jurisdiction—municipality for police departments, and unincorporated service area for sheriffs' departments.

Here are examples of the types of questions included in the survey:

1. How many youth gangs were active in your jurisdiction?
2. How many active youth gang members were in your jurisdiction?
3. In your jurisdiction, what percentage of street sales of drugs were made by youth gang members? (followed by list: powder cocaine, crack cocaine, marijuana, heroin, methamphetamine, other)
4. Does your agency have the following? (list of special youth gang units)

Notice the different units of analysis embedded in these questions. Seven are stated or implied:

1. Gangs: item 1
2. Gang members: items 2, 3
3. Jurisdiction (city or part of county area): items 1, 2, 3
4. Street sales of drugs: item 3
5. Drug types: item 3
6. Agency: item 4
7. Special unit: item 4

Now consider some quotes from a summary report on the 1997 survey (National Youth Gang Center 1999). Which ones do or do not reasonably reflect the actual units of analysis from the survey?

- "Fifty-one percent of survey respondents indicated that they had active youth gangs in their jurisdictions in 1997." (page 7)

- "Thirty-eight percent of jurisdictions in the Northeast, and 26 percent of jurisdictions in the Middle Atlantic regions reported active youth gangs in 1997." (extracted from Table 3, page 10)

- "Results of the 1997 survey revealed that there were an estimated 30,533 youth gangs and 815,986 gang members active in the United States in 1997." (page 13)

- "The percentage of street sales of crack cocaine, heroin, and methamphetamine conducted by youth gang members varied substantially by region…. Crack cocaine sales involving youth gang members were most prevalent in the Midwest (38 percent), heroin sales were most prevalent in the Northeast (15 percent), and methamphetamine sales were most prevalent in the West (21 percent)." (page 27)

- "The majority (66 percent) of respondents indicated that they had some type of specialized unit to address the gang problem." (page 33)

The youth gang survey report includes a number of statements and tables that inaccurately describe units of analysis. You probably detected examples of this in some of the statements shown here. Other statements accurately reflect units of analysis measured in the survey.

If you read the 1997 survey report and keep in mind our discussion of units of analysis, you will find more misleading statements and tables. This will enhance your understanding of units of analysis.

*Source: Information drawn from National Youth Gang Center (1999).*

the National Youth Gang Survey" offers examples of using inappropriate units of analysis. It also illustrates that lack of clarity about units of analysis in criminal justice results in part from difficulties in directly measuring the concepts we want to study.

To test your grasp of the concept of units of analysis, here are some examples of real research topics. See if you can determine the unit of analysis in each. (The answers are given later in the chapter, on page 71.)

1. "Taking into account preexisting traffic fatality trends and several other relevant factors, the implementation of the emergency cellular telephone program resulted in a substantial and permanent reduction in the monthly percentage of alcohol-related fatal crashes." (D'Alessio, Stolzenberg, and Terry 1999, 463–464)

2. "The survey robbery rate was highest in Canada and the Netherlands, and lowest in Scotland.... In 1999 the survey robbery rate was lowest in the United States." (Farrington et al. 2004, xii)

3. "On average, probationers were 31 years old, African American, male, and convicted of drug or property offenses. Most lived with family, and although they were not married, many were in exclusive relationships (44 percent) and had children (47 percent)." (MacKenzie et al. 1999, 433)

4. "Seventy-five percent (n = 158) of the cases were disposed at district courts, and 3 percent (n = 6) remained pending. One percent of the control and 4 percent of the experimental cases were referred to drug treatment court." (Taxman and Elis 1999, 42)

5. "The department's eight Field Operations Command substations (encompassing 20 police districts and 100 patrol beats) comprised the study's cross-sectional units. From January 1986 through July 1989, a period of 43 months, data were collected monthly from each substation for a total of 344 cases." (Kessler 1999, 346)

## THE TIME DIMENSION

*Because time order is a requirement for causal inferences, the time dimension of research requires careful planning.*

We saw earlier in this chapter how the time sequence of events and situations is a critical element in determining causation. In general, observations may be made more or less at one time point or they may be deliberately stretched over a longer period. Observations made at more than one time point can look forward or backward.

### Cross-Sectional Studies

Many criminal justice research projects are designed to study a phenomenon by taking a cross section of it at one time and analyzing that cross section carefully. Exploratory and descriptive studies are often **cross-sectional**. A single U.S. census, for instance, is a study aimed at describing the U.S. population at a given time. A single wave of the National Crime Victimization Survey (NCVS) is a descriptive cross-sectional study that estimates how many people have been victims of crime in a given time.

A cross-sectional exploratory study might be conducted by a police department in the form of a survey that examines what residents believe to be the sources of crime problems in their neighborhood. In all likelihood, the study will ask about crime problems in a single time frame, with the findings used to help the department explore various methods of introducing community policing.

Cross-sectional studies for explanatory or evaluation purposes have an inherent problem. Typically their aim is to understand causal processes that occur over time, but their conclusions are based on observations made at only one time. For example, a survey might ask respondents whether their home has been burglarized and whether they have any special locks on their doors, hoping to explain whether special locks prevent burglary. Because the questions about burglary victimization and door locks are asked at only one time, it is not possible to determine whether burglary victims installed locks after a burglary or whether special locks were already in place but did not prevent the crime. Some of the ways we can deal with the difficult problem of determining time order will be discussed in the section on approximating longitudinal studies.

## Longitudinal Studies

Research projects known as **longitudinal studies** are designed to permit observations over an extended period. An example is a researcher who observes the activities of a neighborhood anticrime organization from the time of its inception until its demise. Analyses of newspaper stories about crime or numbers of prison inmates over time are other examples. In the latter instances, it is irrelevant whether the researcher's observations are made over the course of the actual events under study or at one time—for example, examining a year's worth of newspapers in the library or 10 years of annual reports on correctional populations.

Three types of longitudinal studies are common in criminal justice research: *trend, cohort,* and *panel studies. Trend studies* look at changes within some general population over time. An example is a comparison of Uniform Crime Report figures over time, showing an increase in reported crime from 1960 through 1993 and then a general pattern of decline through 2010. Or a researcher might want to know whether changes in sentences for certain offenses were followed by increases in the number of people imprisoned in state institutions. In this case, a trend study might examine annual figures for prison population over time, comparing totals for the years before and after new sentencing laws took effect.

*Cohort studies* examine more specific populations (cohorts) as they change over time. Typically, a cohort is an age group, such as those people born in 1983, but it can also be based on some other time grouping. Cohorts are often defined as a group of people who enter or leave an institution at the same time, such as persons entering a drug treatment center during July, offenders released from custody in 2009, or high school seniors in March 2010.

In what is probably the best-known cohort study, Marvin Wolfgang and associates (Wolfgang, Figlio, and Sellin 1972) studied all males born in 1945 who lived in the city of Philadelphia from their 10th birthday through age 18 or older. The researchers examined records from police agencies and public schools to determine how many boys in the cohort had been charged with delinquency or arrested, how old they were when first arrested, and what differences there were in school performance between delinquents and nondelinquents.

*Panel studies* are similar to trend and cohort studies except that observations are made on the same set of people on two or more occasions. The NCVS is a good example of a descriptive panel study. A member of each household selected for inclusion in the survey is interviewed seven times at six-month intervals. The NCVS serves many purposes, but it was developed initially to estimate how many people were victims of various types of crimes each year. It is designed as a panel study so that persons can be asked about crimes that occurred in the previous six months, and two waves of panel data are combined to estimate the nationwide frequency of victimization over a one-year period.

## Approximating Longitudinal Studies

It is sometimes possible to draw conclusions about processes that take place over time even when only cross-sectional data are available. It is worth noting some of the ways to do that.

**Logical Inferences** Cross-sectional data sometimes imply processes that occur over time on the basis of simple logic. Consider a study of gun ownership and violence by Swiss researcher Martin Killias (1993). Killias compared rates of gun ownership as reported in an international crime survey to rates of homicide and suicide committed with guns. He was interested in the possible effects of gun availability on violence: do nations with higher rates of gun ownership also have higher rates of gun violence?

Killias reasoned that inferring causation from a cross-sectional comparison of gun ownership and homicides committed with guns would be ambiguous. Gun homicide rates could be high in countries with high gun-ownership rates because the availability of guns was higher. Or people in countries with high gun-ownership rates could have bought guns to protect themselves, in response to rates of homicide. Cross-sectional analysis would not make it possible to sort out the time order of gun ownership and gun homicides.

But does that reasoning hold for gun suicides? Killias argued that the time order in a relationship between gun ownership and gun suicides is less ambiguous. It makes much more sense that suicides involving guns are at least partly a result of gun availability. But it is not reasonable to assume that people might buy guns in response to high gun-suicide rates.

Logical inferences may also be made whenever the time order of variables is clear. If we discover in a cross-sectional study of high school students that males are more likely than females to smoke marijuana, we can conclude that gender affects the propensity to use marijuana, not the other way around. Thus, even though our observations are made at only one time, we are justified in drawing conclusions about processes that take place across time.

**Retrospective Studies**   Research that asks people to recall their pasts, called retrospective research, is a common way of approximating observations over time. In a study of recidivism, for example, we might select a group of prison inmates and analyze their history of delinquency or crime. Or suppose we are interested in whether college students convicted of drunk driving are more likely to have parents with drinking problems than college students with no drunk-driving record. Such a study is retrospective because it focuses on the histories of college students who have or have not been convicted of drunk driving.

The danger in this technique is evident. Sometimes people have faulty memories; sometimes they lie. Retrospective recall is one way of approximating observations across time, but it must be used with caution. Retrospective studies that analyze records of past arrests or convictions suffer from different problems: records may be unavailable, incomplete, or inaccurate.

A more fundamental issue in retrospective research hinges on how subjects are selected and how

subject selection affects the kinds of questions such studies can address.

Imagine that you are a juvenile court judge and you're troubled by what appears to be a large number of child abuse cases in your court. Talking with a juvenile caseworker, you wonder whether the parents of these children were abused or neglected during their own childhood. Together, you formulate a hypothesis about the intergenerational transmission of violence: victims of childhood abuse later abuse their own children. How might you go about investigating that hypothesis?

Given your position as a judge who regularly sees abuse victims, you will probably consider a retrospective approach that examines the backgrounds of families appearing in your court. Let's say you and the caseworker plan to investigate the family backgrounds of 20 abuse victims who appear in your court during the next three months. The caseworker consults with a clinical psychologist from the local university and obtains copies of a questionnaire, or protocol, that has been used by researchers to study the families of child abuse victims. After interviewing the families of 20 victims, the caseworker reports to you that 18 of the 20 child victims have a mother or father who was abused as a child. It seems safe to conclude that your hypothesis about the intergenerational transmission of violence is strongly supported, because 90 percent (18 out of 20) of abuse or neglect victims brought before your court come from families with a history of child abuse.

Think for a moment about how you approached the question of whether child abuse breeds child abuse. You began with abuse victims and retrospectively established that many of their parents had been abused. However, this is different from the question of how many victims of childhood abuse later abuse their own children. That question requires a prospective approach, in which you begin with childhood victims and then determine how many of them later abuse their own children.

To clarify this point, let's shift from the hypothetical study to actual research that illustrates the difference between prospective and retrospective approaches to the same question. Rosemary Hunter and Nancy Kilstrom (1979) conducted a study of 255 infants and their parents. The researchers began by selecting families of premature infants in a newborn intensive care unit. Interviews with the parents of 255 infants revealed that either the mother or the father in 49 of the families had been the victim of abuse or neglect; 206 families revealed no history of abuse. In a prospective follow-up study, Hunter and Kilstrom found that within one year 10 of the 255 infants had been abused. Nine of those 10 infant victims were from the 49 families with a history of abuse, and 1 abused infant was from the 206 families with no background of abuse.

Figure 3.5 illustrates these prospective results graphically. Infants in 18 percent (9 out of 49) of families with a history of abuse showed signs of abuse within one year of birth, whereas less than 1 percent of infants born to parents with no history of abuse were abused within one year. Although that is a sizable difference, notice that the 18 percent figure for continuity of abuse is very similar to the 19 percent rate of abuse discovered in the histories of all 255 families.

Now consider what Hunter and Kilstrom would have found if they had begun with the 10 abused infants at Time 2 and then checked their family backgrounds. Figure 3.6 illustrates this retrospective approach. A large majority of the 10 infant victims (90 percent) had parents with a history of abuse.

You probably realize by now that the prospective and retrospective approaches address fundamentally different questions, even though the questions may appear similar on the surface:

*Prospective*: What percentage of abuse victims later abuse their children? (18 percent; Figure 3.5)

*Retrospective*: What percentage of abuse victims have parents who were abused? (90 percent; Figure 3.6)

In a study of how child abuse and neglect affect drug use, Cathy Spatz Widom and associates (Widom, Weiler, and Cotler 1999) present a similar contrast of prospective and retrospective analysis. Looking backward, 75 percent of subjects with a

drug abuse diagnosis in semiclinical interviews were victims of childhood abuse or neglect. Looking forward, 35 percent of childhood victims and 34 percent of nonvictims had a drug abuse diagnosis.

More generally, Robert Sampson and John Laub (1993, 14) comment on how retrospective and prospective views yield different interpretations about patterns of criminal offending over time:

> Looking *back* over the careers of adult criminals exaggerates the prevalence of stability. Looking *forward* from youth reveals the success and failures, including adolescent delinquents who go on to be normal functioning adults [emphasis in original]. This is the paradox noted [by Lee Robins] earlier: adult criminality seems to be always preceded by childhood misconduct, but most conduct-disordered children do not become antisocial or criminal adults.

Notice how the time dimension is linked to how research questions are framed. A retrospective approach is limited in its ability to reveal how causal processes unfold over time. A retrospective approach is therefore not well suited to answer questions such as how many childhood victims of abuse or neglect later abuse their own children. A retrospective study can be used, however, to compare whether childhood victims are more likely than nonvictims to have a history of abuse in their family background.

## The Time Dimension Summarized

Joel Devine and James Wright (1993, 19) offer a clever metaphor that distinguishes longitudinal studies from cross-sectional ones. Think of a cross-sectional study as a snapshot, a trend study as a slide show, and a panel study as a motion picture. A cross-sectional study, like a snapshot, produces an image at one point in time. This can provide useful information about crime—burglary, for example—at a single time, perhaps in a single place. A trend study is akin to a slide show—a series of snapshots in sequence over time. By viewing a slide show, we can tell how some indicator—change in burglary rates—varies

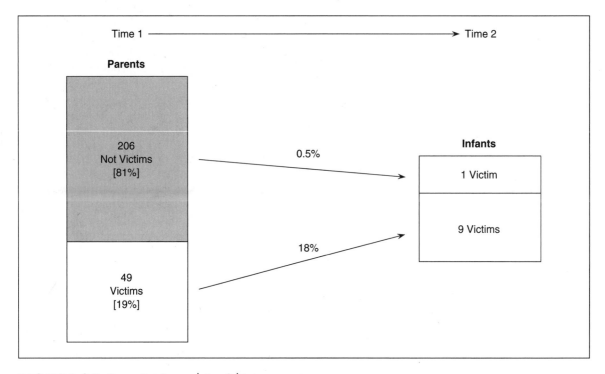

**FIGURE 3.5** Prospective Approach to a Subject
*Source:* Adapted from Hunter and Kilstrom (1979), as suggested by Widom (1989).

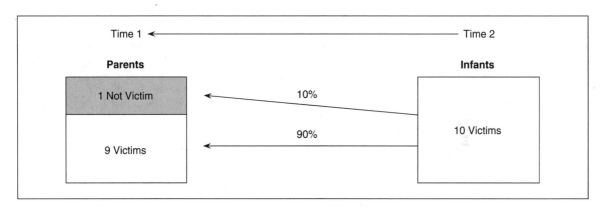

**FIGURE 3.6** Retrospective Approach to a Subject
*Source:* Adapted from Hunter and Kilstrom (1979), as suggested by Widom (1989).

over time. But a trend study is usually based on aggregate information. It can tell us something about aggregations of burglary over time, but not, for instance, whether the same people are committing burglaries at an increasing or decreasing rate or whether there are more or fewer burglars with a relatively constant rate of crime commission. A panel study, like a motion picture, can capture moving images of the same individuals and give us information about individual rates of offending over time.

## ANSWERS TO THE UNITS-OF-ANALYSIS EXERCISE

1. Social artifacts (alcohol-related fatal crashes)
2. Groups (countries)
3. Individuals (probationers)
4. Social artifacts (court cases)
5. Organizations (police substations)

## SUMMARY

- Social science involves three fundamental aspects: theory, data collection, and data analysis.

- Social scientific theory addresses what is, not what should be.

- Theory guides research. In grounded theory, observations contribute to theory development.

- Social scientists are interested in explaining aggregates, not individuals.

- Although social scientists observe people, they are primarily interested in discovering relationships that connect variables.

- Explanations may be idiographic or nomothetic.

- Theories may be inductive or deductive.

- Data may be quantitative or qualitative.

- Explanatory scientific research centers on the notion of cause and effect.

- Most explanatory social research uses a probabilistic model of causation. $X$ may be said to cause $Y$ if it is seen to have some influence on $Y$.

- Three basic requirements determine a causal relationship in scientific research: (1) the independent variable must occur before the dependent variable, (2) the independent and dependent variables must be empirically related to each other, and (3) the observed relationship cannot be explained away as the effect of another variable.

- When scientists consider whether causal statements are true or false, they are concerned with the validity of causal inference.

- A scientific realist approach to examining mechanisms in context bridges idiographic and nomothetic approaches to causation.

- Units of analysis are the people or things whose characteristics researchers observe, describe, and explain. The unit of analysis in criminal justice research is often the individual person, but it may also be a group, organization, or social artifact.

- Researchers sometimes confuse units of analysis, resulting in the ecological fallacy or the individualistic fallacy.

- Cross-sectional studies are those based on observations made at one time. Although such studies are limited by this characteristic, inferences can often be made about processes that occur over time.

- Longitudinal studies are those in which observations are made at many times. Such observations may be made of samples drawn from general populations (trend studies), samples drawn from more specific subpopulations (cohort studies), or the same sample of people each time (panel studies).

- Retrospective studies can sometimes approximate longitudinal studies, but retrospective approaches must be used with care.

## KEY TERMS

aggregates, p. 50

attributes, p. 51

cross-sectional study, p. 66

deductive reasoning, p. 56

dependent variable, p. 54

ecological fallacy, p. 64

hypothesis, p. 49

hypothesis testing, p. 50

idiographic, p. 55

independent variable, p. 54

inductive reasoning, p. 56

longitudinal study, p. 67

nomothetic, p. 55

probabilistic, p. 50

scientific realism, p. 60

theory, p. 47

units of analysis, p. 62

validity, p. 58

validity threats, p. 59

variables, p. 51

## REVIEW QUESTIONS AND EXERCISES

1. Discuss one of the following statements in terms of what you have learned about the criteria of causation and threats to the validity of causal inference. What cause-and-effect relationships are implied? What are some alternative explanations?

    a. Guns don't kill people; people kill people.

    b. Capital punishment prevents murder.

    c. Marijuana is a gateway drug that leads to the use of other drugs.

2. In describing different approaches to the time dimension, criminologist Lawrence Sherman (1995) claimed that cross-sectional studies can show differences and that longitudinal studies can show change. How does this statement relate to the three criteria for inferring causation?

3. William Julius Wilson (1996, 167) cites the following example of why it's important to think carefully about units and time. Imagine a 13-bed hospital, in which 12 beds are occupied by the same 12 people for one year. The other hospital bed is occupied by 52 people, each staying one week. At any given time, 92 percent of beds are occupied by long-term patients (12 out of 13), but over the entire year, 81 percent of patients are short-term patients (52 out of 64). Discuss the implications of a similar example, using jail cells instead of hospital beds.

## ADDITIONAL READINGS

Farrington, David P., Lloyd E. Ohlin, and James Q. Wilson, *Understanding and Controlling Crime: Toward a New Research Strategy* (New York: Springer-Verlag, 1986). Three highly respected criminologists describe the advantages of longitudinal studies and policy experiments for criminal justice research. The book also presents a research agenda for studying the causes of crime and the effectiveness of policy responses.

Gottfredson, Michael R., and Travis Hirschi, "The Methodological Adequacy of Longitudinal Research on Crime," *Criminology* 25 (1987): 581–614. Two *other* highly respected criminologists point to some of the shortcomings of longitudinal studies.

Maxwell, Joseph A., *Qualitative Research Design: An Interactive Approach*, 2nd ed. (Thousand Oaks, CA: Sage, 2005). Despite the word *qualitative* in the title, this book offers excellent advice in progressing from general interests or thoughts to more specific plans for actual research. Each chapter concludes with exercises that incrementally help readers develop research plans.

Pawson, Ray, and Nick Tilley, *Realistic Evaluation* (Thousand Oaks, CA: Sage, 1997). The authors propose an alternative way of thinking about cause, in the context of what they call "scientific realism." Although they criticize traditional social science approaches to inferring cause, Pawson and Tilley supplement the classic insights of Shadish, Cook and Campbell.

Sampson, Robert J., and John H. Laub, *Crime in the Making: Pathways and Turning Points through Life* (Cambridge, MA: Harvard University Press, 1993); Laub, John H., and Robert J. Sampson, *Shared Beginnings, Divergent Lives: Delinquent Boys to Age 70* (Cambridge, MA: Harvard University Press, 2003). The highly acclaimed research described in these two volumes illustrates the longitudinal approach to explanatory research, beginning with juveniles and following their lives through age 70. Sampson and Laub are also attentive to possible validity threats to their findings.

# CHAPTER 4

# Concepts, Operationalization, and Measurement

*It's essential to specify exactly what we mean (and don't mean) by the terms we use. This is the first step in the measurement process, and we'll cover it in depth.*

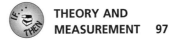

## INTRODUCTION

*Because measurement is difficult and imprecise, researchers try to describe the measurement process explicitly.*

This chapter describes the progression from having a vague idea about what we want to study to being able to recognize it and measure it in the real world. We begin with the general issue of conceptualization, which sets up a foundation for our examination of operationalization and measurement. We then turn to different approaches to assessing measurement quality. The chapter concludes with an overview of strategies for combining individual measures into more complex indicators.

As you read this chapter, keep in mind a central theme: communication. Ultimately, criminal justice and social scientific research seek to communicate findings to an audience, such as professors, classmates, journal readers, or coworkers in a probation services agency. Moving from vague ideas and interests to a completed research report, as we described in Chapter 3, involves communication at every step—from general ideas to more precise definitions of critical terms. With more precise definitions, we can begin to develop measures to apply in the real world.

## CONCEPTIONS AND CONCEPTS

*Clarifying abstract mental images is an essential first step in measurement.*

If you hear the word *recidivism*, what image comes to mind? You might think of someone who has served time for burglary and who breaks into a house soon after being released from prison. Or, in contrast to that rather specific image, you might have a more general image of a habitual criminal. Someone who works in a criminal justice agency might have a different mental image. Police officers might think of a specific individual they have arrested repeatedly for a variety of offenses, and a judge might think of a defendant who has three prior convictions for theft.

Ultimately, *recidivism* is simply a term we use in communication—a word representing a collection of related phenomena that we have either observed or heard about somewhere. It's as though we have file drawers in our minds containing thousands of sheets of paper, and each sheet has a label in the upper right-hand corner. One sheet of paper in your file drawer has the term *recidivism* on it, and the person who sits next to you in class has one, too.

The technical name for those mental images, those sheets of paper in our file drawers, is **conception**. Each sheet of paper is a conception—a subjective thought about things that we encounter in daily life. But those mental images cannot be communicated directly. There is no way we can directly reveal what is written on our mental images. Therefore we use the terms written in the upper right-hand corners as a way of communicating about our conceptions and the things we observe that are related to those conceptions.

For example, the word *crime* represents our conception about certain kinds of behavior. But individuals have different conceptions; they may think of different kinds of behavior when they hear the word *crime*. Police officers in most states would include possession of marijuana among their conceptions of crime, whereas members of the advocacy group National Organization for the Reform of Marijuana Laws (NORML) would not. Recent burglary victims might recall their own experiences in their conceptions of crime, whereas more fortunate neighbors might think about the murder story in yesterday's newspaper.

Because conceptions are subjective and cannot be communicated directly, we use the words and symbols of language as a way of communicating about our conceptions and the things we observe that are related to those conceptions.

**Concepts** are the words or symbols in language that we use to represent these mental images. We use concepts to communicate with one another, to share our mental images. Although a common language enables us to communicate, it is important to recognize that the words and phrases we use represent abstractions. Concepts are abstract because they are independent of the labels we assign to them. Crime as a concept is abstract, meaning that in the English language this label represents mental images of illegal acts. Of course, actual crimes are real events, and our mental images of crime may be based on real events (or the stuff of TV drama). However, when we talk about crime, without being more specific, we are talking about an abstraction. Thus, for example, the concept of crime proposed by Michael Gottfredson and Travis Hirschi (1990, 15)—using force or fraud in pursuit of self-interest—is abstract. Crime is the symbol, or label, they have assigned to this concept.

Let's discuss a specific example. What is your conception of *serious crime*? What mental images come to mind? Most people agree that airplane hijacking, rape, bank robbery, and murder are serious crimes. What about a fist fight that results in a concussion and facial injuries? Many of us would classify it as a serious crime but not if the incident took place in a boxing ring. Is burglary a serious crime? It doesn't rank up there with drive-by shooting, but we would probably agree that it is more serious than shoplifting. What about drug use or drug dealing?

Our mental images of serious crime may vary depending on our backgrounds and experiences. If your home has ever been burglarized, you might be more inclined than someone who has not suffered that experience to rate it as a serious crime. If you have been both burglarized and robbed at gunpoint, you would probably think the burglary was less serious than the robbery.

Disagreement over the seriousness of drug use continues. Younger people, whether or not they have used drugs, may be less inclined to view drug use as a serious crime, whereas police and other public officials might rank drug use as very serious. California, Michigan, New Jersey, and Oregon are among states that have legalized the use of marijuana for medical purposes. However, during the administration of George Bush, the U.S. Department of Justice viewed all marijuana use as a crime, challenging state laws and raiding San Francisco medical marijuana dispensaries (Murphy 2005).

*Serious crime* is an abstraction, a label we use to represent a concept. However, we must be careful to distinguish the label we use for a concept from the reality that the concept represents. There are real robberies, and robbery is a serious crime, but the concept of crime seriousness is not real.

The concept of serious crime, then, is a construct created from your conception of it, our conception of it, and the conceptions of all those who have ever used the term. The concept of serious crime cannot be observed directly or indirectly. We can, however, meaningfully discuss the concept, observe examples of serious crime, and measure it indirectly.

## Conceptualization

Day-to-day communication is made possible through general but often vague and unspoken agreements about the use of terms. Often other people do not understand exactly what we wish to communicate, but they get the general drift of our meaning. Although we may not fully agree about the meaning of the term *serious crime*, it's safe to assume that the crime of bank robbery is more serious than the crime of bicycle theft. A wide range of misunderstandings is the price we pay for our imprecision, but somehow we muddle through. Science, however, aims at more than muddling, and it cannot operate in a context of such imprecision.

**Conceptualization** is the process by which we specify precisely what we mean when we use particular terms. Suppose we want to find out whether violent crime is more serious than nonviolent crime. Most of us would probably assume that is true, but it might be interesting to find out whether it's really so. Notice that we can't meaningfully study the issue, let alone agree on the answer, without some precise working agreements about the meanings of the terms we are using. They are working agreements in the sense that they allow us to work on the question.

We begin by clearly differentiating violent and nonviolent crime. In violent crimes, an offender uses force or threats of force against a victim. Nonviolent crimes either do not involve any direct contact between a victim and an offender or involve contact but no force. For example, pickpockets have direct contact with their victims but use no force. In contrast, robbery involves at least the threat to use force on victims. Burglary, auto theft, shoplifting, and the theft of unattended personal property such as bicycles are examples of nonviolent crimes. Assault, rape, robbery, and murder are violent crimes.

## Indicators and Dimensions

The end product of the conceptualization process is the specification of a set of indicators of what we have in mind, indicating the presence or absence of the concept we are studying. To illustrate this process, let's discuss the more general concept of *crime seriousness*. This concept is more general than *serious crime* because it implies that some crimes are more serious than others.

One good indicator of crime seriousness is harm to the crime victim. Physical injury is an example of harm, and physical injury is certainly more likely to result from violent crime than from nonviolent crime. What about other kinds of harm? Burglary victims suffer economic harm from property loss and perhaps damage to their homes. Is the loss of $800 in a burglary an indicator of more serious crime than a $10 loss in a robbery in which the victim was not injured? Victims of both violent crime and nonviolent crime may suffer psychological harm. Or people might feel a sense of personal violation after discovering that their home has been burglarized. Other types of victim harm can be combined into groups and subgroups as well.

The technical term for such groupings is **dimension**—some specifiable aspect of a concept. Thus we might speak of the "victim harm dimension" of crime seriousness. This dimension could include indicators of physical injury, economic loss, or psychological consequences. And we can easily think of other indicators and dimensions related to the general concept of crime seriousness. If we consider the theft of $20 from an unemployed person to be more serious than the theft of $20,000 from a wealthy oil company chief executive officer, victim wealth might be another dimension. Also

consider a victim identity dimension. Killing a burglar in self-defense would not be as serious as threatening to kill the president of the United States.

It is possible to subdivide the concept of crime seriousness into several dimensions. Specifying dimensions and identifying the various indicators for each of those dimensions are both parts of conceptualization.

Specifying the different dimensions of a concept often paves the way for a better understanding of what we are studying. We might observe that fist fights among high school students result in thousands of injuries per year but that the annual costs of auto theft cause direct economic harm to hundreds of insurance companies and millions of auto insurance policyholders. Recognizing the many dimensions of crime seriousness, we cannot say that violent crime is more serious than nonviolent crime in all cases.

## Creating Conceptual Order

The design and execution of criminal justice research requires that we clear away the confusion over concepts and reality. To this end, logicians and scientists have found it useful to distinguish three kinds of definitions: real, conceptual, and operational. With respect to the first of these, Carl G. Hempel (1952, 6) cautioned:

> A "real" definition, according to traditional logic, is not a stipulation determining the meaning of some expression but a statement of the "essential nature" or the "essential attributes" of some entity. The notion of essential nature, however, is so vague as to render this characterization useless for the purposes of rigorous inquiry.

A *real* or *essential nature* definition is inherently subjective. The specification of concepts in scientific inquiry depends instead on conceptual and operational definitions. A **conceptual definition** is a working definition specifically assigned to a term. In the midst of disagreement and confusion over what a term really means, the scientist specifies a working definition for the purposes of the inquiry. Wishing to examine socioeconomic status (SES), we may simply specify that we are going to treat it as a combination of income and educational attainment. With that definitional decision, we rule out many other possible aspects of SES: occupational status, money in the bank, property, lifestyle, and so forth.

The specification of conceptual definitions does two important things. First, it serves as a specific working definition we present so that readers will understand exactly what we mean by a concept. Second, it focuses our observational strategy. Notice that a conceptual definition does not directly produce observations; rather, it channels our efforts to develop actual measures.

As a next step, we must specify exactly what we will observe, how we will do it, and what interpretations we will place on various possible observations. These further specifications make up the **operational definition** of the concept—a definition that spells out precisely how the concept will be measured. Strictly speaking, an operational definition is a description of the operations undertaken in measuring a concept.

Pursuing the definition of SES, we might decide to ask the people we are studying three questions:

1. What was your total household income during the past 12 months?

2. How many persons are in your household?

3. What is the highest level of school you have completed?

Next, we need to specify a system for categorizing the answers people give us. For income, we might use the categories "under $25,000" and "$25,000–$35,000." Educational attainment might be similarly grouped into categories, and we might simply count the number of people in each household. Finally, we need to specify a way to combine each person's responses to these three questions to create a measure of SES.

The end result is a working and workable definition of SES. Others might disagree with our conceptualization and operationalization, but the

definition has one essential scientific virtue: it is absolutely specific and unambiguous. Even if someone disagrees with our definition, that person will have a good idea of how to interpret our research results because what we mean by SES—reflected in our analyses and conclusions—is clear.

Here is a diagram showing the progression of measurement steps from our vague sense of what a term means to specific measurements in a scientific study:

Conceptualization

↓

Conceptual definition

↓

Operational definition

↓

Measurements in the real world

To test your understanding of these measurement steps, return to the beginning of the chapter, where we asked you what image comes to mind in connection with the word *recidivism*. Recall your own mental image, and compare it with Tony Fabelo's discussion in the box titled "What Is Recidivism?"

## OPERATIONALIZATION CHOICES

*Describing how to obtain empirical measures begins with operationalization.*

Recall from Chapter 1 that the research process is not usually a set of steps that proceed in order from first to last. This is especially true of operationalization, the process of developing operational definitions. Although we begin by conceptualizing what we wish to study, once we start to consider operationalization, we may revise our conceptual definition. Developing an operational definition also moves us closer to measurement, which requires that we think about selecting a data collection method as well. In other words, operationalization does not proceed according to a systematic checklist.

To illustrate this fluid process, let's return to the issue of crime seriousness. Suppose we want to conduct

## WHAT IS RECIDIVISM?

Tony Fabelo

The Senate Criminal Justice Committee will be studying the record of the corrections system and the use of recidivism rates as a measure of performance for the system. The first task for the committee should be to clearly define recidivism, understand how it is measured, and determine the implications of adopting recidivism rates as measures of performance.

**Defining Recidivism**

Recidivism is the recurrence of criminal behavior. The rate of recidivism refers to the proportion of a specific group of offenders (for example, those released on parole) who engage in criminal behavior within a given period of time. Indicators of criminal behavior are rearrests, reconvictions, or reincarcerations.

Each of these indicators depends on contact with criminal justice officials and will therefore underestimate the recurrence of criminal behavior. However, criminal behavior that is unreported and not otherwise known to officials in justice agencies is difficult to measure in a consistent and economically feasible fashion.

In 1991, the Criminal Justice Policy Council recommended to the Texas legislature and state criminal justice agencies that recidivism be measured in the following way:

> Recidivism rates should be calculated by counting the number of prison releases or number of offenders placed under community supervision who are reincarcerated for a technical violation or new offense within a uniform period of at-risk street time.
>
> The at-risk street time can be one, two, or three years, but it must be uniform for the group being tracked so that results are not distorted by uneven at-risk periods.
>
> Reincarceration should be measured using data from the "rap sheets" collected by the Texas Department of Public Safety in their Computerized Criminal History system. A centralized source of information reduces reporting errors.

**Systemwide Recidivism Rates**

Recidivism rates can be reported for all offenders in the system—for all offenders released from prison or for all offenders placed on probation. This I call systemwide recidivism rates. Approxi-

mately 48 percent of offenders released from prison on parole or mandatory supervision, or released from county jails on parole, in 1991 were reincarcerated by 1994 for a new offense or a parole violation.

For offenders released from prison in 1991 the reincarceration recidivism rates three years after release from prison by offense of conviction are listed below:

| | | | |
|---|---|---|---|
| Burglary | 56% | Assault | 44% |
| Robbery | 54% | Homicide | 40% |
| Theft | 52% | Sexual assault | 39% |
| Drugs | 43% | Sex offense | 34% |

For the same group, the reincarceration recidivism rate three years after release by age group is listed below:

| | |
|---|---|
| 17–25 | 56% |
| 26–30 | 52% |
| 31–35 | 48% |
| 36–40 | 46% |
| 41 or older | 35% |

**The Meaning of Systemwide Recidivism Rates**

The systemwide recidivism rate of prison releases should not be used to measure the performance of institutional programs. There are many socioeconomic factors that can affect systemwide recidivism rates.

For example, the systemwide recidivism rate of offenders released from prison in 1995 declined because of changes in the characteristics of the population released from prison. Offenders are receiving and serving longer sentences, which will raise the average age at release. Therefore performance in terms of systemwide recidivism will improve but not necessarily because of improvements in the delivery of services within the prison system.

On the other hand, the systemwide recidivism rate of felons released from state jail facilities should be expected to be relatively high, because state jail felons are property and drug offenders who tend to have high recidivism rates.

*Source: Adapted from Fabelo (1995).*

a descriptive study that shows which crimes are more serious and which crimes are less serious.

One obvious dimension of crime seriousness is the penalties that are assigned to different crimes by

law. Let's begin with this conceptualization. Our conceptual definition of crime seriousness is therefore the level of punishment that a state criminal code authorizes for different crimes. Notice that this definition has the distinct advantage of being unambiguous, which leads us to an operational definition something like this:

> Consult the Texas Criminal Code. (1) Those crimes that may be punished by death will be judged most serious. (2) Next will be crimes that may be punished by a prison sentence of more than one year. (3) The least serious crimes are those with jail sentences of less than a year, fines, or both.

The operations undertaken to measure crime seriousness are specific. Our data collection strategy is also clear: go to the library, make a list of crimes described in the Texas Code, and classify each crime into one of the three groups.

Note that we have produced rather narrow conceptual and operational definitions of crime seriousness. We might presume that penalties in the Texas Code take into account additional dimensions such as victim harm, offender motivation, and other circumstances of individual crimes. However, the three groups of crimes include very different types of incidents and so do not tell us much about crime seriousness.

An alternative conceptualization of crime seriousness might center on what people think of as serious crime. In this view, crime seriousness is based on people's beliefs, which may reflect their perceptions of harm to victims, offender motivation, or other dimensions. Conceptualizing crime seriousness in this way suggests a different approach to operationalization: you will present descriptions of various crimes to other students in your class and ask them to indicate how serious they believe the crimes are. If crime seriousness is operationalized in this way, a questionnaire is the most appropriate data collection method.

Think of some examples of the process. Your instructor assigns number or letter grades to exams and papers to represent your mastery of course material. You count the number of pages in this week's history assignment to represent how much time you will have to spend studying. The American Bar Association rates nominees to the U.S. Supreme Court as qualified, highly qualified, or not qualified. You might rank last night's date on the proverbial scale of 1 to 10, reflecting whatever conceptual properties are important to you.

## Measurement as Scoring

Another way to think of measurement is in terms of scoring. Your instructor scores exams by counting the right answers and assigning some point value to each answer. Referees keep score at basketball games by counting the number of one-point free throws and two- and three-point field goals for each team. Judges or juries score persons charged with crime by pronouncing "guilty" or "not guilty." City murder rates are scored by counting the number of murder victims and dividing by the number of city residents.

Many people consider measurement to be the most important and difficult phase of criminal justice research. It is difficult, in part, because so many basic concepts in criminal justice are not easy to define as specifically as we would like. Without being able to settle on a conceptual definition, we find operationalizing and measuring things challenging. This is illustrated by the box titled "Jail Stay."

In addition to being challenging, different operationalization choices can produce different results. In the box titled "What Is Recidivism?" Tony Fabelo argues that the at-risk period for comparing recidivism for different groups of offenders should be uniform. It's possible to examine one-, two-, or three-year rates, but comparisons should use standard at-risk periods. Varying the at-risk period produces, as we might expect, differences in recidivism rates. Evaluating a Texas program that provided drug abuse treatment, Michael Eisenberg (1999, 8) reports rates for different at-risk periods:

|  | 1-Year | 2-Year | 3-Year |
|---|---|---|---|
| All participants | 14% | 37% | 42% |

Note that the difference between one- and two-year rates is much larger than that between two- and three-year rates. Operationalizing "recidivism" as a one-year failure rate would be much less accurate than operationalizing the concept as a two-year rate, because recidivism rates seem to stabilize at the two-year point.

**JAIL STAY**

Recall from Chapter 1 that two of the general purposes of research are description and explanation. The distinction between them has important implications for the process of definition and measurement. If you have formed the opinion that description is a simpler task than explanation, you may be surprised to learn that definitions can be more problematic for descriptive research than for explanatory research. To illustrate this, we present an example based on an attempt by one of the authors to describe what he thought was a simple concept.

In the course of an evaluation project, Maxfield wished to learn the average number of days people stayed in the Marion County (Indiana) jail. This concept was labeled *jail stay*. People can be in the county jail for three reasons: (1) They are serving a sentence of one year or less. (2) They are awaiting trial. (3) They are being held temporarily while awaiting transfer to another county or state, or to prison. The third category includes people who have been sentenced to prison and are waiting for space to open up, or those who have been arrested and are wanted for some reason in another jurisdiction.

Maxfield vaguely knew these things but did not recognize how they complicated the task of defining and ultimately measuring jail stay. So the original question—"What is the average jail stay?"—was revised to "What is the average jail stay for persons serving sentences and for persons awaiting trial?"

Just as people can be in jail for different reasons, an individual can be in jail for more than one reason. Let's consider a hypothetical jail resident we'll call Allan. He was convicted of burglary in July 2002 and sentenced to a year in jail. All but 30 days of his sentence were suspended, meaning that he was freed but could be required to serve the remaining 11 months if he got into trouble again. It did not take long. Two months after being released, Allan was arrested for robbery and returned to jail.

Now it gets complicated. A judge imposes the remaining 11 months of Allan's suspended sentence. Allan is denied bail and must wait for his trial in jail. It is soon learned that Allan is wanted by police in Illinois for passing bad checks. Many people would be delighted to send Allan to Illinois; they tell officials in that state they can have him, pending resolution of the situation in Marion County.

Allan is now in jail for three reasons: (1) serving his sentence for the original burglary, (2) awaiting trial on a robbery charge, and (3) waiting for transfer to Illinois.

Is this one jail stay or three? In a sense, it is one jail stay because one person, Allan, is occupying a jail cell. But let's say Allan's trial on the robbery charge is delayed until after he completes his sentence for the burglary. He stays in jail and begins a new jail stay. When he comes up for trial, the prosecutor asks to waive the robbery charges against Allan in hopes of exporting him to the neighboring state, and a new jail stay begins as Allan awaits his free trip to Illinois.

You may recognize this as a problem with units of analysis. Is the unit the person who stays in jail? Or are the separate reasons Allan is in jail—which are social artifacts—the units of analysis? After some thought, Maxfield decided that the social artifact was the more appropriate unit because he was interested in whether jail cells are more often occupied by people serving sentences or people awaiting trial. But that produced a new question of how to deal with people like Allan. Do we double-count the overlap in Allan's jail stays, so that he accounts for two jail stays while serving his suspended sentence for burglary and waiting for the robbery trial? This seemed to make sense, but then Allan's two jail stays would count the same as two other people with one jail stay each. In other words, Allan would appear to occupy two jail beds at the same time. This was neither true nor helpful in describing how long people stay in jail for different reasons.

## Exhaustive and Exclusive Measurement

Briefly revisiting terms introduced in Chapter 3, an attribute is a characteristic or quality of something. *Female* is an example, as are *old* and *student*. Variables, in contrast, are logical sets of attributes. Thus, *gender* is a variable traditionally composed of the attributes *female* and *male*. The conceptualization and operationalization processes can be seen as the specification of variables and the attributes composing them. Thus, *employment status* is a variable that has the attributes *employed* and *unemployed*, or the list of attributes could be expanded to include other possibilities such as *employed part time*, *employed full time*, and *retired*.

Every variable should have two important qualities. First, the attributes composing it should be *exhaustive*. If the variable is to have any utility in research, researchers must be able to classify every observation in terms of one of the attributes composing the variable. We will run into trouble if we conceptualize the variable *sentence* in terms of the attributes *prison* and *fine*. After all, some convicted persons are assigned to probation, some have a portion of their prison sentence suspended, and others may receive a mix of prison term, probation, suspended sentence, or perhaps community service. Notice that we could make the list of attributes exhaustive by adding *other* and *combination*. Whatever approach we take, we must be able to classify every observation.

At the same time, attributes composing a variable must be *mutually exclusive*. Researchers must be able to classify every observation in terms of one and only one attribute. Thus, for example, we need to define *prison* and *fine* in such a way that nobody can possess both attributes at the same time. That means we must be able to handle the variables for a person whose sentence includes both a prison term and a fine. In this case, attributes could be defined more precisely by specifying *prison only*, *fine only*, and *both prison and fine*.

## Levels of Measurement

Attributes composing any variable must be mutually exclusive and exhaustive. Attributes may be related in other ways as well. Of particular interest is that variables may represent different levels of measurement: nominal, ordinal, interval, and ratio. Levels of measurement tell us what sorts of information we can gain from the scores assigned to the values of a variable.

**Nominal Measures**   Variables whose attributes have only the characteristics of exhaustiveness and mutual exclusiveness are **nominal measures**. Examples are gender, city of residence, college major, Social Security number, and marital status. The attributes composing each of these variables—male and female for the variable gender—are distinct from one another and pretty much cover the traditional possibilities among people. Nominal measures merely offer names or labels for characteristics.

Imagine a group of people being characterized in terms of a nominal variable and physically grouped by the appropriate attributes. Suppose we are at a convention attended by hundreds of state court judges. At a social function, we ask them to stand together in groups according to the states in which they live: all those from Vermont in one group, those from California in another, and so forth. The variable is *state of residence*; the attributes are *live in Vermont*, *live in California*, and so on. All the people standing in a given group have at least one thing in common; the people in any one group differ from the people in all other groups in that same regard. Where the individual groups are formed, how close they are to one another, and how they are arranged in the room is irrelevant. All that matters is that all the members of a given group share the same state of residence and that each group has a different shared state of residence.

**Ordinal Measures**   Variables whose attributes may be logically rank ordered are **ordinal measures**. The different attributes represent relatively more or less of the variable. Examples of variables that can be ordered in some way are opinion of police, occupational status, crime seriousness, and fear of crime.

Let's pursue the earlier example of grouping state court judges at a social gathering and imagine that we ask all those who have sat on appellate courts to stand in one group, all those serving felony trial courts to stand in another group, and all those who sit on misdemeanor trial courts to stand in a third group. This manner of grouping people satisfies the requirements for exhaustiveness and mutual exclusiveness. In addition, however, we might logically arrange the three groups in terms of the level of court where they serve (the shared attribute). We might arrange the three groups in a row, ranging from highest court to lowest court. This arrangement provides a physical representation of an ordinal measure. If we know which groups two individuals are in, we can determine what level of court they sit on.

Note that in this example it is irrelevant how close or far apart the court groups are from one another. They might stand 5 feet apart or 500 feet apart; the appellate and felony trial court groups could be 5 feet apart, and the misdemeanor trial court group might be 500 feet farther down the line. These physical distances have no meaning. The felony group, however, should be between the misdemeanor group and the appellate group, or else the rank order is incorrect.

**Interval Measures**  When the actual distance that separates the attributes composing some variables does have meaning, the variables are **interval measures**. The logical distance between attributes can then be expressed in meaningful standard intervals.

Interval measures commonly used in social scientific research are constructed measures such as standardized intelligence tests. The interval that separates IQ scores of 100 and 110 is the same as the interval that separates scores of 110 and 120 by virtue of the distribution of the observed scores of the many thousands of people who have taken the test over the years. Criminal justice researchers often combine individual nominal and ordinal measures to produce a composite interval measure.

**Ratio Measures**  Most of the social scientific variables that meet the minimum requirements for interval measures also meet the requirements for **ratio measures**. In ratio measures, the attributes that compose a variable, besides having all the structural characteristics mentioned previously, are based on a true zero point. Examples from criminal justice research are age, dollar value of property loss from burglary, number of prior arrests, blood alcohol content, and length of incarceration.

Returning to the example of various ways to classify judges, we might ask them to group themselves according to years of experience in their present position. All those new to their job would stand together, as would those with one year of experience, those with two years on the job, and so forth. The facts that members of each group share the same years of experience and that each group has a different shared length of time satisfy the minimum requirements for a nominal measure. Arranging the several groups in a line from those with the least to those with the most experience meets the additional requirements for an ordinal measure and permits us to determine whether one person is

more experienced, is less experienced, or has the same level of experience as another. If we arrange the groups so that there is the same distance between each pair of adjacent groups, we satisfy the additional requirements of an interval measure and can say how much more experience one chief has than another. Finally, because one of the attributes included—experience—has a true zero point (judges just appointed or elected to their job), the phalanx of hapless convention goers also meets the requirements for a ratio measure, permitting us to say that one person is twice as experienced as another.

## Implications of Levels of Measurement

To review this discussion and to illustrate why level of measurement may make a difference, consider Table 4.1. It presents information on crime seriousness adapted from a survey of crime severity conducted for the Bureau of Justice Statistics (Wolfgang et al. 1985). The survey presented brief descriptions of more than 200 different crimes to a sample of 60,000 people. Respondents were asked to assign a score to each crime based on how serious they thought the crime was compared with bicycle theft (scored at 10).

The first column in Table 4.1 lists some of the crimes described. The second column shows a nominal measure that identifies the victim in the crime: home, person, business, or society. Type of victim is an attribute of each crime. The third column lists seriousness scores computed from survey results, ranging from 0.6 for trespassing to 35.7 for murder. These seriousness scores are interval measures because the distance between, for example, auto theft (at 8.0) and accepting a bribe (at 9.0) is the same as that between accepting a bribe (at 9.0) and obstructing justice (at 10.0). Seriousness scores are not ratio measures; there is no absolute zero point, and three instances of obstructing justice (at 10.0) do not equal one rape with injury (at 30.0).

The fourth column shows the ranking for each of the 17 crimes in the table; the most serious crime, murder, is ranked 1, followed by rape with

**TABLE 4.1** Crime Seriousness and Levels of Measurement

| Crime | Victim | Seriousness Score | Rank | Value of Property Loss |
|-------|--------|-------------------|------|------------------------|
| Accepting a bribe | Society | 9.0 | 9 | 0 |
| Arson | Business | 12.7 | 6 | $10,000 |
| Auto theft | Home | 8.0 | 10 | $12,000 |
| Burglary | Business | 15.5 | 5 | $100,000 |
| Burglary | Home | 9.6 | 8 | $1,000 |
| Buying stolen property | Society | 5.0 | 12 | 0 |
| Heroin sales | Society | 20.6 | 4 | 0 |
| Heroin use | Society | 6.5 | 11 | 0 |
| Murder | Person | 35.7 | 1 | 0 |
| Obstructing justice | Society | 10.0 | 7 | 0 |
| Public intoxication | Society | 0.8 | 15 | 0 |
| Rape and injury | Person | 30.0 | 2 | 0 |
| Robbery and injury | Person | 21.0 | 3 | $1,000 |
| Robbery attempt | Person | 3.3 | 13 | 0 |
| Robbery, no injury | Person | 8.0 | 10 | $1,000 |
| Shoplifting | Business | 2.2 | 14 | $10 |
| Trespassing | Home | 0.6 | 16 | 0 |

*Source:* Adapted from Wolfgang, Figlio, Tracy, and Singer (1985).

injury, and so on. The rankings express only the order of seriousness, however, because the difference between murder (ranked 1) and rape (ranked 2) is smaller than the distance between rape and robbery with injury (ranked 3).

Finally, the crime descriptions presented to respondents indicated the value of property loss for each offense. This is a ratio measure with a true zero point, so that 10 burglaries with a loss of $1,000 each have the same property value as one arson offense with a loss of $10,000.

Specific analytic techniques require variables that meet certain minimum levels of measurement. For example, we could compute the average property loss from the crimes listed in Table 4.1 by adding up the individual numbers in the fifth column and dividing by the number of crimes listed (17). However, we would not be able to compute the average victim type because that is a nominal variable. In that case, we could report the modal—the

most common—victim type, which is society in Table 4.1.

Researchers may treat some variables as representing different levels of measurement. Ratio measures are the highest level, followed by interval, ordinal, and nominal. A variable that represents a given level of measurement—say, ratio—may also be treated as representing a lower level of measurement—say, ordinal. For example, age is a ratio measure. If we wish to examine only the relationship between age and some ordinal-level variable, such as delinquency involvement (high, medium, or low), we might choose to treat age as an ordinal-level variable as well. We might characterize the subjects of our study as being young, middle age, or old, specifying the age range for each of those groupings. Finally, age might be used as a nominal-level variable for certain research purposes. Thus, people might be grouped as baby boomers if they were born between 1945 and 1955.

The analytic uses planned for a given variable, then, should determine the level of measurement to be sought, with the realization that some variables are inherently limited to a certain level. If a variable is to be used in a variety of ways that require different levels of measurement, the study should be designed to achieve the highest level possible. Although ratio measures such as number of arrests can later be reduced to ordinal or nominal ones, it is not possible to convert a nominal or ordinal measure to a ratio one. More generally, you cannot convert a lower-level measure to a higher-level one. That is a one-way street worth remembering.

## CRITERIA FOR MEASUREMENT QUALITY

*The key standards for measurement quality are reliability and validity.*

Measurements can be made with varying degrees of precision, which refers to the fineness of the distinctions made between the attributes that compose a variable. Saying that a woman is 43 years old is more precise than saying that she is in her forties. Describing a felony sentence as 18 months is more precise than describing it as more than one year.

As a general rule, precise measurements are superior to imprecise ones, as common sense would suggest. Precision is not always necessary or desirable, however. If knowing that a felony sentence is more than one year is sufficient for your research purpose, then any additional effort invested in learning the precise sentence would be wasted. The operationalization of concepts, then, must be guided partly by an understanding of the degree of precision required. If your needs are not clear, be more precise rather than less.

But don't confuse precision with accuracy. Describing someone as "born in Stowe, Vermont" is more precise than "born in New England," but suppose the person in question was actually born in Boston? The less precise description, in this instance, is more accurate; it's a better reflection of the real world. This is a point worth keeping in mind. Many criminal justice measures are impre-

cise, so reporting approximate values is often more accurate.

Precision and accuracy are obviously important qualities in research measurement, and they probably need no further explanation. When criminal justice researchers construct and evaluate measurements, they pay special attention to two technical considerations: reliability and validity.

### Reliability

Fundamentally, **reliability** is a matter of whether a particular measurement technique, applied repeatedly to the same thing, will yield the same result each time. In other words, measurement reliability is roughly the same as measurement consistency or stability. Imagine a police officer standing on the street, guessing the speed of cars that pass by and issuing speeding tickets based on that judgment. If you received a ticket from this officer and went to court to contest it, you would almost certainly win your case. The judge would no doubt reject this way of measuring speed, regardless of the police officer's experience. The reliability or consistency of this method of measuring vehicle speed is questionable at best. If the same police officer used a laser speed detector, however, it is doubtful that you would be able to beat the ticket. The laser device is judged a much more reliable way of measuring speed.

Reliability, though, does not ensure accuracy any more than precision does. The speedometer in your car may be a reliable instrument for measuring speed, but it is common for speedometers to be off by a few miles per hour, especially at higher speeds. If your speedometer shows 55 miles per hour when you are actually traveling at 60, it gives you a consistent but inaccurate reading that might attract the attention of police officers with more accurate laser guns.

Measurement reliability is often a problem with indicators used in criminal justice research. For example, forensic DNA evidence is increasingly being used in violent crime cases. National Research Council studies (1996; 2009) found a variety of errors in laboratory procedures, including sample mishandling, evidence contamination, and analyst bias. These are measurement reliability problems that can lead to unwarranted exclusion of evidence or to the conviction of innocent people (Roth 2010).

Reliability problems crop up in many forms. Reliability is a concern every time a single observer is the source of data because we have no way to guard against that observer's subjectivity. We can't tell for sure how much of what's reported represents true variation and how much is due to the observer's unique perceptions.

Reliability can also be an issue when more than one observer makes measurements. Survey researchers have long known that different interviewers get different answers from respondents as a result of their own attitudes and demeanor. Or we may want to classify a few hundred community anticrime groups into a set of categories created by the National Institute of Justice. A police officer and a neighborhood activist are unlikely to classify all those groups into the same categories; such inconsistency would be an example of reliability problems.

How do we create reliable measures? Because the problem of reliability is a basic one in criminal justice measurement, researchers have developed a number of techniques for dealing with it.

**The Test–Retest Method**   Sometimes it is appropriate to make the same measurement more than once. If there is no reason to expect the information to change, we should expect the same response every time. If answers vary, however, then the measurement method is, to the extent of that variation, unreliable. Here's an illustration.

In their classic research on delinquency in England, Donald West and David Farrington (1977) interviewed a sample of 411 males from a working-class area of London at age 16 and again at age 18. The subjects were asked to describe a variety of aspects of their lives, including educational and work history, leisure pursuits, drinking and smoking habits, delinquent activities, and experience with police and courts.

West and Farrington assessed reliability in several ways. One was to compare responses from the inter-view at age 18 with those from the interview at age 16. For example, in each interview, the youths were asked at what age they left school. In most cases, there were few discrepancies in stated age from one interview to the next, which led the authors to conclude, "There was therefore no systematic tendency for youths either to increase or lessen their claimed period of school attendance as they grew older, as might have occurred if they had wanted either to exaggerate or to underplay their educational attainments" (1977, 76–77). If West and Farrington had found less consistency in answers to this and other items, they would have had good reason to doubt the truthfulness of responses to more sensitive questions. The test–retest method suggested to the authors that memory lapses were the most common source of minor differences.

Although this method can be a useful reliability check, it is limited in some respects. Faulty memory may produce inconsistent responses if there is a lengthy gap between the initial interview and the retest. In their study of childhood victimization, Christine Walsh et al. (2008) addressed this problem by asking their respondents about experiences of violence and then retesting by repeating the questions to their sample only four weeks later. A different problem can arise in trying to use the test–retest method to check the reliability of attitude or opinion measures. If the test–retest interval is short, then answers given in the second interview may be affected by earlier responses if subjects try to be consistent.

**Interrater Reliability**   It is also possible for measurement unreliability to be generated by research workers—for example, interviewers and coders. To guard against interviewer unreliability, it is common practice in surveys to have a supervisor call a subsample of the respondents on the telephone and verify selected information. West and Farrington (1977, 173) checked interrater reliability in their study of London youths and found few significant differences in results obtained from different interviewers.

Comparing measurements from different raters works in other situations as well. Michael Geerken

(1994) presents an important discussion of reliability problems that researchers are likely to encounter in measuring prior arrests through police rap sheets. Duplicate entries, the use of aliases, and the need to transform official crime categories into a smaller number of categories for analysis are among the problems Geerken cites. One way to increase consistency in translating official records into research measures—a process often referred to as coding—is to have more than one person code a sample of records and then compare the consistency of coding decisions made by each person. This approach was used by Michael Maxfield and Cathy Spatz Widom (1996) in their analysis of adult arrests of child abuse victims.

In general, whenever researchers are concerned that measures obtained through coding may not be classified reliably, they should have each independently coded by different people. A great deal of disagreement among coders would most likely be due to ambiguity in operational definitions.

The reliability of measurements is a fundamental issue in criminal justice research, and we'll return to it in the chapters to come. For now, however, we hasten to point out that even total reliability doesn't ensure that our measures actually measure what we think they measure. That brings us to the issue of validity.

## Validity

In Chapter 3, we discussed validity in connection with the accuracy of causal inference. We are also interested in validity as a criterion for measurement quality—whether an empirical measure adequately reflects the meaning of the concept under consideration. Put another way, measurement validity involves whether you are really measuring what you say you are measuring. Recall that an operational definition specifies the operations you will perform to measure a concept. Does your operational definition accurately reflect the concept you are interested in? If the answer is yes, you have a valid measure. A radar gun is a valid measure of vehicle speed, but a wind velocity indicator is not because it measures total wind speed, not vehicle speed with respect to the ground.

Although methods for assessing reliability are relatively straightforward, it is more difficult to demonstrate that individual measures are valid. Because concepts are not real, but abstract, we cannot directly demonstrate that measures, which are real, are actually measuring an abstract concept. Nevertheless, researchers have some ways of dealing with the issue of validity.

**Face Validity** First, there's something called **face validity**. Particular empirical measures may or may not jibe with our common agreements and our individual mental images about a particular concept. We might debate the adequacy of measuring satisfaction with police services by counting the number of citizen complaints registered by the mayor's office, but we'd surely agree that the number of citizen complaints has something to do with levels of satisfaction. If someone suggested that we measure satisfaction with police by finding out whether people like to watch police dramas on TV, we would probably agree that the measure has no face validity; it simply does not make sense.

Second, there are many concrete agreements among researchers about how to measure certain basic concepts. The Census Bureau, for example, has created operational definitions of such concepts as family, household, and employment status that seem to have a workable validity in most studies using those concepts.

**Criterion-Related Validity** A more formal way to assess validity is to compare a measure with some external criterion, known as **criterion-related validity**. A measure can be validated by showing that it predicts scores on another measure that is generally accepted as valid; this is sometimes referred to as *convergent validity*. The validity of College Board exams, for example, is shown in their ability to predict the success of students in college.

Timothy Heeren and associates (Heeren et al. 1985) offer a good example of criterion-related validity in their efforts to validate a measure of alcohol-related auto fatalities. Of course, conducting a blood alcohol laboratory test on everyone killed in auto accidents would be a valid measure. Not all states regularly do this, however, so Heeren and colleagues tested the validity of an alternative measure: single-vehicle fatal accidents involving male drivers occurring between 8:00 p.m. and 3:00 a.m. The validity of this measure was shown by comparing it with the blood alcohol test results for all drivers killed in states that reliably conducted such tests in fatal accidents. Because the two measures agreed closely, Heeren and associates claimed that the proxy, or surrogate, measure would be valid in other states.

Another approach to criterion-related validity is to show that our measure of a concept is different from measures of similar but distinct concepts. This is called *discriminant validity*, meaning that measures can discriminate between different concepts.

Sometimes it is difficult to find behavioral criteria that can be used to validate measures as directly as described here. In those instances, however, we can often approximate such criteria by considering how the variable in question ought, theoretically, to relate to other variables.

**Construct Validity** **Construct validity** is based on the logical relationships among variables. Let's suppose that we are interested in studying fear of crime—its sources and consequences. As part of our research, we develop a measure of fear of crime, and we want to assess its validity.

In addition to our measure, we will also develop certain theoretical expectations about the way the variable fear of crime relates to other variables. For instance, it's reasonable to conclude that people who are afraid of crime are less likely to leave their homes at night for entertainment than people who are not afraid of crime. If our measure of fear of crime relates to how often people go out at night in the expected fashion, that constitutes evidence of our measure's construct validity. However, if people who are afraid of crime are just as likely to go out at night as people who are not afraid, that challenges the validity of our measure. This and related points about measures of fear are nicely illustrated by Jason Ditton and Stephen Farrall in their analysis of data from England (2007).

Tests of construct validity, then, can offer a weight of evidence that our measure either does or does not tap the quality we want it to measure, without providing definitive proof.

**Multiple Measures** Another approach to validation of an individual measure is to compare it with alternative measures of the same concept. The use of multiple measures is similar to establishing criterion validity. However, the use of multiple measures does not necessarily assume that the criterion measure is always more accurate. For example, many crimes never result in an arrest, so arrests are not good measures of how many crimes are committed by individuals. Self-report surveys have often been used to measure delinquency and criminality. But how valid are survey questions that ask people how many crimes they have committed?

The approach used by West and Farrington (and by others) is to ask people, for example, how many times they have committed robbery and how many times they have been arrested for that crime. Those who admit to having been arrested for robbery are asked when and where the arrest occurred. Self-reports can then be validated by checking police arrest records. This works two ways: (1) it is possible to validate individual reports of being arrested for robbery, and (2) researchers can check police records for all persons interviewed to see if there are any records of robbery arrests that subjects do not disclose to interviewers.

Figure 4.1 illustrates the difference between validity and reliability. Think of measurement as analogous to hitting the bull's-eye on a target. A reliable measure produces a tight pattern, regardless of where it hits, because reliability is a function of consistency. Validity, in contrast, relates to the arrangement of shots around the bull's-eye. The failure of reliability in the figure can be seen as a random error; the failure of validity is a systematic error. Notice that neither an unreliable nor an invalid measure is likely to be very useful.

## MEASURING CRIME

*Different approaches to measuring crime illustrate basic principles in conceptualization and measurement.*

By way of illustrating basic principles in measurement, we now focus more narrowly on different

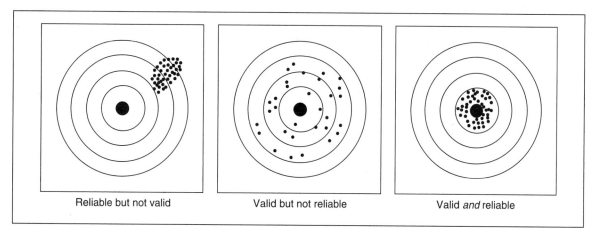

| Reliable but not valid | Valid but not reliable | Valid *and* reliable |

**FIGURE 4.1**  Analogy to Validity and Reliability

ways of measuring crime. Crime is a fundamental dependent variable in criminal justice and criminology. Explanatory studies frequently seek to learn what causes crime, whereas applied studies often focus on what actions might be effective in reducing crime. Descriptive and exploratory studies may simply wish to count how much crime there is in a specific area, a question of obvious concern to criminal justice officials as well as researchers.

Crime can also be an independent variable— for example, in a study of how crime affects fear or other attitudes, or of whether people who live in high-crime areas are more likely than others to favor long prison sentences for drug dealers. Sometimes crime can be both an independent and a dependent variable, as in a study about the relationship between drug use and other offenses.

### General Issues in Measuring Crime

At the outset, we must consider two general questions that influence whatever approach we might take to measuring crime: (1) How will we conceptualize *crime*? and (2) What units of analysis should be used?

**Conceptualization**  Let's begin by proposing a conceptual definition of crime—one that will enable us to decide what specific types of crime we'll measure. Recall a definition from Gottfredson and

Hirschi (1990, 15), mentioned earlier: "acts of force or fraud undertaken in pursuit of self-interest." This is an interesting definition, but it is better suited to an extended discussion of theories of crime than to our purposes in this chapter. For example, we would have to clarify what was meant by *self-interest*, a term that has engaged philosophers and social scientists for centuries.

James Q. Wilson and Richard Herrnstein (1985, 22) propose a different definition that should get us started: "A crime is any act committed in violation of a law that prohibits it and authorizes punishment for its commission." Although other criminologists (such as Gottfredson and Hirschi) might not agree with this conceptual definition, it has the advantage of being reasonably specific. We could be even more specific by consulting a state or federal code and listing the types of acts for which the law provides punishment.

Our list would be very long. In fact, one of the principal difficulties we encounter when we try to measure crime is that many different types of behaviors and actions are included in our conceptualization of crime as an *act committed in violation of a law that prohibits it and authorizes punishment for its commission*, but we may be interested in only a small subset of things included under such a broad definition. Different measures tend to focus on different types of crime, primarily because not all crimes can be measured the same way with any degree of reliability or validity. Therefore, one important step in selecting a measure is deciding what crimes will be included.

**What Units of Analysis?**   Recall that units of analysis are the specific entities researchers collect information about. Chapter 3 considered individuals, groups, social artifacts, and other units of analysis. Deciding how to measure crime requires that we once again think about these units.

Crimes involve four elements that are often easier to recognize in the abstract than they are to actually measure: offender, victim, offense, and incident. The most basic of these elements is the offender. Without an offender, there's no crime, so a crime must, at a minimum, involve an offender. The offender is therefore one possible unit of analysis. We might decide to study burglars, auto thieves, bank robbers, child molesters, drug dealers, or people who have committed many different types of offenses.

Crimes also require some sort of victim, the second possible unit of analysis. We could study victims of burglary, auto theft, bank robbery, or assault. Notice that this list of victims includes different types of units: households or businesses for burglary, car owners for auto theft, banks for bank robbery, and individuals for assault. Some of these units are organizations (banks, businesses), some are individual people, some are abstractions (households), and some are ambiguous (individuals or organizations can own automobiles).

What about so-called victimless crimes like drug use, bookmaking, or prostitution? In a legal sense, victimless crimes do not exist because crimes are acts that injure society, organizations, or individuals. But studying crimes in which only society is the victim—prostitution, for example—presents special challenges, and specialized techniques have been developed to measure certain types of victimless crimes.

The final two elements of crimes—offense and incident—are closely intertwined and so will be discussed together. An offense is defined as an individual act of burglary, auto theft, bank robbery, and so on. The FBI defines incident as "one or more offenses committed by the same offender, or group of offenders *acting in concert, at the same time and place*" (Federal Bureau of Investigation 2000, 17; emphasis in original).

Think about the difference between offense and incident for a moment. A single incident can include multiple offenses, but it's not possible to have one offense and multiple incidents.

To illustrate the different units of analysis—offenders, victims, offenses, and incidents—consider the examples in the box titled "Units of Analysis and Measuring Crime." These examples help distinguish units from each other and illustrate the links among different units. Notice that we have said nothing about aggregate units of analysis, a topic we examined in Chapter 3. We have considered only individual units, even though measures of crime are often based on aggregate units of analysis—neighborhoods, cities, counties, states, and so on.

We cover units at some length because they play a critical, and often overlooked, role in developing operational definitions, to which our attention now turns.

## Measures Based on Crimes Known to Police

The most widely used measures of crime are based on police records and are commonly referred to as *crimes known to police*. This phrase is at the core of police-based operational definitions and has important implications for understanding what police records do and do not measure. The most obvious implication is that crimes not known to police cannot be measured by consulting police records. Other features of measures based on police records can best be understood by considering specific examples.

**Uniform Crime Reports**   Police measures of crime form the basis for the FBI's Uniform Crime Reports (UCR), a data series that has been collected since 1930 and has been widely used by criminal justice researchers. But certain characteristics and procedures related to the UCR affect its suitability as a measure of crime. Most of our comments highlight shortcomings in this regard, but keep in mind that the UCR is and will continue

## UNITS OF ANALYSIS AND MEASURING CRIME

Figuring out the different units of analysis in counting crimes can be difficult and confusing at first. Much of the problem comes from the possibility of what database designers call one-to-many and many-to-many relationships. The same incident can have multiple offenses, offenders, and victims or just one of each. Fortunately, thinking through some examples usually clarifies the matter. Our two examples are adapted from an FBI publication (2000, 18).

### Example 1

Two males entered a bar. The bartender was forced at gunpoint to hand over all money from the cash register. The offenders also took money and jewelry from three customers. One of the offenders used his handgun to beat one of the customers, thereby causing serious injury. Both offenders fled on foot.

> One incident
>> One robbery offense
>> Two offenders
>> Four victims (bar owner, three patrons)
>
> One aggravated assault offense
>> Two offenders
>> One victim

Even though only one offender actually assaulted the bar patron, the other offender would be charged with assisting in the offense because he prevented others from coming to the aid of the assault victim.

### Example 2

Two males entered a bar. The bartender was forced at gunpoint to hand over all the money from the cash register. The offenders also took money and jewelry from two customers. One of the offenders, in searching for more people to rob, found a customer in a back room and raped her there, outside the view of the other offender. When the rapist returned, both offenders fled on foot.

This example includes two incidents because the rape occurred in a different place and the offenders were not acting in concert. And because they were not acting in concert in the same place, only one offender was associated with the rape incident.

> Incident 1
>> One robbery offense
>> Two offenders
>> Three victims (bar owner, two patrons)
>
> Incident 2
>> One rape offense
>> One offender
>> One victim

to be a very useful measure for researchers and public officials.

The UCR does not even try to count all crimes reported to police. What are referred to as Part I offenses are counted if these offenses are reported to police (and recorded by police). Part I offenses include murder and non-negligent manslaughter, forcible rape, robbery, aggravated assault, burglary, larceny-theft, and motor vehicle theft (Federal Bureau of Investigation 2010). Other offenses, referred to as Part II crimes, are counted only if a person has been arrested and charged with a crime. The UCR therefore does not include such offenses as shoplifting, drug sale or use, fraud, prostitution, simple assault, vandalism, receiving stolen property, and all other nontraffic offenses unless someone is arrested. This means that a large number of crimes reported to police are not measured in the UCR.

Another source of measurement error in the UCR is produced by the hierarchy rule used by police agencies and the FBI to classify crimes. Under the hierarchy rule, if multiple crimes are committed in a single incident, only the most serious is counted in the UCR. For example, if a burglar breaks into a home, stabs one of the occupants, and flees in the homeowner's car, at least three crimes are committed—burglary, aggravated assault, and vehicle theft. Under the FBI hierarchy rule, however, only the most serious crime, aggravated assault, is counted in the UCR, even though the offender could be charged with all three offenses. In the examples described in the box "Units of Analysis and Measuring Crime," the UCR would count one offense in each incident: a single robbery in the first example and rape in the second.

Before we move on to other approaches to measuring crime, consider another important way units of analysis figure into UCR data. The UCR system produces what is referred to as a **summary-based measure** of crime. This means that UCR data include summary, or total, crime counts from reporting agencies—cities or counties. UCR summary data therefore represent groups as units of analysis. Crime reports are available for cities or counties, and these may be aggregated upward to measure crime for states or regions of the United States. But UCR data available from the FBI cannot represent individual crimes, offenders, or victims as units.

Recall that it is possible to aggregate units of analysis to higher levels, but it is not possible to disaggregate grouped data to the individual level. Because UCR data are aggregates, they cannot be used in descriptive or explanatory studies that focus on individual crimes, offenders, or victims. UCR data are therefore restricted to the analysis of such units as cities, counties, states, or regions.

**Incident-Based Police Records**   The U.S. Department of Justice sponsors two series of crime measures that are based on incidents as units of analysis. The first of these **incident-based measures**, Supplementary Homicide Reports (SHR), was begun in 1961 and is part of the UCR program, as implied by *supplementary*.

Local law enforcement agencies submit detailed information about individual homicide incidents under the SHR program. This includes information about victims and, if known, offenders (age, gender, race); the relationship between victim and offender; the weapon used; the location of the incident; and the circumstances surrounding the killing. Notice how the SHR relates to our discussion of units of analysis. Incidents are the basic unit and can include one or more victims and offenders; because the series is restricted to homicides, offense is held constant.

Because the SHR is an incident-based system, investigators can use SHR data to conduct descriptive and explanatory studies of individual events. For example, it's possible to compare the relationship between victim and offender for male victims and female victims or to compare the types of weapons used in killings by strangers and killings by nonstran-

gers. Such analyses are not possible if we are studying homicide using UCR summary data.

Crime measures based on incidents as units of analysis therefore have several advantages over summary measures. It's important to keep in mind, however, that SHR data still represent crimes known to police and recorded by police.

**The National Incident-Based Reporting System**   A relatively new development in police-based measures at the national level is the ongoing effort by the FBI and the Bureau of Justice Statistics (BJS) to convert the UCR to a National Incident-Based Reporting System (NIBRS, pronounced "nybers"). Planning for replacement of the UCR began in the mid-1980s, but because NIBRS represents major changes, law enforcement agencies have shifted only gradually to the new system.

About 17,000 law enforcement agencies report UCR summary data each year; that's 17,000 annual observations, one for each reporting agency. In 2007, 106 agencies in Idaho reported UCR data, so Idaho submitted a maximum of 106 observations for 2007. Under NIBRS, Idaho reported over 89,000 incidents in 2007. So, for Idaho, shifting from the summary UCR system for measuring crime to the incident-based NIBRS system meant shifting from 106 units (UCR reporting jurisdictions) to more than 89,000 units. In other words, rather than reporting 106 summary crime counts for eight UCR Part I offenses, Idaho reported detailed information on 89,410 individual incidents. And this is Idaho, which ranked 39th among the states in 2009 resident population (Idaho State Police 2008)!

In addition, NIBRS guidelines call for gathering information about a much broader array of offenses. Whereas the UCR reports information about eight Part I offenses, NIBRS is designed to collect detailed information on 46 "Group A" offenses. Table 4.2 shows what kinds of information are collected for offenses, victims, and offenders under NIBRS. Table 4.3 shows NIBRS crime data for Idaho in 2007. Compare the top part of the table, reporting crime counts for Part I offenses, to the bottom part. Additional NIBRS Group A offenses

**TABLE 4.2**  Selected Information in National Incident-Based Reporting System Records

| Administrative Segment | Offense Segment |
|---|---|
| Incident date and time | Offense type |
| Reporting agency ID | Attempted or completed |
| Other ID numbers | Offender drug/alcohol use |
| | Location type |
| | Weapon use |

| Victim Segment | Offender Segment |
|---|---|
| Victim ID number | Offender ID number |
| Offense type | Offender age, gender, race |
| Victim age, gender, race | |
| Resident of jurisdiction? | |
| Type of injury | |
| Relationship to offender | |
| Victim type: | |
|    Individual person | |
|    Business | |
|    Government | |
|    Society/public | |

*Source:* Adapted from Federal Bureau of Investigation (2000, 6–8, 90).

**TABLE 4.3**  Crime in Idaho, 2007

**UCR Part I Offenses**

| | |
|---|---|
| Murder, non-negligent manslaughter | 55 |
| Rape | 586 |
| Robbery | 234 |
| Aggravated assault | 2,749 |
| Burglary | 6,799 |
| Larceny | 24,812 |
| Motor vehicle theft | 2,201 |
| Arson | 340 |
|   Subtotal | 37,776 |

**Additional NIBRS Group A Offenses**

| | |
|---|---|
| Simple assault | 13,978 |
| Intimidation | 1,667 |
| Bribery | 2 |
| Counterfeit/forgery | 1,275 |
| Destruction of property | 14,052 |
| Drug violations | 7,131 |
| Drug equipment violations | 6,272 |
| Embezzlement | 328 |
| Extortion/blackmail | 16 |
| Fraud | 3,202 |
| Gambling | 3 |
| Kidnapping/abduction | 269 |
| Pornography/obscene material | 79 |
| Prostitution | 14 |
| Forcible sex offenses | 1,269 |
| Nonforcible sex offenses | 261 |
| Stolen property | 559 |
| Weapons violations | 1,257 |
|   Subtotal | 51,634 |
|   Group A total | 89,410 |

*Source:* Adapted from Idaho Department of Law Enforcement, "Crime in Idaho, 2007," http://www.isp.idaho.gov/identification/ucr/crimeinidaho2007.html

more than double the number of crimes "known to police" in Idaho (37,776 UCR Part I, plus 51,634 additional Group A). Simple assault and destruction of property (vandalism) are by far the most common of these additional offenses, but drug violations accounted for over 13,000 offenses in 2007 (drug violations plus drug equipment violations).

Collecting detailed information on each incident for each offense, victim, and offender, and doing so for a large number of offense types, represents the most significant changes in NIBRS compared with the UCR. Dropping the hierarchy rule is also a major change, but that is a consequence of incident-based reporting.

In the future, incident-based police records will become more readily available and will cover a larger number of law enforcement agencies. In fact, many agencies have developed their own incident-based

records systems independent of NIBRS, largely because of major advances in computing technology (Maxfield 1999). Furthermore, researchers are beginning to analyze NIBRS data, something that is certain to prompt other researchers to do the same. For examples, see studies of child prostitution (Finkelhor and Ormrod 2004), child abuse (Snyder 2000), hate crimes (Nolan, Akiyama, and Berhanu 2002), and domestic violence (Vazquez, Stohr, and Purkiss 2005).

## Victim Surveys

Conducting a **victim survey** that asks people whether they have been the victim of a crime is an alternative approach to operationalization. In principle, measuring crime through surveys has several advantages. Surveys can obtain information on crimes that were not reported to police. Asking people about victimizations can also measure incidents that police may not have officially recorded as crimes. Finally, asking people about crimes that may have happened to them provides data on victims and offenders (individuals) and on the incidents themselves (social artifacts). Like an incident-based reporting system, a survey can therefore provide more disaggregated units of analysis.

**The National Crime Victimization Survey**  The U.S. Census Bureau has conducted the NCVS since 1972, the longest continuous crime survey in the world. The NCVS is based on a nationally representative sample of households and uses uniform procedures to select and interview respondents, which enhances the reliability of crime measures. Because individual people living in households are interviewed, the NCVS can be used in studies in which individuals or households are the unit of analysis. And the NCVS uses a panel design, interviewing respondents from the same household seven times at six-month intervals.

The NCVS cannot measure all crimes, however, in part because of the procedures used to select victims. Because the survey is based on a sample of households, it cannot count crimes in which businesses or commercial establishments are the victims. Bank robberies, gas station holdups, shoplifting, embezzlement, and securities fraud are examples of crimes that cannot be systematically counted by interviewing household members. Samples of banks, gas stations, retail stores, business

establishments, or stockbrokers would be needed to measure those crimes. In much the same fashion, crimes directed at homeless victims cannot be counted by surveys of households like the NCVS.

What about victimless crimes? For example, think about how you would respond to a Census Bureau interviewer who asked whether you had been the victim of a drug sale. If you have bought illegal drugs, you might think of yourself as a customer rather than as a victim. Or if you lived near a park where drug sales were common, you might think of yourself as a victim even though you did not participate in a drug transaction. The point is that victim surveys are not good measures of victimless crimes because the respondents can't easily be conceived as victims.

Measuring certain forms of delinquency through victim surveys presents similar problems. Status offenses such as truancy and curfew violations do not have identifiable victims who can be included in samples based on households. Homicide and manslaughter are other crimes that are not well measured by victim surveys, for obvious reasons.

Since its inception, the NCVS has served as a measure to monitor the volume of crime, including crimes not reported to police. In a regular series of publications, the BJS reports annual victimization data together with analysis of victimization for special topics such as carjackings (Klaus 2004), intimate partner violence (Rand and Rennison 2005), and contacts between individuals and the police (Durose, Smith, and Langan 2007). In addition, the NCVS is a valuable tool for researchers who take advantage of detailed information about individual victimizations to examine such topics as victimization in public schools (Dinkes et al. 2007), identity theft (Langton and Planty 2010), and why domestic violence victimizations may or may not be reported to police (Felson et al. 2002).

**Community Victimization Surveys**  Following the initial development of victim survey methods in the late 1960s, the Census Bureau completed a series of city-level surveys. These were discontinued for a variety of reasons, but researchers and officials in the BJS occasionally conducted city-level victim surveys in specific communities. In 1998, the BJS and the Office of Community Oriented Policing Services (COPS) launched pilot surveys in 12 large- and medium-sized cities (Smith et al. 1999).

The city-level initiative underscores one of the chief advantages of measuring crime through victim surveys—obtaining counts of incidents not reported to police. In large part, city-level surveys were promoted by BJS and COPS to enable local law enforcement agencies to better understand the scope of crime—reported and unreported—in their communities. Notice also the title of the first report: "Criminal Victimization and *Perceptions* of Community Safety in 12 Cities, 1998." We emphasize perceptions to illustrate that city-level surveys can be valuable tools for implementing community policing, a key component of the 1994 Crime Bill that provided billions of dollars to hire new police officers nationwide. It is significant that the Department of Justice recognized the potential value of survey measures of crime and perceptions of community safety to develop and evaluate community policing.

The initial BJS/COPS effort was a pilot test of new methods for conducting city-level surveys. In 2010, the BJS began new efforts to develop local-level estimates of victimization for selected areas through a redesign of the NCVS (Cantor et al. 2010).

## Surveys of Offending

Just as survey techniques can measure crime by asking people to describe their experiences as victims, **self-report surveys** ask people about crimes they may have committed. We might initially be skeptical of this technique: how truthful are people when asked about crimes they may have committed? Our concern is justified in one sense. Many people do not wish to disclose illegal behavior to interviewers even if they are assured of confidentiality. Others might deliberately lie to interviewers and exaggerate the number of offenses they have committed.

Self-report surveys are the best method available for trying to measure certain crimes that are poorly represented by other techniques. Thinking about the other methods we have discussed—crimes known to

police and victimization surveys—suggests several examples. Crimes such as prostitution and drug abuse are excluded from victimization surveys and underestimated by police records of people arrested for these offenses. Public order crimes and delinquency are other examples. A third class of offenses that might be better counted by self-report surveys is crimes that are rarely reported to or observed by police—shoplifting and drunk driving are examples.

Think of it this way: As we saw earlier, all crimes require an offender. Not all crimes have clearly identifiable victims who can be interviewed, however, and not all crimes are readily observed by police, victims, or witnesses. If we can't observe the offense and can't interview a victim, what's the next logical step?

There are no nationwide efforts to systematically collect self-report measures on a variety of offenses, as is the case with the UCR and NCVS. Instead, periodic surveys yield information either on specific types of crime or on crimes committed by a specific target population. We will briefly consider two ongoing self-report surveys here.

**National Survey on Drug Use and Health** Like the NCVS, the National Survey on Drug Use and Health (NSDUH) is based on a national sample of households. Currently sponsored by the Substance Abuse and Mental Health Services Administration in the U.S. Department of Health and Human Services, the NSDUH samples households and household residents ages 12 and older. In the 2009 sample, about 67,500 individuals responded to questions regarding their use of illegal drugs, alcohol, and tobacco (Substance Abuse and Mental Health Services Administration 2010). Because it has been conducted for more than three decades, the NSDUH provides information on trends and changes in drug use among respondents. The 2009 survey was designed to obtain statistically reliable samples from the eight largest states in addition to the overall national sample.

Think for a moment about what sorts of questions we would ask to learn about people's experience in using illegal drugs. Among other things, we would probably want to distinguish someone who tried marijuana once from daily users. The drug use survey does this by including questions to distinguish lifetime use (ever used) of different drugs from current use (used within the past month). You may or may not agree that use in the past month represents current use, but it is the standard used in regular reports on NSDUH results. That's the operational definition of current use.

**Monitoring the Future**   Our second example is different in two respects: (1) it targets a specific population, and (2) it asks sampled respondents a broader variety of questions.

Since 1975, the National Institute on Drug Abuse has sponsored an annual survey of high school seniors, Monitoring the Future: A Continuing Study of the Lifestyles and Values of Youth, or the MTF for short. As its long title implies, the MTF survey is intended to monitor the behaviors, attitudes, and values of young people. The MTF includes several samples of high school students and other groups, totaling about 46,000 respondents in 2008 (Johnston et al. 2009).

Each spring between 120 and 140 high schools are sampled within particular geographic areas. In larger high schools, samples of up to 350 seniors are selected; in smaller schools, all seniors may participate. Students fill out computer scan sheets containing batteries of questions that include self-reported use of alcohol, tobacco, and illegal drugs. In most cases, students record their answers in classrooms during normal school hours.

The core sample of the MTF—surveys of high school seniors—thus provides a cross section for measuring annual drug use and other illegal acts. Now recall our discussion of the time dimension in Chapter 3. Each year, both the MTF and the NSDUH survey drug use for a cross section of high school seniors and adults in households, thus providing a snapshot of annual rates of self-reported drug use. Examining annual results from the MTF and the NSDUH over time provides a time series, or trend study, that enables researchers and policy makers to detect changes in drug use among high school seniors and adults. Finally, a series of follow-up samples of MTF respondents constitute a series of panel studies whereby changes

in drug use among individual respondents can be studied over time. Thomas Mieczkowski (1996) presents an excellent discussion of these two surveys and compares self-reported drug use from each series over time.

## Measuring Crime Summary

Table 4.4 summarizes the strengths and weaknesses of different measures of crime. The UCR and SHR provide the best counts for murder and crimes in which the victim is a business or a commercial establishment. Crimes against persons or households that are not reported to police are best counted by the NCVS. Usually these are less serious crimes, many of them UCR Part II incidents that are counted only if a suspect is arrested. Recent changes in NCVS procedures have improved counts of sexual assault and other violent victimizations. Compared with the UCR, NIBRS potentially provides much greater detail for a broader range of offenses. NIBRS complements the NCVS by including disaggregated incident-based reports for state and local areas and by recording detailed information on crimes against children younger than age 12.

Self-report surveys are best at measuring crimes that do not have readily identifiable victims and that are less often observed by or reported to police. The two self-report surveys listed in Table 4.4 sample different populations and use different interview procedures.

Don't forget that all crime measures are selective, so it's important to understand the selection process. Despite their various flaws, the measures of crime available to you can serve many research purposes. Researchers are best advised to be critical and careful users of whatever measure of crime best suits their research purpose.

# COMPOSITE MEASURES

*Combining individual measures often produces more valid and reliable indicators.*

Sometimes it is possible to construct a single measure that captures the variable of interest. For example, asking auto owners whether their car has been

**TABLE 4.4**    Measuring Crime Summary

|  | Units | Target Population | Crime Coverage | Best Count for |
|---|---|---|---|---|
| **Known to police** | | | | |
| UCR | Aggregate: reporting agency | All law enforcement agencies; 98% reporting | Limited number reported and recorded crimes | Commercial and business victims |
| SHR | Incident | All law enforcement agencies; 98% reporting | Homicides only | Homicides |
| NIBRS | Incident | All law enforcement agencies; limited reporting | Extensive | Details on local incidents; victims under age 12 |
| **Surveys** | | | | |
| NCVS | Victimization, individuals and households | Individuals in households | Household and personal crimes | Household and personal crimes not reported to police |
| NSDUH | Individual respondent, offender | Individuals in households | Drug use | Drug use by adults in households |
| MTF | Individual respondent, offender | High school seniors; follow-up on sample | Substance use, delinquency, offending | Drug use by high school seniors |

stolen in the previous six months is a straightforward way to measure auto-theft victimization. But other variables may be better measured by more than one indicator. A "property crime" index might combine burglary, larceny, and motor vehicle theft; a "violent crime" index would be a composite of murder, rape, robbery, and assault.

Composite measures are frequently used in criminal justice research for three reasons. First, despite carefully designing studies to provide valid and reliable measurements of variables, the researcher is often unable to develop single indicators of complex concepts. That is especially true with regard to attitudes and opinions that are measured through surveys. For example, measuring fear of crime through a question that asks about feelings of safety on neighborhood streets measures some dimensions of fear but certainly not all of them. This leads us to question the validity of using that single question to measure fear of crime.

 **THEORY AND MEASUREMENT**

Opportunity-based theories of crime argue that offenders will evaluate specific situations before selecting crime targets. Thus, theory suggests that auto thieves will search for unlocked cars, and burglars try to find properties that are unoccupied. What about parrot poachers—people who steal parrots to sell on illegal markets? Finding little previous research on parrot poaching, Stephen Pires and Ronald Clarke (2011) reasoned that parrot thieves in Mexico would target birds that nested close to ground level. So nesting location was an important variable for assessing the vulnerability of different species to poaching. Nesting location was a measure derived from opportunity-based theory.

Second, we may wish to use a rather refined ordinal measure of a variable, arranging cases in several ordinal categories from very low to very high according to a variable such as degree of parental supervision. A single data item might not have enough categories to provide the desired range of variation, but an index or scale formed from several items would.

Finally, indexes and scales are *efficient* devices for data analysis. If a single data item gives only a rough indication of a given variable, considering several data items may give us a more comprehensive and more accurate indication. For example, the results of a single drug test would give us some indication of drug use by a probationer. Examining results from several drug tests would give us a better indication, but the manipulation of several data items simultaneously can be very complicated. In contrast, composite measures are efficient data reduction devices. Several indicators may be summarized in a single numerical score, even while very nearly maintaining the specific details of all the individual indicators.

## Typologies

Researchers combine variables in different ways to produce different composite measures. The simplest of these is a **typology**, sometimes called a taxonomy. Typologies are produced by the intersection of two or more variables to create a set of categories or types. We may, for example, wish to classify people according to the range of their experience in criminal court. Assume we have asked a sample of people whether they have ever served as a juror and whether they have ever testified as a witness in criminal court. Table 4.5 shows how the yes and no responses to these two questions can be combined into a typology of experience in court.

Typologies can be more complex—combining scores on three or more measures or combining scores on two measures that take many different values. For an example of a complex typology, consider research by Rolf Loeber and associates (Loeber et al. 1991) on patterns of delinquency over time. The researchers used a longitudinal design in which a sample of boys was selected from Pittsburgh public schools and interviewed many times. Some questions asked about their

**TABLE 4.5**    Typology of Court Experience

|  |  | Serve on Jury? | |
|---|---|---|---|
|  |  | **No** | **Yes** |
| **Testify as Witness?** | **No** | A | B |
|  | **Yes** | C | D |

Typology
A: No experience with court
B: Experience as juror only
C: Experience as witness only
D: Experience as juror and witness

involvement in delinquency and criminal offending. This approach made it possible to distinguish boys who reported different types of offending at different times.

Loeber and associates first classified delinquent and criminal acts into the following ordinal seriousness categories (1991, 44):

*None*: No self-reported delinquency

*Minor*: Theft of items worth less than $5, vandalism, fare evasion

*Moderate*: Theft of more than $5, gang fighting, carrying weapons

*Serious*: Car theft, breaking and entering, forced sex, selling drugs

Next, to measure changes in delinquency over time, the researchers compared reports of delinquency from the first screening interview with reports from follow-up interviews. These two measures—delinquency at time 1 and delinquency at time 2—formed the typology, which they referred to as a "dynamic classification of offenders" (1991, 44). Table 4.6 summarizes this typology.

The first category in the table, nondelinquent, includes those boys who reported committing no offenses at both the screening and follow-up interviews. Starters reported no offenses at screening and then minor, moderate, or serious delinquency at follow-up, whereas desistors were just the opposite. Those who committed the same types of offenses at both times were labeled stable; deescalators reported committing less serious offenses at follow-up; and escalators moved on to more serious offenses.

**TABLE 4.6**  Typology of Change in
Juvenile Offending

| | Juvenile Offending | |
|---|---|---|
| **Typology** | **Screening (Time 1)** | **Follow-Up (Time 2)** |
| A. Nondelinquent | 0 | 0 |
| B. Starter | 0 | 1, 2, or 3 |
| C. Desistor | 1, 2, or 3 | 0 |
| D. Stable | 1 | 1 |
| D. Stable | 2 | 2 |
| D. Stable | 3 | 3 |
| E. Deescalator | 3 | 2 |
| E. Deescalator | 2 or 3 | 1 |
| F. Escalator | 1 | 2 or 3 |
| F. Escalator | 2 | 3 |

Juvenile Offending Typology
0:  None
1:  Minor
2:  Moderate
3:  Serious

*Source:* Adapted from Loeber and associates (1991, 43-46).

Notice the efficiency of this typology. Two variables (delinquency at screening and follow-up) with four categories each are reduced to a single variable with six categories. Furthermore, the two measures of delinquency are themselves composite measures, produced by summarizing self-reports of a large number of individual offenses. Finally, notice also how this efficiency is reflected in the clear meaning of the new composite measure. This dynamic typology summarizes information about time, offending, and offense seriousness in a single measure.

## An Index of Disorder

"What is disorder, and what isn't?" asks Wesley Skogan (1990a) in his book on the links between crime, fear, and social problems such as public drinking, drug use, litter, prostitution, panhandling, dilapidated buildings, and groups of boisterous youths. In an influential article titled "Broken Windows," James Q. Wilson and George Kelling (1982) describe disorder as a sign of crime that

may contribute independently to fear and crime itself. The argument goes something like this: Disorder is a symbol of urban decay that people associate with crime. Signs of disorder can produce two related problems. First, disorder may contribute to fear of crime, as urban residents believe that physical decay and undesirables are symbols of crime. Second, potential offenders may interpret evidence of disorder as a signal that informal social control mechanisms in a neighborhood have broken down and that the area is fair game for mayhem and predation.

We all have some sort of mental image (conception) of disorder, but, to paraphrase Skogan's question: how do we measure it? Let's begin by distinguishing two conceptions of disorder. First, we can focus on the physical presence of disorder—whether litter, public drinking, public drug use, and the like are evident in an urban neighborhood. We might measure the physical presence of disorder through a series of systematic observations. This is the approach used by Robert Sampson and Stephen Raudenbush (1999) in their study of links between disorder and crime in Chicago. Unfortunately, these authors observed very few examples of disorder and altogether ignored the question of whether such behaviors were perceived as problematic by residents of Chicago neighborhoods.

That brings us to the second conception, one focusing on the *perception* of disorder. Thus, some people might view public drinking as disorderly, whereas others (New Orleans residents, for example) consider public drinking to be perfectly acceptable. Questionnaires and survey methods are best suited for measuring perceived disorder.

Skogan used questions about nine different examples of disorder and classified them into two groups representing what he calls social and physical disorder (Skogan 1990a, 51, 191):

| **Social Disorder** | **Physical Disorder** |
|---|---|
| Groups of loiterers | Abandoned buildings |
| Drug use and sales | Garbage and litter |
| Vandalism | Junk in vacant lots |
| Gang activity | |
| Public drinking | |
| Street harassment | |

Questions corresponding to each of these examples of disorder asked respondents to rate them as a big problem (scored 2), some problem (scored 1), or almost no problem (scored 0) in their neighborhood. Together, these nine items measure different types of disorder and appear to have reasonable face validity. However, examining the relationship between each individual item and respondents' fear of crime or experience as a crime victim would be unwieldy at best. So Skogan created two indexes, one for social disorder and one for physical disorder, by adding up the scores for each item and dividing by the number of items in each group. Figure 4.2 shows a hypothetical sample questionnaire for these nine items, together with the scores that would be produced for each index.

This example illustrates how several related variables can be combined to produce an index that has three desirable properties. First, a composite index is a more valid measure of disorder than is a single question. Second, computing and averaging across all items in a category create more variation in the index than we could obtain in any single item. Finally, two indexes are more parsimonious than nine individual variables; data analysis and interpretation can be more efficient.

## MEASUREMENT SUMMARY

We have covered substantial ground in this chapter, introducing the important and often complex issue of measurement in criminal justice research. More than a step in the research process, measurement involves continuous thinking about what conceptual properties we wish to study, how we

---

Introduction:

Now I'm going to read you a list of crime-related problems that may be found in some parts of the city. For each one, please tell me how much of a problem it is in your neighborhood. Is it a big problem, some problem, or almost no problem?

| | Big problem | Some problem | No problem |
|---|---|---|---|
| (S) Groups of people loitering | ② | 1 | 0 |
| (S) People using or selling drugs | 2 | ① | 0 |
| (P) Abandoned buildings | 2 | 1 | ⓪ |
| (S) Vandalism | 2 | ① | 0 |
| (P) Garbage and litter on street | ② | 1 | 0 |
| (S) Gangs and gang activity | 2 | 1 | ⓪ |
| (S) People drinking in public | ② | 1 | 0 |
| (P) Junk in vacant lots | 2 | 1 | ⓪ |
| (S) People making rude or insulting remarks | 2 | ① | 0 |

(S) Social = 2 + 1 + 1 + 0 + 2 + 1 = 7

    Index score = $7/6$ = 1.16

(P) Physical = 0 + 2 + 0 = 2

    Index score = $2/3$ = 0.67

**FIGURE 4.2** Index of Disorder

will operationalize those properties, and how we will develop measures that are reliable and valid. Often some type of composite measure better represents underlying concepts and thus enhances validity.

Subsequent chapters will pursue issues of measurement further. Part Three of this book will describe data collection—how we go about making actual measurements. And the next chapter will focus on different approaches to measuring crime.

## SUMMARY

- Concepts are mental images we use as summary devices for bringing together observations and experiences that seem to have something in common.

- Our concepts do not exist in the real world, so they can't be measured directly.

- In operationalization, we specify concrete empirical procedures that will result in measurements of variables.

- Operationalization begins in study design and continues throughout the research project, including the analysis of data.

- Categories in a measure must be mutually exclusive and exhaustive.

- Higher levels of measurements specify categories that have ranked order or more complex numerical properties.

- *Precision* refers to the exactness of the measure used in an observation or description of an attribute.

- Reliability and validity are criteria for measurement quality. Valid measures are true indicators of underlying concepts. A reliable measure is consistent.

- Crime is a fundamental concept in criminal justice research. Different approaches to measuring crime illustrate general principles of conceptualization, operationalization, and measurement. We have different measures of crime because each measure has its strengths and weaknesses.

- Different measures of crime are based on different units of analysis. Uniform Crime Reports (UCRs) are summary measures that report totals for individual agencies. Other measures use offenders, victims, incidents, or offenses as the units of analysis.

- Crimes known to police have been the most widely used measures. UCR data are available for most of the 20th century; more detailed information about homicides was added to the UCR in 1961. Most recently, the FBI has developed an incident-based reporting system that is gradually being adopted.

- Surveys of victims reveal information about crimes that are not reported to police. The NCVS includes detailed information about personal and household incidents, but it does not count crimes against businesses or individual victims under age 12.

- Self-report surveys were developed to measure crimes with unclear victims that are less often detected by police. Two surveys estimate drug use among high school seniors and adults.

- The creation of specific, reliable measures often seems to diminish the richness of meaning our general concepts have. A good solution is to use multiple measures, each of which taps different aspects of the concept.

- Composite measures, formed by combining two or more variables, are often more valid measures of complex criminal justice concepts.

## KEY TERMS

conception, p. 75

concepts, p. 75

conceptualization, p. 76

dimension, p. 77

conceptual definition, p. 77

operational definition, p. 78

nominal measures, p. 82

ordinal measures, p. 82

interval measures, p. 83

ratio measures, p. 83

reliability, p. 85

face validity, p. 87

criterion-related validity, p. 87

construct validity, p. 88

summary-based measure, p. 92

incident-based measures, p. 92

victim survey, p. 94

self-report surveys, p. 95

typology, p. 98

## REVIEW QUESTIONS AND EXERCISES

1. Review the box titled "What Is Recidivism?" on page 79. From that discussion, write conceptual and operational definitions for recidivism. Summarize how Fabelo proposes to measure the concept. Finally, discuss possible reliability and validity issues associated with Fabelo's proposed measure.

2. We all have some sort of mental image of the pace of life. In a fascinating book titled *A Geography of Time*, Robert Levine (1997) operationalized the pace of life in cities around the world with a composite measure of the following:

   a. How long it took a single pedestrian to walk 60 feet on an uncrowded sidewalk

   b. What percentage of public clocks displayed the correct time

   c. How long it took to purchase the equivalent of a first-class postage stamp with the equivalent of a $5 bill

   Discuss possible reliability and validity issues with these indicators of the pace of life. Be sure to specify a conceptual definition for pace of life.

3. Measuring gang-related crime is an example of trying to measure a particular dimension of crime: motive. Other examples are hate crimes, terrorism, and drug-related crimes. Specify conceptual and operational definitions for at least one of these types. Find one newspaper story and one research report that present an example.

## ADDITIONAL READINGS

Best, Joel, *Damned Lies and Statistics: Untangling Numbers from the Media, Politicians, and Activists* (Berkeley: University of California Press, 2001). Despite the title, much of this entertaining and informative book describes problems with measurement. For example, page 45 tells us: "Measuring involves deciding how to go about counting." Best emphasizes how ambiguity in measures of social problems makes it easy for advocates to exaggerate the frequency of such problems. Mass media often report

and perpetuate errorful measures. The result, Best informs us, are mutant statistics.

Bureau of Justice Statistics, *Performance Measures for the Criminal Justice System* (Washington, DC: U.S. Department of Justice, Office of Justice Programs, Bureau of Justice Statistics, 1993). This collection of essays by prominent criminal justice researchers focuses on developing measures for evaluation uses. The discussion of general measurement issues as encountered in different types of justice agencies is uncommonly thoughtful. You will find this a provocative discussion of how to measure important constructs in corrections, trial courts, and policing. See especially the general essays by John DiIulio and James Q. Wilson.

Gaes, Gerald G., Scott D. Camp, Julianne B. Nelson, and William G. Saylor, *Measuring Prison Performance: Government Privatization and Accountability* (Walnut Creek, CA: AltaMira Press, 2004). This book stemmed partly from the BJS report, as an effort to expand how to measure the various dimensions of prisons. Another stated goal of the authors is to devise a system for comparing the performance of public and private correctional facilities. This is an excellent resource for anyone interested in corrections.

Hough, Mike, and Mike Maxfield (eds.), *Surveying Crime in the 21st Century*, Crime Prevention Studies, vol. 22 (Monsey, NY: Criminal Justice Press, 2007). This collection of essays was produced to commemorate the 25th anniversary of the British Crime Survey. Contributors describe what they have learned from crime surveys in many research areas. In the concluding essay, the editors (with Pat Mayhew) suggest how crime surveys should be revised.

Moore, Mark H., and Anthony Braga, *The "Bottom Line" of Policing: What Citizens Should Value (and Measure) in Police Performance* (Washington, DC: Police Executive Research Forum, 2003). Although somewhat long-winded, the authors offer an exceptionally thoughtful discussion of measuring different dimensions of police performance.

# CHAPTER 5

# Experimental and Quasi-Experimental Designs

*We'll learn about the experimental approach to social scientific research. We'll consider a wide variety of experimental and other designs available to criminal justice researchers.*

## INTRODUCTION

*Experimentation is an approach to research best suited for explanation and evaluation.*

Research design in the most general sense involves devising a strategy for finding out something. We'll first discuss the experiment as a mode of scientific observation in criminal justice research. At base, experiments involve (1) taking action, and (2) observing the consequences of that action. Social scientific researchers typically select a group of subjects, do something to them, and observe the effect of what was done.

It is worth noting at the outset that experiments are often used in nonscientific human inquiry as well. We experiment copiously in our attempts to develop a more generalized understanding about the world we live in. We learn many skills through experimentation: riding a bicycle, driving a car, swimming, and so forth. Students discover how much studying is required for academic success through experimentation. Professors experiment to learn how much preparation is required for successful lectures.

Experimentation is especially appropriate for hypothesis testing and evaluation. Suppose we are interested in studying alcohol abuse among college students and in discovering ways to reduce it. We might hypothesize that acquiring an understanding about the health consequences of binge drinking and long-term alcohol use will have the effect of reducing alcohol abuse. We can test this hypothesis experimentally. To begin, we might ask a group of experimental subjects how much beer, wine, or spirits they drank on the previous day and how frequently, in an average week, they consume alcohol for the specific purpose of getting drunk. Next, we might show these subjects a video depicting the various physiological effects of chronic drinking and binge drinking. Finally—say, one month later—we might again ask the subjects about their use of alcohol in the previous week to determine whether watching the video reduced alcohol use.

You might typically think of experiments as being conducted in laboratories under carefully controlled conditions. Although this may be true in the natural sciences, few social scientific experiments take place in laboratory settings. The most notable exception to this occurs in the discipline of psychology, in which laboratory experiments are common. Criminal justice experiments are almost always conducted in field settings outside the laboratory.

## THE CLASSICAL EXPERIMENT

*Variables, time order, measures, and groups are the central features of the classical experiment.*

Like much of the vocabulary of research, the word *experiment* has acquired both a general and a specialized meaning. So far, we have referred to the general meaning, defined by David Farrington, Lloyd Ohlin, and James Q. Wilson (1986, 65) as "a systematic attempt to test a causal hypothesis about the effect of variations in one factor (the independent variable) on another (the dependent variable).... The defining feature of an experiment lies in the control of the independent variable by the experimenter." In a narrower sense, the term *experiment* refers to a specific way of structuring research, usually called the **classical experiment**. In this section, we examine the requirements and components of the classical experiment. Later in the chapter we will consider designs that can be used when some of the requirements for classical experiments cannot be met.

The most conventional type of experiment in the natural and the social sciences involves three major pairs of components: (1) independent and dependent variables, (2) pretesting and posttesting, and (3) experimental and control groups. We will now consider each of those components and the way they are put together in the execution of an experiment.

### Independent and Dependent Variables

Essentially, an experiment examines the effect of an **independent variable** on a **dependent variable**. Typically the independent variable takes the form of an experimental stimulus that is either present or absent—that is, having two attributes. In the example concerning alcohol abuse, how often subjects used alcohol is the dependent variable and exposure to a video about alcohol's effects is the independent variable. The researcher's hypothesis suggests that levels of alcohol use depend, in part, on understanding its physiological and health effects. The purpose of the experiment is to test the validity of this hypothesis.

The independent and dependent variables appropriate to experimentation are nearly limitless. It should be noted, moreover, that a given variable might serve as an independent variable in one experiment and as a dependent variable in another. Alcohol use is the dependent variable in our example, but it might be the independent variable in an experiment that examines the effects of alcohol abuse on academic performance.

Recalling our discussion of cause and effect in Chapter 3, the independent variable is the cause and the dependent variable is the effect. Thus we might say that watching the video causes a change in alcohol use or that reduced alcohol use is an effect of watching the video.

It is essential that both independent and dependent variables be operationally defined for the purposes of experimentation. Such operational definitions might involve a variety of observation methods. Responses to a questionnaire, for example, might be the basis for defining self-reported alcohol use on the previous day. Alternatively, alcohol use by subjects could be measured with a Breathalyzer® or other blood alcohol test.

### Pretesting and Posttesting

In the simplest experimental design, subjects are measured on a dependent variable (pretested), exposed to a stimulus that represents an independent variable, and then remeasured on the dependent variable (posttested). Differences noted between the first and second measurements on the dependent variable are then attributed to the influence of the independent variable.

In our example of alcohol use, we might begin by pretesting the extent of alcohol use among our experimental subjects. Using a questionnaire, we measure the extent of alcohol use reported by each

individual and the average level of alcohol use for the whole group. After showing subjects the video on the effects of alcohol, we administer the same questionnaire again. Responses given in this posttest permit us to measure the subsequent extent of alcohol use by each subject and the average level of alcohol use of the group as a whole. If we discover a lower level of alcohol use on the second administration of the questionnaire, we might conclude that the video indeed reduced the use of alcohol among the subjects.

In the experimental examination of behaviors such as alcohol use, we face a special practical problem relating to validity. As you can imagine, the subjects might respond differently to the questionnaires the second time, even if their level of drinking remained unchanged. During the first administration of the questionnaire, the subjects might have been unaware of its purpose. By the time of the second measurement, however, they might have figured out the purpose of the experiment, become sensitized to the questions about drinking, and changed their answers. Thus the video might *seem* to have reduced alcohol abuse although, in fact, it did not.

This is an example of a more general problem that plagues many forms of criminal justice research: the very act of studying something may change it. Techniques for dealing with this problem in the context of experimentation are covered throughout the chapter.

### Experimental and Control Groups

The traditional way to offset the effects of the experiment itself is to use a **control group**. Social scientific experiments seldom involve only the observation of an **experimental group**, to which a stimulus has been administered. Researchers also observe a control group, to which the experimental stimulus has not been administered.

In our example of alcohol abuse, two groups of subjects are examined. To begin, each group is administered a questionnaire designed to measure their alcohol use in general and binge drinking in particular. Then only one of the groups—the experimental group—is shown the video. Later, the researcher

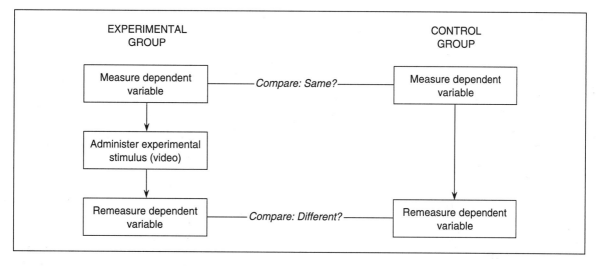

**F I G U R E 5.1** Basic Experimental Design

administers a posttest of alcohol use to both groups. Figure 5.1 illustrates this basic experimental design.

Using a control group allows the researcher to control for the effects of the experiment itself. If participation in the experiment itself, rather than the treatment, leads the subjects to report less alcohol use, then the effects of participation should occur in both the experimental and the control groups. If, on the one hand, the overall level of drinking exhibited by the control group decreases between the pretest and posttest as much as for the experimental group, then the apparent reduction in alcohol use must be a function of some external factor, not a function of watching the video specifically. In this situation, we can conclude that the video did not cause any change in alcohol use.

If, on the other hand, drinking decreases only in the experimental group, then we can be more confident in saying that the reduction is a consequence of exposure to the video (because that's the only difference between the two groups). Alternatively, if drinking decreases more in the experimental group than in the control group, then that too is grounds for assuming that watching the video reduced alcohol use.

The need for control groups in experimentation has been most evident in medical research. Patients who participate in medical experiments appear to improve, but it can be unclear how much of the improvement came from the experimental treatment and how much from the experiment. Now, in testing the effects of new drugs, medical researchers frequently administer a placebo (for example, sugar pills) to a control group. Thus the control group patients believe that they, like members of the experimental group, are receiving an experimental drug—and they often improve. If the new drug is effective, however, those who receive that drug will improve more than those who receive the placebo.

In criminal justice experiments, control groups are important as a guard against the effects of not only the experiments themselves but also events that may occur outside the laboratory during the course of experiments. Suppose the alcohol use experiment was being conducted on your campus and at that time a popular athlete was hospitalized for acute alcohol poisoning after he and a chum drank a bottle of rum. This event might shock the experimental subjects and thereby decrease their reported drinking. Because such an effect should happen about equally for members of the control and experimental groups, lower levels of reported alcohol use in the experimental group than in the control group would again demonstrate the impact of the experimental stimulus: watching the video that describes the health effects of alcohol abuse.

Sometimes an experimental design requires more than one experimental or control group. In the case of the alcohol video, we might also want to examine the impact of participating in group discussions about why college students drink alcohol, with the intent of demonstrating that peer pressure may promote drinking by people who would otherwise abstain. We might design our experiment around three experimental groups and one control group. One experimental group would see the video and participate in the group discussions, another would only see the video, and still another would only participate in group discussions; the control group would do neither. With this kind of design, we could determine the impact of each stimulus separately, as well as their combined effect.

## Double-Blind Experiments

As we saw with medical experimentation, patients sometimes improve when they think they are receiving a new drug; thus it is often necessary to administer a placebo to a control group.

Sometimes experimenters have this same tendency to prejudge results. In medical research, the experimenters may be more likely to "observe" improvements among patients who receive the experimental drug than among those receiving the placebo. That would be most likely, perhaps, for the researcher who developed the drug. A double-blind experiment eliminates this possibility because neither the subjects nor the experimenters know which is the experimental group and which is the control. In medical experiments, those researchers who are responsible for administering the drug and for noting improvements are not told which subjects receive the drug. Thus both researchers and subjects are blind with respect to who is receiving the experimental drug and who is getting the placebo. Another researcher knows which subjects are in which group, but that person is not responsible for administering the experiment.

## Selecting Subjects

Before beginning an experiment, we must make two basic decisions about who will participate. First, we must decide on the target population—the group to which the results of our experiment will apply. If our experiment is designed to determine, for example, whether restitution is more effective than probation in reducing recidivism, our target population is some group of persons convicted of crimes. In our hypothetical experiment about the effects of watching a video on the health consequences of alcohol abuse, the target population might be college students.

Second, we must decide how particular members of the target population will be selected for the experiment. In most cases, the methods used to select subjects must meet the scientific norm of generalizability; it should be possible to generalize from the sample of subjects studied to the population those subjects represent.

Aside from the question of generalizability, the cardinal rule of subject selection and experimentation is the comparability of the experimental and control groups. Ideally, the control group represents what the experimental group would have been like if it had not been exposed to the experimental stimulus. It is essential, therefore, that the experimental and control groups be as similar as possible.

## Randomization

Having recruited, by whatever means, a group of subjects, we randomly assign those subjects to either the experimental or the control group. This might be accomplished by numbering all the subjects serially and selecting numbers by means of a random-number table. Or we might assign the odd-numbered subjects to the experimental group and the even-numbered subjects to the control group.

**Randomization** is a central feature of the classical experiment. The most important characteristic of randomization is that it produces experimental and control groups that are statistically equivalent. Put another way, randomization reduces possible sources of systematic bias in assigning subjects to groups. The basic principle is simple: if subjects are assigned to experimental and control groups through a random process such as flipping a coin, the assignment process is said to be unbiased and the resultant groups are equivalent.

Although the rationale underlying this principle is a bit complex, understanding how randomization produces equivalent groups is a key point. David Farrington and associates (Farrington, Ohlin, and Wilson 1986, 66) compare randomization in criminal justice research to laboratory controls in the natural sciences:

> The control of extraneous variables by randomization is similar to the control of extraneous variables in the physical sciences by holding physical conditions (e.g., temperature, pressure) constant. Randomization insures that the average unit in [the] treatment group is approximately equivalent to the average unit in another [group] before the treatment is applied.

You've surely heard the expression "All other things being equal." Randomization makes it possible to assume that all other things are equal.

## EXPERIMENTS AND CAUSAL INFERENCE

*Experiments potentially control for many threats to the validity of causal inference, but researchers must remain aware of these threats.*

The central features of the classical experiment are independent and dependent variables, pretesting and posttesting, and experimental and control groups created through random assignment. Think of these features as building blocks of a research design to demonstrate a cause-and-effect relationship. This point will become clearer by comparing the criteria for causality, discussed in Chapter 3, to the features of the classical experiment, as shown in Figure 5.2.

The experimental design ensures that the cause precedes the effect in time by taking posttest measurements of the dependent variable after introducing the experimental stimulus. The second criterion for causation—an empirical correlation between the cause-and-effect variables—is determined by comparing the pretest (in which the experimental stimulus is not present) to the posttest for the experimental group (after the experimental stimulus is administered). A change in pretest to posttest measures demonstrates correlation.

The final requirement is to show that the observed correlation between cause and effect is not due to the influence of a third variable. The classical experiment makes it possible to satisfy this criterion for cause in two ways. First, the posttest measures for the experimental group (stimulus present) are compared with those for the control group (stimulus not present). If the observed correlation between the stimulus and the dependent variable is due to some other factor, then the two posttest scores will be similar. Second, random assignment produces experimental and control groups that are

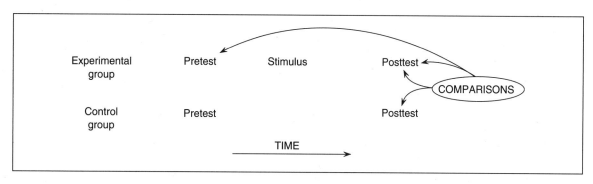

**FIGURE 5.2** Another Look at the Classical Experiment

equivalent and will not differ on some other variable that could account for the empirical correlation between cause and effect.

## Experiments and Threats to Validity

The classical experiment is designed to satisfy the three requirements for demonstrating cause-and-effect relationships. But what about threats to the validity of causal inference? We mentioned validity threats in Chapter 3. Here, we consider different types of validity threats and describe how the classical experiment reduces many of them. Our discussion draws mostly on the book by William Shadish, Thomas Cook, and Donald Campbell (2002). We present these threats in a slightly different order than those authors, beginning with threats to internal validity.

## Threats to Internal Validity

The problem of threats to **internal validity** refers to the possibility that conclusions drawn from experimental results may not accurately reflect what went on in the experiment itself. Put differently, conclusions about cause and effect may be biased in some systematic way. Shadish, Cook, and Campbell (2002, 54–60) pointed to several sources of the problem. As you read about these different threats to internal validity, keep in mind that each is an example of a simple point: possible ways researchers might be wrong in inferring causation.

**History**    Historical events may occur during the course of the experiment that confound the experimental results. The hospitalization of a popular athlete for acute alcohol poisoning during an experiment on reducing alcohol use is an example.

**Maturation**    People are continually growing and changing, whether in an experiment or not, and those changes affect the results of the experiment. In a long-term experiment, the fact that the subjects grow older may have an effect. In shorter experiments, they may become tired, sleepy, bored, or hungry, or change in other ways that affect their behavior in the experiment. A long-term study of alcohol abuse might reveal a decline in binge drinking as the subjects mature.

History and maturation are similar in that they represent a correlation between cause and effect that is due to something other than the independent variable. They're different in that history represents something that's outside the experiment altogether, whereas maturation refers to change within the subjects themselves.

**Testing**    Often the process of testing and retesting influences people's behavior and thereby confounds the experimental results. Suppose we administer a questionnaire to a group as a way of measuring their alcohol use. Then we administer an experimental stimulus and remeasure their alcohol use. By the time we conduct the posttest, the subjects may have gotten more sensitive to the issue of alcohol use and so provide different answers. In fact, they may believe we are trying to determine whether they drink too much. Because excessive drinking is frowned on by university authorities, our subjects will be on their best behavior and give answers that they think we want or that will make them look good.

**Instrumentation**    Thus far we haven't said much about the process of measurement in pretesting and posttesting, and it's appropriate to keep in mind the problems of conceptualization and operationalization discussed in Chapter 4. If we use different measures of the dependent variable (say, different questionnaires about alcohol use), how can we be sure that they are comparable? Perhaps alcohol use seems to have decreased simply because the pretest measure was more sensitive than the posttest measure.

Or if the measurements are being made by the experimenters, their procedures may change over the course of the experiment. You probably recognize this as a problem with reliability. Instrumentation is always a potential problem in criminal justice research that uses secondary sources of information such as police records about crime or court records about probation violations. There may be changes in how probation violations are defined or changes in the record-keeping practices of police departments.

In general, testing refers to changes in how subjects respond to measurement, whereas instrumentation is concerned with changes in the measurement process itself. If police officers respond differently to pretest and posttest questionnaires about prejudice, for example, that is a testing problem. However, if different questionnaires about prejudice are used in pretest and posttest measurements, instrumentation is a potential threat.

**Statistical Regression**   Sometimes it's appropriate to conduct experiments on subjects who start out with extreme scores on the dependent variable. Many sentencing policies, for example, target chronic offenders. Commonly referred to as *regression to the mean*, this threat to validity can emerge whenever researchers are interested in extreme cases. As a simple example, statisticians often point out that extremely tall people as a group are likely to have children shorter than themselves, and extremely short people as a group are likely to have children taller than themselves. The danger, then, is that changes occurring by virtue of subjects starting out in extreme positions will be attributed erroneously to the effects of the experimental stimulus.

Statistical regression can also be at work in aggregate analysis of changes in crime rates. For example, some researchers initially viewed declines in crime rates throughout U.S. cities in the 1990s as a return to more normal levels of crime after abnormally high rates in the 1980s.

**Selection Biases**   Randomization eliminates the potential for systematic bias in selecting subjects, but subjects may be chosen in other ways that threaten validity. Volunteers are often solicited for experiments conducted on college campuses. Students who volunteer for an experiment may not be typical of students as a whole, however. Volunteers may be more interested in the subject of the experiment and more likely to respond to a stimulus.

A common type of selection bias in applied criminal justice studies results from the natural caution of public officials. Let's say you are a bail commissioner in a large city, and the mayor wants to try a new program to increase the number of arrested

persons who are released on bail. The mayor asks you to decide what kinds of defendants should be eligible for release and informs you that staff from the city's criminal justice services agency will be evaluating the program. In establishing eligibility criteria, you will probably try to select defendants who will not be arrested again while on bail and defendants who will most likely show up for scheduled court appearances. In other words, you will try to select participants who are least likely to fail. This is a threat to validity because the low-risk persons selected for release, although most likely to succeed, do not represent the jail population as a whole.

**Experimental Mortality**   Experimental subjects often drop out of an experiment before it is completed, and that can affect statistical comparisons and conclusions. This is termed *experimental mortality*, also known as *attrition*. In the classical experiment involving an experimental and a control group, each with a pretest and a posttest, suppose that the heavy drinkers in the experimental group are so turned off by the video on the health effects of binge drinking that they tell the experimenter to forget it and leave. Those subjects who stick around for the posttest were less heavy drinkers to start with, and the group results will thus reflect a substantial "decrease" in alcohol use.

Mortality may also be a problem in experiments that take place over a long period (people may move away) or in experiments that require a substantial commitment of effort or time by subjects; they may become bored with the study or simply decide it's not worth the effort.

**Ambiguous Causal Time Order**   In criminal justice research, there may be ambiguity about the time order of the experimental stimulus and the dependent variable. Whenever this occurs, the research conclusion that the stimulus caused the dependent variable can be challenged with the explanation that the "dependent" variable actually caused changes in the stimulus. Many early studies of the relationship between different types of punishments and rates of offending exhibited this threat to validity by relying on single interviews with subjects who were asked how they viewed alternative punishments and whether they had committed any crimes.

## Ruling Out Threats to Internal Validity

The classical experiment, coupled with proper subject selection and assignment, can *potentially* handle each of these threats to internal validity. Let's look again at the classical experiment, presented graphically in Figure 5.2.

Pursuing the example of the educational video as an attempt to reduce alcohol abuse, if we use the experimental design shown in Figure 5.2, we should expect two findings. For the experimental group, the frequency of drinking measured in their posttest should be less than in their pretest. In addition, when the two posttests are compared, the experimental group should have less drinking than the control group.

This design guards against the problem of history because anything occurring outside the experiment that might affect the experimental group should also affect the control group. There should still be a difference in the two posttest results. The same comparison guards against problems of maturation as long as the subjects have been randomly assigned to the two groups. Testing and instrumentation should not be problems because both the experimental and the control groups are subject to the same tests and experimenter effects. If the subjects have been assigned to the two groups randomly, statistical regression should affect both equally, even if people with extreme scores on drinking (or whatever the dependent variable is) are being studied. Selection bias is ruled out by the random assignment of subjects.

Experimental mortality can be more complicated to handle because dropout rates may be different between the experimental and control groups. The experimental treatment itself may increase mortality in the group exposed to the video. As a result, the group of experimental subjects that received the posttest will differ from the group that received the pretest. In our example of the alcohol video, it would probably not be possible to handle

this problem by administering a placebo, for instance. In general, however, the potential for mortality can be reduced by shortening the time between pretest and posttest, by emphasizing to subjects the importance of completing the posttest, or perhaps by offering cash payments for participating in all phases of the experiment.

The remaining problems of internal invalidity can be avoided through the careful administration of a controlled experimental design. We emphasize *careful administration*. Random assignment, pretest and posttest measures, and use of control and experimental groups do not automatically rule out threats to validity. This caution is especially true in field studies and evaluation research, in which subjects participate in natural settings and uncontrolled variation in the experimental stimulus may be present. Control over experimental conditions is the hallmark of this approach, but conditions in field settings are usually more difficult to control.

For example, Richard Berk and associates (2003) randomly assigned several thousand inmates entering California prisons to an experimental or traditional (control) procedure for classifying inmate risk. That was a straightforward intervention that was easily administered and unlikely to vary much; classification also took place over a short period of time. In contrast, Denise Gottfredson and colleagues (2006) conducted a classical experiment to assess the effects of drug courts in reducing recidivism. Drug courts involve a range of interventions that are more difficult to standardize. The treatment—drug-court participation—can take place over a long period of time. Researchers examined how long individuals stayed in drug-court treatment, but they acknowledged that the quality of treatment was more difficult to control and could have varied quite a lot.

## Generalizability and Threats to Validity

Potential threats to internal validity are only some of the complications faced by experimenters. They also have the problem of generalizing from experimental findings to the real world. Even if the results of an experiment are an accurate gauge of what happened during that experiment, do they really tell us anything about life in the wilds of society? With our examination of cause and effect in Chapter 3 in mind, we consider two dimensions of **generalizability**: construct validity and external validity.

**Threats to Construct Validity** In the language of experimentation, **construct validity** is the correspondence between the empirical test of a hypothesis and the underlying causal process that the experiment is intended to represent. Construct validity is thus concerned with generalizing from our observations in an experiment to causal processes in the real world. In our hypothetical example, the educational video is how we operationalize the construct of understanding the health effects of alcohol abuse. Our questionnaire represents the dependent construct of actual alcohol use.

Are these reasonable ways to represent the underlying causal process in which understanding the effects of alcohol use causes people to reduce excessive or abusive drinking? It's a reasonable representation but also one that is certainly incomplete. People develop an understanding of the health effects of alcohol use in many ways. Watching an educational video is one way; having personal experience, talking to friends and parents, taking other courses, and reading books and articles are others. Our video may do a good job of representing the health effects of alcohol use, but it is an incomplete representation of that construct. Alternatively, the video may be poorly produced, too technical, or incomplete. Then the experimental stimulus may not adequately represent the construct we are interested in—educating students about the health effects of alcohol use. There may also be problems with our measure of the dependent variable: questionnaire items on self-reported alcohol use.

By this time, you should recognize a similarity between construct validity and some of the measurement issues discussed in Chapter 4. Almost any empirical example or measure of a construct is incomplete. Much of construct validity involves how completely an empirical measure can represent a construct or how well we can generalize from a measure to a construct.

A related issue in construct validity is whether a given level of treatment is sufficient. Perhaps showing a single video to a group of subjects would have little effect on alcohol use, but administering a series of videos over several weeks would have a greater impact. We could test this experimentally by having more than one experimental group and varying the number of videos seen by different groups.

**Threats to External Validity** Will an experimental study, conducted with the kind of control we have emphasized here, produce results that would also be found in more natural settings? Can an intensive probation program shown to be successful in Minneapolis achieve similar results in Miami? **External validity** represents a slightly different form of generalizability, one in which the question is whether results from experiments in one setting (time and place) will be obtained in other settings or whether a treatment found to be effective for one population will have similar effects on a different group.

Threats to external validity are greater for experiments conducted under carefully controlled conditions. If the alcohol education experiment reveals that drinking decreased among students in the experimental group, then we can be confident that viewing the video led to reduced alcohol use among our experimental subjects. But will the video have the same effect on high school students or adults if it is broadcast on television? We cannot be certain because the carefully controlled conditions of the experiment might have had something to do with the video's effectiveness.

In contrast, criminal justice field experiments are conducted in more natural settings. Real probation officers in different local jurisdictions deliver intensive supervision to real probationers. This is not to say that external validity is never a problem in field experiments. But one of the advantages of field experiments in criminal justice is that, because they take place under real-world conditions, results are more likely to be valid in other real-world settings as well.

You may have detected a fundamental conflict between internal and external validity. Threats to internal validity are reduced by conducting experiments under carefully controlled conditions. But such conditions do not reflect real-world settings, and this restricts our ability to generalize results. Field experiments generally have greater external validity, but their internal validity may suffer because such studies are more difficult to monitor than those taking place in more controlled settings. John Eck describes this trade-off as a diabolical dilemma (Eck 2002, 104).

Shadish, Cook, and Campbell (2002, 98–101) offer some useful advice for resolving the potential for conflict between internal and external validity. Explanatory studies that test cause-and-effect theories should place greater emphasis on internal validity, whereas applied studies should be more concerned with external validity. This is not a hard and fast rule because internal validity must be established before external validity becomes an issue. That is, applied researchers must have confidence in the internal validity of their cause-and-effect relationships before they ask whether similar relationships would be found in other settings.

### Threats to Statistical Conclusion Validity

**Statistical conclusion validity** refers to whether we are able to determine if two variables are related. Statistical conclusion validity most often becomes an issue when findings are based on small samples of cases. Because experiments can be costly and time consuming, they are frequently conducted with relatively small numbers of subjects. In such cases, only large differences between experimental and control groups on posttest measures can be detected with any degree of confidence.

In practice, this means that finding cause-and-effect relationships through experiments depends on two related factors: (1) the number of subjects, and (2) the magnitude of posttest differences between the experimental and control groups. Experiments with large numbers of cases may be able to reliably detect small differences, but experiments with smaller numbers can detect only large differences.

Threats to statistical conclusion validity can be magnified by other difficulties in field experiments. Unreliable measurement is one such problem that is often encountered in criminal justice research. More generally, David Weisburd and associates (1993) concluded, after reviewing a large number of criminal justice experiments, that failure to maintain control over experimental conditions reduces statistical conclusion validity even for studies with large numbers of subjects.

## VARIATIONS IN THE CLASSICAL EXPERIMENTAL DESIGN

*The basic experimental design is adapted to meet different research applications.*

We now turn to a more systematic consideration of variations on the classical experiment that can be produced by manipulating the building blocks of experiments.

Slightly restating our earlier remarks, four basic building blocks are present in experimental designs: (1) the number of experimental and control groups, (2) the number and variation of experimental stimuli, (3) the number of pretest and posttest measurements, and (4) the procedures used to select subjects and assign them to groups. By way of illustrating these building blocks and the ways they are used to produce different designs, we adopt the widely used system of notation introduced by Donald Campbell and Julian Stanley (1966). Figure 5.3 presents this notation and shows how it is used to represent the classical experiment and examples of variations on this design.

In Figure 5.3, the letter $O$ represents observations or measurements, and $X$ represents an experimental stimulus or treatment. Different time points are displayed as $t$, with a subscript number to represent time order. Thus for the classical experiment shown in Figure 5.3, $O$ at $t_1$ is the pretest, $O$ at $t_3$ is the posttest, and the experimental stimulus, $X$, is administered to the experimental group at $t_2$, between the pretest and posttest. Measures are taken for the control group at times $t_1$ and $t_3$, but the

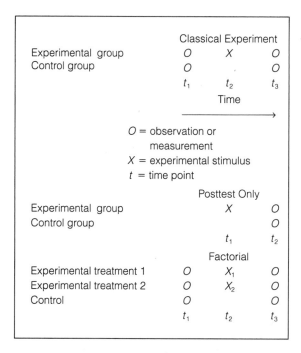

**FIGURE 5.3** Variations in the Experimental Design

experimental stimulus is not administered to the control group.

Now consider the design labeled "Posttest Only." As implied by its name, no pretest measures are made on either the experimental or the control group. Thinking for a moment about the threats to internal validity, we can imagine situations in which a posttest-only design is appropriate. Testing and retesting might especially influence subjects' behavior if measurements are made by administering a questionnaire, with subjects' responses to the posttest potentially affected by their experience in the pretest. A posttest-only design can reduce the possibility of testing being a threat to validity by eliminating the pretest.

Without a pretest, it is obviously not possible to detect change in measures of the dependent variable, but we can still test the effects of the experimental stimulus by comparing posttest measures for the experimental group with posttest measures for the control group. For example, if we are concerned about the possibility of sensitizing subjects in a study of an alcohol education video, we might

eliminate the pretest and examine the posttest differences between the experimental and control groups. Randomization is the key to the posttest-only design. If subjects are randomly assigned to experimental and control groups, we expect them to be equivalent. Any posttest differences between the two groups on the dependent variable can then be attributed to the influence of the video.

In general, posttest-only designs are appropriate when researchers suspect that the process of measurement may bias subjects' responses to a questionnaire or other instrument. This is more likely when only a short time elapses between pretest and posttest measurements. The number of observations made on subjects is a design building block that can be varied as needed. We emphasize here that random assignment is essential in a posttest-only design.

Figure 5.3 also shows a factorial design, which has two experimental groups that receive different treatments, or different levels of a single treatment, and one control group. This design is useful for comparing the effects of different interventions or different amounts of a single treatment. In evaluating a probation program, we might wish to compare how different levels of contact between probation officers and probation clients affect recidivism. In this case, subjects in one experimental group might receive weekly contact ($X_1$), the other experimental group be seen by probation officers twice each week ($X_2$), and control-group subjects have normal contact (say, monthly) with probation officers. Because more contact is more expensive than less contact, we would be interested in seeing how much difference in recidivism was produced by monthly, weekly, and twice-weekly contacts.

Thus an experimental design may have more than one group receiving different versions or levels of experimental treatment. We can also vary the number of measurements made on dependent variables. No hard and fast rules exist for using these building blocks to design a given experiment. A useful rule of thumb, however, is to keep the design as simple as possible to control for potential threats to validity. The specific design for any particular study depends on the research purpose, available resources, and unavoidable constraints in designing and actually carrying out the experiment.

One very common constraint is how subjects or units of analysis are selected and assigned to experimental or control groups. This building block brings us to the subject of quasi-experimental designs.

# QUASI-EXPERIMENTAL DESIGNS

*When randomization is not possible, researchers can use different types of quasi-experimental designs.*

By now, the value of random assignment in controlling threats to validity should be apparent. However, it is often impossible to randomly select subjects for experimental and control groups and satisfy other requirements. Most often, there may be practical or administrative obstacles. There may also be legal or ethical reasons randomization cannot be used in criminal justice experiments.

When randomization is not possible, the next-best choice is often a **quasi-experiment**. The prefix *quasi-*, meaning "to a certain degree," is significant—a quasi-experiment is, to a certain degree, an experiment. In most cases, quasi-experiments do not randomly assign subjects and therefore may suffer from the internal validity threats that are so well controlled in true experiments. Without random assignment, the other building blocks of experimental design must be used creatively to reduce validity threats. We group quasi-experimental designs into two categories: (1) nonequivalent-groups designs, and (2) time-series designs. Each can be represented with the same *O, X,* and *t* notation used to depict experimental designs.

## Nonequivalent-Groups Designs

The name for this family of designs is also meaningful. The main strength of random assignment is that it allows us to assume equivalence in experimental and control groups. When it is not possible to create groups through randomization, we must use some other procedure, one that is not random. If we construct groups

through a nonrandom procedure, however, we cannot assume that the groups are equivalent—hence the label *nonequivalent-groups design.*

Whenever experimental and control groups are not equivalent, we should select subjects in a way that makes the two groups as comparable as possible. Often the best way to achieve comparability is through a matching process in which subjects in the experimental group are matched with subjects in a comparison group. The term *comparison group* is commonly used, rather than *control group*, to highlight the nonequivalence of groups in quasi-experimental designs. A comparison group does, however, serve the same function as a control group.

Some examples of research that use nonequivalent-groups designs illustrate various approaches to matching and the creative use of experimental design building blocks. Examples include studies of child abuse (Widom 1989), obscene phone calls (Clarke 1997a), and video cameras for crime prevention (Gill and Spriggs 2005). Figure 5.4 shows a diagram of each design using the *X, O,* and *t* notation. The solid line that separates treatment and comparison groups in the figure signifies that subjects have been placed in groups through some nonrandom procedure.

**Child Abuse and Later Arrest**  Cathy Spatz Widom studied the long-term effects of child abuse—whether abused children are more likely to be charged with delinquent or adult criminal offenses than children who were not abused. Child abuse was the experimental stimulus, and the number of subsequent arrests was the dependent variable.

Of course, it is not possible to assign children randomly to groups in which some are abused and others are not. Widom's design called for selecting a sample of children who, according to court records, had been abused. She then matched each abused subject with a comparison subject—of the same gender, race, age, and approximate socioeconomic status (SES)—who had not been abused. The assumption with these matching criteria was that age at the time of abuse, gender, race, and SES differences might confound any observed relationship between abuse and subsequent arrests.

**Widom (1989)**

| | | |
|---|---|---|
| Treatment group | $X$ | $O$ |
| Comparison group | | $O$ |
| | $t_1$ | $t_2$ |

$X$ = official record of child abuse
$O$ = counts of juvenile or adult arrest

**Clarke (1997a)**

| | | | |
|---|---|---|---|
| Treatment group | $O$ | $X$ | $O$ |
| Comparison group | $O$ | | $O$ |
| | $t_1$ | $t_2$ | $t_3$ |

$X$ = caller identification and call tracing
$O$ = customer complaints of obscene calls

**Gill and Spriggs (2005)**

| | | | |
|---|---|---|---|
| Target area 1 | $O$ | $X_1$ | $O$ |
| Comparison area 1 | $O$ | | $O$ |
| Target area 2 | $O$ | $X_2$ | $O$ |
| Comparison area 2 | $O$ | | $O$ |
| Target area 13 | $O$ | $X_{13}$ | $O$ |
| Comparison area 13 | $O$ | | $O$ |
| | $t_1$ | $t_2$ | $t_3$ |

$X_i$ = CCTV installation in area $i$
$O$ = Police crime data, survey data on fear of crime

**FIGURE 5.4** Quasi-Experimental Design Examples

You may be wondering how a researcher selects important variables to use in matching experimental and comparison subjects. We cannot provide a definitive answer to that question, any more than we can specify what particular variables should be used in a given experiment. The answer ultimately depends on the nature and purpose of the experiment. As a general rule, however, the two groups should be comparable in terms of variables that are likely to be related to the dependent variable under study. Widom matched on gender, race, and SES because these variables are correlated with juvenile and adult arrest rates. Age at the time of reported abuse was also an important variable because children abused at a younger age had a longer "at-risk" period for delinquent arrests.

Widom produced experimental and comparison groups matching individual subjects. It is also possible to construct experimental and comparison groups through aggregate matching, in which the average characteristics of each group are comparable. This is illustrated in our next example.

**Deterring Obscene Phone Calls** In 1988, the New Jersey Bell telephone company introduced caller identification (ID) and instant call tracing in a small number of telephone exchange areas. Now ubiquitous in mobile phones, caller ID was a new technology in 1988. Instant call tracing allows the recipient of an obscene or threatening call to automatically initiate a procedure to trace the source of the call.

Ronald Clarke (1997a) studied the effects of these new technologies in deterring obscene phone calls. Clarke expected that obscene calls would decrease in areas where the new services were available. To test this, he compared records of formal customer complaints about annoying calls in the New Jersey areas that had the new services to formal complaints in other New Jersey areas where caller ID and call tracing were not available. One year later, the number of formal complaints had dropped sharply in areas serviced by the new technology; no decline was found in other New Jersey Bell areas.

In this study, telephone service areas with new services were the treatment group, and areas without the services were the comparison group. Clarke's matching criterion was a simple one: telephone service by New Jersey Bell, assuming the volume of obscene phone calls was relatively constant within a single phone service area. Of course, matching on telephone service area cannot eliminate the possibility that the volume of obscene phone calls varies from one part of New Jersey to another, but Clarke's choice of a comparison group was straightforward and certainly more plausible than comparing New Jersey to, say, New Mexico.

Clarke's study is a good example of a natural field experiment. The experimental stimulus—caller ID and call tracing—was not specifically introduced by Clarke, but he was able to obtain measures for the dependent variable before and after the experimental stimulus was introduced. This design made it possible for Clarke to infer with reasonable confidence that caller ID and call tracing reduced the number of formal complaints about obscene phone calls.

**Cameras and Crime Prevention** U.S. residents have probably become accustomed to seeing closed-circuit television (CCTV) cameras in stores and at ATMs, but this technology is less used in public spaces such as streets and parking lots. With an estimated 4 million cameras deployed, CCTV is widely used as a crime prevention and surveillance tool in the United Kingdom (McCahill and Norris 2003). CCTV enabled the London Metropolitan Police to quickly identify suspects in the Underground bombing attacks that took place in 2005. Cameras are increasingly used to monitor traffic and even to record license plates of cars running traffic lights. But does CCTV have any effect in reducing crime?

Martin Gill and associates (Gill and Spriggs 2005; Gill et al. 2005) conducted an evaluation of 13 CCTV projects installed in a variety of residential and commercial settings in England. These were a mix of smaller and large-scale CCTV projects involving multiple cameras. One area on the outskirts of London included more than 500 cameras installed to reduce thefts of and from vehicles in parking facilities. Five projects in London and other urban areas placed 10 to 15 cameras in low-income housing areas, seeking to reduce burglary and robbery. Researchers examined two types of dependent variables before and after cameras were installed: crimes reported to police and fear of crime. Fear was measured through surveys of people living in residential areas and interviews with people on local streets for commercial areas and parking facilities.

Measuring police data and fear of crime before and after cameras were installed made it possible for Gill and associates to satisfy two criteria for cause—time order and covariation between the independent variable (CCTV) and dependent variables. However, they were not able to randomly assign some areas to receive the CCTV intervention while other areas did not. This was because the intervention was planned for only a small number of locations of each type (residential, commercial, parking) and also because CCTV was carefully tailored to each site. Instead, the researchers created two types of comparison areas. First, comparison areas were similar on sociodemographic and geographical characteristics, together with types of crime problems. The second type of comparison was "buffer zones," defined as an area in a one-mile radius from the edge of the target area where CCTV cameras were installed; buffer zones were defined only for CCTV areas.

The rationale for comparison areas is clear. If CCTV is effective in reducing crime, we should expect declines in target areas, but not in comparison areas. Alternatively, if post-treatment measures of crime went down in both treatment and comparison areas, we might expect greater declines in the CCTV sites. But what about buffer areas? After defining buffer areas, researchers then subdivided them into concentric rings around a target area, shown as $T$ in Figure 5.5. The stated purpose was to assess any movement of crime around the target area. If CCTV was effective in reducing crime, any reduction should be greatest in the target area; the size of the reduction should decline moving outward from the target area.

Short-term results found some reduction of some types of crime in some CCTV areas. In other treatment areas, some crimes increased more than in comparison areas. In particular, Gill and Spriggs found that public order offenses such as drunkenness tended to *increase* more in CCTV target areas. Overall, significant drops in crime were found in just 2 of 13 target areas. Fear and related attitudes declined in all target and comparison areas, but the authors believed this was largely due to declining crime in all areas.

This example illustrates why nonequivalent comparison groups are important. Because crime

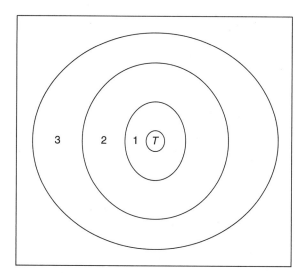

**FIGURE 5.5**  Buffer Zones in CCTV Quasi-Experiment
*Source:* Adapted from Gill and Spriggs (2005, 40).

declined in most areas and fear declined in all, a simple comparison of pre-and post-intervention measures would have been misleading. That strategy would have suggested that CCTV was responsible for reduced crime and fear. Only by adding the comparison and buffer areas to their research were Gill and Spriggs able to learn that CCTV was probably not the cause of declines, since similar patterns were found in many areas where CCTV systems were not installed.

Together, these three studies illustrate different approaches to research design when it is not possible to randomly assign subjects to treatment and control groups. Lacking random assignment, researchers must use creative procedures for selecting subjects, constructing treatment and comparison groups, measuring dependent variables, and exercising other controls to reduce possible threats to validity.

## Cohort Designs

Chapter 3 mentioned cohort studies as examples of longitudinal designs. We can also view cohort studies as a type of nonequivalent-groups design. Recall from Chapter 3 that a cohort may be defined as a group of subjects who enter or leave an institution at the same time. For example, a class of police officers who graduate from a training academy at the same time could be considered a cohort. Or we might view all persons who were sentenced to probation in May as a cohort.

Now think of a cohort that is exposed to some experimental stimulus. The May probation cohort might be required to complete 100 hours of community service in addition to meeting other conditions of probation. If we are interested in whether probationers who receive community service sentences are charged with fewer probation violations, we can compare the performance of the May cohort with that of the April cohort, or the June cohort, or some other cohort not sentenced to community service.

Cohorts that do not receive community service sentences serve as comparison groups. The groups are not equivalent because they were not created by random assignment. But if we assume that a comparison cohort does not systematically differ from a treatment cohort on important variables, we can use this design to determine whether community service sentences reduce probation violations.

That last assumption is very important, but it may not be viable. Perhaps a criminal court docket is organized to schedule certain types of cases at the same time, so a May cohort would be systematically different from a June cohort. But if the assumption of comparability can be met, cohorts may be used to construct nonequivalent comparison and experimental groups by taking advantage of the natural flow of cases through an institutional process.

## Time-Series Designs

Time-series designs are common examples of longitudinal studies in criminal justice research. As the name implies, a time-series design involves examining a series of observations on some variable over time. A simple example is examining trends in arrests for drunk driving over time to see whether the number of arrests is increasing, decreasing, or staying constant. A police executive might be interested in keeping track of arrests for drunk driving, or for other offenses, as a way of monitoring the performance of patrol officers. Or state corrections officials might want to study trends in prison admissions as a way of predicting the future need for correctional facilities.

An interrupted time series is a special type of time-series design that can be used in cause-and-effect studies. A series of observations is compared before and after an intervention is introduced. For example, a researcher might want to know whether roadside sobriety checkpoints cause a decrease in fatal automobile accidents. Trends in accidents could be compared before and after the roadside checkpoints are established.

Interrupted time-series designs can be very useful in criminal justice research, especially in applied studies. They do have some limitations, however, just like other ways of structuring research. Shadish, Cook, and Campbell (2002) describe the strengths and limitations of different approaches to time-series designs. We will introduce these approaches with a hypothetical example and then describe some specific criminal justice applications.

Continuing with the example of sobriety checkpoints, Figure 5.6 presents four possible patterns of alcohol-related automobile accidents. The vertical line in each pattern shows the time when the roadside checkpoint program was introduced. Which of these patterns indicates that the new program caused a reduction in car accidents?

If the time-series results looked like Pattern 1 in Figure 5.6, we might think initially that the checkpoints caused a reduction in alcohol-related accidents, but there seems to be a general downward trend in accidents that continues after the intervention. It's safer to conclude that the decline would have continued even without the roadside checkpoints.

Pattern 2 shows that an increasing trend in auto accidents has been reversed after the intervention, but this appears to be due to a regular pattern in which accidents have been bouncing up and down. The intervention was introduced at the peak of an upward trend, and the later decline may be an arti-

fact of the underlying pattern rather than of the new program.

Patterns 1 and 2 exhibit some outside trend, rather than an intervention, that may account for a pattern observed over time. We may recognize this as an example of history as a validity threat to the inference that the new checkpoint program caused a change in auto accidents. The general decline in Pattern 1 may be due to reduced drunk driving that has nothing to do with sobriety checkpoints. Pattern 2 illustrates what is referred to as *seasonality* in a time series—a regular pattern of change over time. In our example, the data might reflect seasonal variation in alcohol-related accidents that occurs around holidays or maybe on football weekends near a college campus.

Patterns 3 and 4 lend more support to the inference that sobriety checkpoints caused a decline in alcohol-related accidents, but the two patterns are different in a subtle way. In Pattern 3, accidents decline more sharply from a general downward trend immediately after the checkpoint program was introduced, whereas Pattern 4 displays a sharper decline sometime after the new program was established. Which pattern provides stronger support for the inference?

In framing your answer, recall what we have said about construct validity. Think about the underlying causal process these two patterns represent, or consider possible mechanisms that might be at work. Pattern 3 suggests that the program was immediately effective and supports what we might call an incapacitation mechanism: roadside checkpoints enabled police to identify and arrest drunk drivers, thereby getting them off the road and reducing accidents. Pattern 4 suggests a deterrent mechanism: as drivers learned about the checkpoints, they less often drove after drinking, and accidents eventually declined. Either explanation is possible given the evidence presented. This illustrates an important limitation of interrupted time-series designs: they operationalize complex causal constructs in simple ways. Our interpretation depends in large part on how we understand this causal process.

The classic study by Richard McCleary and associates (McCleary, Nienstedt, and Erven 1982)

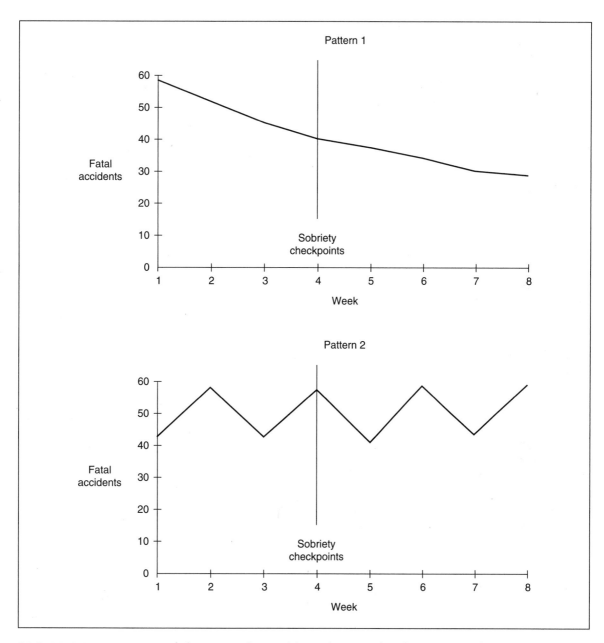

**F I G U R E 5.6** Four Patterns of Change in Fatal Automobile Accidents (Hypothetical Data) (*continued*)

illustrates the need to think carefully about how well time-series results reflect underlying causal patterns. McCleary and colleagues reported a sharp decline in burglaries immediately after a special

burglary investigation unit was established in a large city. This finding was at odds with their understanding of how police investigations could reasonably be expected to reduce burglary. A special unit

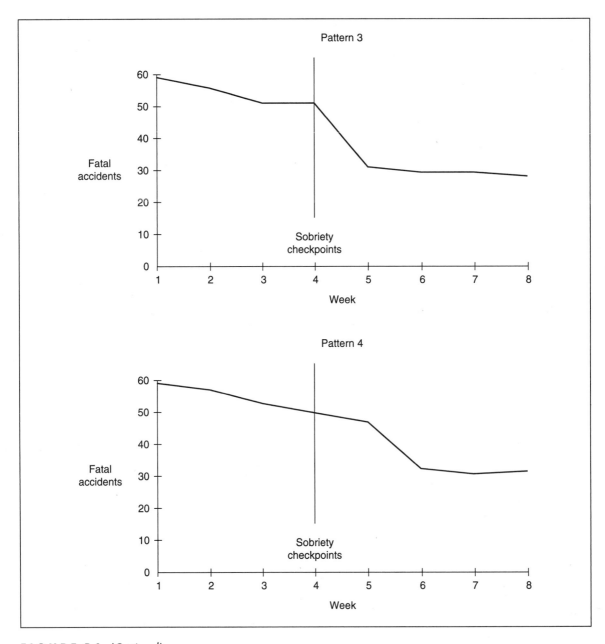

**FIGURE 5.6** *(Continued)*

might eventually be able to reduce the number of burglaries after investigating incidents over a period of time and making arrests. But it is highly unlikely that changing investigative procedures would have an immediate impact. This discrepancy prompted McCleary and associates to look more closely at the policy change and led to their conclusion that the apparent decline in burglaries was produced by changes in record-keeping practices. No evidence existed of any decline in the actual number of burglaries.

This example illustrates our discussion of instrumentation earlier in this chapter. Changes in the way police counted burglaries produced what appeared to be a reduction in burglary. Instrumentation can be a particular problem in time-series designs for two reasons. First, observations are usually made over a relatively long time period, which increases the likelihood of changes in measurement instruments. Second, time-series designs often use measures that are produced by an organization such as a police department, criminal court, probation office, or corrections department. There may be changes or irregularities in the way data are collected by these agencies that are not readily apparent to researchers and that are, in any case, not subject to their control.

## Variations in Time-Series Designs

If we view the basic interrupted time-series design as an adaptation of basic design building blocks, we can consider how modifications can help control for many validity problems. The simplest time-series design studies one group—the treatment group—over time. Rather than making one pretest and one posttest observation, the interrupted time-series design makes a longer series of observations before and after introducing an experimental treatment.

What if we considered the other building blocks of experimental design? Figure 5.7 presents the basic design and some variations using the familiar O, X, and t notation. In the basic design, shown at the top of Figure 5.7, many pretest and posttest observations are made on a single group that receives some type of treatment.

We could strengthen this design by adding a comparison series of observations on a group that does not receive the treatment. If, for example, roadside sobriety checkpoints were introduced all over the state of Ohio but were not used at all in Michigan, then we could compare auto accidents in Ohio (the treatment series) with auto accidents in Michigan (the comparison series). If checkpoints

caused a reduction in alcohol-related accidents, we would expect to see a decline in Ohio following the intervention, but there should be no change or a lesser decline in Michigan over the same time period. The second part of Figure 5.7 shows this design—an interrupted time series with a nonequivalent comparison group. The two series are not equivalent because we did not randomly assign drivers to Ohio or Michigan. Wesley Skogan and associates (2008) present a good example of this design in their analysis of police problem solving in Chicago. They compared changes in crime for police beats where specific problems were identified and addressed to comparison beats where no crime-specific interventions were developed.

A single-series design may be modified by introducing and then removing the intervention, as shown in the third part of Figure 5.7. We might test sobriety checkpoints by setting them up every weekend for a month and then not setting them up for the next few months. If the checkpoints

| Simple Interrupted Time Series | | | | | | | | |
|---|---|---|---|---|---|---|---|---|
| O | O | O | O | X | O | O | O | O |
| $t_1$ | $t_2$ | $t_3$ | $t_4$ | | $t_5$ | $t_6$ | $t_7$ | $t_8$ |

Interrupted Time Series with
Nonequivalent Comparison Group

| O | O | O | O | X | O | O | O | O |
|---|---|---|---|---|---|---|---|---|
| O | O | O | O | | O | O | O | O |
| $t_1$ | $t_2$ | $t_3$ | $t_4$ | | $t_5$ | $t_6$ | $t_7$ | $t_8$ |

Interrupted Time Series
with Removed Treatment

| O | O | X | O | O | O | –X | O | O | O |
|---|---|---|---|---|---|---|---|---|---|
| $t_1$ | $t_2$ | | $t_3$ | $t_4$ | $t_5$ | | $t_6$ | $t_7$ | $t_8$ |

Interrupted Time Series
with Switching Replications

| O | O | O | X | O | O | O | O | O |
|---|---|---|---|---|---|---|---|---|
| O | O | O | O | O | X | O | O | O |
| $t_1$ | $t_2$ | $t_3$ | $t_4$ | | $t_5$ | $t_6$ | $t_7$ | $t_8$ |

**F I G U R E  5.7**  Interrupted Time-Series Designs

caused a reduction in alcohol-related accidents, we might expect an increase after they were removed. Or the effects of weekend checkpoints might persist even after we removed them.

Because different states or cities sometimes introduce new drunk-driving programs at different times, we might be able to use what Shadish, Cook, and Campbell (2002, 192) called a "time-series design with switching replications." The bottom of Figure 5.7 illustrates this design. For example, assume that Ohio begins using checkpoints in May 2009 and Michigan introduces them in July of the same year. A switching-replications design could strengthen our conclusion that checkpoints reduce accidents if we saw that a decline in Ohio began in June and a similar pattern was found in Michigan beginning in August. The fact that similar changes occurred in the dependent variable in different states at different times, corresponding to when the program was introduced, would add to our confidence in stating that sobriety checkpoints reduced auto accidents.

# VARIABLE-ORIENTED RESEARCH, CASE STUDIES, AND SCIENTIFIC REALISM

*Case studies measure many variables for a small number of cases.*

Another way to think about a time-series design is as a study of one or a few cases with many observations. If we design a time-series study of roadside checkpoints in Ohio, we will be examining one case (Ohio) with many observations of auto accidents. Or a design that compares Ohio and Michigan will examine many observations for two cases. Thinking once again about design building blocks, notice how we have slightly restated one of those building blocks. Instead of considering the number of experimental and control *groups,* our attention centers on the number of subjects or *cases* in our study. In Figure 5.7, the first and third time-series designs have one case each, while the second and fourth designs examine two cases each.

Classical experiments and quasi-experiments with large numbers of subjects are examples of what Charles Ragin (2000) terms **case-oriented research**, in which many cases are examined to understand a small number of variables. Time-series designs and case studies are examples of **variable-oriented research**, in which a large number of variables are studied for a small number of cases or subjects. Suppose we wish to study inmate-on-inmate assaults in correctional facilities. With a case-oriented approach, we might send a questionnaire to a sample of 500 correctional facilities, asking facility staff to provide information about assaults, facility design, inmate characteristics, and housing conditions. Here, we are gathering information on a few variables from a large number of correctional facilities. Using a variable-oriented approach, we might visit one or a few facilities to conduct in-depth interviews with staff, observe the condition of facilities, and gather information from institutional records. Here, we are collecting information on a wide range of variables from a small number of institutions.

**Case studies** are examples of variable-oriented research. Here, the researcher's attention centers on an in-depth examination of one or a few cases on many dimensions. Robert Yin (2008) points out that the terms *case* and *case study* are used broadly. Cases can be individual people, neighborhoods, correctional facilities, courtrooms, or other aggregations.

Robert Yin cautions that the case-study design is often misunderstood as representing "qualitative" research or participant observation study. Instead, Yin advises that the case study is a design strategy and that the labels *qualitative* and *quantitative* are not useful ways to distinguish design strategies. Case studies might appear qualitative because they focus on one or a small number of units. But many case studies employ sophisticated statistical techniques to examine many variables for those units. An example illustrates how misleading it can be to associate case studies with qualitative research.

In what has come to be known as the "Boston Gun Project," Anthony Braga and associates (Braga et al. 2001) studied violence by youth gangs in Boston neighborhoods. Theirs was an applied explanatory

## THEORY AND DESIGN

Robert Yin (2008) describes the key role of theory in designing case studies, whether for descriptive or explanatory research. Theory describes what researchers think is going on, and *rival* theories provide alternative explanations. For example, Ronald Clarke and associates (Clarke, Contre, and Petrossian 2010) structured their evaluation of fare evasion in a mass transit system to assess alternative theories of how modifying penalties and enforcement would affect rates of violation. Much of their thinking and design drew on classical theories of deterrence.

Even more generally, Alex Hirschfield (2005, 634) summarizes how different theories of crime distribution offer different implications for analysis. Routine activity theory, for example, requires designing research to assess guardianship and the locations of potential victims and offenders. In crime pattern theory, the movement of victims and offenders in time and space plays a central role. Accordingly, designs that compare different areas are most appropriate.

Finally, consider our description of time-series design with nonequivalent variable comparison groups as a type of theory, something Shadish, Cook, and Campbell (2002) describe as *pattern matching*. When Wesley Skogan and associates (2008) compared change in crime rates within areas where specific police problem solving was introduced to areas where there was no such police action, they specified a theory-based pattern of effects that was supported by their analysis. Their expectations and analysis were based on a theory of action that described expected impacts of police deployment.

study. They worked with local officials to better understand gang violence, develop ways to reduce it, and eventually assess the effects of their interventions. Neither a classical experiment nor a nonequivalent-groups design was possible. Researchers sought to understand and reduce violence by all gangs in the city. Their research centered on gangs, not individuals, though some interventions targeted particular gang members.

Researchers collected a large amount of information about gangs and gang violence from several sources. They used network analysis to examine relationships between gangs in different neighborhoods and conflicts over turf within neighborhoods. Police records of homicides, assaults, and shootings were studied. Based on extensive data on a small number of gangs, researchers collaborated with public officials, neighborhood organizations, and a coalition of religious leaders—the "faith community." A variety of interventions were devised, but most were crafted from a detailed understanding of the specific nature of gangs and gang violence as they existed in Boston neighborhoods. David Kennedy (1998) summarizes these using the label "pulling levers," signifying that key gang members were vulnerable to intensive monitoring via probation or parole. The package

of strategies was markedly successful: youth homicides were reduced from about 35 to 40 each year in the 20 years preceding the program to about 15 per year in the first 5 postintervention years (Braga 2008).

The Boston research is also a good example of the scientific realist approach of Ray Pawson and Nick Tilley (1997). Researchers examined a small number of subjects—gangs and gang members—in a single city and in the context of specific neighborhoods where gangs were active. Extensive data were gathered on the mechanisms of gang violence. Interventions were tailored to those mechanisms in their context.

Braga and associates (2001) emphasize that the success of the Boston efforts was due to the *process* by which researchers, public officials, and community members collaboratively studied gang violence and then developed appropriate policy actions based on their analyses. Other jurisdictions mistakenly tried to reproduce Boston's interventions, with limited or no success, failing to recognize that the interventions were developed specifically for Boston. In case-study language, researchers examined many variables for one site and based policy decisions on that analysis. In the words of scientific realism, researchers studied the gang violence mechanism in the Boston context. In other contexts (Baltimore or Minneapolis, for example), gang violence operated as a different mechanism; the "levers" pulled in Boston did not work elsewhere. Braga and associates emphasize that the problem-solving process is exportable to other settings but that the interventions used in Boston are not (2001, 220).

How do case studies address threats to validity? In the most general sense, case studies attempt to isolate causal mechanisms from possible confounding influences by studying very precisely defined subjects. Donald Campbell (2003, ix–x) likened this to laboratory experiments in the natural sciences, in which researchers try to isolate causal variables from outside influences. Case-study research takes place in natural field settings, not in laboratories. But the logic of trying to isolate causal mechanisms by focusing on one or a few cases is a direct descendant of the rationale for experimental isolation in laboratories.

Figure 5.8 summarizes advice from Yin (2008, 40-41) on how to judge the quality of case-study designs in language that should now be familiar. Construct validity is established through multiple sources of evidence, the establishment of chains of causation that connect independent and dependent variables, and what are termed *member checks*— asking key informants to review tentative conclusions about causation. Examples of techniques for strengthening internal validity are theory-based pattern matching and time-series analysis. The first technique follows Shadish, Cook, and Campbell (2002), calling on researchers to make specific theory-based predictions about what pattern of results will support hypothesized causal relationships. Alternative explanations, also termed *rival hypotheses*, are less persuasive when specific predictions of results are actually obtained.

For example, Braga and associates (2001) predicted that gun killings among male Boston residents under age 25 would decline following implementation of the package of interventions in the Boston gun strategy. Although other explanations are possible for the sharp observed declines, the specific focus of the researchers' interventions and the concomitant results undermine the credi-

bility of rival hypotheses. Having many measures of variables over time strengthens internal validity if observations support our predicted expectations about cause. We saw earlier how nonequivalent time-series comparisons and switching replications can enhance findings. This is also consistent with pattern matching—we make specific statements about what patterns of results we expect in our observations over time.

Finally, a single case study is vulnerable to external validity threats because it is rooted in the context of a specific site. Conducting multiple case studies in different sites illustrates the principle of replication. By replicating research findings, we accumulate evidence. We may also find that causal relationships are different in different settings, as did researchers who tried to transplant specific interventions from the Boston Gun Project. Although such findings can undermine the generalizability of causality, they also help us understand how causal mechanisms can operate differently in different settings.

Time-series designs and case studies are examples of variable-oriented research. A case study with many observations over time can be an example of a time-series design. Adding one or more other cases offers opportunities to create nonequivalent comparisons. Time-series designs, case studies, and nonequivalent comparisons are quasi-experimental designs—they are conducted in the manner of experiments, using design building blocks in different ways.

| Construct validity | Multiple sources of evidence |
| --- | --- |
| | Establishment of chains of causation |
| | Member checks |
| Internal validity | Pattern matching |
| | Time-series analysis |
| External validity | Replication through multiple case studies |

**FIGURE 5.8** Case Studies and Validity
*Source: Adapted from Yin (2008, 40–41).*

## EXPERIMENTAL AND QUASI-EXPERIMENTAL DESIGNS SUMMARIZED

*Understanding the building blocks of research design and adapting them accordingly works better than trying to apply the same design to all research questions.*

By now it should be clear that there are no simple formulas or recipes for designing an experimental or quasi-experimental study. Researchers have an almost infinite variety of ways of varying the number and composition of groups of subjects, selecting subjects, determining how many observations to make, and deciding what types of experimental stimuli to introduce or study.

Variations on experimental and quasi-experimental designs are constructed for basic and applied explanatory studies. As we stated earlier in this chapter, experiments are best suited to topics that involve well-defined concepts and proposi-

tions. Experiments and quasi-experiments also require that researchers be able to exercise, or at least approximate, some degree of control over an experimental stimulus. Finally, these designs depend on the ability to unambiguously establish the time order of experimental treatments and observations on the dependent variable. Often it is not possible to achieve the necessary degree of control.

In designing research projects, researchers should be alert to opportunities for using experimental designs. Researchers should also be aware of how quasi-experimental designs can be developed when randomization is not possible. Experiments and quasi-experiments lend themselves to a logical rigor that is often much more difficult to achieve in other modes of observation. The building blocks of research design can be used in creative ways to address a variety of criminal justice research questions. Careful attention to design issues, and to how design elements can reduce validity threats, is essential to the research process.

## SUMMARY

- Experiments are excellent vehicles for the controlled testing of causal processes. Experiments may also be appropriate for evaluation studies.

- The classical experiment tests the effect of an experimental stimulus on some dependent variable through the pretesting and posttesting of experimental and control groups.

- It is less important that a group of experimental subjects be representative of some larger population than that experimental and control groups be similar to each other.

- Randomization is the best way to achieve comparability in the experimental and control groups.

- The classical experiment with random assignment of subjects guards against most of the threats to internal invalidity.

- Because experiments often take place under controlled conditions, results may not be gen-

eralizable to real-world constructs. Or findings from an experiment in one setting may not apply to other settings.

- The classical experiment may be modified to suit specific research purposes by changing the number of experimental and control groups, the number and types of experimental stimuli, and the number of pretest or posttest measurements.

- Quasi-experiments may be conducted when it is not possible or desirable to use an experimental design.

- Nonequivalent-groups and time-series designs are two general types of quasi-experiments.

- Time-series designs and case studies are examples of variable-oriented research, in which a large number of variables are examined for one or a few cases.

- Not all research purposes and questions are amenable to experimental or quasi-experimental designs because researchers may not be able to exercise the required degree of control.

- Both experiments and quasi-experiments may be customized by using design building blocks to suit particular research purposes.

## KEY TERMS

case-oriented research, p. 124

case studies, p. 124

classical experiment, p. 105

construct validity, p. 113

dependent variable, p. 105

control group, p. 106

experimental group, p. 106

external validity, p. 113

generalizability, p. 113

independent variable, p. 105

internal validity, p. 110

quasi-experiment, p. 116

randomization, p. 108

statistical conclusion validity, p. 114

variable-oriented research, p. 124

## REVIEW QUESTIONS AND EXERCISES

1. If you do not remember participating in DARE—Drug Abuse Resistance Education— you have probably heard or read something about it. Describe an experimental design to test the causal hypothesis that DARE reduces drug use. Is your experimental design feasible? Why or why not?

2. Experiments are often conducted in public health research where a distinction is made between an efficacy experiment and an effectiveness experiment. Efficacy experiments focus on whether a new health program works under ideal conditions; effectiveness experiments test the program under typical conditions that

health professionals encounter in their day-to-day work. Discuss how efficacy experiments and effectiveness experiments reflect concerns about internal validity threats on the one hand and generalizability on the other.

3. Crime hot spots are areas where crime reports, calls for police service, or other measures of crime are especially common. Police in departments with a good analytic capability routinely identify hot spots and launch special tactics to reduce crime in these areas. What kinds of validity threats should researchers be especially attentive to in studying the effects of police interventions on hot spots?

## ADDITIONAL READINGS

Campbell, Donald T., and Julian Stanley, *Experimental and Quasi-Experimental Designs for Research* (Chicago: Rand McNally, 1966). This short book provides an excellent analysis of the logic and methods of experimentation in social research and is widely cited as the classic discussion of validity threats.

Pawson, Ray, and Nick Tilley, *Realistic Evaluation* (Thousand Oaks, CA: Sage, 1997). We mentioned this book in Chapter 3. Pawson and Tilley argue that experiments and quasi-experiments focus too narrowly on threats to internal validity. Instead, they propose a different view of causation and different approaches to assessing cause.

Piquero, Alex, and David Weisburd (eds.), *Handbook of Quantitative Criminology* (New York: Springer, 2010). This new compendium includes 35 chapters on advanced methods in criminological research. Several chapters in Parts II and III address topics we have briefly introduced here.

Shadish, William R., Thomas D. Cook, and Donald T. Campbell, *Experimental and Quasi-Experimental Designs for Generalized Causal Inference* (Boston: Houghton Mifflin, 2002). An update of the definitive guide to quasi-experimentation, this book focuses on basic principles of research design. In addition to numerous pointers on designing research, the authors stress that designing out validity threats is much preferred to trying to control them through later statistical analysis.

Yin, Robert K., *Case Study Research: Design and Methods*, 4th ed. (Thousand Oaks, CA: Sage, 2008). Many people incorrectly associate case studies with qualitative research. Yin describes a variety of case-study designs as quasi-experiments. In doing so, he is consistent with how Shadish, Cook, and Campbell (2002) describe case studies.

# PART 3

# Modes of Observation

Having covered the basics of structuring research, from general issues to research design, let's dive into the various observational techniques available for criminal justice research.

Chapter 6 examines how social scientists go about selecting people or things for observation. Our discussion of sampling addresses the fundamental scientific issue of generalizability. As we'll see, it is possible for us to select a few people or things for observation and then apply what we observe to a much larger group of people or things than we actually observed. It is possible, for example, to ask a thousand people how they feel about "three strikes and you're out" laws and then accurately predict how tens of millions of people feel about it.

Chapter 7 describes survey research and other techniques for collecting data by asking people questions. We'll cover different ways of asking questions and discuss the various uses of surveys and related techniques in criminal justice research.

Chapter 8, on field research, examines what is perhaps the most natural form of data collection: the direct observation of phenomena in natural settings. As we will see, observations can be highly structured and systematic (such as counting pedestrians who walk by a specified point) or less structured and more flexible.

Chapter 9 discusses ways to take advantage of some of the data available all around us. Researchers often examine data collected by criminal justice and other public agencies. Content analysis is a method of collecting data through carefully specifying and counting communications such as news stories, court opinions, or even recorded visual images. Criminal justice researchers may also conduct secondary analysis of data collected by others.

# CHAPTER 6

# Sampling

*Sampling makes it possible to select a few hundred or thousand people for study and discover things that apply to many more people who are not studied.*

# INTRODUCTION

*How we collect representative data is fundamental to criminal justice research.*

Much of the value of research depends on how data are collected. A critical part of criminal justice research is deciding what will be observed and what won't. If you want to study drug users, for example, which drug users should you study? This chapter discusses the logic and fundamental principles of sampling and then describes different general approaches for selecting subjects or other units.

Sampling is the process of selecting observations. Sampling is ordinarily used to select observations for one of two related reasons. First, it is often not possible to collect information from all persons or other units we wish to study. We may wish to know what proportion of all persons arrested in U.S. cities have recently used drugs, but collecting all that data would be virtually impossible. Thus, we have to look at a sample of observations.

The second reason for sampling is that it is often not necessary to collect data from all persons or other units. Probability sampling techniques enable us to make relatively few observations and then generalize from those observations to a much wider population. If we are interested in what proportion of high school students have used marijuana, collecting data from a probability sample of a few thousand students will serve just as well as trying to study every high school student in the country.

Although probability sampling is central to criminal justice research, it cannot be used in many situations of interest. A variety of nonprobability sampling techniques are available in such cases. Nonprobability sampling has its own logic and can provide useful samples for criminal justice inquiry. In this chapter, we examine both the advantages and the shortcomings of such methods, and we discuss where they fit in the larger picture of sampling and collecting data. Keep in mind one important goal of all sampling: to reduce, or at least understand, the potential biases that may be at work in selecting subjects.

# THE LOGIC OF PROBABILITY SAMPLING

*Probability sampling helps researchers generalize from observed cases to unobserved ones.*

In selecting a group of subjects for study, social science researchers often use some type of sampling. Sampling in general refers to selecting part of a population. In selecting **samples**, we want to do two related things. First, we select samples to represent some larger population of people or other things. If we are interested in attitudes about a prisoner reentry facility, we might draw a sample of neighborhood residents, ask them some questions, and use their responses to represent the attitudes of all neighborhood residents. Or, in studying cases in a criminal court, we may not be able to examine all cases, so we select a sample to represent that population of all cases processed through some court.

Second, we may want to generalize from a sample to an unobserved population the sample is intended to represent. If we interview a sample of community residents, we may want to generalize our findings to all community residents—those we interviewed and those we did not. We might similarly expect that our sample of criminal court cases can be generalized to the population of all criminal court cases.

A special type of sampling that enables us to generalize to a larger population is known as **probability sampling**, a method of selection in which each member of a population has a known chance or probability of being selected. Knowing the probability that any individual member of a population could be selected makes it possible for us to make predictions that our sample accurately represents the larger population.

If all members of a population are identical in all respects—demographic characteristics, attitudes, experiences, behaviors, and so on—there is no need for careful sampling procedures. Any sample will be sufficient. In this extreme case of homogeneity, in fact, a single case will be sufficient as a sample to study characteristics of the whole population.

In reality, of course, the human beings who make up any real population are heterogeneous,

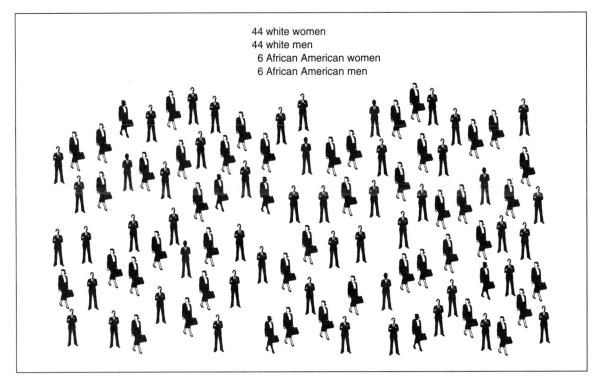

44 white women
44 white men
6 African American women
6 African American men

**F I G U R E  6.1**  A Population of 100 People

varying in many ways. Figure 6.1 offers a simplified illustration of a heterogeneous population: the 100 members of this small population differ by gender and race. We'll use this hypothetical micropopulation to illustrate various aspects of sampling.

A sample of individuals from a population, if it is to provide useful descriptions of the total population, must contain essentially the same variations that exist in the population. This is not as simple as it might seem. Let's look at some of the possible biases in selection or ways researchers might go astray. Then we will see how probability sampling provides an efficient method for selecting a sample that should adequately reflect variations that exist in the population.

## Conscious and Unconscious Sampling Bias

At first glance, it may seem as if sampling is a rather straightforward matter. To select a sample of 100

lawyers, a researcher might simply go to a courthouse and interview the first 100 lawyers who walk through the door. This kind of sampling method is often used by untrained researchers, but it is subject to serious biases. In connection with sampling, *bias* simply means that those selected are not "typical" or "representative" of the larger populations they have been chosen from. This kind of bias is virtually inevitable when a researcher picks subjects casually.

Figure 6.2 illustrates what can happen when we simply select people who are convenient for study. Although women make up only 50 percent of our micropopulation, those closest to the researcher (people in the upper right-hand corner of Figure 6.2) happen to be 70 percent women. Although the population is 12 percent African American, none were selected into this sample of people who happened to be conveniently situated near the researcher.

Moving beyond the risks inherent in simply studying people who are convenient, we need to

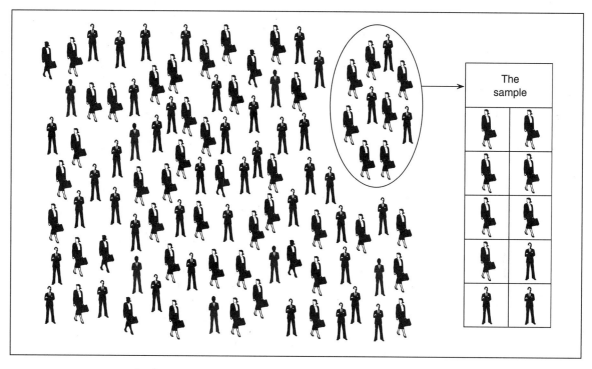

**F I G U R E 6.2**  A Sample of Convenience: Easy, but Not Representative

consider other potential problems as well. To begin, our own personal leanings or biases may affect the sample selected in this manner; hence, the sample will not truly represent the population of lawyers. Suppose a researcher is a little intimidated by lawyers who look particularly prosperous, believing that they might ridicule his research effort. He might consciously or unconsciously avoid interviewing them. Or he might believe that the attitudes of "establishment" lawyers are irrelevant to his research purposes and avoid interviewing them.

Even if the researcher seeks to interview a "balanced" group of lawyers, he won't know the exact proportions of different types of lawyers who make up such a balance and won't always be able to identify the different types merely by watching them walk by.

The researcher might make a conscious effort to interview, say, every 10th lawyer who enters the courthouse, but he still cannot be sure of a representative sample because different types of lawyers visit the courthouse with different frequencies, and

some never go to the courthouse at all. Thus, the resulting sample will overrepresent lawyers who visit the courthouse more often.

As another example, "call-in polls"—in which radio stations ask people to call specified telephone numbers to register their opinions—cannot be trusted to represent the general population. At the very least, not everyone in the population is even aware of the poll. Those who are aware of it have some things in common simply because they listen to the same radio station. As market researchers understand very well, a classical music station has a different audience than a hard rock station. Adding even more bias to the sample, those who are motivated to take part in the poll are probably different from others who are not so motivated.

A similar problem affects polls linked to weblogs or mass e-mail. Blogs tend to be selective; people regularly visit blogs that present views on personal and political issues they endorse (McKenna and Pole 2008). As a result, the population of people who respond to weblog polls can only represent the population of people who regularly visit individual blogs. As a general principle, the more self-selection is involved, the more bias will be introduced into the sample.

The possibilities for inadvertent sampling bias are endless and not always obvious. Fortunately, some techniques can help us avoid bias.

## Representativeness and Probability of Selection

Although the term *representativeness* has no precise, scientific meaning, it carries a commonsense meaning that makes it useful in the discussion of sampling. As we'll use the term here, a sample is *representative* of the population from which it is selected if the aggregate characteristics of the sample closely approximate those same aggregate characteristics in the population. If the population, for example, contains 50 percent women, a representative sample will also contain "close to" 50 percent women. Later in this chapter, we'll discuss "how close" in detail. Notice that samples need not be representative in all respects; representativeness is limited to those characteristics that are relevant to the substantive interests of the study.

A basic principle of probability sampling is that a sample will be representative of the population from which it is selected if all members of the population have an equal chance of being selected in the sample. Samples that have this quality are often labeled **equal probability of selection method (EPSEM)** samples.

Even carefully selected EPSEM samples are seldom, if ever, perfectly representative of the populations from which they are drawn. Nevertheless, probability sampling offers two special advantages. First, probability samples, though never perfectly representative, are typically more representative than other types of samples because they avoid the biases discussed in the preceding section. In practice, there is a greater likelihood that a probability sample will be representative of the population from which it is drawn than that a nonprobability sample will be.

Second, and more importantly, probability sampling permits us to estimate the accuracy or representativeness of the sample. Conceivably, a researcher might wholly by chance select a sample that closely represents the larger population. The odds are against doing so, however, and we cannot estimate the likelihood that a haphazard sample will achieve representativeness. The probability sample can provide an accurate estimate of success or failure, because probability samples enable us to draw on probability theory.

## PROBABILITY THEORY AND SAMPLING DISTRIBUTION

*Probability theory permits inferences about how sampled data are distributed around the value found in a larger population.*

With a basic understanding of the logic of probability sampling in hand, we can examine how probability sampling works in practice. We will then be able to devise specific sampling techniques and assess the results of those techniques. To do so, we first need to understand four important concepts.

A **sample element** is that unit about which information is collected and that provides the basis of analysis. Typically, in survey research, elements are people or certain types of people. However, other kinds of units can be the elements for criminal justice research—correctional facilities, police beats, or court cases, for example. Elements and units of analysis are often the same in a given study, although the former refers to sample selection and the latter to data analysis.

A **population** is the theoretically specified grouping of study elements. Whereas the vague term *delinquents* might describe the target for a study, a more precise description of the population includes the definition of the element *delinquents* (for example, a person charged with a delinquent offense), the time referent for the study (charged with a delinquent offense in the previous six months), and often a particular area (in the city of Los Angeles). Translating the abstract *adult drug addicts* into a workable population requires specifying the age that defines adult and the level of drug use that constitutes an addict. Specifying *college student* includes a consideration of full- and part-time students, degree and nondegree candidates, undergraduate and graduate students, and so on.

A **population parameter** is the value for a given variable in a population. The average income of all families in a city and the age distribution of the city's population are parameters. An important portion of criminal justice research involves estimating population parameters on the basis of sample observations.

The summary description of a given variable in the sample is called a **sample statistic**. Sample statistics are used to make estimates of population parameters. Thus, the average income computed from a sample and the age distribution of that sample are statistics, and those statistics are used to estimate income and age parameters in a population.

The ultimate purpose of sampling is to select a set of elements from a population in such a way that descriptions of those elements (sample statistics) accurately portray the parameters of the total population from which the elements are selected. Probability sampling enhances the likelihood of accomplishing this aim and also provides methods for estimating the degree of probable success.

The key to this process is random selection. In random selection, each element has an equal chance of being selected independent of any other event in the selection process. Flipping a coin is the most frequently cited example: the "selection" of a head or a tail is independent of previous selections of heads or tails.

There are two reasons for using random selection methods. First, this procedure serves as a check on conscious or unconscious bias on the part of the researcher. The researcher who selects cases on an intuitive basis might choose cases that will support his or her research expectations or hypotheses. Random selection erases this danger. Second, and more importantly, with random selection we can draw on probability theory, which allows us to estimate population parameters and to estimate how accurate our statistics are likely to be.

## The Sampling Distribution of 10 Cases

Suppose there are 10 people in a group, and each person has a certain amount of money in his or her pocket. To simplify, let's assume that one person has no money, another has $1, another has $2, and so forth up to the person who has $9. Figure 6.3 illustrates this population of 10 people.

**F I G U R E  6.3**  A Population of 10 People with $0 to $9

Our task is to determine the average amount of money one person has—specifically, the mean number of dollars. If you simply add up the money shown in Figure 6.3, the total is $45, so the mean is $4.50 (45 ÷ 10). Our purpose in the rest of this example is to estimate that mean without actually observing all 10 individuals. We'll do that by selecting random samples from the population and using the means of those samples to estimate the mean for the whole population.

To start, suppose we select—at random—a sample of only 1 person from the 10. Depending on which person we select, we will estimate the group's mean as anywhere from $0 to $9. Figure 6.4 shows a display of those 10 possible samples. The 10 dots shown on the graph represent the 10 "sample" means we will get as estimates of the population. The range of the dots on the graph is the **sampling distribution**, defined as the range of sample statistics we will obtain if we select many samples. Figure 6.4 shows how all of our possible

samples of 1 are distributed. Obviously, it is not a good idea to select a sample of only 1 because we stand a good chance of missing the true mean of $4.50 by quite a bit.

What if we take samples of 2 each? As you can see from Figure 6.5, increasing the sample size improves our estimations. Once again, each dot represents a possible sample. There are 45 possible samples of two elements: $0/$1, $0/$2, . . . , $7/$8, $8/$9. Moreover, some of these samples produce the same means. For example, $0/$6, $1/$5, and $2/$4 all produce means of $3. In Figure 6.5, the three dots shown above the $3 mean represent those 3 samples.

Notice that the means we get from the 45 samples are not evenly distributed. Rather, they are somewhat clustered around the true value of $4.50. Only 2 samples deviate by as much as $4 from the true value ($0/$1 and $8/$9), whereas 5 of the samples give the true estimate of $4.50, and another 8 samples miss the mark by only $.50 (plus or minus).

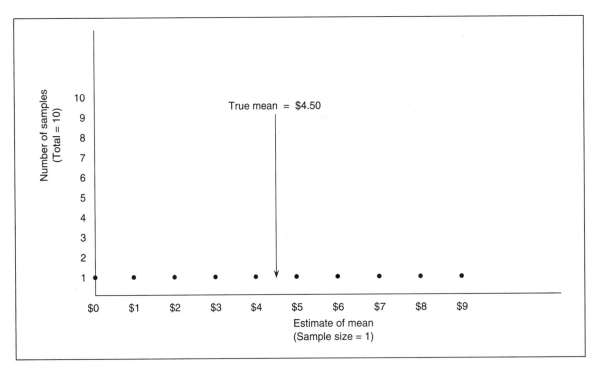

**FIGURE 6.4**   The Sampling Distribution of Samples of 1

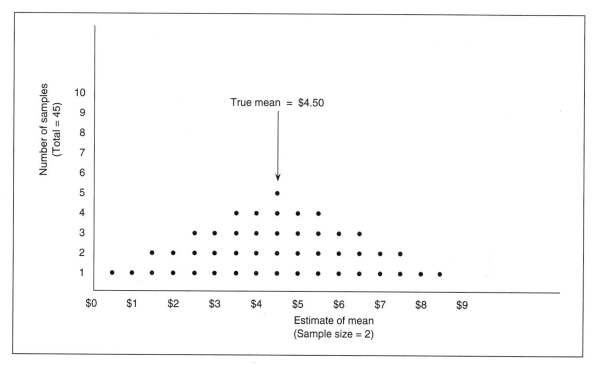

**FIGURE 6.5** The Sampling Distribution of Samples of 2

Now suppose we select even larger samples. What will that do to our estimates of the mean? Figure 6.6 presents the sampling distributions of samples of 3, 4, 5, and 6. The progression of the sampling distributions is clear. Every increase in sample size improves the distribution of estimates of the mean in two related ways. First, in the distribution for samples of 5, for example, no sample means are at the extreme ends of the distribution. Why? Because it is not possible to select five elements from our population and obtain an average of less than $2 or greater than $7. The second way sampling distributions improve with larger samples is that sample means cluster more and more around the true population mean of $4.50. Figure 6.6 clearly shows this tendency.

## From Sampling Distribution to Parameter Estimate

Let's turn now to a more realistic sampling situation and see how the notion of sampling distribution applies. Assume that we wish to study the population of Placid Coast, California, to assess the levels of approval or disapproval of a proposed law to ban possession of assault rifles within the city limits.

Our target population is all adult residents. In order to draw an actual sample, we need some sort of list of elements in our population; such a list is called a **sampling frame**. Assume our sampling frame is a voter registration list of, say, 20,000 registered voters in Placid Coast. The elements are the individual registered voters.

The variable under consideration is attitudes toward the proposed law: approve or disapprove. Measured in this way, attitude toward the law is a **binomial variable**; it can have only two values. We'll select a random sample of, say, 100 persons for the purpose of estimating the population parameter for approval of the proposed law.

Figure 6.7 presents all the possible values of this parameter in the population—from 0 percent approval to 100 percent approval. The midpoint of

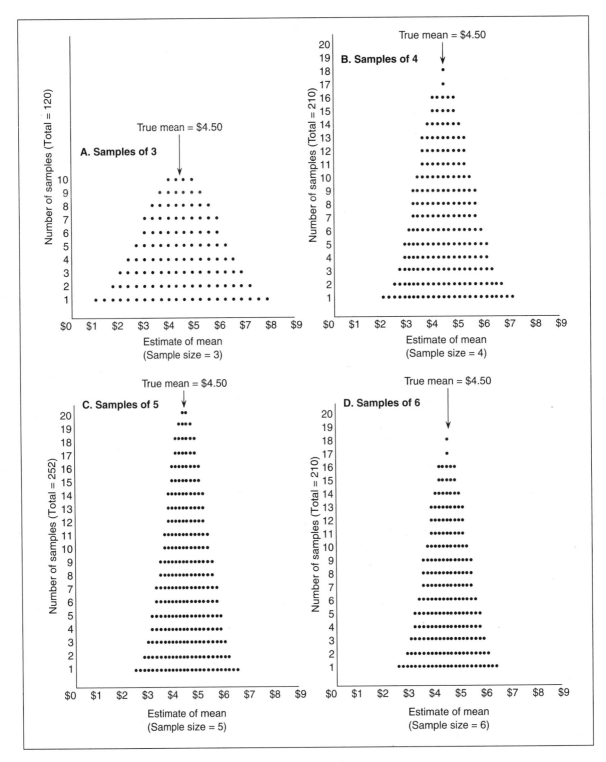

**FIGURE 6.6**   The Sampling Distribution of Samples of 3, 4, 5, and 6

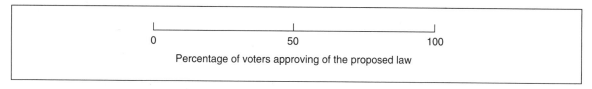

**FIGURE 6.7**  The Range of Possible Sample Study Results

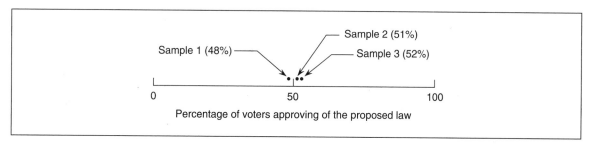

**FIGURE 6.8**  Results Produced by Three Hypothetical Samples

the line—50 percent—represents half the voters approving of the assault rifle ban and the other half disapproving.

To choose our sample, we assign each person on the voter registration list a number and use a computer program to generate 100 random numbers. Then we interview the 100 people whose numbers have been selected and ask for their attitudes toward the assault rifle ban: whether they approve or disapprove. Suppose this operation gives us 48 people who approve of the law and 52 who disapprove. We present this statistic by placing a dot at the point representing 48 percent, as shown in Figure 6.8.

Now suppose we select another sample of 100 people in exactly the same fashion and measure their approval or disapproval of the proposed law. Perhaps 51 people in the second sample approve of the law. We place another dot in the appropriate place on the line in Figure 6.8. Repeating this process once more, we may discover that 52 people in the third sample approve banning assault rifles; we add a third dot to Figure 6.8.

Figure 6.8 now presents the three different sample statistics that represent the percentages of

people in each of the three random samples who approved of the proposed law. Each of the random samples, then, gives us an estimate of the percentage of people in the total population of registered voters who approve of the assault rifle law. Unfortunately, we now have three separate estimates.

To rescue ourselves from this dilemma, let's draw more and more samples of 100 registered voters each, question each of the samples concerning their approval or disapproval, and plot the new sample statistics on our summary graph. In drawing many such samples, we discover that some of the new samples provide duplicate estimates, as in our earlier illustration with 10 cases. Figure 6.9 shows the sampling distribution of hundreds of samples. This is often referred to as a normal or bell-shaped curve.

Notice that by increasing the number of samples selected and interviewed we have also increased the range of estimates provided by the sampling operation. In one sense, we have increased our dilemma in attempting to find the parameter in the population. Fortunately, probability theory provides certain important rules about the sampling distribution shown in Figure 6.9.

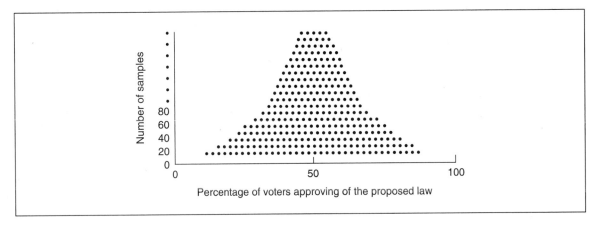

**FIGURE 6.9**  The Sampling Distribution

### Estimating Sampling Error

Probability theory can help resolve our dilemma with some basic statistical concepts. First, if many independent random samples are selected from a population, then the sample statistics provided by those samples will be distributed around the population parameter in a known way. Thus, although Figure 6.9 shows a wide range of estimates, more of them are in the vicinity of 50 percent than elsewhere in the graph. Probability theory tells us, then, that the true value is in the vicinity of 50 percent.

Second, probability theory gives us a formula for estimating how closely the sample statistics are clustered around the true value:

$$s = \sqrt{\frac{p \times q}{n}}$$

where $s$ is the **standard error**—defined as a measure of sampling error—$n$ is the number of cases in each sample, and $p$ and $q$ are the population parameters for the binomial. If 60 percent of registered voters approve of the ban on assault rifles and 40 percent disapprove, then $p$ and $q$ are 60 percent and 40 percent, or 0.6 and 0.4, respectively.

To see how probability theory makes it possible for us to estimate sampling error, suppose that in reality 50 percent of the people approve of the proposed law and 50 percent disapprove. These are the population parameters we are trying to estimate

with our samples. Recall that we have been selecting samples of 100 cases each. When these numbers are plugged into the formula, we get:

$$s = \sqrt{\frac{.5 \times .5}{100}} = .05$$

The standard error equals 0.05, or 5 percent.

In probability theory, the standard error is a valuable piece of information because it indicates how closely the sample estimates will be distributed around the population parameter. A larger standard error indicates that sample estimates are widely dispersed, while a smaller standard error means that estimates are more clustered around a population parameter. Probability theory tells us that approximately 34 percent (0.3413) of the sample estimates will fall within one standard error increment above the population parameter, and another 34 percent will fall within one standard error increment below the parameter. In our example, the standard error increment is 5 percent, so we know that 34 percent of our samples will give estimates of approval between 50 percent (the parameter) and 55 percent (one standard error above); another 34 percent of the samples will give estimates between 50 and 45 percent (one standard error below the parameter). Taken together, then, we know that roughly two-thirds (68 percent) of the samples will give estimates between 45 and 55 percent, which is within 5 percent of the parameter.

The standard error is also a function of the sample size—an inverse function. This means that as the sample size increases, the standard error decreases. And as the sample size increases, the several samples will be clustered nearer to the true value. Figure 6.6 illustrates this clustering. Another rule of thumb is evident in the formula for the standard error: because of the square root operation, the standard error is reduced by half if the sample size is quadrupled. In our example, samples of 100 produce a standard error of 5 percent; to reduce the standard error to 2.5 percent, we would have to increase the sample size to 400.

All of this information is provided by established probability theory in reference to the selection of large numbers of random samples. If the population parameter is known and many random samples are selected, probability theory allows us to predict how many of the samples will fall within specified intervals from the parameter.

Of course, this discussion illustrates only the *logic* of probability sampling. It does not describe the way research is actually conducted. Usually, we do not know the parameter; we conduct a sample survey precisely because we want to estimate that value. Moreover, we don't actually select large numbers of samples; we select only one sample. What probability theory does is provide the basis for making inferences about the typical research situation. Knowing what it would be like to select thousands of samples allows us to make assumptions about the one sample we do select and study.

## Confidence Levels and Confidence Intervals

Probability theory specifies that 68 percent of that fictitious large number of samples will produce estimates that fall within one standard error of the parameter. As researchers, we can turn the logic around and infer that any single random sample has a 68 percent chance of falling within that range. In this regard, we speak of **confidence levels**: we are 68 percent confident that our sample estimate is within one standard error of the parameter. Or we may say that we are 95 percent confident that the

sample statistic is within two standard errors of the parameter, and so forth. Quite reasonably, our confidence level increases as the margin for error is extended. We are virtually positive (99.9 percent) that our statistic is within three standard errors of the true value.

Although we may be confident (at some level) of being within a certain range of the parameter, we seldom know what the parameter is. To resolve this dilemma, we substitute our sample estimate for the parameter in the formula; lacking the true value, we substitute the best available guess.

The result of these inferences and estimations is that we are able to estimate a population parameter and also the expected degree of error on the basis of one sample drawn from a population. We begin with this question: what percentage of the registered voters in Placid Coast approve of the proposed assault rifle ban? We select a random sample of 100 registered voters and interview them. We might then report that our best estimate is that 50 percent of registered voters approve of the gun ban and that we are 95 percent confident that between 40 and 60 percent (plus or minus two standard errors) approve. The range from 40 to 60 percent is called the **confidence interval**. At the 68 percent confidence level, the confidence interval is 45 to 55 percent.

The logic of confidence levels and confidence intervals also provides the basis for determining the appropriate sample size for a study. Once we decide on the sampling error we can tolerate, we can calculate the number of cases needed in our sample.

## Probability Theory and Sampling Distribution Summed Up

This, then, is the basic logic of probability sampling. Random selection permits the researcher to link findings from a sample to the body of probability theory so as to estimate the accuracy of those findings. All statements of accuracy in sampling must specify both a confidence level and a confidence interval. The researcher must report that he or she is *x* percent confident that the population parameter is between two specific values.

In this example, we have demonstrated the logic of sampling error using a binomial variable—a variable analyzed in percentages. A different statistical procedure would be required to calculate the standard error for a mean, but the overall logic is the same.

Notice that nowhere in this discussion did we consider the size of the population being studied. This is because the population size is almost always irrelevant. A sample of 2,000 respondents drawn properly to represent residents of Vermont will be no more accurate than a sample of 2,000 drawn properly to represent residents in the United States, even though the Vermont sample would be a substantially larger proportion of that small state's residents than would the same number chosen to represent the nation's residents. The reason for this counterintuitive fact is that the equations for calculating sampling error assume that the populations being sampled are infinitely large, so all samples would equal zero percent of the whole.

Two cautions are in order before we conclude this discussion of the basic logic of probability sampling. First, the survey uses of probability theory as discussed here are technically not wholly justified. The theory of sampling distribution makes assumptions that almost never apply in survey conditions. The exact proportion of samples contained within specified increments of standard errors mathematically assumes an infinitely large population, an infinite number of samples, and sampling with replacement—that is, every sampling unit selected is "thrown back into the pot" and could be selected again. Second, our discussion has greatly oversimplified the inferential jump from the distribution of several samples to the probable characteristics of one sample.

We offer these cautions to provide perspective on the uses of probability theory in sampling. Researchers in criminal justice and other social sciences often appear to overestimate the precision of estimates produced by the use of probability theory. Variations in sampling techniques and nonsampling factors may further reduce the legitimacy of such estimates. For example, those selected in a sample who fail or refuse to participate further detract from the representativeness of the sample.

Nevertheless, the calculations discussed in this section can be extremely valuable to you in understanding and evaluating your data. Being familiar with the basic logic underlying the calculations can help you react sensibly both to your own data and to those reported by others.

## PROBABILITY SAMPLING

*Different types of sampling designs can be used alone or in combination for different research purposes.*

As researchers and as consumers of research we need to understand the theoretical foundations of sampling. It is no less important to appreciate the less-than-perfect conditions that exist in the field. Most of what we have considered so far assumes we are using simple random sampling. In reality researchers have a number of options in choosing their sampling method, each with its own advantages and disadvantages.

### Populations and Sampling Frames

Our discussion begins with a more practical consideration of one key feature of all probability sampling designs: the relationship between populations and sampling frames.

A sampling frame is the list or quasi-list of elements from which a probability sample is selected. Put another way, a sampling frame is a list or quasi-list of our target population. We say "quasi-list" because, even though an actual list might not exist, we can draw samples as if there were a list. Properly drawn samples provide information appropriate for describing the population of elements that compose the sampling frame—nothing more. This point is important in view of the common tendency for researchers to select samples from a particular sampling frame and then make assertions about a population that is similar, but not identical, to the study population defined by the sampling frame.

For example, if we want to study the attitudes of corrections administrators toward determinant sentencing policies, we might select a sample by consulting the membership roster of the American Correctional Association. In this case, the membership roster is our sampling frame, and corrections administrators are the population we wish to describe. However, unless all corrections administrators are members of the American Correctional Association and all members are listed in the roster, it would be incorrect to generalize results to all corrections administrators.

Studies of organizations are often the simplest from a sampling standpoint because organizations typically have membership lists. In such cases, the list of members may be an acceptable sampling frame. If a random sample is selected from a membership list, then the data collected from that sample may be taken as representative of all members—if all members are included in the list. It is, however, imperative that researchers learn how complete or incomplete such lists might be and limit their generalizations to listed sample elements rather than to an entire population. The membership lists of organizations now often include e-mail addresses. In such cases organizations are especially well suited to web-based sampling and e-mail contacts.

Other lists of individuals may be especially relevant to the research needs of a particular study. Lists of licensed drivers, automobile owners, welfare recipients, taxpayers, holders of weapons permits, and licensed professionals are just a few examples. Although it may be difficult to gain access to some of these lists, they provide excellent sampling frames for specialized research purposes.

Telephone directories are frequently used for "quick and dirty" public opinion polls. Undeniably, they are easy and inexpensive to use, and that is no doubt the reason for their popularity. Still, they have several limitations. A given directory will not include new subscribers or those who have requested unlisted numbers. Sampling is further complicated by the inclusion of nonresidential listings in directories. Moreover, telephone directories are sometimes taken to be a listing of a city's population, which is simply not the case. Lower-income people are less likely to have telephones, and higher-income people may have more than one line. A growing number of households are served only by wireless phone service

and so are not listed in directories. A national study conducted in 2010 reported that about 25 percent of households had only wireless phones (Blumberg and Luke 2010). Telephone companies may not publish listings for temporary residents such as students. And persons who live in institutions or group quarters—dormitories, nursing homes, rooming houses, and the like—are not listed in phone directories.

Street directories and tax maps may be used as sampling frames for households, but they may also suffer from incompleteness and possible bias. For example, illegal housing units such as basement apartments are unlikely to appear on official records. As a result, such units have no chance for selection, and sample findings will not be representative of those units, which are often substandard and overcrowded.

In a more general sense, it's worth viewing sampling frames as operational definitions of a study population. Just as operational definitions of variables describe how abstract concepts will be measured, sampling frames serve as a real-world version of an abstract study population. For example, we may want to study how criminologists deal with ethical issues in their research. We don't know how many criminologists exist out there, but we could develop a general idea about the population of criminologists. We could also operationalize the concept by using the membership directory for the American Society of Criminology (ASC)—that list is our operational definition of the population of criminologists. Since most criminologists use e-mail extensively, a sample of e-mail addresses from the ASC directory would suit our purposes nicely.

## Simple Random Sampling

Simple random sampling forms the basis of probability theory and the statistical tools we use to estimate population parameters, standard error, and confidence intervals. More accurately, such statistics assume unbiased sampling, and simple random sampling is the foundation of unbiased sampling.

Once a sampling frame has been established in keeping with the guidelines we presented, to use simple random sampling, the researcher assigns a single number to each element in the list, not skipping any number in the process. A table of random numbers, or a computer program for generating them, is then used to select elements for the sample.

If the sampling frame is a computerized database or some other form of electronic data, a **simple random sample** can be selected by computer. In effect, the computer program numbers the elements in the sampling frame, generates its own series of random numbers, and prints out the list of elements selected.

## Systematic Sampling

Simple random sampling is seldom used in practice, primarily because it is not usually the most efficient method, and it can be tedious if done manually. It typically requires a list of elements. And when such a list is available, researchers usually use **systematic sampling** rather than simple random sampling.

In systematic sampling, the researcher chooses all elements in the list for inclusion in the sample. If a list contains 10,000 elements and we want a sample of 1,000, we select every 10th element for our sample. To ensure against any possible human bias, we should select the first element at random. Thus, to systematically select 1,000 from a list of 10,000 elements, we begin by selecting a random number between 1 and 10. The element having that number, plus every 10th element following it, is included in the sample. This method technically is referred to as a systematic sample with a random start.

In practice, systematic sampling is virtually identical to simple random sampling. If the list of elements is indeed randomized before sampling, one might argue that a systematic sample drawn from that list is, in fact, a simple random sample.

Systematic sampling has one danger. A periodic arrangement of elements in the list can make systematic sampling unwise; this arrangement is usually called *periodicity*. If the list of elements is arranged in a cyclical pattern that coincides with the sampling interval, a biased sample may be drawn. Suppose we select a sample of apartments in an apartment build-ing. If the sample is drawn from a list of apartments arranged in numerical order (for example, 101, 102, 103, 104, 201, 202, and so on), there is a danger of the sampling interval coinciding with the number of apartments on a floor or some multiple of it. Then the samples might include only northwest-corner apartments or only apartments near the elevator. If these types of apartments have some other particular characteristic in common (for example, higher rent), the sample will be biased. The same potential danger would apply in a systematic sample of houses in a subdivision arranged with the same number of houses on a block.

In considering a systematic sample from a list, then, we need to carefully examine the nature of that list. If the elements are arranged in any particular order, we have to figure out whether that order will bias the sample to be selected and take steps to counteract any possible bias.

In summary, systematic sampling is usually superior to simple random sampling, in terms of convenience if nothing else. Problems in the ordering of elements in the sampling frame can usually be remedied quite easily.

## Stratified Sampling

We have discussed two methods of selecting a sample from a list: random and systematic. **Stratification** is not an alternative to these methods, but it represents a possible modification in their use. Simple random sampling and systematic sampling both ensure a degree of representativeness and permit an estimate of the sampling error present. Stratified sampling is a method for obtaining a greater degree of representativeness—decreasing the probable sampling error. To understand why that is the case, we must return briefly to the basic theory of sampling distribution.

Recall that sampling error is reduced by two factors in the sample design: (1) a large sample produces a smaller sampling error than a small sample does, and (2) a homogeneous population produces samples with smaller sampling errors than a heterogeneous population does. If 99 percent of the population agrees with a certain statement, it is extremely unlikely that any probability sample will greatly misrepresent the extent of agreement. If the population is split 50–50 on the statement, then the sampling error will be much greater.

Stratified sampling is based on this second factor in sampling theory. Rather than selecting our sample from the total population at large, we select appropriate numbers of elements from homogeneous subsets of that population. To get a stratified sample of university students, for example, we first organize our population by college class and then draw appropriate numbers of freshmen, sophomores, juniors, and seniors. In a nonstratified sample, representation by class is subject to the same sampling error as other variables. In a sample stratified by college class, the sampling error on that variable is reduced to zero.

Even more complex stratification methods are possible. In addition to stratifying by class, we might also stratify by gender, grade point average, and so forth. In this fashion, we could ensure that our sample contains the proper numbers of freshman men with a 4.0 average, freshman women with a 4.0 average, and so forth.

The ultimate function of stratification, then, is to organize the population into homogeneous subsets (with heterogeneity between subsets) and to select the appropriate number of elements from each. To the extent that the subsets are homogeneous on the stratification variables, they may also be homogeneous on other variables. Because age is usually related to college class, a sample stratified by class will be more representative in terms of age as well.

The choice of stratification variables typically depends on what variables are available and what variables might help reduce sampling error for a particular study. Gender can often be determined in a list of names. Many local government sources of information on housing units are arranged geographically. Age, race, education, occupation, and other variables are often included on lists of persons who have had contact with criminal justice officials.

In selecting stratification variables, however, we should be concerned primarily with those that are presumably related to the variables we want to represent accurately. Because gender is related to many behavioral variables and is often available for stratification, it is frequently used. Age and race are related to many variables of interest in criminal justice research. Income is also related to many variables, but it is often not available for stratification. Geographic location within a city, state, or nation is related to many things. Within a city, stratification by geographic location usually increases representativeness in social class and ethnicity.

Stratified sampling ensures the proper representation of the stratification variables to enhance representation of other variables related to them. Taken as a whole, then, a stratified sample is likely to be more representative on a number of variables than a simple random sample is.

## Disproportionate Stratified Sampling

Another use of stratification is to purposively produce samples that are not representative of a population on some variable, referred to as **disproportionate stratified sampling**. Because the purpose of sampling, as we have been discussing, is to represent a larger population, you may wonder why anyone would want to intentionally produce a sample that was not representative.

To understand the logic of disproportionate stratification, consider again the role of population homogeneity in determining sample size. If members of a population vary widely on some variable of interest, then larger samples must be drawn to adequately represent the larger sampling error in that population. Similarly, if only a small number of people in a population exhibit some attribute or characteristic of interest, then a large sample must be drawn to produce adequate numbers of elements that exhibit the uncommon condition. Disproportionate stratification is a way of obtaining sufficient numbers of these rare cases by selecting a number disproportionate to their representation in the population.

The best example of disproportionate sampling in criminal justice is a national crime survey in which one goal is to obtain some minimum number of crime victims in a sample. Because crime victimization for certain offenses—such as robbery or aggravated assault—is relatively rare on a national scale, persons who live in large urban areas, where serious crime is more common, are disproportionately sampled.

The British Crime Survey (BCS) is a nationwide survey of people ages 16 and over in England and Wales. Over its first 20 years (since 1982), the BCS selectively oversampled people or areas to yield larger numbers of designated subjects than would result from proportionate random samples of the population of England and Wales. Beginning in 2004, the BCS disproportionately oversampled areas served by smaller police forces to produce a large enough number of cases to statistically represent rural areas (Smith and Hoare 2009).

## Multistage Cluster Sampling

The preceding sections have described reasonably simple procedures for sampling from lists of elements. Unfortunately, however, many interesting research problems require the selection of samples from populations that cannot easily be listed for sampling purposes—that is, sampling frames are not readily available. Examples are the population of a city, state, or nation and all police officers in the United States. In such cases, the sample design must be much more complex. Such a design typically involves the initial sampling of groups of elements—clusters—followed by the selection of elements within each of the selected clusters. This procedure yields multistage **cluster samples**.

Cluster sampling may be used when it is either impossible or impractical to compile an exhaustive list of the elements that compose the target population, such as all law enforcement officers in the United States. Often, however, population elements are already grouped into subpopulations, and a list of those subpopulations either exists or can be created.

Population elements, or aggregations of those elements, are referred to as **sampling units**. In the simplest forms of sampling, elements and units are the same thing—usually people. But in cases in which a listing of elements is not available, we can often use some other unit that includes a grouping of elements.

Because U.S. law enforcement officers are employed by individual cities, counties, or states, it is possible to create lists of those political units. For cluster sampling, then, we could sample the list of cities, counties, and states in some manner as discussed previously (for example, a systematic sample stratified by population). Next, we could obtain lists of law enforcement officers from agencies in each of the selected jurisdictions. We could then sample each of the lists to provide samples of police officers for study.

Another typical situation concerns sampling among population areas such as a city. Although there is no single list of a city's population, citizens reside on discrete city blocks or census blocks. It is possible, therefore, to select a sample of blocks initially, create a list of persons who live on each of the selected blocks, and then sample persons from that list. In this case, blocks are treated as the primary sampling unit.

In a more complex design, we might sample blocks, list the households on each selected block, sample the households, list the persons who reside in each household, and, finally, sample persons within each selected household. This multistage sample design will lead to the ultimate selection of a sample of individuals without requiring the initial listing of all individuals in the city's population.

Multistage cluster sampling, then, involves the repetition of two basic steps: listing and sampling. The list of primary sampling units (city blocks) is compiled and perhaps stratified for sampling. Next, a sample of those units is selected. The list of secondary sampling units is then sampled, and the process continues.

Cluster sampling is highly recommended for its efficiency, but the price of that efficiency is a less accurate sample. A simple random sample drawn from a population list is subject to a single sampling error, but a two-stage cluster sample is subject to two sampling errors. First, the initial sample of clusters represents the population of clusters only within a range of sampling error. Second, the sample of elements selected within a given cluster represents all the elements in that cluster only within a range of sampling error. Thus, for example, we run a certain risk of selecting a sample of disproportionately wealthy city blocks, plus a sample of disproportionately wealthy households within those blocks. The best solution to this problem involves the number of clusters selected initially and the number of elements selected within each cluster.

A good general guideline for cluster design is to maximize the number of clusters selected while decreasing the number of elements within each cluster. But this scientific guideline must be balanced against an administrative constraint. The efficiency of cluster sampling is based on the ability to minimize the list of population elements. By initially selecting clusters, we need only list the elements that make up the selected clusters, not all elements in the entire population. Increasing the number of clusters, however, reduces this efficiency in cluster sampling. A small number of clusters may be listed more quickly and more cheaply than a large number. Remember that all the elements in a selected cluster must be listed, even if only a few are to be chosen in the sample.

The final sample design will reflect these two constraints. In effect, we will probably select as many clusters as we can afford. So as not to leave this issue too open-ended, here is a rule of thumb: population researchers conventionally aim for the selection of 5 households per census block. If a total of 2,000 households are to be interviewed, researchers select 400 blocks and interview 5 households on each. Figure 6.10 presents a graphic overview of this process.

As we turn to more detailed procedures in cluster sampling, keep in mind that this method almost inevitably involves a loss of accuracy. First, as noted earlier, a multistage sample design is subject to a sampling error at each stage. Because the sample size is necessarily smaller at each stage than the total sample size, the sampling error at each stage will be greater than would be the case for a single-stage random sample of elements. Second, sampling error is estimated on the basis of observed variance among the sample elements. When those elements are drawn from relatively homogeneous clusters, the estimated sampling error will be too optimistic and so must be corrected in light of the cluster sample design.

## Multistage Cluster Sampling with Stratification

Thus far we have looked at cluster sampling as though a simple random sample were selected at each stage of the design. In fact, we can use stratification techniques to refine and improve the sample being selected. The basic options available are essentially the same as those possible in single-stage sampling from a list. In selecting a national sample of law enforcement officers, we might initially stratify our list of agencies by type (state, county, municipal), geographic region, size, and rural or urban location.

Once the primary sampling units (law enforcement agencies) have been grouped according to the relevant, available stratification variables, either simple random or systematic sampling techniques can be used to select the sample. We might select a specified number of units from each group or stratum, or we might arrange the stratified clusters in a continuous list and systematically sample that list.

To the extent that clusters are combined into homogeneous strata, the sampling error at this stage will be reduced. The primary goal of stratification, as before, is homogeneity.

In principle, stratification can take place at each level of sampling. The elements listed within a selected cluster might be stratified before the next stage of sampling. Typically, however, that is not done because we strive for relative homogeneity within clusters. If clusters are sufficiently similar, it is not necessary to stratify again.

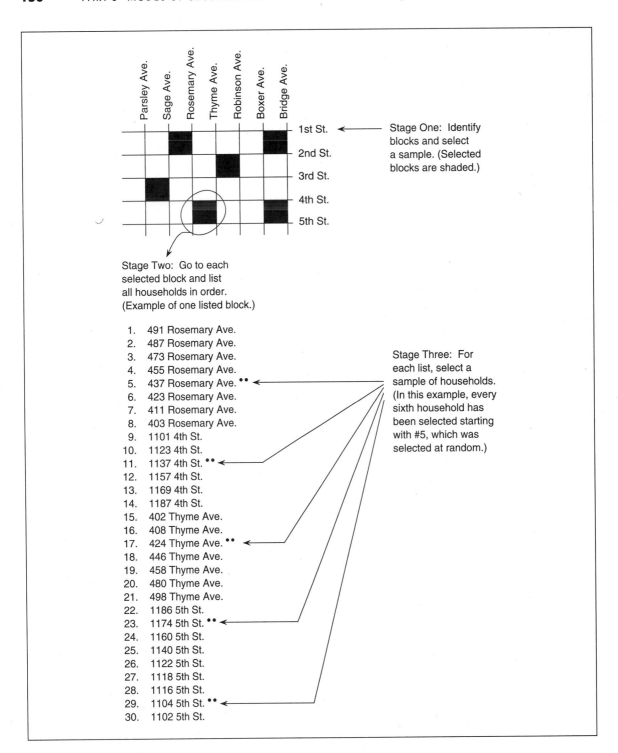

**FIGURE 6.10** Multistage Cluster Sampling

## THEORY AND SAMPLING

Theories of offending often describe why different types of people begin committing crimes, what sorts of paths or trajectories they follow over time, and what things might be associated with desistance, or ending criminal involvement. Collectively, this is often referred to as "crime through the life course" (Sampson and Laub 2005).

If you wanted to study people at different stages of offending, what sorts of samples would you draw? Stated somewhat differently, what are some possible sampling frames for studying crime through the life course? Think about some appropriate study populations and sampling frames for addressing questions like the following:

- What is the rate of involvement in crime among high school students?
- How many property and personal offenses are committed in the year before entering a state prison?
- Among former offenders, what is the effect of being married on criminal involvement?

## ILLUSTRATION: TWO NATIONAL CRIME SURVEYS

*Two national crime surveys show different ways of designing samples to achieve desired results.*

Our discussion of sampling designs suggests that researchers can combine many different techniques of sampling and their various components in different ways to suit various needs. In fact, the different components of sampling can be tailored to specific purposes in much the same way that research design principles can be modified to suit various needs. Because sample frames suitable for simple random sampling are often unavailable, researchers use multistage cluster sampling to move from aggregate sample units to actual sample elements. We can add stratification to ensure that samples are representative of important variables. And we can design samples to produce elements that are proportionate or disproportionate to the population.

Two national crime surveys illustrate how these various building blocks may be combined in complex ways: (1) the National Crime Victimization Survey (NCVS), conducted by the U.S. Census Bureau; and (2) the British Crime Survey (BCS). Each is a multistage cluster sample, but the two surveys use different strategies for sampling to produce sufficient numbers of respondents in different categories. Our summary description is adapted

from Bureau of Justice Statistics (2008) for the NCVS and from Sarah Tipping and associates (2010) for the BCS.

### The National Crime Victimization Survey

Although various parts of the NCVS have been modified since the surveys were begun in 1972, the basic sampling strategies have remained relatively constant. The most significant changes have been fluctuations in sample size and a shift to telephone interviewing, with samples of telephone number listings eventually leading to households.

The NCVS seeks to represent the nationwide population of persons ages 12 and over who are living in households. The phrase "living in households" is significant. NCVS procedures are not designed to sample homeless persons or people who live in institutional settings such as military group housing, temporary housing, or correctional facilities. Also, because the sample targets persons who live in households, it cannot provide estimates of crimes in which a commercial establishment or business is the victim.

Because there is no national list of households in the United States, multistage cluster sampling must be used to proceed from larger units to households and their residents. The national sampling frame used in the first stage defines primary sampling units (PSUs) as large metropolitan areas, non-metropolitan counties, or groups of contiguous counties (to represent rural areas).

The largest 93 PSUs are specified as "self-representing" and are automatically included in the first stage of sampling. The remaining PSUs are stratified by size, population density, reported crimes, and other variables. An additional 110 non-self-representing PSUs are then selected with a probability proportionate to the population of the PSU. Thus, for example, if one stratum includes Bugtussle, Texas (population 7000), Punkinseed, Indiana (5000), and Rancid, Missouri (3000), the probability that each PSU will be selected is 7 in 15 for Bugtussle, 5 in 15 for Punkinseed, and 3 in 15 for Rancid.

The second stage of sampling involves designating four different sampling frames within each PSU. Each of these frames is used to select different types of subsequent units. First, the housing unit frame lists addresses of housing units from census records. Second, a group quarters frame lists group quarters such as dormitories and rooming houses from census records. Third, a building permit frame lists newly constructed housing units from local government sources. Finally, an area frame lists census blocks (physical geographic units), from which independent address lists are generated and sampled. Notice that these four frames are necessary because comprehensive, up-to-date lists of residential addresses are not available in this country.

For the 2008 NCVS, these procedures yielded a sample of approximately 42,000 housing units. Completed interviews were obtained from almost 78,000 individuals living in households (Rand 2009, 2). The sample design for the NCVS is an excellent illustration of the relationship between sample size and variation in the target population. Because serious crime is a relatively rare event when averaged across the entire U.S. population, very large samples must be drawn. And because no single list of the target population exists, samples are drawn in several stages.

For further information, consult NCVS documentation maintained by the Bureau of Justice Statistics (http://bjs.ojp.usdoj.gov/index.cfm?ty=dcdetail&iid=245). Also see the "National Crime Victimization Survey Resource Guide," maintained at the National Archive of Criminal Justice Data (http://icpsr.umich.edu/nacjd/ncvs).

## The British Crime Survey

We have seen that NCVS sampling procedures begin with demographic units and work down to selection of housing units. BCS sampling is simplified by the existence of a national list of something close to addresses. The Postcode Address File (PAF) lists postal delivery points nationwide and is further subdivided to distinguish "small users," those addresses receiving less than 50 items per day. Even though 50 pieces of mail might still seem like quite a bit, this classification makes it easier to distinguish household addresses from commercial ones.

Postcode sectors, roughly corresponding to U.S. five-digit zip codes, are easily defined clusters of addresses from the PAF. Samples of addresses are then selected from within these sectors.

In addition to the core PAF sample, BCS researchers devised "booster samples" to increase the number of respondents who were ethnic minorities or ages 16 to 24. Victimization experiences of ethnic minorities were of special interest to police and other public officials. Young people were oversampled to complete a special questionnaire of self-report behavior items.

The ethnic minority booster was accomplished by first selecting respondents using formal sampling procedures. Interviewers then sought information about four housing units adjacent to the selected unit in an effort to determine if any residents were nonwhite. If adjacent units housed minority families, one was selected to be interviewed for the ethnic minority booster sample. This is an example of what Steven Thompson (1997) calls "adaptive sampling": probability samples are first selected, then those respondents are used to identify other individuals who meet some criterion. Increasing the number of respondents ages 16 to 24 was simpler—interviewers sought additional respondents in that age group within sampled households.

One final sampling dimension reflected the regional organization of police in England and Wales into 43 police areas. The BCS was further stratified to produce about 1,000 interviews in each police area to support analysis within those areas.

Apart from the young-person booster, once individual households were selected, one person age 16 or over was randomly chosen to provide information for all household members. Since 2009, children ages 10 to 15 have been sampled from some households. Sampling procedures initially produced about 60,000 addresses for the 2008–2009 BCS. Interviews were completed with 46,286 individuals for a response rate of about 76 percent.

Although sampling designs for both the BCS and the NCVS are more complex than we have represented in this discussion, the important point is how multistage cluster sampling is used in each. Notice two principal differences between the samples. First, the NCVS uses proportionate sampling to select a large number of respondents who may then represent the relatively rare attribute of victimization. The BCS samples a disproportionate number of minority and young residents, who are more likely to be victims of crime. Second, sampling procedures for the BCS are somewhat simpler than those for the NCVS, largely because a suitable sampling frame exists at the national level. Stratification and later-stage sampling are conducted to more efficiently represent each police area and to oversample minority respondents.

## Probability Sampling in Review

Depending on the field situation, probability sampling can be very simple or extremely complex, time consuming, and expensive. Whatever the situation, however, it is usually the preferred method for selecting study elements. It's worth restating the two main reasons for this.

First, probability sampling avoids conscious or unconscious biases in element selection on the part of the researcher. If all elements in the population have an equal (or unequal and subsequently weighted) chance of selection, there is an excellent chance that the sample so selected will closely represent the population of all elements.

Second, probability sampling permits estimates of sampling error. Although no probability sample will be perfectly representative in all respects, controlled selection methods permit the researcher to estimate the degree of expected error.

Despite these advantages, it is sometimes impossible to use standard probability sampling methods. Sometimes, it isn't even appropriate to do so. In those cases, researchers turn to nonprobability sampling.

## NONPROBABILITY SAMPLING

*In many research applications, nonprobability samples are necessary or advantageous.*

You can no doubt envision situations in which it would be either impossible or unfeasible to select the kinds of probability samples we have described. Suppose we want to study auto thieves. There is no list of all auto thieves, nor are we likely to be able to create anything other than a partial and highly selective list. Moreover, probability sampling is sometimes inappropriate even if it is possible. In many such situations, **nonprobability sampling** procedures are called for. Recall that probability samples are defined as those in which the probability that any given sampling element will be selected is known. Conversely, in nonprobability sampling, the likelihood that any given element will be selected is not known.

We'll examine four types of nonprobability samples in this section: (1) purposive or judgmental sampling, (2) quota sampling, (3) the reliance on available subjects, and (4) snowball sampling.

### Purposive Sampling

Occasionally, it may be appropriate to select a sample on the basis of our own knowledge of the population, its elements, and the nature of our research aims—in short, based on our judgment and the purpose of the study. Such a sample is called a **purposive sample**.

We may wish to study a small subset of a larger population in which many members of the subset are easily identified but the enumeration of all of them would be nearly impossible. For example, we might want to study members of community crime prevention groups; many members are easily visible, but it is not feasible to define and sample all members of community crime prevention organizations. In studying a sample of the most visible members, however, we may collect data sufficient for our purposes.

Criminal justice research often compares practices in different jurisdictions—cities or states, for example. In such cases, study elements may be selected because they exhibit some particular attribute. For example, Michael Leiber and Jayne Stairs (1999) were interested in how economic inequality combined with race to affect sentencing practices in Iowa juvenile courts. After controlling for economic status, they found that African American defendants received more restrictive sentences than white defendants did. Leiber and Stairs purposively selected three jurisdictions to obtain sample elements with adequate racial diversity in the state of Iowa. The researchers then selected over 5,000 juvenile cases processed in those three courts.

Researchers may also use purposive or judgmental sampling to represent patterns of complex variation. In their study of closed-circuit television (CCTV) systems, Martin Gill and Angela Spriggs (2005) describe how sites were sampled to reflect variation in type of area (residential, commercial, city center, large parking facilities). Some individual CCTV projects were selected because of certain specific features—they were installed in a high-crime area, or the CCTV setup was notably expensive. One element of this study involved interviews to assess changes in fear of crime following CCTV installation. Angela Spriggs and associates (2005) sampled passersby on city-center streets. They first selected purposive samples of areas and spread their interviews across four day and time periods. This was done to reflect variation in the types of people encountered on different streets at different times. Sampling strategies were thus adapted because of an expected heterogeneity that would have been difficult to capture with random selection.

One of the best-known social science applications of judgmental sampling is the selection of voting precincts for exit polls on election days. On the basis of previous voting results in a given area (city, state, nation), TV networks select voting precincts that, in combination, produce results similar to those of the entire area. The theory is that the selected precincts represent a cross section of the entire electorate. Each time an election is held, analysts evaluate the adequacy of selected precincts and make revisions, additions, or deletions. The goal is to update the group of precincts to ensure that it provides a good representation of all precincts.

Pretesting a questionnaire is another situation in which purposive sampling is common. If, for example, we plan to study people's attitudes about court-ordered restitution for crime victims, we might want to test the questionnaire on a sample of crime victims. Instead of selecting a probability sample of the general population, we might select some number of known crime victims, perhaps from court records.

## Quota Sampling

Like probability sampling, **quota sampling** addresses the issue of representativeness, although the two methods approach the issue quite differently. Quota sampling begins with a matrix or table describing the characteristics of the target population we wish to represent. To do this, we need to know, for example, what proportion of the population is male or female and what proportions fall into various age categories, education levels, ethnic groups, and so forth. In establishing a national quota sample, we need to know what proportion of the national population is, say, urban, eastern, male, under 25, white, working-class, and all the combinations of these attributes.

Once we have created such a matrix and assigned a relative proportion to each cell in the matrix, we can collect data from people who have all the characteristics of a given cell. We then assign all the persons in a given cell a weight appropriate to their portion of the total population. When all the sample elements are weighted in this way, the overall data should provide a reasonable representation of the total population.

Although quota sampling may resemble probability sampling, it has two inherent problems. First, the quota frame (the proportions that different cells represent) must be accurate, and it is often difficult to get up-to-date information for this purpose. A quota sample of auto thieves or teenage vandals would obviously suffer from this difficulty. Second, biases may exist in the selection of sample elements within a given cell—even though its proportion of the population is accurately estimated. An interviewer, instructed to interview five persons who meet a given complex set of characteristics, may still avoid people who live at the top of seven-story walk-ups, have particularly run-down homes, or own vicious dogs.

Quota and purposive sampling may be combined to produce samples that are intuitively, if not statistically, representative. For example, David Farrington, Trevor Bennett, and Brandon Welsh (2007) designed an experimental evaluation of CCTV impact on perceptions of crime and disorder in Cambridge, England. They wished to represent several characteristics of people who spent time outside in certain areas of the city. A probability sample was rejected because the authors wished to represent characteristics of city-center residents who used city streets, not necessarily people who lived in the city. So researchers selected passersby in target areas of Cambridge to meet quotas of 52 percent male, 40 percent between the ages of 16 and 29, and 92 percent white (2007, 190).

## Reliance on Available Subjects

Relying on available subjects—that is, stopping people at a street corner or some other location—is sometimes misleadingly called "convenience sampling." University researchers frequently conduct surveys among the students enrolled in large lecture classes. The ease and economy of such a method explain its popularity; however, it seldom produces data of any general value. It may be useful to pretest a questionnaire, but it should not be used for a study purportedly describing students as a whole.

Reliance on available subjects can be an appropriate sampling method in some situations. It is generally best justified if the researcher wants to study the characteristics of people who are passing the sampling point at some specified time. For example, in her study of street lighting as a crime prevention strategy, Kate Painter (1996) interviewed samples of pedestrians as they walked through specified areas of London just before and 6 weeks after improvements were made in lighting conditions. Painter clearly understood the scope and limits of this sampling technique. Her findings are described as applying to people who actually use area streets after dark, while recognizing that this population may be quite different from the population of area residents. Interviewing a sample of available evening pedestrians is an appropriate sampling technique for generalizing to the population of evening pedestrians, and the population of pedestrians will not be the same as the population of residents. Unlike Farrington and associates, Painter had no specific quotas for subjects in her sample.

In a more general sense, samples like Painter's select elements of a *process*—the process that generates evening pedestrians—rather than elements of a *population*. If we can safely assume that no systematic pattern generates elements of a process, then a sample of available elements as they happen to pass by can be considered to be representative. So, for example, if you are interested in studying crimes reported to police, then a sample of, say, every seventh crime report over a two-month period will be representative of the general population of crime reports over that two-month period.

Sometimes nonprobability and probability sampling techniques can be combined. For example, most attempts to sample homeless or street people rely on available subjects found in shelters, parks, or other locations. Salaam Semaan, Jennifer Lauby, and Jon Liebman (2002) suggest that once areas are located where homeless people congregate, individuals found there can be enumerated and then sampled. Here's a semihypothetical example.

In recent years, Michael Maxfield has casually observed that many people who appear to be homeless congregate at the corner of 9th Avenue and 41st

**TABLE 6.1**   Systematic Sampling of Available Subjects

| Time | People Present | Interviews | Sampling Fraction |
|------|------|------|------|
| 10:00 a.m. | 15 | 5 | 1/3 |
| 11:00 a.m. | 20 | 5 | 1/4 |
| 12:00 p.m. | 15 | 5 | 1/3 |
| 1:00 p.m. | 30 | 5 | 1/6 |
| 2:00 p.m. | 20 | 5 | 1/4 |
| 3:00 p.m. | 50 | 5 | 1/5 |
| Total | 135 | 30 | 1/4 |

Street in Manhattan. An efficient strategy for interviewing samples of homeless people would be a time-space sample where, for example, each hour individuals would be counted and some fraction sampled. Let's say we wished to interview 30 people and we spread those interviews over a six-hour period; we would try to interview five people per hour. So each hour we would count the number of people within some specific area (say, 30 at 1:00 p.m.), then divide that number by five to obtain a sampling fraction (6 in this case). Recalling our earlier discussion of systematic probability sampling, we would then select a random starting point to identify the first person to interview. Then we would select the sixth person after that, and so on. This approach would yield an unbiased sample that represented the population of street people on one Manhattan corner over a six-hour period. Table 6.1 illustrates how we could complete our 30 interviews, selecting varying fractions of those present at different times.

As it happens, 41st Street and 9th Avenue in Manhattan is the rear entrance to the Port Authority bus terminal. Marcus Felson and associates (1996) described efforts to reduce crime and disorder in the Port Authority terminal, a place they claim is the world's busiest bus station. Among the most important objectives were to reduce perceptions of crime problems and to improve how travelers felt about the Port Authority terminal. These are research questions appropriate to some sort of survey. Because more than 170,000 passengers pass through the bus station on an average spring day, obtaining a sufficiently large sample of users presents no difficulty. The problem was how to select a sample. Felson and associates point out that stopping passengers on their way to or from a bus was out of the question. Most passengers are commuters whose journey to and from work is timed to the minute, with none to spare for interviewers' questions. Here's how Felson and associates describe the solution and the sampling strategy it embodied (1996, 90–91):

> Response rates would have been low if the Port Authority had tried to interview rushing customers or to hand out questionnaires to be returned later. Their solution was ingenious. The Port Authority drew a sample of outgoing buses … and placed representatives aboard. After the bus had departed, he or she would hand out a questionnaire to be completed during the trip … [and] collect these questionnaires as each customer arrived at the destination. This procedure produced a very high response rate and high completion rate for each item.

## Snowball Sampling

Another type of nonprobability sampling that closely resembles the available-subjects approach is called **snowball sampling**. Commonly used in field observation studies or specialized interviewing, snowball sampling begins by identifying a single subject or small number of subjects and then asking the subject(s) to identify others like him or her who might be willing to participate in a study.

Criminal justice research on active criminals or deviants frequently uses snowball sampling techniques. The researcher often makes an initial contact by consulting criminal justice agency records to identify, say, someone convicted of auto theft and placed on probation. That person is interviewed and asked to suggest other auto thieves whom researchers could contact. Stephen Baron and Timothy Hartnagel (1998) studied violence among homeless youths in Edmonton, Canada, identifying their sample through snowball techniques. Similarly, snowball sampling is often used to study drug users and dealers. Martin Bouchard (2007) began with contacts from colleagues to identify marijuana growers in Quebec, Canada, who then referred him to other active cultivators. Bruce Jacobs and Jody Miller (1998) accumulated a sample of 25 female crack dealers in St. Louis to study specific techniques to avoid arrest.

Contacting an initial subject or informant who will then refer the researcher to other subjects can be especially difficult in studies of active offenders. As in most aspects of criminal justice research, the various approaches to initiating contacts for snowball sampling have advantages and disadvantages. Beginning with subjects who have a previous arrest or conviction is usually the easiest method for researchers, but it suffers from potential bias by depending on offenders who are known to police or other officials (Jacobs, Topalli, and Wright 2003).

Because snowball samples are used most commonly in field research, we'll return to this method of selecting subjects in Chapter 8 on field methods and observation. In the meantime, recent studies by researchers at the University of Missouri–St. Louis offer good examples of snowball samples of offenders that are not dependent on contacts with criminal justice officials. Beginning with a street-savvy ex-offender, these researchers identified samples of burglars (Wright and Decker 1994), members of youth gangs (Decker and Van Winkle 1996), and armed robbers (Wright and Decker 1997). It's especially difficult to identify active offenders as research subjects, but these examples illustrate notably clever uses of snowball sampling techniques.

## Nonprobability Sampling in Review

Snowball samples are essentially variations on purposive samples (we want to sample juvenile gang members) and on samples of available subjects (sample elements identify other sample elements that are available to us). Each of these is a nonprobability sampling technique. And, like other types of nonprobability samples, snowball samples are most appropriate when it is impossible to determine the probability that any given element will be selected in a sample. Furthermore, snowball sampling and related techniques may be necessary when the target population is difficult to locate or even identify. Approaching pedestrians who happen to pass by, for example, is not an efficient way to select a sample of prostitutes or juvenile gang members. In contrast, approaching pedestrians *is* an appropriate sampling method for studying pedestrians, whereas drawing a probability sample of urban residents to identify people who walk in specific areas of the city would be costly and inefficient.

Like other elements of criminal justice research, sampling plans must be adapted to specific research applications. When it's important to make estimates of the accuracy of our samples, and when suitable sampling frames are possible, we use probability sampling techniques. When no reasonable sampling frame is available, and we cannot draw a probability sample, we cannot make estimates about sample accuracy. Fortunately, in such situations, we can make use of a variety of approaches for drawing nonprobability samples.

## SUMMARY

- The logic of probability sampling forms the foundation for representing large populations with small subsets of those populations.

- The chief criterion of a sample's quality is the degree to which it is representative—the extent

to which the characteristics of the sample are the same as those of the population from which it was selected.

- The most carefully selected sample is almost never a perfect representation of the population from which it was selected. Some degree of sampling error always exists.

- Probability sampling methods provide one excellent way of selecting samples that will be quite representative. They make it possible to estimate the amount of sampling error that should be expected in a given sample.

- The chief principle of probability sampling is that every member of the total population must have some known nonzero probability of being selected in the sample.

- Our ability to estimate population parameters with sample statistics is rooted in the sampling distribution and probability theory. If we draw a large number of samples of a given size, sample statistics will cluster around the true population parameter. As sample size increases, the cluster becomes tighter.

- A variety of sampling designs can be used and combined to suit different populations and research purposes. Each type of sampling has its own advantages and disadvantages.

- Simple random sampling is logically the most fundamental technique in probability sampling, although it is seldom used in practice.

- Systematic sampling involves using a sampling frame to select units that appear at some specified interval—for example, every 8th, or 15th, or 1,023rd unit. This method is functionally equivalent to simple random sampling.

- Stratification improves the representativeness of a sample by reducing the sampling error.

- Disproportionate stratified sampling is especially useful when we want to select adequate numbers of certain types of subjects who are relatively rare in the population we are studying.

- Multistage cluster sampling is frequently used when there is no list of all the members of a population.

- The NCVS and the BCS are national crime surveys based on multistage cluster samples. Sampling methods for each survey illustrate different approaches to representing relatively rare events.

- Nonprobability sampling methods are less statistically representative and less reliable than probability sampling methods. However, they are often easier and cheaper to use.

- Purposive sampling is used when researchers wish to select specific elements of a population. This may be because the elements are believed to be representative of extreme cases or because they represent the range of variation expected in a population.

- In quota sampling, researchers begin with a detailed description of the characteristics of the total population and then select sample members in a way that includes the different composite profiles that exist in the population.

- When it is not possible to draw nonprobability samples through other means, researchers often rely on available subjects. Professors sometimes do this—students in their classes are available subjects.

- Snowball samples accumulate subjects through chains of referrals and are most commonly used in field research.

## KEY TERMS

## REVIEW QUESTIONS AND EXERCISES

1. Discuss possible study populations, elements, sampling units, and sampling frames for drawing a sample to represent the populations listed here. You may wish to limit your discussion to populations in a specific state or other jurisdiction.

   a. Municipal police officers

   b. Felony court judges

   c. Auto thieves

   d. Licensed automobile drivers

   e. State police superintendents

   f. Persons incarcerated in county jails

3. What steps would be involved in selecting a multistage cluster sample of undergraduate students taking criminal justice research methods courses in U.S. colleges and universities?

4. Describe two examples of target populations that might be readily sampled using lists of e-mail addresses.

## ADDITIONAL READINGS

Kish, Leslie, *Survey Sampling* (New York: Wiley, 1965). Unquestionably the definitive work on sampling in social research. Kish's coverage ranges from the simplest matters to the most complex and mathematical. He is both highly theoretical and downright practical. Easily readable and difficult passages intermingle as Kish dissects everything you could want or need to know about each aspect of sampling.

Patton, Michael Quinn, *Qualitative Research and Evaluation Methods,* 3rd ed. (Thousand Oaks, CA: Sage, 2002). Though its focus is evaluation, this book presents one of the best discussions of nonprobability sampling available. Patton covers a wide range of variations on purposive sampling.

Semaan, Salaam, Jennifer Lauby, and Jon Liebman, "Street and Network Sampling in Evaluation Studies of HIV Risk-Reduction Interventions," *AIDS Reviews* 4 (2002): 213-223. Many techniques used in public health research can cross over nicely for criminal justice studies. This is a good example of creative sampling techniques for finding hard-to-find people.

Weisel, Deborah, *Conducting Community Surveys: A Practical Guide for Law Enforcement Agencies* (Washington, DC: U.S. Department of Justice, Office of Justice Programs, Bureau of Justice Statistics, 1999). This short handbook offers good, basic advice on drawing samples for community-level victimization surveys. The information on estimating sample size is especially good.

# CHAPTER 7

# Survey Research and Other Ways of Asking Questions

We'll examine how mail, interview, and telephone surveys can be used in criminal justice research. We'll also consider other ways of collecting data by asking people questions.

## INTRODUCTION

*Asking people questions is the most common data collection method in social science.*

A little-known survey was attempted among French workers in 1880. A German political sociologist mailed some 25,000 questionnaires to workers to determine the extent of their exploitation by employers. The rather lengthy questionnaire included items such as these:

> Does your employer or his representative resort to trickery in order to defraud you of a part of your earnings? If you are paid piece rates, is the quality of the article made a pretext for fraudulent deductions from your wages?

The survey researcher in this case was not George Gallup but Karl Marx (1880, 208). Although 25,000 questionnaires were mailed out, there is no record of any being returned. And you need not know much about survey methods to recognize the loaded questions posed by Marx.

Survey research is perhaps the most frequently used mode of observation in sociology and political science, and surveys are often used in criminal justice research as well. You have no doubt been a respondent in a survey, and you may have conducted a **survey** yourself.

We begin this chapter by discussing the criminal justice topics that are most appropriate for survey methods. Next, we cover the basic principles of how to ask people questions for research purposes, including some of the details of questionnaire construction. We describe the three basic ways of administering questionnaires—self-administration, face-to-face interviews, and telephone interviews—and summarize the strengths and weaknesses of each method. After discussing more specialized interviewing techniques, such as focus groups, we conclude the chapter with some advice on the benefits and pitfalls of conducting your own surveys.

## TOPICS APPROPRIATE TO SURVEY RESEARCH

*Surveys have a wide variety of uses in basic and applied criminal justice research.*

Surveys may be used for descriptive, explanatory, exploratory, and applied research. They are best suited for studies that have individual people as the units of analysis. They are often used for other units of analysis as well, such as households or organizations. Even in these cases, however, one or more individual people act as **respondent** or informant.

For example, researchers sometimes use victimization incidents as units of analysis in examining data from crime surveys. The fact that some people may be victimized more than once and others not at all means that victimization incidents are not the same units as individuals. However, a survey questionnaire must still be administered to people who provide information about victimization incidents. In a similar fashion, the National Jail Census, conducted every five or so years by the Census Bureau, collects information about local detention facilities. Jails are the units of analysis, but information about each jail is provided by individuals. The national youth gang survey has been conducted for many years. Though it seeks information about gangs, the survey is sent to law enforcement agencies and the questionnaire is completed by individuals in police departments.

We now consider some broad categories of research applications in which survey methods are especially appropriate.

### Counting Crime

We touched on this use of surveys in Chapter 4. Asking people about victimization is a measure of crime that adjusts for some of the limitations of data collected by police. Of course, survey measures have their own shortcomings. Most of these difficulties, such as recall error and reluctance to discuss victimization with interviewers, are inherent in survey methods. Nevertheless, victim surveys have become important sources of data about the volume of crime in the United States and in other countries.

### Self-Reports

Surveys that ask people about crimes they may have committed were also discussed in Chapter 4. For research that seeks to explore or explain why people commit criminal, delinquent, or deviant acts, asking questions is the best method available.

Within the general category of self-report surveys, two different applications are distinguished by their target population and sampling methods. Studies of offenders select samples of respondents known to have committed crimes, often prisoners. Typically the focus is on the *frequency* of offending—how many crimes of various types are committed by active offenders over a period of time.

The other type of self-report survey focuses on the *prevalence* of offending—how many people commit crimes, in contrast to how many crimes are committed by a target population of offenders. Such surveys typically use samples that represent a broader population, such as U.S. households, adult males, or high school seniors. The Monitoring the Future survey, briefly described in Chapter 4, is a self-report survey that centers on measuring the prevalence of offending among high school seniors.

General-population surveys and surveys of offenders tend to present different types of difficulties in connection with the validity and reliability of self-reports. Recall error and the reporting of fabricated offenses may be problems in a survey of high-rate offenders (Roberts et al. 2005), whereas respondents in general-population self-report surveys may be reluctant to disclose illegal behavior. When we discuss questionnaire construction later in this chapter, we will present examples and suggestions for creating self-report items.

## Perceptions and Attitudes

Another application of surveys in criminal justice is to learn how people feel about crime and criminal justice policy. Public views about sentencing policies, gun control, police performance, and drug abuse are often solicited in opinion polls. Begun in 1972, the General Social Survey is an ongoing survey of social indicators in the United States. Questions about fear of crime and other perceptions of crime problems are regularly included. Since the 1970s, a growing number of explanatory studies have been conducted on public perceptions of crime and crime problems. A large body of research on fear of crime has grown, in part, from the realization that fear and its behavioral consequences

are much more widespread among the population than is actual criminal victimization (Ditton and Farrall 2007).

## Targeted Victim Surveys

Victim surveys that target individual cities or neighborhoods are important tools for evaluating policy innovations. Many criminal justice programs seek to prevent or reduce crime in a specific area, but crimes reported to police cannot be used to evaluate many types of programs.

To see why this is so, consider a hypothetical community policing program that encourages neighborhood residents to report all suspected crimes to the police. Results from the National Crime Victimization Survey (NCVS) have consistently shown that many minor incidents are not reported because victims believe that police will not want to be bothered. But if a new program stresses that police actually want to be bothered, the proportion of crimes reported may increase, resulting in what appears to be an increase in crime.

The solution is to conduct targeted victim surveys before and after introducing a policy change. Such victim surveys are especially appropriate for evaluating any policy that may increase crime reporting as a side effect.

Consider also that large-scale surveys such as the NCVS cannot be used to evaluate local crime prevention programs. This is because the NCVS is designed to represent the national population of persons who live in households. Although NCVS data for the 11 largest states can be analyzed separately (Lauritsen and Schaum 2005), the NCVS is not representative of any particular local jurisdiction. It is not possible to identify the specific location of victimizations from NCVS data.

The community victim surveys designed by the Bureau of Justice Statistics (BJS) and the Office of Community Oriented Police Services (COPS) help with each of these needs. Local surveys can be launched specifically to evaluate local crime prevention efforts. Or innovative programs can be timed to correspond to regular cycles of local surveys. In each case, the BJS-COPS guide (Weisel

1999) presents advice on drawing samples to represent local jurisdictions.

Another type of targeted victim survey is one that focuses on particular types of incidents that might target more narrowly defined population segments. A good example is the National Violence Against Women Survey, a joint effort of the National Institute of Justice and a violence prevention bureau in the National Institutes of Health (Tjaden and Thoennes 2000). Screening questions presented explicit descriptions of sexual and other violence with the specific purpose of providing better information about these incidents that have proved difficult to measure through general-purpose crime surveys.

## Other Evaluation Uses

Other types of surveys may be appropriate for applied studies. A good illustration of this is a continuing series of neighborhood surveys to evaluate community policing in Chicago. Here's an example of how the researchers link their information needs to surveys (Chicago Community Policing Evaluation Consortium 2004, 2):

> Because it is a participatory program, CAPS [Chicago's Alternative Policing Strategy] depends on the effectiveness of campaigns to bring it to the public's attention and on the success of efforts to get the public involved in beat meetings and other district projects. The surveys enable us to track the public's awareness and involvement in community policing in Chicago.

In general, surveys can be used to evaluate policy that seeks to change attitudes, beliefs, or perceptions. Consider a program designed to promote victim and witness cooperation in criminal court by reducing case-processing time. At first, we might consider direct measures of case-processing time as indicators of program success. If the program goal is to increase cooperation, however, a survey that asks how victims and witnesses perceive case-processing time will be more appropriate.

## GUIDELINES FOR ASKING QUESTIONS

*How questions are asked is the single most important feature of survey research.*

A defining feature of survey methods is that research concepts are operationalized by asking people questions. Several general guidelines can assist in framing and asking questions that serve as excellent operationalizations of variables. It is important also to be aware of pitfalls that can result in useless and even misleading information. We'll begin with some of the options available for creating a questionnaire.

### Open-Ended and Closed-Ended Questions

In asking questions, researchers have two basic options, and each can accommodate certain variations. The first is the **open-ended question**, in which the respondent is asked to provide his or her own answers. For example, the respondent may be asked, "What do you feel is the most important crime problem facing the police in your city today?" and be provided with a space to write in the answer (or be asked to report it orally to an interviewer). The other option is a **closed-ended question**, in which the respondent is asked to select an answer from among a list provided by the researcher.

Closed-ended questions are especially useful because they provide more uniform responses and are more easily processed. They often can be transferred directly into a data file. Open-ended responses, in contrast, must be coded before they can be processed for analysis. This coding process often requires that the researcher interpret the meaning of responses, which opens up the possibility of misunderstanding and researcher bias. Also, some respondents may give answers that are essentially irrelevant to the researcher's intent.

The chief shortcoming of closed-ended questions lies in the researcher's structuring of responses. When the relevant answers to a given question are relatively clear, there should be no problem. In some cases, however, the researcher's list of responses may fail to include some important answers. When we ask about "the most important crime problem facing the police in your city today," for example, our checklist might omit certain crime problems that respondents consider important.

In constructing closed-ended questions, we are best guided by two of the requirements for operationalizing variables stated in Chapter 4. First, the response categories provided should be exhaustive: they should include all the possible responses that might be expected. Often, researchers ensure this by adding a category labeled something like "Other (Please specify: ___)." Second, the answer categories must be mutually exclusive: the respondent should not feel compelled to select more than one. In some cases, researchers solicit multiple answers, but doing so can create difficulties in subsequent data processing and analysis. To ensure that categories are mutually exclusive, we should carefully consider each combination of categories, asking whether a person could reasonably choose more than one answer. In addition, it is useful to add an instruction that respondents should select the one best answer. However, this is still not a satisfactory substitute for a carefully constructed set of responses.

## Questions and Statements

The term **questionnaire** suggests a collection of questions, but a typical questionnaire probably has as many statements as questions. This is because researchers often are interested in determining the extent to which respondents hold a particular attitude or perspective. Researchers try to summarize the attitude in a fairly brief statement; then they present that statement and ask respondents whether they agree or disagree with it. Rensis Likert formalized this procedure through the creation of the Likert scale, a format in which respondents are asked whether they strongly agree, agree, disagree, or strongly disagree, or perhaps strongly approve, approve, and so forth.

Both questions and statements may be used profitably. Using both in a questionnaire adds flexibility in the design of items and can make the questionnaire more interesting as well.

## Make Items Clear

It should go without saying that questionnaire items must be clear and unambiguous, but the broad proliferation of unclear and ambiguous questions in surveys makes the point worth stressing here. Researchers commonly become so deeply involved in the topic that opinions and perspectives that are clear to them will not be at all clear to respondents, many of whom have given little or no thought to the topic. Or researchers may have only a superficial understanding of the topic and so may fail to specify the intent of a question sufficiently. The question "What do you think about the governor's decision concerning prison furloughs?" may evoke in the respondent some counter-questions: "Which governor's decision?" "What are prison furloughs?" "What did the governor decide?" Questionnaire items should be precise so that the respondent knows exactly what the researcher wants an answer to.

Frequently, researchers ask respondents for a single answer to a combination question. Such double-barreled questions seem to occur most often when the researcher has personally identified with a complex question. For example, the researcher might ask respondents to agree or disagree with the statement "The Department of Corrections should stop releasing inmates for weekend furloughs and concentrate on rehabilitating criminals." Although many people will unequivocally agree with the statement and others will unequivocally disagree, still others will be unable to answer. Some might want to terminate the furlough program and punish—not rehabilitate—prisoners. Others might want to expand rehabilitation efforts while maintaining weekend furloughs; they can neither agree nor disagree without misleading the researcher.

## Short Items Are Best

In the interest of being unambiguous and precise and pointing to the relevance of an issue, researchers often create long, complicated items. That should be avoided. In the case of questionnaires that respondents complete themselves, they are often unwilling to study an item to understand it. The respondent should be able to read an item quickly, understand its intent, and select or provide an answer without difficulty. In general, it's safe to assume that respondents will read items quickly and give quick answers; therefore short, clear items that will not be misinterpreted under those conditions are best. Questions read to respondents in person or over the phone should be similarly brief.

## Avoid Negative Items

A negation in a questionnaire item paves the way for easy misinterpretation. Asked to agree or disagree with the statement "Drugs such as marijuana should not be legalized," many respondents will overlook the word *not* and answer on that basis. Thus some will agree with the statement when they are in favor of legalizing marijuana and others will agree when they oppose it. And we may never know which is which.

## Biased Items and Terms

Recall from the earlier discussion of conceptualization and operationalization that there are no ultimately true meanings for any of the concepts we typically study in social science. This same general principle applies to the responses we get from persons in a survey.

The meaning of a given response to a question depends in large part on the wording of the question. That is true of every question and answer. Some questions seem to encourage particular responses more than other questions. In the context of questionnaires, **bias** refers to any property of a question that encourages respondents to answer in a particular way. Most researchers recognize the likely effect of a question such as "Do you support the president's use of intensive interrogation to promote the safety and security of all Americans?" and no reputable researcher would use such an item. The biasing effect of items and terms is far subtler than this example suggests, however.

The mere identification of an attitude or position with a prestigious (or unpopular) person or agency

can bias responses. For example, an item that starts with "Do you agree or disagree with the recent Supreme Court decision that…" might have this effect. We are not suggesting that such wording will necessarily produce consensus or even a majority in support of the position identified with the prestigious person or agency. Rather, support will likely be greater than what would have been obtained without such identification.

Sometimes, the impact of different forms of question wording is relatively subtle. For example, Kenneth Rasinski (1989) analyzed the results of several General Social Survey studies of attitudes toward government spending. He found that the way programs were identified had an impact on the amount of public support they received. Here are some comparisons:

| More Support | Less Support |
|---|---|
| "Assistance to the poor" | "Welfare" |
| "Halting the rising crime rate" | "Law enforcement" |
| "Dealing with drug addiction" | "Drug rehabilitation" |

In 1986, for example, 63 percent of respondents said too little money was being spent on "assistance to the poor," while in a matched survey that year, only 23 percent said we were spending too little on "welfare."

The main guidance we offer for avoiding bias is that researchers imagine how they would feel giving each of the answers they offer to respondents. If they would feel embarrassed, perverted, inhumane, stupid, irresponsible, or anything like that, then they should give some serious thought to whether others will be willing to give those answers. Researchers must carefully examine the purpose of their inquiry and construct items that will be most useful to it.

We also need to be generally wary of what researchers call the *social desirability* of questions and answers. Whenever we ask people for information, they answer through a filter of what will make them look good. That is especially true if they are being interviewed in a face-to-face situation.

The Centers for Disease Control and Prevention (Choi and Pak 2005) provides an excellent analysis of both obvious and not-so-obvious ways in which your choice of terms can bias and otherwise confuse responses to questionnaires. Among other things, they warn against using ambiguous, technical, uncommon, or vague words. Their thorough analysis includes many concrete illustrations.

## Designing Self-Report Items

Social desirability is one of the problems that plagues self-report crime questions in general population surveys. Adhering to the ethical principles of confidentiality and anonymity, as well as convincing respondents that we are doing so, is one way of getting more truthful responses to self-report items. Other techniques can help us avoid or reduce problems with self-report items.

One method, used in earlier versions of the British Crime Survey (BCS), is to introduce a group of self-report items with a disclaimer and to sanitize the presentation of offenses. The self-report section of the 1984 BCS began with this introduction:

> There are lots of things which are actually crimes, but which are done by lots of people, and which many people do not think of as crimes. On this card [printed card handed to respondents] are a list of eight of them. For each one, can you tell me how many people you think do it— most people, a lot of people, or no one.

Respondents then read a card, shown in Figure 7.1, that presented descriptions of various offenses. Interviewers first asked respondents how many people they thought ever did X, where X corresponded to the letter for an offense shown in Figure 7.1. Next, respondents were asked whether they had ever done X. Interviewers then moved on down the list of letters for each offense on the card.

This procedure incorporates three techniques to guard against the socially desirable response of not admitting to having committed a crime. First, the disclaimer seeks to reassure respondents that "many people" do not really think of various acts as crimes. Second, respondents are asked how many people they think commit each offense before being asked whether they have done so themselves.

| | |
|---|---|
| A. | Taken office supplies from work (such as stationery, envelopes, and pens) when not supposed to. |
| B. | Taken things other than office supplies from work (such as tools, money, or other goods) when not supposed to. |
| C. | Fiddled expenses [fiddled is the Queen's English equivalent of fudged]. |
| D. | Deliberately traveled [on a train] without a ticket or paid too low a fare. |
| E. | Failed to declare something at customs on which duty was payable. |
| F. | Cheated on tax. |
| G. | Used cannabis (hashish, marijuana, ganga, grass). |
| H. | Regularly driven a car when they know they have drunk enough to be well above the legal limit. |

**F I G U R E  7.1**  Showcard for Self-Report Items, 1984 British Crime Survey

Source: Adapted from the 1984 British Crime Survey (NOP Market Research Limited 1985).

This takes advantage of a common human justification for engaging in certain kinds of behavior— other people do it. Third, asking whether they "have ever done X" is less confrontational than asking whether they "have ever cheated on an expense account." Again, the foibles of human behavior are at work here, in much the same way that people use euphemisms such as *restroom* for "toilet" and *sleep together* for "have sexual intercourse." It is, of course, not realistic to expect that such ploys will reassure all respondents. Furthermore, disclaimers about serious offenses such as rape or bank robbery would be ludicrous. But such techniques illustrate how thoughtful wording and introductions can be incorporated into sensitive questions.

Self-report surveys of known offenders encounter different problems. Incarcerated persons may be reluctant to admit committing crimes because of the legal consequences. High-rate offenders may have difficulty distinguishing among a number of different crimes or remembering even approximate dates. Sorting out dates and details of individual crimes among high-rate offenders requires different strategies.

One technique that is useful in surveys of active offenders is to interview subjects several times at regular intervals. Other research asks offenders to complete "crime calendars" on which they make records of weekly or monthly offenses committed. Jennifer Roberts and associates (2005) found that more frequent interviews were necessary for use by high-rate offenders, and that crime calendars were best suited for tracking more serious offenses.

Obtaining valid and reliable results from self-report items is challenging, but self-report survey techniques are important tools for addressing certain types of criminal justice research questions. For this reason, researchers are constantly striving to improve self-report items. See the collection of essays by Joel Kennet and Joseph Gfroerer (2005) for a detailed discussion of issues involved in measuring self-reported drug use through the National Household Survey on Drug Abuse. A National Research Council report (2001) discusses self-report survey measures more generally.

Computer technology has made it possible to significantly improve self-reported items. David Matz (2007) describes advances in self-report items from recent surveys that supplement the British Crime Survey. We present examples later in the chapter when we focus on different modes of survey administration.

# QUESTIONNAIRE CONSTRUCTION

*After settling on question content, researchers must consider the format and organization of all items in a questionnaire.*

Because questionnaires are the fundamental instruments of survey research, we now turn our attention to some of the established techniques for constructing them. The following sections are best considered as a continuation of our theoretical discussions in Chapter 4 of conceptualization and measurement.

## General Questionnaire Format

The format of a questionnaire is just as important as the nature and wording of the questions. An improperly laid-out questionnaire can cause respondents to miss questions, confuse them about

the nature of the data desired, and even lead them to throw the questionnaire away.

As a general rule, the questionnaire should be uncluttered. Inexperienced researchers tend to fear that their questionnaire will look too long, so they squeeze several questions onto a single line, abbreviate questions, and try to use as few pages as possible. Such efforts are ill-advised and even counterproductive. Putting more than one question on a line will cause some respondents to miss the second question altogether. Some respondents will misinterpret abbreviated questions. And, more generally, respondents who have spent considerable time on the first page of what seemed a short questionnaire will be more demoralized than respondents who quickly completed the first several pages of what initially seemed a long form. Moreover, the latter will have made fewer errors and will not have been forced to reread confusing, abbreviated questions. Nor will they have been forced to write a long answer in a tiny space.

## Contingency Questions

Quite often in questionnaires, certain questions are clearly relevant to only some of the respondents and irrelevant to others. A victim survey, for example, presents batteries of questions about victimization incidents that are meaningful only to crime victims.

Frequently, this situation—realizing that the topic is relevant only to some respondents—arises when we wish to ask a series of questions about a certain topic. We may want to ask whether respondents belong to a particular organization and, if so, how often they attend meetings, whether they have held office in the organization, and so forth. Or we might want to ask whether respondents have heard anything about a certain policy proposal, such as opening a youth shelter in the neighborhood, and then investigate the attitudes of those who have heard of it.

The subsequent questions in series such as these are called *contingency questions*; whether they are to be asked and answered is *contingent* on the response to the first question in the series. The proper use of contingency questions can make it easier for respondents to complete the questionnaire because they do not have to answer questions that are irrelevant to them.

Contingency questions can be presented in several formats on printed questionnaires. The one shown in Figure 7.2 is probably the clearest and most effective. Note that the questions shown in the figure could have been dealt with in a single question: "How many times, if any, have you smoked marijuana?" The response categories then would be: "Never," "Once," "2 to 5 times," and so forth. This single question would apply to all respondents, and each would find an appropriate answer category. Such a question, however, might put pressure on some respondents to report having smoked marijuana, because the main question asks how many times they have smoked it. The contingency question format illustrated in Figure 7.2 reduces the subtle pressure on respondents to report having smoked marijuana. This discussion shows how seemingly theoretical issues of validity and reliability are involved in so mundane a matter as how to format questions on a piece of paper.

Used properly, even complex sets of contingency questions can be constructed without confusing respondents. Sometimes a set of contingency questions is long enough to extend over several pages. Victim surveys typically include many contingency questions. Figure 7.3 presents a few questions from the NCVS questionnaire used in 2004. All respondents are asked a series of screening questions to reveal possible victimizations. Persons who answer yes to any of the screening questions then complete a crime incident report that presents a large number of items designed to measure details of the victimization incident.

As Figure 7.3 shows, the crime incident report itself also contains contingency questions. You might notice that even this brief adaptation from the NCVS screening and crime incident report questionnaires is rather complex. NCVS questionnaires are administered primarily through computer-assisted telephone interviews in which the flow of contingency questions is more or less automated. It would be difficult to construct a self-administered victimization questionnaire with such complicated contingency questions.

## Matrix Questions

Often researchers want to ask several questions that have the same set of answer categories. This happens whenever the Likert response categories are used. Then it is often possible to construct a matrix of items and answers, as illustrated in Figure 7.4.

This format has three advantages. First, it uses space efficiently. Second, respondents probably find it easier to complete a set of questions presented in this fashion. Third, this format may make it easier for the respondent as well as the researcher to compare responses given to different questions. Because respondents can quickly review their answers to earlier items in the set, they might choose between, say, "strongly agree" and "agree" on a given statement by comparing their strength of agreement with their earlier responses in the set.

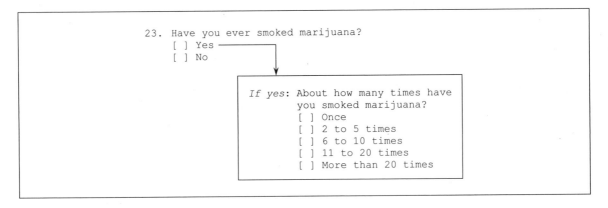

```
        23. Have you ever smoked marijuana?
            [ ] Yes ─────────┐
            [ ] No           │
                             ▼
                  ┌─────────────────────────────────────────┐
                  │ If yes: About how many times have        │
                  │         you smoked marijuana?            │
                  │         [ ] Once                          │
                  │         [ ] 2 to 5 times                  │
                  │         [ ] 6 to 10 times                 │
                  │         [ ] 11 to 20 times                │
                  │         [ ] More than 20 times            │
                  └─────────────────────────────────────────┘
```

**FIGURE 7.2** Contingency Question Format

*Screening Question:*

36a.  I'm going to read you some examples that will give you an idea of the kinds of crimes this study covers. As I go through them, tell me if any of these happened to you in the last 6 months, that is, since [date].

Was something belonging to YOU stolen, such as

(a)  Things that you carry, like luggage, a wallet, purse, briefcase, book

(b)  Clothing, jewelry or calculator

(c)  Bicycle or sports equipment

(d)  Things in your home—like a TV, stereo, or tools

(e)  Things outside your home, such as a garden hose or lawn furniture

(f)  Things belonging to children in the household

(g)  Things from a vehicle, such as a package, groceries, camera, or tapes
OR

(h)  Did anyone ATTEMPT to steal anything belonging to you?

*Crime Incident Report:*

20a.  Were you or any other member of this household present when this incident occurred?

____ Yes [ask item 20b]

____ No [skip to 56, page 8]

20b.  Which household members were present?

____ Respondent only [ask item 21]

____ Respondent and other household member(s) [ask item 21]

____ Only other household member(s) [skip to 59, page 8]

21.  Did you personally see an offender?

____ Yes

____ No

. . . . . . . . .

56.  Do you know or have you learned anything about the offender(s)—for instance, whether there was one or more than one offender involved, whether it was someone young or old, or male or female?

____ Yes [ask 57]

____ No [skip to 88, page 11]

**F I G U R E  7.3**  NCVS Screening Questions and Crime Incident Report

*Source:* Adapted from National Crime Victimization Survey, NCVS-1 Basic Screen Questionnaire, 9/16/2004 version, http://bjs.ojp.usdoj.gov/content/pub/pdf/ncvs104.pdf, National Crime Victimization Survey, NCVS-2 Crime Incident Report, 9/16/2004 version, http://bjs.ojp.usdoj.gov/content/pub/pdf.ncvs204.pdf.

Some dangers are inherent in using this format, as well. Its advantages may promote structuring an item so that the responses fit into the matrix format when a different, more idiosyncratic, set of responses might be more appropriate. Also, the matrix question format can generate a response set among some respondents. This

17. Beside each of the statements presented below, please indicate whether you Strongly Agree (SA), Agree (A), Disagree (D), Strongly Disagree (SD), or are Undecided (U).

| | | SA | A | D | SD | U |
|---|---|---|---|---|---|---|
| a. | What this country needs is more law and order. | [ ] | [ ] | [ ] | [ ] | [ ] |
| b. | Police in America should not carry guns. | [ ] | [ ] | [ ] | [ ] | [ ] |
| c. | Repeat drug dealers should receive life sentences. | [ ] | [ ] | [ ] | [ ] | [ ] |

**FIGURE 7.4**  Matrix Question Format

means that respondents may develop a pattern of, say, agreeing with all the statements, without really thinking about what the statements mean. That is especially likely if the set of statements begins with several that indicate a particular orientation (for example, a conservative political perspective) and then offers only a few subsequent ones that represent the opposite orientation. Respondents might assume that all the statements represent the same orientation and, reading quickly, might misread some of them, thereby giving the wrong answers. This problem can be reduced somewhat by alternating statements that represent different orientations and by making all statements short and clear.

A more difficult problem is when responses are generated through respondent boredom or fatigue. This can be avoided by keeping matrix questions and the entire questionnaire as short as possible. Later in this chapter, in the section on comparing different methods of questionnaire administration, we will describe a useful technique for avoiding response sets generated by respondent fatigue.

## Ordering Items in a Questionnaire

The order in which questions are asked can also affect the answers given. The content of one question can affect the answers given to later ones. If several questions ask about the dangers of illegal drug use and then a question (open-ended) asks respondents to volunteer what they believe to be the most serious crime problems in U.S. cities, drug use will receive more mentions than would otherwise be the case. In this situation, it is preferable to ask the open-ended question first.

If respondents are asked to rate the overall effectiveness of corrections policy, they will answer subsequent questions about specific aspects of correctional institutions in a way that is consistent with their initial assessment. The converse is true as well: if respondents are first asked specific questions about prisons and other correctional facilities, their subsequent overall assessment will be influenced by the earlier question.

The best solution is sensitivity to the problem. Although we cannot avoid the effect of question order, we should attempt to estimate what that effect will be. Then we will be able to interpret results in a meaningful fashion. If the order of questions seems an especially important issue in a given study, we could construct several versions of the questionnaire that contain the different possible orderings of questions. We could then determine the effects of ordering. At the very least, different versions of the questionnaire should be pretested.

The desired ordering of questions differs somewhat between self-administered questionnaires and interviews. In the former, it is usually best to begin the questionnaire with the most interesting questions. Potential respondents who glance casually at the first few questions should want to answer them. Perhaps the questions involve opinions that they are aching to express. At the same time, however, the initial questions should be neither threatening nor sensitive. It might be a bad idea to begin with questions about sexual behavior or drug use. Requests for demographic data (age, gender, and the like) should generally be placed at the end of a self-administered questionnaire. Placing these questions

**DON'T START FROM SCRATCH!**

It's always easier to modify an existing questionnaire for a particular research application than it is to start from scratch. It's also difficult to imagine asking questions that nobody has asked before. Here are examples of websites that present complete questionnaires or batteries of questionnaire items.

- Bureau of Justice Statistics (BJS; http://bjs .ojp.usdoj.gov/index.cfm). In addition to administering the NCVS, the BJS collects information from a variety of justice organizations. Copies of recent questionnaires for all BJS-sponsored surveys are available on the Bureau's website. Look for a ribbon of links near the top of the page. Mouse over "Data Collections" to find a series (e.g., corrections, courts and sentencing, law enforcement, victims) and then click on one of interest. Browse through collections and follow links to find questionnaires for the series.

- California Healthy Kids Survey (http://chks.wested .org/administer/download). This set of questionnaires is useful for assessing behavior routines. Most include items on alcohol, tobacco, and other drug use; fighting; and other behaviors of potential interest for school-based interventions.

English and Spanish versions are available for elementary, middle, and high school.

- Centers for Disease Control and Prevention (CDC; http://www.cdc.gov/nchs/surveys.htm). Various centers within the CDC regularly collect a variety of health-related data through questionnaires and other data collection systems. Copies of instruments are available at the CDC website.

- The Measurement Group. (http://www .themeasurementgroup.com/evaluationtools/ evaluation_tools.htm). This provides links to questionnaires designed for use in public health studies, but many of these include items of potential interest to treatment-related initiatives.

- University of Delaware Survey Questionnaire Archive (http://www.cadsr.udel.edu/sqa/index. htm). The Questionnaire Archive includes links to complete questionnaires for a wide variety of surveys conducted mostly in the United States. Over 150 documents were included as of January 2010. You can either search or browse through recent additions. You can find a master list of surveys, or you can browse questionnaires by topic.

at the beginning, as many inexperienced researchers are tempted to do, might make the questionnaire appear overly intrusive, so the person who receives it may not want to complete it.

Finally, it's common for less experienced researchers to assume that questionnaires must be newly constructed for each application. In contrast, it's almost always possible—and usually preferable—to use an existing questionnaire as a point of departure. See the box "Don't Start from Scratch!" for more on this.

## SELF-ADMINISTERED QUESTIONNAIRES

*Self-administered questionnaires are generally the least expensive and easiest to complete.*

Although the mail survey is the typical method used in self-administered studies, several other methods

are also possible. In some cases, it may be appropriate to administer the questionnaire to a group of respondents gathered at the same place at the same time, such as police officers at roll call or prison inmates at some specially arranged assembly. The Monitoring the Future survey (see Chapter 4) has high school seniors complete self-administered questionnaires in class.

Some experimentation has been conducted on the home delivery of questionnaires. A research worker delivers the questionnaire to the home of sample respondents and explains the study. Then the questionnaire is left for the respondent to complete, and the researcher picks it up later.

Home delivery and the mail can be used in combination as well. Questionnaires can be mailed to families, and then research workers may visit the homes to pick up the questionnaires and check them for completeness. In the opposite approach, survey packets are hand-delivered by research workers with a request that the respondents mail the completed questionnaires to the research office. In general, when a research worker delivers the questionnaire, picks it up, or both, the completion rate is higher than for straightforward mail surveys.

The Internet has made it possible to have respondents complete self-administered questionnaires online. Before discussing web-based questionnaires, let us turn our attention to the fundamentals of mail surveys, which might still be used for people without Internet access.

## Mail Distribution and Return

The basic method for collecting data through the mail is transmittal of a questionnaire accompanied by a letter of explanation and a self-addressed, stamped envelope for returning the questionnaire. You have probably received a few. As a respondent, you are expected to complete the questionnaire, put it in the envelope, and mail it back. If, by any chance, you have received such a questionnaire and failed to return it, it would be a valuable exercise for you to recall your reasons for not returning it—and keep those in mind any time you plan to send questionnaires to others.

Timing is important to consider in the actual mailing of questionnaires. In most cases, the holiday months of November, December, and January should be avoided. Overall mail volume is greatest during those periods, which can substantially slow down the process of both distribution and return of questionnaires. And because a greater volume of mail is flowing through post offices, people receive more mail of all types. If a questionnaire arrives in the company of glossy gift catalogs, holiday greetings, bills, and assorted junk mail, respondents will be more likely to discard the survey packet.

## Warning Mailings and Cover Letters

Warning mailings can be used to verify who lives at sampled addresses and to increase response rates. Warning mailings work like this: After researchers generate a sample, they send a postcard to each selected respondent, with the notation "Address correction requested" printed on the postcard. If the addressee has moved and left a forwarding address, the questionnaire is sent to the new address. When someone has moved and not left a forwarding address, or more than a year has elapsed and the post office no longer has information about a new address, the postcard is returned marked something like "Addressee unknown." Selected persons who still reside at the original listed address are warned in suitable language to expect a questionnaire in the mail. In such cases, postcards should briefly describe the purpose of the survey for which the respondent has been selected.

Warning letters can be more effective than postcards in increasing a survey's **response rate**, the percentage of people contacted who actually participate. Letters printed on letterhead stationery can present a longer description of the survey's purpose and a more reasoned explanation of why it is important for everyone to respond.

Cover letters accompanying the questionnaire offer a similar opportunity to increase response rates. Two features of cover letters warrant some attention. First, the content of the letter is obviously important. The message should communicate why a survey is being conducted, how and why the respondent was selected, and why it is important for the respondent to complete the questionnaire. In line with our discussion of the protection of human subjects in Chapter 2, the cover letter should also assure respondents that their answers will be confidential.

Second, the cover letter should identify the institutional affiliation or sponsorship of the survey. The two alternatives are (1) an institution that the respondent respects or can identify with, or (2) a neutral but impressive-sounding affiliation. For example, if we are conducting a mail survey of police chiefs, printing our cover letter on International Association of Chiefs of Police (IACP) stationery and having the letter signed by an official in the IACP might increase the response rate. Of course, we cannot adopt such a procedure unless the survey is endorsed by the IACP.

By the same token, it is important to avoid controversial affiliations or those inappropriate for the target population. The National Organization for the Reform of Marijuana Laws, for instance, is not suitable for most target populations. A university affiliation is appropriate in many cases, unless the university is on bad terms with the target population.

## Follow-Up Mailings

Follow-up mailings may be administered in a number of ways. In the simplest, nonrespondents are sent a letter of additional encouragement to participate. A better method, however, is to send a new copy of the survey questionnaire with the follow-up letter. If potential respondents have not returned their questionnaires after two or three weeks, the questionnaires probably have been lost or misplaced. In general, the longer a potential respondent delays replying, the less likely he or she is to do so at all. Properly timed follow-up mailings provide additional stimuli to respond.

The effects of follow-up mailings may be seen by monitoring the number of questionnaires received over time. Initial mailings will be followed by a rise in and subsequent subsiding of returns, and follow-up mailings will spur a resurgence of returns. In practice, three mailings (an original and two follow-ups) are most effective.

## Acceptable Response Rates

A question frequently asked about mail surveys concerns the percentage return rate that should be achieved. Note that the body of inferential statistics used in connection with survey analysis assumes that *all* members of the initial sample complete and return their questionnaires. Because this almost never happens, response bias becomes a concern. Researchers must test (and hope for) the possibility that respondents look essentially like a random sample of the initial sample and thus a somewhat smaller random sample of the total population. For example, if the gender of all people in the sample is known, a researcher can compare the percentages of males and females indicated on returned questionnaires with the percentages for the entire sample.

Nevertheless, overall response rate is one guide to the representativeness of the sample respondents. If the response rate is high, there is less chance of significant response bias than if the rate is low. As a rule of thumb, a response rate of at least 50 percent is adequate for analysis and reporting. A response rate of at least 60 percent is good, and a response rate of 70 percent is very good. Bear in mind that these are only rough guides; they have no statistical basis, and a demonstrated lack of response bias is far more important than a high response rate. Response rates tend to be higher for surveys that target a narrowly defined population, whereas general population surveys yield lower response rates.

Don Dillman (2007) has undertaken an extensive review of the various techniques survey researchers use to increase return rates on mail surveys, and he evaluates the impact of each. More importantly, Dillman stresses the necessity of paying attention to all aspects of the study—what he calls the "total design method"—rather than one or two special gimmicks.

## Computer-Based Self-Administration

Advances in computer and telecommunications technology over the past several decades have produced additional options for distributing and collecting self-administered questionnaires. As the Internet and web have permeated work and leisure activities, different types of computer-assisted self-administered surveys have become more common.

David Shannon and associates (Shannon et al. 2002) describe three general types of electronic surveys. The first is a disk-based survey. Respondents load a questionnaire from a disk or CD into their own computer, key in responses to survey items, and then either mail the disk back to researchers or transmit the information electronically. As the earliest form of electronic survey, the disk-based survey is a relic of stand-alone personal computers. Disk-based surveys are now virtually obsolete because personal computers are routinely connected to the web in one way or another.

The second type, e-mail surveys, has a few variations. Researchers can include a few simple questions in an e-mail message and ask respondents to reply by e-mail. More elaborate versions can embed complex formatted questionnaires in e-mail messages. Respondents might be asked to open an attached file that contains a questionnaire, or they might be directed to another web page that contains a formatted questionnaire. That brings us to the third type of electronic survey described by Shannon and associates—a questionnaire posted on a web page.

The advantages of this method are obvious. Responses are automatically recorded in computer files, saving time and money. Web-page design tools make it possible to create attractive questionnaires that include contingency questions, matrixes, and other complex tools for presenting items to respondents. Don Dillman, long recognized for his total design approach to conducting mail surveys, has written a comprehensive guide to conducting mail, web-based, and other self-administered surveys (Dillman 2007).

All electronic versions of self-administered questionnaires face a couple of problems. The first concerns representativeness: will the people who can be surveyed online be representative of meaningful populations, such as all U.S. adults, all registered voters, or all residents of particular urban neighborhoods? This criticism has also been raised with regard to surveys via fax and, in the mid-20th century, with regard to telephone surveys. Put in terms that should be familiar from the previous chapter, how closely do available sampling frames for electronic surveys match possible target populations? If, for example, our target population is university students, how can we obtain a list of e-mail addresses or other identifiers that will enable us to survey a representative sample? It's easy to think of other target populations of interest to criminal justice researchers that might be difficult to reach via e-mail or web-based questionnaires.

The second problem is an unfortunate consequence of the rapid growth of e-mail and related technologies. Just as junk mail clutters our physical mailboxes with all sorts of advertising, "spam" and other kinds of unwanted messages pop up all too often in our virtual mailboxes. The proliferation of junk e-mail has led to the development of anti-spam filters that screen out unwanted correspondence. Unfortunately, such programs can also screen out unfamiliar but well-meaning mail such as e-mail questionnaires. Similar problems with telemarketing have made it increasingly difficult to conduct surveys by telephone.

In yet another example of technology advances being accompanied by new threats, the spread of computer viruses and other "malware" has made people even more cautious about opening e-mail or attachments from unfamiliar sources. This problem, and the electronic version of junk mail, can be addressed in a manner similar to warning mailings for printed questionnaires. One solution is a version of the warning letter described above for mail surveys. In the electronic adaptation, researchers distribute e-mail messages from trusted sources to warn recipients to expect to receive a questionnaire or link in a later message.

We should keep one basic principle in mind when considering whether a self-administered questionnaire can be distributed electronically: web-based surveys depend on access to the web, which, of course, implies having a computer. The use of computers and the web continues to increase rapidly. Although access to this technology still is unequally distributed across socioeconomic classes, web-based surveys can be readily conducted for many target populations of interest to criminal justice researchers.

For example, in their recommendations for rethinking crime surveys, Michael Maxfield and associates argue that web-based surveys are well suited for learning more about victims of computer-facilitated fraud. Since only people with Internet access are possible victims, an Internet-based sample is ideal (Maxfield, Hough, and Mayhew 2007). Mike Sutton (2007) describes other examples of nontraditional crimes where Internet samples of computer users are appropriate.

Recalling our discussion in Chapter 6, the correspondence between a sampling frame and target population is a crucial feature of sampling. Most justice professionals and criminal justice organizations routinely use the web and e-mail. Lower-cost but generalizable victim surveys can use web-based samples of university students to distribute questionnaires. Or printed warning letters can be mailed, inviting respondents to complete either traditional or e-mail self-administered questionnaires. Just as e-mail, electronic bill-paying, and other transactions have replaced letters, check-writing, and other correspondence, self-administered surveys will increasingly be conducted on web-based computers. At the end of this chapter, we list a small sample of resources for conducting web-based surveys.

## IN-PERSON INTERVIEW SURVEYS

*Face-to-face interviews are best for complex questionnaires and other specialized needs.*

The in-person **interview survey** is an alternative method of collecting survey data. Rather than asking respondents to read questionnaires and enter their own answers, researchers send interviewers to ask the questions orally and record respondents' answers. Most interview surveys require more than one interviewer, although a researcher might undertake a small-scale interview survey alone.

### The Role of the Interviewer

In-person interview surveys typically attain higher response rates than mail surveys. Respondents seem more reluctant to turn down an interviewer who is standing on their doorstep than to throw away a mail questionnaire. A properly designed and executed interview survey ought to achieve a completion rate of at least 80 to 85 percent.

The presence of an interviewer generally decreases the number of "don't know" and "no answer" responses. If minimizing such responses is important to the study, the interviewer can be instructed to probe for answers ("If you had to pick one of the answers, which do you think would come closest to your feelings?"). The interviewer can also help respondents with confusing questionnaire items. If the respondent clearly misunderstands the intent of a question, the interviewer can clarify matters and thereby obtain a relevant response. Such

clarifications must be strictly controlled, however, through formal specifications.

Finally, the interviewer can observe as well as ask questions. For example, the interviewer can make observations about the quality of the respondent's dwelling, the presence of various possessions, the respondent's ability to speak English, or the respondent's general reactions to the study. Interviewers for the BCS routinely make observations of the physical conditions outside each respondent's home and in the surrounding area (Bolling, Grant, and Donovan 2009).

Survey research is, of necessity, based on an unrealistic stimulus–response theory of cognition and behavior. That is, it is based on the assumption that a questionnaire item will mean the same thing to every respondent, and every given response must mean the same thing when given by different respondents. Although this is an impossible goal, survey questions are drafted to approximate the ideal as closely as possible. The interviewer also plays a role in this ideal situation. The interviewer's presence should not affect a respondent's perception of a question or the answer given. The interviewer, then, should be a neutral medium through which questions and answers are transmitted. If this goal is met, different interviewers will obtain the same responses from a given respondent, an example of reliability in measurement (see Chapter 4).

**Familiarity with the Questionnaire** The interviewer must be able to read the questionnaire items to respondents without stumbling over words and phrases. A good model for interviewers is the actor reading lines in a play or film. The interviewer must read the questions as though they are part of a natural conversation, but that "conversation" must precisely follow the language set down in the question.

By the same token, the interviewer must be familiar with the specifications for administering the questionnaire. Inevitably, some questions will not exactly fit a given respondent's situation, and the interviewer must determine how those questions should be interpreted in that situation. The specifications provided to the interviewer should include adequate guidelines in such cases, but the interviewer must know the organization and content of the specifications well enough to refer to them efficiently.

**Probing for Responses** Probes are frequently required to elicit responses to open-ended questions. For example, to a question about neighborhood crime problems, the respondent might simply reply, "Pretty bad." The interviewer could obtain an elaboration on this response through a variety of probes. Sometimes, the best probe is silence; if the interviewer sits quietly with pencil poised, the respondent will probably fill the pause with additional comments. Appropriate verbal probes are "How is that?" and "In what ways?" Perhaps the most generally useful probe is "Anything else?"

In every case, however, it is imperative that the probe be completely neutral. The probe must not in any way affect the nature of the subsequent response. If we anticipate that a given question may require probing for appropriate responses, we should write one or more useful probes next to the item in the questionnaire. This practice has two important advantages. First, it allows for more time to devise the best, most neutral probes. Second, it ensures that all interviewers will use the same probes as needed. Thus even if the probe is not perfectly neutral, the same stimulus is presented to all respondents. This is the same logical guideline as for question wording. Although a question should not be loaded or biased, it is essential that every respondent be presented with the same question, even if a biased one.

## Coordination and Control

Whenever more than one interviewer will administer a survey, it is essential that the efforts be carefully coordinated and controlled. Two ways to ensure this control are by (1) training interviewers, and (2) supervising them after they begin work.

Whether the researchers will be administering a survey themselves or paying a professional firm to do it for them, they should be attentive to the importance of training interviewers. The interviewers usually should know what the study is all about. Even though the interviewers may be involved only in the data collection phase of the project,

they should understand what will be done with the information they gather and what purpose will be served.

Obviously, training should ensure that interviewers understand the questionnaire. Interviewers should also understand procedures to select respondents from among household members. And interviewers should recognize circumstances in which substitute sample elements may be used in place of addresses that no longer exist, families who have moved, or persons who simply refuse to be interviewed.

Training should include practice sessions in which interviewers administer the questionnaire to one another. The final stage of the training should involve some real interviews conducted under conditions like those in the survey.

While interviews are being conducted, it is a good idea to review questionnaires as they are completed. This may reveal questions or groups of questions that respondents do not understand. By reviewing completed questionnaires, it is also possible to determine if interviewers are completing items accurately.

## Computer-Assisted In-Person Interviews

Just as e-mail and web-based surveys apply new technology to the gathering of survey data through self-administration, laptop and hand-held computers are increasingly being used to conduct in-person interviews. Different forms of **computer-assisted interviewing (CAI)** offer major advantages in the collection of survey data. At the same time, CAI has certain disadvantages that must be considered. We'll begin by describing an example of how this technology was adopted in the BCS, one of the earliest uses of CAI in a general-purpose crime survey.

**Computer-Assisted Interviewing in the BCS** Early waves of the BCS, a face-to-face interview survey, asked respondents to complete a self-administered questionnaire about drug use, printed as a small booklet that was prominently marked "Confidential." Beginning with the 1994 survey, respondents answered self-report questions on laptop computers. The BCS includes two related versions of CAI. In computer-assisted personal interviewing (CAPI), interviewers read questions from computer screens, instead of printed questionnaires, and then key in respondents' answers. For self-report items, interviewers hand the computers to subjects, who then key in the responses themselves. This approach is known as computer-assisted self-interviewing (CASI). In addition, CASI as used in the BCS is supplemented with audio instructions—respondents listen to interview prompts on headphones connected to the computer. After subjects key in their responses to self-report items, the answers are scrambled so the interviewer cannot access them. Notice how this feature of CASI enhances the researcher's ethical obligation to keep responses confidential.

Malcolm Ramsay and associates (2001) report that CASI had at least two benefits. First, respondents seemed to sense a greater degree of confidentiality when they responded to questions on a computer screen as opposed to questions on a written form. Second, the laptop computers were something of a novelty that stimulated respondents' interest; this was especially true for younger respondents.

Examining results from the BCS reveals that CASI techniques produced higher estimates of illegal drug use than those revealed in previous surveys. Table 7.1 compares self-reported drug use from the 1998 BCS (Ramsey and Partridge 1999) with results from the 1992 BCS (Mott and Mirrlees-Black 1995), in which respondents answered questions in printed booklets. We present results for only three drugs here, together with tabulations about the use of any drug. For each drug, the survey measured lifetime use ("Ever used?") and use in the past 12 months.

Notice that rates of self-reported use were substantially higher in 1998 than in 1992, with the exception of "semeron" use, reported by very few respondents in 1992 and none in 1998. If you've never heard of semeron, you're not alone. It's a fictitious drug, included in the list of real drugs to detect untruthful or exaggerated responses. If someone confessed to using semeron, his or her responses to other self-reported items would be suspect. Notice in Table 7.1 that CASI use in

**TABLE 7.1**  Self-Reported Drug Use, 1992 and 1998 British Crime Survey

|  | Percentage of Respondents Ages 16–29 Who Report Use | |
|---|---|---|
|  | **1992** | **1998** |
| Marijuana or cannabis | | |
| Ever used? | 24 | 42 |
| Used in previous 12 months? | 12 | 23 |
| Amphetamines | | |
| Ever used? | 9 | 20 |
| Used in previous 12 months? | 4 | 8 |
| Semeron | | |
| Ever used? | 0.3 | 0.0 |
| Used in previous 12 months? | 0.1 | 0.0 |
| Any drug | | |
| Ever used? | 28 | 49 |
| Used in previous 12 months? | 14 | 25 |

*Source:* 1992 data adapted from Mott and Mirrlees-Black (1995, 41–42); 1998 data adapted from Ramsay and Partridge (1999, 68–71).

1998 reduced the number of respondents who admitted using a drug that doesn't exist.

CASI has also been used in the BCS since 1996 to measure domestic violence committed by partners and ex-partners of males and females aged 16 to 59. Catriona Mirrlees-Black (1999) reports that CASI techniques reveal higher estimates of domestic violence victimization among both females and males.

**Advantages and Disadvantages**  Different types of CAI offer a number of advantages for in-person interviews. The BCS and other surveys that include self-report items indicate that CAI is more productive in that self-reports of drug use and other offending tend to be higher. In 1999, the National Household Survey on Drug Abuse (now the National Household Survey on Drug Use and Health) shifted completely to CAI (Wright et al. 2002). Other advantages include the following:

- Responses can be quickly keyed in and automatically reformatted into data files for analysis.

- Complex sequences of contingency questions can be automated. Instead of printing many examples of "If answer is yes, go to question 43a; if no…," computer-based questionnaires automatically jump to the next appropriate question contingent on responses to earlier ones.

- CAI offers a way to break up the monotony of a long interview by shifting from verbal interviewer prompts to self-interviewing, with or without an audio supplement.

- Questionnaires for self-interviewing can be programmed in different languages, readily switching to the language appropriate for a particular respondent.

- Audio-supplemented CASI produces a standardized interview, avoiding any bias that might emerge from interviewer effects.

- Audio supplements, in different languages, facilitate self-interviews of respondents who cannot read.

At the same time, CAI has certain disadvantages that preclude its use in many survey applications:

- Although computers become more of a bargain each day, doing a large-scale in-person interview survey requires providing computers for each interviewer. Costs can quickly add up. CAI also requires specialized software to format and present on-screen questionnaires.

- Although CAI reduces costs in data processing, it requires more up-front investment in programming questionnaires, skip sequences, and the like.

- Automated skip sequences for contingency questions are great, but if something goes wrong with the programmed questionnaire, all sorts of subsequent problems are possible. As Emma Forster and Alison McCleery (1999) point out, such question-routing mistakes might mean that whole portions of a questionnaire are skipped. Whereas occasional random errors are possible with pen-and-paper interviews, large-scale systematic error can happen with CAI technology.

- Proofreading printed questionnaires is straightforward, but it can be difficult to audit a computerized questionnaire. Doing so might require special technical skills.

- It can be difficult to print and archive a complex questionnaire used in CAI. This was a problem with early applications of CAI technology, but improvements in software are helping to solve it.

- Batteries of laptops run down, and computers and software are more vulnerable to malfunctions and random weirdness than are stacks of printed questionnaires.

In sum, CAI can be costly and requires some specialized skills. As a result, these and related technologies are best suited for use by professional survey researchers or research centers that regularly conduct large-scale in-person interviews. We will return to this issue in the concluding section of this chapter.

## TELEPHONE SURVEYS

*Telephone surveys are fast and relatively low cost.*

Telephone surveys have many advantages that make them a popular method. Probably the greatest advantages involve money and time. In a face-to-face household interview, a researcher may drive several miles to a respondent's home, find no one there, return to the research office, and drive back the next day—possibly finding no one there again.

When interviewing by telephone, researchers can dress any way they please, and it will have no effect on the answers respondents give. Respondents may also be more honest in giving socially disapproved answers if they don't have to look the questioner in the eye. Similarly, it may be possible to probe into more sensitive areas, although that is not necessarily the case. People are, to some extent, more suspicious when they can't see the person asking them questions—perhaps a consequence of telemarketing and salespeople conducting bogus surveys before making sales pitches.

In computer-assisted telephone interviewing (CATI), interviewers wearing telephone headsets sit at computer workstations. Computer programs dial sampled phone numbers, which can be either generated through random-digit dialing (RDD) or extracted from a database of phone numbers compiled from some source. As soon as phone contact is made, the computer screen displays an introduction ("Hello, my name is … calling from the Survey Research Center at Ivory Tower University") and the first question to be asked, which is often a query about the number of residents who live in the household. As interviewers key in answers to each question, the computer program displays a new screen that presents the next question, until the end of the interview is reached. Perhaps you've occasionally marveled at newspaper stories that report the results of a nationwide opinion poll the day after some major speech or event. The speed of CATI technology makes these instant poll reports possible.

Telephone surveys can give a researcher greater control over data collection if several interviewers are engaged in the project. If all the interviewers are calling from the research office, they can get clarification from the supervisor whenever problems occur, as they inevitably do. Alone in the field, an interviewer may have to wing it between weekly visits with the interviewing supervisor.

A related advantage is rooted in the growing diversity of U.S. cities. Because many major cities have growing immigrant populations, interviews may need to be conducted in different languages. Telephone interviews are usually conducted from a central site so that one or more multilingual interviewers can be quickly summoned if an English-speaking interviewer makes contact with, say, a Spanish-speaking respondent. In-person interview surveys present much more difficult logistical problems in handling multiple languages. And mail surveys require printing and distributing questionnaires in different languages.

Telephone interviewing has its problems, however. Telephone surveys are limited by definition to people who own telephones. Years ago, this method produced a substantial social class bias by excluding poor people. Over time, however, the telephone has become a standard fixture in almost all American homes. The Centers for Disease Control and Prevention says that 98.3 percent of all households now have telephones, so the earlier class

bias has been substantially reduced (Blumberg and Luke 2010). The NCVS, traditionally an in-person interview, has increased its use of telephone interviews as part of the crime survey's redesign.

A related sampling problem involves unlisted numbers. If the survey sample is selected from the pages of a local telephone directory, it totally omits all those people who have requested that their numbers not be published. Similarly, those who recently moved and transient residents are not well represented in published telephone directories. This potential bias has been eliminated through RDD, a technique that has advanced telephone sampling substantially.

RDD samples use computer algorithms to generate lists of random telephone numbers—usually the last four digits. This procedure gets around the sampling problem of unlisted telephone numbers but may substitute an administrative problem. Randomly generating phone numbers produces numbers that are not in operation or that serve a business establishment or pay phone. In most cases, businesses and pay phones are not included in the target population; dialing these numbers and learning that they're out of scope will take time away from producing completed interviews with the target population.

Another developing problem is the increasing number of households that have mobile phone service only. Steven Blumberg and Julian Luke (2010) report that about 25 percent of households in a U.S. national sample drawn in 2010 had only mobile phones.

The ease with which people can hang up is, of course, another shortcoming of telephone surveys. Once a researcher is inside someone's home for an interview, that person is unlikely to order the researcher out of the house in mid-interview. It's much easier to terminate a telephone interview abruptly, saying something like "Whoops! Someone's at the door. Gotta go" or simply hanging up.

Partly as a result of extensive telemarketing in past years, completion rates for telephone surveys have declined (Cantor and Lynch 2007). Though commercial telemarketing is sharply reduced, people still commonly receive solicitations from charitable organizations, college alumni groups, aggressive political campaigns, and other "soft" telemarketers.

People who are weary of bothersome calls are less inclined to complete telephone interviews, especially those lasting longer than a couple of minutes (Tourangeau 2004).

## COMPARISON OF THE THREE METHODS

*Cost, speed, and question content are issues to consider in selecting a survey method.*

We've now examined three ways of collecting survey data: self-administered questionnaires, in-person interviews, and telephone surveys. We have also considered some recent advances in each mode of administration. Although we've touched on some of the relative advantages and disadvantages of each, let's take a minute to compare them more directly.

Self-administered questionnaires are generally cheaper to use than interview surveys. Moreover, for self-administered e-mail or web-based surveys, it costs no more to conduct a national survey than a local one. Obviously, the cost difference between a local and a national in-person interview survey is considerable. The cost of telephone surveys continues to decline, as Internet-based calling services eliminate long-distance toll charges. Mail surveys typically require a small staff. One person can conduct a reasonable mail survey, although it is important not to underestimate the work involved. Web-based surveys can be very inexpensive, particularly because they combine data collection and tabulation.

Up to a point, cost and speed are inversely related. In-person interview surveys can be completed very quickly if a large pool of interviewers is available and funding is adequate to pay them. In contrast, if a small number of people are conducting a larger number of face-to-face interviews, costs are generally lower, but the survey takes much longer to complete. Telephone surveys that use CATI technology are easily the fastest. In comparing different modes of self-administered surveys, Nojin Kwak and Barry Radler (2002) report faster responses from web-based surveys but higher completion rates from mailed questionnaires.

Self-administered surveys may be more appropriate to use with especially sensitive issues if the surveys offer complete anonymity. Respondents are sometimes reluctant to report controversial or deviant attitudes or behaviors in interviews, but they may be willing to respond to an anonymous self-administered questionnaire. However, the successful use of computers for self-reported items in the BCS and the National Household Survey on Drug Use and Health indicates that interacting with a machine can promote more candid responses. This is supported by experimental research comparing different modes of questionnaire administration (Tourangeau and Smith 1996).

Interview surveys have many advantages, too. For example, in-person or telephone surveys are more appropriate when respondent literacy may be a problem. Interview surveys also result in fewer incomplete questionnaires. Respondents may skip questions in a self-administered questionnaire, but interviewers are trained not to do so. CAI offers a further check on this in telephone and in-person surveys.

Self-administered questionnaires may be more effective in dealing with sensitive issues, but interview surveys are definitely more effective in dealing with complicated ones. Interviewers can explain complex questions to respondents and use visual aids that are not possible in mail or phone surveys.

In-person interviews, especially with computer technology, can also help reduce response sets. Respondents (like students?) eventually become bored listening to a lengthy series of similar types of questions. It's easier to maintain individuals' interest by changing the kind of stimulation they are exposed to. A mix of questions verbalized by a person, presented on a computer screen, and heard privately through earphones is more interesting for respondents and reduces fatigue.

Interviewers who question respondents face to face are also able to make important observations aside from responses to questions asked in the interview. In a household interview, they may summarize characteristics of the neighborhood, the dwelling unit, and so forth. They may also note characteristics of the respondents or the quality of their interaction with the respondents—whether the respondent had difficulty communicating, was hostile, seemed to be lying, and so on. Finally, when the safety of interviewers is an issue, a mail or phone survey may be the best option.

Ultimately, researchers must weigh all these advantages and disadvantages of the three methods against research needs and available resources.

## STRENGTHS AND WEAKNESSES OF SURVEY RESEARCH

*Surveys tend to be high on reliability and generalizability, but validity can often be a weak point.*

Like other modes of collecting data in criminal justice research, surveys have strengths and weaknesses. It is important to consider these in deciding whether the survey format is appropriate for a specific research purpose.

Surveys are particularly useful in describing the characteristics of a large population. The NCVS has become an important tool for researchers and public officials because of its ability to describe levels of crime. A carefully selected probability sample, in combination with a standardized questionnaire, allows researchers to make refined descriptive statements about a neighborhood, a city, a nation, or some other large population.

Standardized questionnaires have an important advantage in regard to measurement. Earlier chapters discussed the ambiguous nature of concepts: they ultimately have no real meanings. One person's view about, say, crime seriousness or punishment severity is quite different from another's. Although we must be able to define concepts in ways that are most relevant to research goals, it's not always easy to apply the same definitions uniformly to all subjects. Nevertheless, the survey researcher is bound to the requirement of having to ask exactly the same questions of all subjects and having to impute the same intent to all respondents giving a particular response.

At the same time, survey research has its weaknesses. First, the requirement for standardization might mean that we are trying to fit round pegs into square holes. Standardized questionnaire items often represent the least common denominator in assessing people's attitudes, orientations, circumstances, and experiences. By designing questions that are at least minimally appropriate to all respondents, we may miss what is most appropriate to many respondents. In this sense, surveys often appear superficial in their coverage of complex topics.

Using surveys to study crime and criminal justice policy presents special challenges. The target population frequently includes lower-income, transient persons who are difficult to contact through customary sampling methods. For example, homeless persons are excluded from any survey that samples households, but people who live on the street no doubt figure prominently as victims and offenders. Michael Maxfield (1999) describes how new data from the National Incident-Based Reporting System suggest that a number of "non-household-associated" persons are systematically undercounted by sampling procedures used in the NCVS. Research by Census Bureau staff has tried to document how many individuals might be missed in household-based surveys, finding that young males and minorities appear to be most undercounted (Martin 1999).

Crime surveys such as the NCVS and the BCS have been deficient in getting information about crimes of violence when the victim and offender have some prior relationship. This is particularly true for domestic violence, although Michael Rand and Callie Rennison report some advantages of large surveys in this regard (2005).

Underreporting of domestic violence appears to be due, in part, to the very general nature of large-scale crime surveys. Catriona Mirrlees-Black (1995, 8) of the British Home Office summarizes the trade-offs of using survey techniques to learn about domestic violence:

> Measuring domestic violence is difficult territory. The advantage of the BCS is that it is based on a large nationally representative sample, has a relatively high response rate, and collects information on enough incidents to provide reliable details of their

nature. One disadvantage is that domestic violence is measured in the context of a crime survey, and some women may not see what happened to them as "crime," or be reluctant to do so. Also, there is little time to approach the topic "gently." A specially designed questionnaire with carefully selected interviewers may well have the edge here.

An experimental use of computer-assisted self-interviewing in the BCS produced higher estimates of victimization prevalence among women as well as the first measurable rates of domestic violence victimization for males (Mirrlees-Black 1999). The BCS now routinely uses CASI to get better estimates of violent victimization.

Survey research is generally weaker on validity and stronger on reliability. In comparison with field research, for instance, the artificiality of the survey format puts a strain on validity. As an illustration, most researchers agree that fear of crime is not well measured by the standard question "How safe do you feel, or would you feel, out alone in your neighborhood at night?" Survey responses to that question are, at best, approximate indicators of what we have in mind when we conceptualize fear of crime.

Reliability is a different matter. By presenting all subjects with a standardized stimulus, survey research goes a long way toward eliminating unreliability in observations made by the researcher.

However, even this statement is subject to qualification. Critics of survey methods argue that questionnaires for standard crime surveys and many specialized studies embody a narrow, legalistic conception of crime that cannot reflect the perceptions and experiences of minorities and women. Survey questions typically are based on male views and do not adequately tap victimization or fear of crime among women (Straus 1999; Tjaden and Thoennes 2000). Concern that survey questions might mean different things to different respondents raises important questions about reliability and about the generalizability of survey results across subgroups of a population.

As with all methods of observation, a full awareness of the inherent or probable weaknesses

of survey research may partially resolve them. Ultimately, though, we are on the safest ground when we can use several different research methods to study a given topic.

# OTHER WAYS OF ASKING QUESTIONS

*Specialized interviews and focus groups are alternative ways of gathering question-based data.*

Sample surveys are perhaps the best-known application of asking questions as a data-gathering strategy for criminal justice research. Often, however, more specialized interviewing techniques are appropriate. Such specialized interviews, sometimes referred to as qualitative interviews, are usually conducted with a few individuals or small groups.

## Specialized Interviewing

No precise definition of the term *survey* enables us to distinguish a survey from other types of interview situations. As a rule of thumb, a sample survey (even one that uses nonprobability sampling methods) is an interview-based technique for generalizing to a larger population using a standardized questionnaire. In contrast, specialized interviewing focuses on the views and opinions of only those individuals who are interviewed.

Let's say we are interested in how mental health professionals view different drug treatment programs for prison inmates. One approach is to conduct a sample survey of psychologists who work in state correctional facilities in which each sampled psychologist completes a structured questionnaire concerning drug treatment programs. This approach will enable us to generalize to the population of state prison psychologists.

Another approach is to study one or two (or some other small number) correctional institutions intensively. We might interview a psychologist in each institution and present questions about various approaches to drug treatment therapy. In all likelihood, we will use not a highly structured questionnaire, but rather a list of questions or topics we wish to discuss with each subject. And we will treat the interview as more of a directed conversation than a formal interview. Of course, we cannot generalize from interviews with one or two prison psychologists to any larger population. However, we will gain an understanding (and probably a more detailed one) of how staff psychologists in specific institutions feel about different drug treatment programs.

Specialized interviewing asks questions of a small number of subjects, typically using an interview schedule that is much less structured than that in sample surveys. Michael Quinn Patton (2002) distinguishes two variations of specialized interviews. The less structured alternative is to prepare a general interview guide that includes the issues, topics, or questions the researcher wishes to cover. Issues and items are not presented to respondents in any standardized order. The interview guide is more like a checklist than an interview schedule, ensuring that planned topics are addressed at some point in the interview. The standardized open-ended interview, in contrast, is more structured, using specific questions arranged in a particular order. The researcher presents each respondent with the same questions in the same sequence (subject to any contingency questions). The questions are open-ended, but their format and presentation are standardized.

To underscore the flexibility of specialized interviewing, Patton describes how the two approaches can be used in combination (2002, 347):

> A conversational strategy can be used within an interview guide approach, or you can combine a guide approach. This combined strategy offers the interviewer flexibility in probing and in determining when it is appropriate to explore certain subjects in greater depth, or even to pose questions about new areas of inquiry that were not originally anticipated in the interview instrument's development.

Open-ended questions are ordinarily used because they capture rich detail better. The primary disadvantage of open-ended questions—having to categorize responses—is not a problem in specialized interviewing because of the small number of subjects

and because researchers are more interested in describing than in generalizing.

Specialized interviewing can be incorporated into any research project as a supplementary source of information. If, for example, we are interested in the effects of determinant sentencing on prison populations, we can analyze data from the Census of State Adult Correctional Facilities, conducted by the BJS. We might also interview a small number of corrections administrators, perhaps asking them to react to our data analysis. Evaluation studies and other applied research projects frequently use specialized interviewing techniques, alone or in combination with other sources of data.

## Focus Groups

Like sample surveys, focus group techniques were refined by market research firms in the years following World War II. As the name implies, market research explores questions about the potential for sales of consumer products. Because a firm may spend millions of dollars developing, advertising, and distributing some new item, market research is an important tool to test consumer reactions before large sums of money are invested in a product.

Surveys have two disadvantages in market research. First, a nationwide or large-scale probability survey can be expensive. Second, it may be difficult to present advertising messages or other product images in a survey format. Focus groups have proved to be more suitable for many market research applications. In recent years, focus groups have commonly been used as substitutes for surveys in criminal justice and other social scientific research.

In a **focus group**, 8 to 15 people are brought together in a room to engage in a guided group discussion of some topic. Although focus groups cannot be used to make statistical estimates about a population, members are nevertheless selected to represent a target population. Richard Krueger and Mary Anne Casey (2000) describe focus groups, their applications, and their advantages and disadvantages in detail.

For example, the location of community correctional facilities such as work-release centers and halfway houses often prompts a classic "Not in my backyard!" (NIMBY) response from people who live in neighborhoods where proposed facilities will be built. Recognizing this, a mayor who wants to find a suitable site without annoying neighborhood residents (voters) is well-advised to convene a focus group that includes people who live in areas near possible facility locations. A focus group can test the "market acceptability" of a work-release center, which might include the best way to package and sell the product. Such an exercise might reveal that an appeal to altruism ("We all have to make sacrifices in the fight against crime") is much less effective in gaining support than an alternative sales pitch that stresses potential economic benefits ("This new facility will provide jobs for neighborhood residents").

Focus groups may also be used in combination with survey research in one of two ways. First, a focus group can be valuable in questionnaire development. When researchers are uncertain how to present items to respondents, a focus group discussion about the topic can generate possible item formats. For instance, James Nolan and Yoshio Akiyama (1999) studied police routines for making records of hate crimes. In a general sense, they knew what concepts they wanted to measure but were unsure how to operationalize them. They convened five focus groups in different cities, including police administrators, mid-level managers, patrol officers, and civilian employees, to learn about different perspectives on

hate-crime recording. Analyzing focus group results, Nolan and Akiyama prepared a self-administered questionnaire that was sent to a large number of individuals in four police departments.

Second, after a survey has been completed and preliminary results tabulated, focus groups may be used to guide the interpretation of some results. After a citywide survey in which we find, for example, that recent immigrants from Southeast Asian countries are least supportive of community policing, we might conduct a focus group of Asian residents to delve more deeply into their concerns.

Focus groups are flexible and can be adapted to many uses in basic and applied research. Keep in mind, however, two key elements expressed in the name of this data collection technique. *Focus* means that researchers present specific questions or issues for directed discussion. Having a free-for-all discussion about hate crime, for example, would not have yielded much useful insight for Nolan and Akiyama to develop a survey instrument. *Group* calls our attention to potential participants in the focused discussions. Like market researchers, we should select participants from a specific target population that relates to our research questions. If we're interested in how residents of a specific neighborhood will feel about opening a work-release center, we should select group participants who live in the target neighborhood or one very much like it.

## SUMMARY

- Survey research, a popular social research method, involves the administration of questionnaires to a sample of respondents selected from some population.

- Survey research is especially appropriate for descriptive or exploratory studies of large populations, but surveys have many other uses in criminal justice research.

- Surveys are the method of choice for obtaining self-reported offending data. Continuing efforts to improve self-report surveys include using

confidential computer-assisted personal interviews.

- Questions may be open-ended or closed-ended. Each technique for formulating questions has advantages and disadvantages.

- Short items in a questionnaire are usually better than long ones.

- Bias in questionnaire items encourages respondents to answer in a particular way or to support a particular point of view. It should be avoided.

- Questionnaires are administered in three basic ways: self-administered questionnaires, face-to-face interviews, and telephone interviews. Each mode of administration can be varied in a number of ways.

- Computers can be used to enhance each type of survey. Computer-assisted surveys have many advantages, but they often require special skills and equipment.

- It is generally advisable to plan follow-up mailings for self-administered questionnaires, sending new questionnaires to respondents who fail to respond to the initial appeal.

- The essential characteristic of interviewers is that they be neutral; their presence in the data collection process must not have any effect on the responses given to questionnaire items.

- Surveys conducted over the telephone are fast and flexible.

- Each method of survey administration has a variety of advantages and disadvantages.

- Survey research has the weaknesses of being somewhat artificial and potentially superficial. It is difficult to gain a full sense of social processes in their natural settings through the use of surveys.

- Specialized interviews with a small number of people and focus groups are additional ways of collecting data by asking questions.

## KEY TERMS

bias, p. 165

closed-ended question, p. 163

computer-assisted interviewing (CAI), p. 176

focus group, p. 183

interview survey, p. 175

open-ended question, p. 163

questionnaire, p. 164

respondent, p. 161

response rate, p. 172

survey, p. 161

## REVIEW QUESTIONS AND EXERCISES

1. Find a questionnaire on the Internet. Bring the questionnaire to class and critique it. Critique other aspects of the survey design as well.

2. For each of the open-ended questions listed, construct a closed-ended question that could be used in a questionnaire.

   a. What was your family's total income last year?

   b. How do you feel about shock incarceration or "boot camp" programs?

   c. How do people in your neighborhood feel about the police?

   d. What do you feel is the biggest problem facing this community?

   e. How do you protect your home from burglary?

3. Prepare a brief questionnaire to study perceptions of crime near your college or university. Include questions asking respondents to describe a nearby area where they either are afraid to go after dark or think crime is a problem. Then use your questionnaire to interview at least 10 students.

## ADDITIONAL READINGS

Babbie, Earl, *Survey Research Methods*, 2nd ed. (Belmont, CA: Wadsworth, 1990). A comprehensive overview of survey methods, this textbook covers many aspects of survey techniques that are omitted here.

Dillman, Don A., *Mail and Internet Surveys: The Tailored Design Method 2007 Update,* 2nd ed. (New York: Wiley, 2007). This update of a classic reference on self-administered surveys includes a variety of web-based techniques. Dillman makes many good suggestions for improving response rates.

General Accounting Office, *Using Structured Interviewing Techniques* (Washington, DC: General Accounting Office, 1991). This is another useful handbook in the GAO series on evaluation methods. In contrast to Patton (below), the GAO emphasizes getting comparable information from respondents through structured interviews. This is a very useful step-by-step guide.

Krueger, Richard A., and Mary Anne Casey, *Focus Groups: A Practical Guide for Applied Research,* 3rd ed. (Thousand Oaks, CA: Sage, 2000). A clear and comprehensive introduction to focus groups, this book really lives up to its title, describing basic principles of focus groups and giving numerous practical tips.

Patton, Michael Quinn, *Qualitative Research and Evaluation Methods*, 3rd ed. (Thousand Oaks, CA: Sage, 2002). This is a thorough discussion of specialized interviewing. Patton's advice will also be useful in constructing questionnaires for surveys in general.

Weisel, Deborah, *Conducting Community Surveys: A Practical Guide for Law Enforcement Agencies* (Washington, DC: U.S. Department of Justice, Office of Justice Programs, Bureau of Justice Statistics, and Office of Community Oriented Police Services, 1999). Another practical guide, this brief publication is prepared for use by public officials, not researchers. As such, it's a very good description of the nuts and bolts of doing telephone surveys.

# CHAPTER 8

# Field Research

*The techniques described in this chapter focus on observing life in its natural habitat—going where the action is and watching. We'll consider how to prepare for the field, how to observe, how to make records of what is observed, and how to recognize the relative strengths and weaknesses of field research.*

## INTRODUCTION

*Field research includes qualitative techniques for observation and interviewing together with structured observations.*

We turn now to what may seem like the most obvious method of making observations: field research. If researchers want to know about something, why not simply go where it's happening and watch it happen?

Field research encompasses two different methods of obtaining data: (1) making direct observation and (2) asking questions. This chapter concentrates primarily on observation, although we expand somewhat on techniques for specialized interviewing in field studies introduced in Chapter 7.

Most of the observation methods discussed in this book are designed to produce data appropriate for *quantitative* analysis. Surveys provide data to calculate things like the percentage of crime victims in a population or the mean value of property lost in burglaries. Field research may yield *qualitative* data—observations not easily reduced to numbers—in addition to quantitative data. For example, a field researcher who is studying burglars may note how many times subjects have been arrested (quantitative), as well as whether individual burglars tend to select certain types of targets (qualitative).

Qualitative field research is often a theory- or hypothesis-generating activity, as well. In many types of field studies, researchers do not have precisely defined hypotheses to be tested. Field observation may be used to make sense out of an ongoing process that cannot be predicted in advance. This process involves making initial observations, developing tentative general conclusions that suggest further observations, making those observations, revising the prior conclusions, and so forth.

For example, Ross Homel and associates (Homel, Tomsen, and Thommeny 1992) conducted a field study of violence in bars in Sydney, Australia, and found that certain situations tended to trigger violent incidents. Subsequent studies tested a series of hypotheses about the links between certain situations and violence (Homel and Clark 1994) and how interior design

was related to aggression in dance clubs (Macintyre and Homel 1996). Later research by James Roberts (2002) expanded these findings by examining management and serving practices in New Jersey bars and clubs. Barney Glaser and Anselm Strauss (1967) refer to this process as **grounded theory**, which we mentioned in Chapter 3. Rather than following the deductive approach to theory building, grounded theory is based on (or grounded in) experience, usually through observations made in the field. Building grounded theory is a common purpose of qualitative field research.

By now, especially if you have experience as a criminal justice professional, you may be thinking that field research is not much different from what police officers and many other people do every day—make observations in the field and ask people questions. Police may also collect data about particular crime problems, take action, and monitor results. So what's new here?

Compared with criminal justice professionals, researchers tend to be more concerned with making generalizations and then using systematic field research techniques to support those generalizations. Consider the different goals and approaches used by two people who might observe shoplifters: a retail store security guard and a criminal justice researcher. The security guard wishes to capture a thief and prevent the loss of shop merchandise. Toward those ends, he or she adapts surveillance techniques to the behavior of a particular suspected shoplifter. The researcher's interests are different; perhaps she or he estimates the frequency of shoplifting, describes characteristics of shoplifters, or evaluates some specific measure to prevent shoplifting. In all likelihood, researchers use more standardized methods of observation aimed toward a generalized understanding.

This chapter examines field research methods in some detail, providing a logical overview and suggesting some specific skills and techniques that make scientific field research more useful than the casual observation we all engage in. As we cover the various applications and techniques of field research, it's useful to recall the distinction we made, way back in Chapter 1, between ordinary human inquiry and social scientific research. Field methods illustrate how the common techniques of observation that we all use in ordinary inquiry can be deployed in systematic ways. Also recall our discussion, from Chapter 3, of how qualitative and quantitative approaches can often be combined.

## TOPICS APPROPRIATE TO FIELD RESEARCH

*When conditions or behavior must be studied in natural settings, field research is usually the best approach.*

One of the key strengths of field research is the comprehensive perspective it gives the researcher. This aspect of field research enhances its validity. By going directly to the phenomenon under study and observing it as completely as possible, we can develop a deeper and fuller understanding of it. This mode of observation, then, is especially (though not exclusively) appropriate to research topics that appear to defy simple quantification. The field researcher may recognize nuances of attitude, behavior, and setting that escape researchers using other methods.

For example, Clifford Shearing and Phillip Stenning (1992, 251) describe how Disney World employs subtle but pervasive mechanisms of informal social control that are largely invisible to millions of theme park visitors. It is difficult to imagine any technique other than direct observation that could produce these insights:

> Control strategies are embedded in both environmental features and structural relations. In both cases control structures and activities have other functions which are highlighted so that the control function is overshadowed. For example, virtually every pool, fountain, and flower garden serves both as an aesthetic object and to direct visitors away from, or towards, particular locations. Similarly, every Disney employee, while visibly and primarily engaged in other functions, is also engaged in the maintenance of order.

For another, grittier, example of direct observations used to understand conditions in field conditions, see the box "Port Operations and Stolen Vehicles."

Many of the different uses of field observation in criminal justice research are nicely summarized by George McCall. Comparing the three principal ways of collecting data—observing, asking questions, and consulting written records—McCall (1978, 8–9) states that observation is most appropriate for obtaining information about physical or social settings, behaviors, and events.

Field research is especially appropriate for topics that can best be understood within their natural settings. Surveys may be able to measure behaviors and attitudes in somewhat artificial settings, but not all behavior is best measured this way. For example, field research is a superior method for studying how street-level drug dealers interpret behavioral and situational cues to distinguish potential customers, normal street traffic, and undercover police officers. It would be difficult to study these skills through a survey.

Field research on actual crimes involves obtaining information about events. McCall (1978) points out that observational studies of vice—such as prostitution and drug use—are much more common than observational studies of other crimes, largely because these behaviors depend at least in part on being visible and attracting customers. One notable exception is research on shoplifting. A classic study by Terry Baumer and Dennis Rosenbaum (1982) had two goals: (1) to estimate the incidence of shoplifting in a large department store, and (2) to assess the effectiveness of different store security measures. Each objective required devising some measure of shoplifting, which Baumer and Rosenbaum obtained through direct observation. Samples of persons were followed by research staff from the time they entered the store until they left. Observers, posing as fellow shoppers, watched for any theft by the person they had been assigned to follow.

Many aspects of physical settings are probably best studied through direct observation. The prevalence and patterns of gang graffiti in public places could not be reliably measured through surveys,

## PORT OPERATIONS AND STOLEN VEHICLES

With colleague Ronald Clarke and graduate students at Rutgers, Michael Maxfield conducted an extensive study of auto theft and efforts to reduce it by requiring that certain auto parts be specially marked. This research used data from a variety of sources, including field observations and qualitative interviews in a variety of domains, including auto body repair shops. The fieldwork described here was undertaken to learn more about the export of stolen vehicles through large seaports.

Maxfield and Clarke had learned that over 380,000 vehicles were shipped abroad from Port Newark, New Jersey, in 2008. According to vehicle theft records, just under 1 percent of those, about 3,750, had been reported as stolen. For an additional 104,800 vehicles, some irregularity was found with vehicle identification numbers (VINs). So the researchers arranged to visit a large shipping terminal at Port Newark, one of the busiest seaports in the United States. Their general objective was to understand port and shipping operations in an effort to learn more about the export of stolen vehicles. Their role was strictly as observers.

They toured the huge facility, a modern port that is engaged exclusively in container handling. A shipping container is basically a semitrailer truck without its tractor or wheels. Thousands of containers move in and out of Port Newark each day, coming by train or truck. Observations began at a portal where all container trucks were weighed and documents were presented. Port and shipping company security staff explained how containers were processed. Incoming containers passed through the portal on their way to an outgoing ship. Outgoing containers had arrived by ship and were leaving the port by truck or train destined to other parts of the United States. In addition to weighing and checking documents, the process for outgoing containers included inspection to screen for contraband and dangerous materials.

Maxfield and Clarke were most interested in containers coming into the port on trucks, bound for export. Cars to be exported were in containers when they arrived at the port; each container was large enough to hold up to three autos. Incoming containers were shuttled around several acres where they were stacked five containers high. Small trucks fetched the containers for loading on an outbound container ship. At one point, Maxfield and Clarke boarded a 950-foot ship from China to observe loading and unloading operations. Three crane-towers worked the ship's length, simultaneously moving containers on and off the ship. This was quite a sight. The "round trip"—pick up → load-on-ship → pick up → place-on-dock—took only about 90 seconds.

From one morning at the shipping terminal coupled with unstructured interviews of security and other port staff, the researchers learned several things that appeared to facilitate the export of stolen vehicle through the port:

- An enormous number of containers moved in and out of the port.

- From 800 to 1,000 autos were shipped out each day. Some containers included a car with other types of goods; other containers included only two or three cars.

- Some stolen vehicles mixed with other cargo were not listed as contents of a container.

- Documents for outbound autos were inspected, but rarely compared to VIN numbers identifying individual cars, because:

  - Containers with cars were mixed with other containers and were difficult to access.

  - Adding to their large number, containers were frequently moved around the shipping yard.

  - Cars and other goods presented for outbound shipment were available for inspection for 72 hours before being loaded on a ship. But constraints on Immigration and Customs Enforcement staff meant that only a small fraction of containers could be inspected during this period.

  - New technology has been developed to "see" inside containers, much like the evolving full-body-scan technology at airports, but only one such machine was available and rarely used.

  - Since the September 11 attacks on the United States, security officials have devoted extensive resources to screening cargo shipped into the country, which undermines the capacity to screen exports.

These are not conclusive findings. Instead, the observations helped Maxfield and Clarke develop tentative explanations for things that contribute to the export of stolen vehicles. Without these observations, they could not have understood how the enormous scale of operations at the port offers cover for stolen cars comingled among the thousands of other containers handled each day at Port Newark. One Rutgers graduate student on their project, Steven Block, is conducting his dissertation research on this problem.

You can get a tiny feel for what a modern port is like by typing "port Newark" into Google Earth or a mapping program. Scroll around and zoom in to see a forest of shipping containers. You might also be interested in Marc Levinson's book (2007) on the history of the shipping container. Among other things, Levinson points out how containerized cargo reduced many forms of cargo theft.

unless the goal was to measure perceptions of graffiti. The work of Oscar Newman (1972, 1996), Ray Jeffery (1977), and Patricia and Paul Brantingham (Brantingham and Brantingham 1991) on the relationship between crime and environmental design depends crucially on field observation of settings. If opportunities for crime vary by physical setting, then observation of the physical characteristics of a setting is required.

An evaluation of street lighting as a crime prevention tool in two areas of London illustrates how observation can be used to measure both physical settings and behavior. Kate Painter (1996) was interested in the relationships between street lighting, certain crime rates (measured by victim surveys), fear of crime, and nighttime mobility. Improvements in street lighting were made in selected streets; surveys of pedestrians and households in the affected areas were conducted before and after the lighting improvements. Survey questions included items about victimization, perceptions of crime problems and lighting quality, and reports about routine nighttime behavior in areas affected by the lighting.

Although the pretest and posttest survey items could have been used to assess changes in attitudes and behavior associated with improved lighting, field observations provided better measures of behavior. Painter observed pedestrians in areas both before and after street lighting was enhanced. Observations like these are better measures of such behavior than are survey items because people often have difficulty recalling actions such as how often they walk through some area after dark.

## THE VARIOUS ROLES OF THE OBSERVER

*Field observer roles range from full participation to fully detached observation.*

The term *field research* is broader and more inclusive than the common term **ethnography**. Field researchers need not always participate in what they are studying, although they usually will study it directly at the scene of the action. As Catherine Marshall and Gretchen Rossman (2006, 72) point out:

The researcher may plan a role that entails varying degrees of "participantness"—that is, the degree of actual participation in daily life. At one extreme is the full participant, who goes about ordinary life in a role or set of roles constructed in the setting. At the other extreme is the complete observer, who engages not at all in social interaction and may even shun involvement in the world being studied. And, of course, all possible complementary mixes along the continuum are available to the researcher.

The full participant, in this sense, may be a genuine participant in what he or she is studying (for example, a participant in a demonstration against capital punishment)—or at least pretend to be a genuine participant. In any event, if you are acting as a full participant, you let people see you only as a participant, not as a researcher.

That raises an ethical question: is it ethical to deceive the people we are studying in the hope that they will confide in us as they would not confide in an identified researcher? Do the interests of science—the scientific values of the research—offset any ethical concerns?

Related to this ethical consideration is a scientific one. No researcher deceives his or her subjects solely for the purpose of deception. Rather, it is done in the belief that the data will be more valid and reliable, that the subjects will be more natural and honest if they do not know the researcher is doing a research project. If the people being studied know they are being studied, they might reject the researcher or modify their speech and behavior to appear more respectable than they otherwise would. In either case, the process being observed might radically change.

On the other side of the coin, if we assume the role of complete participant, we may affect what we are studying. To play the role of participant, we must participate, yet our participation may affect the social process we are studying. Additional problems may emerge in any participant observation study of active criminals. Legal and physical risks, mentioned in Chapter 2, present obstacles to the complete participant in field research among active offenders or delinquents.

Finally, complete participation in field studies of criminal justice institutions is seldom possible. Although it is common for police officers to become criminal justice researchers, practical constraints on the official duties of police present major obstacles to simultaneously acting as researcher and police officer. Similarly, the responsibilities of judges, prosecutors, probation officers, and corrections workers are not normally compatible with collecting data for research. For a notable exception to this general rule, see the book *Cop in the Hood*, in which Peter Moskos describes how he became a sworn police officer in Baltimore in order to conduct field research for his dissertation (Moskos 2009).

Because of these considerations—ethical, scientific, practical, and safety—field researchers most often choose a different role. The researcher taking the role *participant-as-observer* participates with the group under study but makes it clear that he or she is also undertaking research. If someone has been convicted of some offense and has been placed on probation, for example, that might present an opportunity to launch a study of probation officers.

McCall (1978) suggests that field researchers who study active offenders may comfortably occupy positions around the periphery of criminal activity. Acting as a participant in certain types of leisure activities, such as frequenting selected bars or dance clubs, may be appropriate roles. This approach was used by Dina Perrone (2009) in her research on drug use in New York dance clubs (see the box in Chapter 2). Furthermore, McCall describes how making one's role as a researcher known to criminals and becoming known as a "right square" is more acceptable to subjects than an unsuccessful attempt to masquerade as a colleague. There are dangers in this role also, however. The people being studied may shift their attention to the research project, and the process being observed may no longer be typical. Conversely, a researcher may come to identify too much with the interests and viewpoints of the participants. This is referred to as *going native* and results in loss of the detachment necessary for social science.

The *observer-as-participant* identifies himself or herself as a researcher and interacts with the participants in the course of their routine activities but makes no pretense of actually being a participant. Many observational studies of police patrol are examples of this approach. Researchers typically accompany police officers on patrol, observing routine activities and interactions between police and citizens. Spending several hours in the company of a police officer also affords opportunities for unstructured interviewing.

The *complete observer*, at the other extreme, observes a location or process without becoming a part of it in any way. The subjects of study might not even realize they are being studied because of the researcher's unobtrusiveness. An individual making observations while sitting in a courtroom is an example. Although the complete observer is less likely to affect what is being studied and less likely to go native than the complete participant, he or she may also be less able to develop a full appreciation of what is being studied. A courtroom observer, for example, witnesses only the public acts that take place in the courtroom, not private conferences between judges and attorneys.

McCall (1978, 45) points out an interesting and often unnoticed trade-off between the role observers adopt and their ability to learn from what they see. If their role is *covert* (complete participation) or *detached* (complete observation), they are less able to ask questions to clarify what they observe. As complete participants, they take pains to conceal their observations and must exercise care in querying subjects. Similarly, complete observation means that it is generally not possible to interact with the persons or things being observed.

Researchers have to think carefully about the trade-off. If it is most important that subjects not be affected by their role as observer, known as **reactivity**, then complete participation or observation is preferred. If being able to ask questions about what they observe is important, then some role that combines participation and observation is better.

More generally, the appropriate role for observers hinges on what they want to learn and how their inquiry is affected by opportunities and constraints.

Different situations require different roles for researchers. Unfortunately, there are no clear guidelines for making this choice; field researchers rely on their understanding of the situation, their judgment, and their experience. In making a decision, researchers must be guided by both methodological and ethical considerations. Because these often conflict, deciding on the appropriate role may be difficult. Often, researchers find that their role limits the scope of their study.

## ASKING QUESTIONS

*Field researchers frequently supplement observations by interviewing subjects.*

Field research might involve going where the action is and simply watching and listening. Researchers can learn a lot merely by being attentive to what's going on. Field research can also involve more active inquiry. Sometimes, it's appropriate to ask people questions and record their answers. Richard Wright and Trevor Bennett (1990) describe observing and interviewing as two complementary ways to study offenders.

We examined interviewing in Chapter 9 on survey research. The interviewing normally done in connection with field observation falls into the category of specialized interviewing. This is sometimes referred to as a **qualitative interview**, which is based on a set of topics to be discussed in depth rather than based on the use of standardized questions.

Qualitative interviews are usually much less structured than survey interviews. At one extreme, an interview can be essentially a conversation in which the interviewer establishes a general direction for the conversation and pursues specific topics raised by the respondent. Ideally, the respondent does most of the talking. Michael Patton (2002) refers to this type as an "informal conversational interview," which is especially well suited to in-depth probing.

Qualitative interviews are most appropriate when researchers have little knowledge about a topic and when it's reasonable for them to have a casual conversation with a subject. This is a good strategy for interviewing active criminals. Qualita-

tive interviews are also appropriate when researchers and subjects are together for an extended time, such as a researcher accompanying police on patrol.

One of the special strengths of field research is its flexibility in the field. Even during structured interviews with public officials, the answers evoked by initial questions should shape subsequent ones.

For example, Michael Maxfield and Carsten Andresen (2002) studied the use by the New Jersey State Police of video recording equipment to document traffic stops. Very little published research existed on the use of video equipment by police or even the ways they go about doing traffic enforcement. Part of the research involved semistructured field interviews with commanders, supervisors, and troopers. Figure 8.1 shows the interview guide Maxfield and Andresen used with supervisors. This guide was just that—a guide. Some subjects were friendly and wanted to talk, so the interview became more of a conversation that eventually yielded answers to the queries in the guide. Others were wary, probably because the agency had been subject to criticism over racial profiling and other discriminatory practices. Interviews with such persons were brief, and they followed the guide very closely.

Another example is research on human trafficking conducted by Galma Jahic for her graduate study at Rutgers University, which included interviews with law enforcement officers and other experts in Bosnia and Herzegovina. She describes a different type of experience (2009, 190–191):

> I often felt that I had to navigate very complicated turfs of power and influence where I was the powerless and the participants the powerful ones.... [I]t was often difficult to direct the interview, as experts did not always answer my questions, but talked about issues they thought were relevant or important. It was often difficult to insist on asking questions that were not responded to without creating [a] hostile atmosphere. In such situations, I did not insist on obtaining answers, but simply moved on.

---

1. What do you feel are the main uses of the mobile video system (MVS) for supervisors? [probe contingent on responses]

2. Please describe how you use tapes from the MVS system to periodically review officer performance. [probes]

   ▪ Compare tapes with incident reports.

   ▪ Review tapes from certain types of incidents. [probe: Please describe types and why these types.]

   ▪ Keep an eye on individual officers. [probe: Please describe what might prompt you to select individual officers. I do not want you to name individuals. Instead, can you describe the reasons why you might want to keep an eye on specific individuals?]

3. For routine review, how do you decide which tapes to select for review?

   ▪ Does it vary by shift?

   ▪ Do you try to review a certain number of incidents?

   ▪ Or do you scan through tapes sort of at random?

4. Think back to when the system first became operational in cars at this station. What were some questions, concerns, or problems that officers might have had at the beginning?

5. How do officers under your command feel about the system now?

6. What, if any, technical problems seem to come up regularly? Occasionally?

7. Have you encountered any problems, or do you have any concerns about the MVS? [probe: operational issues; tape custody issues; other]

8. Please describe any specific ways you think the system can or should be improved.

9. If you want to find the tape for an individual officer on a specific day, and for a specific incident, would you say that's pretty easy, not difficult, or somewhat difficult? Do you have any suggestions for changing the way tapes are filed and controlled?

10. I would like to view some sample tapes. Can we go to the tape cabinet and find a tape for [select date from list]?

---

**FIGURE 8.1** Interview Guide for Field Study of State Police
*Source:* Adapted from Maxfield and Andresen (2002).

Justice officials can be busy, powerful people with little tolerance for what they feel are trivial or self-evident questions. The flexibility of field research can be important in adapting to varied circumstances.

The discussion of probes in Chapter 7 offers useful guidelines for getting more in-depth answers without biasing later answers. Researchers must learn the skill of being a good listener, of being more interested than interesting. They learn to say things like "How is that?" "In what ways?" "How do you mean that?" and "What would be an example of that?" They learn to look and listen expectantly and to let the person they are interviewing break the silence.

At its best, a field research interview is much like normal conversation. Because of this, it is essential to keep reminding ourselves that we are not having a normal conversation. In normal conversations, each of us wants to come across as an interesting, worthwhile person. Often we don't really hear each other because we're too busy thinking of what we'll say next. As an interviewer, the desire to appear interesting is counter-productive to the task. We need to make the other person seem interesting by being interested ourselves.

## GAINING ACCESS TO SUBJECTS

*Arranging access to subjects in formal organizations or subcultures begins with an initial contact.*

Suppose you decide to undertake field research on a community corrections agency in a large city. Let's assume that you do not know a great deal about the agency and that you will identify yourself as a researcher to staff and other people you encounter. Your research interests are primarily descriptive: you want to observe the routine operations of the agency in the office and elsewhere. In addition, you want to interview agency staff and persons who are serving community corrections sentences. This section will discuss some of the ways you might prepare before you conduct your interviews and direct observations.

## THEORY AND QUALITATIVE RESEARCH

Qualitative research frequently aims to inductively build grounded theory: theory that is grounded in observations and interviews obtained though fieldwork. Elijah Anderson's (1999) qualitative fieldwork that produced *The Code of the Street* is a well-known example. Several other examples of research on active offenders have contributed to the development of theories of offending in recent years.

Qualitative field research also draws on existing theory. In an interesting example that applies situational crime prevention theory to active offenders, Scott Jacques and Danielle Reynald (2012, forthcoming) examine how offenders seek to avoid victimization by other criminals and arrest by police. In the same way, individuals can prevent victimization by not carrying large sums of cash or carelessly displaying valuables. Drug dealers, for example, are careful to protect cash and drugs that may be targets of theft by others. Offenders take similar precautions to avoid arrests. Citing Clarke's typology (1997b) of techniques for crime prevention, Jacques and Reynald describe the following ways in which offenders avoid arrest and "rip-offs" by others:

- Increasing the effort required by police and offenders
- Increasing the risks by threatening retaliation against potential thieves
- Reducing the rewards by concealing cash and other targets of theft
- Reducing provocations though behavior to avoid undue attention from police
- Removing excuses that adversaries or police might exploit

Jacques and Reynald draw on qualitative interviews with active offenders to illustrate examples of these preventive actions.

As usual, you are well advised to begin with a search of the relevant literature, filling in your knowledge of the subject, and learning what others have said about it.

### Gaining Access to Formal Organizations

Any research on a criminal justice institution, or on persons who work either in or under the supervision of an institution, normally requires a formal request and approval. One of the first steps in preparing for the field, then, is to arrange access to the community corrections agency.

Obtaining initial approval can be confusing and frustrating. Many criminal justice agencies in large cities have a complex organization, combining a formal hierarchy with a bewildering variety of informal organizational cultures. Criminal courts are highly structured organizations in which a presiding judge may oversee court assignments and case scheduling for judges and many support personnel. At the same time, courts are chaotic organizations in which three constellations of professionals—prosecutors, defense attorneys, and judges—episodically interact to process large numbers of cases.

Continuing with the example of your research on community corrections, the best strategy in gaining access to virtually any other formal criminal justice organization is to use a four-step procedure: sponsor, letter, phone call, and meeting. Our discussion of these steps assumes that you will begin your field research by interviewing the agency executive director and gaining that person's approval for subsequent interviews and observations.

**Sponsor**   The first step is to find a sponsor—a person who is personally known to and respected by the executive director. Ideally, a sponsor will be able to advise you on a person to contact, that person's formal position in the organization, and her or his informal status, including her or his relationships with other key officials. Such advice can be important in helping you initiate contact with the right person while avoiding people who have bad reputations.

Finding the right sponsor is often the most important step in gaining access. It may require a couple of extra steps, because you might first need to ask a professor whether she or he knows someone. You could then contact that person (with the sponsorship of your professor) and ask for further assistance. For purposes of illustration, we will assume that your professor is knowledgeable, well connected, and happy to act as your sponsor.

**Letter**  Next, write a letter to the executive director. Your letter should have three parts: introduction, brief statement of your research purpose, and action request. See Figure 8.2 for an example. The introduction begins by naming your sponsor, thus immediately establishing your mutual acquaintance.

Next, describe your research purpose succinctly. This is not the place to give a detailed description as you would in a proposal. If possible, keep the description to one or two paragraphs, as in Figure 8.2. If a longer description is necessary to explain what you will be doing, you should *still* include only a brief description in your introductory letter, referring the reader to a separate attachment in which you summarize your research.

The action request describes what immediate role you are asking the contact person to play in your research. You may simply be requesting an interview, or you may want the person to help

---

Jane Adams
Executive Director
Chaos County Community Corrections
Anxiety Falls, Colorado

1 May 2009

Dear Ms. Adams:

My colleague, Professor Marcus Nelson, suggested I contact you for assistance in my research on community corrections. I will be conducting a study of community corrections programs and wish to include the Chaos County agency in my research.

Briefly, I am interested in learning more about the different types of sentences that judges impose in jurisdictions with community corrections agencies. As you know, Colorado's community corrections statute grants considerable discretion to individual counties in arranging locally administered corrections programs. Because of this, it is generally believed that a wide variety of corrections programs and sentences have been developed throughout the state. My research seeks to learn more about these programs as a first step toward developing recommendations that may guide the development of programs in other states. I also wish to learn more about the routine administration of a community corrections program such as yours.

I would like to meet with you to discuss what programs Chaos County has developed, including current programs and those that were considered but not implemented. In addition, any information about different types of community corrections sentences that Chaos County judges impose would be very useful. Finally, I would appreciate your suggestions on further sources of information about community corrections programs in Chaos County and other areas.

I will call your office at about 10:00 a.m. on Monday, May 8, to arrange a meeting. If that time will not be convenient, or if you have any questions about my research, please contact me at the number below.

Thanks in advance for your help.

Sincerely,

Alfred Nobel
Research Assistant
Institute for Advanced Studies
(201) 555-1212

---

**FIGURE 8.2**  Sample Letter of Introduction

you gain access to other officials. Notice how the sample in Figure 8.2 mentions both an interview and "suggestions on further sources of information about community corrections." In any case, you will usually want to arrange to meet or at least talk with the contact person. That leads to the third step.

**Phone Call** You probably already know that it can be difficult to arrange meetings with public officials (and often professors) or even to reach people by telephone. You can simplify this task by concluding your letter with a proposal for this step: arranging a phone call.

When you make the call, the executive director will have some idea of who you are and what you want. She will also have had the opportunity to contact your sponsor if she wants to verify any information in your introductory letter.

Even if you are not able to talk with the executive director personally, you will probably be able to talk to an assistant and make an appointment for a meeting (the next step). Again, this will be possible because your letter described what you eventually want—a meeting with the executive director—and established your legitimacy by naming a sponsor.

**Meeting** The final step is meeting with or interviewing the contact person. Because you have used the letter–phone call–meeting procedure, the contact person may have already taken preliminary steps to help you. For example, because the letter in Figure 8.2 indicates that you wish to interview the executive director about different types of community corrections sentences, she may have assembled some procedures manuals or reports in preparation for your meeting.

This procedure generally works well in gaining initial access to public officials or other people who work in formal organizations. Once initial access is gained, it is up to the researcher to use interviewing skills and other techniques to elicit the desired information. This is not as difficult as it might seem to novice (or apprentice) researchers for a couple of reasons.

First, most people are at least a bit flattered that their work, ideas, and knowledge are of interest to a researcher. And researchers can take advantage of this with the right words of encouragement. Second, criminal justice professionals are often happy to talk about their work with a knowledgeable outsider. Police, probation officers, and corrections workers usually encounter only their colleagues and their clients on the job. Interactions with colleagues become routine and suffused with office politics, and interactions with clients are common sources of stress. Talking with an interested and knowledgeable researcher is often seen as a pleasant diversion.

By the same token, Richard Wright and Scott Decker (1994) report that most members of their sample of active burglars were both happy and flattered to discuss the craft of burglary. Because they were engaged in illegal activities, burglars had to be more circumspect about sharing their experiences, unlike the way many people talk about events at work. As a result, burglars enjoyed the chance to describe their work to interested researchers who both promised confidentiality and treated them "as having expert knowledge normally unavailable to outsiders" (1994, 26).

## Gaining Access to Subcultures

Research by Wright and Decker illustrates how gaining access to subcultures in criminal justice—such as active criminals, deviants, and juvenile gangs—requires tactics that differ in some respects from those used to meet with public officials. Letters, phone calls, and formal meetings are usually not appropriate for initiating field research among active offenders. However, the basic principle of using a sponsor to gain initial access operates in much the same way, although the word *informant* is normally used to refer to someone who helps make contact with subcultures.

Informants may be people whose job involves working with criminals—such as police, juvenile caseworkers, probation officers, attorneys, and counselors at drug clinics. Lawyers who specialize in criminal defense work can be especially useful sources of information about potential subjects. Frances Gant and Peter Grabosky (2001) contacted a private investigator to help locate car thieves and people working in auto-related businesses who were reputed to deal in stolen parts.

Wright and Decker (1994) were fortunate to encounter a former offender who was well connected with active criminals. The ex-offender helped researchers in two related ways. First, he referred them to other people, who in turn found active burglars willing to participate in the study. Second, he was well known and respected among burglars, and his sponsorship of the researchers made it possible for them to study a group of naturally suspicious subjects.

A different approach for gaining access to subcultures is to hang around places where criminals hang out. Wright and Decker rejected that strategy as a time-consuming and uncertain way to find burglars, in part because they were not sure where burglars hung out. In contrast, Bruce Jacobs (1999) initiated contact with street-level drug dealers by hanging around and being noticed in locations known for crack availability. Consider how this tactic might make sense for finding drug dealers, whose illegal work requires customers. In contrast, the offense of burglary is more secretive, and it's more difficult to imagine how one would find an area known for the presence of burglars.

Reviewing field research in several cities, Scott Jacques and Richard Wright (2008) offer general advice on recruiting active offenders. First, more informal social interaction between researchers, criminals, and informants increases the likelihood that offenders will participate. Second, it often helps to pay a small fee in gaining cooperation from offenders who are recruited through a chain of referrals. Third,

> criminals who are closest in relational distance to the researcher, especially those who have done previous interviews, are the ones most likely to produce the greatest amount of valid data and are thus the most appropriate persons with whom to discuss the most serious crimes (Jacques and Wright 2008, 35).

The next section offers further guidance on the importance of referrals for recruiting active offenders.

Whatever techniques are used to identify subjects among subcultures, it is usually not possible to produce a probability sample, and so the sample cannot be assumed to represent some larger population in the kind of statistical sense we discussed in Chapter 6. Although we can't make probability statements about samples of active offenders, such samples may be representative of a subculture or target population. For example, in his study of drug trafficking in a region of Burma, Ko-lin Chin and associates interviewed 300 opium farmers (Chin 2009). Chin acknowledges that his sample is not statistically representative, but nonetheless it provides valuable information about opium growing in a region of Burma.

## Selecting Cases for Observation

This brings us to the more general question of how to select cases for observation in field research. The techniques used by Chin and by Wright and Decker, as well as by many other researchers who have studied active criminals, combine the use of informants and what is called **snowball sampling**. As we mentioned in Chapter 6, with snowball sampling, initial research subjects (or informants) identify other persons who might also become subjects, who in turn suggest more potential subjects, and so on. In this way, a group of subjects is accumulated through a series of referrals.

Wright and Decker's (1994) study provides a good example. The ex-offender contacted a few active burglars and a few streetwise noncriminals, who referred researchers to additional subjects, and so on. This process is illustrated in Figure 8.3, which shows the chain of referrals that accumulated a snowball sample of 105 individuals.

Starting at the top of Figure 8.3, the ex-offender put researchers in contact with two subjects directly (001 and 003), a small-time criminal, three streetwise noncriminals, a crack addict, a youth worker, and someone serving probation. Continuing downward, the small-time criminal was especially helpful, identifying 12 subjects who participated in the study (005, 006, 008, 009, 010, 021, 022, 023, 025, 026, 030, 032). Notice how the

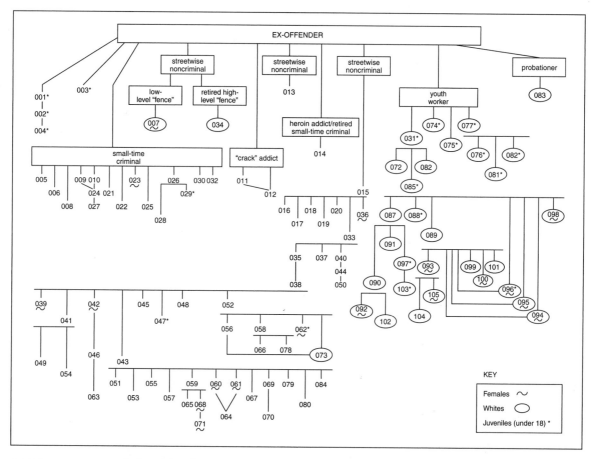

**FIGURE 8.3** Snowball Sample Referral Chart

*Source:* Reprinted from Richard T. Wright and Scott H. Decker, *Burglars on the Job: Streetlife and Residential Break-ins* (Boston: Northeastern University Press, 1994). Reprinted by permission of Northeastern University Press.

snowball effect continues, with subject 026 identifying subjects 028 and 029. Notice also that some subjects were themselves "nominated" by more than one source. In the middle of the bottom row in Figure 8.3, for example, subject 064 was mentioned by subjects 060 and 061.

As an illustration, consider the potential selection biases involved in a field study of deviants. Let's say we want to study a small number of drug dealers. We have a friend who works in the probation department of a large city and is willing to introduce us to people convicted of drug dealing and sentenced to probation. What selection problems

might result from studying subjects identified in this way? How might our subjects not be representative of the general population of drug dealers? If we work our way backward from the chain of events that begins with a crime and ends with a criminal sentence, the answers should become clear.

First, drug dealers sentenced to probation may be first-time offenders or persons convicted of dealing small amounts of "softer" drugs. Repeat offenders and kingpin cocaine dealers will not be in this group. Second, it is possible that people initially charged with drug dealing were convicted of simple possession through a plea bargain; because of our focus on people convicted of dealing, our selection procedure will miss this group as well. Finally, by selecting dealers who have been arrested and convicted, we may be gaining access only to those less skilled dealers who were caught. More skilled or experienced dealers may be less likely to be arrested in the first place; they may be different in important ways from the dealers we wish to study. Also, if dealers in street drug markets are more likely to be arrested than dealers who work through social networks of friends and acquaintances, a sample based on arrested dealers could be biased in more subtle ways.

To see why this raises an important issue in selecting cases for field research, let's return again to the sample of burglars studied by Wright and Decker. Notice that their snowball sample began with an ex-offender and that they sought out *active* burglars. An alternative approach would be to select a probability or other sample of convicted burglars, perhaps in prison or on probation. But Wright and Decker rejected this strategy for sampling because of the possibility that they would overlook burglars who had not been caught. After accumulating their sample, the researchers were in a position to test this assumption by examining arrest records for their subjects. Only about one-fourth of the active burglars had ever been convicted of burglary; an additional one-third had been arrested for burglary but not convicted. More than 40 percent had no burglary arrests, and 8 percent had never been arrested for any offense (1994, 12).

Putting all this together, Wright and Decker concluded that about three-fourths of their subjects would not have been eligible for inclusion if the researchers had based their sample on persons convicted of burglary. Thus little overlap exists between the population of active burglars and the population of convicted burglars.

## Purposive Sampling in Field Research

Sampling in field research tends to be more complicated than in other kinds of research. In many types of field studies, researchers attempt to observe everything within their field of study; thus, in a sense, they do not sample at all. In reality, of course, it is impossible to observe everything. To the extent that field researchers observe only a portion of what happens, what they do observe is a de facto sample of all the possible observations that might have been made. We can seldom select a controlled sample of such observations. But we can keep in mind the general principles of representativeness and interpret our observations accordingly.

The ability to systematically sample cases for observation depends on the degree of structure and predictability of the phenomenon being observed. This is more of a general guideline than a hard-and-fast rule. The actions of youth gangs, burglars, and auto thieves are less structured and predictable than those of police officers. It is possible to select a probability sample of police officers for observation because the behavior of police officers in a given city is structured and predictable in many dimensions. Because the population of active criminals is unknown, it is not possible to select a probability sample for observation.

This example should call to mind our discussion of sampling frames in Chapter 6. A roster of police officers and their assignments to patrol sectors and shifts could serve as a sampling frame for selecting subjects to observe. No such roster of gang members, burglars, and auto thieves is available.

Now consider the case in which a sampling frame is less important than the regularity of a process. The regular, predictable passage of people on city sidewalks makes it possible to systematically select a sample of cases for observation. There is no sampling frame of pedestrians, but studies such as Painter's research (1996) on the effects of street lighting can depend on the reliable flow of passersby who may be observed.

In an observational study such as Painter's, we might also make observations at a number of different locations on different streets. We could pick the sample of locations through standard probability methods, or more likely, we could use a rough quota system, observing wide streets and narrow ones, busy streets and quiet ones, or samples from different times of day. In a study of pedestrian traffic, we might also observe people in different types of urban neighborhoods—

comparing residential and commercial areas, for example. Since she was interested specifically in drug use among patrons of rave dance clubs, sampling dance clubs was a natural strategy for Dina Perrone.

Table 8.1 summarizes different sampling dimensions that might be considered in planning field research. The behavior of people, together with the characteristics of people and places, can vary by population group, location, time, and weather. We touched on the first two in this chapter and in the example of New York City homeless people described in Chapter 6. Now we will briefly discuss how sampling plans might consider time and weather dimensions.

People tend to engage in more out-of-door activities in fair weather than in wet or snowy conditions. In northern cities, people are outside more when the weather is warm. Any study of outdoor activity should therefore consider the potential effects of variation in the weather. For example, in Painter's study of pedestrian traffic before and after improvements in street lighting, it was important to consider weather conditions during the times observations were made.

Behavior also varies by time, presented as micro and macro dimensions in Table 8.1. City streets in a central business district are busiest during working hours, whereas more people are in residential areas at other times. And, of course, people do different things on weekends than during the workweek.

Seasonal variation, the macro time dimension, may also be important in criminal justice research. Daylight lasts longer in summer months, which affects the amount of time people spend outdoors. Shopping peaks from Thanksgiving to Christmas, increasing the number of shoppers, who along with their automobiles may become targets for thieves.

In practice, controlled probability sampling is seldom used in field research. Different types of purposive samples are much more common. Patton (2002, 230; emphasis in original) describes a broad range of approaches to purposive sampling and offers a useful comparison of probability and purposive samples:

> The logic and power of probability sampling derive from statistical probability theory. A random and statistically representative sample permits confident generalization from a sample to a larger population. The logic and power of purposeful sampling lies in selecting *information rich cases* for study in depth.

Nonetheless, if researchers understand the principles and logic of more formal sampling methods, they are likely to produce more effective purposive sampling in field research.

## RECORDING OBSERVATIONS

*Many different methods are available for collecting and recording field observations.*

Just as there is great variety in the types of field studies we might conduct, we have many options for making records of field observations. In conducting field interviews, researchers almost certainly write notes of some kind, but they might also tape-record interviews. Video recording may be useful in field interviews to capture visual images of dress and body language. Photographs or videotapes can be used to make records of visual images such as a block of apartment buildings before and after some physical design change or to serve as a pretest for an experimental neighborhood cleanup campaign. This technique was used by Robert Sampson

**TABLE 8.1**  Sampling Dimensions in Field Research

| Sampling Dimension | Variation in |
|---|---|
| Population | Behavior and characteristics |
| Space | Behavior |
| | Physical features of locations |
| Time, micro | Behavior by time of day, day of week |
| | Lighting by time of day |
| | Business, store, entertainment activities by time of day, day of week |
| Time, macro | Behavior by season, holiday |
| | Entertainment by season, holiday |
| Weather | Behavior by weather |

and Stephen Raudenbush (1999) in connection with probability samples of city blocks in Chicago. Videotapes were made of sampled blocks, and the recordings were then viewed to assess physical and social conditions in those areas.

We can think of a continuum of methods for recording observations. At one extreme is traditional field observation and note taking with pen and paper, such as we might use in field interviews. The opposite extreme includes various types of automated and remote measurement, such as videotapes, devices that count automobile traffic, or computer tabulations of mass transit users. In between is a host of methods that have many potential applications in criminal justice research.

Of course, the methods selected for recording observations are directly related to issues of measurement—especially how key concepts are operationalized. Thinking back to our discussion of measurement in Chapter 4, you should recognize why this is so. If we are interested in policies to increase nighttime pedestrian traffic in some city, we might want to know why people do or do not go out at night and how many people stroll around different neighborhoods. Interviews—perhaps in connection with a survey—can determine people's reasons for going out or not, whereas video recordings of passersby can provide simple counts. By the same token, a traffic-counting device can produce information about the number of automobiles that pass a particular point on the road, but it cannot measure what the blood alcohol levels of drivers are, whether riders are wearing seat belts, or how fast a vehicle is traveling.

## Cameras and Voice Recorders

Video cameras may be used in public places to record relatively simple phenomena, such as the passage of people or automobiles, or more complex social processes. For several years, London police have monitored traffic conditions at dozens of key intersections using video cameras mounted on building rooftops. In fact, the *2007 Road Atlas for Britain* includes the locations of stationary video cameras on its maps. Since 2003, video cameras have monitored all traffic

entering central London as part of an effort to reduce traffic. The license plates of vehicles that do not register paying a toll are recorded, and violation notices are sent to owners.

Still photographs may be appropriate to record some types of observations, such as graffiti or litter. Photos have the added benefit of preserving visual images that can later be viewed and coded by more than one person, thus facilitating interrater reliability checks. If we are interested in studying pedestrian traffic on city streets, we might gather data about what types of people we see and how many there are. As the number and complexity of our observations increase, it becomes more difficult to reliably record how many males and females we see, how many adults and juveniles, and so on. Taking photographs of sampled areas will enable us to be more confident in our measurements and will also make it possible for another person to check on our interpretation of the photographs.

This approach was used by James Lange and associates (Lange, Johnson, and Voas 2005) in their study of speeding on the New Jersey Turnpike. The researchers deployed radar devices and digital cameras to measure the speed of vehicles and to take photos of drivers. Equipment was housed in an unmarked van parked at sample locations on the turnpike. The race of drivers was later coded by teams of researchers who studied the digital images. Agreement by at least two of three coders was required to accept the photos for further analysis.

In addition to their use in interviews, audio recording is useful for dictating observations. For example, a researcher interested in patterns of activity on urban streets can dictate observations while riding through selected areas in an automobile. It is possible to dictate observations in an unstructured manner, describing each street scene as it unfolds. Or a voice recorder can be used more like an audio checklist, with observers noting specified items seen in preselected areas.

## Field Notes

Even tape recorders and cameras cannot capture all the relevant aspects of social processes. Most field researchers make some records of observations as written notes, perhaps in a field journal. Field notes should include both empirical observations and interpretations of them. They should record what we "know" we have observed and what we "think" we have observed. It is important, however, that these different kinds of notes be identified for what they are. For example, we might note that person $X$ approached and handed something to person $Y$—a known drug dealer—that we think this was a drug transaction, and that we think person $X$ was a new customer.

Every student is familiar with the process of taking notes. Good note taking in field research requires more careful and deliberate attention and involves some specific skills. Three guidelines are particularly important.

First, don't trust your memory any more than you have to; it's untrustworthy. Even if you pride yourself on having a photographic memory, it's a good idea to take notes, either during the observation or as soon afterward as possible. If you are taking notes during the observation, do it unobtrusively because people are likely to behave differently if they see you writing down everything they say or do.

Second, it's usually a good idea to take notes in stages. In the first stage, you may need to take sketchy notes (words and phrases) to keep abreast of what's happening. Then remove yourself and rewrite your notes in more detail. If you do this soon after the events you've observed, the sketchy notes will help you recall most of the details. The longer you delay, the less likely you are to recall things accurately and fully. James Roberts (2002), in his study of aggression in New Jersey nightclubs, was reluctant to take any notes while inside clubs, so he retired to his car to make sketchy notes about observations, then wrote them up in more detail later. Dina Perrone (2009) wrote up preliminary notes from her study of dance clubs while riding home, then fleshed them out no later than three days after completing her field observations.

Third, you will inevitably wonder how much you should record. Is it really worth the effort to write out all the details you can recall right after the observation session? The basic answer is yes. In field research, you can't really be sure what's important and unimportant until you've had a chance to review and analyze a great volume of information, so you should record even things that don't seem important at the time. They may turn out to be significant after all. In addition, the act of recording the details of something unimportant may jog your memory on something that is important.

## Structured Observations

Field notes may be recorded on highly structured forms in which observers mark items in much the same way a survey interviewer marks a closed-ended questionnaire. For example, Stephen Mastrofski and associates (1998, 11) describe how police performance can be recorded on field observation questionnaires:

> Unlike ethnographic research, which relies heavily on the field researcher to make choices about what to observe and how to interpret it, the observer using [structured observation] is guided by … instruments designed by presumably experienced and knowledgeable police researchers.

Training for such efforts is extensive and time consuming. But Mastrofski and associates compared structured observation to closed-ended questions on a questionnaire. If researchers can anticipate in advance that observers will encounter a limited number of situations in the field, those situations can be recorded on structured observation forms. And, like closed-ended survey questions, structured observations have higher reliability.

In a long-term study, Ralph Taylor (1999) developed forms to code a range of physical characteristics in a sample of Baltimore neighborhoods. Observers recorded information on closed-ended items about housing layout, street length and width, traffic volume, type of nonresidential land use, graffiti, persons hanging out, and so forth. Observations were completed in the same neighborhoods in 1981 and 1994.

Because structured field observation forms often resemble survey questionnaires, the use of such forms has the benefit of enabling researchers to generate numeric measures of conditions observed in the field. The Bureau of Justice Assistance has produced a handbook containing guidelines for conducting structured field observations, called **environmental surveys**. The name is significant because observers record information about the conditions of a specified environment:

> [Environmental] surveys seek to assess, as systematically and objectively as possible, the overall physical environment of an area. That physical environment comprises the buildings, parks, streets, transportation facilities, and overall landscaping of an area as well as the functions and conditions of those entities (Bureau of Justice Assistance 1993, 43).

Environmental surveys have come to be an important component of problem-oriented policing and situational crime prevention. Figure 8.4 is adapted from an environmental survey form used by the Philadelphia Police Department in drug enforcement initiatives. Environmental surveys are conducted to plan police strategy in drug enforcement in small areas and to assess changes in conditions following targeted enforcement. Notice that the form can be used to record both information about physical conditions (street width, traffic volume, streetlights) and counts of people and their activities.

Like interview surveys, environmental surveys require that observers be carefully trained in what to observe and how to interpret it. For example, the instructions that accompany the environmental survey excerpted in Figure 8.4 include guidance on coding abandoned automobiles:

> Count as abandoned if it appears non-drivable (i.e., has shattered windows, dismantled body parts, missing tires, missing license plates). Consider it abandoned if it appears that it has not been driven for some time and that it is not going to be for some time to come.

Other instructions provide details on how to count drivable lanes, what sorts of activities constitute "playing" and "working," how to estimate the ages of people observed, and so on.

## Linking Field Observations and Other Data

Although criminal justice research may use field methods or sample surveys exclusively, a given project will often collect data from several sources. This is consistent with general advice about using appropriate measures and data collection methods. Simply saying, "I am going to conduct an observational study of youth gangs" restricts the research focus at the outset to the kinds of information that can be gathered through observation. Such a study may be useful and interesting, but a researcher is better advised to consider what data collection methods are necessary in any particular study.

Recognizing the role of disorder and antisocial behavior as law enforcement problems, the Home Office Research unit in England has developed a guide for collecting data that combines surveys, field observations, and official records. Surveys provide measures of how people perceive problems of disorder, while official records (which we examine in Chapter 9) document problems that have been reported to police and others. More standard measures of disorder can be produced by observational "audits" of behavior and physical conditions. Sally Harrandine and associates (2004) provide a detailed guide to completing such audits and to comparing the data produced with measures obtained through surveys and official records.

A long-term research project on community policing in Chicago draws on data from surveys, field observation, and police records (Chicago Community Policing Evaluation Consortium 2003). As just one example, researchers studied what sorts of activities and discussions emerged at community meetings in 130 of the city's 270 police beats that covered residential areas. Observers attended meetings, making detailed notes and completing structured observation forms. One section of the form, shown in Figure 8.5, instructed observers to make notes of specific types of neighborhood problems that were discussed at the meeting (Bennis, Skogan, and Steiner 2003). Here is an excerpt from the narrative notes that supplemented this section of the form:

> They ... had very serious concerns in regard to a dilapidated building in their block that

Date:_____ Day of week:_____ Time:_____

Observer:_____

Street name:_____

Cross streets:_____

1.  Street width

    Number of drivable lanes                    ____
    Number of parking lanes                     ____
    Median present? (yes = 1, no = 2)           ____

2.  Volume of traffic flow: (check one)

    a. very light                               ____
    b. light                                    ____
    c. moderate                                 ____
    d. heavy                                    ____
    e. very heavy                               ____

3.  Number of street lights                     ____
4.  Number of broken street lights              ____
5.  Number of abandoned automobiles             ____
6.  List all the people on the block and their activities:

| Males | Hanging out | Playing | Working | Walking | Other |
|---|---|---|---|---|---|
| Young (up to age 12) | ____ | ____ | ____ | ____ | ____ |
| Teens (13 – 19) | ____ | ____ | ____ | ____ | ____ |
| Adult (20 – 60) | ____ | ____ | ____ | ____ | ____ |
| Seniors (61+) | ____ | ____ | ____ | ____ | ____ |
| Females | | | | | |
| Young (up to age 12) | ____ | ____ | ____ | ____ | ____ |
| Teens (13 – 19) | ____ | ____ | ____ | ____ | ____ |
| Adult (20 – 60) | ____ | ____ | ____ | ____ | ____ |
| Seniors (61+) | ____ | ____ | ____ | ____ | ____ |

**FIGURE 8.4** Example of Environmental Survey

*Source:* Adapted from Bureau of Justice Assistance (1993, Appendix B).

was being used for drug sales. The drug seller's people were also squatting in the basement of the building. The main concern was that the four adults who were squatting also had three children under the age of four with them. (Chicago Community Policing Evaluation Consortium 2003, 37)

In addition, observers distributed questionnaires to community residents and police officers attending each meeting. Items asked how often people attended beat meetings, what sorts of other civic activities they pursued, and whether they thought various other issues were problems in their neighborhood. As an example, the combination of field observation

5. Location code (circle one)

1. Police station
2. Park building
3. Library
4. Church
5. Bank
6. Other government

7. Hospital
8. Public housing facility
9. Private facility
10. Restaurant
11. Other not-for-profit

*Count the house 30 minutes after the meeting. Exclude police in street clothes ... and others that you can identify as non-residents.*

8. _____ Total number residents attending

**Note Problems Discussed**

1. Drugs (include possibles)

____ ____    Street sales or use
big    small   Building used for drugs
               Drug-related violence

9. Physical decay

____ ____    Abandoned buildings
big    small   Run-down buildings
               Abandoned cars
               Graffiti and vandalism
               Illegal dumping

**FIGURE 8.5** Excerpts from Chicago Beat Meeting Observation Form
*Source:* Adapted from Bennis, Skogan, and Steiner (2003, Appendix 1).

data and survey questionnaires enabled researchers to assess the degree of general social activism among those who attended beat meetings.

Field research can also be conducted after a survey. For example, a survey intended to measure fear of crime and related concepts might ask respondents to specify any area near their residence that they believe is particularly dangerous. Follow-up field visits to the named areas could then be conducted, during which observers record information about physical characteristics, land use, numbers of people present, and so forth.

The type of environmental survey that focuses on security and safety of places is often called a **safety audit**. The box titled "Conducting a Safety Audit" describes how structured field observations were combined with a focus group discussion to assess the scope of environmental design changes in Toronto, Canada. Safety audits, coupled with surveys or focus groups, are becoming more widely used to assess women's security in public places (Whitzman et al. 2009). Mangai Natarajan (2009) describes her research on sexual harassment of college women in India, known as "eve teasing." Interviews with college students and police were followed by safety audits of specific areas around students' campuses.

The flexibility of field methods is one reason observation and field interviews can readily be incorporated into many research projects. And field observation often provides a much richer understanding of a phenomenon that is imperfectly revealed through a survey questionnaire.

---

 **CONDUCTING A SAFETY AUDIT**

Gisela Bichler-Robertson
California State University
at San Bernardino

A safety audit involves a careful inventory of specific environmental and situational factors that may contribute to feelings of discomfort, fear of victimization, or crime itself. The goal of a safety audit is to devise recommendations that will improve a specific area by reducing fear and crime.

Safety audits combine features of focus groups and structured field observations. To begin, the researcher assembles a small group of individuals (10 or fewer) considered to be vulnerable. Examples include: senior citizens, physically challenged individuals, young women who travel alone, students, youth, and parents with young children. Assembling diverse groups helps to identify a greater variety of environmental and situational factors for the particular area.

After explaining safety audit procedures, an audit leader then takes the group on a tour of the audit site. Since perceptions differ by time of day, at least two audits are conducted for each site—one during daylight and one after dark.

When touring audit sites, individuals do not speak to one another. The audit leader instructs group members to imagine that they are walking through the area alone. Each person is equipped with a structured form for documenting their observations and perceptions. Forms vary, depending on the group and site. In general, however, safety audit participants are instructed to document the following items:

1. Before walking through the area, briefly describe the type of space you are reviewing (e.g., a parking deck, park, shopping district). Record the number of entrances, general volume of users, design of structures, materials used in design, and type of lighting.
2. Complete the following while walking through the area.

**General feelings of safety:**
- Identify the places in which you feel unsafe and uncomfortable.
- What is it about each place that makes you feel this way?
- Identify the places in which you feel safe.
- What is it about each place that makes you feel this way?

**General visibility:**
- Can you see very far in front of you?
- Can you see behind you?
- Are there any structures or vegetation that restrict your sightlines?
- How dense are the trees/bushes?
- Are there any hiding spots or entrapment zones?
- Is the lighting adequate? Can you see the face of someone 15 meters in front of you?
- Are the paths/hallways open or are they very narrow?
- Are there any sharp corners (90° angles)?

**Perceived control over the space:**
- Could you see danger approaching with enough time to choose an alternative route?
- Are you visible to others on the street or in other buildings?
- Can you see any evidence of a security system?

**Presence of others:**
- Does the area seem to be deserted?
- Are there many women around?
- Are you alone in the presence of men?
- What do the other people seem to be doing?
- Are there any undesirables—vagrants (homeless or beggars), drunks, etc.?
- Do you see people you know?
- Are there any police or security officers present?

**General safety:**
- Do you have access to a phone or other way of summoning help?
- What is your general perception of criminal behavior?
- Are there any places where you feel you could be attacked or confronted in an uncomfortable way?

**Past experience in this space:**
- Have you been harassed in this space?
- Have you heard of anyone who had a bad experience in this place (any legends or real experiences)?

*(continued)*

- Is it likely that you may be harassed here (e.g., drunk young men coming out of the pub)?

- Have you noticed any social incivilities (minor deviant behavior—i.e., public drinking, vandalism, roughhousing, or skateboarding)?

- Is there much in the way of physical incivilities (broken windows, litter, broken bottles, vandalism)?

Following the site visit, the group finds a secure setting for a focused discussion of the various elements they identified. Harvesting observations about good and bad spaces helps to develop recommendations for physical improvement. Group members may also share perceptions and ideas about

personal safety. This process should begin with a brainstorming discussion and finish with identifying the key issues of concern and most reasonable recommendations for addressing those issues.

This method of structured observation has proven to be invaluable. Much of the public space in Toronto, including university campuses, public parks, transportation centers, and garages, has been improved through such endeavors.

*Source:* Adapted from materials developed by the Metro Action Committee on Public Violence Against Women and Children (METRAC) (Toronto, Canada: METRAC, 1987, http://www.metrac.org/programs/safety/safety.htm#training). Used by permission.

## ILLUSTRATIONS OF FIELD RESEARCH

*Examples illustrate different applications of field research to study speeding, traffic enforcement, and violence in bars.*

Let's now examine some illustrations of field research in action. These descriptions will provide a clearer sense of how researchers use field observations and interviews in criminal justice research.

### Field Research on Racial Profiling, Speeding, and Traffic Enforcement

Field research has been an important element in studies of racial profiling for two reasons. First, field research has provided measures of driver behavior that are not dependent on police records. As we have seen in earlier chapters, it is important to compare police records of stops to some other source of information. Second, field research has provided insights into traffic enforcement, an area of policing not much studied by researchers. Field research has also covered the wide range of applications from highly structured counting to less structured field observation and interviews.

**Field Measures of Speed**   Studies of racial profiling in three states used highly structured techniques to measure the speed of vehicles. The most sophisticated

equipment was used by Lange and associates in New Jersey. Here's how the authors described their setup:

> The digital photographs were captured by a TC-2000 camera system, integrated with an AutoPatrol PR-100 radar system, provided by Transcore, Inc. The equipment, other than two large strobe lights, was mounted inside an unmarked van, parked behind preexisting guide rails along the turnpike. The camera and radar sensor pointed out of the van's back window toward oncoming traffic. The two strobe lights were mounted on tripods behind the van and directed toward oncoming traffic. Transcore's employees operated the equipment. (2005, 202)

Equipment was programmed to photograph every vehicle exceeding the speed limit by 15 or more miles per hour. Operators also photographed and timed samples of 25 to 50 other vehicles per hour. Elsewhere we have described the other element of observation—coding the appearance of driver race from photographs.

Pennsylvania researchers also used radar to measure the speed of vehicles in selected locations throughout the state. Their procedures were less automated, relying on teams of two observers in a car parked on the side of sampled roadways. Undergraduate students at Pennsylvania State University served as observers. They were trained by Pennsylvania state police in the use of radar equipment, completing the same classroom training that was required of troopers. Additional training for observers was conducted on samples of roadways by the project director. State police were trained to operate radar equipment, but not to combine it with systematic field observation of driver characteristics. That was an important research task, however. Engel and associates describe training and field procedures in detail. Their simple field observation form is included in an appendix to their report (2005, 229).

William Smith and associates (Smith et al. 2003) tried but rejected stationary observation as a technique for recording speed and observing drivers, citing the high speed of passing vehicles and glare from windows as problems. Instead, a research team used mobile observation techniques—observing drivers and timing cars that passed them. Radar was also considered and rejected because it was feared that vehicles with radar detectors, said to be common in North Carolina, would slow down when nearing the research vehicle. Worse, Smith and associates report that truck drivers quickly broadcasted word of detected radar, thus eroding the planned unobtrusive measure.

As you can see, the observational component of research in these three states varied quite a lot. Reading the detailed reports from each study offers valuable insights into the kinds of things field researchers must consider.

**Observing New Jersey State Police**  Other research in New Jersey used less structured field observation techniques because the research purpose was less structured—learning about the general nature of traffic enforcement on New Jersey highways. In a series of studies, researchers from Rutgers University (Maxfield and Kelling 2005; Maxfield and Andresen 2002; Andresen 2005) were interested in the mechanics of making traffic stops and what kinds of things troopers considered in deciding which vehicles to stop. Researchers have long accompanied municipal police on patrol, and a number of studies have documented their efforts. But, as Andresen points out, only a handful of studies have examined traffic enforcement, and even fewer considered state police.

To study video recording cameras in state police cars, Maxfield and Andresen (2002) rode with state police and watched the equipment in use. They learned that sound quality of recordings was often poor, for a variety of reasons associated with microphones and wireless transmittal. It was initially hoped that video records might make it possible to classify the race of drivers, but after watching in car video monitors the researchers confirmed that poor image quality undermined the potential reliability of that approach. Moreover, although the Rutgers researchers expected that troopers would be on their best behavior, on a few occasions troopers avoided recording sound and/or images. Even though people behave differently when accompanied by researchers, it's not uncommon for police to let their guard down a little.

Andresen accompanied troopers on 57 patrols overall, conducting unstructured interviews during the several hours he spent with individual troopers. He adopted the common practice of using an interview guide, a list of simple questions he planned to ask in the field. He took extensive notes while riding and repeatedly told troopers they could examine his notes. Andresen observed more than 150 traffic stops, writing field notes to document who was involved, reasons for the stop, what actions troopers took, and what comments they made after the stops. He reports that most troopers seemed to enjoy describing their work. And, as you might imagine, troopers' commentary about traffic enforcement was very interesting.

## Bars and Violence

Researchers in the first example conducted systematic observations for specific purposes and produced quantitative estimates of speeding traffic stops. Field research is commonly used in more qualitative studies as well, in which precise quantitative estimates are neither available nor needed. A fascinating series of studies of violence in Australian bars by Ross Homel and associates provides an example (Homel, Tomsen, and Thommeny 1992; Homel and Clark 1994; Macintyre and Homel 1996).

Homel and associates set out to learn how various situational factors related to public drinking might promote or inhibit violence in Australian bars and nightclubs. Think for a moment about how you might approach their research question: "whether alcohol consumption itself contributes in some way to the likelihood of violence, or whether aspects of the drinkers or of the drinking settings are the critical factors" (1992, 681). Examining police records might reveal that assault reports are more likely to come from bars than from, say, public libraries. Or a survey might find that self-reported bar patrons were more likely to have witnessed or participated in violence than respondents who did not frequent bars or nightclubs. But neither of these approaches will yield measures of the setting or situational factors that might provoke violence. Field research can produce direct observation of barroom settings and is well suited to addressing the question framed by Homel and associates.

Researchers began by selecting 4 high-risk and 2 low-risk sites on the basis of Sydney police records and preliminary scouting visits. These 6 sites were visited five or more times, and an additional 16 sites were visited once in the course of scouting.

Visits to bars were conducted by pairs of observers who stayed two to six hours at each site. Their role is best described as complete participant because they were permitted one alcoholic drink per hour and otherwise played the role of bar patron. Observers made no notes while onsite. As soon as possible after leaving a bar, they wrote up separate narrative accounts. Later, at group meetings of observers and research staff, the narrative accounts were discussed and any discrepancies resolved. Narratives were later coded by research staff to identify categories of situations, people, and activities that seemed to be associated with the likelihood of violence. These eventually included physical and social atmosphere, drinking patterns, characteristics of patrons, and characteristics of staff.

The researchers began their study by assuming that some thing or things distinguished bars in which violence was common from those in which it was less common. After beginning their fieldwork, however, Homel and associates (1992, 684) realized that circumstances and situations were the more important factors:

During field research it soon became apparent that the violent premises are for most

of the time not violent. Violent occasions in these places seemed to have characteristics that clearly marked them out from nonviolent times.... This unexpectedly helped us refine our ideas about the relevant situational variables, and to some extent reduced the importance of comparisons with the premises selected as controls.

In other words, the research question was partly restated. What began as a study to determine why some bars in Sydney were violent was revised to determine what situations seemed to contribute to violence.

This illustrates one of the strengths of field research—the ability to make adjustments while in the field. You may recognize this as an example of inductive reasoning. Learning that even violent clubs were peaceful most of the time, Homel and associates were able to focus observers' attention on looking for more specific features of the bar environment and staff and patron characteristics. Such adjustments on the fly would be difficult, if not impossible, if you were doing a survey.

Altogether, field observers made 55 visits to 23 sites for a total of about 300 hours of field observation. During these visits, observers witnessed 32 incidents of physical violence. Examining detailed field notes, researchers attributed violent incidents to a variety of interrelated factors.

With respect to patrons, violence was most likely to break out in bars frequented by young, working-class males. However, these personal characteristics were deemed less important than the flow of people in and out of bars. Violent incidents were often triggered when groups of males entered a club and encountered other groups of males they did not know.

Physical features mattered little unless they contributed to crowding or other adverse characteristics of the social atmosphere. Chief among social features associated with violence were discomfort and boredom. A crowded, uncomfortable bar with no entertainment spelled trouble.

Drinking patterns made a difference; violent incidents were most common when bar patrons were very drunk. More importantly, certain management practices seemed to produce more drunk patrons. Fewer customers were drunk in bars that had either a restaurant or a snack table. Bars with high cover charges and cheap drinks produced a high density of drunk patrons and violence. The economics of this situation are clear: if you must pay to enter a bar that serves cheap drinks, you'll get more for your money by drinking a lot.

The final ingredient found to contribute to violence was aggressive bouncers. "Many bouncers seem poorly trained, obsessed with their own machismo (relating badly to groups of male strangers), and some of them appear to regard their employment as a license to assault people" (1992, 688). Rather than reducing violence by rejecting unruly patrons, bouncers sometimes escalated violence by starting fights.

Field observation was necessary to identify what situations produce violence in bars. No other way of collecting data could have yielded the rich and detailed information that enabled Homel and associates to diagnose the complex relationships that produce violence in bars:

> Violent incidents in public drinking locations do not occur simply because of the presence of young or rough patrons or because of rock bands, or any other single variable. Violent occasions are characterized by subtle interactions of several variables. Chief among these are groups of male strangers, low comfort, high boredom, high drunkenness, as well as aggressive and unreasonable bouncers and floor staff. (1992, 688)

## STRENGTHS AND WEAKNESSES OF FIELD RESEARCH

*Validity is usually a strength of field research, but reliability and generalizability are sometimes weaknesses.*

As we have seen, field research is especially effective for studying the subtle nuances of behavior and for examining processes over time. For these reasons,

the chief strength of this method is the depth of understanding it permits.

Flexibility is another advantage of field research. Researchers can modify their research design at any time. Dina Perrone stated, "I consistently reevaluated my methodology to ensure the highest level of credibility, dependability, and transferability of the data. Coding methods, sampling, observational techniques and [my] interview guide evolved with the research" (2009, 37).

Most significantly, qualitative research is a superior method for studying active offenders in field settings. Qualitative interviews and observations combine offenders' perspectives and systematic measures collected by researchers. A growing body of research has provided rich detail on the motives of offenders, how they select targets, and what sorts of things they are attentive to as incidents unfold. Researchers have studied drug dealers, robbers, burglars, gang members, carjackers, sex workers, and individuals engaged in a variety of other offenses. Although it's possible to study arrested or convicted offenders in other settings, field research offers many advantages for learning about criminal activity that is untainted by official intervention.

By the same token, field research offers advantages for studying justice officials in natural settings. Scholars have long recognized that the view of police work through a car's windshield offers much richer information about police work than the statistical analysis of arrests or crime reports. Similarly, researchers have interviewed corrections officers for many studies. Ted Conover tried that approach but was denied access to interview corrections workers in New York state prisons. So he became a corrections officer in New York and wrote up his experiences after working for two years in Sing Sing. His book, *Newjack: Guarding Sing Sing*, provides insights into life on the job that are unobtainable through any other research method (Conover 2000).

Field research has its weaknesses, too. First, qualitative studies seldom yield precise descriptive statements about a large population. Observing casual discussions among corrections officers in a cafeteria, for example, does not yield trustworthy estimates about prison conditions. Nevertheless, it could provide important insights into some of the problems facing staff and inmates in a specific institution.

Second, field observation can produce systematic counts of behaviors and reasonable estimates for a large population of behaviors beyond those actually observed. However, because it is difficult to know the total population of given phenomena—shoppers or drivers, for example—precise probability samples cannot normally be drawn. In designing a quantitative field study or assessing the representativeness of some other study, researchers must think carefully about the density and predictability of what will be observed. Then they must decide whether sampling procedures are likely to tap representative instances of cases they will observe.

More generally, the advantages and disadvantages of different types of field studies can be considered in terms of their validity, reliability, and generalizability. As we have seen, validity and reliability are both qualities of measurements. *Validity* concerns whether measurements actually measure what they are supposed to, not something else. *Reliability* is a matter of dependability: if researchers make the same measurement again and again, will they get the same result? Note that some examples we described in this chapter included special steps to improve reliability. Finally, *generalizability* refers to whether specific research findings apply to people, places, and things not actually observed. Let's see how field research stacks up in these respects.

## Validity

Recall our discussion in Chapter 7 of some of the limitations of using survey methods to study domestic violence. An alternative is a field study in which the researcher interacts at length with victims of domestic violence. The relative strengths of each approach are nicely illustrated in a pair of articles that examine domestic violence in England. Chapter 7 quoted from Catriona Mirrlees-Black's (1995) article on domestic violence as measured in the British Crime Survey. John Hood-Williams and Tracey Bush (1995) provide a different perspective through their study published in the same issue of the *Home Office Research Bulletin*.

Tracey Bush lived in a London public housing project (termed *housing estate* in England) for about five years. This enabled her to study domestic violence in a natural setting: "The views of men and women on the estate about relationships and domestic violence have been gathered through the researcher's network of friends, neighbours, acquaintances, and contacts" (Hood-Williams and Bush 1995, 11). Through long and patient fieldwork, Bush learned that women sometimes normalize low levels of violence, seeing it as an unfortunate but unavoidable consequence of their relationship with a male partner. When violence escalates, victims may blame themselves. Victims may also remain in an abusive relationship in hopes that things will get better:

> She reported that she wanted the companionship and respect that she had received at the beginning of the relationship. It was the earlier, nonviolent man, whom she had met and fallen in love with, that she wanted back. (1995, 13)

Mirrlees-Black (1995) notes that measuring domestic violence is "difficult territory" in part because women may not recognize assault by a partner as a crime. Field research such as that by Hood-Williams and Bush offers an example of this phenomenon and helps us understand why it exists.

In field research, validity often refers to whether the intended meaning of the things observed or people interviewed has been accurately captured. In the case of interviews, Joseph Maxwell (2005) suggests getting feedback on the measures from the people being studied. For example, Wright and Decker (1994) conducted lengthy semistructured interviews with their sample of burglars. The researchers recognized that their limited understanding of the social context of burglary may have produced some errors in interpreting what they learned from subjects. To guard against this, Wright and Decker had some of their subjects review what they thought they had learned:

> As the writing proceeded, we read various parts of the manuscript to selected members of our sample. This allowed us to check our interpretations against those of

insiders and to enlist their help in reformulating passages they regarded as misleading or inaccurate. The result of using this procedure, we believe, is a book that faithfully conveys the offender's perspective on the process of committing residential burglaries. (1994, 33–34)

This approach is possible only if subjects are aware of the researcher's role as a researcher. In that case, having informants review draft field notes or interview transcripts can be an excellent strategy for improving validity.

## Reliability

Qualitative field research can have a potential problem with reliability. Suppose you characterize your best friend's political orientations based on everything you know about him or her. There's certainly no question that your assessment of that person's politics is at least somewhat idiosyncratic. The measurement you arrive at will appear to have considerable validity. We can't be sure, however, that someone else will characterize your friend's politics the same way you do, even with the same amount of observation.

Field research measurements—even in-depth ones—are also often very personal. If, for example, you wished to conduct a field study of bars and honky-tonks near your campus, you might judge levels of disorder on a Friday night to be low or moderate. In contrast, older adults might observe the same levels of noise and commotion and rate levels of disorder as intolerably high. How we interpret the phenomena we observe depends very much on our own experiences and preferences. Dina Perrone (2009, 36) acknowledges that her dislike for "hot, sweaty places" affected the areas she observed in her study of dance clubs, and thus the kinds of behavior she was able to describe.

The reliability of quantitative field studies can be enhanced by careful attention to the details of observation. Environmental surveys in particular can promote reliable observations by including detailed instructions on how to classify what is observed. Reliability can be strengthened by reviewing the products of field observations. Homel and associates sought to increase the reliability of observers' narrative descriptions by having group discussions about discrepancies in reports by different observers.

In a more general sense, reliability will increase as the degree of interpretation required in making actual observations decreases. Participant observation or unstructured interviews may require a considerable degree of interpretation on the part of the observer, and most of us draw on our own experiences and backgrounds in interpreting what we observe. At another extreme, electronic devices and machines can produce very reliable counts of persons who enter a store or of cars that pass some particular point. Somewhere in the middle are field-workers who observe motorists or pedestrians and tabulate a specific behavior.

## Generalizability

One of the chief goals of social science is generalization. We study particular situations and events to learn about life in general. Generalizability can be a problem for qualitative field research. It crops up in two forms.

First, the personal nature of the observations and measurements made by the researcher can produce results that will not necessarily be replicated by another independent researcher. If the observation depends in part on the individual observers, it is more valuable as a source of particular insight than as a general truth. You may recognize the similarity between this and the more general issue of reliability.

Second, because field researchers get a full and in-depth view of their subject matter, they can reach an unusually comprehensive understanding. By its very comprehensiveness, however, this understanding is less generalizable than results based on rigorous sampling and standardized measurements.

For example, Maxfield's observational research with the New Jersey State Police took several forms. One experience involved learning about radar speed enforcement on a 50-mile segment of the New Jersey Turnpike. Maxfield accompanied troopers on a thorough tour of this segment, identifying where radar units were routinely stationed (termed *fishing holes* by troopers). In his fieldwork, he also examined physical characteristics of the roadway; patterns of in-state and out-of-state travel; and areas where entrance ramps, slight upward grades, and other features affected vehicle speed. Finally, he gained extensive information on priorities and patterns in speed enforcement—learning what affects troopers' decisions to stop certain vehicles.

As a result, Maxfield has detailed knowledge about that 50-mile segment of the New Jersey Turnpike. How generalizable is that knowledge? In one sense, learning about fishing holes in very specific terms can help identify such sites on other roads. And learning how slight upward grades can slow traffic in one situation may help us understand traffic on other upward grades. But a detailed, idiosyncratic understanding of 50 miles of highway is just that—idiosyncratic. Knowing all there is to know about a straight, largely level stretch of limited-access toll road with few exits is not generalizable to other roadways—winding roads in mountainous areas with many exits, for example.

At the same time, some field studies are less rooted in the local context of the subject under study. Wright and Decker (1994) studied burglars in St. Louis, and it's certainly reasonable to wonder whether their findings apply to residential burglars in St. Petersburg, Florida. The actions and routines of burglars might be affected by local police strategies, differences in the age or style of dwelling units, or even the type and amount of vegetation screening buildings from the street. However, Wright and Decker draw general conclusions about how burglars search for targets, what features of dwellings signal vulnerability, how opportunistic knowledge can trigger an offense, and what strategies exist for fencing stolen goods. It's likely that their findings about the technology and incentives that affect St. Louis burglars apply generally to residential burglars in other cities.

Perrone (2009) describes the generalizability of her field research in terms of *transferability*—whether she might obtain similar findings if she had studied different dance clubs in different settings. She conducted 45 field observations in New York City, Miami, and beach resort towns in New York and New Jersey. She argues that observing similar behavior in different settings enhanced the transferability of her research.

In reviewing reports of field research projects, it's important to determine where and to what extent the researcher is generalizing beyond her or his specific observations to other settings. Such generalizations may be in order, but it is necessary to judge that. Nothing in this research method guarantees it.

As we've seen, field research is a potentially powerful tool for criminal justice research, one that provides a useful balance to surveys.

## SUMMARY

- Field research is a data collection method that involves the direct observation of phenomena in their natural settings.

- Field research in criminal justice may produce either qualitative or quantitative data. Grounded theory is typically built from qualitative field observations. Observations that can be quantified may produce measures for hypothesis testing.

- Field observation is usually the preferred data collection method for obtaining information about physical or social settings, behavior, and events.

- Qualitative field research is the preferred method for studying many types of active offenders, especially those with no recorded arrests or convictions for particular crimes.

- Observations made through field research can often be integrated with data collected from other sources. In this way, field observations can help researchers interpret other data.

- Field researchers may or may not identify themselves as researchers to the people they are observing. Being identified as a researcher may have some effect on what is observed.

- Asking questions through qualitative interviewing is often integrated with field observation.

- Preparing for the field involves negotiating or arranging access to subjects. Specific strategies depend on whether formal organizations, subcultures, or something in between are being studied.

- Controlled probability sampling techniques are not usually possible in field research.

- Snowball sampling is a method for acquiring an ever-increasing number of sample observations. One participant is asked to recommend others for interviewing, and each of these other participants is asked for more recommendations.

- If field observations will be made on a phenomenon that occurs with some degree of regularity, purposive sampling techniques can be used to select cases for observation.

- Alternatives for recording field observations range from video, audio, and other equipment to unstructured field notes. In between are observations recorded on structured forms, such as environmental surveys.

- Field notes should be planned in advance to the greatest extent possible. However, note taking should be flexible enough to make records of unexpected observations.

- Compared with surveys, qualitative field research is stronger on validity but weaker on reliability. Field research results can have general applicability beyond the specific settings observed. However, findings cannot be formally generalized to the same extent as findings based on rigorous sampling and standardized questionnaires.

## KEY TERMS

environmental surveys, p. 204
ethnography, p. 191
grounded theory, p. 188

qualitative interview, p. 193
reactivity, p. 192
safety audit, p. 206

snowball sampling, p. 198

## REVIEW QUESTIONS AND EXERCISES

1. Think of some group or activity you participate in or are familiar with. In two or three paragraphs, describe how an outsider might effectively go about studying that group or activity. What should he or she read, what contacts should be made, and so on?

2. Review the box titled "Conducting a Safety Audit" by Gisela Bichler-Robertson on page 207.

Try conducting a safety audit on your campus or in an area near your campus.

3. Many police departments encourage citizen ride-alongs as a component of community policing. If this is the case for a police or sheriff's department near you, take advantage of this excellent opportunity to test your observation and unstructured interviewing skills.

## ADDITIONAL READINGS

Bureau of Justice Assistance, *A Police Guide to Surveying Citizens and Their Environment* (Washington, DC: U.S. Department of Justice, Office of Justice Programs, Bureau of Justice Assistance, 1993). Intended for use in community policing initiatives, this publication is a useful source of ideas about conducting structured observations. Appendixes include detailed examples of environmental surveys. You can also download this publication in text form (no drawings) from the web (www.ncjrs.gov/pdffiles/polc .pdf).

Felson, Marcus, *Crime and Everyday Life*, 3rd ed. (Thousand Oaks, CA: Sage, 2002). We mentioned this book in Chapter 2 as an example of criminal justice theory. Many of Felson's explanations of how everyday life is linked to crime describe physical features of cities and other land use patterns. This entertaining book suggests many opportunities for conducting field research.

Miller, Joel, *Profiling Populations Available for Stops and Searches*. Police Research Series, paper 131 (London: Home Office Policing and Reducing Crime Unit, 2000). Race-biased policing has been a concern in England for many years. This report presents a thorough description of observation to produce baseline measures of populations eligible to be stopped by police. Similar efforts have been under way in many U.S. states and cities. (http://webarchive.nationalarchives.gov.uk/20110218135832/rds.homeoffice.gov.uk/rds/prgpdfs/prs131 .pdf).

Patton, Michael Quinn, *Qualitative Research and Evaluation Methods*, 3rd ed. (Thousand Oaks, CA: Sage, 2002). We mentioned this book in Chapter 7 as a good source of guidance on questionnaire construction. Patton also offers in-depth information on observation techniques, along with tips on conducting unstructured and semistructured field interviews. In addition, Patton describes a variety of purposive sampling techniques for qualitative interviewing and field research.

Smith, Steven K., and Carolyn C. DeFrances, *Assessing Measurement Techniques for Identifying Race, Ethnicity, and Gender: Observation-Based Data Collection in Airports and at Immigration Checkpoints* (Washington, DC: Bureau of Justice Statistics, 2003). Racial profiling and the September 11, 2001, attacks on New York and Washington prompted researchers and public officials to consider observational studies of drivers and others. This report by the Bureau of Justice Statistics describes experiments to test observation methods.

# CHAPTER 9

# Agency Records, Content Analysis, and Secondary Data

*We will examine three sources of existing data: agency records, content analysis, and data collected by other researchers. Data from these sources have many applications in criminal justice research.*

## INTRODUCTION

*Agency records, secondary data, and content analysis do not require direct interaction with research subjects.*

Except for the complete observer role in field research, the modes of observation discussed so far require the researcher to intrude to some degree into whatever he or she is studying. This is most obvious with survey research. Even the field researcher, as we've seen, can change things in the process of studying them.

Other ways of collecting data do not involve intrusion by observers. In this chapter, we'll consider three different approaches to using information that has been collected by others, often as a routine practice.

First, a great deal of criminal justice research uses data collected by state and local agencies such as police, criminal courts, probation offices, juvenile authorities, and corrections departments. Government agencies gather a vast amount of crime and criminal justice data, probably rivaled only by efforts to produce economic and public health indicators. We refer to such information as "data from agency records." In this chapter, we will describe different types of such data that are available for criminal justice research, together with the promise and potential pitfalls of using information from agency records.

Second, in content analysis, researchers examine a class of social artifacts—written documents or other types of messages. Suppose you want to contrast the importance of criminal justice policy and health care policy for Americans in 2001 and 2011. One option is to examine public-opinion polls from these years. Another method is to analyze articles from newspapers published in each year. The latter is an example of content analysis: the analysis of communications.

Finally, information collected by others is frequently used in criminal justice research, which in this case involves **secondary analysis** of existing data. Investigators who conduct research funded by federal agencies such as the National Institute of Justice are usually obliged to release their data

for public use. Thus, if you were interested in developing sentence reform proposals for your state, you might analyze data collected by Nancy Merritt, Terry Fain, and Susan Turner in the study of Oregon's efforts to increase sentence length for certain types of offenders (Merritt, Fain, and Turner 2006).

Keep in mind that most data we might obtain from agency records or research projects conducted by others are secondary data. Someone else gathered the original data, usually for purposes that differ from ours.

## TOPICS APPROPRIATE FOR AGENCY RECORDS AND CONTENT ANALYSIS

*Agency records support a wide variety of research applications.*

Data from agency records or archives may have originally been gathered in any number of ways, from sample surveys to direct observation. Because of this, such data may, in principle, be appropriate for just about any criminal justice research topic.

Published statistics and agency records are most commonly used in descriptive or exploratory studies. This is consistent with the fact that many of the criminal justice data published by government agencies are intended to describe something. For instance, the Bureau of Justice Statistics (BJS) publishes annual figures on prison populations. If we are interested in describing differences in prison populations between states or changes in prison populations from 1990 through 2010, a good place to begin is with the annual data published by BJS. Or, if we wish to learn more about cases of identity theft, we could consult the annual *Consumer Network Data Book,* which summarizes known cases of identity theft and related frauds (Federal Trade Commission 2010). Similarly, published figures on crimes reported to police, criminal victimization, felony court caseloads, drug use by high school seniors, and a host of other measures are available over time—for 25 years or longer in many cases.

Agency records may also be used in explanatory studies. Nancy Sinauer and colleagues (1999) examined medical examiner records for more than 1,000 female homicide victims in North Carolina to understand the relationship between female homicide and residence in urban versus rural counties. They found that counties on the outskirts of cities had higher female homicide rates than either urban or rural counties.

Agency records are frequently used in applied studies as well. Evaluations of new policies that seek to reduce recidivism might draw on arrest or conviction data for measures of recidivism. For example, a study of drug courts as an alternative way to process defendants with substance abuse problems traced arrest records for experimental and control subjects (Gottfredson et al. 2006). In another study, researchers used data from public sex offender registries in New York to examine the impact of laws restricting where sex offenders could live (Berenson and Appelbaum 2010). Sometimes, records obtained from private firms can be used in applied studies; Gisela Bichler and Ronald Clarke (1996) examined records of international telephone calls in their evaluation of efforts to reduce telephone fraud in New York City.

In a different type of applied study, James Austin and associates (2007) combined data on prison releases and capacities, reincarcerations, and general-population forecasts to develop a mathematical model that predicts future prison populations. This is an example of forecasting, in which past relationships among arrest rates and prison sentences for different age groups are compared with estimates of future population by age group. Assuming that past associations between age, arrest, and prison sentence will remain constant in future years, demographic models of future population can be used to predict future admissions to prison.

Topics appropriate to research using content analysis center on the important links between communication, perceptions of crime problems, individual behavior, and criminal justice policy. The prevalence of violence on fictional television dramas has long been a concern of researchers and public officials (Anderson and Bushman 2002). Niyazi Ekici (2008) used content analysis to learn about how terrorists were recruited in Turkey. Mass media also play an important role in affecting

policy action by public officials. Many studies have examined the influence of media in setting the agenda for criminal justice policy (see, for example, Chermak and Weiss 1997).

Research data collected by other investigators, through surveys or field observation, may be used for a broad variety of later studies. National Crime Victimization Survey (NCVS) data have been used by a large number of researchers in countless descriptive and explanatory studies since the 1970s. In a notably ambitious use of secondary data, Robert Sampson and John Laub (1993) recovered life history data on 500 delinquents and 500 nondelinquents originally collected by Sheldon and Eleanor Glueck in the 1940s. Taking advantage of theoretical and empirical advances in criminological research over the ensuing 40 years, Sampson and Laub produced a major contribution to knowledge of criminal career development in childhood.

Existing data may also be considered as a supplemental source of data. For example, a researcher planning to survey correctional facility administrators about their views on the need for drug treatment programs will do well to examine existing data on the number of drug users sentenced to prison terms. Or, if we are evaluating an experimental morale-building program in a probation services department, statistics on absenteeism will be useful in connection with the data our own research will generate.

This is not to say that agency records and secondary data can always provide answers to research questions. If this were true, much of this book would be unnecessary. The key to distinguishing appropriate and inappropriate uses of agency records, content analysis, and secondary data is understanding how these written records are produced. We cannot emphasize this point too strongly. Much of this chapter will underscore the importance of learning where data come from and how they are gathered.

## TYPES OF AGENCY RECORDS

*Researchers use a variety of published statistics and nonpublic agency records.*

Information collected by or for public agencies usually falls into one of three general categories: (1) published statistics, (2) nonpublic agency records routinely collected for internal use, and (3) new data collected by agency staff for specific research purposes. Each category varies in the extent to which data are readily available to the researcher and in the researcher's degree of control over the data collection process.

## Published Statistics

Most government organizations routinely collect and publish compilations of data, which we refer to collectively as **published statistics**. Examples are the Census Bureau, the FBI, the Administrative Office of U.S. Courts, the Federal Bureau of Prisons, and the BJS. Two of these organizations merit special mention. First, the Census Bureau conducts enumerations and sample surveys for several other federal organizations. Notable examples are the NCVS, Census of Children in Custody, Survey of Inmates in Local Jails, Correctional Populations in the United States, and Survey of Justice Expenditure and Employment.

Second, the BJS compiles data from several sources and publishes annual and special reports on most data series. For example, *Criminal Victimization in the United States* reports summary data from the NCVS each year. Table 9.1 presents a sample breakdown of victimization rates by race and home ownership from the report for 2004. The BJS also issues reports on people under correctional supervision. These are based on sample surveys and enumerations of jail, prison, and juvenile facility populations. Sample tabulations of females serving sentences in state and federal prison in 2004 are shown in Table 9.2. And the series *Federal Criminal Case Processing* reports detailed data on federal court activity.

The most comprehensive BJS publication on criminal justice data is the annual *Sourcebook of Criminal Justice Statistics*. Since 1972, this report has summarized hundreds of criminal justice data series, ranging from public perceptions about crime to characteristics of criminal justice agencies, to tables on how states execute capital offenders. Data from private sources such as the Gallup Poll are included with statistics collected by government agencies. Each year's *Sourcebook* concludes with notes on data sources, appendixes summarizing data collection procedures for major series, and addresses of organizations that either collect or archive original data.

Compilations of published data on crime and criminal justice are readily available from many sources. For example, the *Sourcebook* is available on the web (www.albany.edu/sourcebook). The companion website to this book presents a more comprehensive list, together with some guidelines on how to get more information from the BJS and other major sources. At this point, however, we

**TABLE 9.1** Victimization Rates by Type of Crime, Form of Tenure, and Race of Head of Household, 2004 (rates per 1,000 households)

| | Household Crimes | | | |
| --- | --- | --- | --- | --- |
| | **Burglary** | **Motor Vehicle Theft** | **Theft** | **Total Number of Households** |
| Race of Head of Household | | | | |
| White | 27.6 | 7.6 | 121.6 | 95,605,550 |
| Black | 44.3 | 15.6 | 130.6 | 13,376,960 |
| Home Ownership | | | | |
| Owned | 24.9 | 7.1 | 110.8 | 79,511,410 |
| Rented | 39.9 | 12.5 | 148.9 | 36,264,170 |

*Source:* Adapted from Bureau of Justice Statistics (2006: Tables 16 and 56).

**T A B L E 9.2**   Female Prisoners under Jurisdiction of State and Federal Correctional Authorities

|  | Total 2004 | Percent Change 2003–2004 |
|---|---|---|
| Northeast | 8,910 | –2.2 |
| Connecticut | 1,488 | –3.9 |
| Maine | 125 | 0.8 |
| Massachusetts | 741 | 4.7 |
| New Hampshire | 119 | 1.7 |
| New Jersey | 1,470 | –3.1 |
| New York | 2,789 | –4.3 |
| Pennsylvania | 1,827 | 0.2 |
| Rhode Island | 208 | –6.3 |
| Vermont | 143 | 5.9 |
| Midwest | 16,545 | 5.5 |
| South | 44,666 | 3.7 |
| West | 22,563 | 5.1 |

*Source:* Adapted from Harrison and Beck (2005: Table 5).

want to suggest some possible uses, and limits, of what Herbert Jacob (1984, 9) refers to as being "like the apple in the Garden of Eden: tempting but full of danger . . . [for] the unwary researcher."

Referring to Tables 9.1 and 9.2, you may recognize that published data from series such as the NCVS or *Correctional Populations in the United States* are summary data, as discussed in Chapter 4. This means that data are presented in highly aggregated form and cannot be used to analyze the individuals from or about whom information was originally collected. For example, Table 9.2 shows that in 2004 a total of 2,789 women were serving sentences of one year or more in state and federal correctional institutions in New York. By comparing that figure with figures from other states, we can make some descriptive statements about prison populations in different states. We can also consult earlier editions of *Correctional Populations* to examine trends in prison populations over time or to compare rates of growth from state to state.

Summary data cannot, however, be used to reveal anything about individual correctional facilities, let alone facility inmates. Individual-level data about inmates and institutions are available from the Census Bureau in electronic form, but published tabulations present only summaries.

This is not to say that published data are useless to criminal justice researchers. Highly aggregated summary data from published statistical series are frequently used in descriptive, explanatory, and applied studies. For example, Eric Baumer and colleagues (Baumer et al. 1998) examined Uniform Crime Report (UCR), Drug Abuse Warning Network (DAWN), and Drug Use Forecasting (DUF) data for 142 U.S. cities from 1984 to 1992. Interested in the relationship between crack cocaine use and robbery, burglary, and homicide rates, the researchers found that high levels of crack cocaine use in the population were found in cities that also had high rates of robbery. In contrast, burglary rates were lower in cities with high levels of crack cocaine use.

Ted Robert Gurr used published statistics on violent crime dating back to 13th-century England to examine how social and political events affected patterns of homicide through 1984. A long-term decline in homicide rates has been punctuated by spikes during periods of social dislocation, when

> significant segments of a population have been separated from the regulating institutions that instill and reinforce the basic Western injunctions against interpersonal violence. They may be migrants, demobilized veterans, a growing population of resentful young people for whom there is no social or economic niche, or badly educated young black men trapped in the decaying ghettos of an affluent society. (1989, 48–49)

Published data can therefore address questions about highly aggregated patterns or trends—drug use and crime, the covariation in two estimates of crime, or epochal change in fatal violence. Published data also have the distinct advantage of being readily available; a web search or a trip to the library can quickly place several data series at your disposal. You can obtain copies of most publications by the BJS and other Justice Department offices on the Internet; most documents published since about

1994 are available electronically. Many formerly printed data reports are now available only in electronic format.

Electronic formats have many advantages. Data fields may be read directly into statistical or graphics computer programs for analysis. Many basic crime data can be downloaded from the BJS website in spreadsheet formats or read directly into presentation software. More importantly, complete data series are available in electronic formats. Although printed reports of the NCVS limit you to summary tabulations such as those in Table 9.1, electronic and optical media include the original survey data from 60,000 or more respondents.

Of course, before using either original data or tabulations from published sources, researchers must consider the issues of validity and reliability and the more general question of how well these data meet specific research purposes. It would make little sense to use only FBI data on homicides in a descriptive study of domestic violence because murder records measure only incidents of fatal violence. Or data from an annual prison census would not be appropriate for research on changes in sentences to community corrections programs.

## Nonpublic Agency Records

Despite the large volume of published statistics in criminal justice, those data represent only the tip of the proverbial iceberg. The FBI publishes the summary UCR, but each of the nation's several thousand law enforcement agencies produces an incredible volume of data not routinely released for public distribution. The BJS series *Correctional Populations in the United States* presents statistics on prison inmates collected from annual surveys of correctional facilities, but any given facility also maintains detailed case files on individual inmates. *Court Caseload Statistics*, published by the National Center for State Courts, contains summary data on cases filed and disposed in state courts, but any courthouse in any large city houses files on thousands of individual defendants.

Although we have labeled this data source "nonpublic agency records," criminal justice organizations quite often make such data available to criminal justice researchers. But obtaining agency records is not as simple as scrolling through a list of publications on the BJS website, or clicking a download button to get data from the Census Bureau. Obtaining access to nonpublic records involves many of the same steps we outlined in Chapter 8 for gaining entry for field research.

At the outset, we want to emphasize that the potential promise of agency records is not without cost. Jacob's caution about the hidden perils to unwary researchers who uncritically accept published data applies to nonpublic agency records as well. On the one hand, we could devote an entire book to describing the potential applications of agency records in criminal justice research, together with advice on how to use and interpret such data. On the other hand, we can summarize that unwritten book with one piece of advice: understand how agency records are produced. Restated slightly, researchers can find the road to happiness in using agency records by following the paper trail.

By way of illustrating this humble maxim, we present two types of examples. First, we describe a study in which nonpublic agency records were used to reveal important findings about the etiology of crime. Second, we briefly review two studies in which the authors recognized validity and reliability problems but still were able to draw conclusions about the behavior of criminal justice organizations. At the end of this section, we summarize the promise of agency records for research and note cautions that must be exercised if such records are to be used effectively.

**Child Abuse, Delinquency, and Adult Arrests**   In earlier chapters, we described Cathy Spatz Widom's research on child abuse as an example of a quasi-experimental design. For present purposes, her research illustrates the use of several different types of agency records.

Widom (1989) identified cases of child abuse and neglect by consulting records from juvenile and adult criminal courts in a large midwestern city. Unlike adult courts, juvenile court proceedings are not open to the public, and juvenile records may not be released. However, after obtaining institutional review board approval, Widom was granted access to these files for research purposes by court authorities. From juvenile court records, she selected 774 cases of neglect, physical abuse, or sexual abuse. Cases of extreme abuse were processed in adult criminal court, where charges were filed against the offender. Criminal court records yielded an additional 134 cases.

As described in Chapter 5, Widom constructed a comparison group of nonabused children through individual matching. Comparison subjects were found from two different sources of agency records. First, abused children who were age 6 to 11 at the time of the abuse were matched to comparison subjects by consulting public school records. An abused child was matched with a comparison child of the same sex, race, and age (within six months) who attended the same school. Second, children who were younger than 6 years old at the time of abuse were matched on similar criteria by consulting birth records and selecting a comparison subject born in the same hospital.

These two types of public records and matching criteria—attending the same public school and being born in the same hospital—were used in an attempt to control for socioeconomic status. Although such criteria may be viewed with skepticism today, Widom (1989, 360), points out that during this time period (1967 to 1971) school busing was not used in the area where her study was conducted, and "elementary schools represented very homogeneous neighborhoods." Similarly, in the late 1960s, hospitals tended to serve local communities, unlike contemporary medical-industrial complexes that advertise their services far and wide. Widom assumed that children born in the same hospital were more likely to be from similar socioeconomic backgrounds than children born in different hospitals.

Though far from perfect, school and birth records enabled Widom to construct approximate matches on socioeconomic status, which illustrates our earlier advice to be creative while being careful.

Widom's research purpose was explanatory—to examine the link between early child abuse and later delinquency or adult criminal behavior. These two dependent variables were measured by consulting additional agency records for information on arrests of abused subjects and comparison subjects

for the years 1971 through 1986. Juvenile court files yielded information on delinquency. Adult arrests were measured from criminal history files maintained by local, state, and national law enforcement agencies. In an effort to locate as many subjects as possible, Widom searched state Department of Motor Vehicles files for current addresses and Social Security numbers. Finally, "marriage license bureau records were searched to find married names for the females" (Widom 1989, 371).

Findings revealed modest but statistically significant differences between abused and comparison subjects. As a group, abused subjects were more likely to have records of delinquency or adult arrests (Maxfield and Widom 1996). However, Widom (1992) also found differences in these dependent variables by race and gender.

Now let's consider two potential validity and reliability issues that might be raised by Widom's use of nonpublic agency records. First, data from juvenile and adult criminal courts reveal only cases of abuse that come to the attention of public officials. Unreported and unsubstantiated cases of abuse or neglect are excluded, and this raises a question about the validity of Widom's measure of the independent variable. Second, dependent variable measures are similarly flawed because juvenile and adult arrests do not reflect all delinquent or criminal behavior.

Recognizing these problems, Widom is careful to point out that her measure of abuse probably reflects only the most severe cases, those that were brought to the attention of public officials. She also notes that cases in her study were processed before officials and the general public had become more aware of the problem of child abuse. Widom understood the limits of official records and qualified her conclusions accordingly: "These findings, then, are not generalizable to unreported cases of abuse or neglect. Ours are also the cases in which agencies have intervened, and in which there is little doubt of abuse or neglect. Thus, these findings are confounded with the processing factor" (1989, 365–366).

**Agency Records as Measures of Decision Making**  Research by Richard McCleary and associates (McCleary, Nienstedt, and Erven 1982) illustrates why it's essential to learn about agency record-keeping practices when using official data. McCleary and associates discovered that an apparent reduction in burglary rates was, in fact, due to changes in record-keeping practices. When a police department assigned officers from a special unit to investigate burglaries, it was learned that earlier investigative procedures sometimes resulted in double counts of a single incident; the special unit also reduced misclassification of larcenies as burglaries.

McCleary and colleagues became suspicious of police records when they detected an immediate decline in burglary rates following the introduction of the special unit, a pattern that was not reasonable given the technology of burglary. Following the paper trail, they were able to discover how changes in procedures affected these measures. In the same article, they describe additional examples—how replacement of a police chief and changes in patrol dispatch procedures produced apparent increases in crime and calls for service. However, after carefully investigating how these records were produced, they were able to link changes in the indicators to changes in agency behavior rather than changes in the frequency of crime.

In a similar type of study, Hugh Whitt (2006) examined mortality data for New York City over 16 years. While deaths by homicide and accidents varied little from year to year between 1976 and 1992, the number of suicides dropped dramatically from 1984 through 1988, then rose sharply in 1989 to match the numbers in earlier years. Reasoning that such sharp changes in a short period are unlikely to reflect natural variation in suicide, Whitt traced the deviation to a series of personnel and policy changes in the city medical examiner's office. So the sharp, short-term variation was due to changes in how deaths were recorded, not changes in the manner of death.

## New Data Collected by Agency Staff

Thus far we have concentrated on the research uses of information routinely collected by or for public agencies. Such data are readily available, but researchers have little control over the actual data collection process. Furthermore, agency procedures and definitions may not correspond with the needs of researchers.

It is sometimes possible to use a hybrid source of data in which criminal justice agency staff collect information for specific research purposes. We refer to this as a "hybrid" source because it combines the collection of new data—through observation or interviews—with day-to-day criminal justice agency activities. Virtually all criminal justice organizations routinely document their actions, from investigating crime reports to housing convicted felons. By slightly modifying forms normally used for recording information, researchers may be able to have agency staff collect original data for them.

For example, in their study of traffic enforcement in Pennsylvania, Robin Shepard Engel and associates (Engel et al. 2005) worked with troopers from the state police to develop special forms to collect data on traffic stops. The research team first worked with agency command staff to gain approval. They then included line officers and union representatives in a collaborative effort to design new data collection forms and procedures. One of the chief concerns was whether individual troopers would be identified on the stop records. All confidentiality procedures were approved by troopers—the people who prepared the traffic stop records. Researchers believed this was an important component of their efforts to enhance the accuracy of the data they collected.

Incorporating new data collection procedures into agency routine has two major advantages. First, and most obvious, having agency staff collect data for us is much less costly than fielding a team of research assistants. It is difficult to imagine how original data on all traffic stops made by Pennsylvania State Police could be collected in any other way.

Second, we have more control over the measurement process than we would by relying on agency definitions. Instead of adapting existing measures on traffic stops, Engel and associates were able to tailor data collection to meet their specific research needs.

The box by Marie Mele, titled "Improving Police Records of Domestic Violence," gives another example of this approach to gathering new data from agency records. You should recognize the importance of collaboration in this example. Less obvious, but equally important, is a lesson we will return to later in this chapter: agency records are not usually intended for research purposes and, as a consequence, are not always well suited to researchers' needs. Sometimes, as was the case for Marie Mele, some subtle tweaking can transform unusable mounds of paper files into computer-based record systems. In any event, researchers are well advised to be careful, not to assume that existing data will meet their needs, but to also be creative in seeking ways to improve the quality of agency data.

 **IMPROVING POLICE RECORDS OF DOMESTIC VIOLENCE**

### Marie Mele

An interest in domestic violence led me to learn more about repeat victimization. Research conducted in England has indicated that repeated domestic violence involving the same victim and offender is quite common (Hanmer, Griffiths, and Jerwood 1999; Farrell et al. 2000). For example, combining data from four British Crime Surveys, Pease (1998, 3) reports that about 1 percent of respondents had four or more personal victimizations and that these victims accounted for 59 percent of all personal victimization incidents disclosed to BCS interviewers. Other studies in England have shown that many other types of offenses are disproportionately concentrated among small groups of victims. Identifying repeat victims and directing prevention and enforcement resources to them has the potential to produce a large decrease in crime rates.

My interest centered on determining the distributions of incidents, victims, and offenders in cases of domestic violence reported to police in a large city in the northeastern United States. Partly this was exploratory research, but I also wished to make policy recommendations to reduce repeat victimization. Working with Michael Maxfield, my initial inquiries found that, although data on assaults and other offenses were available in paper files, it was not possible to efficiently count the number of repeat incidents for victims and offenders. However, seeing the potential value of gathering more systematic information on repeat offenders and victims, senior department staff collaborated with Maxfield and me to produce a database that reorganized existing data on domestic violence incidents. A pilot data system was developed in November 2001. Plans called for the database to be maintained by the department's domestic violence and sexual assault unit (DVSAU); staff would begin entering new incidents in January 2002. In the meantime, I proposed to test the database and its entry procedures by personally entering incidents from August through December 2001. After ironing out a few kinks, the final system was established, and I continued entering new incident reports for a period of time.

This is an admittedly brief description of a process that unfolded over several months. The process began as an attempt to obtain what we thought were existing data. Finding that suitable data were not available, Maxfield had sufficient access to the department to begin discussions of how to supplement existing record-keeping practices to tabulate repeat victimization. Many public agencies will accommodate researchers if such accommodation does not unduly burden the agency. Collecting new data for researchers does qualify as unduly burdensome for most public organizations. The key here was collaboration in a way that helped both the researchers and the host organization.

It's obvious that my research benefited from having the department design and ultimately assume responsibility for tabulating repeat victimization. The department benefited in three ways. First, DVSAU staff recognized how a data file that identified repeat offenders and victims could produce information that would aid their investigations of incidents. I emphasize offenders here because, all other things being equal, police are more interested in offenders than they are in victims. So the database was designed to track people (offenders) of special interest to police and people (victims) of special interest to my research. Second, recognizing that setting up a new data system is especially difficult in a tradition-bound organization, I was able to ease the transition somewhat by initially entering data myself. One intentional by-product of this was to establish quality-control procedures during a shakedown period. As a criminal justice researcher, I knew that the reliability of data-gathering procedures was important and I was able to establish reliable data-entry routines for the department.

The DVSAU staff benefited in yet another way that was probably most important of all. This department had incorporated its version of Compstat for about three years. Two important components of Compstat are timely data and accountability. Each week, the DVSAU commander was required to present a summary of the unit's activity and was held accountable for the performance of unit staff. Before the database was developed, the DVSAU commander spent several hours compiling data to prepare for each week's Compstat meeting. After the database was operational, preparation time was reduced to minutes. In addition, the DVSAU commander was able to introduce new performance measures—repeat offenders and victims—that came to be valued by the department's chief.

This approach to data collection has many potential applications. Probation officers or other court staff in many jurisdictions complete some type of presentence investigation on convicted offenders. A researcher might be able to supplement standard interview forms with additional items appropriate for some specific research interest.

At the same time, having agencies collect original research data has some disadvantages. An obvious one is the need to obtain the cooperation of organizations and staff. The difficulty of this varies in direct proportion to the intrusiveness of data collection. Cooperation is less likely if some major additional effort is required of agency personnel or if data collection activities disrupt routine operations. The potential benefit to participating agencies is a related point. If a research project or an experimental program is likely to economize agency operations or improve staff performance, as was the case for Marie Mele's research, it will be easier to enlist their assistance.

Researchers have less control over the data collection process when they rely on agency staff. Staff in criminal justice agencies have competing demands on their time and naturally place a lower priority on data collection than on their primary duties. If you were a probation officer serving a heavy caseload and were asked to complete detailed 6- and 12-month reports on services provided to individual clients, would you devote more attention to keeping up with your clients or filling out data collection forms?

## RELIABILITY AND VALIDITY

*Understanding the details of how agency records are produced is the best guard against reliability and validity problems.*

The key to evaluating the reliability and validity of agency records, as well as the general suitability of those data for a research project, is to understand as completely as possible how the data were originally collected. Doing so can help researchers identify potential new uses of data and be better able to detect potential reliability or validity problems in agency records.

Any researcher who considers using agency records will benefit from a careful reading of Herbert Jacob's invaluable little guide *Using Published Data: Errors and Remedies* (1984). In addition to warning readers about general problems with reliability and validity, such as those we discussed in Chapter 4, Jacob cautions users of these data to be aware of other potential errors that can be revealed by scrutinizing source notes. Clerical errors, for example, are unavoidable in such large-scale reporting systems as the UCR. These errors may be detected and reported in correction notices appended to later reports.

Users of data series collected over time must be especially attentive to changes in data collection procedures or changes in the operational definitions of key indicators. As you might expect, such changes are more likely to occur in data series that extend over several years. David Cantor and James Lynch (2005) describe how changes in the NCVS, especially the redesign elements introduced in 1992, should be kept in mind for any long-term analysis of NCVS data. In earlier chapters, we described the NCVS redesign that was completed in 1994. If we plan to conduct research on victimization over time, we will have to consider how changes in sample size and design, increased use of telephone interviews, and questionnaire revisions might affect our findings.

Longitudinal researchers must therefore diligently search for modifications of procedures or definitions over time to avoid attributing some substantive meaning to a change in a particular measure. Furthermore, as the time interval under investigation increases, so does the potential for change in measurement. Ted Robert Gurr (1989, 24) cites a good example:

> In the first two decades of the 20th century many American police forces treated the fatalities of the auto age as homicides. The sharp increase in "homicide" rates that followed has led to some dubious conclusions. Careful study of the sources and their historical and institutional context is necessary to identify and screen out the potentially misleading effects of these factors on long-term trends.

The central point is that researchers who analyze criminal justice data produced by different cities or states or other jurisdictions must be alert to variations in the definitions and measurement of key variables. Even when definitions and measurement seem straightforward, they may run into problems. For example, Craig Perkins and Darrell Gilliard (1992, 4)—statisticians at the Bureau of Justice Statistics—caution potential users of corrections data:

> Care should be exercised when comparing groups of inmates on sentence length and time served. Differences may be the result of factors not described in the tables, including variations in the criminal histories of each group, variations in the offense composition of each group, and variations among participating jurisdictions in their sentencing and correctional practices.

Fortunately, most published reports on regular data series present basic information on definitions and collection procedures. The BJS website includes copies of questionnaires used in surveys and enumerations. Researchers should, however, view summary descriptions in printed reports as no more than a starting point in their search for information on how data were collected.

## Sources of Reliability and Validity Problems

We conclude this section on agency records by discussing some general characteristics of record keeping by public agencies. Think carefully about each of the features we mention, considering how each might apply to specific types of criminal justice research. It will also be extremely useful for you to think of some examples in addition to those we mention, perhaps discussing them with your instructor or others in your class.

**Social Production of Data**   Virtually all criminal justice record keeping is a social process. By this we mean that indicators of, say, arrests, juvenile probation violations, court convictions, or rule infractions by prison inmates reflect decisions made by criminal justice officials in addition to the actual behavior of juvenile or adult offenders. As Baumer and associates state, "Researchers must realize that performance measures are *composites* of offenders' behavior, organizational capacity to detect behavior, and decisions about how to respond to offenders' misbehavior" (1993, 139; emphasis added). For example, Richard McCleary (1992) describes the social production of data by parole officers. A small number of classic articles have described the **social production of data** in the form of crime records by police (Black 1970; Kitsuse and Cicourel 1963; Seidman and Couzens 1974), showing that police may fail to record minor infractions to avoid paperwork or, alternatively, may keep careful records of such incidents in an effort to punish troublesome parolees by returning them to prison.

Discretionary actions by criminal justice officials and others affect the production of virtually all agency records. Police neither learn about all crimes nor arrest all offenders who come to their attention. Similarly, prosecutors, probation officers, and corrections staff are selectively attentive to charges filed or to rule violations by probationers and inmates. At a more general level, the degree of attention state legislatures and criminal justice officials devote to various crime problems varies over time. Levels of tolerance of such behaviors as child abuse, drug use, acquaintance rape, and even alcohol consumption have changed over the years.

**Agency Data Are Not Designed for Research**   In many cases, criminal justice officials collect data because the law requires them to do so. More generally, agencies tend to collect data for their own use, not for the use of researchers. Court disposition records are maintained in part because of legal mandates, and such records are designed for the use of judges, prosecutors, and other officials. Record-keeping procedures reflect internal needs and directives from higher authorities. As a consequence, researchers sometimes find it difficult to adapt agency records for a specific research purpose.

For example, Michael Maxfield once wished to trace court dispositions for arrests made by individual police officers in Louisville, Kentucky. "No problem," he was assured by a deputy prosecutor, "we keep all disposition records on the computer." Following this electronic version of a paper trail to the county data-processing facility, Maxfield discovered that only the previous year's cases were maintained on computer tape, the most common bulk storage medium in the 1970s. Such tapes were said to be expensive (about $17), and nobody had authorized the data processing staff to buy new tapes for each year's files. Instead, voluminous computer printouts from the previous year were microfilmed and saved, whereas the "costly" computer tape was erased for the new year. Maxfield abandoned the project after realizing that data collection would involve viewing literally hundreds of thousands of microfilmed case files, instead of running a quick-and-easy computer search.

Keep in mind that research needs may not be congruent with agency record-keeping practices. Courts or police departments commonly use idiosyncratic definitions or methods of classifying information that make such records difficult to use. Also recognize that conceptual and operational definitions of key concepts, however thoughtful and precise, will seldom be identical to actual measures maintained by criminal justice agencies.

For another example of how definitional differences can be traced to different agency needs, see the box titled "How Many Parole Violators Were There Last Month?"

**Tracking People, Not Patterns**  At the operational level, officials in criminal justice organizations are generally more interested in keeping track of individual cases than in examining patterns. Police patrol officers and investigators deal with individual calls for service, arrests, or case files. Prosecutors and judges are most attentive to court dockets and the clearing of individual cases, and corrections officials maintain records on individual inmates. Although each organization produces summary reports on weekly, monthly, or annual activity, officials tend to be much more interested in individual cases. Michael Geerken (1994) makes this point clearly in his discussion of problems that researchers are likely to encounter in analyzing police arrest records. Few rap-sheet databases are regularly re-

viewed for accuracy; rather, they simply accumulate arrest records submitted by individual officers. Joel Best (2008) offers additional examples of how small errors in case-by-case record keeping can accumulate to produce compound errors in summary data.

With continued advances in computer and telecommunications technology, more criminal justice agencies are developing the capability to analyze data in addition to tracing individual cases. Crime analysis by police tracks spatial patterns of recent incidents; prosecutors are attentive to their scorecards; state correctional intake facilities consider prison capacity, security classification, and program availability in deciding where to send new admissions.

As problem-oriented and community approaches to policing become more widely adopted, many law enforcement agencies have improved their record-keeping and crime analysis practices. New York City's reduction in reported crime has been attributed to police managers' use of timely, accurate crime data to plan and evaluate specific anticrime tactics (Bratton 1999). This illustrates an important general principle about the accuracy of agency-produced data: when agency managers routinely use data to make decisions, they will be more attentive to data quality. The box describing Marie Mele's research offers another example: when domestic violence detectives realized how a database would help them prepare for weekly command staff meetings, they endorsed the effort to improve their record-keeping procedures.

However, record-keeping systems used in most cities today are still designed more to track individual cases for individual departments than to produce data for management or research purposes. Individual agencies maintain what are sometimes called *silo databases*, a colorful label that refers to stacks of data that are isolated from each other. Similar problems have been linked to the failure of intelligence agencies to share information about suspicious activities leading up to the 9/11 attacks (Farmer 2009; National Commission on Terrorist Attacks upon the United States 2004).

This does not mean that computerized criminal history, court disposition, or prison intake records are

## HOW MANY PAROLE VIOLATORS WERE THERE LAST MONTH?

John J. Poklemba
New York State Division of
Criminal Justice Services

Question: How many parole violators were there last month? Answer: It depends. More accurately, it depends on which agency is asked. Each of the three answers below is right in its own way:

| | |
|---|---|
| New York State Commission of Correction | 611 |
| New York Department of Correctional Services | 670 |
| New York Division of Parole | 356 |

The State Commission of Correction (SCOC) maintains daily aggregate information on the local under-custody population. Data are gathered from local sheriffs, using a set of common definitions. The SCOC defines a parole violator as follows: an alleged parole violator being held as a result of allegedly having violated a condition of parole—for example, a new arrest. This makes sense for local jails; a special category is devoted to counting alleged parole violators with new arrests. However, New York City does not distinguish between parole violators with and without new arrests, so the SCOC figure includes violators from upstate New York only.

The Department of Correctional Services (DOCS) is less interested in why people are in jail; its concern centers on the backlog of inmates whom it will soon need to accommodate. Furthermore, as far as DOCS is concerned, the only true parole violator is a technical parole violator. This makes sense for DOCS, because a parole violator convicted of a new crime will enter DOCS as a new admission, who—from an administrative standpoint—will be treated differently than a parolee returned to prison for a technical violation.

The Division of Parole classifies parole violators into one of four categories: (1) those who have violated a condition of parole, (2) those who have absconded, (3) those who have been arrested for a new crime, and (4) those who have been convicted of a new crime. Once again, this makes sense, because the Division of Parole is responsible for monitoring parolee performance and wishes to distinguish different types of parole violations. The Division also classifies a parole violation as either alleged (yet to be confirmed by a parole board) or actual (the violation has been confirmed and entered into the parolee's file). Further differences in the fluid status of parolees and their violations, together with differences between New York City and other areas, add to the confusion.

Taking the varying perspectives and roles of these three organizations into account, answers to the "how many" question can be made more specific:

*SCOC:* Last month, there were 611 alleged parole violators who were believed to have violated a condition of their parole by being arrested for a new offense and are being held in upstate New York jails.

*DOCS:* Last month, there were 670 actual parole violators who were judged to have violated a condition of their parole and are counted among the backlog of persons ready for admission to state correctional facilities.

*Parole Division:* Last month, 356 parolees from the Division's aggregate population were actually removed from the Division's caseload and were en route to DOCS.

One of the major reasons that agency counts do not match is that agency information systems have been developed to meet internal operational needs. A systemwide perspective is lacking. Questions that depend on data from more than one agency are often impossible to answer with confidence. Recognize also that the availability and quality of state data depend on data from local agencies.

As stated above, the best answer to the question is: it depends.

*Source:* Adapted from Poklemba (1988, 11–13).

---

of little use to researchers. However, researchers must be aware that even state-of-the-art systems may not be readily adaptable for research purposes.

**Error Increases with Volume** The potential for clerical errors increases as the number of clerical entries increases. This seemingly obvious point is nonetheless important to keep in mind when analyzing criminal justice records. Lawrence Sherman and Ellen Cohn (1989, 34) describe the "mirror effect" of duplicate calls-for-service (CFS) records. Handling a large volume of CFS, phone operators in Minneapolis, or any large city for that matter, are not always able to distinguish duplicate reports of the same incident. An updated report about a CFS may be treated as a new incident. In either case, duplicate data result.

The relationship between the volume of data entry and the potential for error can be especially troublesome for studies of relatively rare crimes or incidents. Although murder is rare compared with other crimes, information about individual homicides might be keyed into a computer by the same clerk who inputs data on parking violations. If a murder record is just one case among hundreds of parking tickets and petty thefts awaiting a clerk, there is no guarantee that the rare event will be treated any differently than the everyday ones.

While preparing a briefing for an Indianapolis commission on violence, Maxfield discovered that a single incident in which four people had been murdered in a rural area appeared twice in computerized FBI homicide records. This was traced to the fact that officers from two agencies—sheriff's deputies and state police—investigated the crime, and each agency filed a report with the FBI. But the thousands of murders entered into FBI computer files for that year obscured the fact that duplicate records had been keyed in for one multiple murder in a rural area of Indiana.

In concluding our discussion of agency records, we do not mean to leave you with the impression that data produced by and for criminal justice organizations are fatally flawed. Thousands of studies making appropriate use of such data are produced each year. It is, however, essential that researchers understand potential sources of reliability and validity problems, as well as ways they can be overcome. Public agencies do not normally collect information for research purposes. The data they do collect often reflect discretionary decisions by numerous individuals. And, like any large-scale human activity, making observations on large numbers of people and processes inevitably produces some error.

# CONTENT ANALYSIS

*Content analysis involves the systematic study of messages.*

The Office of Community Oriented Policing Services (COPS) was established by the 1994 Crime Bill to promote community policing by providing funds to local law enforcement agencies. In addition to being concerned about the effectiveness of these efforts, COPS staff wanted to know something about the public image of community policing as presented in local newspapers. Stephen Mastrofski and Richard Ritti conducted a content analysis of stories about community policing in newspapers serving 26 cities. The researchers found more than 7,500 stories from 1993 through 1997, with most focusing on a small number of themes: "community, resources, and producing real results for the community. Stories that offer a viewpoint on community policing are nearly always overwhelmingly positive" (1999, 10–11).

This is an example of **content analysis**, the systematic study of messages and the meaning those messages convey. For the COPS office, the study by Mastrofski and Ritti was satisfying—many stories about community policing were published in urban newspapers, and most stories presented positive images.

Content analysis methods may be applied to virtually any form of communication. Among the possible artifacts for study are books, magazines, films, songs, speeches, television programs, letters, laws, and constitutions, as well as any components or collections of these. Content analysis is particularly well suited to answering the classic questions of communications research: who says what, to whom, why, how, and with what effect? As a mode of observation, content analysis requires a considered handling of the *what*, and the analysis of data collected in this mode, as in others, addresses the *why* and *with what effect*.

## Coding in Content Analysis

Content analysis is essentially a coding operation, and of course, coding represents the measurement process in content analysis. Communications—oral, written, or other—are coded or classified according to some conceptual framework. Thus, for example, newspaper editorials might be coded as liberal or conservative. Radio talk shows might be coded as bombastic or not. Novels might be coded as detective fiction or not. Political speeches might be coded as containing unsupported rhetoric about crime or not. Recall that terms such as these are subject to many interpretations, and the researcher must specify definitions clearly.

Coding in content analysis involves the logic of conceptualization and operationalization we considered in Chapter 4. In content analysis, as in other research methods, researchers must refine their conceptual framework and develop specific methods for observing in relation to that framework.

For all research methods, conceptualization and operationalization typically involve the interaction of theoretical concerns and empirical observations. If, for example, you believe some newspaper editorials support liberal crime policies and others support conservative ones, ask yourself why you think so. Read some editorials, asking which ones are liberal and which ones are conservative. Is the political orientation of a particular editorial most clearly indicated by its manifest content or by its overall tone? Is your decision based on the use of certain terms (such as *moral decay* or *need for rehabilitation*) or on the support or opposition given to a particular issue, such as mandatory prison sentences versus treatment programs for drug users?

As in other decisions relating to measurement, the researcher faces a fundamental choice between depth and specificity of understanding. The survey researcher must decide whether specific closed-ended questions or more general open-ended questions will better suit her or his needs. By the same token, the content analyst has a choice between searching for manifest or for latent content. Coding the **manifest content**—the visible, surface content—of a communication more closely approximates the use of closed-ended items in a survey questionnaire. Alternatively, coding the **latent content** of the communication—its underlying meaning—is an option. In the most general sense, manifest and latent content can be distinguished by the degree of interpretation required in measurement.

Throughout the process of conceptualizing manifest- and latent-content coding procedures, remember that the operational definition of any variable is composed of the attributes included in it. Such attributes, moreover, should be mutually exclusive and exhaustive. A newspaper editorial, for example, should not be described as both liberal and conservative, although we should probably allow for some to be middle-of-the-road. It may be sufficient to code TV programs as being violent or not violent, but it is also possible that some programs could be antiviolence.

No coding scheme should be used in content analysis unless it has been carefully pretested. We must decide what manifest or latent contents of communications will be regarded as indicators of the different attributes that make up our research variables, write down these operational definitions, and use them in the actual coding of several units of observation. If we plan to use more than one coder in the final project, each of them should independently code the same set of observations so that we can determine the extent of agreement. In any event, we'll want to take special note of any difficult cases—observations that were not easily classified using the operational definition. Finally, we should review the overall results of the pretest to ensure that they are appropriate to our analytic concerns. If, for example, all of the pretest newspaper editorials have been coded as liberal, we should certainly reconsider our definition of that attribute.

Before beginning to code newspapers, crime dramas on TV, or detective fiction, we need to make plans to assess the reliability of coding. Fortunately, reliability in content analysis can readily be tested, if not guaranteed, in two related ways. First, interrater reliability can be determined by having two different people code the same message and then computing the proportion of items coded the same. If 20 attributes of newspaper stories about crime are being coded and two coders score 18 attributes identically, their reliability is 90 percent.

The second way to assess coding reliability is the test–retest method, in which one person codes the same message twice. Of course, some time should elapse between the two coding operations. Test–retest procedures can be used when only one person is doing the coding; reliability can be computed in the same way as if the interrater method were being used.

## Illustrations of Content Analysis

We now turn to examples of content analysis in action. The first illustration describes content analysis of violence in video games. The second demonstrates how extracting information from police records is a form of content analysis.

**Violence in Video Games**  It seems that whenever some new technology or musical idiom becomes popular, someone becomes interested in linking it to behavior. Examples include television and violence, pornography and sexual assault, and suggestive lyrics in popular music and sexual behavior. It is always difficult to establish causality in such cases, and we will say nothing more about that. But content analysis is the appropriate research tool for classifying content as violent or sexually explicit.

Kimberly Thompson and Kevin Haninger examined the contents of video games rated in categories "E" (suitable for everyone) and "T" (teens, aged 13 and up) by the Entertainment Software Rating Board (ESRC). Their first study (Thompson and Haninger 2001) sampled 55 of more than 600 E-rated games available at the time. An undergraduate college student "with considerable video gaming experience" was assigned to play all games for 90 minutes or until the game reached a natural conclusion. Videotapes of the game-player formed the basis for content analysis. One researcher (also described as being an experienced player) and the game-player reviewed the video, coding several dimensions of what was depicted.

Coders counted the number of violent incidents depicted while the game was being played and also timed the duration of each violent incident. Violence was defined as "acts in which the aggressor causes or attempts to cause physical injury or death to another character." This is an example of latent content. The duration of violent acts was manifest content, though researchers had to distinguish short pauses between violent acts. Additional variables coded included the number of deaths; the presence of drugs, alcohol, or tobacco; profanity and sexual behavior; weapon use; and whether any music was included that itself was rated as explicit. Comparing the duration of violent acts and the number of deaths to how long each game was played yielded two standardized measures: violent minutes as a percentage of all minutes, and number of deaths per minute.

Results showed quite a lot of violence. Action games ranged from 3.3 percent (*Sonic Adventure*) to 91 percent (*Nuclear Strike*) violence as a portion of total time. *Paperboy* depicted no deaths, but *Rat Attack* averaged 8.4 deaths per minute. Games classified as "sports" rarely showed violence.

Later research used similar methods to examine violence in a larger number of games rated as suitable for teens (Haninger and Thompson 2004). These games displayed a wider variety of behaviors in the general domains of violence, obscenity, substance use, and sexual behavior. Again, the authors did not attempt to link such content with behavior. Their content analysis centered on systematically classifying what sorts of things were depicted in video games, thus providing information independent of industry ratings. Of their findings, the authors highlight that ESRC ratings did not mention several examples of violence in almost half of the games reviewed.

**Classifying Gang-Related Homicides**  When is a homicide gang-related? Are there different types of gang-related homicides? These two questions guided research by Rosenfeld and associates (Rosenfeld, Bray, and Egley 1999) to understand how gang membership might facilitate homicide in different ways. To address these questions, the researchers conducted a content analysis of police case files for homicides in St. Louis over a 10-year period.

By now, you should recognize the importance of conceptualization in most criminal justice research. Rosenfeld and associates began by further specifying the ambiguous term *gang-related*. They distinguished *gang-motivated* and *gang-affiliated* homicides. Gang-motivated killings "resulted from gang behavior or relationships, such as an initiation ritual, the 'throwing' of gang signs, or a gang fight" (1999, 500). Gang-affiliated homicides involved a gang member as victim or offender, but with no indication of specific gang activity; a gang member killing a nongang person during a robbery is an example. A third category, nongang youth homicide, included all other murders in which no evidence of gang activity was available and the suspected offender was between ages 10 and 24.

Because St. Louis police did not apply the labels *gang-affiliated* or *gang-motivated*, it was necessary for researchers to code each case into one of the three categories using information from case files.

This was a form of content analysis—systematically classifying the messages contained in homicide case files. Homicide case files are good examples of police records that are not maintained for research purposes. Recognizing this, Rosenfeld and associates coded the files in a two-stage process, building reliability checks into each stage.

First, one person coded each case as either gang-related or not gang-related. This might seem a step backwards, but it focused researchers' measurement on the separate dimensions of homicide that were of interest to them by simplifying the coding process. It was relatively easy to determine whether any evidence of gang activity or membership was present; if not, the case was classified as a nongang youth killing and set aside. Cases that had some evidence of gang involvement were retained for the second coding stage. During this stage, a second researcher randomly selected a 10 percent sample of cases and coded them again, without knowing how the first coder had classified the sampled cases. You will recognize this as an example of interrater reliability.

The second coding stage involved the finer and more difficult classification of cases as either gang-motivated or gang-affiliated. Interrater reliability checks were again conducted, this time on a 25 percent sample of cases. More cases were selected because reliability was lower in this stage—the two coders exhibited less agreement on how to classify gang homicides. Cases in which independent coding produced discrepancies were reviewed and discussed by the two coders until they agreed on how the homicide should be classified.

For another example that combines content analysis and the use of specialized agency records, see the box "Terrorist Recruitment."

## TERRORIST RECRUITMENT

Dr. Niyazi Ekici used agency records and content analysis in his research on recruitment by two terrorist organizations in Turkey (Ekici 2008). A high-ranking officer in the Turkish National Police, Ekici had access to official records during his graduate study at Rutgers University. His interests centered on how terrorist organizations initiated contact with potential members, together with what sorts of factors entered into the selection process.

Several organizations that employ terrorist tactics have been active in Turkey. Ekici selected two groups with very different ideologies, expecting that the groups would seek recruits with different qualities. The Revolutionary People's Liberation Party/Front (DHKP/C) is fueled by a Marxist ideology, while Turkish Hezbollah is a religious extremist group.

Two sources were used to gather data about active terrorists and those who aspired to join the two groups. Data on active terrorists were obtained from police records of 70 individuals in each of the two organizations who had been arrested and convicted of terroristic offenses. The second source was unique—documents written by individuals who sought to join the organizations, something similar to a letter of application. These documents, seized in police raids of terrorist cells over a 10-year period, provided information on an individual's family, political and religious beliefs, and reasons for wishing to join the organization. In earlier chapters we discussed the validity and reliability of self-reports. Ekici writes that these documents are likely to be accurate because

"the terrorist organization will not hesitate to kill members who are found to be lying" (2008, 92).

Ekici used content analysis to systematically extract information from both police records of active terrorists and seized documents of recruits. He then compared a variety of measures for recruits and active members in Turkish Hezbollah and DHKP/C.

Compared to convicted terrorists, candidate terrorists in both organizations were more likely

- to have criminal records;
- to have family members with criminal records;
- to have associated with other terrorist organizations.

Ekici interprets these findings as some measure of selectivity, showing that loyalty and not being known to police are valued by these two terrorist groups and affect the kinds of people who become members.

This is an unusual example of research based on agency records. However, it applies many of the principles of research using agency records and content analysis discussed in this chapter. A police officer as well as a researcher, Dr. Niyazi Ekici used the tools of social science research to systematically analyze documents maintained by the Turkish National Police and to add to knowledge about terrorist recruitment.

## THEORY AND DATA COLLECTION FROM AGENCY RECORDS

Jacqueline Berenson and Paul Appelbaum (2010) frame their study of sex offender residency restrictions on spatially based theories that include the principle of *distance decay*, meaning that offenders tend to commit crime near where they work or live. As the distance from an offender residence increases, the likelihood that the offender will commit a crime decreases. An example is research by George Rengert and associates on distance decay and burglary (Rengert, Piquero, and Jones 1999).

Distance decay underlies laws restricting where sex offenders can live. For example, New York state law prohibits sex offenders from living within 1,000 to 2,000 feet of locations such as parks, schools, playgrounds, and child-care facilities. The assumption is that if sex offenders lived close to such places, children would be at greater risk of victimization.

Distance decay led Berenson and Appelbaum to publicly available data from sex offender registries. State laws in recent years have required that information about where sex offenders live be made available to the public. For example, if you do an Internet search on the phrase "sex offender residence [state]" and input any specific state, with only a few clicks on links that show up you'll be able to do a place-based search for registered sex offenders.

Berenson and Appelbaum compiled a geographically coded data file of registered sex offender home addresses for two counties in New York State. They then obtained publicly available data on the locations of schools, licensed child-care providers, and other facilities that were named in residency restrictions for sex offenders in New York. Computing the distances between where sex offenders lived and sites named in residency restrictions, the researchers found that 89 percent of sex offenders in Erie County and 90 percent in Schenectady County lived within a restricted zone. In other words, for these two counties in New York, only about 10 percent of registered sex offenders were in compliance with residential restrictions.

From these very different examples, we expect that you can think of many additional applications of content analysis in criminal justice research. You might wish to consult Ray Surette's (2006) excellent book *Media, Crime, and Justice: Images, Realities, and Policies* to learn more about the scope of topics for which content analysis can be used. The General Accounting Office (renamed the Government Accountability Office in 2004) has an excellent guide to content analysis generally (1996).

## SECONDARY ANALYSIS

*Data collected by other researchers are often used to address new research questions.*

Our final topic encompasses all sources of criminal justice data we have described in this and preceding chapters: content analysis, agency records, field observation, and surveys. We begin with an example of an unusually ambitious use of secondary data by a prolific criminal justice scholar.

For almost three decades, Wesley Skogan has examined the influence of crime on the lives of urban residents. In most cases, his research has relied on sample surveys to investigate questions about fear of crime (Skogan and Maxfield 1981), community crime prevention (Skogan 1974), and the relationships between urban residents and police (Skogan 1990b), among others. He has long recognized the importance of incivilities—symbols of social disorder—as indicators of neighborhood crime problems and as sources of fear for urban residents.

In 1990, Skogan published a comprehensive study of incivilities, drawing on his own research as well as studies by others (Skogan 1990a). However, instead of conducting new surveys to collect original data, Skogan's findings were based on secondary analysis of 40 surveys conducted in six cities from 1977 through 1983. He aggregated responses from about 13,000 individuals and examined questions about the sources of disorder, its impact, and the scope of action by individuals and police.

Secondary analysis of data collected by other researchers has become an increasingly important tool. Like Skogan, numerous criminal justice researchers have reanalyzed data collected by others. Several factors contribute to this practice, including the high cost of collecting original data through surveys or other means. More important, however, is that data for secondary analysis are readily available. We describe two important sources below.

Suppose you are interested in the relationship between delinquency, drug use, and school performance among adolescents. The National Youth Survey (NYS), which includes responses from 1,725 youths interviewed nine times from 1975 through 2004, might suit your needs nicely. NYS data were originally collected by Delbert Elliott and associates (for example, Elliott, Huizinga, and Ageton 1985). However, like Cesar Rebellon and Karen Van Gundy (2005), who used the NYS to examine links between child maltreatment and delinquency, you may be able to reanalyze the survey data to address your own research questions.

Or perhaps you wish to learn whether there are differences in the sentencing decisions of black and white judges. Cassia Spohn (1990) addressed this question using data originally collected by Milton Heumann and Colin Loftin (1979), who were interested in the effect of a new Michigan law on plea bargaining. Spohn was able to conduct a secondary analysis of the same data to answer a different research question. Let's examine these examples more closely to see how they illustrate the uses and advantages of secondary analysis.

Original NYS data were collected by Elliott and associates (1985, 91) for three related research purposes: (1) to estimate the prevalence and incidence of delinquency and drug use among U.S. adolescents, (2) to assess causal relationships between drug use and delinquency, and (3) to test a comprehensive theory of delinquency. The NYS was designed as a panel survey, in which a nationally representative sample of youths aged 11 to 17 in 1976 was interviewed once each year from 1976 through 1989. As we described in Chapter 3, this is an example of a longitudinal study, and it is especially well suited to disentangling the time ordering of such behaviors as drug use and delinquency.

Rebellon and Van Gundy (2005) were interested in the time order of somewhat different behaviors—physical abuse in childhood and delinquency—that were not directly addressed by the original researchers. A longitudinal design was equally important in this secondary analysis. Given this research interest,

they faced two choices: collect original data by conducting a new panel survey, or reanalyze existing data from a panel survey that included questions on victimization and self-reported delinquency. Because the NYS included questions appropriate for their research purpose, Rebellon and Van Gundy were spared the need and (considerable) expense of conducting a new panel study.

## Sources of Secondary Data

As a college student, you probably would not be able to launch a nine-wave panel study of a national sample of adolescents or even gather records from some 2,600 felony cases in Michigan. You do, however, have access to the same data used in those studies, together with data from thousands of other research projects, through the **Interuniversity Consortium for Political and Social Research (ICPSR)** at the University of Michigan.

Since 1962, the ICPSR has served as a central repository of machine-readable data collected by social science researchers. In the early 1960s, "machine-readable" meant punch cards and paper tape. Current online holdings include data from thousands of studies conducted by researchers all over the world.

Of particular interest to criminal justice researchers is the **National Archive of Criminal Justice Data (NACJD)**, established by the BJS in cooperation with the ICPSR. Here you will find the NYS, Heumann and Loftin's sentencing data, and each of the 40 surveys analyzed by Skogan for the book we mentioned earlier. There's more, including surveys on criminal justice topics by national polling firms, the NCVS from 1972 to the present, periodic censuses of juvenile detention and correctional facilities, a study of thefts from commercial trucks in New York City, and data from the classic study of a Philadelphia birth cohort by Marvin Wolfgang and colleagues (Wolfgang, Figlio, and Sellin 1972). Data from the growing National Incident-Based Reporting System (NIBRS) are now available, with an expanding number of participating agencies dating from 1996. Data from selected studies are even available for online data analysis. The possibilities are almost endless and grow each year as new data are added to the archives.

One of the most useful websites for aggregate secondary data is maintained by the BJS. Summary tabulations for many published data series are presented as graphs or tables. In addition, it's possible to download summary data in spreadsheet format to easily conduct additional analysis, to display graphs in different forms, and even to prepare transparencies for presentations.

Other sites on the Internet offer a virtually unlimited source of secondary data. You can obtain documentation for most data archived by the ICPSR and the NACJD, as well as health statistics, census data, and other sources limited only by your imagination. Find the NACJD website at http://www.icpsr.umich.edu/icpsrweb/NACJD/.

## Advantages and Disadvantages of Secondary Data

The advantages of secondary analysis are obvious and enormous: it is cheaper and faster than collecting original data, and depending on who did the original study, you may benefit from the work of topflight professionals and esteemed academics. Many criminal justice researchers spend their entire careers in secondary data analysis.

Potential disadvantages must be kept in mind, however. The key problem involves the recurrent question of validity. When one researcher collects data for one particular purpose, you have no assurance that those data will be appropriate to your research interests. Typically you'll find that the original researcher collected data that come close to measuring what you are interested in, but you may wish key variables had been operationalized just a little differently. The question, then, is whether secondary data provide valid measures of the variables you want to analyze.

This closely resembles one of the key problems in the use of agency records. Perhaps a particular set of data does not provide a totally satisfactory measure of what interests you, but other sets of data are available. Even if no one set of data provides totally valid measures, you can build up a weight of evidence by analyzing all the possibilities. If each of the imperfect measures points to the same research conclusion, you will have developed considerable support for its accuracy. The use of replication lessens the problem.

In general, secondary data are least useful for evaluation studies. This is because evaluations are designed to answer specific questions about specific programs. It is always possible to reanalyze data from evaluation studies, but secondary data cannot be used to evaluate an entirely different program. Thus, for example, a number of researchers have reexamined data collected for a series of domestic violence experiments conducted by Lawrence Sherman and others in several cities (see Sherman 1992 for a summary). In most cases, these secondary researchers (such as Maxwell, Garner, and Fagan 2001) wished to verify or reassess findings from the original studies. But it is not possible to use those data to answer questions about domestic violence interventions other than arrest or to evaluate arrest policies in new cities where the experiments did not take place.

In this book, the discussion of secondary analysis has a special purpose. As we conclude our examination of modes of observation in criminal justice research, you should have developed a full appreciation for the range of possibilities available in finding the answers to questions about crime and criminal justice policy. No single method of getting information unlocks all puzzles, yet there is no limit to the ways you can find out about things. And, more powerfully, you can zero in on an issue from several independent directions, gaining an even greater mastery of it.

## SUMMARY

- Data and records produced by formal organizations may be the most common source of data in criminal justice research.

- Many public organizations produce statistics and data for the public record, and these data are often useful for criminal justice researchers.

- All organizations keep nonpublic records for internal operational purposes, and these records are valuable sources of data for criminal justice research.

- Public organizations can sometimes be enlisted to collect new data—through observation or interviews—for use by researchers.

- Although agency records have many potential research uses, because they are produced for purposes other than research they may be unsuitable for a specific study.

- Researchers must be especially attentive to possible reliability and validity problems when they use data from agency records.

- "Follow the paper trail" and "expect the expected" are two general maxims for researchers to keep in mind when using agency records in their research.

- Content analysis is a research method appropriate for studying human communications. Because communication takes many forms, content analysis can study many other aspects of behavior.

- Units of communication, such as words, paragraphs, and books, are the usual units of analysis in content analysis.

- Coding is the process of transforming raw data—either manifest or latent content—into a standardized, quantitative form.

- Secondary analysis refers to the analysis of data collected earlier by another researcher for some purpose other than the topic of the current study.

- Archives of criminal justice and other social data are maintained by the ICPSR and the NACJD for use by other researchers.

- The advantages and disadvantages of using secondary data are similar to those for agency records—data previously collected by a researcher may not match our own needs.

## KEY TERMS

content analysis, p. 230

Interuniversity Consortium for Political and Social Research (ICPSR), p. 235

latent content, p. 231

manifest content, p. 231

National Archive of Criminal Justice Data (NACJD), p. 235

published statistics, p. 220

secondary analysis, p. 218

social production of data, p. 227

## REVIEW QUESTIONS AND EXERCISES

1. Each year, the BJS publishes the *Sourcebook of Criminal Justice Statistics*, a compendium of data from many different sources. Consult the online edition of the *Sourcebook* (www.albany.edu/sourcebook) and select a table of interest to you. After consulting the appropriate source annotations, describe how the data presented in that table were originally collected.

2. In New York City, police officers assigned to a specialized gang squad pay special attention to graffiti, or tagging. In doing so, they conduct a type of content analysis to study actions, threats, and other messages presented in this form of communication. Describe how you would plan a formal content analysis of graffiti. Be sure to distinguish manifest and latent content, units of analysis, and coding rules for your study.

## ADDITIONAL READINGS

Bureau of Justice Statistics, *Data Quality Guidelines* (Washington, DC: U.S. Department of Justice, Bureau of Justice Statistics, 2002). In 2001, the U.S. Office of Management and Budget directed that all federal agencies develop guidelines to maximize the quality of information they collect and disseminate. This publication describes how the BJS complied with that directive. It provides an excellent overview of validity and reliability issues in series of data often used by criminal justice researchers.

Geerken, Michael R., "Rap Sheets in Criminological Research: Considerations and Caveats," *Journal of Quantitative Criminology* 10 (1994): 3-21. You won't find a more thorough or interesting discussion of how police arrest records are produced and what that means for researchers. Anyone who uses arrest data should read this very carefully.

General Accounting Office, *Content Analysis: A Methodology for Structuring and Analyzing Written Material,* Transfer Paper 10.3.1. (Washington, DC: U.S. General Accounting Office, 1996). As an agency conducting evaluation studies for the U.S. Congress, the GAO (now named the Government Accountability Office) uses a variety of research methods. One of a series of "transfer papers" that describe GAO methods, this book presents an excellent overview of content analysis applications and methods.

Jacob, Herbert, *Using Published Data: Errors and Remedies* (Thousand Oaks, CA: Sage, 1984). We have often referred to this small book. It is an extremely valuable source of insight into the promise and pitfalls of using agency records.

# PART 4

# Application and Analysis

This final section of the book draws on concepts and ideas from earlier chapters to bring you closer to the actual process of criminal justice research. Having examined the role of theory, cause and effect, measurement, experiments, and different ways of collecting data, we are now ready to see how these pieces come together.

Criminal justice research can be conducted in many ways to answer many different types of questions. We have touched on various research purposes throughout the text, but the first chapter in this section examines a specific research purpose more closely. Because crime is an important and seemingly intractable social problem, applied research is attracting growing interest from researchers and public officials alike. Chapter 10 describes evaluation research and problem analysis. As we will see, carefully specifying concepts and being attentive to measures are as important for applied research as they are for other research purposes.

Chapter 11 takes up the question of analysis. After we have designed a research project, specified measures, and collected data, our attention will turn to a search for patterns and relationships for description, explanation, or evaluation, depending on the research purpose. In Chapter 11, we take a preliminary look at descriptive and inferential statistics. Our goal is to establish a familiarity with the principles of basic statistical analysis.

# CHAPTER 10

# Evaluation Research and Problem Analysis

*In this chapter, our attention centers on applied criminal justice research. Evaluation studies are conducted to learn whether (and why) programs have succeeded or failed. Problem analysis helps officials plan their actions and anticipate the possible effects of new programs.*

## INTRODUCTION

*Evaluation research and problem analysis are increasingly important activities for researchers and public officials alike.*

**Evaluation research**—sometimes called *program evaluation*—refers to a research purpose rather than a specific research method. Its special purpose is to evaluate the effects of policies such as mandatory arrest for domestic violence, innovations in probation, and new sentencing laws. Another type of evaluation study, **problem analysis**, helps public officials plan and select alternative actions. Virtually all types of designs, measures, and data collection techniques can be used in evaluation research and problem analysis.

Growth of evaluation research over the last several years no doubt reflects desire on the part of criminal justice researchers to actually make a difference in the world. At the same time, we cannot discount the influence of two additional factors: (1) increased federal requirements for program evaluations to accompany the implementation of new programs, and (2) the availability of research funds to meet that requirement.

By the same token, increased interest in program evaluation and problem analysis has followed heightened concern for the accountability of public officials and public policy. Criminal justice agencies are expected to justify the effectiveness and cost of their actions. If traditional approaches to probation supervision, for example, do not deter future law-breaking, new approaches should be developed and their effectiveness assessed. Or if using temporary detention facilities fabricated from recycled semitrailers is less costly than constructing new jails, public officials should consider whether the lower-cost alternative will meet their needs for pretrial detention and short-term incarceration.

Justice agencies have come to rely more on **evidence-based policy**, in which the actions of justice agencies are linked to evidence used for planning and evaluation. Traditional practices are being reevaluated against evidence provided by social science research. The *Problem-Oriented Guides* series summarizes evidence concerning responses by police and others to problems ranging from acquaintance rape of college students (Sampson 2002) to witness intimidation (Johnson 2006). CompStat and its variations base police actions on evidence about the location and circumstances of crime problems. Corrections policies are increasingly evaluated to sort out those that do in fact reduce reoffending (Cullen and Sundt 2003). This trend represents an expansion of applied research that moves beyond collaborations between justice professionals and professional researchers.

## TOPICS APPROPRIATE FOR EVALUATION RESEARCH AND PROBLEM ANALYSIS

*Problem analysis and evaluation are used to develop justice policy and determine its impact.*

Evaluation research is appropriate whenever some policy intervention occurs or is planned. A policy intervention is an action taken for the purpose of producing some intended result. In its simplest sense, evaluation research is a process of determining whether the intended result was produced. Problem analysis focuses more on deciding what intervention should be pursued. Given alternative courses of action, which is likely to be least costly, most effective, or least difficult to implement? Our focus, of course, is on the analysis and evaluation of criminal justice policy and criminal justice agencies. However, it will be useful to first consider a simple general model of the policy-making process in order to understand various topics appropriate to evaluation and problem analysis.

### The Policy Process

Figure 10.1 presents our model, adapted from Robert Lineberry's (1977, 42–43) classic summary of a policy system. A similar type of input–output model is described in a National Institute of Justice publication on evaluation guidelines (McDonald and Smith 1989). Although we will examine each

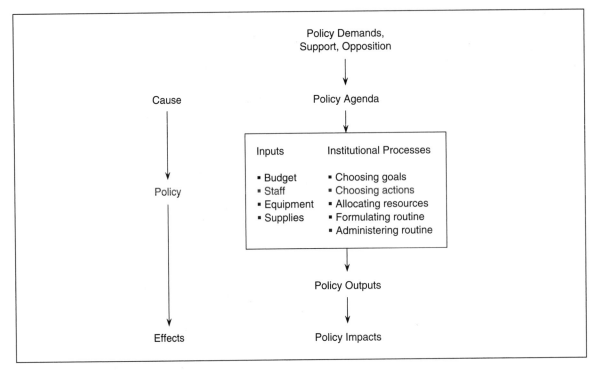

**FIGURE 10.1** The Policy Process
*Source:* Adapted from Lineberry (1977, 24–43).

step in turn, it is important to recognize that the policy process, like the research process generally (see Chapter 1), is fluid and does not always start at the beginning and conclude at the end.

The policy process begins with a demand that normally appears as support for a new course of action or opposition to existing policy. Such demands can emerge from within a public organization or from outside sources. Newspaper stories alleging racial discrimination in drug sentencing can generate demand for revised sentencing policies, or a prosecutor may independently decide to review all sentence recommendations made by deputies who prosecute drug cases. Before any action can be taken, demands must find a place on the policy agenda.

The next step, as shown in Figure 10.1, actually encompasses several steps. Policy makers consider ultimate goals they wish to accomplish and different means of achieving those goals. Does our prosecutor

seek absolute equality in sentences recommended for all white and African American drug defendants, or should there be ranges of permissible variation based on criminal history, severity of charges, and so on? Resources must be allocated from available inputs, including personnel, equipment, supplies, and even time. Who will review sentence recommendations? How much time will that take, and will additional staff be required? Because the word *policy* implies some standard course of action about how to respond to a recurring problem or issue, routine practices and decision rules must be formulated. Will sentence recommendations for each case be reviewed as they are prepared, or is it sufficient to review all cases on a weekly basis?

Policy outputs refer to what is actually produced, in much the same manner that a manufacturer of office supplies produces paper clips and staples. In our hypothetical example, the prosecutor's policy produces the routine review of sentence recommendations in drug cases. Or, to consider a different example, a selective traffic enforcement program intended to reduce auto accidents on a particular roadway may produce a visible police presence together with traffic citations for speeding.

In the final stage, we consider the impact of policy outputs. Does the prosecutor's review process actually eliminate disparities in sentences? Are auto accidents reduced in the targeted enforcement area?

The distinction between policy outputs and their impacts is important for understanding applications of evaluation to different stages of the policy process. Unfortunately, this difference is often confusing to both public officials and researchers. *Impacts* are fundamentally related to policy goals; they refer to the basic question of what a policy action is trying to achieve. *Outputs* embody the means to achieve desired policy goals. The prosecutor seeks to achieve equality in sentence recommendations (impact), so a review process is produced as a means to achieve that goal (output). Or a police executive allocates officers, patrol cars, and overtime pay to produce traffic citations (outputs) in the expectation that citations will achieve the goal of reducing auto accidents (impact).

Now consider the left side of Figure 10.1. Our policy model can be expressed as a simple cause-and-effect process such as we considered in earlier chapters. A cause has produced the variation in sentences for African American and white defendants, or a cause has produced a concentration of auto accidents. Policies are formulated to produce an effect or impact. In this sense, a policy can be viewed as a hypothesis in which an independent variable is expected to produce change in a dependent variable. Sentence review procedures are expected to produce a reduction in sentence disparities; targeted enforcement is expected to produce a reduction in auto accidents. Goal-directed public policies may therefore be viewed as if-then statements: if some policy action is taken, then we expect some result to be produced.

## Linking the Process to Evaluation

If we compare this simple model with a general definition of program evaluation given in one of the most widely used texts on the subject (Rossi, Freeman, and Lipsey 1999), the topics appropriate to applied research will become clearer. Peter Rossi and associates (1999, 4; emphasis in original) define program evaluation as

> *the use of social science research procedures to systematically assess the effectiveness of social intervention programs.* More specifically, evaluation researchers (evaluators) use social research methods to study, appraise, and help improve social programs in all their aspects, including the diagnosis of the social problems they address, their conceptualization and design, their implementation and administration, their outcomes, and their efficiency.

We have been discussing systematic social scientific research procedures throughout this book. Now let's substitute *criminal justice* for *social programs* and see how this definition and Figure 10.1 help us understand program evaluation applications.

**Problem Analysis** Activities listed under "Institutional Processes" in Figure 10.1 refer to conceptualization and design. For example, faced with a court order to maintain prison populations within established capacity, corrections officials might begin by conceiving and designing different ways to achieve this demand. Problem analysis is an example of a social scientific research procedure that can help corrections officials evaluate alternative actions, choose among them, and formulate routine practices for implementing policy to comply with a court order.

One approach might be to increase rated capacity through new construction or conversion of existing facilities. Another might be to devise a program to immediately reduce the existing population. Still another might be to cut back on the admission of newly sentenced offenders. A more general goal that would certainly be considered is the need to protect public safety. Each goal implies different types of actions, together with different types and levels of resources, that would be considered within constraints implied by the need to protect public safety. If officials from other organizations—prosecutors, judges, or state legislators—were involved in conceptualization and design, then additional goals, constraints, and policies might be considered.

Increasing capacity by building more prisons would be the most costly approach in financial terms, but it might also be viewed as the most certain way to protect public safety. Early release of current inmates would be cheaper and faster than building new facilities, but this goal implies other decisions, such as how persons would be selected and whether they would be released to parole or to halfway houses. Each of these alternatives requires some organizational capacity to choose inmates for release, place them in halfway houses, or supervise compliance with parole. Refusing new admissions would be least costly. Political support must be considered for each possible approach. Each alternative—spending money on new construction, accepting responsibility for early release, or tacitly passing the problem on to jails that must house inmates refused admission to state facilities—requires different types of political influence or courage.

Many other topics in criminal justice research are appropriate for problem analysis. Police departments use such techniques to help determine the boundaries of patrol beats and the allocation of other resources. In most large cities, analysts examine the concentration of calls for service in terms of space and time and consider how street layout and obstacles might facilitate or impede patrol car mobility.

A growing number of law enforcement agencies are using computerized crime maps to detect emerging patterns in crime and develop appropriate responses. Producing computer-generated maps that display reported crimes within days after they have occurred is one of the most important policy planning tools for the New York City Police Department (Silverman 1999). Other departments have taken advantage of funding and technical assistance made available by federal funding to enhance mapping and other crime analysis capabilities (Boba 2005).

**Program Evaluation** Problem analysis takes place in the earlier stages of the policy process. In contrast, program evaluation studies are conducted in later stages and seek answers to two types of questions: (1) Are policies being implemented as planned? and (2) Are policies achieving their intended goals? Evaluation, therefore, seeks to link the intended actions and goals of criminal justice policy to empirical evidence that policies are being carried out as planned and are having the desired effects. These two types of questions correspond to two related types of program evaluations: process evaluation and impact assessment. Returning to our example of policies to reduce prison population, we will first consider impact assessment and then process evaluation.

Let's assume that corrections department analysts select an early-release program to reduce the population of one large institution. Inmates who have less than 120 days remaining on their sentence and who were committed for nonviolent offenses will be considered for early release. Further assume that of those inmates selected for early release, some will be assigned to parole officers, and some will serve their remaining sentence in halfway houses—working at jobs during the week but spending evenings and weekends in a community-based facility.

The program has two general goals: (1) to reduce prison population to the court-imposed ceiling and (2) to protect public safety. Whereas the first goal is fairly straightforward, the second is uncomfortably vague. What do we mean by "protecting public safety"? For now, let's say we will conclude that the program is successful in this regard if, after six months, persons in the two early-release conditions have aggregate rates of arrest for new offenses equal to or less than a comparison group of inmates released after completing their sentences.

**TABLE 10.1** Hypothetical Results of Early-Prison-Release Impact Assessment

| | Percent New Arrests After 6 Months | Number of Persons |
|---|---|---|
| Normal release | 26% | 142 |
| Early release to halfway houses | 17% | 25 |
| Early parole | 33% | 46 |
| Subtotal early release | 27% | 71 |
| Total | 26% | 213 |

*Note:* Preprogram population = 1,578; actual population after implementation = 1,402; court-imposed population cap = 1,350.

Our **impact assessment** would examine data on the prison population before and after the new program was implemented, together with arrest records for the two types of early releases and a comparison group. We might obtain something like the hypothetical results shown in Table 10.1.

Did the program meet its two goals? Your initial reaction might be that it did not, but Table 10.1 presents some interesting findings. The prison population certainly was reduced, but it did not reach the court-imposed cap of 1,350. Those released to halfway houses had lower arrest rates than others, but persons placed on early parole had higher arrest rates. Averaging arrest rates for all three groups shows that the total figure is about the same as that for persons released early. Notice also that almost twice as many people were released to early parole as were placed in halfway houses.

The impact assessment results in Table 10.1 would have been easier to interpret if we had conducted a **process evaluation**. A process evaluation focuses on program outputs, as represented in Figure 10.1, seeking answers to the question of whether the program was implemented as intended. If we had conducted a process evaluation of this early-release program, we might have discovered that something was amiss in the selection process. Two pieces of evidence in Table 10.1 suggest that one of the selection biases we considered in Chapter 5 might be at work in this program. Recall the natural tendency of public officials to choose experimental subjects least likely to

fail. In this case, selectivity is indicated by the failure of the early-release program to meet its target number, the relatively small number of persons placed in halfway houses, and the lower re-arrest rates for these persons. A process evaluation would have monitored selection procedures and probably revealed evidence of excessive caution on the part of corrections officials in releasing offenders to halfway houses.

Ideally, impact assessments and process evaluations are conducted together. Our example illustrates the important general point that process evaluations make impact assessments more interpretable. In other cases, process evaluations may be conducted when an impact assessment is not possible. To better understand how process evaluations and impact assessments complement each other, let's now look more closely at how evaluations are conducted.

## GETTING STARTED

*Learning policy goals is a key first step in doing evaluation research.*

Several steps are involved in planning any type of research project. This is especially true in applied studies, for which even more planning may be required. In evaluating a prison early release program, we need to think about design, measurement, sampling, data collection procedures, analysis, and so on. We also have to address such practical problems as obtaining access to people, information, and data needed in an evaluation.

In one sense, however, evaluation research differs slightly in the way research questions are developed and specified. Recall that we equated program evaluation with hypothesis testing; policies are equivalent to if-then statements postulating that an intervention will have the desired impact. Preliminary versions of research questions, therefore, will already have been formulated for many types of evaluations. Problem analysis usually considers a limited range of alternative choices; process evaluations focus on whether programs are carried out according to plans; and impact assessments evaluate whether specified goals are attained.

This is not to say that evaluation research is a straightforward business of using social scientific methods to answer specific questions that are clearly stated by criminal justice officials. It is often difficult to express policy goals in the form of if-then statements that are empirically testable. Another problem is the presence of conflicting goals. Many issues in criminal justice are complex, involving different organizations and people. And different organizations and people may have different goals that make it difficult to define specific evaluation questions. Perhaps most common and problematic are vague goals. Language describing criminal justice programs may optimistically state goals of enhancing public safety by reducing recidivism without clearly specifying what is meant by that objective.

In most cases, researchers have to help criminal justice officials formulate testable goals, something that is not always possible. Other obstacles may interfere with researchers' access to important information. Because of these and similar problems, evaluation researchers must first address the question of whether to evaluate at all.

## Evaluability Assessment

An evaluability assessment is described by Rossi and associates (1999, 157) as sort of a "preevaluation," in which a researcher determines whether conditions necessary for conducting an evaluation are present. One obvious condition is support for the study from organizations delivering program components that will be evaluated. The word *evaluation* may be threatening to public officials, who fear that their own job performance is being rated. Even if officials do not feel personally threatened by an impact assessment or other applied study, evaluation research can disrupt routine agency operations. Ensuring agency cooperation and support is therefore an important part of evaluability assessment. Even if no overt opposition exists, officials may be ambivalent about evaluation.

This might be the case, for example, if an evaluation is required as a condition of launching a new program. This and other steps in evaluability assessment may be accomplished by scouting a program

and interviewing key personnel (Rossi, Freeman, and Lipsey 1999, 135). The focus in scouting and interviewing should be on obtaining preliminary answers to questions that eventually will have to be answered in more detail as part of an evaluation. What are general program goals and more specific objectives? How are these goals translated into program components? What kinds of records and data are readily available? Who will be the primary consumers of evaluation results? Do other persons or organizations have a direct or indirect stake in the program? Figure 10.2 presents a partial menu of questions that can guide information gathering for the evaluability assessment and later stages.

---

1. Goals
   a. What is the program intended to accomplish?
   b. How do staff determine how well they have attained their goals?
   c. What formal goals and objectives have been identified?
   d. Which goals or objectives are most important?
   e. What measures of performance are currently used?
   f. Are adequate measures available, or must they be developed as part of the evaluation?

2. Clients
   a. Who is served by the program?
   b. How do they come to participate?
   c. Do they differ in systematic ways from nonparticipants?

3. Organization and Operation
   a. Where are the services provided?
   b. Are there important differences among sites?
   c. Who provides the services?
   d. What individuals or groups oppose the program or have been critical of it in the past?

4. History
   a. How long has the program been operating?
   b. How did the program come about?
   c. Has the program grown or diminished in size and influence?
   d. Have any significant changes occurred in the program recently?

**F I G U R E  10.2**  Evaluation Questions
*Source: Adapted from Stecher and Davis (1987, 58–59).*

The answers to these and similar questions should be used to prepare a program description. Although official program descriptions may be available, evaluation researchers should always prepare their own description, one that reflects their own understanding of program goals, elements, and operations. Official documents may present incomplete descriptions or ones intended for use by program staff, not evaluators. Even more importantly, official program documents often do not contain usable statements about program goals. As we will see, formulating goal statements that are empirically testable is one of the most important components of evaluation research.

Douglas McDonald and Christine Smith (1989, 1) describe slightly different types of questions to be addressed by criminal justice officials and evaluators in deciding whether to evaluate state-level drug control programs:

- How central is the project to the state's strategy?
- How costly is it relative to others?
- Are the project's objectives such that progress toward meeting them is difficult to estimate accurately with existing monitoring procedures?

Such questions are related to setting both program and evaluation priorities. On the one hand, if a project is not central to drug control strategies or if existing information can help determine project effectiveness, then an evaluation should probably not be conducted. On the other hand, costly projects that are key elements in antidrug efforts should be evaluated so that resources can be devoted to new programs if existing approaches are found to be ineffective.

## Problem Formulation

We mentioned that evaluation research questions may be defined for you. This is true in a general sense, but formulating applied research problems that can be empirically evaluated is an important and often difficult step. Evaluation research is a matter of finding out whether something is or is not there, whether something did or did not happen. To conduct evaluation research, we must be able to operationalize, observe, and recognize the presence or absence of what is under study.

This process normally begins by identifying and specifying program goals. The difficulty of this task, according to Rossi and associates (1999, 167), revolves around the fact that formal statements of goals are often abstract statements about ideal outcomes. Here are some examples of goal statements paraphrased from actual program descriptions:

- Equip individuals with life skills to succeed (a state-level shock incarceration program; MacKenzie, Shaw, and Gowdy 1993).
- Provide a safe school environment conducive to learning (a school resource officer program; Johnson 1999).
- Encourage participants to accept the philosophy and principles of drug-free living (an urban drug court; Finn and Newlyn 1993).
- Provide a mechanism that engages local citizens and community resources in the problem-solving process (a probation-police community corrections program; Wooten and Hoelter 1998).

Each statement expresses a general program objective that must be clarified before we can formulate research questions to be tested empirically. We can get some idea of what the first example means, but this goal statement raises several questions. The objective is for individuals to succeed, but succeed at what? What is meant by "life skills"—literacy, job training, time management, self-discipline? We might also ask whether the program focuses on outputs (equipping people with skills) or on impacts (promoting success among people who are equipped with the skills). On the one hand, an evaluation of program outputs might assess individual learning of skills, without considering whether the skills enhance chances for success. On the other hand, an evaluation of program impacts might obtain measures of success such as stable employment or not being arrested within some specified time period.

In all fairness, these goal statements are taken somewhat out of context; source documents expand on program goals in more detail. They are, however, typical of stated goals or initial responses we might get to the question "What are the goals of this program?" Researchers require more specific statements of program objectives.

Wesley Skogan (1985) cautions that official goal statements frequently oversell what a program might realistically be expected to accomplish. It's natural for public officials to be positive or optimistic in stating goals, and overselling may be evident in goal statements. Another reason officials and researchers embrace overly optimistic goals is that they fail to develop a micromodel of the program production process (Weiss 1995). That is, they do not adequately consider just how some specified intervention will work. Referring to Figure 10.1, we can see that developing a micromodel can be an important tool for laying out program goals and understanding how institutional processes are structured to achieve those goals. Skogan (1985, 38; emphasis in original) describes a micromodel as

> part of what is meant by a "theory-driven" evaluation. Researchers and program personnel should together consider just how each element of a program should affect its targets. If there is not a good reason why "X" *should* cause "Y" the evaluation is probably not going to find that it did! Micromodeling is another good reason for monitoring the actual implementation of programs.

A micromodel can also reveal another problem that sometimes emerges in applied studies: inconsistent goals.

For example, Michael Maxfield and Terry Baumer (1992) evaluated a pretrial home detention program in which persons awaiting trial for certain types of offenses were released from jail and placed on home detention with electronic monitoring. Five different criminal justice organizations played roles in implementation or had stakes in the program. The county sheriff's department (1) faced pressure to reduce its jail population. Under encouragement from the county prosecutor (2), the pretrial release program was established. Criminal court judges (3) had the ultimate authority to release defendants to home detention, following recommendations by bail commissioners in a county criminal justice services agency (4). Finally, a community corrections department (5) was responsible for actually monitoring persons released to home detention.

Maxfield and Baumer interviewed persons in each of these organizations and discovered that different agencies had different goals. The sheriff's department was eager to release as many people as possible to free up jail space for convicted offenders and pretrial defendants who faced more serious charges. Community corrections staff, charged with the task of monitoring pretrial clients, were more cautious and sought only persons who presented a lower risk of absconding or committing more offenses while on home detention. The county prosecutor viewed home detention as a way to exercise more control over some individuals who would otherwise be released under less restrictive conditions. Some judges refused to release people on home detention, whereas others followed prosecutors' recommendations. Finally, bail commissioners viewed pretrial home detention as a form of jail resource management, adding to the menu of existing pretrial dispositions (jail, bail, or release on recognizance).

The different organizations involved in the pretrial release program comprised multiple **stakeholders**—persons and organizations with a direct interest in the program. Each stakeholder had different goals for and different views on how the program should actually operate—who should be considered for pretrial home detention, how they should be monitored, and what actions should be taken against those who violated various program rules. After laying out these goals and considering different measures of program performance, Maxfield and Baumer (1992, 331) developed a micromodel of home detention indicating that electronic monitoring is suitable for only a small fraction of defendants awaiting trial.

Clearly specifying program goals, then, is a fundamental first step in conducting evaluation studies. If officials are not certain about what a program is expected to achieve, it is not possible to determine whether goals are reached. If multiple stakeholders embrace different goals, evaluators must specify different ways to assess those goals. Michael Maxfield (2001) describes a number of different approaches to specifying clear goals, a crucial first step in the evaluation process.

## Measurement

After we identify program goals, our attention turns to measurement, considering first how to measure a program's success in meeting goals. Obtaining evaluable statements of program goals is conceptually similar to the measurement process, in which program objectives represent conceptual definitions of what a program is trying to accomplish.

**Specifying Outcomes** If a criminal justice program is intended to accomplish something, we must be able to measure that something. If we want to reduce fear of crime, we need to be able to measure fear of crime. If we want to increase consistency in sentences for drug offenses, we need to be able to measure that. Notice, however, that although outcome measures are derived from goals, they are not the same as goals. Program goals represent desired outcomes, whereas outcome measures are empirical indicators of whether those desired outcomes are achieved. Furthermore, if a program pursues multiple goals, then researchers may have to either devise multiple outcome measures or select a subset of possible measures to correspond with a subset of goals.

Keeping in mind our program-as-hypothesis simile, outcome measures correspond to dependent variables—the $Y$ in a simple $X \rightarrow Y$ causal hypothesis. Because we have already considered what's involved in developing measures for dependent variables, we can describe how to formulate outcome measures. Pinning down program goals and objectives results in a conceptual definition. We then specify an operational definition by describing empirical indicators of program outcomes.

In our earlier example, Maxfield and Baumer (1992) translated the disparate interests of organizations involved in pretrial home detention into three more specific objectives: (1) ensure appearance at trial, (2) protect public safety, and (3) relieve jail crowding. These objectives led to corresponding outcome measures: (1) failure-to-appear rates for persons released to pretrial home detention, (2) arrests while on home detention, and (3) estimates of the number of jail beds made available, computed by multiplying the number of persons on pretrial home detention by the number of days each person served on the program. Table 10.2 summarizes the goals, objectives, and measures defined by Maxfield and Baumer.

**Measuring Program Contexts** Measuring the dependent variables directly involved in an impact assessment is only a beginning. As Ray Pawson and Nick Tilley (1997, 69) point out, it is usually necessary to measure the context within which the program is conducted. These variables may appear to be external to the experiment itself, yet they still affect it.

Consider, for example, an evaluation of a job-skills training program coupled with early prison

**TABLE 10.2** Pretrial Home Detention with Electronic Monitoring: Goals, Objectives, and Measures

| Actor/Organization | Goals |
|---|---|
| Sheriff | Release jail inmates |
| Prosecutor | Increase supervision of pretrial defendants |
| Judges | Protect public safety |
| Bail commission | Provide better jail resource management |
| Community corrections | Monitor defendant compliance |
| | Return violators to jail |

| Objectives | Measures |
|---|---|
| Ensure court appearance | Failure-to-appear counts |
| Protect public safety | Arrests while on program |
| Relieve jail crowding | $N$ defendants $X$ days served |

*Source:* Adapted from Maxfield and Baumer (1992, 321).

release to a halfway house. The primary outcome measure might be the participants' success at gaining employment after completing the program. We will, of course, observe and calculate the subjects' employment rates. We should also be attentive to what has happened to the employment and unemployment rates of the community and state where the program is located. A general slump in the job market should be taken into account in assessing what might otherwise seem to be a low employment rate for subjects. Or if all the experimental subjects get jobs following the program, that might result more from a general increase in available jobs than from the value of the program itself.

There is no magic formula or set of guidelines for selecting measures of program context, any more than there is for choosing control variables in some other type of research. Just as we read what other researchers have found with respect to some topic we are interested in—say, explanatory research—we should also learn about the production process for some criminal justice program before conducting an evaluation.

**Measuring Program Delivery**   In addition to making measurements relevant to the outcomes of a program, it is necessary to measure the program intervention—the experimental stimulus or independent variable. In some cases, this measurement will be handled by assigning subjects to experimental and control groups, if that's the research design. Assigning a person to the experimental group is the same as scoring that person "yes" on the intervention, and assignment to the control group represents a score of "no." In practice, however, it's seldom that simple.

Let's continue with the job-training example. Some inmates will participate in the program through early release; others will not. But imagine for a moment what job-training programs are actually like. Some subjects will participate fully; others might miss sessions or fool around when they are present. So we may need measures of the extent or quality of participation in the program. And if the program is effective, we should find that those who

participated fully have higher employment rates than those who participated less.

Other factors may further confound the administration of the experimental stimulus. Suppose we are evaluating a new form of counseling designed to cure drug addiction. Several counselors administer it to subjects composing an experimental group. We can compare the recovery rate of the experimental group with that of a control group (a group that received some other type of counseling or none at all). It might be useful to include the names of the counselors who treat specific subjects in the experimental group, because some may be more effective than others. If that turns out to be the case, we must find out why the treatment works better for some counselors than for others. What we learn will further elaborate our understanding of the therapy itself.

Obtaining measures that reflect actual delivery of the experimental intervention is very important for many types of evaluation designs. Variation in the levels of treatment delivered by a program can be a major threat to the validity of even randomized evaluation studies. Put another way, uncontrolled variation in treatment is equivalent to unreliable measurement of the independent variable.

**Specifying Other Variables**   It is usually necessary to measure the population of subjects involved in the program being evaluated. In particular, it is important to define those for whom the program is appropriate. In evaluation studies, such persons are referred to as the program's *target population*. If we are evaluating a program that combines more intensive probation supervision with periodic urine testing for drug use, it's probably appropriate for convicted persons who are chronic users of illegal drugs, but how should we define and measure chronic drug use more specifically? The job-skills training program mentioned previously is probably appropriate for inmates who have poor employment histories, but a more specific definition of employment history is needed.

This process of definition and measurement has two aspects. First, the program target population must be specified. This is usually done in a manner similar to the process of defining program goals. Drawing on questions like those in Figure 10.2, evaluators consult program officials to identify the intended targets or beneficiaries of a particular program. Because the hypothetical urine-testing program is combined with probation, its target population will include persons who might receive suspended sentences with probation. However, offenders convicted of crimes that carry nonsuspendable sentences will not be in the target population. Prosecutors and other participants may specify additional limits to the target population—employment or no previous record of probation violations, for example.

Most evaluation studies that use individual people as units of analysis also measure such background variables as age, gender, educational attainment, employment history, and prior criminal record. Such measures are made to determine whether experimental programs work best for males, those older than 25, high school graduates, persons with fewer prior arrests, and so forth.

Second, in providing for the measurement of these different kinds of variables, we need to choose whether to create new measures or use ones already collected in the course of normal program operation. If our study addresses something that's not routinely measured, the choice is easy. More commonly, at least some of the measures we are interested in will be represented in agency records in some form or other. We then have to decide whether agency measures are adequate for our evaluation purposes.

Because we are talking about measurement here, our decision to use our own measures or those produced by agencies should, of course, be based on an assessment of measurement reliability and validity. If we are evaluating the program that combined intensive probation with urinalysis, we will have more confidence in the reliability and validity of basic demographic information recorded by court personnel than in court records of drug use. In this case, we might want to obtain self-report measures of drug use and crime commission from subjects themselves, rather than relying on official records.

By now, it should be abundantly clear that measurement must be taken very seriously in evaluation research. Evaluation researchers must carefully determine all the variables to be measured and obtain appropriate measures for each. However, such decisions are typically not purely scientific ones. Evaluation researchers often must work out their measurement strategy with the people responsible for the program being evaluated.

## DESIGNS FOR PROGRAM EVALUATION

*Designs used in basic research are readily adapted for use in evaluation research.*

Chapter 5 introduced a variety of experimental and other designs that researchers use in studying criminal justice. Recall that randomly assigning research subjects to experimental or control groups controls for many threats to internal validity. Here our attention turns specifically to the use of different designs in program evaluation.

### Randomized Evaluation Designs

To illustrate the advantages of random assignment, consider this dialogue from Lawrence Sherman's book *Policing Domestic Violence: Experiments and Dilemmas* (1992, 67):

> When the Minneapolis domestic violence experiment was in its final planning stage, some police officers asked: "Why does it have to be a randomized experiment? Why can't you just follow up the people we arrest anyway, and compare their future violence risks to the people we don't arrest?"
>
> Since this question reveals the heart of the logic of controlled experiments, I said, "I'm glad you asked. What kind of people do you arrest now?" "Assholes," they replied. "People who commit aggravated POPO."
>
> "What is aggravated POPO?" I asked.

"Pissing off a police officer," they answered. "Contempt of cop. But we also arrest people who look like they're going to be violent, or who have caused more serious injuries."

"What kind of people do you not arrest for misdemeanor domestic assault?" I continued.

"People who act calm and polite, who lost their temper but managed to get control of themselves," came the answer.

"And which kinds of people do you think would have higher risks of repeat violence in the future?" I returned.

"The ones we arrest," they said, the light dawning.

"But does that mean arrest caused them to become more violent?" I pressed.

"Of course not—we arrested them because they were more trouble in the first place," they agreed.

"So just following up the ones you arrest anyway wouldn't tell us anything about the effects of arrest, would it?" was my final question.

"Guess not," they agreed. And they went on to perform the experiment.

Sherman's dialogue portrays the obvious problems of selection bias in routine police procedures for handling domestic violence. In fact, one of the most important benefits of randomization is to avoid the selectivity that is such a fundamental part of criminal justice decision making. Police selectively arrest people, prosecutors selectively file charges, judges and juries selectively convict defendants, and offenders are selectively punished. In a more general sense, randomization is the great equalizer: through probability theory, we can assume that groups created by random assignment will be statistically equivalent.

Randomized designs are not suitable for evaluating all experimental criminal justice programs. Certain requirements of randomized studies mean that this design cannot be used in many situations. A review of those requirements illustrates many of the limits of randomized designs for applied studies.

**Program and Agency Acceptance** Random assignment of people to receive some especially desirable or punitive treatment may not be possible for legal, ethical, and practical reasons. We discussed ethics and legal issues in Chapter 2. Sometimes practical obstacles may also be traced to a misunderstanding of the meaning of random assignment. It is crucial that public officials understand why randomization is desirable and that they fully endorse the procedure.

Richard Berk and associates (2003) describe how researchers obtained cooperation for an evaluation of a new inmate classification system in the California Department of Corrections (CDC) by appealing to the needs of agency managers. Preliminary research suggested that the experimental classification system would increase inmate and staff safety at lower cost than classification procedures then in use. In addition:

> Plans for the study were thoroughly reviewed by stakeholders, including CDC administrators, representatives of prison employee bargaining unions, ... California State legislative offices, and a wide variety of other interested parties. There was widespread agreement that the study was worth doing. (Berk et al. 2003, 211)

At the same time, justice agencies have expanding needs for evaluations of smaller-scale programs. John Eck (2002) explains how designs that are less elaborate are more likely to be accepted by public agencies.

**Minimization of Exceptions to Random Assignment** In any real-world delivery of alternative programs or treatments to victims, offenders, or criminal justice agency staff, exceptions to random assignment are all but inevitable. In a series of experiments on police responses to domestic violence, officers responded to incidents in one of three ways, according to a random assignment procedure (Sherman et al. 1992). The experimental treatment was arrest; control treatments included simply separating parties to the dispute or attempting to advise and mediate. Although patrol officers and police administrators accepted the random procedure, exceptions were made as warranted in individual cases, subject to an officer's discretionary judgment.

As the number of exceptions to random assignment increases, however, the statistical equivalence of experimental and control groups is threatened. When police (or others) make exceptions to random assignment, they are introducing bias into the selection of experimental and control groups. Randomized experiments are best suited for programs in which such exceptions can be minimized. The prison classification study by Berk and associates (2003, 224–225) offers a good example. Random assignment was automatic—inmates having odd identification numbers at intake were assigned to the treatment group, while those having even numbers were in the control group. This procedure produced treatment and control groups that were virtually identical in size: 9,662 in treatment and 9,656 controls.

**Adequate Case Flow for Sample Size**    In Chapter 6, we examined the relationship between sample size and accuracy in estimating population characteristics. As sample size increases (up to a point), estimates of population means and standard errors become more precise. By the same token, the number of subjects in groups created through random assignment is related to the researcher's ability to detect significant differences in outcome measures between groups. If each group has only a small number of subjects, statistical tests can detect only very large program effects or differences in outcome measures between the two groups. This is a problem with statistical conclusion validity and sample size, as we discussed in Chapters 5 and 6.

Case flow represents the process through which subjects are accumulated in experimental and control groups. In Sherman's domestic violence evaluations, cases flowed into experimental and control groups as domestic violence incidents were reported to police. Evaluations of other types of programs will generate cases through other processes—for example, offenders sentenced by a court or inmates entering a correctional facility. In a drug court evaluation by Denise Gottfredson and associates (Gottfredson et al. 2006), it took 18 months to accumulate 235 cases for the treatment group (drug court). Berk and associates (2003) accumulated their 9,662 treatment subjects in 6 months.

If relatively few cases flow through some process and thereby become eligible for random assignment, it will take longer to obtain sufficient numbers of cases. The longer it takes to accumulate cases, the longer it will take to conduct an experiment and the longer experimental conditions must be maintained. Imagine filling the gas tank of your car with a small cup: it would take a long time, it would test your patience, and you would probably tarnish the paint with spilled gasoline as the ordeal dragged on. In a similar fashion, an inadequate flow of cases into experimental groups risks contaminating the experiment through other problems. Getting information about case flow in the planning stages of an evaluation is a good way to diagnose possible problems with numbers of subjects.

**Maintaining Treatment Integrity**    Treatment integrity refers to whether an experimental intervention is delivered as intended. Sometimes called *treatment consistency*, treatment integrity is therefore roughly equivalent to measurement reliability. Experimental designs in applied studies often suffer from problems related to treatment inconsistencies. If serving time in jail is the experimental treatment in a program designed to test different approaches to sentencing drunk drivers, treatment integrity will be threatened if some defendants are sentenced to a weekend in jail while others serve 30 days or longer.

Criminal justice programs can vary considerably in the amount of treatment applied to different subjects in experimental groups. For example, Gottfredson and associates (2006) acknowledge that the drug-court treatment in Baltimore County was unevenly implemented. Only about half of those assigned to the experimental group received certified drug treatment. In contrast, the classification system tested by Berk and associates (2003) was a relatively simple treatment that was readily standardized. There was no danger of treatment dilution as in the drug-court experiment.

Midstream changes in experimental programs can also threaten treatment integrity. Rossi and associates (1999, 297) point out that the possibility of midstream changes means that randomized designs are usually not appropriate for evaluating programs in early stages of development, when such changes are more likely. For example, assume we are evaluating an intensive supervision probation program with randomized experimental and control groups. Midway through the experiment, program staff decide to require weekly urinalysis for everyone in the experimental group (those assigned to intensive supervision). If we detect differences in outcome measures between the experimental and control groups (say, arrests within a year after release), we will not know how much of the difference is due to intensive supervision and how much might be due to the midstream change of adding urine tests.

**Summing Up the Limits of Randomized Designs** Randomized experiments therefore require that certain conditions be met. Staff responsible for program delivery must accept random assignment and further agree to minimize exceptions to randomization. Case flow must be adequate to produce enough subjects in each group so that statistical tests will be able to detect significant differences in outcome measures. Finally, experimental interventions must be consistently applied to treatment groups and withheld from control groups.

These conditions, and the problems that may result if they are not met, can be summarized as two overriding concerns in field experiments: (1) equivalence between experimental and control groups before an intervention, and (2) the ability to detect differences in outcome measures after an intervention is introduced. If there are too many exceptions to random assignment, experimental and control groups may not be equivalent. If there are too few

cases, or inconsistencies in administering a treatment, or treatment spillovers to control subjects, outcome measures may be affected in such a way that researchers cannot detect the effects of an intervention.

Let's now look at an example that illustrates both the strengths of random experiments and constraints on their use in criminal justice program evaluations.

## Home Detention: Two Randomized Studies

Terry Baumer and Robert Mendelsohn conducted two random experiments to evaluate programs that combine home detention with electronic monitoring (ELMO). In earlier chapters, we examined how different features of these studies illustrated measurement principles; here our focus is on the mechanics of random assignment and program delivery.

In their first study, Baumer and Mendelsohn evaluated a program that targeted adult offenders convicted of nonviolent misdemeanor and minor felony offenses (Baumer and Mendelsohn 1990; also summarized in Baumer, Maxfield, and Mendelsohn 1993). The goal of the program was to provide supervision of offenders that was more enhanced than traditional probation but less restrictive and less costly than incarceration. Several measures of outcomes and program delivery were examined, as we have described in earlier chapters.

Baumer and Mendelsohn selected a randomized posttest-only design, in which the target population was offenders sentenced to probation. Subjects were randomly assigned to an experimental group in which the treatment was electronically monitored home detention or to a control group sentenced to home detention without electronic monitoring. Figure 10.3 summarizes case flow into the evaluation experiment. After a guilty plea or trial conviction, probation office staff reviewed offenders' backgrounds and criminal records for the purpose of recommending an appropriate sentence. The next step was a hearing, at which sentences were imposed by a criminal court judge.

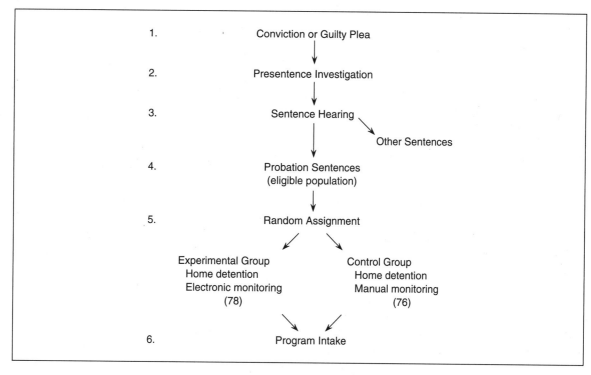

1. Conviction or Guilty Plea

2. Presentence Investigation

3. Sentence Hearing
   Other Sentences

4. Probation Sentences
   (eligible population)

5. Random Assignment

   Experimental Group
   Home detention
   Electronic monitoring
   (78)

   Control Group
   Home detention
   Manual monitoring
   (76)

6. Program Intake

**F I G U R E 10.3** Home Detention for Convicted Adults: Case Flow and Random Assignment

Persons sentenced to probation were eligible for inclusion in the experiment. Their case files were forwarded to staff in the community corrections agency responsible for administering the home detention programs. On receiving an eligible case file, community corrections staff telephoned the evaluation researchers, who, having prepared a random list of case numbers, assigned subjects to either the treatment or control group. Subject to two constraints, this process produced 78 treatment subjects and 76 control subjects.

Thinking back on our consideration of ethics in Chapter 2, you should be able to think of one constraint: informed consent. Researchers and program staff explained the evaluation project to subjects and obtained their consent to participate in the experiment. Those who declined to participate in the evaluation study could nevertheless be assigned to home detention as a condition of their proba-

tion. The second constraint was made necessary by the technology of ELMO: subjects could not be kept in the treatment group if they did not have a telephone that could be connected to the ELMO equipment.

Notice that random assignment was made after sentencing. Baumer and Mendelsohn began their evaluation by randomizing subjects between stages 2 and 3 in Figure 10.3. This produced problems because judges occasionally overruled presentence investigation recommendations to probation, thus overriding random assignment. After detecting this problem, Baumer and Mendelsohn (1990, 27–29) moved randomization downstream, so that judicial decisions could not contaminate the selection process.

Baumer and Mendelsohn (1990, 26) obtained agreement from community corrections staff, prosecutors, and judges to use random assignment by getting all parties to accept an assumption of "no difference":

> That is, in the absence of convincing evidence to the contrary, they were willing to assume that there was no difference between the … methods of monitoring. This allowed the prosecutor to negotiate and judges to assign home detention as a condition of probation only, while permitting the community corrections agency to make the monitoring decision.

Convinced of the importance of random assignment, the community corrections agency delegated to researchers the responsibility for making the monitoring decision, a "decision" that was randomized.

In this example, the experimental condition—ELMO—was readily distinguished from the control condition, home detention without ELMO. There was no possibility of treatment spillover; control subjects could not unintentionally receive ELMO because they had neither the bracelet nor the home-base unit that embodied the treatment. ELMO could therefore be readily delivered to subjects in the experimental group and withheld from control subjects.

The second ELMO evaluation conducted by Baumer and Mendelsohn reveals how program delivery problems can undermine the strengths of random assignment (Baumer, Maxfield, and Mendelsohn 1993). In their study of juvenile burglars, they used similar procedures for randomization, but eligible subjects were placed in one of four groups, as illustrated in this table:

|  | **Electronic Monitoring?** | |
| --- | --- | --- |
| **Police Visits?** | **No** | **Yes** |
| **No** | C | E1 |
| **Yes** | E2 | E3 |

Juvenile burglars could be randomly assigned to three possible treatments: ELMO only (E1), police visits to their home after school only (E2), or ELMO and police visits (E3). Subjects in the control group (C) were sentenced to home detention only. As in the adult study, outcome measures included arrests after release.

Although there were no problems with random assignment, inconsistencies in the delivery of each of the two experimental treatments produced uninterpretable results (Maxfield and Baumer 1991, 5):

> Observations of day-to-day program operations revealed that, compared with the adult program, the juvenile court and cooperating agencies paid less attention to delivering program elements and using information from … the electronic monitoring equipment. Staff were less well trained in operating the electronic monitoring equipment, and police visits were inconsistent.

The box titled "Home Detention" in Chapter 1 elaborates on differences in the operation of these two programs and a third ELMO program for pretrial defendants. However, the lesson from these studies bears repeating here: *randomization does not control for variation in treatment integrity and program delivery.*

Randomized experiments can be powerful tools in criminal justice program evaluations. However, it is often impossible to maintain the desired level of control over experimental conditions. This is especially true for complex interventions that may change while an evaluation is under way. Experimental conditions are also difficult to maintain when different organizations work together in delivering some service—a community-based drug treatment provider coupled with intensive probation, for example.

Largely because of such problems, evaluation researchers are increasingly turning to other types of designs that are less fragile—less subject to problems if rigorous experimental conditions cannot be maintained.

## Quasi-Experimental Designs

Quasi-experiments are distinguished from true experiments by the lack of random assignment of subjects to an experimental and a control group.

Random assignment of subjects is often impossible in criminal justice evaluations. Rather than forgo evaluation altogether in such instances, it is usually possible to create and execute research designs that will permit evaluation of the program in question.

Quasi-experiments may also be nested into experimental designs as backups should one or more of the requisites for a true experiment break down. For example, William Shadish, Thomas Cook, and Donald Campbell (2002) describe how time-series designs can be nested into a series of random experiments. In the event that case flow is inadequate or random assignment to enhanced or standard counseling regimens breaks down, the nested time-series design will salvage a quasi-experiment.

We considered different classes of quasi-experimental designs—nonequivalent groups, cohorts, and time series—in Chapter 5, together with examples of each type. Each of these designs has been used extensively in criminal justice evaluation research.

**Nonequivalent-Groups Designs** As we saw in Chapter 5, quasi-experimental designs lack the built-in controls for selection bias and other threats to internal validity. Nonequivalent-groups designs, by definition, cannot be assumed to include treatment and comparison subjects who are statistically equivalent. For this reason, quasi-experimental program evaluations must be carefully designed and analyzed to rule out possible validity problems.

For evaluation designs that use nonequivalent groups, attention should be devoted to constructing experimental and comparison groups that are as similar as possible on important variables that might account for differences in outcome measures. Rossi and associates (1999) caution that procedures for constructing such groups should be grounded in a theoretical understanding of what individual and group characteristics might confound evaluation results. In a study of recidivism by participants in shock incarceration programs, we certainly want to ensure that equal numbers of men and women are included in groups assigned to shock incarceration and groups that received another sentence.

Alternatively, we can restrict our analysis of program effects to only men or only women.

One common reason for using nonequivalent-groups designs is that some experimental interventions are intended to affect all persons in a larger unit—a neighborhood crime prevention program, for example. It may not be possible to randomly assign some neighborhoods to receive the intervention while withholding it from others. And we are usually unable to control which individuals in a neighborhood are exposed to the intervention.

Different types of quasi-experimental designs can be used in such cases. In a Kansas City program to reduce gun violence, police targeted extra patrols at gun crime hot spots (Sherman, Shaw, and Rogan 1995). Some beats were assigned to receive the extra patrols, while comparison beats—selected for their similar frequency of gun crimes—did not get the special patrols. Several outcome measures were compared for the two types of areas. After 29 weeks, gun seizures in the target area increased by more than 65 percent and gun crimes dropped by 49 percent. There were no significant changes in either gun crimes or gun seizures in the comparison beat. Drive-by shootings dropped from 7 to 1 in the target area and increased from 6 to 12 in the comparison area. Homicides declined in the target area but not in the comparison area. Citizen surveys showed less fear of crime and more positive feelings about the neighborhood in the target area than in the comparison area.

**Time-Series Designs** Interrupted time-series designs require attention to certain validity threats because researchers cannot normally control how reliably the experimental treatment is implemented. Foremost among these issues are instrumentation, history, and construct validity. In many interrupted time-series designs, conclusions about whether an intervention produced change in an outcome measure rely on simple indicators that represent complex causal processes.

In their evaluation of legislation to provide for mandatory minimum sentences in Oregon, Nancy Merritt and associates (Merritt, Fain, and Turner 2006) examined changes in sentences for different types of offenses. They found that sentences for offenses clearly covered by the law did in fact increase in the first five years after its passage. However, they also found declines in the number of cases filed that were clearly included in the mandatory provisions. Meanwhile, more charges were filed for offenses covered by discretionary provisions. Of course, criminal case prosecution and sentencing are complex processes. The authors could not directly control for different circumstances surrounding cases processed before and after the law took effect. However, their time-series analysis does clearly show changes in case filings, suggesting that prosecutors exercised discretion to evade the mandatory provisions of Oregon's legislation.

Understanding the causal process that produces measures used in time-series analysis is crucial for interpreting results. Such understanding can come in two related ways. First, we should have a sound conceptual grasp of the underlying causal forces at work in the process we are interested in. Second, we should understand how the indicators used in any time-series analysis are produced.

Patricia Mayhew and associates (Mayhew, Clarke, and Elliott 1989) concluded that laws requiring motorcycle riders to wear helmets produced a reduction in motorcycle theft. This might seem puzzling until we consider the causal constructs involved in stealing motorcycles. Assuming that most motorcycle thefts are crimes of opportunity, Mayhew and associates argue that few impulsive thieves stroll about carrying helmets. Even thieves are sufficiently rational to recognize that a helmetless motorcycle rider will be unacceptably conspicuous—an insight that deters them from stealing motorcycles. Mayhew and colleagues considered displacement as an alternative explanation for the decline in motorcycle theft, but they found no evidence that declines in motorcycle theft were accompanied by increases in either stolen cars or bicycles. By systematically thinking through the causal process of motorcycle theft, Mayhew and associates were able to conclude that helmet laws were unintentionally effective in reducing theft. For another study of vehicle theft, see the box "Evaluating Vehicle Security."

The figure also shows vertical lines that correspond to government action regarding electronic immobilizers:

- In 1999, immobilizers were required for *all cars* less than 12 years old registered in Western Australia.

- In 2001, immobilizers were required for *all new cars* sold throughout Australia.

You can see a clear downward trend in the two series after immobilizer requirements were introduced in different places at different times. The declines correspond roughly with the requirements that were introduced in different years.

This figure presents an example of an *interrupted time series*, a type of evaluation often used to assess whether change follows some new law. We describe this and other approaches to evaluation in this chapter. Keep this example in mind as you read our discussion of different types of applied research.

## Other Types of Evaluation Studies

Earlier in this chapter, we noted how process evaluations are distinct from impact assessments. Whereas the latter seek answers to questions about program effects, process evaluations monitor program implementation, asking whether programs are being delivered as intended.

Process evaluations can be invaluable aids in interpreting results from an impact assessment. We described how Baumer and Mendelsohn were better able to understand outcome measures in their evaluation of ELMO for juvenile burglars because they had monitored program delivery. Similarly, process evaluations were key elements of CCTV evaluations reported by Martin Gill and Angela Spriggs (2005), discussed in Chapter 5. They were able to describe whether cameras were placed and monitored as intended. In many cases, camera placement was modified, something the authors suggest was related to the relative success of different CCTV installations. Without a process evaluation, information about program implementation cannot be linked to outcome measures.

## EVALUATING VEHICLE SECURITY

Graham Farrell and associates (2011) investigated vehicle theft trends for Australia, Canada, England and Wales, and the United States. This was part of a research project undertaken by Michael Maxfield and Ronald Clarke (2009) on the effectiveness of marking auto parts in the United States.

Because vehicle theft had been persistently high in Australia for many years, officials were prompted to take a variety of measures to reduce the problem (Carroll 2004). Farrell and associates took advantage of the staged introduction of security measures in different parts of Australia to conduct an evaluation of the effectiveness of electronic engine immobilizers. These devices prevent a vehicle's engine from being

started unless an electronic key code matches the code installed in the vehicle.

The figure below shows trends in motor vehicle theft for Western Australia, one of the country's states and territories, and for the other seven states and territories. Data points are an index set at 100 for the year 1997. Thefts in subsequent years are expressed as change in that base. For example, the value for Western Australia in 1998 was 118, which means that vehicle theft had increased 18 percent in 1998 compared to the previous year. By the year 2008, the index for Western Australia had declined to about 40, which means that vehicle theft had dropped by about 60 percent from 1997 through 2008.

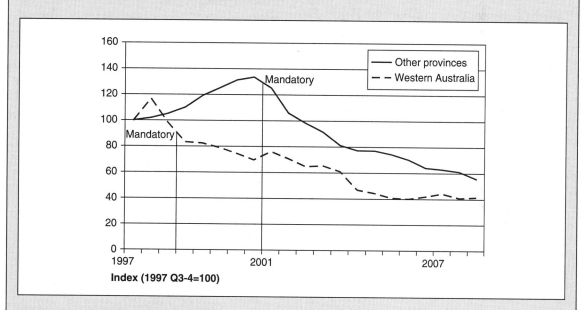

Trends in Australian Vehicle Theft 1997–2007

*Source:* Adapted from Farrell et al. (2011).

Process evaluations can also be useful for criminal justice officials whose responsibility centers more on the performance of particular tasks than on the overall success of some program. For example, police patrol officers are collectively responsible for public safety in their beat, but their routine actions focus more on performing specific tasks such as responding to a call for service or, in community policing, diagnosing the concerns of neighborhood residents. Police supervisors are attentive to traffic tickets written, arrests made, and complaints against individual officers. Probation and parole officers are, of course, interested in the ultimate performance of their clients, but they are also task-oriented in their use of records to keep track of client contacts, attendance at substance abuse sessions, or job performance. Process evaluations center on measures of task performance—on the assumption that tasks are linked to program outcomes. So process evaluations can be valuable in their own right, as well as important for diagnosing measures of program effects.

# PROBLEM ANALYSIS AND SCIENTIFIC REALISM

*Problem analysis, coupled with scientific realism, helps public officials use research to select and assess alternative courses of action.*

Program evaluation differs from problem analysis with respect to the time dimension and where each activity takes place in the policy process. Problem analysis is used to help design alternative courses of action and to choose among them.

In reality, there is not much of a difference between these two types of applied research. Similar types of research methods are used to address problem analysis questions (What would happen? What should we do?) as are brought to bear on program evaluation questions (What did happen? What have we done?). Consider, for example, a definition of a similar approach, policy analysis, from a prominent text: "Attempting to bring modern science and technology to bear on society's problems, policy analysis searches for feasible courses of action, generating information and marshalling evidence of the benefits and other consequences that would follow their adoption and implementation" (Quade 1989, 4). Except for the form of the verb ("would follow"), this is not too different from the way we defined program evaluation.

Results from program evaluations are frequently considered in choosing among future courses of action. Problem analysis and policy analysis depend just as much on clearly specifying goals and objectives as does program evaluation. And the achievement of goals and objectives worked out through problem analysis can be tested through program evaluation. Measurement is also a fundamental concern in both types of applied studies.

## Problem-Oriented Policing

More than an alternative approach to law enforcement, the core of problem-oriented policing is applying problem analysis methods to public safety problems. Problem-oriented policing depends on identifying problems, planning and taking appropriate action, and then assessing whether those actions achieved intended results.

This approach centers on problems, not individual incidents. For example, traditional policing responds to reports of auto thefts, writing up details about the incident to support an insurance claim, then moving on to the next incident. Let's consider this *incident-oriented policing*. In contrast, **problem-oriented policing** would begin by analyzing a number of auto theft reports. Reports would be examined for similarities, such as where and when they occurred, types of autos stolen, whether stolen cars were eventually recovered, and if so in what condition. Such analysis would define a more general problem of auto theft. Subsequent steps would consider what kinds of actions might be taken to address the problem.

A fundamental tool in problem-oriented policing is **problem solving**. As initially defined by Ronald Clarke and John Eck, problem solving involves four analytic steps:

(1) carefully define specific problems ...;
(2) conduct in-depth analysis to understand their causes; (3) undertake broad searches for solutions to remove these causes and bring about lasting reductions in problems; (4) evaluate how successful these activities have been. (2005, step 7-1)

You can easily see how problem solving merges the application of problem analysis and evaluation (assessment) of the effects of interventions.

Problem-oriented policing is an especially useful example of applied research because a large number of resources are available. We'll briefly describe three types of such resources: how-to-do-it guides, problem and response guides, and case studies. Most of the first two categories have been prepared with support from the Community Oriented

Policing Services (COPS) office in the U.S. Department of Justice. Resources are available at the Center for Problem-Oriented Policing website (www.popcenter.org).

**How-to-Do-It Guides** Ronald Clarke and John Eck (2005) have prepared a general guide to crime analysis to support problem-oriented policing. Adapted from a document originally prepared for the Jill Dando Institute of Crime Science in London, this publication offers succinct guidance on analysis and reporting results. The COPS office has also sponsored guides that provide more detail on different problem analysis tools. Examples include assessment and evaluation (Eck 2003a); understanding the process of repeat victimization (Weisel 2005); interviewing offenders (Decker 2005); and analyzing crime displacement (Guerette 2009).

Crime mapping and other methods of space-based analysis are important tools in problem-oriented policing. *GIS and Crime Mapping* by Spencer Chainey and Jerry Ratcliffe (2005) is an excellent general guide. John Eck and associates (2005) focus on the use of mapping to identify crime hot spots.

**Problem and Response Guides** In an earlier chapter, we mentioned that justice agencies frequently adopt programs that appear to have been successful in other jurisdictions. While this can sometimes be advisable, a key principle of problem-oriented policing is to base local actions on an understanding of local problems. Instead of trying an off-the-shelf program or so-called "best practice," appropriate interventions should be considered only after analyzing the data.

This principle is evident in two series of guides that describe what is known about effective responses based on past experience. *Problem guides* describe how to analyze very specific types of problems (for example, "Exploitation of Trafficked Women") and what are known to be effective or ineffective responses to each problem. *Response guides* describe very general kinds of actions that might be undertaken to address different types of problems (for example, "Sting Operations").

**Case Studies and Other Research** One of the hallmarks of applied research is to use research to change practice. The two groups of guides discussed so far were prepared for use by criminal justice professionals, but they were developed following many years of research. Many examples of research that contributed to changes in justice policy have been published in the series *Crime Prevention Studies*. We now turn to an example that illustrates the application of problem analysis, as well as other research principles presented in this and earlier chapters.

## Auto Theft in Chula Vista

Chula Vista is a medium-sized city of just under 200,000 residents, bordered by the Pacific Ocean on the west and sandwiched by San Diego on the north and southwest; the city is about seven miles north of the U.S.-Mexico border. Nanci Plouffe and Rana Sampson (2004) began their analysis of vehicle theft by comparing Chula Vista to other southern California cities. After noting that theft rates tended to increase for cities closer to the border, they began to disaggregate the problem by searching for areas where vehicle thefts and break-ins were concentrated. Deborah Weisel (2003) refers to this as "parsing," or breaking down a large-area measure to examine smaller areas.

Plouffe and Sampson first determined that 10 parking lots accounted for 25 percent of thefts and 20 percent of break-ins in the city. Furthermore, 6 of those 10 lots were also among the top 10 calls-for-service locations in Chula Vista. This meant that auto-theft hot spots also tended to be hot spots for other kinds of incidents. Continuing their analysis, the analysts found some notable patterns:

- Recovery rates for stolen cars and trucks were lower in Chula Vista than in areas to the north.
- Recovery rates in 4 of the 10 hot parking lots were especially low, under 40 percent.
- Smaller pick-up trucks and older Toyota Camrys had even lower recovery rates.
- High-risk lots were close to roads that led to the Mexico border.

Together these findings suggested that many cars stolen from the high-risk areas were being driven into Mexico.

Plouffe and Sampson next moved beyond using existing data from police records. This is again consistent with the methods of problem analysis: use existing data to identify problems and their general features, then collect additional data to better understand the mechanisms of problems. For Plouffe and Sampson that meant conducting environmental surveys of high-risk parking lots, observing operations and interviewing officials at U.S.–Mexico border crossings, and interviewing a small number of individuals arrested for auto theft from target lots. They sought to understand why particular lots were targeted and whether stolen cars could be easily driven into Mexico.

We described environmental surveys in Chapter 8. In conducting theirs, Plouffe and Sampson discovered that the highest-risk lot was a two-minute drive from vehicle entry points into Mexico. The lot served a midrange general shopping mall with typical open parking. Access was easy and thieves could expect that vehicles would be unguarded for some time. Information gathered from the border crossing confirmed that few cars entering Mexico were stopped and vehicle identification documents were rarely requested.

In-person interviews with auto thieves used a 93-item questionnaire, asking about target selection, techniques, and other routines. Thieves preferred older cars because they could be easily stolen—steering column locks wear out and can be broken with simple tools. They watched people entering stores, judged that their vehicle would be unguarded for a time, and then drove the few minutes into Mexico. Cars were rarely stolen from parking garages because thieves would have to produce a ticket in order to exit.

With this and other information, Plouffe and Sampson discussed strategies with Chula Vista police and security staff at parking lots and shopping malls. More diligent screening at the border was rejected, largely because most vehicles had been driven into Mexico before the theft was even discovered. They recommended that high-risk shopping malls install gates at entrance and exit points for parking lots. Drivers would take a ticket upon entering and would have to produce it when leaving. This, it was argued, would substantially increase the effort required to steal vehicles from parking lots near the border.

## Other Applications of Problem Analysis

Partly because it has proved helpful in law enforcement applications, problem analysis is being adopted by other criminal justice agencies. Veronica Coleman and associates describe how local and federal prosecutors in several U.S. cities have formed planning teams to identify crime problems and develop appropriate interventions. Teams include U.S. attorneys, researchers, and other criminal justice professionals who pursue a form of problem analysis labeled Strategic Approaches to Community Safety Initiatives (SACSI). SACSI involves five steps, four of which should look familiar (Coleman et al. 1999, 18):

1. Form an interagency working group.
2. Gather information and data about a local crime problem.
3. Design a strategic intervention to tackle the problem.
4. Implement the intervention.
5. Assess and modify the strategy as the data reveal effects.

We have only scratched the surface of problem analysis applications in criminal justice. This is an area of applied research that is growing daily. Other examples draw on methods of systems analysis, operations research, and economics for such purposes as cost-benefit studies, police patrol allocation, and decisions about hiring probation officers. Cost-benefit analysis, in particular, is used to assess the relative value and expense of alternative policies. Although the mathematical tools that form the basis of problem analysis can be sophisticated, the underlying logic is relatively simple. For example, police departments traditionally used pin maps to represent the spatial and temporal concentrations of reported crime.

## Space- and Time-Based Analysis

Pin maps are examples of "low-tech" problem analysis that are nonetheless conceptually identical to computer models of hot spots used in many departments to plan police deployment. Growing numbers of justice agencies, especially police and sheriff's departments, have taken advantage of rapid advances in computing and telecommunications. Computerized mapping systems now permit police to monitor changes in crime patterns on a daily or hourly basis and to develop responses accordingly. Furthermore, simultaneous advances in computing power and declines in the cost of that power make it possible for even small agencies to use mapping tools (Harries 1999). The ongoing technological advances in mapping have fueled the application of statistical models to geographic clusters of crime problems. Thomas Rich (1999) describes this as *analytic mapping*, whereby statistical tools supplement the "eyeballing" approach to locating concentrations of crime.

Crime maps usually represent at least four different things: (1) one or more crime types, (2) a space or area, (3) some time period, and (4) some dimension of land use, usually streets. The most useful crime maps will show patterns that can help analysts and police decide what sort of action to take. That's part of applied research. An example will illustrate some basic features of crime maps.

Figure 10.4 shows four crime maps prepared by Shuryo Fujita, a graduate student at the Rutgers University School of Criminal Justice, for a mid-sized city in the northeast United States. All four maps show completed auto theft, but for different areas and time periods. The map in panel A shows auto thefts for the year 2005 in one of four police precincts in the city. About 1,750 completed thefts are represented, about 33 percent of all thefts in the city. You will probably notice two things about panel A. First, car theft seems to be everywhere in this area, except for blank spots in the center and on

the right side of the map—a large park and a river, respectively. Second, because car theft seems to be everywhere, the map is not especially useful. Much of the district appears to be a hot spot. Panel B changes the time reference, showing the 30 car thefts that occurred in the first week of August 2005. You might think this is somewhat more useful, showing more theft in the southern part of the district. But while panel A shows too much, panel B shows smaller numbers that don't seem to cluster very much.

Panel C shifts the geographic focus to one sector within the district, to the left of the park. This sector happens to have the highest volume of car theft, 464 completed thefts in 2005; it's the hottest sector in the hottest precinct in the city. Again, car theft seems to be all over the sector. A closer look shows more dots on the longer north-south streets than on cross streets. This is more clear in panel D, which shows a crime density map of the sector. Crime density is a numerical value showing how close some dots are to each other and how distant those clusters are from outlying dots. These values are mapped, showing patterns much more clearly than simple dots. The darker areas of panel D represent more dense concentrations of car theft. There seem to be two corridors of car theft, running north-south below the diagonal street that bisects the map. These corridors are sort of connected in the middle, showing a rough H-shape. This shape happens to correspond with some major thoroughfares in the area. You might be able to imagine cruising up, across, and down, looking for cars to steal. That's useful information a crime analyst can provide for police managers. During the summer months of 2006, police in this city deployed special patrols on the streets within the H-shaped area depicted in panel D.

Tools for mapping crime and other problems are similar to the tools of statistical analysis, a topic we consider in the final chapter. Maps and statistics are most useful when we seek to understand patterns in a large number of observations. Very small police departments that report very few incidents need neither statistical nor geographic analysis to understand crime problems. But departments

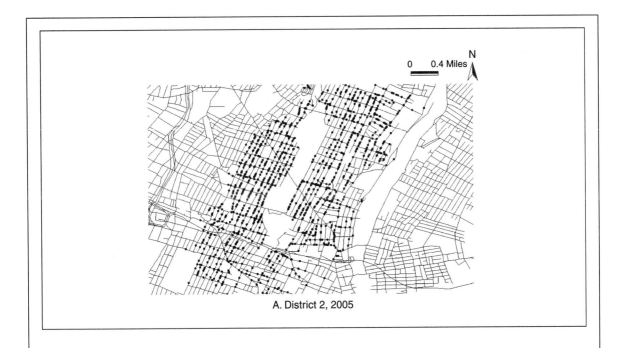

A. District 2, 2005

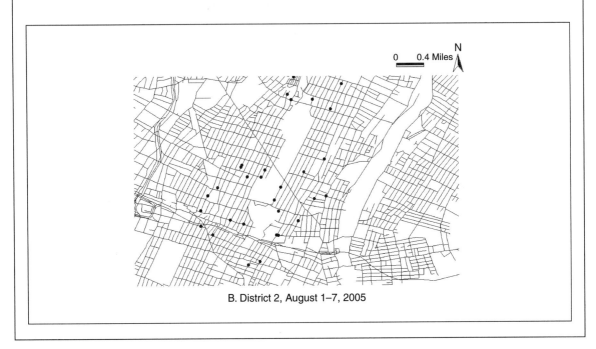

B. District 2, August 1–7, 2005

**FIGURE 10.4** Mapping Auto Theft

*Source:* Maps prepared by Shuryo Fujita.

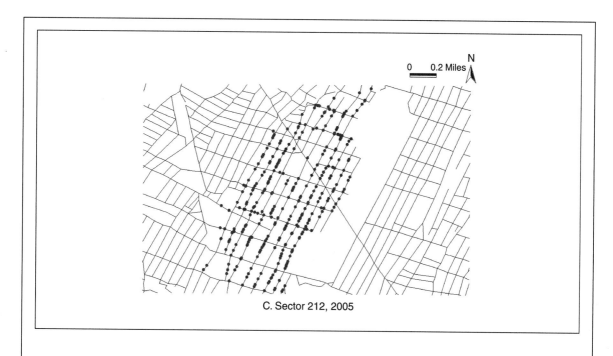

C. Sector 212, 2005

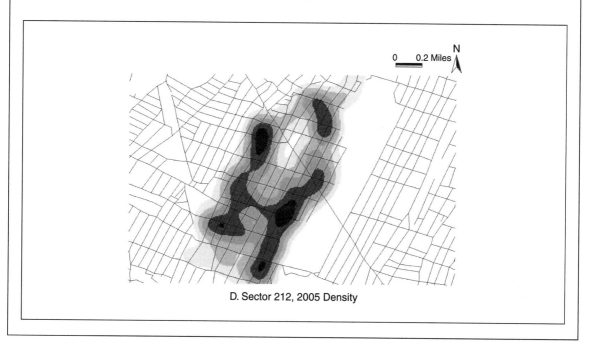

D. Sector 212, 2005 Density

**F I G U R E  10.4**  (*Continued*)

serving cities like the one in Figure 10.4 can really benefit from space-based analytic tools like crime mapping and density analysis.

Computerized crime mapping has been used for many years in a small number of departments and is spreading to many large and midsized cities. Software is more powerful, and web-based mapping programs have been used to make crime maps generally available. More published guides are appearing that describe how to combine maps with other analysis programs and sources of data. Jerry Ratcliffe (2004) describes how to classify crime concentrations across space and time dimensions to produce a hot spot matrix.

Crime mapping and other types of problem analysis illustrate another advantage of incident-based data—the potential for use in the kind of problem analysis we have described. Most crime mapping and similar tools are developed and used by individual departments, reflecting the fact that crime analysis is based on locally generated data. With incident-based reporting, crime analysis can be conducted on larger units. For example, Donald Faggiani and Colleen McLaughlin (1999) describe how National Incident-Based Reporting System (NIBRS) data can show state or regional patterns in drug arrests and offenses. Using NIBRS data for Virginia, the authors demonstrate differences in types of arrests and drugs for different areas of the state.

## Scientific Realism and Applied Research

Traditional research and evaluation are based on the model of cause and effect we considered in Chapters 3 and 5. An independent variable (cause) produces some change in a dependent variable (effect). Experimental and quasi-experimental designs seek to isolate this causal process from the possible effects of intervening variables. Designs thus try to control for the possible effects of intervening variables.

Problem analysis as we have described it represents a bridge between traditional research approaches and applied research that is the foundation of scientific realism. Ray Pawson and Nick Tilley (1997) propose that, instead of trying to explain cause in a traditional sense, evaluators should search for mechanisms acting in context to explain outcomes. As we have seen, experiments do this by producing pretest statistical equivalence between groups of subjects who receive an intervention and groups of subjects who do not. Quasi-experiments using nonequivalent groups might seek to control intervening variables by holding possible intervening variables constant. So, for example, if we believe that employment status might be an intervening variable in the relationship between arrest and subsequent domestic violence, we will try to structure an evaluation to hold employment status constant between treatment and control groups.

Scientific realism treats employment status as the *context* in which an arrest *mechanism* operates on the *outcome* of repeat domestic violence. Rather than try to control for employment status, a scientific realist will study the mechanism in context and conclude, for example, that arrest is effective in reducing subsequent violence in situations in which an offender is employed but is not effective when the offender is unemployed. This finding will be no different from what Sherman and associates (1992) conclude in their assessment of a series of randomized experiments.

What is different is that the scientific realist approach is rooted in the principle that similar interventions can naturally be expected to have different outcomes in different contexts. Most notably, this approach is more compatible with the realities of evaluation than is the experimental approach. Pawson and Tilley (1997, 81) put it this way: "Ultimately, realist evaluation would be *mechanism-* and *context-driven* rather than program-led" (emphasis in original). This means that interventions should not be designed as comprehensive programs that apply equally in all situations. Instead, interventions should be developed for specific contexts, and evaluations of those interventions must consider context as a key factor in whether the intervention achieves the desired outcome.

Situational crime prevention (Clarke 1997b) is an example of the scientific realist approach that bridges problem analysis and evaluation because it focuses on what mechanisms operate for highly specific types of crime in specific situations. So, for example, rather than develop and evaluate large-scale programs intended to reduce auto theft generally, situational crime prevention seeks specific interventions that will be effective in reducing particular types of auto theft. Ronald Clarke and Patricia Harris (1992) distinguish several types of auto theft by their purposes: joyriding, temporary transportation, resale or stripping, or insurance fraud. Theft of certain models for joyriding may be reduced by modest increases in security, while theft of expensive cars for resale or export requires different approaches. Many types of auto theft can be reduced by placing attendants at the exits of parking garages, but car break-ins may not be affected by that intervention.

As we mentioned in Chapter 5, the realist approach resembles a case-study approach. Both are *variable-oriented* strategies for research—they depend on measures of many variables to understand and assess a small number of cases. Detailed data and information are gathered about specific interventions, often in very small areas. Whereas an experimental evaluation uses probability theory to control for intervening variables, the case-study approach depends on detailed knowledge to understand the context in which mechanisms operate.

In his discussion of applied research tools for problem solving, Eck (2002, 2003b), makes the case even more strongly. Public officials, he argues, are more interested in solving local problems than in identifying robust cause-and-effect relationships. Both problem solving and evaluation are concerned with answering the question "Did the problem decline?" But eliminating alternative explanations for a decline, which is the central concern of internal validity and the rationale for stronger evaluation designs, is important only if officials wish to use the same intervention elsewhere.

In what Eck terms "small-claim, small-area problem solving," analysts develop appropriate interventions for problems in context. This is the essence of the problem-solving process. Like Eck, we emphasize *process*—systematically studying a problem,

developing appropriate interventions, and seeing if those interventions have the intended effect. This is quite different from what Eck terms "large-claim interventions"—such as Drug Abuse Resistance Education (DARE) or corrections boot camps—that are developed to apply in a wide variety of settings. Because small-claim, small-scale interventions are tailored to highly specific settings, they cannot easily be transferred intact to different settings. However, the *process* of diagnosing local problems, selecting appropriate interventions, and then assessing the effects of those interventions can be generally applied. Anthony Braga (2008) offers more examples of this reasoning. Gloria Laycock presents an even stronger case for scientific realism in applied criminal justice research generally (2002) and in making specific plans for crime prevention (Tilley and Laycock 2002).

Randomized or quasi-experimental evaluations should be conducted when such designs are appropriate. But it is important to recognize the formidable requirements for deploying these designs. The scientific realist approach to evaluation is flexible and may be appropriate in many situations. A scientific realist evaluation or case study can be especially useful in smaller-scale evaluations in which interest centers on solving some particular problem in a specific context more than on finding generalizable scientific truths. In any case, a variety of approaches can satisfy the definition of program evaluation that we discussed earlier in this chapter by systematically applying social science research procedures to an individual program or agency.

Our general advice in this regard is simple: do the best you can. This requires two things: (1) understanding the strengths and limits of social science research procedures, and (2) carefully diagnosing what is needed and what is possible in a particular application. Only by understanding possible methods and program constraints can we properly judge whether any kind of evaluation study is worth undertaking with an experimental, quasi-experimental, or nonexperimental design, or whether an evaluation should not be undertaken at all.

## THEORY AND APPLIED RESEARCH

Although it may seem that theory has little to contribute to applied research, the opposite is true. Routine activity theory (Cohen and Felson 1979) and crime pattern theory (Brantingham and Brantingham 2009) are frequently cited in problem analysis and evaluation research. Routine activity theory describes a crime triangle in which suitable victims and motivated offenders come together in the absence of capable guardians. Crime pattern theory predicts where crimes will occur by studying where offenders and victims are active, the travel routes that connect them, and the types of facilities where they may come in contact.

Each has played a major role in problem-oriented policing, as illustrated by the large collection of problem guides produced by the Center for Problem-Oriented Policing. By way of illustration, we describe selected features of the guide *Spectator Violence in Stadiums* by Tamara Madensen and John Eck (2008).

Madensen and Eck first consider how three different clusters of characteristics might contribute to spectator violence. Here are examples:

| Venue | Staff | Event |
|---|---|---|
| Performance proximity | Training | Performer behavior |
| Noise level | Experience | Alcohol availability |
| Seating arrangements | Communication | Crowding |

Drawing on routine activity theory, the role of each factor in potentially contributing to spectator violence is considered.

Next is a consideration of stakeholders—the people and organizations that have some interest in spectator violence or the things that might contribute to it. This list of stakeholders includes stadium owners, event planners and managers, emergency medical service providers, insurance companies, police, and the community near a stadium.

Problem analysis requires collecting data, so Madensen and Eck describe what kind of information should be collected about victims, locations, and circumstances of violent incidents. After getting a detailed understanding of local problems and settings, appropriate responses are considered and selected. Finally, data are collected to assess the effectiveness of responses.

The guide by Madensen and Eck lays out each of these steps in detail, ending with a summary table that lists responses, how they work, and things to be considered in applying responses to specific stadiums and events. Reviewing this guide, it's easy to see how routine activity theory plays a major role in applied research.

## THE POLITICAL CONTEXT OF APPLIED RESEARCH

*Public policy involves making choices, and that involves politics.*

Applied researchers bridge the gap between the body of research knowledge about crime and the practical needs of criminal justice professionals—a process that has potential political, ideological, and ethical problems. In the final section of this chapter, we turn our attention to the context of applied research, describing some of the special problems that can emerge in such studies.

Some similarities are evident between this material and our discussion of ethics in Chapter 2. Although ethics and politics are often closely intertwined, the ethics of criminal justice research focuses on the methods used, whereas political issues are more concerned with the substance and use of research findings. Ethical and political aspects of applied research also differ in that there are no formal codes of accepted political conduct comparable to the codes of ethical conduct we examined earlier. Although some ethical norms have political aspects—for example, not harming subjects relates to protection of civil liberties—no one has developed a set of political norms that can be agreed on by all criminal justice researchers.

### Evaluation and Stakeholders

Most applied studies involve multiple stakeholders—people who have a direct or indirect interest in the program or evaluation results (Rossi, Freeman, and Lipsey 1999, 204–205). Some stakeholders may be enthusiastic supporters of an experimental program, others may oppose it, and still others may be neutral. Different stakeholder interests in programs can produce conflicting perspectives on evaluations of those programs.

Emil Posavec and Raymond Carey (2002) describe such problems as dysfunctional attitudes toward program evaluation. Program supporters may have unrealistic expectations that evaluation results will document dramatic success. Conversely, they may worry that negative results will lead to program termination. Agency staff may feel that day-to-day experience in delivering a program imparts a qualitative understanding of its success that cannot be documented by a controlled experiment. Staff and other stakeholders may object that an evaluation consumes scarce resources better spent on actually delivering a program.

We have two bits of advice in dealing with such problems. First, identify program stakeholders, their perspectives on the program, and their likely perspectives on the evaluation. In addition to agency decision makers and staff, stakeholders include program beneficiaries and competitors. For example, store owners in a downtown shopping district might benefit from an experimental program to deploy additional police on foot patrol, whereas people who live in a nearby residential area might argue that additional police should be assigned to their neighborhood.

Second, educate stakeholders about why an evaluation should be conducted. This is best done by explaining that applied research is conducted to determine what works and what does not. The National Institute of Justice (NIJ) and the Office of Community Oriented Policing Services (COPS) have issued brief documents that describe how evaluation can benefit criminal justice agencies by rationalizing their actions (Eck 2003a; Maxfield 2001). Such publications, together with examples of completed evaluations, can be valuable tools for winning the support of stakeholders.

Also keep in mind that applied research is very much a cooperative venture. Accordingly, researchers and program staff are mutual stakeholders in designing and executing evaluations. Evaluators' interest in a strong design that will meet scientific standards must be balanced against the main concern of program sponsors—obtaining information that is useful for developing public policy.

The flip side of being cautious about getting caught in stakeholder conflict is the benefit of applied research in influencing public policy. Evaluation studies can provide support for continuing or expanding successful criminal justice programs, or evidence that ineffective programs should be modified or terminated. And problem analysis results can sometimes be used to influence actions by public officials. For an example, see the box titled "When Politics Accommodates Facts," in which Tony Fabelo describes how problem analysis dissuaded Texas legislators from costly, ineffective lawmaking.

## Politics and Objectivity

Politics and ideology can color research in ways even more subtle than those described by Fabelo. You may consider yourself an open-minded and unbiased person who aspires to be an objective criminal justice researcher. However, you may have strong views about different sentencing policies, believing that probation and restitution are to be preferred over long prison sentences. Because there is no conclusive evidence to favor one approach over the other, your beliefs would be perfectly reasonable.

Now, assume that one of the requirements for the course you are taking is to write a proposal for an evaluation project on corrections policy. In all likelihood, you will prepare a proposal to study a probation program rather than, say, a program on the use of portable jails to provide increased detention capacity. That is natural, and certainly legitimate, but your own policy preferences will affect the topic you choose.

Ronald Clarke (1997b, 28) describes political objections to applied studies of situational crime prevention: "Conservative politicians regard it as an irrelevant response to the breakdown in morality that has fueled the postwar rise in crime. Those on the left criticize it for neglecting issues of social

## WHEN POLITICS ACCOMMODATES FACTS

### Tony Fabelo

The 1994 federal anticrime bill, and related politics emanating from this initiative, put pressure on the states to adopt certain sentencing policies as a condition for receiving federal funds. Among these policies is the adoption of a "three strikes and you're out" provision establishing a no-parole sentence for repeat violent offenders. Facts have prevented a criminal justice operational gridlock in Texas by delineating to policy makers the operational and fiscal impact of broadly drafted policies in this area. Facts established through policy analysis by the Criminal Justice Policy Council (CJPC) have clearly stated that a broad application of the "three strikes and you're out" policy will have a tremendous fiscal impact.

Therefore, state policy makers have carefully drafted policies in this area. For example, during the last legislative session, the adoption of life with no parole for repeat sex offenders was considered. State policy makers, after considering facts presented by the CJPC, adopted a policy that narrowly defined the group of offenders for whom the law is to apply. They also adopted a 35-year minimum sentence that must be served before parole eligibility, rather than a life sentence with no parole. The careful drafting of this policy limited its fiscal impact while still accomplishing the goal of severely punishing the selected group of sex offenders.

Unlike Texas, politics did not accommodate facts in California, where lawmakers adopted a fiscally unsustainable "three strikes and you're out" policy.

For my part, I need to maintain personal integrity and the integrity of the CJPC in defining the facts for policy makers. I have to be judged not only by "objectivity," which is an elusive concept, but by my judgment in synthesizing complex information for policy makers. To do this, I follow and ask my staff to follow these rules:

1. Consider as many perspectives as possible in synthesizing the meaning of information, including the perspectives of those stakeholders who will be affected.
2. State the limits of the facts and identify areas where drawing conclusions is clearly not possible.
3. Consult with your peers to verify methodological assumptions and meet accepted criteria to pass the scrutiny of the scientific community.
4. Provide potential alternative assumptions behind the facts.
5. Set clear expectations for reviewing reports and releasing information so that facts are not perceived as giving advantage to any particular interest group.
6. Judge the bottom-line meaning of the information for policy action based on a frame of reference broader than that of any particular party or constituency.
7. Finally, if the above are followed, never succumb to political pressure to change your judgment. Integrity cannot be compromised even once. In the modern crowded marketplace of information, your audience will judge you first for your motives and then for your technical expertise.

*Source:* Adapted from Fabelo (1997, 2, 4).

---

justice and for being too accepting of the definitions of crime of those in power." By the same token, ELMO is distrusted for being simultaneously too lenient by allowing offenders to do time at home and too close to a technological nightmare by enabling the government to spy on individuals. Evaluations of situational crime prevention or ELMO programs may be criticized for tacitly supporting either soft-on-crime or heavy-handed police state ideologies (Lilly 2006; Nellis 2006).

It is difficult to claim that criminal justice research, either applied or basic, is value-free. Our own beliefs and preferences affect the topics we choose to investigate. Political preferences and ideology may also influence criminal justice research agendas by making funds available for some projects but not others. For example, in 2004, the National Insti-

tute of Justice awarded money for projects to study these topics: "Chinese Connection: Changing Patterns of Drug Trafficking in the Golden Triangle" and "Assessment of Risk Factors Associated with Sexual Violence in the Texas Prison System." No funds were awarded, however, for such projects as "The Scope of Institutionalized Racism in the War on Drugs" or "Exploratory Research on Torture in Federal Detention Camps." It is, of course, possible for researchers—consciously or unconsciously—to become instruments for achieving political or policy objectives in applied research.

It may sometimes seem difficult to maintain an acceptable level of objectivity about or distance from evaluation results in criminal justice research. This task can be further complicated if you have strong views one way or another about a particular program or policy. Researchers who evaluate, say, an experimental program to prevent offenders from repeating probably sincerely hope that the program will work. However, substantially less consensus exists about other criminal justice problems and policies. For example, how do you feel about a project to test the effects of restrictive handgun laws or mandatory jail sentences for abortion protesters? We conclude this chapter with one final example that we expect will make you think about some of the political issues involved in applied research.

In 1990, the elected prosecutor of Marion County, Indiana—in which Indianapolis is located—was sharply criticized in a series of newspaper stories that claimed to present evidence of racial disparity in drug sentences handed down in the county. Convicted minority offenders, it was asserted, received longer prison terms than white offenders. The prosecutor immediately responded, criticizing the data collected and the methods used by the investigative reporter. He also contacted Michael Maxfield and asked him to conduct an independent analysis of drug cases accepted for prosecution.

In the first place, the prosecutor claimed, he had had previous feuds with the author of the newspaper stories. Second, he categorically denied any discriminatory policies in making sentence requests in drug cases. Third, he said he knew that the data and methods reported in the newspaper stories were deficient even though the reporter would not reveal details about his sources and information. Finally, if any pattern of racial disparity existed, it was certainly inadvertent, and the prosecutor wanted to know about it so that the problem could be fixed. Maxfield accepted the project and was paid to produce a report.

How do you feel about this example? Did Maxfield sell out? How would you feel if Maxfield turned up clear evidence of disparity in sentences? Or no evidence of disparity? What about political party affiliation—would it make a difference if the prosecutor and Maxfield identified with the same party? With different parties?

## SUMMARY

- Evaluation research and problem analysis are examples of applied research in criminal justice.

- Different types of evaluation activities correspond to different stages in the policy process—policy planning, process evaluation, and impact evaluation.

- An evaluability assessment may be undertaken as a scouting operation or a preevaluation to determine whether it is possible to evaluate a particular program.

- A careful formulation of the problem, including relevant measurements and criteria of success or failure, is essential in evaluation research.

- Organizations may not have clear statements or ideas about program goals. In such cases, researchers must work with agency staff to formulate mutually acceptable statements of goals before proceeding.

- Evaluation research may use experimental, quasi-experimental, or nonexperimental designs. As in studies with other research purposes, designs that offer the greatest control over experimental conditions are usually preferred.

- The use of randomized field experiments requires careful attention to random assignment, case flow, and treatment integrity.

- Randomized designs cannot be used for evaluations that begin after a new program has been implemented or for full-coverage programs in which it is not possible to withhold an experimental treatment from a control group.

- Process evaluations can be undertaken independently or in connection with an impact assessment. Process evaluations are all but essential for interpreting results from an impact assessment.

- Problem analysis is more of a planning technique. However, problem analysis draws on the same social science research methods used in program evaluation. Many variations on problem analysis are used in applied criminal justice research.

- The scientific realist approach to applied research focuses on mechanisms in context, rather than generalizable causal processes.

- Criminal justice agencies are increasingly using problem analysis tools for tactical and strategic planning. Crime mapping and other space-based procedures are especially useful applied techniques.

- Problem solving, evaluation, and scientific realism have many common elements.

- Evaluation research entails special logistical, ethical, and political problems because it is embedded in the day-to-day events of public policy and real life.

## KEY TERMS

evaluation research, p. 241

evidence-based policy, p. 241

impact assessment, p. 245

problem analysis, p. 241

problem-oriented policing, p. 260

problem solving, p. 260

process evaluation, p. 245

stakeholders, p. 248

## REVIEW QUESTIONS AND EXERCISES

1. In presentations to justice practitioners, Michael Maxfield describes evaluation as answering two questions: "Did you get what you expected?" and "Compared to what?" Discuss how particular sections of this chapter relate to those two questions.

2. When programs do not achieve their expected results, it's due to one of two things: the program was not a good idea to begin with, or it was a good idea but was not implemented properly. Discuss why it is necessary to conduct both a process and an impact evaluation to learn why a program failed.

3. What are the principal advantages and disadvantages of randomized designs for field experiments? Are such designs used in problem analysis? Explain your answer.

## ADDITIONAL READINGS

Clarke, Ronald V., and John Eck, *Crime Analysis for Problem Solvers in 60 Small Steps* (Washington, DC: U.S. Department of Justice, Office of Community Oriented Policing, 2005; www.popcenter.org/learning/60steps/). This guide assumes some knowledge of crime mapping and some experience in doing crime analysis. But it is still a source of countless (well, maybe just 60) tips about doing applied research in crime prevention.

Eck, John E., *Assessing Responses to Problems: An Introductory Guide for Police Problem-Solvers* (Washington, DC: U.S. Department of Justice, Office of Community Oriented Policing Services, 2003;

www.popcenter.org/tools/assessing_responses/). This highly recommended guide was written to accompany a series of problem-solving guides that aid police in addressing a wide range of problems. Eck summarizes key elements of user-oriented evaluation.

Pawson, Ray, and Nick Tilley, *Realistic Evaluation* (Thousand Oaks, CA: Sage, 1997). The authors describe scientific realism and apply it to the evaluation of crime prevention and other criminal justice policy. This book also presents an interesting critique on the inappropriate use of experimental and quasi-experimental designs in criminal justice evaluation.

Rossi, Peter H., Howard E. Freeman, and Mark W. Lipsey, *Evaluation: A Systematic Approach,* 6th ed.

(Thousand Oaks, CA: Sage, 1999). Of the many available "handbooks" on evaluation methods, this is the most widely read. Although the book is uneven in its coverage of recent developments, the authors provide a good general foundation in evaluation methods.

Tilley, Nick (ed.), *Analysis for Crime Prevention: Crime Prevention Studies,* vol. 13 (Monsey, NY: Criminal Justice Press, 2002); *Evaluation for Crime Prevention: Crime Prevention Studies,* vol. 14 (Monsey, NY: Criminal Justice Press, 2002). These companion volumes present innovative thinking about how problem analysis and program evaluation can be used by public officials in preventing crime. Some of the articles will be controversial. All are interesting and mostly fun to read.

# CHAPTER 11

# Interpreting Data

*We'll examine a few simple statistics frequently used in criminal justice research. We'll also cover the fundamental logic of multivariate analysis. You'll come away from this chapter able to perform simple, though powerful, analyses to describe data and reach research conclusions.*

## INTRODUCTION

*Empirical research usually uses some type of statistical analysis.*

Many people are intimidated by empirical research because they feel uncomfortable with mathematics and statistics. And, indeed, many research reports are filled with otherwise unspecified computations. The role of statistics in criminal justice research is very important, but it is equally important for that role to be seen in its proper perspective.

Empirical research is, first and foremost, a logical rather than a mathematical operation. Mathematics is not much more than a convenient and efficient language for accomplishing the logical operations inherent in good data analysis. Statistics is the applied branch of mathematics especially appropriate to a variety of research analyses.

We'll be looking at two types of statistics: descriptive and inferential. **Descriptive statistics** are used to summarize and otherwise describe data in manageable forms. **Inferential statistics** help researchers form conclusions from their observations; typically that involves forming conclusions about a population from the study of a sample drawn from it.

Before considering any numbers, we want to assure you that the level of statistics used in this chapter has been proven safe for humans. The underlying logic and fundamental techniques of statistics are not at all complicated. It's mostly counting and comparing.

We assume that you are taking a course in research methods for criminology and criminal justice because you are interested in the subjects of crime and criminal justice policy. We suggest that you approach this chapter by thinking about statistics as tools for describing and explaining crime and criminal justice policy. Learning how to use these tools will help you better understand this fascinating subject. And learning how to summarize and interpret data about a subject you find inherently interesting is the least painful and most rewarding way to become acquainted with statistics.

## UNIVARIATE DESCRIPTION

*The simplest statistics describe some type of average and dispersion for a single variable.*

Descriptive statistics represent a method for presenting quantitative descriptions in a manageable form. Sometimes we want to describe single variables; this procedure is known as **univariate analysis**. Other times we want to describe the associations that connect one variable with another. **Bivariate analysis** refers to descriptions of two variables, and **multivariate analysis** examines relationships among three or more variables.

Univariate analysis examines the distribution of cases on only one variable at a time. We'll begin with the logic and formats for the analysis of univariate data.

## Distributions

The most basic way to present univariate data is to report all individual cases—that is, to list the attribute for each case under study in terms of the variable in question. Suppose we are interested in the ages of criminal court judges; our data might come from a directory of judges prepared by a state bar association. The most direct manner of reporting the ages of judges is to simply list them: 63, 57, 49, 62, 80, 72, 55, and so forth. Such a report will provide readers with complete details of the data, but it is too cumbersome for most purposes. We could arrange our data in a somewhat more manageable form without losing any of the detail by reporting that 5 judges are 38 years old, 7 are 39, 18 are 40, and so forth. Such a format avoids duplicating data on this variable.

For an even more manageable format—with a certain loss of detail—we might report judges' ages as marginals, which are **frequency distributions** of grouped data: 24 judges under 45 years of age, 51 between 45 and 50 years of age, and so forth. Our readers will have less data to examine and interpret, but they will not be able to reproduce fully the original ages of all the judges. Thus, for example, readers will have no way of knowing how many judges are 41 years old.

The preceding example presented marginals in the form of raw numbers. An alternative form is the use of percentages. We might report that $x$ percent of the judges are younger than 45, $y$ percent are between 45 and 50, and so forth. Table 11.1 shows an example.

In computing percentages, it is necessary to determine the base from which to compute—the number that represents 100 percent. In the most straightforward situation, the base is the total number of cases under study. A problem arises, however, whenever some cases have missing data. Let's consider a survey in which respondents are asked to report their ages. If some respondents fail to answer that question, we have two alternatives. First, we might still base our percentages on the total number of respondents, reporting those who

**TABLE 11.1** Ages of Criminal Court Judges (Hypothetical)

| Age | Percent |
|---|---|
| Under 35 | 9% |
| 36–45 | 21 |
| 46–55 | 45 |
| 56–65 | 19 |
| 65 and older | 6 |
| Total | 100% = 433 |
| No data | 18 |

fail to give their ages as a percentage of the total. Second, we might use the number of persons who give an answer as the base from which to compute the percentages; this approach is illustrated in Table 11.1. We will still report the number who do not answer, but they will not figure in the percentages.

The choice of a base depends entirely on the purposes of the analysis. If we wish to compare the age distribution of a survey sample with comparable data on the population from which the sample was drawn, we will probably want to omit the "no answers" from the computation. Our best estimate of the age distribution of all respondents is the distribution for those who answered the question. Because "no answer" is not a meaningful age category, its presence among the base categories will only confuse the comparison of sample and population figures.

## Measures of Central Tendency

Beyond simply reporting marginals, researchers often present data in the form of summary **averages**, or measures of **central tendency**. Options in this regard include the **mode** (the most frequent attribute, either grouped or ungrouped), the arithmetic **mean** (the sum of values for all observations, divided by the number of observations), and the **median** (the middle attribute in the ranked distribution of observed attributes). Here's how the three averages are calculated from a set of data.

Suppose we are conducting an experiment that involves teenagers as subjects. They range in age from 13 to 19, as indicated in this frequency distribution:

| Age | Number |
|---|---|
| 13 | 3 |
| 14 | 4 |
| 15 | 6 |
| 16 | 8 |
| 17 | 4 |
| 18 | 3 |
| 19 | 3 |

Now that we know the ages of the 31 subjects, how old are these subjects in general, or on average? Let's look at three different ways we might answer that question.

The easiest average to calculate is the mode, the most frequent value. The distribution of our 31 subjects shows there are more 16-year-olds (eight of them) than any other age, so the modal age is 16, as indicated in Figure 11.1.

Figure 11.1 also demonstrates the calculation of the mean. There are three steps: (1) multiply each age by the number of subjects who are that age, (2) total the results of all those multiplications, and (3) divide that total by the number of subjects. As indicated in Figure 11.1, the mean age in this illustration is 15.87.

The median represents the middle value; half are above it and half below. If we had the precise age of each subject (for instance, 17 years and 124 days), we could arrange all 31 subjects in order by age, and the median for the whole group would be the age of the middle subject.

We do not, however, know precise ages; our data constitute grouped data in this regard. Three people who are not precisely the same age have been grouped in the category "13 years old," for example.

Figure 11.1 illustrates the logic of calculating a median for grouped data. Because there are 31 subjects altogether, the middle subject is number 16

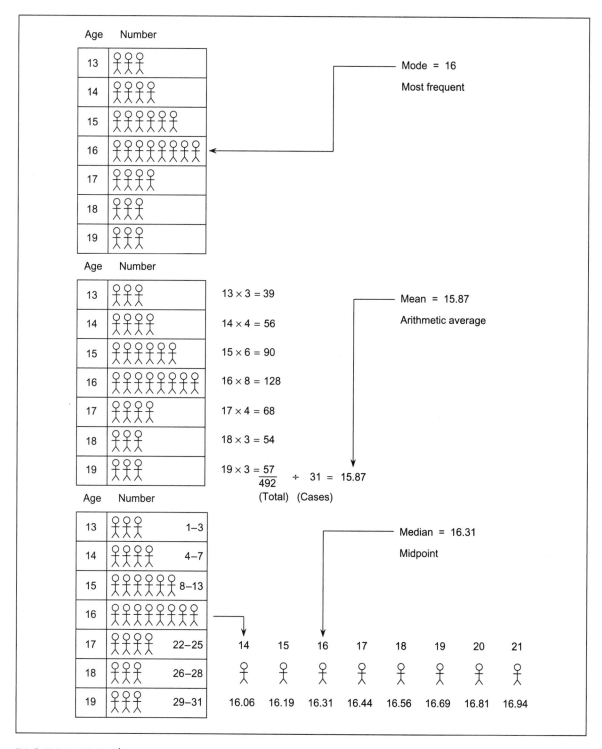

**FIGURE 11.1**   Three "Averages"

when they are arranged by age—15 are younger and 17 are older. The bottom portion of Figure 11.1 shows that the middle person is one of the eight 16-year-olds. In the enlarged view of that group, we see that number 16 is the third from the left.

## Measures of Dispersion

In the research literature, we find both means and medians presented. Whenever means are presented, we must be aware that they are susceptible to extreme values: a few very large or very small numbers can change the mean dramatically. Because of this, it is usually important to examine measures of **dispersion** about the mean.

The simplest measure of dispersion is the **range**: the distance separating the highest from the lowest value. Thus, besides reporting that our subjects have a mean age of 15.87, we might also indicate that their ages range from 13 to 19. A somewhat more sophisticated measure of dispersion is the **standard deviation**, which can be described as the average amount of variation about the mean. If the mean is the average value of all observations in a group, then the standard deviation represents the average amount each individual observation varies from the mean. Table 11.2 presents some hypothetical data on the ages of persons in juvenile and adult court that will help illustrate the concepts of deviation and average deviation. Let's first consider the top of Table 11.2.

The first column shows the age for each of 10 juvenile court defendants. The mean age for these 10 juveniles is 14. The second column shows how much each individual's age deviates from the mean. Thus the first juvenile is two years younger than the mean, the second is one year older, and the third is the same age as the mean.

You might first think that the average deviation is calculated in the same way as the mean—add up all individual deviations for each case and divide by the number of cases. We did that in Table 11.2, but notice that the total deviation is zero; therefore the average deviation is zero. In fact, the sum of deviations from the mean will always be zero. This is because some individual deviations will be negative

and some will be positive—and the positive and negative values will always cancel each other out.

Largely for this reason, the standard deviation measure of dispersion is based on the squared deviations from the mean. Squaring any number always produces a positive value, so when we add all the squared deviations together, we will not get zero for the total. Summing these squared deviations in the top of Table 11.2 produces a total of 20, and dividing by the number of observations produces an average deviation of 2. This quantity—the sum of squared deviations from the mean divided by the number of cases—is called the *variance*. Taking the square root of the variance produces the standard deviation, which is 1.41 for juveniles in Table 11.2.

How should we interpret a standard deviation of 1.41, or any other such value, for that matter? By itself, any particular value for the standard deviation has no intuitive meaning. This measure of dispersion is most useful in a comparative sense. Comparing the relative values for the standard deviation and the mean indicates how much variation there is in a group of cases, relative to the average. Similarly, comparing standard deviations for different groups of cases indicates relative amounts of dispersion within each group.

In our example of juvenile court cases, the standard deviation of 1.41 is rather low relative to the mean of 14. Now compare the data for juvenile court with the bottom half of Table 11.2, which presents ages for a hypothetical group of adult court defendants. The mean is higher, of course, because adults are older than juveniles. More important for illustrating the standard deviation, there is greater variation in the distribution of adult court defendants, as illustrated by the standard deviation and the columns that show raw deviations and squared deviations from the mean of 28. The standard deviation for adult cases (10.61) is much higher relative to the mean of 28 than are the relative values of the standard deviation and mean for juvenile cases. In this hypothetical example, the substantive reason for this is obvious: there is much greater age variation in adult court than in juvenile court because the range for ages of adults is potentially greater (18 to whatever) than the

**TABLE 11.2**    Standard Deviation for Two Hypothetical Distributions

| | Juvenile Court | | |
|---|---|---|---|
| | **Age** | **Deviation from Mean** | **Squared Deviation from Mean** |
| | 12 | −2 | 4 |
| | 15 | 1 | 1 |
| | 14 | 0 | 0 |
| | 13 | −1 | 1 |
| | 15 | 1 | 1 |
| | 14 | 0 | 0 |
| | 16 | 2 | 4 |
| | 16 | 2 | 4 |
| | 12 | −2 | 4 |
| | 13 | −1 | 1 |
| Sum | 140 | 0 | 20 |
| Average | 14 | (0) | (2) |
| Standard deviation | | | 1.41 |

| | Adult Court | | |
|---|---|---|---|
| | **Age** | **Deviation from Mean** | **Squared Deviation from Mean** |
| | 18 | −10 | 100 |
| | 37 | 9 | 81 |
| | 23 | −5 | 25 |
| | 22 | −6 | 36 |
| | 25 | −3 | 9 |
| | 43 | −15 | 225 |
| | 19 | −9 | 81 |
| | 50 | 22 | 484 |
| | 21 | −7 | 49 |
| | 22 | −6 | 36 |
| Sum | 280 | 0 | 1,126 |
| Average | 28 | (0) | (112.6) |
| Standard deviation | | | 10.61 |

range for ages in juveniles (1 to 17). As a result, the standard deviation for adult defendants indicates greater variation than the same measure for juvenile defendants.

In addition to providing a summary measure of dispersion, the standard deviation plays a role in the calculation of other descriptive statistics, some of which we will touch on later in this chapter. The standard deviation is also a central component of many inferential statistics used to make generalizations from a sample of observations to the population from which the sample was drawn.

## Comparing Measures of Dispersion and Central Tendency

Other measures of dispersion can help us interpret measures of central tendency. One useful indicator that expresses both dispersion and grouping of cases is the percentile, which indicates what percentage of cases fall at or below some value. For example, scores on achievement tests such as the SAT are usually reported in both percentiles and raw scores.

Thus a raw score of 630 might fall in the 80th percentile, indicating that 80 percent of persons who take the SAT achieve scores of 630 or less; alternatively, the 80th percentile means that 20 percent of scores were higher than 630. Percentiles may also be grouped into quartiles, which give the cases that fall in the first (lowest), second, third, and fourth (highest) quarters of a distribution.

Table 11.3 presents a distribution of prior arrests for a hypothetical population of, say, probationers to illustrate different measures of central tendency and dispersion. Notice that, although the number of prior arrests ranges from 0 to 55, cases cluster in the lower end of this distribution. Half the cases have 4 or fewer prior arrests, as

**T A B L E  11.3**    Hypothetical Data on Distribution of Prior Arrests

| Number of Prior Arrests | Number of Cases | Percentage of Cases | Percentile/ Quartile |
|---|---|---|---|
| 0 | 1 | 0.56% | |
| 1 | 16 | 8.89 | |
| 2 | 31 | 17.22 | 25th/1st |
| 3 | 23 | 12.78 | |
| 4 | 20 | 11.11 | 50th/2nd |
| 5 | 16 | 8.89 | |
| 6 | 19 | 10.56 | |
| 7 | 18 | 10.00 | 75th/3rd |
| 8 | 11 | 6.11 | |
| 9 | 14 | 7.78 | |
| 10 | 5 | 2.78 | |
| 30 | 3 | 1.67 | |
| 40 | 2 | 1.11 | |
| 55 | 1 | 0.56 | |
| Total | 180 | 100.00% | |
| Mode | 2 | | |
| Median | 4 | | |
| Mean | 5.76 | | |
| Range | 0–55 | | |
| Standard deviation | 6.64 | | |

indicated by three descriptive statistics in Table 11.3: median, 50th percentile, and second quartile. Only one-fourth of the cases have 8 or more prior arrests.

Notice also the different values for our three measures of central tendency. The mode for prior arrests is 2, and the mean or average number is 5.76. Whenever the mean is much higher than the mode, it indicates that the mean is distorted by a small number of persons with many prior arrests. The standard deviation of 6.64 further indicates that our small population has quite a bit of variability. Figure 11.2 presents a graphic representation of the dispersion of cases and the different values for the three measures of central tendency.

Distributions such as those shown in Table 11.3 and Figure 11.2 are known as *skewed distributions*.

Although most cases cluster near the low end, a few are spread out over very high values for prior arrests. Many variables of interest to criminal justice researchers are skewed in similar ways, especially when examined for a general population. Most people have no prior arrests, but a small number of persons have many. Similarly, most people suffer no victimization from serious crime in any given year, but a small number of persons are repeatedly victimized.

In an appropriately titled article, "Deviating from the Mean," Michael Maltz (1994) cautions that criminologists, failing to recognize high levels of variation, sometimes report means for populations that exhibit a great deal of skewness. When reading reports of criminal justice research, researchers are advised to look closely at measures of

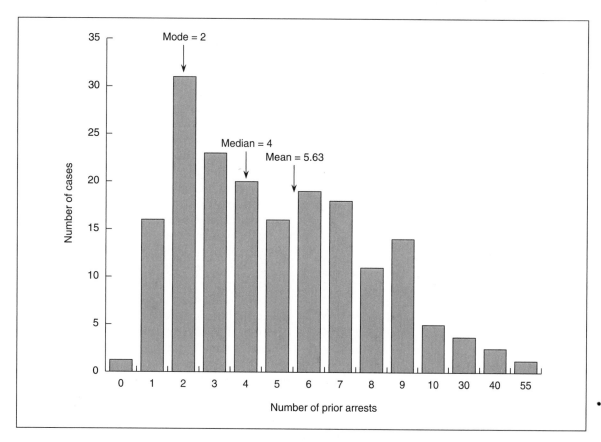

**FIGURE 11.2** Graphic Representation of a Distribution of Prior Arrests (Hypothetical Data)

both dispersion and central tendency. When the numerical value of the standard deviation is high and that for the mean is low, the mean is not a good measure of central tendency.

The preceding calculations are not appropriate for all variables. To understand this, we must examine two types of variables: continuous and discrete. Age and number of prior arrests are continuous ratio variables; they increase steadily in tiny fractions instead of jumping from category to category as does a discrete variable such as gender or marital status. If discrete variables are being analyzed—a nominal or ordinal variable, for example—then some of the techniques discussed previously are not applicable.

Strictly speaking, medians and means should be calculated for only interval and ratio data, respectively. If the variable in question is gender, for instance, raw numbers or percentage marginals are appropriate and useful measures. Calculating the mode is a legitimate tool of analysis, but reports of mean, median, or dispersion summaries would be inappropriate.

## Computing Rates

Rates are fundamental descriptive statistics in criminal justice research. In most cases, rates are used to standardize some measure for comparative purposes. For example, the following table shows Uniform Crime Report (UCR) figures on total murders for 2008 in four states.

**Total Murders in Four States, 2008**

|  | Total Murders | Population |
|---|---|---|
| California | 2,142 | 36,758,000 |
| Louisiana | 527 | 4,411,000 |
| Missouri | 455 | 5,912,000 |
| New York | 836 | 19,490,000 |

Source: Federal Bureau of Investigation 2009.

Obviously, California had far more murders than the other three states, but these figures are difficult to interpret because of large differences in the states' total populations. Computing rates enables us

to standardize by population size and make more meaningful comparisons, as the next table shows.

**Murder Rates per 100,000 Population, 2008**

| California | 5.8 |
|---|---|
| Louisiana | 11.9 |
| Missouri | 7.7 |
| New York | 4.3 |

We can see that Louisiana, even with the second fewest murders in 2008 (among the states reported here), had the highest murder rate. California and New York, although they had the largest number of murders, had the lowest rates among these four states. Notice also that the murder rate is expressed as the number of murders per 100,000 population. This is a common convention in reporting rates of crime and other rare events. To get the rate of murder *per person*, move the decimal point five places to the left in each of the figures in the second table. By doing that you can clearly see which version is easier to interpret.

The arithmetic of calculating rates could not be much easier. What is not so simple, and in any event requires careful consideration, is deciding on the two basic components of rates: numerator and denominator. The numerator represents the central concept we are interested in measuring, so selecting the numerator involves all the considerations of measurement we have discussed elsewhere. Murder rates, arrest rates, conviction rates, and incarceration rates are common examples in which the numerator is a relatively straightforward count.

Choosing the right denominator is important. In most cases, we should compute rates to standardize according to some population eligible to be included in the numerator. Sometimes, the choice is fairly obvious, as in our use of each state's total population to compute murder rates. To compute rates of rape or sexual assault, we should probably use the population of adult women in the denominator, although we should also consider how to handle rapes with male victims. Because households are at risk of residential burglary, burglary rates should be computed using some count of households. Similarly,

## IDENTITY THEFT

We have all heard about identity theft, often from media reports about how it is a growing problem. But how common is it? Or, for that matter, what is identity theft, and what forms does it take? The National Crime Victimization Survey (NCVS) added questions on identity theft in 2004. Here we report some basic descriptive statistics on results from the 2005 NCVS (Baum 2007).

The first table estimates the number of households that experienced different forms of identity theft in 2005. The survey counted victimization for three types of incidents:

- Unauthorized use or attempted use of existing credit cards

- Unauthorized use or attempted use of other existing accounts, such as checking or savings

- Misuse of personal identification to obtain new accounts or loans, or to commit other crimes

The last category is what many people think of when they hear the phrase "identity theft." The other two categories are more common, and might just as easily be labeled "credit card fraud" or "checking account fraud." By whatever name, about 5.5 percent of households experienced one or more of these three types.

| Total | Estimated Number of Households | Percent of Households |
|---|---|---|
| | 117,110,800 | 100.0% |
| ID theft | 6,426,200 | 5.5% |
| Credit card | 2,966,200 | 2.5 |
| Other accounts | 1,586,500 | 1.4 |
| Personal information | 1,083,100 | 0.9 |
| Multiple types | 790,200 | 0.7 |

Source: Baum 2007, 1.

As is the case for other types of crimes, some variation exists in victimization. The next table shows what percent of households were victimized, by age of household head and income. As with many other types of crime, younger people are at greater risk of identity theft. Victimization risk for those aged 65 or older is one-half or less that for other age groups.

Patterns for income are different from those for other offenses. With the exception of households earning less than $7,500 per year, victimization increases with income. Almost 10 percent of households in the highest income category reported identity theft in 2005.

| Age of household head | Percent of Households Victimized |
|---|---|
| 18–24 | 7.0% |
| 25–34 | 6.1 |
| 35–49 | 6.1 |
| 50–64 | 5.9 |
| 65 or older | 3.0 |
| **Household income** | |
| Less than $7,500 | 4.7% |
| $7,500–14,999 | 3.7 |
| $15,000–24,999 | 3.9 |
| $25,000–34,999 | 4.9 |
| $35,000–49,999 | 5.5 |
| $50,000–74,999 | 6.8 |
| $75,000 or more | 9.6 |

Source: Baum 2007, 2–3.

These simple tables offer examples of univariate statistics (in the first table) and bivariate statistics. The univariate table shows the distribution of victimization across households in the United States. The bivariate table shows relationships between identity theft victimization and two other variables—age and income. Think about why these patterns exist: Unauthorized use of credit cards is much more common than other types of identity theft; victimization decreases with age, but increases with income.

If you wish to compute other statistics of your own, you can get copies of the tables Baum reports in spreadsheet form at this URL: http://bjs.ojp.usdoj.gov/index.cfm?ty=pbdetail&iid=971

---

commercial burglaries should be based on a count of commercial establishments, and auto theft on an indicator of registered autos.

More difficult problems can arise in computing rates to express a characteristic of a mobile popula-tion. For example, residents of Miami are at risk of criminal victimization in that city, but so are tourists and other visitors. Because many nonresidents visit or pass through the city in any given year, a measure of Miami's crime rate based on only the city's resident population (such as the U.S. Census) will tend to overestimate the number of crimes standardized by the population at risk; many people at risk will not be counted in the denominator. Or what about estimating the crime rate on a subway system? The population at risk here is users, who, in New York City, amount to millions of persons per day.

Rates are very useful descriptive statistics that may be easily computed. It is important, however, to be careful in selecting numerators and denominators. Recognize that this caution applies as much to questions of making measurements as it does to questions of computing descriptive statistics. The box titled "Murder on the Job," presented later in this chapter, gives an example of confusion about the meaning of rates.

The "Identity Theft" box offers an example of victimization rates for identity theft, showing what percentage of households were victimized, together with selected characteristics of victims. Notice how expressing characteristics of incidents and victims as percentages—rate per 100—helps us to understand the problem in ways that simple counts would not. This example also leads us into a more extended consideration of using percentages in univariate and bivariate analysis.

## DESCRIBING TWO OR MORE VARIABLES

*Descriptive statistics applied to two or more variables are tools to understand relationships among those variables.*

Univariate analyses describe the units of analysis of a study and, if they are a sample drawn from some larger population, allow us to make descriptive inferences about the larger population. Bivariate and multivariate analyses are aimed primarily at explanation.

Often it's appropriate to describe subsets of cases, subjects, or respondents. Table 11.4, for example, presents hypothetical data on sentence length for offenders grouped by prior felony record. In some situations, the researcher presents subgroup comparisons purely for descriptive purposes. More often, the purpose of subgroup descriptions is

comparative. In this case, comparing sentences for subgroups of convicted offenders implies some causal connection between prior felony record and sentence length. Similarly, if we compare sentence lengths for men and women, it implies that something about gender has a causal effect on sentence length.

### Bivariate Analysis

In contrast to univariate analysis, subgroup comparisons constitute a kind of bivariate analysis in that two variables are involved. In such situations, we are usually interested in relationships among the variables. Thus univariate analysis and subgroup comparisons focus on describing the people (or other units of analysis) under study, whereas bivariate analysis focuses more on the variables themselves.

Notice, then, that Table 11.5 can be regarded as a subgroup comparison: it independently describes gun ownership among male and female respondents in the 2000 General Social Survey. It shows—comparatively and descriptively—that fewer females than males report owning a gun.

**TABLE 11.4** Hypothetical Illustration of Subgroup Comparisons: Length of Prison Sentence by Felony Criminal History

| Felony Criminal History | Median Sentence Length |
|---|---|
| No arrests or convictions | 6 months |
| Prior arrests only | 11 months |
| Prior convictions | 23 months |

**TABLE 11.5** Gun Ownership Among Male and Female Respondents, 2000

| | Male | Female |
|---|---|---|
| **Own a Gun?** | | |
| Yes | 42% | 25% |
| No | 58 | 75 |
| 100% = | (817) | (1,040) |

*Source: 2000 General Social Survey (available at http://sda.berkeley.edu/archive.htm.*

The same table viewed as an explanatory bivariate analysis tells a somewhat different story. It suggests that the variable *gender* has an effect on the variable *gun ownership*. The behavior is seen as a dependent variable that is partially determined by the independent variable, gender. Explanatory bivariate analyses, then, involve the variable language we introduced in Chapter 1. In a subtle shift of focus, we are no longer talking about male and female as different subgroups but about gender as a variable—a variable that has an influence on other variables.

The logic of causal relationships among variables has an important implication for the construction and reading of percentage tables. Novice data analysts often have difficulty in deciding on the appropriate direction of "percentaging" for any given table. In Table 11.5, for example, we divided the group of subjects into two subgroups—male and female—and then described the behavior of each subgroup. That is the correct way to construct this table.

Notice, however, that it would have been possible, though inappropriate, to construct the table differently. We could have first divided the subjects into different categories of gun ownership and then described each of those subgroups by the percentage of male and female subjects in each. This method would make no sense in terms of explanation, however; owning a gun does not make someone male or female.

Table 11.5 suggests that gender affects gun ownership. Had we used the other method of construction, the table would have suggested that gun ownership affects whether someone is male or female—which is nonsense.

Another, related problem complicates the lives of novice data analysts: how do you read a percentage table? There is a temptation to read Table 11.5 as "Among females, only 25 percent owned a gun, and 75 percent did not; therefore, being female makes you less likely to own a gun." That is not the correct way to read the table, however. The conclusion that gender—as a variable—has an effect on gun ownership must hinge on a comparison between males and females. Specifically, we compare the 25 percent of females with the 42 percent of males and note that women are less likely than men to own a gun. The appropriate comparison of subgroups, then, is essential in reading an explanatory bivariate table.

**Percentaging a Table** In constructing and presenting Table 11.5, we have used a convention called *percentage down*. This means that we can add the percentages down each column to total 100 percent. We read this form of table across a row. For the row labeled "Yes," what percentage of the males own a gun? What percentage of the females?

The percentage-down convention is just that—a conventional practice; some researchers prefer to percentage across. They would organize Table 11.5 with "Male" and "Female" on the left side of the table, identifying the two rows, and "Yes" and "No" at the top, identifying the columns. The actual numbers in the table would be moved around accordingly, and each row of percentages would total 100 percent. In that case, we would make our comparisons between males and females by reading down, within table columns, still asking what percentage of males and females owned guns. The logic and the conclusion would be the same in either case; only the form would be different.

In reading a table that someone else has constructed, it's therefore necessary to find out in which direction it has been percentaged. Usually that will be apparent from the labeling of the table or the logic of the variables being analyzed. Sometimes, however, tables are not clearly labeled. In such cases, the reader should add the percentages in each column and each row. If each of the columns totals 100 percent, the table has been percentaged down. If the rows total 100 percent each, the table has been percentaged across. Follow these rules of thumb:

- If the table is percentaged down, read across.
- If the table is percentaged across, read down.

Here's another example: Suppose we are interested in investigating newspaper editorial policies regarding the legalization of marijuana. We undertake a content analysis of editorials on this subject that have appeared during a given year in a sample of daily newspapers across the nation. Each editorial has been classified as favorable, neutral, or unfavorable with regard to the legalization of marijuana. Perhaps we wish to examine the relationship between editorial policies and the types of communities in which the newspapers are published, thinking that rural newspapers might be more conservative than urban ones. Thus each newspaper (and so, each editorial) is classified in terms of the population of the community in which it is published.

Table 11.6 presents some hypothetical data describing the editorial policies of rural and urban newspapers. Note that the unit of analysis in this example is the individual editorial. Table 11.6 tells us that there were 127 editorials about marijuana in our sample of newspapers published in communities with populations less than 100,000. (Note: This choice of 100,000 is for simplicity of illustration and does not mean that rural refers to a community of less than 100,000 in any absolute sense.) Of these, 11 percent (14 editorials) were favorable toward the legalization of marijuana, 29 percent were neutral, and 60 percent were unfavorable. Of the 438 editorials that appeared in our sample of newspapers published in communities with more than 100,000 residents, 32 percent (140 editorials) were favorable toward legalizing marijuana, 40 percent were neutral, and 28 percent were unfavorable.

When we compare the editorial policies of rural and urban newspapers in our imaginary study, we find—as expected—that rural newspapers are less favorable toward the legalization of marijuana than are urban newspapers. That is determined by noting that a larger percentage (32 percent) of the urban editorials than the rural ones (11 percent) were favorable. We might note, as well, that more rural than urban editorials were unfavorable (60 percent versus 28 percent). Note, too, that this table assumes that the size of a community might affect its newspaper's editorial policies on this issue, rather than that editorial policy might affect the size of communities.

**Constructing and Reading Tables**   Before introducing multivariate analysis, let's review the steps involved in the construction of explanatory bivariate tables:

1. Divide the cases into groups according to attributes of the independent variable.

2. Describe each of these subgroups in terms of attributes of the dependent variable.

3. Read the table by comparing the independent variable subgroups with one another in terms of a given attribute of the dependent variable.

In the example of editorial policies regarding the legalization of marijuana, the size of a community is the independent variable, and a newspaper's editorial policy is the dependent variable. The table is constructed as follows:

1. Divide the editorials into subgroups according to the sizes of the communities in which the newspapers are published.

2. Describe each subgroup of editorials in terms of the percentages favorable, neutral, or unfavorable toward the legalization of marijuana.

3. Compare the two subgroups in terms of the percentages favorable toward the legalization of marijuana.

**Bivariate Table Formats**   Tables such as those we've been examining are commonly called **contingency tables**: values of the dependent variable are contingent on values of the independent variable. Although contingency tables are commonly used

**T A B L E   11.6**   Newspaper Editorials on the Legalization of Marijuana

| Editorial Policy Toward Legalizing Marijuana | Community Size | |
|---|---|---|
| | Under 100,000 | Over 100,000 |
| Favorable | 11% | 32% |
| Neutral | 29 | 40 |
| Unfavorable | 60 | 28 |
| 100% = | (127) | (438) |

in criminal justice research, their format has never been standardized. As a result, a variety of formats will be found in the research literature. As long as a table is easy to read and interpret, there is probably no reason to strive for standardization; however, the following guidelines should be followed in the presentation of most tabular data:

1.  Provide a heading or a title that succinctly describes what is contained in the table.

2.  Present the original content of the variables clearly—in the table itself if at all possible or in the text with a paraphrase in the table. This information is especially critical when a variable is derived from responses to an attitudinal question because the meaning of the responses will depend largely on the wording of the question.

3.  Clearly indicate the attributes of each variable. Complex categories need to be abbreviated, but the meaning should be clear in the table, and of course, the full description should be reported in the text.

4.  When percentages are reported in the table, identify the base on which they are computed. It is redundant to present all the raw numbers for each category, because these could be reconstructed from the percentages and the bases. Moreover, the presentation of both numbers and percentages often makes a table more difficult to read.

5.  If any cases are omitted from the table because of missing data ("no answer," for example), indicate their numbers in the table.

By following these guidelines and thinking carefully about the kinds of causal and descriptive relationships they want to examine, researchers address many policy and research questions in criminal justice. We want to emphasize, however, the importance of thinking through the logic of contingency tables. Descriptive statistics—contingency tables, measures of central tendency, or rates—are sometimes misrepresented or misinterpreted. See the box titled "Murder on the Job" for an example of this.

## Multivariate Analysis

A great deal of criminal justice research uses multivariate techniques to examine relationships among several variables. Like much statistical analysis, the logic of multivariate analysis is straightforward, but the actual use of many multivariate statistical techniques can be complex. A full understanding requires a solid background in statistics and is beyond the scope of this book. In this section, we briefly discuss the construction of multivariate tables—those constructed from three or more variables—and the comparison of multiple subgroups.

Multivariate tables can be constructed by following essentially the same steps outlined previously for bivariate tables. Instead of one independent variable and one dependent variable, however, we will have more than one independent variable. And instead of explaining the dependent variable on the basis of a single independent variable, we'll seek an explanation through the use of more than one independent variable. Let's consider an example from research on victimization.

**Multivariate Tables: Lifestyle and Street Crime** If we consult any source of published statistics on victimization (see Chapter 9), we will find several tables that document a relationship between age and personal crime victimization—younger people are more often victims of assault and robbery, for example. A classic book by Michael Hindelang and associates (Hindelang, Gottfredson, and Garofalo 1978) suggested a lifestyle explanation for this relationship. The lifestyle of many younger people—visiting bars and clubs for evening entertainment, for example—exposes them to street crime and potential predators more than does the less active lifestyle of older people. This is certainly a sensible hypothesis, and Hindelang and associates found general support for the lifestyle explanation in their analysis of data from early versions of the National Crime Victimization Survey (NCVS). But the U.S. crime survey data did not include direct measures of lifestyle concepts.

Questionnaire items in the British Crime Survey (BCS) provided better measures of individual behaviors. Using these data, Ronald Clarke and

**MURDER ON THE JOB**

"High Murder Rate for Women on the Job," read the headline for a brief story in the *New York Times*, reporting on a study released by the U.S. Department of Labor. The subhead was equally alarming, and misleading, to casual readers: "40 percent of women killed at work are murdered, but the figure for men is only 15 percent." Think about this statement, in light of our discussion of how to percentage a table. You should be able to imagine something like the following:

**Cause of Death at Work**

|        | Women | Men  |
|--------|-------|------|
| Murder | 40%   | 15%  |
| Other  | 60    | 85   |
| Total  | 100%  | 100% |

This table indicates that of those women who die while at work, 40 percent are murdered, and the table is consistent with the opening paragraphs of the story. Notice that so far nothing has been said about how many women and men are murdered, or how many women and men die on the job from all causes. Later on, the story provides more details:

> Vehicle accidents caused the most jobrelated deaths, 18 percent or 1,121 of the 6,083 work-related deaths in 1992.... Homicides, including shootings and stabbings, were a close second with 17 percent, or 1,004 deaths, said the study by the department's Bureau of Labor Statistics.

This information enables us to supplement the table by adding row totals: 6,083 people died on the job in 1992, 1,004 of them were murdered, and 5,079 (6,083 − 1,004) died from other causes.

One more piece of information is needed to construct a contingency table: the total number of men and women killed on the job. The story does not tell us that directly, but it provides enough information to approximate the answer: "Although men are 55 percent of the workforce, they comprise 93 percent of all job-related deaths." Men must therefore be 93 percent of the 6,083 total workplace deaths, or approximately 5,657; this leaves approximately 426 deaths of women on the job. "Approximately" is an important qualifier here, because computing numbers of cases from percentages creates some inconsistencies due to rounding off percentages reported in the newspaper story. Let's now construct a contingency table to look at the numbers of workplace deaths. The next table shows computed numbers in parentheses. Notice that with the exception of "Total" all numbers have been estimated from the newspaper story's percentages for men and women.

**Cause of Death at Work**

|        | Women (est.) | Men (est.) | Total | Total (est.) |
|--------|--------------|------------|-------|--------------|
| Murder | (170)        | (849)      | 1,004 | (1,019)      |
| Other  | (256)        | (4,808)    | 5,079 | (5,064)      |
| Total  | (426)        | (5,657)    | 6,083 |              |

The results are interesting. Although a greater *percentage* of women than men are murdered, a much larger *number* of men than women are murdered.

Now, recall the story's headline, "High Murder *Rate*." This implies that the *number* of women murdered on the job, divided by the total number of women at risk of murder on the job, is higher than the same computed rate for men. We need more information than the story provides to verify this claim, but there is a clue. Women are about 45 percent of the workforce, so there are about 1.2 men in the workforce for every woman (55 percent ÷ 45 percent). But about five times as many men as women are murdered on the job (849 ÷ 170).

This should tip you off that the headline is misleading. If the ratio of male-to-female murders is 5 to 1, but the ratio of male-to-female workers is 1.2 to 1, how could the murder rate for women be higher? You could compute actual rates of murder on the job by finding a suitable denominator; in this case, the number of men and women in the workforce would be appropriate. Consulting the Census Bureau publication *Statistical Abstract of the United States* would provide this information and enable you to compute rates, as in our final table:

|                                      | Women  | Men    |
|--------------------------------------|--------|--------|
| Civilian workforce (1,000s)          | 53,284 | 63,593 |
| Murdered at work                     | 170    | 849    |
| On-the-job murder rate per 100,000 workers | 0.319  | 1.335  |

So the *New York Times* got it wrong; there is a higher murder rate for men on the job. Women are less often killed on the job by any cause, including murder. But women who die on the job (in much smaller numbers than men) are more likely to die from murder than are men who die on the job. A murder rate expresses the number of people murdered divided by the population at risk.

Rates are often computed with inappropriate denominators. But it is less common to find the term *rate* used so inaccurately.

*Source:* "High Murder Rate for Women on the Job" (1993); U.S. Bureau of the Census (1992).

associates (Clarke et al. 1985) examined the link between exposure to risk and victimization, while holding age and gender constant. Specifically, Clarke and colleagues hypothesized that older persons are less often victims of street crime because they spend less time on the streets. The 1982 BCS asked respondents whether they had left their homes in the previous week (that is, the week before they were interviewed) for any evening leisure or social activities. Those who responded "yes" were asked which nights they had gone out and what they had done.

Hypothesizing that some types of evening activities are more risky than others, Clarke and associates restricted their analysis to leisure pursuits away from respondents' homes, such as visiting a pub, nightclub, or theater. Their dependent variable—street crime victimization—was also carefully defined to include only crimes against persons (actual and attempted assault, robbery, rape, and theft) that occurred away from victims' homes or workplaces or the homes of friends. Furthermore, because the leisure behavior questions asked about evening activities, only street crime victimizations that took place between 6:00 p.m. and midnight were included.

Clarke and associates therefore proposed a very specific hypothesis that involves three carefully defined concepts and variables: older persons are less often victims of street crime because they less often engage in behavior that exposes them to risk of street crime. Tables 11.7A through 11.7C present cross-tabulations for the three possible bivariate relationships among these variables: evening street crime victimization by age and by evening leisure pursuits, and evening leisure pursuits by age.

The relationships illustrated in these tables are consistent with the lifestyle hypothesis of personal crime victimization. First, victimization was more common for younger people (ages 16 to 30) and for those who pursued leisure activities outside their home three or more evenings in the previous week (Tables 11.7A and 11.7B). Second, as shown in Tables 11.7C, the attributes of young age and frequent exposure to risk were positively related: about 41 percent of the youngest group had gone

**TABLE 11.7A**  Evening Street Crime Victimization by Age

| Street Crime Victim | 16–30 | 31–60 | 61+ |
|---|---|---|---|
| Yes | 4.8% | 1.0% | 0.3% |
| No | 95.2 | 99.0 | 99.7 |
| 100% = | (2,738) | (4,460) | (1,952) |

**TABLE 11.7B**  Evening Street Crime Victimization by Evenings Out During Previous Week

| Street Crime Victim | None | 1 or 2 | 3+ |
|---|---|---|---|
| Yes | 1.2% | 1.6% | 3.8% |
| No | 98.9 | 98.4 | 96.2 |
| 100% = | (3,252) | (3,695) | (2,203) |

**TABLE 11.7C**  Evenings Out During Previous Week by Age

| Evenings Out | 16–30 | 31–60 | 61+ |
|---|---|---|---|
| None | 20.6% | 35.2% | 57.2% |
| 1 or 2 | 38.6 | 44.9 | 32.5 |
| 3+ | 40.9 | 19.8 | 10.2 |
| 100% = | (2,738) | (4,460) | (1,952) |

**TABLE 11.7D**  Evening Street Crime Victimization by Age and Evenings Out

| Evenings Out | Percentage of Victims | | |
|---|---|---|---|
| | 16–30 | 31–60 | 61+ |
| None | 3.9 | 1.0 | 0.2 |
| | (563) | (1,572) | (1,117) |
| 1 or 2 | 3.8 | 0.9 | 0.2 |
| | (1,056) | (2,004) | (635) |
| 3+ | 6.2 | 1.4 | 1.1 |
| | (1,119) | (884) | (200) |
| Total N = | (2,738) | (4,460) | (1,952) |

*Note:* Percentages and numbers of cases computed from published tabulations.
*Source:* Adapted from Clarke, Ekblom, Hough, and Mayhew (1985, Tables 1, 2, and 3).

out three or more nights, compared with 20 percent of those ages 31 to 60 and only 10 percent of those over age 60.

However, because we are interested in the effects of two independent variables—lifestyle and age—on victimization, we must construct a table that includes all three variables.

Several of the tables we have presented in this chapter are somewhat inefficient. When the dependent variable—street crime victimization—is dichotomous (two attributes), knowing one attribute permits us to easily reconstruct the other. Thus if we know from Table 11.7A that 1 percent of respondents ages 31 to 60 were victims of street crime, then we know automatically that 99 percent were not victims. So reporting the percentages for both values of a dichotomy is unnecessary. On the basis of this recognition, Table 11.7D presents the relationship between victimization and two independent variables in a more efficient format.

In Table 11.7D, the percentages of respondents who reported a street crime victimization are shown in the cells at the intersections of the two independent variables. The numbers presented in parentheses below each percentage are the numbers of cases on which the percentages are based. Thus we know that 563 people ages 16 to 30 did not go out for evening leisure in the week before their interview and that 3.9 percent of them were victims of street crime in the previous year. We can calculate from this that 22 of those 563 people were victims and the other 541 people were not victims.

Let's now interpret the results presented in this table:

- Within each age group, persons who pursue outside evening leisure activities three or more times per week are more often victimized.

- There is not much difference between those who go out once or twice per week and those who stay home.

- Within each category for evening leisure activities, street crime victimization declines as age increases.

- Exposure to risk through evenings out is less strongly related to street crime victimization than is age.

- Age and exposure to risk have independent effects on street crime victimization. Within a given attribute of one independent variable, different attributes of the second are still related to victimization.

- Similarly, the two independent variables have a cumulative effect on victimization. Younger people who go out three or more times per week are most often victimized.

Returning to the lifestyle hypothesis, what can we conclude from Table 11.7D? First, this measure of exposure to risk is, in fact, related to street crime victimization. People who go out more frequently are more often exposed to risk and more often victims of street crime. As Clarke and associates point out, however, differences in exposure to risk do not account for lower rates of victimization among older persons: within categories of exposure to risk, victimization still declines with age. So lifestyle is related to victimization, but this measure of behavior—exposure to risk of street crime—does not account for all age-related differences in victimization. Furthermore, what we might call lifestyle intensity plays a role here. Going out once or twice a week does not have as much impact on victimization as going out more often. The most intensely active night people ages 30 or younger are most often victims of street crime.

Multivariate contingency tables are powerful tools for examining relationships between a dependent variable and multiple independent variables measured at the nominal or categorical level. Contingency tables can, however, become cumbersome and difficult to interpret if independent variables have several categories or if more than two independent variables are included. In practice, criminal justice researchers often employ more sophisticated techniques for multivariate analysis of discrete or nominal variables. Although the logic of such analysis is not especially difficult, most people learn these techniques in advanced courses in statistics.

## THEORY AND DATA ANALYSIS

Our final example of how theory permeates virtually all stages of the research process draws on economic theory that explains how prices and demand are related. The same sort of logic that links increases in the price of oil to higher demand for oil can help understand patterns of theft. Economist Gary Becker (1968) was among the first to apply economic principles to crime. Criminologists have begun to examine how criminals may similarly respond to changes in prices and markets.

Aiden Sidebottom and associates (Sidebottom et al. 2011) studied how increases in the price of copper on scrap metal markets was related to increases in theft of copper wiring from railway networks in England, Scotland, and Wales. They described scrap metals as examples of price-volatile markets, arguing that "theft levels are influenced by price shifts as the product of supply and demand dynamics" (2011, 17). Copper appeared especially vulnerable to theft because it is widely used in large quantities by electric-powered railways. The British railway network had suffered increasing thefts of copper, ranging from lengths of signal wire to coils stored in unguarded facilities throughout the system.

As an independent variable, the authors used average monthly market prices for copper on the London Metals Exchange. Their dependent variable was incidents of copper theft recorded by British Transport Police.

The researchers drew on another principle from economic theory in structuring their analysis by *lagging* the relationship between prices and thefts. It did not make sense to assume that copper theft would increase and decrease immediately with corresponding changes in prices. Instead, the researchers assumed that changes in prices would have a delayed, or lagged, effect on theft.

Sidebottom and associates conducted a multivariate analysis, comparing the effects of changes in copper prices to changes in two other independent variables: unemployment and other types of theft. They summarized their findings as follows:

A significant positive correlation was found between higher prices of copper and increases in copper cable theft.... [T]here was little or no relationship between the volume of copper cable theft and other thefts and with monthly variation in U.K. unemployment. (2011, 13)

The authors conclude by suggesting that other research should be conducted on links between theft and the prices of different commodities. Just as economics exerts powerful influences on the behavior of consumers, the value of different goods affects the behavior of thieves.

## INFERENTIAL STATISTICS

*When we generalize from samples to larger populations, we use inferential statistics to test the significance of an observed relationship.*

Many criminal justice research projects examine data collected from a sample drawn from a larger population. A sample of people may be interviewed in a survey; a sample of court records may be coded and analyzed; a sample of newspapers may be examined through content analysis. Researchers seldom, if ever, study samples merely to describe the samples per se; in most instances, their ultimate purpose is to make assertions about the larger population from which the sample has been selected. Frequently, then, we will want to interpret our univariate and multivariate sample findings as the basis for inferences about some population.

This section examines the statistical measures used for making such inferences and their logical bases. We'll begin with univariate data and then move to bivariate.

### Univariate Inferences

The opening sections of this chapter dealt with methods of presenting univariate data. Each summary measure was intended to describe the sample studied. Now we will use those measures to make broader assertions about the population. This section will focus on two univariate measures: percentages and means.

If 50 percent of a sample of people say they received traffic tickets during the past year, then 50 percent is also our best estimate of the proportion of people who received traffic tickets in the total population from which the sample was drawn.

Our estimate assumes a simple random sample, of course. It is rather unlikely, however, that precisely 50 percent of the population got tickets during the year. If a rigorous sampling design for random selection has been followed, we will be able to estimate the expected range of error when the sample finding is applied to the population.

The section in Chapter 6 on sampling theory covered the procedures for making such estimates, so they will be only reviewed here. The quantity

$$s = \sqrt{\frac{p \times q}{n}},$$

where $p$ is a percentage, $q$ equals $1-p$, and $n$ is the sample size, is called the *standard error*. As noted in Chapter 8, this quantity is very important in the estimation of sampling error. We may be 68 percent confident that the population figure falls within plus or minus 1 standard error of the sample figure, 95 percent confident that it falls within plus or minus 2 standard errors, and 99.9 percent confident that it falls within plus or minus 3 standard errors.

Any statement of sampling error, then, must contain two essential components: the confidence level (for example, 95 percent) and the confidence interval (for example, 2.5 percent). If 50 percent of a sample of 1,600 people say they have received traffic tickets during the year, we might say we are 95 percent confident that the population figure is between 47.5 and 52.5 percent.

Recognize in this example that we have moved beyond simply describing the sample into the realm of making estimates (inferences) about the larger population. In doing that, we must be wary of three assumptions.

First, the sample must be drawn from the population about which inferences are being made. A sample taken from a telephone directory cannot legitimately be the basis for statistical inferences about the population of a city.

Second, the inferential statistics assume simple random sampling, which is virtually never the case in actual sample surveys. The statistics assume sampling with replacement, which is almost never done, but that is probably not a serious problem. Although

systematic sampling is used more frequently than random sampling, that, too, probably presents no serious problem if done correctly. Stratified sampling, because it improves representativeness, clearly presents no problem. Cluster sampling does present a problem, however, because the estimates of sampling error may be too small. Clearly, street-corner sampling does not warrant the use of inferential statistics. This standard error sampling technique also assumes a 100 percent completion rate. This problem increases in seriousness as the completion rate decreases.

Third, inferential statistics apply to sampling error only; they do not take account of **nonsampling errors**. Thus, although we might correctly state that between 47.5 and 52.5 percent of the population (95 percent confidence) will report getting a traffic ticket during the previous year, we cannot so confidently guess the percentage that had actually received them. Because nonsampling errors are probably larger than sampling errors in a respectable sample design, we need to be especially cautious in generalizing from our sample findings to the population.

## Tests of Statistical Significance

There is no scientific answer to the question of whether a given association between two variables is significant, strong, important, interesting, or worth reporting. Perhaps the ultimate test of significance rests with our ability to persuade readers (present and future) of the association's significance. At the same time, a body of inferential statistics— known as parametric tests of significance—can assist in this regard. As the name suggests, *parametric statistics* make certain assumptions about the parameters that describe the population from which the sample is selected.

Although **tests of statistical significance** are widely reported in criminal justice literature, the logic underlying them is subtle and often misunderstood. A test of statistical significance is based on the same sampling logic that has been discussed elsewhere in this book. To understand that logic, let's return to the concept of sampling error with regard to univariate data.

Recall that a sample statistic normally provides the best single estimate of the corresponding population parameter, but the statistic and the parameter are seldom identical. Thus we report the probability that the parameter falls within a certain range (confidence interval). The degree of uncertainty within that range is due to normal sampling error. The corollary of such a statement is, of course, that it is improbable that the parameter will fall outside the specified range only as a result of sampling error. Thus, if we estimate that a parameter (99.9 percent confidence) lies between 45 and 55 percent, we say by implication that it is extremely improbable that the parameter is actually, say, 70 percent if our only error of estimation is due to normal sampling.

The fundamental logic of tests of statistical significance, then, is this: faced with any discrepancy between the assumed independence of variables in a population and the observed distribution of sample elements, we may explain that discrepancy in either of two ways. One, we attribute it to an unrepresentative sample, or two, we reject the assumption of independence. The logic and statistics associated with probability sampling methods offer guidance about the varying probabilities of different degrees of unrepresentativeness (expressed as sampling error). Most simply put, there is a high probability of a small degree of unrepresentativeness and a low probability of a large degree of unrepresentativeness.

The **statistical significance** of a relationship observed in a set of sample data, then, is always expressed in terms of probabilities. Significant at the 0.05 level ($p \leq 0.05$) simply means that the probability of a relationship as strong as the observed one being attributable to sampling error alone is no more than 5 in 100. Put somewhat differently, if two variables are independent of each other in the population, and if 100 probability samples were selected from that population, then no more than 5 of those samples should provide a relationship as strong as the one that has been observed.

There is a corollary to confidence intervals in tests of significance, which represents the probability of the measured associations being due to only sampling error. This is called the **level of significance**. Like confidence intervals, levels of

significance are derived from a logical model in which several samples are drawn from a given population. In the present case, we assume that no association exists between the variables in the population, and then we ask what proportion of the samples drawn from that population would produce associations at least as great as those measured in the empirical data. Three levels of significance are frequently used in research reports: 0.05, 0.01, and 0.001. These mean, respectively, that the chances of obtaining the measured association as a result of sampling error are no more than 5 in 100, 1 in 100, and 1 in 1,000.

## Visualizing Statistical Significance

In a Bureau of Justice Statistics publication describing the NCVS for a nontechnical audience, Michael Maltz and Marianne Zawitz (1998) introduced a very informative graphical display to show statistical significance. Recall that the NCVS is a national sample designed to estimate nationwide rates of victimization. Maltz and Zawitz use visual displays of estimates and their confidence intervals to demonstrate the relative precision of victimization rates disclosed by the survey.

Figure 11.3, reproduced from Maltz and Zawitz, presents an example of this approach. The figure shows annual rates of change in all violent victimizations from 1973 through 1996. Notice the vertical line representing no change in violent victimization rates for each year. Estimates of annual rates of change are shown in horizontal bars arrayed along the vertical line. The horizontal bars for each year present parameter estimates for annual change, signified by a dot or square, bracketed by the confidence intervals for each parameter estimate at three confidence levels: 68 percent (1 standard error), 90 percent (1.6 standard errors), and 95 percent (2 standard errors).

Consider first the topmost bar, showing estimates for change from 1973 to 1974. The small dot signifying the point estimate (an increase of 1.24 percent) is just to the right of the no-change vertical line. But notice also that the confidence intervals of 1, 1.6, and 2 standard errors cross over

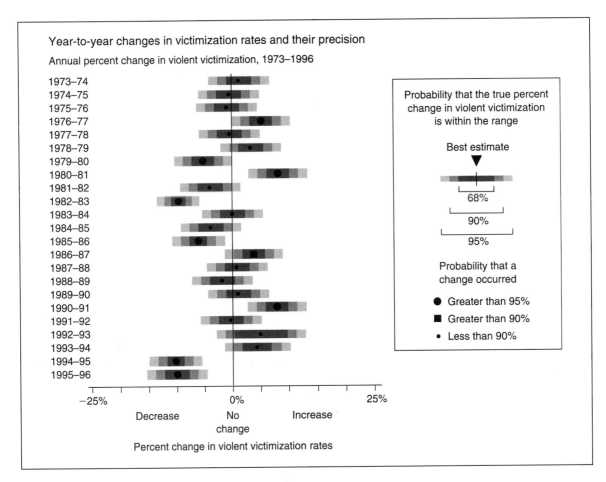

Year-to-year changes in victimization rates and their precision

Annual percent change in violent victimization, 1973–1996

**FIGURE 11.3**  Point Estimates and Confidence Intervals

*Source:* Maltz and Zawitz (1998, 4).

the no-change line; the estimate of a 1.24 percent increase is less than 2 standard errors above zero. This means that, using the 0.05 (2 standard errors) criterion, the estimated increase is not statistically significant. To further emphasize this point, notice the key in Figure 11.3, which shows different probabilities that a change occurred each year; the small dot representing the point estimate for 1973–74 change indicates the probability that a change occurred is less than 90 percent.

Now consider the most recent estimate shown in this figure—change from 1995 to 1996. The point estimate of −9.9 percent is well below the no-change line, and the confidence intervals are well

to the left of this line. Bracketing the point estimate by 2 standard errors produces an interval estimate of between −15.7 percent (point estimate minus 2 standard errors) and −4.05 percent (point estimate plus 2 standard errors). This means we can be 95 percent certain that the violent victimization rate declined from 1995 to 1996 by somewhere between −4.05 and −15.7 percent. Because the point estimate of −9.9 percent is more than 2 standard errors from zero, we can confidently say there was a statistically significant decline in violent victimization.

Displaying point and interval estimates in this way accurately represents the concepts of statistical inference and statistical significance. Sample-based estimates of victimization, or any other variable, are just that—estimates of population values, bounded by estimates of standard error. Statistical significance, in this example, means that our estimates of change are above or below zero, according to some specified criterion for significance.

Studying Figure 11.3 will enhance your understanding of statistical inference. We suggest that you consider the point and interval estimates for each year's change. Pay particular attention to the confidence intervals and their position relative to the no-change line. Then classify the statistical significance (at the .05 level) for change each year into one of three categories: (1) no change, (2) significant increase, and (3) significant decrease. You'll find our tabulation in the exercises at the end of this chapter.

## Chi Square

Chi square $(\chi^2)$ is a different type of significance test that is widely used in criminal justice research. It is based on the **null hypothesis**: the assumption that there is no relationship between two variables in a population. Given the observed distribution of values on two variables in a contingency table, we compute the joint distribution that would be expected if there were no relationship between the two variables. The result of this operation is a set of expected frequencies for all the cells in the contingency table. We then compare this expected distribution with the empirical distribution—cases actually found in the data—and determine the probability that the difference between expected and empirical distributions could have resulted from sampling error alone. Stated simply, chi square compares what you *get* (empirical) with what you *expect* given a null hypothesis of no relationship. An example will illustrate this procedure.

Let's assume we are interested in the possible relationship between gender and whether people avoid areas near their home because of crime, which we will refer to as avoidance behavior. To test this relationship, we select a sample of 100 people at random. Our sample is made up of 40 men and 60 women; 70 percent of our sample report avoidance behavior, and the remaining 30 percent do not.

If there is no relationship between gender and avoidance behavior, then 70 percent of the men in the sample should report avoiding areas near their home, and 30 percent should report no avoidance behavior. Moreover, women should describe avoidance behavior in the same proportion. Table 11.8 (part I) shows that, based on this model, 28 men and 42 women say they avoid areas at night, with 12 men and 18 women reporting no avoidance.

Part II of Table 11.8 presents the observed avoidance behavior for the hypothetical sample of 100 people. Note that 20 of the men say they avoid areas at night, and the remaining 20 say they do not. Among the women in the sample, 50 avoid areas and 10 do not. Comparing the expected and observed frequencies (parts I and II), we note that somewhat fewer men report avoidance behavior than expected, whereas somewhat more women than expected avoid areas near their home at night.

Chi square is computed as follows: for each cell in the tables, we (1) subtract the expected frequency for that cell from the observed frequency, (2) square this quantity, and (3) divide the squared difference by the expected frequency. This procedure is carried out for each cell in the tables, and the results are added. Part III of Table 11.8 presents the cell-by-cell computations. The final sum is the value of chi square—12.70 in this example.

This value is the overall discrepancy between the observed distribution in the sample and the distribution we would expect if the two variables were unrelated. Of course, the mere discovery of a discrepancy does not prove that the two variables are related, because normal sampling error might produce discrepancies even when there is no relationship in the total population. The magnitude of the value of chi square, however, permits us to estimate the probability of that having happened.

To determine the statistical significance of the observed relationship, we must use a standard set of chi-square values. That will require the computation of the degrees of freedom. For chi square, the degrees of freedom are computed as follows: the number of rows in the table of observed frequencies, minus one, is multiplied by the number of columns, minus one. This may be written as

**TABLE 11.8**    Hypothetical Illustration of Chi Square

### I. Expected Cell Frequencies

|                   | Men | Women | Total |
|-------------------|-----|-------|-------|
| Avoid areas*      | 28  | 42    | 70    |
| Do not avoid areas| 12  | 18    | 30    |
| Total             | 40  | 60    | 100   |

### II. Observed Cell Frequencies

|                   | Men | Women | Total |
|-------------------|-----|-------|-------|
| Avoid areas       | 20  | 50    | 70    |
| Do not avoid areas| 20  | 10    | 30    |
| Total             | 40  | 60    | 100   |

### III. (Observed – Expected)$^2$ ÷ Expected

|                    | Men  | Women |                    |
|--------------------|------|-------|--------------------|
| Avoid areas        | 2.29 | 1.52  | Chi sq. = 12.70    |
| Do not avoid areas | 5.33 | 3.56  | $p < 0.001$        |

\* "Is there any area around here—that is, within a city block—that you avoid at night because of crime?"

$(r - 1)$ $(c - 1)$. In the present example, we have two rows and two columns (discounting the totals), so there is 1 degree of freedom.

Turning to a table of chi-square values (see the inside covers of this text), we find that, for 1 degree of freedom and random sampling from a population in which there is no relationship between two variables, 10 percent of the time we should expect a chi square of at least 2.7. Thus, if we select 100 samples from such a population, we should expect about 10 of those samples to produce chi squares equal to or greater than 2.7. Moreover, we should expect chi-square values of at least 6.6 in only 1 percent of the samples and chi-square values of 10.8 in only 0.1 percent of the samples. The higher the chi-square value, the less probable it is that the value can be attributed to sampling error alone.

In our example, the computed value of chi square is 12.70. If there is no relationship between gender and avoidance behavior and a large number of samples were selected and studied, we can expect a chi square of this magnitude in fewer than 0.1 percent of those samples. Thus the probability of obtaining a chi square of this magnitude is less than 0.001 if random sampling has been used and there is no relationship in the population. We report this finding by saying that the relationship is statistically significant at the 0.001 level. Because it is so improbable that the observed relationship could have resulted from sampling error alone, we are likely to reject the null hypothesis and assume that a relationship does, in fact, exist between the two variables.

Many measures of association can be tested for statistical significance in a similar manner. Standard tables of values permit us to determine whether a given association is statistically significant and at what level.

## Cautions in Interpreting Statistical Significance

Tests of significance provide an objective yardstick against which to estimate the significance of associations between variables. They assist us in ruling out associations that may not represent genuine relationships in the population under study. However, the researcher who uses or reads reports of significance tests should be aware of certain cautions in their interpretation.

First, we have been discussing tests of *statistical* significance; there are no objective tests of *substantive* significance. We may be legitimately convinced that a given association is not due to sampling error but still assert, without fear of contradiction, that two variables are only slightly related to each other. Recall that sampling error is an inverse function of sample size: the larger the sample, the smaller the expected error. Thus a correlation of, say, .1 might well be significant (at a given level) if discovered in a large sample, whereas the same correlation between the same two variables would not be significant if found in a smaller sample. Of course, that makes perfect sense if one understands the basic logic of tests of significance: in the larger sample, there is less chance that the correlation is simply the product of sampling error.

The distinction between statistical and substantive significance is perhaps best illustrated by those cases in which there is absolute certainty that observed differences cannot be a result of sampling error. That is the case when we observe an entire population. Suppose we are able to learn the age and gender of every murder victim in the United States for the year 2009. For argument's sake, let's assume that the average age of male murder victims is 25, as compared with, say, 26 for female victims. Because we have the ages of all murder victims, there is no question of sampling error. We know with certainty that the female victims are older than their male counterparts. At the same time, we can say that the difference is of no substantive significance. We conclude, in fact, that they are essentially the same age.

Second, lest you be misled by this hypothetical example, statistical significance should not be calculated on relationships observed in data collected from whole populations. Remember, tests of statistical significance measure the likelihood of relationships between variables being a product of only sampling error, which, of course, assumes that data come from a sample. If there's no sampling, there's no sampling error.

Third, tests of significance are based on the same sampling assumptions we use to compute confidence intervals. To the extent that these assumptions are not met by the actual sampling design, the tests of significance are not strictly legitimate.

In practice, tests of statistical significance are frequently used inappropriately. Michael Maltz (2006) presents several examples of questionable interpretations of significance. If you were to review any given issue of an academic journal in criminal justice, we'd be willing to bet that you would find one or more of these technically improper uses:

- Tests of significance computed for data representing entire populations
- Tests based on samples that do not meet the required assumptions of probability sampling
- Interpretation of statistical significance as a measure of association (a "relationship" of $p \leq 0.001$ is "stronger" than one of $p \leq 0.05$)

We do not mean to suggest a purist approach by these comments. We encourage you to use any statistical technique—any measure of association or any test of significance—on any set of data if it will help you understand your data. In doing so, however, you should recognize what measures of association and statistical significance can and cannot tell you, as well as the assumptions required for various measures. Any individual statistic or measure tells only part of the story, and you should try to learn as much of the story as you can.

## SUMMARY

- Descriptive statistics are used to summarize data under study.

- A frequency distribution shows the number of cases that have each of the attributes of a given variable.

- Measures of central tendency reduce data to an easily manageable form, but they do not convey the detail of the original data.

- Measures of dispersion give a summary indication of the distribution of cases around an average value.

- Rates are descriptive statistics that standardize some measure for comparative purposes.

- Bivariate analysis and subgroup comparisons examine some type of relationship between two variables.

- The rules of thumb in interpreting bivariate percentage tables to make the subgroup comparisons are (1) if percentaged down, then read across, or (2) if percentaged across, then read down.

- Multivariate analysis is a method of analyzing the simultaneous relationships among several variables and may be used to more fully understand the relationship between two variables.

- Inferential statistics are used to estimate the generalizability of findings arrived at in the analysis of a sample to the larger population from which the sample has been selected.

- Inferences about a characteristic of a population—such as the percentage that favors gun control laws—must contain an indication of a confidence interval (the range within which the value is expected to be—for example, between 45 and 55 percent favor gun control) and an indication of the confidence level (the likelihood that the value does fall within that range—for example, 95 percent confidence).

- Tests of statistical significance estimate the likelihood that an association as large as the observed one could result from normal sampling error if no such association exists between the variables in the larger population.

- Statistical significance must not be confused with substantive significance, which means that an observed association is strong, important, or meaningful.

- Tests of statistical significance, strictly speaking, make assumptions about data and methods that are almost never satisfied completely by real social research.

## KEY TERMS

averages, p. 276

bivariate analysis, p. 275

central tendency, p. 276

contingency tables, p. 286

descriptive statistics, p. 275

dispersion, p. 278

frequency distributions, p. 275

inferential statistics, p. 275

level of significance, p. 293

mean, p. 276

median, p. 276

mode, p. 276

multivariate analysis, p. 275

nonsampling errors, p. 292

null hypothesis, p. 295

range, p. 278

standard deviation, p. 278

statistical significance, p. 293

tests of statistical significance, p. 292

univariate analysis, p. 275

## REVIEW QUESTIONS AND EXERCISES

1. Using the data in the accompanying table, construct and interpret tables showing:

   a. The bivariate relationship between age and attitude toward capital punishment

   b. The bivariate relationship between political orientation and attitude toward capital punishment

   c. The multivariate relationship linking age, political orientation, and attitude toward capital punishment

| Age | Political Orientation | Attitude Toward Capital Punishment | Frequency |
|-----|----------------------|-----------------------------------|-----------|
| Young | Conservative | Favor | 90 |
| Young | Conservative | Oppose | 10 |
| Young | Liberal | Favor | 60 |
| Young | Liberal | Oppose | 40 |
| Old | Conservative | Favor | 60 |
| Old | Conservative | Oppose | 10 |
| Old | Liberal | Favor | 15 |
| Old | Liberal | Oppose | 15 |

2. Here are our answers to the question about statistical significance relating to Figure 11.3: Fifteen years show no significant change in violent victimization; significant increases are shown for three years; violent victimization declines significantly in five years. The increase from 1976 to 1977 and the decrease from 1979 to 1980 are close; notice the edge of the 95 percent confidence interval borders the no-change line. We recommend that you read the Maltz and Zawitz publication. It's listed in the references and can be downloaded from the Bureau of Justice Statistics website at http://bjs.ojp.usdoj.gov/content/pub/pdf/dvctue.pdf.

## ADDITIONAL READINGS

Wagner III, William E., Earl Babbie, Fred Halley, and Jeanne Zaino, *Adventures in Social Research*, 7th ed. (Thousand Oaks, CA: Sage, 2010). This book introduces you to data analysis through SPSS, a widely used computer program for statistical analysis. Several of the basic techniques described in this chapter are illustrated and discussed further.

Finkelstein, Michael O., and Bruce Levin, *Statistics for Lawyers*, 2nd ed. (New York: Springer-Verlag, 2001). Law school trains people to be analytic, but few lawyers know much about statistics. This book provides a straightforward explanation of many basic statistical concepts. Examples are drawn from actual cases to illustrate how to calculate and interpret statistics. In addition, readers gain insight into how to reason with statistics.

Miller, Jane E. *The Chicago Guide to Writing about Numbers* (Chicago: University of Chicago Press, 2004). This is an excellent guide to thinking about and interpreting results of data analysis. The book is helpful as an introduction for beginning researchers and a reference for more experienced analysts.

Weisburd, David, and Chester Britt, *Statistics in Criminal Justice,* 3rd ed. (Belmont, CA: Wadsworth, 2009). This text presents an excellent basic introduction to statistics using examples from criminal justice.

# Glossary

**aggregate** Groups of units—people, prisons, courtrooms, or stolen autos, for example. Although criminal justice professionals are usually most concerned with individual units, social science searches for patterns that are reflected in aggregations of units. For example, a probation officer focuses on probation clients as individuals, whereas a social scientist focuses on groups of probation clients, or aggregates. See Chapter 3.

**anonymity** The identity of a research subject is not known, and it is therefore impossible to link data about a subject to an individual's name. Anonymity is one tool for addressing the ethical issue of privacy. Compare with *confidentiality*. See Chapter 2.

**applied research** A type of *explanatory research* purpose (see *explanatory research*) to determine links between justice policy and crime or other problems. Examples include estimating whether prison populations will be reduced from changes in parole standards, or whether requiring steering column locks reduces car theft. See Chapter 1.

**attributes** Characteristics of persons or things. See Chapter 3. See also *variables*.

**average** An ambiguous term that generally suggests typical or normal. The *mean, median,* and *mode* are specific mathematical averages. See Chapter 11.

**Belmont Report** A publication that proposed three ethical principles to guide the protection of human subjects: respect for persons, beneficence, and justice. Federal regulations for the protection of human subjects are based on this report. See Chapter 2.

**bias** That quality of a measurement device that tends to result in a misrepresentation of what is being measured in a particular direction. For example, the questionnaire item "Don't you agree that the president is doing a good job?" would be biased in that it would generally encourage more favorable responses. See Chapter 7.

**binomial variable** A variable that has only two attributes is binomial. *Gender* is an example; it has the attributes *male* and *female*. See Chapter 6.

**bivariate analysis** The analysis of two variables simultaneously for the purpose of determining the empirical relationship between them. The construction of a simple percentage table and the computation of a simple correlation coefficient are examples of bivariate analyses. See Chapter 11.

**case-oriented research** A research strategy in which many cases are examined to understand a comparatively small number of variables. Examples include experiments (Chapter 5) and surveys (Chapter 7).

**case study** A research strategy in which the researcher's attention centers on an in-depth examination of one or a few cases on many dimensions. Case studies can be exploratory, descriptive, or explanatory. Case studies can also be used in evaluation research. See Chapter 5.

**central tendency** Statistical measures that express how observations are clustered in a distribution. See Chapter 11.

**classical experiment** A research design well suited to inferring cause, the classical experiment involves three major pairs of components: (1) independent and dependent variables, (2) pretesting and posttesting, and (3) experimental and control groups, with subjects randomly assigned to one group or the other. See Chapter 5.

**closed-ended questions** Survey questions in which the respondent is asked to select an answer from a list provided by the researcher. Closed-ended questions are especially popular in surveys because they provide a greater uniformity of responses and are more easily analyzed than open-ended questions. See Chapter 7.

**cluster sample** A multistage sample in which natural groups (clusters) are sampled initially, with the members of each selected group being subsampled afterward. For example, you might select a sample of municipal police departments from a directory, get lists of the police officers at all the selected departments, then draw samples of officers from each. See Chapter 6.

**computer-assisted interviewing** Survey research by computer in which questionnaires are presented on computer screens instead of paper. In computer-assisted personal interviewing, an interviewer reads items from the computer screen and keys in responses. In computer-assisted self-interviewing, respondents read items (silently) on the screen of a laptop computer and key in their answers. Another variation is audio-assisted self-interviewing, whereby respondents hear questions through headphones, then key in their answers. Both types of self-interviewing are especially useful for sensitive questions such as those in self-reports. See Chapter 7.

**concept** The words or symbols in language that we use to represent mental images. *Crime*, for example, is a concept that represents our mental images of violence and other acts that are prohibited and punished by government. We use conceptual definitions to specify the meaning of concepts. Compare with *conception*. See Chapter 4.

**conception** The mental images we have that represent our thoughts about things we routinely encounter. We use the word *speeding* (a concept) to represent our mental image (conception) of traveling above the posted speed limit. See Chapter 4.

**conceptual definition** Defining concepts by using other concepts. Concepts are abstract—the words and symbols that are used to represent mental images of things and ideas. This means that a conceptual definition uses words and symbols to define concepts. In practice, conceptual definitions serve as working definitions of what a researcher means by a concept. A conceptual definition of prior record might be "recorded evidence

of one or more convictions for a criminal offense." See Chapter 4. See also *operational definition*.

**conceptualization** The mental process whereby fuzzy and imprecise notions (concepts) are made more specific and precise. So you want to study fear of crime? What do you mean by fear of crime? Are there different kinds of fear? What are they? See Chapters 1 and 4.

**confidence interval** The range of values within which a population parameter is estimated to lie. A survey, for instance, may show that 40 percent of a sample favor a ban on handguns. Although the best estimate of the support that exists among all people is also 40 percent, we do not expect it to be exactly that. We might, therefore, compute a confidence interval (for example, from 35 to 45 percent) within which the actual percentage of the population probably lies. Note that it is necessary to specify a confidence level in connection with every confidence interval. See Chapters 6 and 11.

**confidence level** The estimated probability that a population parameter lies within a given confidence interval. Thus we might be 95 percent confident that between 35 and 45 percent of all residents of California favor an absolute ban on handguns. See Chapters 6 and 11.

**confidentiality** Researchers know the identity of a research subject but promise not to reveal any information that can be attributed to an individual subject. Anonymity is similar, but sometimes researchers need to know subjects' names to link information from different sources. Assuring confidentiality is one way of meeting our ethical obligation to not harm subjects. See Chapter 2.

**construct validity** (1) The degree to which a measure relates to other variables as expected within a system of theoretical relationships. See Chapter 4. (2) How well an observed cause-and-effect relationship represents the underlying causal process a researcher is interested in. See Chapters 4 and 5. See also *validity threats*.

**content analysis** The systematic study of messages and their meaning. Researchers use content analysis to study all forms of communication, including text, pictures, and video recordings. See Chapter 9.

**contingency table** A format for presenting the relationship among variables in the form of percentage distributions. See Chapter 11.

**control group** In experimentation, a group of subjects to whom no experimental stimulus is administered and who should resemble the experimental group in all other respects. The comparison of the control group and the experimental group at the end of the experiment indicates the effect of the experimental stimulus. See Chapter 5.

**criterion-related validity** The degree to which a measure relates to some external criterion. For example, the validity of self-report surveys of drug use can be shown by comparing survey responses to laboratory tests for drug use. See Chapter 4.

**cross-sectional study** A study based on observations that represent a single point in time. Compare with *longitudinal study*. See Chapter 3.

**deductive reasoning** A mode of inquiry using the logical model in which specific expectations of hypotheses are developed on the basis of general principles. Starting from the general principle that all deans are meanies, you might anticipate that your current one won't let you change courses. That anticipation would be the result of deduction. See Chapter 3. See also *inductive reasoning*.

**dependent variable** The variable assumed to depend on or be caused by another variable (called the independent variable). If you find that sentence length is partly a function of the number of prior arrests, then sentence length is being treated as a dependent variable. See Chapters 3 and 5.

**descriptive research** A type of research purpose to systematically describe the scope of a subject under study. Annual reports of the number of people under correctional supervision would be an example. See Chapter 1.

**descriptive statistics** Statistical computations that describe either the characteristics of a sample or the relationship among variables in a sample. Descriptive statistics summarize a set of sample observations, whereas inferential statistics move beyond the description of specific observations to make inferences about the larger population from which the sample observations were drawn. See Chapter 11.

**dimension** A specifiable aspect, or feature, of a concept. See Chapter 4.

**dispersion** The distribution of values around some central value, such as an average. The range is a simple measure of dispersion. Thus we may report that the mean age of a group is 37.9 and the range is from 12 to 89. See Chapter 11.

**disproportionate stratified sampling** Deliberately drawing a sample that overrepresents or underrepresents some characteristic of a population. We may do this to ensure that we obtain a sufficient number of uncommon

cases in our sample. For example, believing violent crime to be more common in large cities, we might oversample urban residents to obtain a specific number of crime victims. See Chapter 6.

**ecological fallacy** Erroneously drawing conclusions about individuals based solely on the observation of groups. See Chapter 3.

**empirical** From experience. Social science is said to be empirical when knowledge is based on what we experience. See Chapter 1.

**environmental survey** Structured observations undertaken in the field and recorded on specially designed forms. Note that interview surveys record a respondent's answers to questions, whereas environmental surveys record what an observer sees in the field. For example, a community organization may conduct periodic environmental surveys to monitor neighborhood parks—whether facilities are in good condition, how much litter is present, and what kinds of people use the park. See Chapter 8.

**equal probability of selection method (EPSEM)** A sample design in which each member of a population has the same chance of being selected in the sample. See Chapter 6.

**ethical** Conforming to norms and standards embraced by a group or profession. Norms regarding ethical behavior for research on human subjects are often described by professional associations of researchers. See Chapter 2.

**ethnography** A report on social life that focuses on detailed and accurate description rather than explanation. See Chapter 8.

**evaluation research** An example of applied research, evaluation involves assessing the effects of some program or policy action, usually in connection with the goals of that action. Determining whether a sex offender treatment program attained its goal of reducing recidivism by participants would be an example. Compare with *problem analysis*. See Chapter 10.

**evidence-based policy** Using data and other sources of information to formulate and evaluate justice policy. This usually means planning justice actions based on evidence of need, such as deploying police patrols to crime hot spots. It also includes assessing the results of justice policy, such as measuring any change in recidivism among a group of offenders processed through drug court. See Chapter 10.

**experimental group** In experimentation, a group of subjects who are exposed to an experimental stimulus.

Subjects in the experimental group are normally compared with subjects in a control group to test the effects of the experimental stimulus. See Chapter 5.

**explanatory research** A type of research purpose that seeks to explain why things happen. This is sometimes referred to as causal research. An example would be research to determine whether increased rates of mortgage foreclosures appear to cause increases in property crime. See Chapter 1.

**exploratory research** A type of research purpose to learn about the basic nature of a research problem or question about which little is known. For example, a researcher might learn how auto body shops screen out parts removed from stolen cars. See Chapter 1.

**external validity** Whether a relationship observed in a specific population, at a specific time, and in a specific place would also be observed in other populations, at other times, and in other places. External validity is concerned with generalizability from a relationship observed in one setting to the same relationship in other settings. Replication enhances external validity. See Chapter 5.

**face validity** The quality of an indicator that makes it seem a reasonable measure of some variable. That sentence length prescribed by law is some indication of crime seriousness seems to make sense without a lot of explanation; it has face validity. See Chapter 4.

**focus group** Small groups (of 12 to 15) engaged in guided discussions of some topic. Participants selected are from a homogeneous population. Although focus groups cannot be used to make statistical estimates about a population, members are nevertheless selected to represent a target population. Focus groups are most useful in two situations: (1) when precise generalization to a larger population is not necessary and (2) when focus group participants and the larger population they are intended to represent are relatively homogeneous. See Chapter 7.

**frequency distribution** A description of the number of times the various attributes of a variable are observed in a sample. The report that 53 percent of a sample were men and 47 percent were women is a simple example of a frequency distribution. Another example is the report that 15 of the cities studied had populations of less than 10,000, 23 had populations between 10,000 and 25,000, and so forth. See Chapter 11.

**generalizability** That quality of a research finding that justifies the inference that it represents something more than the specific observations on which it was based. Sometimes this involves the generalization of findings from a sample to a population. Other times it is a matter of concepts: if you are able to discover why people commit burglaries, can you generalize that discovery to other crimes as well? See Chapter 5.

**grounded theory** A type of inductive theory that is based on (grounded in) field observation. The researcher makes observations in natural settings, then formulates a tentative theory that explains those observations. See Chapter 8.

**hypothesis** An expectation about the nature of things derived from a theory. It is a statement of something that will be observed in the real world if the theory is correct. See Chapter 3. See also *deductive reasoning*.

**hypothesis testing** The determination of whether the expectations that a hypothesis represents are indeed found in the real world. See Chapter 3.

**idiographic** A mode of causal reasoning that seeks detailed understanding of all factors that contribute to a particular phenomenon. Police detectives trying to solve a particular case use the idiographic mode of explanation. Compare with *nomothetic*. See Chapter 3.

**impact assessment** A type of applied research that seeks to answer the question: "Did a public program have the intended effect on the problem it was meant to address?" If, for example, a new burglary prevention program has the goal of reducing burglary in a particular neighborhood, an impact assessment would try to determine whether burglary was, in fact, reduced as a result of the new program. Compare with *process evaluation*. See Chapter 10.

**incident-based measure** Refers to crime measures that express characteristics of individual crime incidents. The FBI Supplementary Homicide Reports are well-known examples, reporting details on each homicide incident. Compare with *summary-based measure*. See Chapter 4.

**independent variable** An independent variable is presumed to cause or determine a dependent variable. If we discover that police cynicism is partly a function of years of experience, then experience is the independent variable and cynicism is the dependent variable. Note that any given variable might be treated as independent in one part of an analysis and dependent in another part of the analysis. Cynicism might become an independent variable in the explanation of job satisfaction. See Chapters 3 and 5.

**inductive reasoning** Uses the logical model in which general principles are developed from specific observations. Having noted that teenagers and crime victims are less supportive of police than older people and nonvictims are, you might conclude that people with more direct police contact are less supportive of police and explain why. That would be an example of induction. See Chapter 3. See also *deductive reasoning*.

**inferential statistics** The body of statistical computations relevant to making inferences from findings on the basis of sample observations to some larger population. See Chapter 11. See also *descriptive statistics*.

**informed consent** Telling research subjects about research goals, procedures, and potential risks before asking them to participate. This standard procedure addresses the norm of voluntary participation, a basic tenet of research ethics. See Chapter 2.

**internal validity** Whether observed associations between two (or more) variables are, in fact, causal associations or are due to the effects of some other variable. The internal validity of causal statements may be threatened by an inability to control experimental conditions. See Chapter 5. See also *validity threats*.

**Interuniversity Consortium for Political and Social Research (ICPSR)** Based at the University of Michigan, ICPSR is an organization that archives and distributes major social science data collections. Most universities and many smaller colleges are member institutions, which gives students and faculty access to vast sources of secondary data. See also the *National Archive of Criminal Justice Data*. See Chapter 9.

**interval measure** A level of measurement that describes a variable whose attributes are rank ordered and have equal distances between adjacent attributes. The Fahrenheit temperature scale is an example because the distance between 17 and 18 is the same as that between 89 and 90. See Chapter 4. See also *nominal measure, ordinal measure*, and *ratio measure*.

**interview survey** Interview surveys use a questionnaire in a systematic way to interview a large number of people. The NCVS is an example. Interview surveys can be face-to-face, over the telephone, or a mix of these two together with computer-assisted interviewing. See Chapter 7. See also *environmental survey*.

**latent content** As used in connection with content analysis, this term describes the underlying meaning of communications as distinguished from their manifest content. See Chapter 9.

**level of significance** In the context of tests of statistical significance, the degree of likelihood that an observed, empirical relationship could be attributable to sampling error. A relationship is significant at the .05 level if the likelihood of its being only a function of sampling error is no greater than 5 out of 100. See Chapter 11.

**longitudinal study** A study design that involves the collection of data at different points in time, as contrasted to a cross-sectional study. See Chapter 3.

**manifest content** In connection with content analysis, the concrete terms contained in a communication, as distinguished from latent content. See Chapter 9.

**mean** An average, computed by summing the values of several observations and dividing by the number of observations. If you now have a grade-point average of 4.0 based on 10 courses, and you get an F in this course, then your new grade-point (mean) average will be 3.6. See Chapter 11.

**median** Another average, representing the value of the middle case in a rank-ordered set of observations. If the ages of five people are 16, 17, 20, 54, and 88, then the median is 20. (The mean is 39.) See Chapter 11.

**methodology** The study of methods used to understand something; the science of finding out. See Chapter 1.

**mode** An average representing the most frequently observed value or attribute. If a sample contains 1,000 residents of California, 275 from New Jersey, and 33 from Minnesota, then California is the modal category for residence. See Chapter 11.

**multivariate analysis** The analysis of the simultaneous relationships among several variables. Simultaneously examining the effects of age, gender, and city of residence on robbery victimization is an example of multivariate analysis. See Chapter 11.

**National Archive of Criminal Justice Data (NACJD)** A special collection within the Interuniversity Consortium of Political and Social Research, the NACJD includes data series of special interest to criminal justice researchers and practitioners. The NCVS, UCR, and data series on correctional populations are included, as are hundreds of other examples of published statistics. The data collection also includes data from most research studies funded by the National Institute of Justice, something that makes the NACJD an excellent source of secondary data. See also the *Interuniversity Consortium of Political and Social Research*. See Chapter 9.

**nominal measure** A variable whose attributes have only the characteristics of exhaustiveness and mutual exclusiveness. In other words, a level of measurement describing a variable that has attributes that are merely different, as distinguished from ordinal, interval, or ratio measures. Gender is an example of a nominal measure. See Chapter 4.

**nomothetic** A mode of causal reasoning that tries to explain a number of similar phenomena or situations. Police crime analysts trying to explain patterns of auto thefts, burglaries, or some other offense use nomothetic reasoning. Compare with *idiographic*. See Chapter 3.

**nonprobability sample** A sample selected in some fashion other than those suggested by probability theory. Examples are *purposive, quota,* and *snowball samples*. See Chapter 6.

**nonsampling error** Imperfections of data quality that are a result of factors other than sampling error. Examples are misunderstandings of questions by respondents, erroneous recordings by interviewers and coders, and data entry errors. See Chapter 11.

**null hypothesis** In connection with hypothesis testing and tests of statistical significance, this is the hypothesis that suggests there is no relationship between the variables under study. You may conclude that the two variables are related after having statistically rejected the null hypothesis. See Chapter 11.

**open-ended questions** Questions for which the respondent is asked to provide his or her own answers. See Chapter 7.

**operational definition** Specifying what operations should be performed to measure a concept. The operational definition of prior record might be "Consult the county (or state or FBI) criminal history records information system. Count the number of times a person has been convicted of committing a crime." See Chapter 4.

**operationalization** One step beyond conceptualization. Operationalization is the process of developing operational definitions by describing how actual measurements will be made. See Chapter 1.

**ordinal measure** A level of measurement that describes a variable whose attributes may be rank ordered along some dimension. An example is socioeconomic status as composed of the attributes high, medium, and low. See Chapter 4. See also *nominal measure, interval measure,* and *ratio measure.*

**population** All people, things, or other elements we wish to represent. Researchers often study only a subset or sample of a population, then generalize from the people, things, or other elements actually observed to the larger population of all people, things, or elements. See Chapter 6.

**population parameter** The summary description of a particular variable in the population. For example, if the mean age of all professors at your college is 43.7, then 43.7 is the population parameter for professors' mean age. Compare with *sample statistic* and *sampling distribution.* See Chapter 6.

**probabilistic** A type of causal reasoning that certain factors make outcomes more or less likely to happen. Having been arrested as a juvenile makes it more likely that someone will be arrested as an adult. See Chapter 3.

**probability sample** The general term for a sample selected in accord with probability theory, typically involving some random selection mechanism. Specific types of probability samples include simple probability sample, *equal probability of selection method (EPSEM), simple random sample,* and *systematic sample.* See Chapter 6.

**problem analysis** Using social science research methods to assess the scope and nature of a problem so that one can plan and select actions to address the problem. For example, examining patterns of auto theft to decide what preventive and enforcement strategies should be pursued is an example of problem analysis. Compare with *evaluation research.* See Chapter 10.

**problem-oriented policing** An approach to policing that depends on analysis to understand patterns of incidents and conditions that police are expected to handle, and then developing responses based on that analysis. It differs from traditional approaches in its focus on patterns rather than individual incidents. See Chapter 10.

**problem solving** An example of applied research that combines elements of evaluation and policy analysis. Problem-oriented policing makes extensive use of problem solving. See Chapter 10.

**process evaluation** A type of applied research that seeks to determine whether a public program was implemented as intended. For example, a burglary prevention program might seek to reduce burglaries by having crime prevention officers meet with all residents of some target neighborhood. A process evaluation would determine whether meetings with neighborhood residents were taking place as planned. Compare with *impact assessment.* See Chapter 10.

**published statistics** Summary data collected by public agencies and routinely made available to the public;

sometimes referred to as "administrative data." Agencies are often required to keep and publish such measures. See Chapter 9.

**purposive sample** A type of nonprobability sample in which you select the units to be observed on the basis of your own judgment about which ones will be best suited to your research purpose. For example, if you were interested in studying community crime prevention groups affiliated with public schools and groups affiliated with religious organizations, you would probably want to select a purposive sample of school- and church-affiliated groups. Most television networks use purposive samples of voting precincts to project winners on election night; precincts that always vote for winners are sampled. See Chapter 6.

**qualitative interview** Contrasted with survey interviewing, the qualitative interview is based on a set of topics to be discussed in depth rather than based on the use of standardized questions. See Chapter 8.

**quasi-experiment** A research design that includes most, but not all, elements of an experimental design. *Quasi* means "sort of," and a quasi-experiment is sort of an experiment. Two general classes of quasi-experiments are nonequivalent groups and time-series designs. Compare with *classical experiment*. See Chapter 5.

**questionnaire** A document that contains questions and other types of items designed to solicit information appropriate to analysis. Questionnaires are used primarily in survey research and also in field research. See Chapter 7.

**quota sample** A type of nonprobability sample in which units are selected in the sample on the basis of prespecified characteristics, so that the total sample will have the same distribution of characteristics as are assumed to exist in the population being studied. See Chapter 6.

**randomization** A technique for randomly assigning experimental subjects to experimental groups and control groups. See Chapter 5.

**range** A measure of dispersion, the distance that separates the highest and lowest values of a variable in some set of observations. In your class, for example, the range of ages might be from 17 to 37. See Chapter 11.

**ratio measure** A level of measurement that describes a variable whose attributes have all the qualities of nominal, ordinal, and interval measures and in addition are based on a true zero point. Length of prison sentence is an example of a ratio measure. See Chapter 4.

**reactivity** The problem that the subjects of social research may react to the fact of being studied, thus altering their behavior from what it would have been normally. See Chapter 8.

**reliability** Consistency of measurement. Measures are reliable if researchers obtain the same results when measuring something more than once. This is not to be confused with validity. See Chapter 4.

**replication** Repeating a research study to test the findings of an earlier study, often under slightly different conditions or for a different group of subjects. Replication results either support earlier findings or cause us to question the accuracy of an earlier study. See Chapter 1.

**respondent** A person who provides data for analysis by responding to a survey questionnaire that is self-completed or administered as an interview. See Chapter 7.

**response rate** The number of people participating in a survey divided by the number selected in the sample, in the form of a percentage. This is also called the completion rate or, in self-administered surveys, the return rate—the percentage of questionnaires sent out that are returned. See Chapter 7.

**safety audit** A type of environmental survey that focuses on security and safety of places. Safety audits are often combined with interviews or focus groups to measure *perceptions* of safety among people who regularly use specific places. See Chapter 8.

**sample** A subset of a population selected according to one or more criteria. Two general types are probability and nonprobability samples. See Chapter 6.

**sample element** The unit about which information is collected and that provides the basis of analysis. Typically, in survey research, elements are people. Other kinds of units can be the elements for criminal justice research—correctional facilities, gangs, police beats, or court cases. See Chapter 6.

**sample statistic** The summary description of a particular variable in a sample. For example, if the mean age of a sample of 100 professors on your campus is 41.1, then 41.1 is the sample statistic for professor age. We usually use sample statistics to estimate population parameters. Compare with *sampling distribution*. See Chapter 6.

**sampling distribution** The range, or array, of sample statistics we would obtain if we drew a very large number of samples from a single population. With random sampling, we expect that the sampling distribution for a particular statistic (mean age, for example) will cluster around the population parameter for mean age.

Furthermore, sampling distributions for larger sample sizes will cluster more tightly around the population parameter. See Chapter 6.

**sampling frame** That list or quasi-list of units composing a population from which a sample is selected. If the sample is to be representative of the population, it is essential that the sampling frame include all (or nearly all) members of the population. See Chapter 6.

**sampling units** Like sampling elements, these are things that may be selected in the process of sampling; often sampling units are people. In some types of sampling, however, we often begin by selecting large groupings of the eventual elements we will analyze. *Sampling units* is a generic term for things that are selected in some stage of sampling but are not necessarily the objects of our ultimate interest. See Chapter 6.

**scientific realism** An approach to evaluation that studies what's called "local causality." Interest focuses more on how interventions and measures of effect are related in a specific situation. This is different from a more traditional social science interest in finding causal relationships that apply generally to a variety of situations. As explained by Ray Pawson and Nick Tilley (1997), scientific realism is especially useful for evaluating justice programs because it centers on analyzing interventions in local contexts. See Chapters 3 and 10.

**secondary analysis** A form of research in which the data collected and processed by one researcher are reanalyzed—often for a different purpose—by another. This is especially appropriate in the case of survey data. Data archives are repositories, or libraries, for the storage and distribution of data for secondary analysis. See Chapter 9.

**self-report survey** Self-report surveys ask people to tell about crimes they have committed. This method is best for measuring drug use and other so-called victimless crimes. Confidentiality is especially important in self-report surveys. See Chapters 4 and 7.

**simple random sample** A type of probability sample in which the units composing a population are assigned numbers, a set of random numbers is then generated, and the units that have those numbers are included in the sample. Although probability theory and the calculations it provides assume this basic sampling method, it is seldom used for practical reasons. An alternative is the systematic sample (with a random start). See Chapter 6.

**snowball sampling** A method for drawing a non-probability sample. Snowball samples are often used in field research. Each person interviewed is asked to sug-

gest additional people for interviewing. See Chapters 6 and 8.

**social production of data** Referring mostly to agency records, data that reflect organization processes and decision rules in addition to the condition measured. Crime reports and probation records are examples. See Chapter 9.

**special populations** Regulations concerning human subjects specify juveniles and prisoners as populations that require special protections. Juveniles are considered unable to grant informed consent, just as juveniles are treated differently in most areas of the law. Special rules apply to prisoners because they may feel compelled to participate in research, or because participation may be especially desirable. See Chapter 2.

**stakeholders** Individuals with some interest, or stake, in a specific program. Any particular program may have multiple stakeholders with different interests and goals. See Chapter 10.

**standard deviation** A measure of dispersion about the mean. Conceptually, the standard deviation represents an average deviation of all values relative to the mean. See Chapter 11.

**standard error** A measure of sampling error, the standard error gives us a statistical estimate of how much a member of a sample might differ from the population we are studying, solely by chance. Larger samples usually result in smaller standard errors. See Chapters 6 and 11.

**statistical conclusion validity** Whether we can find covariation among two variables. This is the first of three requirements for causal inference (see Chapter 3 for the other two). If two variables do not vary together (covariation), there cannot be a causal relationship between them. See Chapter 5 for more on statistical conclusion validity. Chapter 11 describes the role of sample size in finding statistical significance, which is conceptually related to statistical conclusion validity.

**statistical significance** A general term for the unlikeliness that relationships observed in a sample could be attributed to sampling error alone. See Chapter 11. See also *test of statistical significance*.

**stratification** The grouping of the units composing a population into homogeneous groups (or strata) before sampling. This procedure, which may be used in conjunction with simple random, systematic, or cluster sampling, improves the representativeness of a sample, at least in terms of the stratification variables. See Chapter 6.

**summary-based measure** Crime measures that report only total crimes for a jurisdiction or other small area are summary-based measures of crime. The FBI Uniform Crime Reports is one well-known summary measure. Compare with *incident-based measure*. See Chapter 4.

**survey** A method for collecting data by applying a standard instrument in a systematic way to take measures from a large number of units. See Chapter 7. See also *interview survey* and *environmental survey*.

**systematic sampling** A method of probability sampling in which units occurring in some specified interval in a list are selected for inclusion in the sample—for example, every 25th student in the college directory of students. Within certain constraints, systematic sampling is a functional equivalent of simple random sampling and is usually easier to do. Typically the first unit is selected at random. See Chapter 6.

**test of statistical significance** A class of statistical computations that indicate the likelihood that the relationship observed between variables in a sample can be attributed to sampling error only. See Chapter 11. See also *inferential statistics*.

**theory** A systematic explanation for the observed facts and laws that relate to a particular aspect of life. For example, routine activities theory (see Cohen and Felson 1979) explains crime as the result of three key elements coming together: a suitable victim, a motivated offender, and the absence of capable guardians. See Chapter 3.

**typology** Classifying observations in terms of their attributes. Sometimes referred to as taxonomies, typologies are typically created with nominal variables. For example, a typology of thieves might group them according to the types of cars they steal and the types of locations they search to find targets. See Chapter 4.

**units of analysis** The "what" or "who" being studied. Units of analysis may be individual people, groupings of people (a juvenile gang), formal organizations (a probation department), or social artifacts (crime reports). See Chapter 3.

**univariate analysis** The analysis of a single variable for purposes of description. Frequency distributions, averages, and measures of dispersion are examples of univariate analysis, as distinguished from bivariate and multivariate analyses. See Chapter 11.

**validity** (1) Whether statements about cause and effect are true (valid) or false (invalid). (2) A descriptive term used for a measure that accurately reflects what it is intended to measure. For example, police records of auto theft are more valid measures than police records of shoplifting. It is important to realize that the ultimate validity of a measure can never be proved. Yet we may agree as to its relative validity on the basis of face validity, criterion-related validity, and construct validity. This must not be confused with reliability. See Chapters 3 and 5. See also *validity threats*.

**validity threats** Possible sources of invalidity, or making false statements about cause and effect. Four categories of validity threats are linked to fundamental requirements for demonstrating cause: *statistical conclusion validity*, *internal validity*, *construct validity*, and *external validity* (see separate entries in this glossary). In general, statistical conclusion validity and internal validity are concerned with bias; construct validity and external validity are concerned with generalization. See Chapters 3 and 5.

**variable-oriented research** A research strategy whereby a large number of variables are studied for one or a small number of cases or subjects. Time-series designs and case studies are examples. See Chapter 5.

**variables** Logical groupings of attributes. The variable *gender* is made up of the attributes *male* and *female*. See Chapter 3.

**victim survey** A sample survey that asks people about their experiences as victims of crime. Victim surveys are one way to measure crime, and they are especially valuable for getting information about crimes not reported to police. The National Crime Victimization Survey is an example. See Chapters 4 and 7.

# References

Academy of Criminal Justice Sciences. 2000. "Code of Ethics." Greenbelt, MD: Academy of Criminal Justice Sciences. http://acjs.org/pubs/167_671_2922.cfm

Als-Nielsen, Bodil, Wendong Chen, Christian Gluud, and Lise L. Kjaergard. 2003. "Association of Funding and Conclusions in Randomized Drug Trials: A Reflection of Treatment Effect or Adverse Events?" *Journal of the American Medical Association* 290(7): 921–927.

American Association of University Professors. 2006. *Research on Human Subjects: Academic Freedom and the Institutional Review Board (2006).* Report from the Committee on Academic Freedom and Tenure. Washington, DC: American Association of University Professors. http://www.aaup.org/AAUP/comm/rep/A/humansubs.htm

American Psychological Association. 2010. *Ethical Principles of Psychologists and Code of Conduct.* 2002 Code as amended. Washington, DC: American Psychological Association. http://www.apa.org/ethics/code/index.aspx

American Sociological Association. 1999. "Code of Ethics." Washington, DC: American Sociological Association. http://asanet.org/about/ethics.cfm

Anderson, Craig A., and Brad Bushman. 2002. "The Effects of Media Violence on Society." *Science* 295(5564): 2377–2379.

Anderson, Elijah. 1999. *Code of the Street: Decency, Violence, and the Moral Life of the City.* New York: Norton.

Andresen, W. Carsten. 2005. *State Police: Discretion and Traffic Enforcement.* Unpublished Ph.D. dissertation. Newark, NJ: School of Criminal Justice, Rutgers University.

Associated Press. 1993. "High Murder Rate for Women on the Job." *New York Times,* October 3.

Austin, James, Wendy Naro, and Tony Fabelo. 2007. *Public Safety, Public Spending: Forecasting America's Prison Population 2007–2011.* Philadelphia: Pew Charitable Trusts.

Babbie, Earl. 1990. *Survey Research Methods.* 2d ed. Belmont, CA: Wadsworth.

Baron, Stephen W., and Timothy F. Hartnagel. 1998. "Street Youth and Criminal Violence." *Journal of Research in Crime and Delinquency* 35(2): 166–192.

Baum, Katrina. 2007. *Identity Theft, 2005.* BJS Special Report. Washington, DC: U.S. Department of Justice, Office of Justice Programs, Bureau of Justice Statistics, November.

Baumer, Eric, Janet L. Lauritsen, Richard Rosenfeld, and Richard Wright. 1998. "The Influence of Crack Cocaine on Robbery, Burglary, and Homicide Rates: A Cross-City Longitudinal Analysis." *Journal of Research in Crime and Delinquency* 35(3): 316–340.

Baumer, Terry L., Michael G. Maxfield, and Robert I. Mendelsohn. 1993. "A Comparative Analysis of Three Electronically Monitored Home Detention Programs." *Justice Quarterly* 10(1): 121–142.

Baumer, Terry L., and Robert I. Mendelsohn. 1990. *The Electronic Monitoring on Non-Violent Convicted Felons: An Experiment in Home Detention*. Final report to the National Institute of Justice. Indianapolis: Indiana University, School of Public and Environmental Affairs.

Baumer, Terry L., and Dennis Rosenbaum. 1982. *Combating Retail Theft: Programs and Strategies*. Boston: Butterworth.

Becker, Gary S. 1968. "Crime and Punishment: An Economic Approach." *Journal of Political Economy* 76: 169–217.

Bennett, Trevor, and Katy Holloway. 2005. "Association between Multiple Drug Use and Crime." *International Journal of Offender Therapy* 49(1): 63–81.

Bennett, Trevor, Katy Holloway, and David Farrington. 2008. "The Statistical Association between Drug Misuse and Crime: A Meta-Analysis." *Aggression and Violent Behavior* 13(2): 107–118.

Bennis, Jason, Wesley G. Skogan, and Lynn Steiner. 2003. "The 2002 Beat Meeting Observation Study." Community Policing Working Paper 26. Evanston, IL: Center for Policy Research, Northwestern University. www.northwestern.edu/ipr/publications/policing.html

Berenson, Jacqueline A., and Paul S. Appelbaum. 2010. "A Geospatial Analysis of the Impact of Sex Offender Residency Restrictions in Two New York Counties." *Law and Human Behavior*, June 12.

Berk, Richard A., Heather Ladd, Heidi Graziano, and Jong-ho Baek. 2003. "A Randomized Experiment Testing Inmate Classification Systems." *Criminology and Public Policy* 2(2): 215–242.

Best, Joel. 2001. *Damned Lies and Statistics: Untangling Numbers from the Media, Politicians, and Activists*. Berkeley: University of California Press.

Best, Joel. 2008. *Stat-Spotting: A Field Guide to Identifying Dubious Data*. Berkeley: University of California Press.

Bichler, Gisela, and Ronald V. Clarke. 1996. "Eliminating Pay Phone Toll Fraud at the Port Authority Bus Terminal in Manhattan." In *Preventing Mass Transit Crime*, ed. Ronald V. Clarke. *Crime Prevention Studies*, vol. 6. Monsey, NY: Criminal Justice Press.

Black, Donald. 1970. "The Production of Crime Rates." *American Sociological Review* 35(4): 733–748.

Blumberg, Stephen J., and Julian V. Luke. 2010. *Wireless Substitution: Early Release Estimates from the National Health Interview Survey, January–June 2010*. Atlanta, Georgia: Centers for Disease Control, December 21. http://www.cdc.gov/nchs/data/nhis/earlyrelease/wireless201012.htm

Blumstein, Alfred, and Richard Rosenfeld. 1998. "Explaining Recent Trends in U.S. Homicide Rates." *Journal of Criminal Law and Criminology* 88(4): 1175–1216.

Boba, Rachel. 2005. *Crime Analysis and Crime Mapping*. Thousand Oaks, CA: Sage.

Bolling, Keith, Catherine Grant, and Jeri-Lee Donovan. 2009. *2008–9 British Crime Survey (England and Wales) Technical Report*. Vol. I, 2d ed. London: Home Office RDS.

Bouchard, Martin. 2007. "A Capture-Recapture Method to Estimate the Size of Criminal Populations and the Risks of Detection in a Marijuana Cultivation Industry." *Journal of Quantitative Criminology* 23(3): 221–241.

Braga, Anthony A. 2008. *Problem-Oriented Policing and Crime Prevention*. 2d ed. Monsey, NY: Criminal Justice Press.

Braga, Anthony A., David M. Kennedy, Elin J. Waring, and Anne Morrison Piehl. 2001. "Problem-Oriented Policing and Youth Violence: An Evaluation of Boston's Operation Ceasefire." *Journal of Research in Crime and Delinquency* 38(3): 195–225.

Brantingham, Patricia L., and Paul J. Brantingham. 1991. "Notes on the Geometry of Crime." In *Environmental Criminology*, 2d ed., ed. Paul J. Brantingham and Patricia L. Brantingham. Prospect Heights, IL: Waveland.

Brantingham, Paul, and Patricia Brantingham. 2009. "Crime Pattern Theory." In *Evaluating Crime Reduction Initiatives*, ed. Johannes Knutsson and Nick Tilley. *Crime Prevention Studies*, vol. 24. Monsey, NY: Criminal Justice Press.

Bratton, William J. 1999. "Great Expectations: How Higher Expectations for Police Departments Can Lead to a Decrease in Crime." In *Measuring What Matters*. Proceedings from the Policing Research Institute meetings, ed. Robert Langworthy. Washington, DC: U.S. Department of Justice, Office of Justice Programs, National Institute of Justice.

Brown, Rick, and Ronald V. Clarke. 2004. "Police Intelligence and Theft of Vehicles for Export: Recent U.K. Experience." In *Understanding and Preventing Car Theft*, ed. Michael G. Maxfield and Ronald V. Clarke. *Crime Prevention Studies*, vol. 17. Monsey, NY: Criminal Justice Press.

Bureau of Justice Assistance. 1993. *A Police Guide to Surveying Citizens and Their Environment*. Washington, DC: U.S. Department of Justice, Office of Justice Programs, Bureau of Justice Assistance. NCJ-143711.

Bureau of Justice Statistics. 1993. *Performance Measures for the Criminal Justice System*. Discussion papers from the BJS-Princeton project. U.S. Department of Justice, Office of Justice Programs, Bureau of Justice Statistics.

Bureau of Justice Statistics. 2002. *Data Quality Guidelines*. Washington, DC: U.S. Department of Justice, Office of Justice Programs, Bureau of Justice Statistics, October.

Bureau of Justice Statistics. 2006. *Criminal Victimization in the United States, 2004 Statistical Tables*. Washington, DC: U.S. Department of Justice, Office of Justice Programs, Bureau of Justice Statistics. http://bjs.ojp.usdoj.gov/content/pub/pdf/cvus0404.pdf

Bureau of Justice Statistics. 2008. *Criminal Victimization in the United States: Statistical Tables*. Washington, DC: U.S. Department of Justice, Office of Justice Programs, Bureau of Justice Statistics. http://bjs.ojp.usdoj.gov/index.cfm?ty=pbdetail&iid=1094

Campbell, Donald T. 2003. "Introduction." In *Case Study Research: Design and Methods*, 3d ed., ed. Robert K. Yin. Thousand Oaks, CA: Sage.

Campbell, Donald T., and Julian Stanley. 1966. *Experimental and Quasi-Experimental Designs for Research*. Chicago: Rand McNally.

Cantor, David, Tom Krenzke, Diana Stukel, and Lou Rizzo. 2010. *NCVS Task 4 Report: Summary of Options Relating to Local Area Estimations*. Rockville, MD: Westat. http://bjs.ojp.usdoj.gov/content/pub/pdf/westat_lae_5-19-10.pdf

Cantor, David, and James P. Lynch. 2005. "Exploring the Effects of Changes in Design on the Analytical Uses of the NCVS Data." *Journal of Quantitative Criminology* 21(3): 293–319.

Cantor, David, and James P. Lynch. 2007. "Addressing the Challenge of Cost and Error in Victimization Surveys: The Potential of New Technologies and New Methods." In *Surveying Crime in the 21st Century*, ed. Mike Hough and Mike Maxfield. *Crime Prevention Studies*, vol. 22. Monsey, NY: Criminal Justice Press.

Carroll, Ray. 2004. "Preventing Vehicle Crime in Australia Through Partnerships and National Collaboration." In *Understanding and Preventing Car Theft*, ed. Michael G. Maxfield and Ronald V. Clarke. *Crime Prevention Studies*, vol. 17. Monsey, NY: Criminal Justice Press.

Chaiken, Jan M., and Marcia R. Chaiken. 1982. *Varieties of Criminal Behavior*. Santa Monica, CA: RAND Corporation.

Chaiken, Jan M., and Marcia R. Chaiken. 1990. "Drugs and Predatory Crime." In *Crime and Justice: A Review of Research: Vol. 13. Drugs and Crime*, ed. Michael Tonry and James Q. Wilson. Chicago: University of Chicago Press.

Chainey, Spencer, and Jerry Ratcliffe. 2005. *GIS and Crime Mapping*. New York: Wiley.

Chermak, Steven M., and Alexander Weiss. 1997. "The Effects of the Media on Federal Criminal Justice Policy." *Criminal Justice Policy Review* 8(4): 323–341.

Chicago Community Policing Evaluation Consortium. 2003. *Community Policing in Chicago, Years Eight and Nine*. Chicago: Illinois Criminal Justice Information Authority.

Chicago Community Policing Evaluation Consortium. 2004. *Community Policing in Chicago, Year Ten*. Chicago: Illinois Criminal Justice Information Authority.

Chin, Ko-lin. 2009. *The Golden Triangle: Inside Southeast Asia's Drug Trade*. Ithaca, NY: Cornell University Press.

Choi, Bernard C. K., and Anita W. P. Pak. 2005. "A Catalog of Biases in Questionnaires." *Preventing Chronic Disease: Public Health Research, Policy, and Practice* 2(1): 1–13.

Clarke, Ronald V. 1997a. "Deterring Obscene Phone Callers: The New Jersey Experience." In *Situational Crime Prevention: Successful Case Studies*, 2d ed., ed. Ronald V. Clarke. New York: Harrow and Heston.

Clarke, Ronald V. 1997b. "Introduction." In *Situational Crime Prevention: Successful Case Studies*, 2d ed., ed. Ronald V. Clarke. New York: Harrow and Heston.

Clarke, Ronald V., Stephanie Contre, and Gohar Petrossian. 2010. "Deterrence and Fare Evasion: Results of a Natural Experiment." *Security Journal* 23(1): 5–17.

Clarke, Ronald V., and John Eck. 2005. *Crime Analysis for Problem Solvers in 60 Small Steps*. Washington, DC: U.S. Department of Justice, Office of Community Oriented Policing. http://www.popcenter.org/learning/60steps/

Clarke, Ronald, Paul Ekblom, Mike Hough, and Pat Mayhew. 1985. "Elderly Victims of Crime and Exposure to Risk." *The Howard Journal* 24(1): 1–9.

Clarke, Ronald V., and Patricia M. Harris. 1992. "Auto Theft and Its Prevention." In *Crime and Justice: An Annual Review of Research*, vol. 16, ed. Michael Tonry. Chicago: University of Chicago Press.

Clarke, Ronald V., and Graeme R. Newman. 2006. *Outsmarting the Terrorists*. Westport, CT: Praeger Security International.

Clarke, Ronald V., and Phyllis A. Schultze. 2005. *Researching a Problem*. Washington, DC: U.S. Department of Justice, Office of Community Oriented Policing Services. http://popcenter.org/tools/researching/

Cohen, Lawrence E., and Marcus Felson. 1979. "Social Change and Crime Rate Trends: A Routine Activity Approach." *American Sociological Review* 44(4): 588–608.

Coleman, Veronica, et al. 1999. "Using Knowledge and Teamwork to Reduce Crime." *National Institute of Justice Journal*, October, 16–23.

Committee on Science, Engineering, and Public Policy. 2009. *On Being a Scientist: Responsible Conduct in Research*. 3d ed. Washington, DC: National Academy Press.

Conover, Ted. 2000. *Newjack: Guarding Sing Sing*. New York: Random House.

Cullen, Francis T., and Paul Gendreau. 2000. "Assessing Correctional Rehabilitation: Policy, Practice, and Prospects." In *Policies, Processes, and Decisions of the Criminal Justice System*, ed. Julie Horney. *Criminal Justice 2000*, vol. 3. Washington, DC: U.S. Department of Justice, Office of Justice Programs, National Institute of Justice.

Cullen, Francis T., and Jody L. Sundt. 2003. "Reaffirming Evidence-Based Corrections." *Criminology and Public Policy* 2(2): 353–358.

D'Alessio, Stewart J., Lisa Stolzenberg, and W. Clinton Terry. 1999. "'Eyes on the Street': The Impact of Tennessee's Emergency Cellular Telephone Program on Alcohol Related Crashes." *Crime and Delinquency* 45(4): 453–466.

Decker, Scott H. 2005. *Using Offender Interviews to Inform Police Problem Solving*. Problem Solving Tools series. Washington, DC: U.S. Department of Justice, Office of Community Oriented Policing Services.

Decker, Scott H., and Barrik Van Winkle. 1996. *Life in the Gang: Family, Friends, and Violence*. New York: Cambridge University Press.

Dennis, Michael L. 1990. "Assessing the Validity of Randomized Field Experiments: An Example from Drug Abuse Treatment Research." *Evaluation Review* 14: 347–373.

Devine, Joel A., and James D. Wright. 1993. *The Greatest of Evils: Urban Poverty and the American Underclass*. Hawthorne, NY: Aldine de Gruyter.

Dillman, Don A. 2007. *Mail and Internet Surveys: The Tailored Design Method 2007 Update*. 2d ed. New York: Wiley.

Dinkes, Rachel, Emily Forrest Cataldi, Wendy Lin-Kelly, and Thomas D. Snyder. 2007. *Indicators of School Crime and Safety: 2007*. Washington, DC: National Center for Education Statistics, Institute of Education Sciences, U.S. Department of Education, and Bureau of Justice Statistics, Office of Justice Programs, U.S. Department of Justice, December.

Ditton, Jason, and Stephen Farrall. 2007. "The British Crime Survey and the Fear of Crime." In *Surveying Crime in the 21st Century*, ed. Mike Hough and Mike Maxfield. *Crime Prevention Studies*, vol. 22. Monsey, NY: Criminal Justice Press.

Durose, Matthew R., Erica L. Smith, and Patrick A. Langan. 2007. *Contacts between Police and the Public, 2005*. Washington, DC: U.S. Department of Justice, Office of Justice Programs, Bureau of Justice Statistics, April.

Eck, John E. 2002. "Learning from Experience in Problem-Oriented Policing and Situational Prevention: The Positive Functions of Weak Evaluations and the Negative Functions of Strong Ones." In *Evaluation for Crime Prevention*, ed. Nick Tilley. *Crime Prevention Studies*, vol. 14. Monsey, NY: Criminal Justice Press.

Eck, John E. 2003a. *Assessing Responses to Problems: An Introductory Guide for Police Problem-Solvers*. Problem-Oriented Guides for Police. Washington, DC: U.S. Department of Justice, Office of Community Oriented Policing Services.

Eck, John E. 2003b. "Police Problems: The Complexity of Problem Theory, Research and Evaluation." In

*Problem-Oriented Policing: From Innovation to Mainstream*, ed. Johannes Knutsson. *Crime Prevention Studies*, vol. 15. Monsey, NY: Criminal Justice Press.

Eck, John, et al. 2005. *Mapping Crime: Understanding Hot Spots*. NIJ Special Report. Washington, DC: U.S. Department of Justice, Office of Justice Programs, National Institute of Justice.

Eisenberg, Michael. 1999. *Three Year Recidivism Tracking of Offenders Participating in Substance Abuse Treatment Programs*. Austin, TX: Criminal Justice Policy Council.

Ekici, Niyazi. 2008. *The Dynamics of Terrorist Recruitment: The Case of the Revolutionary People's Liberation Party/Front (DHKP/C) and the Turkish Hezbollah*. Unpublished Ph.D. dissertation. Newark, NJ: School of Criminal Justice, Rutgers University.

Elliott, Delbert S., David Huizinga, and Suzanne S. Ageton. 1985. *Explaining Delinquency and Drug Use*. Thousand Oaks, CA: Sage.

Engel, Robin Shepard, et al. 2005. *Project on Police-Citizen Contacts: Year 2 Final Report*. Cincinnati, OH: Criminal Justice Research Center, University of Cincinnati.

Fabelo, Tony. 1995. "What is Recidivism? How Do You Measure It? What Can It Tell Policy Makers?" *Bulletin from the Executive Director* (19). Austin, TX: Criminal Justice Policy Council.

Fabelo, Tony. 1997. "The Critical Role of Policy Research in Developing Effective Correctional Policies." *Corrections Management Quarterly* 1(1): 25–31.

Fagan, Jeffrey, Franklin E. Zimring, and June Kim. 1998. "Declining Homicide in New York City: A Tale of Two Trends." *Journal of Criminal Law and Criminology* 88(4): 1277–1323.

Faggiani, Donald, and Colleen McLaughlin. 1999. "Using National Incident-Based Reporting System Data for Strategic Crime Analysis." *Journal of Quantitative Criminology* 15(2): 181–191.

Farmer, John J. 2009. *The Ground Truth: The Untold Story of America under Attack on 9/11*. New York: Riverhead Books.

Farrell, Graham, Alan Edmunds, Louise Hobbs, and Gloria Laycock. 2000. *RV Snapshot: UK Policing and Repeat Victimisation*. Crime Reduction Research Series. Policing and Reducing Crime Unit, Paper 5. London: Home Office.

Farrell, Graham, Andromachi Tseloni, Jen Mailley, and Nick Tilley. 2011. "The Crime Drop and the Security Hypothesis." *Journal of Research in Crime and Delinquency* 48.

Farrington, David P., Trevor H. Bennett, and Brandon C. Welsh. 2007. "The Cambridge Evaluation of the Effects of CCTV on Crime." In *Imagination for Crime Prevention: Essays in Honour of Ken Pease*, ed. Graham Farrell, Kate J. Bowers, Shane D. Johnson, and Michael Townsley. *Crime Prevention Studies*, vol. 21. Monsey, NY: Criminal Justice Press.

Farrington, David P., Patrick A. Langan, Michael Tonry, and Darrick Jolliffe. 2004. "Introduction." In *Cross-National Studies in Crime and Justice*, ed. David P. Farrington, Patrick A. Langan, and Michael Tonry. Washington, DC: U.S. Department of Justice, Office of Justice Programs, Bureau of Justice Statistics.

Farrington, David P., Lloyd E. Ohlin, and James Q. Wilson. 1986. *Understanding and Controlling Crime: Toward a New Research Strategy*. New York: Springer-Verlag.

Federal Bureau of Investigation. 2000. *National Incident-Based Reporting System. Vol. 1: Data Collection Guidelines*. Washington, DC: U.S. Department of Justice, Federal Bureau of Investigation, August.

Federal Bureau of Investigation. 2009. *Crime in the United States 2008*. Washington, DC: U.S. Department of Justice, Federal Bureau of Investigation. http://www2.fbi.gov/ucr/cius2008/index.html

Federal Bureau of Investigation. 2010. *Crime in the United States 2009*. Washington, DC: U.S. Department of Justice, Federal Bureau of Investigation. http://www2.fbi.gov/ucr/cius2009/index.html

Federal Trade Commission. 2010. *Consumer Sentinel Network Data Book for January–December 2009*. Washington, DC: Federal Trace Commission, February. http://www.ftc.gov/sentinel/reports/sentinel-annual-reports/sentinel-cy2009.pdf

Felson, Marcus. 2002. *Crime and Everyday Life*. 3rd ed. Thousand Oaks, CA: Sage.

Felson, Marcus, et al. 1996. "Redesigning Hell: Preventing Crime and Disorder at the Port Authority Bus Terminal." In *Preventing Mass Transit Crime*, ed. Ronald V. Clarke. *Crime Prevention Studies*, vol. 6. Monsey, NY: Criminal Justice Press.

Felson, Marcus, and Ronald V. Clarke. 1998. *Opportunity Makes the Thief: Practical Theory for Crime Prevention.* Police Research Series, paper 98. London: Home Office, Policing and Reducing Crime Unit, Research, Development and Statistics Directorate.

Felson, Richard B., Steven F. Messner, Anthony W. Hoskin, and Glenn Deane. 2002. "Reasons for Reporting and Not Reporting Domestic Violence to the Police." *Criminology* 40(3): 617–647.

Finkelhor, David, and Richard Ormrod. 2004. *Prostitution of Juveniles: Patterns from NIBRS.* Juvenile Justice Bulletin. Washington, DC: U.S. Department of Justice, Office of Justice Programs, Office of Juvenile Justice and Delinquency Prevention, June.

Finkelstein, Michael O., and Bruce Levin. 2001. *Statistics for Lawyers.* 2d ed. New York: Springer-Verlag.

Finn, Peter, and Andrea K. Newlyn. 1993. *Miami's Drug Court: A Different Approach.* Program Focus. Washington, DC: U.S. Department of Justice, Office of Justice Programs, National Institute of Justice.

Forster, Emma, and Alison McCleery. 1999. "Computer Assisted Personal Interviewing: A Method of Capturing Sensitive Information." *IASSIST Quarterly* 23(2): 26–38. http://iassistdata.org/iq/issue/23/2

Fox, James Alan. 2000. "Demographics and U.S. Homicide." In *The Crime Drop in America*, ed. Alfred Blumstein and Joel Wallman. New York: Cambridge University Press.

Gaes, Gerald G., Scott D. Camp, Julianne B. Nelson, and William G. Saylor. 2004. *Measuring Prison Performance: Government Privatization and Accountability.* Walnut Creek, CA: AltaMira Press.

Gant, Frances, and Peter Grabosky. 2001. *The Stolen Vehicle Parts Market.* Trends and Issues, no. 215. Canberra, Australia: Australian Institute of Criminology (October).

Geerken, Michael R. 1994. "Rap Sheets in Criminological Research: Considerations and Caveats." *Journal of Quantitative Criminology* 10(1): 3–21.

General Accounting Office. 1991. *Using Structured Interviewing Techniques.* Transfer Paper 10.1.5. Washington, DC: General Accounting Office.

General Accounting Office. 1996. *Content Analysis: A Methodology for Structuring and Analyzing Written Material.* Transfer paper 10.3.1. Washington, DC: United States General Accounting Office.

Gill, Martin, and Angela Spriggs. 2005. *Assessing the Impact of CCTV.* Home Office Research Study, 292. London: Her Majesty's Stationery Office.

Gill, Martin, et al. 2005. *Technical Annex: Methods Used in Assessing the Impact of CCTV.* Online Report 17/05. London: Research, Development and Statistics Directorate, Home Office.

Glaser, Barney G., and Anselm Strauss. 1967. *The Discovery of Grounded Theory.* Chicago, IL: University of Chicago Press.

Gottfredson, Denise C., Stacy S. Najaka, Brook W. Kearly, and Carlos M. Rocha. 2006. "Long-Term Effects of Participation in the Baltimore City Drug Treatment Court: Results from an Experimental Study." *Journal of Experimental Criminology* 2: 67–98.

Gottfredson, Michael R., and Travis Hirschi. 1987. "The Methodological Adequacy of Longitudinal Research on Crime," *Criminology* 25(3): 581–614.

Gottfredson, Michael R., and Travis Hirschi. 1990. *A General Theory of Crime.* Stanford, CA: Stanford University Press.

Greenwood, Peter. 1975. *The Criminal Investigation Process.* Santa Monica, CA: RAND Corporation.

Guerette, Rob T. 2009. *Analyzing Crime Displacement and Diffusion.* Problem Solving Tools series. Washington, DC: U.S. Department of Justice, Office of Community Oriented Policing Services.

Guerette, Rob T., and Kate J. Bowers. 2009. "Assessing the Extent of Crime Displacement and Diffusion of Benefits." *Criminology* 47(4): 1331–1368.

Gurr, Ted Robert. 1989. "Historical Trends in Violent Crime: Europe and the United States." In *Violence in America: The History of Crime*, ed. Ted Robert Gurr. Thousand Oaks, CA: Sage.

Haney, Craig, Curtis Banks, and Philip Zimbardo. 1973. "Interpersonal Dynamics in a Simulated Prison." *International Journal of Criminology and Penology* 1: 69–97.

Hanmer, Jalna, Sue Griffiths, and David Jerwood. 1999. *Arresting Evidence: Domestic Violence and Repeat Victimisation.* Police Research Series, Paper 104. London: Home Office.

Haninger, Kevin, and Kimberly M. Thompson. 2004. "Content and Ratings of Teen-Rated Video Games." *Journal of the American Medical Association* 291(7): 856–865.

Harradine, Sally, Jenny Kodz, Francesca Lemetti, and Bethan Jones. 2004. *Defining and Measuring Anti-Social Behaviour*. Home Office Development and Practice Report 26. London: Home Office Research, Development and Statistics Directorate.

Harries, Keith. 1999. *Mapping Crime: Principle and Practice*. Washington, DC: U.S. Department of Justice, Office of Justice Programs, National Institute of Justice.

Harrison, Paige M., and Allen J. Beck. 2005. *Prisoners in 2004*. BJS Bulletin Washington, DC: U.S. Department of Justice, Office of Justice Programs, Bureau of Justice Statistics, October. http://bjs.ojp.usdoj.gov/content/pub/pdf/p04.pdf.

Heeren, Timothy, Robert A. Smith, Suzette Morelock, and Ralph W. Hingson. 1985. "Surrogate Measures of Alcohol Involvement in Fatal Crashes: Are Conventional Indicators Adequate?" *Journal of Safety Research* 16(3): 127–134.

Hempel, Carl G. 1952. "Fundamentals of Concept Formation in Empirical Science." In *International Encyclopedia of Unified Science: Foundations of the Unity of Science*, vol. 2. Chicago: University of Chicago Press.

Hesseling, René B. P. 1994. "Displacement: A Review of the Empirical Literature." In *Crime Prevention Studies*, vol. 3, ed. Ronald V. Clarke. Monsey, NY: Criminal Justice Press.

Heumann, Milton, and Colin Loftin. 1979. "Mandatory Sentencing and the Abolition of Plea Bargaining: The Michigan Felony Firearm Statute." *Law and Society Review* 13(2): 393–430.

Hindelang, Michael J., Michael R. Gottfredson, and James Garofalo. 1978. *Victims of Personal Crime: An Empirical Foundation for a Theory of Personal Victimization*. Cambridge, MA: Ballinger.

Hirschfield, Alex. 2005. "Analysis for Intervention." In *Handbook of Crime Prevention and Community Safety*, ed. Nick Tilley. Cullompton, Devon: Willan Publishing.

Homel, Ross, and Jeff Clark. 1994. "The Prediction and Prevention of Violence in Pubs and Clubs." In *Crime Prevention Studies*, vol. 3, ed. Ronald V. Clarke. Monsey, NY: Criminal Justice Press.

Homel, Ross, Steve Tomsen, and Jennifer Thommeny. 1992. "Public Drinking and Violence: Not Just an Alcohol Problem." *Journal of Drug Issues* 22(3): 679–697.

Hood-Williams, John, and Tracey Bush. 1995. "Domestic Violence on a London Housing Estate." *Home Office Research Bulletin* 37: 11–18.

Hoover, Kenneth R., and Todd Donovan. 2007. *The Elements of Social Scientific Thinking*. 9th ed. Belmont, CA: Wadsworth.

Hough, Mike, and Mike Maxfield, eds. 2007. *Surveying Crime in the 21st Century*. *Crime Prevention Studies*, vol. 22. Monsey, NY: Criminal Justice Press.

Hunter, Rosemary S., and Nancy Kilstrom. 1979. "Breaking the Cycle in Abusive Families." *American Journal of Psychiatry* 136(10): 1318–1322.

Idaho State Police. 2008. *Crime in Idaho 2007*. Meridian: Idaho State Police, Bureau of Criminal Identification, Uniform Crime Reporting Unit. http://www.isp.idaho.gov/identification/ucr/crimeinidaho2007.html

Inciardi, James A. 1993. "Some Considerations on the Methods, Dangers, and Ethics of Crack-House Research." Appendix A. In *Women and Crack Cocaine*, ed. James A. Inciardi, Dorothy Lockwood, and Anne E. Pettieger. New York: Macmillan.

Jacob, Herbert. 1984. *Using Published Data: Errors and Remedies*. Thousand Oaks, CA: Sage.

Jacobs, Bruce A. 1996. "Crack Dealers' Apprehension Avoidance Techniques: A Case of Restrictive Deterrence." *Justice Quarterly* 13(3): 359–381.

Jacobs, Bruce A. 1999. *Dealing Crack: The Social World of Streetcorner Selling*. Boston: Northeastern University Press.

Jacobs, Bruce A., and Jody Miller. 1998. "Crack Dealing, Gender, and Arrest Avoidance." *Social Problems* 45(4): 550–569.

Jacobs, Bruce A., Volkan Topalli, and Richard Wright. 2003. "Carjacking, Streetlife and Offender Motivation." *British Journal of Criminology* 43(4): 673–688.

Jacques, Scott, and Danielle Reynald. 2012 (forthcoming). "The Offenders' Perspective on Prevention: Guarding against Victimization and Law Enforcement." *Journal of Research in Crime and Delinquency* 49.

Jacques, Scott, and Richard Wright. 2008. "Intimacy with Outlaws: The Role of Relational Distance in Recruiting, Paying, and Interviewing Underworld Research Participants." *Journal of Research in Crime and Delinquency* 45(1): 22–38.

Jahic, Galma. 2009. *Analysis of Economic and Social Factors Associated with Trafficking in Women: Thinking Globally, Researching Locally.* Unpublished Ph.D. dissertation. Newark, NJ: School of Criminal Justice, Rutgers University.

Jeffery, C. Ray. 1977. *Crime Prevention through Environmental Design.* 2d ed. Thousand Oaks, CA: Sage.

Johansen, Helle Krogh, and Peter C. Gotzsche. 1999. "Problems in the Design and Reporting of Trials of Antifungal Agents Encountered during Meta-Analysis." *Journal of the American Medical Association* 282(18): 1752–1759.

Johnson, Bruce D., et al. 1985. *Taking Care of Business: The Economics of Crime by Heroin Abusers.* Lexington, MA: Lexington Books.

Johnson, Bruce, Andrew Golub, and Eloise Dunlap. 2000. "The Rise and Decline of Hard Drugs, Drug Markets, and Violence in Inner-City New York." In *The Crime Drop in America*, ed. Alfred Blumstein and Joel Wallman. New York: Cambridge University Press.

Johnson, Ida M. 1999. "School Violence: The Effectiveness of a School Resource Officer Program in a Southern City." *Journal of Criminal Justice* 27(2): 173–192.

Johnson, Kelly Dedel. 2006. *Witness Intimidation.* Problem-Oriented Guides for Police, no. 42. Washington, DC: U.S. Department of Justice, Office of Community Oriented Policing Services.

Johnson, Shane D., Aiden Sidebottom, and Adam Thorpe. 2008. *Bicycle Theft.* Problem-Oriented Guides for Police, no. 52. Washington, DC: U.S. Department of Justice, Office of Community Oriented Policing Services.

Johnston, Lloyd D., Patrick M. O'Malley, Jerald G. Bachman, and John E. Schulenberg. 2009. *Monitoring the Future National Results on Adolescent Drug Use: Overview of Key Findings, 2008.* NIH publication no. 09-7401. Bethesda, MD: National Institute on Drug Abuse.

Kalichman, Seth C. 2000. *Mandated Reporting of Suspected Child Abuse: Ethics, Law, and Policy.* 2d ed. Washington, DC: American Psychological Association.

Karmen, Andrew. 2000. *New York Murder Mystery: The True Story behind the Crime Crash of the 1990s.* New York: New York University Press.

Kelling, George L., and William J. Bratton. 1998. "Declining Crime Rates: Insiders' Views of the New York City Story." *Journal of Criminal Law and Criminology* 88(4): 1217–1231.

Kelling, George L., Tony Pate, Duane Dieckman, and Charles E. Brown. 1974. *The Kansas City Preventive Patrol Experiment: A Technical Report.* Washington, DC: Police Foundation.

Kennedy, David M. 1998. "Pulling Levers: Getting Deterrence Right." *National Institute of Justice Journal* 236(July): 2–8.

Kennet, Joel, and Joseph Gfroerer, eds. 2005. *Evaluating and Improving Methods Used in the National Survey on Drug Use and Health.* Publication no. SMA 03-3768. DHHS Publication No. SMA 05-4044, Methodology Series M-5. Rockville, MD: Office of Applied Studies, Substance Abuse and Mental Health Services Administration. http://oas.samhsa.gov/nsduh/methods.cfm

Kessler, David A. 1999. "The Effects of Community Policing on Complaints against Officers." *Journal of Quantitative Criminology* 15(3): 333–372.

Killias, Martin. 1993. "Gun Ownership, Suicide and Homicide: An International Perspective." *Canadian Medical Association Journal* 148(10): 1721–1725.

Killias, Martin, Marcelo F. Aebi, and Denis Ribeaud. 2000. "Learning through Controlled Experiments: Community Service and Heroin Prescription in Switzerland." *Crime and Delinquency* 46(2): 233–251.

Kish, Leslie. 1965. *Survey Sampling.* New York: Wiley.

Kitsuse, John I., and Aaron V. Cicourel. 1963. "A Note on the Uses of Official Statistics." *Social Problems* 11: 131–138.

Klaus, Patsy. 2004. *Carjacking, 1993–2002.* BJS Special Report. Washington, DC: U.S. Department of Justice, Office of Justice Programs, Bureau of Justice Statistics, July.

Krueger, Richard A., and Mary Anne Casey. 2000. *Focus Groups: A Practical Guide for Applied Research.* 3d ed. Thousand Oaks, CA: Sage.

Kwak, Nojin, and Barry Radler. 2002. "A Comparison between Mail and Web Surveys: Response Pattern, Respondent Profile, and Data Quality." *Journal of Official Statistics* 18(2): 257–273.

Lange, James E., Mark B. Johnson, and Robert B. Voas. 2005. "Testing the Racial Profiling Hypothesis for

Seemingly Disparate Traffic Stops on the New Jersey Turnpike." *Justice Quarterly* 22(2): 193–223.

Langton, Lynn, and Michael Planty. 2010. *Victims of Identity Theft, 2008*. BJS Special Report. Washington, DC: U.S. Department of Justice, Office of Justice Programs, Bureau of Justice Statistics, November.

Laub, John H., and Robert J. Sampson. 2003. *Shared Beginnings, Divergent Lives: Delinquent Boys to Age 70*. Cambridge, MA: Harvard University Press.

Lauritsen, Janet L., and Robin J. Schaum. 2005. *Crime and Victimization in the Three Largest Metropolitan Areas, 1980–98*. Bureau of Justice Statistics Technical Report. Washington, DC: U.S. Department of Justice, Office of Justice Programs, Bureau of Justice Statistics.

Laycock, Gloria. 2002. "Methodological Issues in Working with Policy Advisers and Practitioners." In *Analysis for Crime Prevention*, ed. Nick Tilley. *Crime Prevention Studies*, vol. 13. Monsey, NY: Criminal Justice Press.

Leiber, Michael J., and Jayne M. Stairs. 1999. "Race, Contexts, and the Use of Intake Diversion." *Journal of Research in Crime and Delinquency* 36(1): 56–86.

Lempert, Richard O. 1984. "From the Editor." *Law and Society Review* 18: 505–153.

Levine, Robert. 1997. *A Geography of Time: The Temporal Misadventures of a Social Psychologist*. New York: Basic Books.

Levinson, Marc. 2007. *The Box: How the Shipping Container Made the World Smaller and the World Economy Bigger*. Princeton, NJ: Princeton University Press.

Lilly, J. Robert. 2006. "Issues beyond Empirical EM Reports." *Criminology and Public Policy* 5(1): 93–102.

Lineberry, Robert L. 1977. *American Public Policy*. New York: Harper and Row.

Loeber, Rolf, Magda Stouthamer-Loeber, Welmoet van Kammen, and David P. Farrington. 1991. "Initiation, Escalation and Desistance in Juvenile Offending and Their Correlates." *Journal of Criminal Law and Criminology* 82(1): 36–82.

Macintyre, Stuart, and Ross Homel. 1996. "Danger on the Dance Floor: A Study of the Interior Design, Crowding and Aggression in Nightclubs." In *Policing for Prevention: Reducing Crime, Public Intoxication, and Injury. Crime Prevention Studies*, vol. 7, ed. Ross Homel. Monsey, NY: Criminal Justice Press.

MacKenzie, Doris Layton, Katherine Browning, Stacy B. Skroban, and Douglas A. Smith. 1999. "The Impact of Probation on the Criminal Activities of Offenders." *Journal of Research in Crime and Delinquency* 36(4): 423–453.

MacKenzie, Doris Layton, James W. Shaw, and Voncile B. Gowdy. 1993. *An Evaluation of Shock Incarceration in Louisiana*. Research in Brief. Washington, DC: U.S. Department of Justice, Office of Justice Programs, National Institute of Justice, June.

Madensen, Tamara D., and John E. Eck. 2008. *Spectator Violence in Stadiums*. Problem-Oriented Guides for Police, no. 54. Washington, DC: U.S. Department of Justice, Office of Community Oriented Policing Services.

Maltz, Michael D. 1994. "Deviating from the Mean: The Declining Significance of Significance." *Journal of Research in Crime and Delinquency* 31(4): 434–463.

Maltz, Michael D. 2006. "Some P-Baked Thoughts (P > 0.5) on Experiments and Statistical Significance." *Journal of Experimental Criminology* 2(2): 211–226.

Maltz, Michael D., and Marianne W. Zawitz. 1998. *Displaying Violent Crime Trends Using Estimates from the National Crime Victimization Survey*. Bureau of Justice Statistics Technical Report. Washington, DC: U.S. Department of Justice, Office of Justice Programs, Bureau of Justice Statistics. http://bjs.ojp .usdoj.gov/content/pub/pdf/dvctue.pdf

Marshall, Catherine, and Gretchen B. Rossman. 2006. *Designing Qualitative Research*. 4th ed. Thousand Oaks, CA: Sage.

Martin, Elizabeth. 1999. "Who Knows Who Lives Here? Within-Household Disagreements as a Source of Survey Coverage Error." *Public Opinion Quarterly* 63(2): 220–236.

Marx, Karl. 1880. "Revue Socialist." Reprinted. In *Karl Marx: Selected Writings in Sociology and Social Philosophy*, ed. T. N. Bottomore and Maximilien Rubel. New York: McGraw-Hill.

Mastrofski, Stephen D., et al. 1998. *Systematic Observation of Public Police: Applying Field Research Methods to Policy Issues*. Research Report. Washington, DC: U.S. Department of Justice, Office of Justice Programs, National Institute of Justice, December.

Mastrofski, Stephen D., and R. Richard Ritti. 1999. "Patterns of Community Policing: A View from Newspapers in the United States." COPS Working

Paper #2. Washington, DC: U.S. Department of Justice, Office of Community Oriented Policing Services.

Matz, David. 2007. "Development and Key Results from the First Two Waves of the Offending Crime and Justice Survey." In *Surveying Crime in the 21st Century*, ed. Mike Hough and Mike Maxfield. *Crime Prevention Studies*, vol. 22. Monsey, NY: Criminal Justice Press.

Maxfield, Michael G. 1999. "The National Incident-Based Reporting System: Research and Policy Applications." *Journal of Quantitative Criminology* 15(2): 119–149.

Maxfield, Michael G. 2001. *Guide to Frugal Evaluation for Criminal Justice*. Final report to the National Institute of Justice. Washington, DC: U.S. Department of Justice, Office of Justice Programs, National Institute of Justice. www.ncjrs.org/pdffiles1/nij/187350.pdf

Maxfield, Michael G., and W. Carsten Andresen. 2002. *Evaluation of New Jersey State Police in-Car Mobile Video Recording System*. Final report to the Office of the Attorney General. Newark, NJ: School of Criminal Justice, Rutgers University.

Maxfield, Michael G., and Terry L. Baumer. 1991. "Electronic Monitoring in Marion County Indiana." *Overcrowded Times* 2: 5, 17.

Maxfield, Michael G., and Terry L. Baumer. 1992. "Home Detention with Electronic Monitoring: A Nonexperimental Salvage Evaluation." *Evaluation Review* 16(3): 315–332.

Maxfield, Michael G., and Ronald V. Clarke. 2009. *The Role of Parts-Marking in Reducing Vehicle Theft*. Unpublished final report submitted to the National Highway Traffic Safety Administration. Newark, NJ: Rutgers University.

Maxfield, Michael G., and George L. Kelling. 2005. *New Jersey State Police and Stop Data: What Do We Know, What Should We Know, and What Should We Do?* With the assistance of W. Carsten Andresen, Wayne Fisher, William Sousa, and Michael Wagers. Newark, NJ: Police Institute at Rutgers-Newark, March.

Maxfield, Michael G., and Cathy Spatz Widom. 1996. "The Cycle of Violence: Revisited Six Years Later." *Archives of Pediatrics and Adolescent Medicine* 150: 390–395.

Maxfield, Mike, Mike Hough, and Pat Mayhew. 2007. "Surveying Crime in the 21st Century: Summary and Recommendations." In *Surveying Crime in the 21st Century*, ed. Mike Hough and Mike Maxfield. *Crime Prevention Studies*, vol. 22. Monsey, NY: Criminal Justice Press.

Maxwell, Christopher D., Joel H. Garner, and Jeffrey A. Fagan. 2001. *The Effects of Arrest on Intimate Partner Violence: New Evidence from the Spouse Assault Replication Program. Research in Brief*. Washington, DC: U.S. Department of Justice, Office of Justice Programs, National Institute of Justice (July).

Maxwell, Joseph A. 2005. *Qualitative Research Design: An Interactive Approach*. 2d ed. Thousand Oaks, CA: Sage Publications.

Mayhew, Patricia, Ronald V. Clarke, and David Elliott. 1989. "Motorcycle Theft, Helmet Legislation, and Displacement." *Howard Journal* 28(1): 1–8.

McCahill, Michael, and Clive Norris. 2003. "Estimating the Extent, Sophistication and Legality of CCTV in London." In *CCTV*, ed. Martin Gill. Leicester: Perpetuity Press.

McCall, George J. 1978. *Observing the Law: Field Methods in the Study of Crime and the Criminal Justice System*. New York: Free Press.

McCleary, Richard. 1992. *Dangerous Men: The Sociology of Parole*. 2d ed. New York: Harrow and Heston.

McCleary, Richard, Barbara C. Nienstedt, and James M. Erven. 1982. "Uniform Crime Reports as Organizational Outcomes: Three Time Series Experiments." *Social Problems* 29(4):361–372.

McDonald, Douglas C., and Christine Smith. 1989. *Evaluating Drug Control and System Improvement Projects*. Washington, DC: U.S. Department of Justice, Office of Justice Programs, National Institute of Justice.

McKenna, Laura, and Antoinette Pole. 2008. "What Do Bloggers Do? An Average Day on an Average Political Blog." *Public Choice* 134(1-2): 97–108.

Mele, Marie. 2003. *Repeat Domestic Violence in the City of Newark, NJ: Prevalence and Policy Opportunities*. Unpublished Ph.D. dissertation, Rutgers University School of Criminal Justice. Newark, NJ: School of Criminal Justice, Rutgers University.

Meriam Library. 2010. "Evaluating Information: Applying the CRAAP Test." Web page. Chico: California State University. http://www.csuchico.edu/lins/handouts/eval_websites.pdf

Merritt, Nancy, Terry Fain, and Susan Turner. 2006. "Oregon's Get Tough Sentencing Reform: A Lesson in Justice System Adaptation." *Criminology and Public Policy* 5(1): 5–36.

Metro Action Committee on Public Violence Against Women and Children (METRAC) 1987. "Community Safety Program." Toronto, Canada. http://www.metrac.org/programs/safety/safety.htm#training.

Mieczkowski, Thomas M. 1996. "The Prevalence of Drug Use in the United States." In *Crime and Justice: An Annual Review of Research*, ed. Michael Tonry. Chicago: University of Chicago Press.

Milgram, Lester. 1965. "Some Conditions of Obedience to Authority." *Human Relations* 18(1): 57–76.

Miller, Jane E. 2004. *The Chicago Guide to Writing about Numbers*. Chicago: University of Chicago Press.

Miller, Joel. 2000. *Profiling Populations Available for Stops and Searches*. Police Research Series, paper 131. London: Home Office, Policing and Reducing Crime Unit, Research, Development and Statistics Directorate.

Mirrlees-Black, Catriona. 1995. "Estimating the Extent of Domestic Violence: Findings from the 1992 BCS." *Home Office Research Bulletin* 37: 1–9.

Mirrlees-Black, Catriona. 1999. *Domestic Violence: Findings from a New British Crime Survey Self-Completion Questionnaire*. Home Office Research Study. London: Home Office Research, Development, and Statistics Directorate.

Mitford, Jessica. 1973. *Kind and Usual Punishment: The Prison Business*. New York: Random House.

Monahan, John, et al. 1993. "Ethical and Legal Duties in Conducting Research on Violence: Lessons from the MacArthur Risk Assessment Study." *Violence and Victims* 8(4): 387–396.

Moore, Mark H., and Anthony Braga. 2003. *The 'Bottom Line' of Policing: What Citizens Should Value (and Measure) in Police Performance*. Washington, DC: Police Executive Research Forum.

Moskos, Peter. 2009. *Cop in the Hood*. Princeton: Princeton University Press.

Mott, Joy, and Catriona Mirrlees-Black. 1995. *Self-Reported Drug Misuse in England and Wales: Findings from the 1992 British Crime Survey*. Research and Planning Unit Paper 89. London: Home Office.

Murphy, Dean E. 2005. "Arrests Follow Searches in Medical Marijuana Raid." *New York Times*, June 23.

Natarajan, Mangai. 2009. "Journey to Victimization: A Situational Analysis of Sexual Harassment of Women in Public Places ('Eve Teasing') in Tamil Nadu, India." 19th Environmental Criminology and Crime Analysis Symposium. Brasilia, Brazil, 2009 July.

National Commission for the Protection of Human Subjects of Biomedical and Behavioral Research. 1979. *The Belmont Report: Ethical Principles and Guidelines for the Protection of Human Subjects of Research*. Washington, DC: U.S. Department of Health, Education, and Welfare.

National Commission on Terrorist Attacks upon the United States. 2004. *The 9/11 Commission Report*. Final Report of the National Commission on Terrorist Attacks upon the United States. New York: Norton.

National Institute of Justice. 2010a. *Solicitation: Electronic Crime and Digital Evidence Recovery*. Washington, DC: U.S. Department of Justice, Office of Justice Programs, National Institute of Justice. http://www.ncjrs.gov/pdffiles1/nij/sl000957.pdf

National Institute of Justice. 2010b. *Solicitation: NIJ Ph.D. Graduate Research Fellowship Program FY 2011*. Washington, DC: U.S. Department of Justice, Office of Justice Programs, National Institute of Justice. http://ncjrs.gov/pdffiles1/nij/sl000965.pdf

National Research Council. 1996. *The Evaluation of Forensic DNA Evidence*. Washington, DC: National Academy Press.

National Research Council. 2001. *Informing America's Problem on Illegal Drugs: What We Don't Know Keeps Hurting Us*. Committee on Data and Research for Policy on Illegal Drugs, ed. Charles F. Manski, John V. Pepper, and Carol V. Petrie. Washington, DC: National Academy Press.

National Research Council. 2009. *Strengthening Forensic Science in the United States: A Path Forward*. Washington, DC: National Academy Press.

National Youth Gang Center. 1999. *1997 Youth Gang Survey*. Washington, DC: U.S. Department of Justice, Office of Justice Programs, Office of Juvenile Justice and Delinquency Prevention, December.

Nellis, Mike. 2006. "Surveillance, Rehabilitation, and Electronic Monitoring: Getting the Issues Clear." *Criminology and Public Policy* 5(1): 103–108.

Newman, Oscar. 1972. *Defensible Space*. New York: Macmillan.

Newman, Oscar. 1996. *Creating Defensible Space*. Washington, DC: U.S. Department of Housing and Urban Development, Office of Policy Development and Research.

Nolan, James J., and Yoshio Akiyama. 1999. "An Analysis of Factors That Affect Law Enforcement Participation in Hate Crime Reporting." *Journal of Contemporary Criminal Justice* 15(1): 111–127.

Nolan, James J., Yoshio Akiyama, and Samuel Berhanu. 2002. "The Hate Crime Statistics Act of 1990: Developing a Method for Measuring the Occurrence of Hate Violence." *American Behavioral Scientist* 46 (1): 136–153.

NOP Market Research Limited. 1985. *1984 British Crime Survey Technical Report*. London: NOP Market Research Limited.

Painter, Kate. 1996. "The Influence of Street Lighting Improvements on Crime, Fear and Pedestrian Street Use after Dark." *Landscape and Urban Planning* 35(2-3): 193–201.

Patton, Michael Quinn. 2002. *Qualitative Research and Evaluation Methods*. 3d ed. Thousand Oaks, CA: Sage.

Pawson, Ray, and Nick Tilley. 1997. *Realistic Evaluation*. Thousand Oaks, CA: Sage.

Pease, Ken. 1998. *Repeat Victimisation: Taking Stock*. Crime Prevention and Detection Series, Paper 90. London: Home Office.

Perkins, Craig, and Darrell K. Gilliard. 1992. *National Corrections Reporting Program, 1988*. Washington, DC: U.S. Department of Justice, Office of Justice Programs, Bureau of Justice Statistics.

Perrone, Dina. 2009. *The High Life: Club Kids, Harm and Drug Policy*. Qualitative Studies in Crime and Justice. Monsey, NY: Criminal Justice Press.

Piquero, Alex, and David Weisburd eds. 2010. *Handbook of Quantitative Criminology*. New York: Springer.

Pires, Stephen, and Ronald V. Clarke. 2011. "Are Parrots Craved? An Analysis of Parrot Poaching in Mexico." *Journal of Research in Crime and Delinquency* 48.

Plouffe, Nanci, and Rana Sampson. 2004. "Auto Theft and Theft from Autos in Parking Lots in Chula Vista, CA: Crime Analysis for Local and Regional Action." In *Understanding and Preventing Car Theft*, ed. Michael G. Maxfield and Ronald V. Clarke. *Crime Prevention Studies*, vol. 17. Monsey, NY: Criminal Justice Press.

Poklemba, John J. 1988. *Measurement Issues in Prison and Jail Overcrowding*. Albany, NY: New York Division of Criminal Justice Services, Criminal Justice Information Systems Improvement Program.

Pollock, Joycelyn M. 2006. *Ethical Dilemmas and Decisions in Criminal Justice*. 5th ed. Belmont, CA: Wadsworth.

Posavec, Emil J., and Raymond G. Carey. 2002. *Program Evaluation: Methods and Case Studies*. 6th ed. Englewood Cliffs, NJ: Prentice Hall.

President's Commission on Law Enforcement and Administration of Justice. 1967. *The Challenge of Crime in a Free Society*. Washington, DC: U.S. Government Printing Office.

Pudney, Stephen. 2002. *The Road to Ruin? Sequences of Initiation into Drug Use and Offending by Young People in Britain*. Home Office Research Study, 253. London: Her Majesty's Stationery Office.

Quade, Edward S. 1989. *Policy Analysis for Public Decisions*. 3d ed. Rev. Grace M. Carter. New York: North-Holland.

Ragin, Charles C. 2000. *Fuzzy-Set Social Science*. Chicago: University of Chicago Press.

Ramsay, Malcolm, and Sarah Partridge. 1999. *Drug Misuse Declared in 1998: Results from the British Crime Survey*. Home Office Research Study, 197. London: Her Majesty's Stationery Office.

Ramsay, Malcolm, et al. 2001. *Drug Misuse Declared in 2000: Results from the British Crime Survey*. Home Office Research Study, 224. London: Her Majesty's Stationery Office.

Rand, Michael. 2009. *Criminal Victimization, 2008*. Washington, DC: U.S. Department of Justice, Office of Justice Programs, Bureau of Justice Statistics. http://bjs.ojp.usdoj.gov/content/pub/pdf/cv08.pdf

Rand, Michael R., and Callie M. Rennison. 2005. "Bigger Is Not Necessarily Better: An Analysis of Violence against Women Estimates from the National Crime Victimization Survey and the National Violence Against Women Survey." *Journal of Quantitative Criminology* 21(3): 267–291.

Rasinski, Kenneth A. 1989. "The Effect of Question Wording on Public Support for Government Spending." *Public Opinion Quarterly* 53: 388–394.

Ratcliffe, Jerry H. 2004. "The Hotspot Matrix: A Framework for the Spatio-Temporal Targeting of Crime Reduction." *Police Practice and Research* 5(1): 5–23.

Rebellon, Cesar J., and Karen Van Gundy. 2005. "Can Control Theory Explain the Link between Parental Physical Abuse and Delinquency? A Longitudinal Analysis." *Journal of Research in Crime and Delinquency* 42(3): 247–274.

Rengert, George F., Alex R. Piquero, and Peter R. Jones. 1999. "Distance Decay Reexamined." *Criminology* 37(2): 427–445.

Reuter, Peter, Robert MacCoun, and Patrick Murphy. 1990. *Money from Crime: A Study of the Economics of Drug Dealing in Washington, D.C.* Santa Monica, CA: RAND Corporation.

Reynolds, Paul D. 1979. *Ethical Dilemmas and Social Research*. San Francisco: Jossey-Bass.

Rich, Thomas F. 1999. "Mapping the Path to Problem Solving." *National Institute of Justice Journal* (October): 2–9.

Roberts, James C. 2002. *Serving Up Trouble in the Barroom Environment*. Unpublished Ph.D. dissertation, Rutgers University School of Criminal Justice. Newark, NJ: School of Criminal Justice, Rutgers University.

Roberts, Jennifer, et al. 2005. "A Test of Two Models of Recall for Violent Events." *Journal of Quantitative Criminology* 21(2): 175–193.

Rosenfeld, Richard. 2000. "Patterns in Adult Homicide: 1980–1995." In *The Crime Drop in America*, ed. Alfred Blumstein and Joel Wallman. New York: Cambridge University Press.

Rosenfeld, Richard, Timothy M. Bray, and Arlen Egley. 1999. "Facilitating Violence: A Comparison of Gang-Motivated, Gang-Affiliated, and Nongang Youth Homicides." *Journal of Quantitative Criminology* 15(4): 495–516.

Rossi, Peter H., Howard E. Freeman, and Mark W. Lipsey. 1999. *Evaluation: A Systematic Approach*. 6th ed. Thousand Oaks, CA: Sage.

Roth, Andrea. 2010. "Database-Driven Investigations: The Promise—and Peril—of Using Forensics to Solve 'No-Suspect' Cases." *Criminology and Public Policy* 9(2): 421–428.

Sampson, Rana. 2002. *Acquaintance Rape of College Students*. Problem-Oriented Guides for Police, no. 17. Washington, DC: U.S. Department of Justice, Office of Community Oriented Policing Services.

Sampson, Robert J., and John H. Laub. 1993. *Crime in the Making: Pathways and Turning Points through Life*. Cambridge, MA: Harvard University Press.

Sampson, Robert J., and John H. Laub. 2005. "A Life-Course View of the Development of Crime." *The Annals* 602(1): 12–45.

Sampson, Robert J., and Stephen W. Raudenbush. 1999. "Systematic Social Observation of Public Spaces: A New Look at Disorder in Urban Neighborhoods." *American Journal of Sociology* 105(3): 603–651.

Schuck, Amie M., and Cathy Spatz Widom. 2001. "Childhood Victimization and Alcohol Symptoms in Females: Causal Inferences and Hypothesized Mediators." *Child Abuse and Neglect* 25(8): 1069–1092.

Seidman, David, and Michael Couzens. 1974. "Getting the Crime Rate Down: Political Pressure and Crime Reporting." *Law and Society Review* 8(3): 457–493.

Semaan, Salaam, Jennifer Lauby, and Jon Liebman. 2002. "Street and Network Sampling in Evaluation Studies of HIV Risk-Reduction Interventions." *AIDS Reviews* 4: 213–223.

Shadish, William R., Thomas D. Cook, and Donald T. Campbell. 2002. *Experimental and Quasi-Experimental Designs for Generalized Causal Inference*. Boston: Houghton Mifflin.

Shannon, David M., Todd E. Johnson, Shelby Searcy, and Alan Lott. 2002. "Using Electronic Surveys: Advice from Professionals." *Practical Assessment, Research and Evaluation* 8(1). http://pareonline.net/getvn.asp?v=8&n=1

Shearing, Clifford D., and Phillip C. Stenning. 1992. "From the Panopticon to Disney World: The Development of Discipline." In *Situational Crime Prevention: Successful Case Studies*, ed. Ronald V. Clarke. New York: Harrow and Heston.

Sherman, Lawrence W. 1992. *Policing Domestic Violence: Experiments and Dilemmas*. New York: Free Press.

Sherman, Lawrence W. 1995. "Hot Spots of Crime and Criminal Careers of Places." In *Crime and Place*, ed.

John E. Eck and David Weisburd. *Crime Prevention Studies*, vol. 4. Monsey, NY: Criminal Justice Press.

Sherman, Lawrence W., and Richard A. Berk. 1984. *The Minneapolis Domestic Violence Experiment*. Washington, DC: Police Foundation.

Sherman, Lawrence W., and Ellen G. Cohn 1989. "The Impact of Research on Legal Policy: The Minneapolis Domestic Violence Experiment." *Law and Society Review* 23(1): 117–144.

Sherman, Lawrence W., et al. 1992. "The Variable Effects of Arrest on Criminal Careers: The Milwaukee Domestic Violence Experiment." *Journal of Criminal Law and Criminology* 83: 137–169.

Sherman, Lawrence W., James W. Shaw, and Dennis P. Rogan. 1995. *The Kansas City Gun Experiment. Research in Brief*. Washington, DC: U.S. Department of Justice, Office of Justice Programs, National Institute of Justice (January).

Shweder, Richard A. 2006. "Protecting Human Subjects and Preserving Academic Freedom." *American Ethnologist* 33(4): 507–518.

Sidebottom, Aiden, et al. 2011. "Theft in Price-Volatile Markets: On the Relationship between Copper Price and Copper Theft." *Journal of Research in Crime and Delinquency* 48.

Sieber, Joan E. 2001. *Summary of Human Subjects Protection Issues Related to Large Sample Surveys*. Washington, DC: U.S. Department of Justice, Office of Justice Programs, Bureau of Justice Statistics, June.

Silverman, Eli B. 1999. *NYPD Battles Crime: Innovative Strategies in Policing*. Boston: Northeastern University Press.

Sinauer, Nancy, et al. 1999. "Comparisons among Female Homicides Occurring in Rural, Intermediate, and Urban Counties in North Carolina." *Homicide Studies* 3(2):107–128.

Skogan, Wesley G. 1974. "The Validity of Official Crime Statistics: An Empirical Investigation." *Social Science Quarterly* 55(1): 25–38.

Skogan, Wesley G. 1985. *Evaluating Neighborhood Crime Prevention Programs*. The Hague, Netherlands: Ministry of Justice, Research and Documentation Centre.

Skogan, Wesley G. 1990a. *Disorder and Decline: Crime and the Spiral of Decay in American Neighborhoods*. New York: Free Press.

Skogan, Wesley G. 1990b. *The Police and the Public in England and Wales*. Home Office Research Study, 117. London: Her Majesty's Stationery Office.

Skogan, Wesley G., Susan M. Hartnett, Natalie Bump, and Jill Dubois. 2008. *Evaluation of CeaseFire-Chicago*. Assisted by Ryan Hollon and Danielle Morris. Evanston, IL: Center for Policy Research, Northwestern University. http://www.northwestern.edu/ipr/publications/ceasefire.html

Skogan, Wesley G., and Michael G. Maxfield. 1981. *Coping with Crime: Individual and Neighborhood Reactions*. Thousand Oaks, CA: Sage.

Smith, Kevin, and Jacqueline Hoare. 2009. *Crime in England and Wales 2008/09. Vol. 2: Explanatory Notes and Classifications*. Home Office Statistical Bulletin. London: Research, Development and Statistics Directorate, Home Office.

Smith, Steven K., and Carolyn C. DeFrances. 2003. *Assessing Measurement Techniques for Identifying Race, Ethnicity, and Gender: Observation-Based Data Collection in Airports and at Immigration Checkpoints*. Washington, DC: U.S. Department of Justice, Office of Justice Programs, Bureau of Justice Statistics, January.

Smith, Steven K., Greg W. Steadman, Todd D. Minton, and Meg Townsend. 1999. *Criminal Victimization and Perceptions of Community Safety in 12 Cities, 1998*. Washington, DC: U.S. Department of Justice, Office of Justice Programs, Bureau of Justice Statistics and Office of Community Oriented Police Services, June.

Smith, William R., et al. 2003. *The North Carolina Highway Traffic Study*. Final report to the National Institute of Justice. With Harvey McMurray and C. Robert Fenlon. Raleigh: North Carolina State University, July 21.

Snyder, Howard N. 2000. *Sexual Assault of Young Children as Reported to Law Enforcement: Victim, Incident, and Offender Characteristics*. NIBRS Statistical Report. Washington, DC: U.S. Department of Justice, Office of Justice Programs, Bureau of Justice Statistics, July.

Spelman, William. 2000. "The Limited Importance of Prison Expansion." In *The Crime Drop in America*, ed. Alfred Blumstein and Joel Wallman. New York: Cambridge University Press.

Spohn, Cassia. 1990. "The Sentencing Decisions of Black and White Judges: Expected and Unexpected Similarities." *Law and Society Review* 24(5): 1197–216.

Spriggs, Angela, Javier Argomaniz, Martin Gill, and Jane Bryan. 2005. *Public Attitudes towards CCTV: Results from the Pre-Intervention Public Attitude Survey Carried Out in Areas Implementing CCTV.* Online Report 10/05. London: Research, Development and Statistics Directorate, Home Office.

Spurgeon Hall, Richard A., Carolyn Brown Dennis, and Tere L. Chipman. 1999. *The Ethical Foundations of Criminal Justice.* Boca Raton, FL: CRC Press.

Stecher, Brian M., and W. Alan Davis. 1987. *How to Focus an Evaluation.* Thousand Oaks, CA: Sage Publications.

Straus, Murray A. 1999. "The Controversy over Domestic Violence by Women: A Methodological, Theoretical, and Sociology of Science Analysis." In *Violence in Intimate Relationships,* ed. Ximena Arriaga and Stuart Oskamp. Thousand Oaks, CA: Sage.

Substance Abuse and Mental Health Services Administration. 2010. *Results from the 2009 National Survey of Drug Use and Health: Volume I. Summary of National Findings.* NSDUH Series H-38-A, Publication No. SMA 10-4586. Rockville, MD: U.S. Department of Health and Human Services, Substance Abuse and Mental Health Services Administration, Office of Applied Studies. http://www.oas.samhsa.gov/NSDUH/2k9NSDUH/2k9ResultsP.pdf

Surette, Ray. 2006. *Media, Crime, and Justice: Images, Realities, and Policies.* 3d ed. Belmont, CA: Wadsworth.

Sutton, Mike. 2007. "Improving National Crime Surveys with a Focus on Fraud, High-Tech Crimes, and Stolen Goods." In *Surveying Crime in the 21st Century,* ed. Mike Hough and Mike Maxfield. *Crime Prevention Studies,* vol. 22. Monsey, NY: Criminal Justice Press.

Taxman, Faye S., and Lori Elis. 1999. "Expediting Court Dispositions: Quick Results, Uncertain Outcomes." *Journal of Research in Crime and Delinquency* 36(1): 30–55.

Taylor, Ralph B. 1999. *Crime, Grime, Fear, and Decline: A Longitudinal Look.* Research in Brief. Washington, DC: U.S. Department of Justice, Office of Justice Programs, National Institute of Justice, July.

Thompson, Kimberly M., and Kevin Haninger. 2001. "Violence in E-Rated Video Games." *Journal of the American Medical Association* 286(5): 591–598.

Thompson, Steven K. 1997. *Adaptive Sampling in Behavioral Surveys.* NIDA Monograph no. 167. Bethesda, MD: US Department of Health and Human Services, National Institute of Drug Abuse.

Tilley, Nick, ed. 2002a. *Analysis for Crime Prevention. Crime Prevention Studies,* vol. 13. Monsey, NY: Criminal Justice Press.

Tilley, Nick, ed. 2002b. *Evaluation for Crime Prevention. Crime Prevention Studies,* vol. 14. Monsey, NY: Criminal Justice Press.

Tilley, Nick, and Gloria Laycock. 2002. *Working Out What to Do: Evidence-Based Crime Reduction.* Crime Reduction Research Series, paper 11. London: Home Office, Policing and Reducing Crime Unit, Research, Development and Statistics Directorate.

Tipping, Sarah, David Hussey, Martin Wood, and Jon Hales. 2010. *British Crime Survey: Medthis Review 2009.* Final Report. London: National Centre for Social Research.

Tjaden, Patricia, and Nancy Thoennes. 2000. *Full Report of the Prevalence, Incidence, and Consequences of Violence against Women.* Findings from the National Violence against Women Survey. Research Report. Washington, DC: U.S. Department of Justice, Office of Justice Programs, National Institute of Justice, November.

Tourangeau, Roger. 2004. "Survey Research and Societal Change." *Annual Review of Psychology* 55: 775–801.

Tourangeau, Roger, and Tom W. Smith. 1996. "Asking Sensitive Questions: The Impact of Data Collection Mode, Question Format, and Question Context." *Public Opinion Quarterly* 60(2): 275–304.

Townsley, Michael, Ross Homel, and Janet Chaseling. 2003. "Infectious Burglaries: A Test of the Near Repeat Hypothesis." *British Journal of Criminology* 43: 615–633.

Tremblay, Pierre, Bernard Talon, and Doug Hurley. 2001. "Body Switching and Related Adaptations in the Resale of Stolen Vehicles." *British Journal of Criminology* 41(4): 561–579.

U.S. Bureau of the Census. 1992. *Statistical Abstract of the United States.* Washington, DC: U.S. Government Printing Office.

Van Kirk, Marvin. 1977. *Response Time Analysis.* Washington, DC: U.S. Department of Justice,

National Institute of Law Enforcement and Administration of Justice.

Vazquez, Salvador P., Mary K. Stohr, and Marcus Purkiss. 2005. "Intimate Partner Violence Incidence and Characteristics: Idaho NIBRS 1995 to 2001 Data." *Criminal Justice Policy Review* 16(1): 99–114.

Wagner, III, William E., Earl Babbie, Fred S. Halley, and Jeanne Zaino. 2010. *Adventures in Social Research*. 7th ed. Thousand Oaks, CA: Sage.

Walker, Samuel. 1994. *Sense and Nonsense about Crime and Drugs: A Policy Guide*. 3d ed. Belmont, CA: Wadsworth.

Walsh, Christine A., et al. 2008. "Measurement of Victimization in Adolescence: Development and Validation of the Childhood Experiences of Violence Questionnaire." *Child Abuse and Neglect* 32(11): 1037–1057.

Wartell, Julie, and J. Thomas McEwen. 2001. *Privacy in the Information Age: A Guide for Sharing Crime Maps and Spatial Data*. Crime Mapping Research Center. Washington, DC: U.S. Department of Justice, Office of Justice Programs, National Institute of Justice, February.

Weisburd, David, and Chester Britt. 2009. *Statistics in Criminal Justice*. 3d ed. New York: Springer.

Weisburd, David, Anthony Petrosino, and Gail Mason. 1993. "Design Sensitivity in Criminal Justice Experiments." In *Crime and Justice: An Annual Review of Research,* ed. Michael Tonry. Chicago: University of Chicago Press.

Weisel, Deborah. 1999. *Conducting Community Surveys: A Practical Guide for Law Enforcement Agencies*. Washington, DC: U.S. Department of Justice, Office of Justice Programs, Bureau of Justice Statistics and Office of Community Oriented Police Services, October.

Weisel, Deborah Lamm. 2003. "The Sequence of Analysis in Solving Problems." In *Problem-Oriented Policing: From Innovation to Mainstream,* ed. Johannes Knutsson. *Crime Prevention Studies,* vol. 15. Monsey, NY: Criminal Justice Press.

Weisel, Deborah Lamm. 2005. *Analyzing Repeat Victimization*. Problem Solving Tools series. Washington, DC: U.S. Department of Community Oriented Policing Services.

Weiss, Carol H. 1995. "Nothing as Practical as Good Theory: Exploring Theory-Based Evaluation for Comprehensive Community Initiatives for Children and Families." In *New Approaches to Evaluating Community Initiatives: Concepts, Methods, and Contexts,* ed. James P. Connell, Anne C. Kubisch, Lisbeth B. Schorr, and Carol H. Weiss. Washington, DC: Aspen Institute.

West, Donald J., and David P. Farrington. 1977. *The Delinquent Way of Life*. London: Heinemann.

White, Norman A., and Rolf Loeber. 2008. "Bullying and Special Education as Predictors of Serious Delinquency." *Journal of Research in Crime and Delinquency* 45(4): 380–397.

Whitt, Hugh P. 2006. "Where Did the Bodies Go? The Social Construction of Suicide Data, New York City, 1976–1992." *Sociological Inquiry* 76(2): 166–187.

Whitzman, Carolyn, Margaret Shaw, Caroline Andrew, and Kathryn Travers. 2009. "The Effectiveness of Women's Safety Audits." *Security Journal* 22(3): 205–218.

Widom, Cathy Spatz. 1989. "Child Abuse, Neglect, and Adult Behavior: Research Design and Findings on Criminality, Violence, and Child Abuse." *American Journal of Orthopsychiatry* 59(3): 355–367.

Widom, Cathy Spatz. 1992. *The Cycle of Violence*. Research in Brief. Washington, DC: U.S. Department of Justice, Office of Justice Programs, National Institute of Justice, October.

Widom, Cathy Spatz, Barbara Luntz Weiler, and Linda B. Cotler. 1999. "Childhood Victimization and Drug Abuse: A Comparison of Prospective and Retrospective Findings." *Journal of Consulting and Clinical Psychology* 67(6): 867–880.

Williams, Terry, Eloise Dunlap, Bruce D. Johnson, and Ansley Hamid. 1992. "Personal Safety in Dangerous Places." *Journal of Contemporary Ethnography* 21(3): 343–374.

Wilson, James Q., and Richard J. Herrnstein. 1985. *Crime and Human Nature*. New York: Simon and Schuster.

Wilson, James Q., and George Kelling. 1982. "Broken Windows: The Police and Neighborhood Safety." *Atlantic Monthly* March: 29–38.

Wilson, William Julius. 1996. *When Work Disappears: The World of the New Urban Poor*. New York: Knopf.

Wolfgang, Marvin E., Robert M. Figlio, and Thorsten Sellin. 1972. *Delinquency in a Birth Cohort*. Chicago: University of Chicago Press.

Wolfgang, Marvin E., Robert M. Figlio, Paul E. Tracy, and Simon I. Singer. 1985. *The National Survey of Crime Severity*. Washington, DC: U.S. Department of Justice, Office of Justice Programs, Bureau of Justice Statistics. NCJ-96017.

Woodward, Lianne J., and David M. Fergusson. 2000. "Childhood and Adolescent Predictors of Physical Assault: A Prospective Longitudinal Study." *Criminology* 38(1): 233–261.

Wooten, Harold B., and Herbert J. Hoelter. 1998. "Operation Spotlight: The Community Probation-Community Police Team Process." *Federal Probation* 62(2): 30–35.

Wright, Doug, Peggy Barker, Joseph Gfroerer, and Lanny Piper. 2002. "Summary of NHSDA Design Changes in 1999." Chapter 2. In *Redesigning an Ongoing National Household Survey: Methodological Issues*. Publication no. SMA 03-3768, ed. Joseph Gfroerer, Joe Eyerman, and James Chromy. Rockville, MD: Office of Applied Studies, Substance Abuse and Mental Health Services Administration. http://www.oas.samhsa.gov/redesigningNHSDA.pdf

Wright, Richard T., and Scott H. Decker. 1994. *Burglars on the Job: Streetlife and Residential Break-ins*. Boston: Northeastern University Press.

Wright, Richard T., and Scott H. Decker. 1997. *Armed Robbers in Action: Stickups and Street Culture*. Boston: Northeastern University Press.

Wright, Richard, and Trevor Bennett. 1990. "Exploring the Offender's Perspective: Observing and Interviewing Criminals." In *Measurement Issues in Criminology*, ed. Kimberly L. Kempf. New York: Springer-Verlag.

Yin, Robert K. 2008. *Case Study Research: Design and Methods*. 4th ed. Thousand Oaks, CA: Sage.

Zanin, Nicholas, Jon M. Shane, and Ronald V. Clarke. 2004. *Reducing Drug Dealing in Private Apartment Complexes in Newark, New Jersey*. Final report to the Office of Community Oriented Police Services. Washington, DC: U.S. Department of Justice, Office of Community Oriented Police Services. http://www.popcenter.org/Library/researcherprojects/DrugsApartment.pdf

# Author Index

# Subject Index